WORLDMARK ENCYCLOPEDIA OF THE NATIONS

Volume 1

A practical guide to the geographic, historical,
political, social, & economic status of all nations, their international
relationships, and the United Nations system.

WORLDMARK
ENCYCLOPEDIA
OF THE NATIONS

Editor and Publisher, **MOSHE Y. SACHS**

UNITED NATIONS

WORLDMARK PRESS

HARPER & ROW   NEW YORK

v

Acknowledgments

A basic part of the editorial preparation of the *Worldmark Encyclopedia of the Nations* consists of keeping continuously abreast of the work of governments. The editors wish to express their gratitude to the many government officials the world over who so kindly gave their cooperation. Grateful acknowledgment is made for the invaluable material, used throughout the encyclopedia, drawn from the mass of documents issued by the United Nations and its specialized agencies. Gratitude is expressed to the numerous officials of the United Nations and the specialized agencies and to the inter-governmental organizations for their cooperation in helping to update material concerning their organizations.

The editors are especially thankful to Miss Anita R. Horwich, principal contributing editor, for updating of the majority of entries of the United Nations section, and for her contributions in reorganizing this section; to Mr. Jeffrey P. Rajasooria, associate contributing editor; to Dr. Egon Schwelb for his contribution of *Human Rights;* and to Mr. Harry N. M. Winton for the bibliography.

Deep indebtedness for their contributions is expressed to the Washington Branch of ILO; the FAO; Mrs. Patricia Palmer, Division of Public Information, WHO; the Press Division, UNESCO; the Information Office, IMF; the Information and Public Affairs Department of the World Bank Group; the IAEA Liaison Office at the UN; the Public Information Office, ICAO; the ITU; the UPU; Mr. Colin Goad, secretary-general, IMCO; Mr. F. T. Hannan, WMO; and Mr. Nathaniel O. Abelson, Map Librarian of the United Nations, for flag data.

Errors in the text of the encyclopedia are the responsibility of the editors.

The publisher expresses his appreciation to the staff of Keter Inc. who set, printed and bound this encyclopedia and took great pains over the proofreading and the preparation of the index.

The publisher wishes to acknowledge his gratitude to the late Mr. Simha Amir for having made feasible the establishment of this encyclopedia. Appreciation is expressed to Mr. Joseph R. Vergara of Harper & Row for his advice and encouragement and for helping the encyclopedia to achieve recognition as a basic reference work.

The editors express their appreciation for the labors of Mr. Harry Zam as copy editor of the encyclopedia, Mr. Melvin Wolfson for copy-editing the United Nations volume, Mrs. Mary Jane Alexander for proofreading, Mrs. Adele Sachs for her work on the glossary of intergovernmental organizations, Mr. Rudi Vecerin for graphic work, and Dr. Francis Barkoczy for updating the country maps.

The author of the first edition (1960) of the United Nations System, and the second edition (1963) United Nations, was John H. E. Fried, Professor of Political Science, City University of New York (Lehman College).

Foreword

This encyclopedia is different from all others produced in recent years. It is not simply a collection of miscellaneous facts for ready reference. It resembles more the pioneer work of those encyclopedists who ushered in the era of enlightenment in 18th-century France, in that it mirrors the life of men and nations at a great turning point in history, when the national state system of absolute sovereignties has to find new adjustments under the sovereignty of science. The old safeguards for security—mountains and oceans—no longer hold against the impact of an atomic age. The United Nations is the mirror of this new world in which international life becomes more and more interdependent. The political framework is therefore filled in by a comprehensive survey of the major interests of people everywhere. Such an encyclopedia should prove a valuable guide to the understanding not only of the United Nations but of our time.

JAMES T. SHOTWELL
Chairman, Editorial Advisory Board

Preface

The purpose of this encyclopedia is to offer the reader a portrait of the world—the individual nations and their main meeting ground, the United Nations system. Each country and organization is here viewed as it might be reflected in a world mirror and not as seen from the perspective of any one nation.

The world view was achieved by constantly seeking to adhere to a supranational attitude. Belief in the basic mutuality of interests of the people of all lands and in the work of international organizations guided the editors in their approach to the material and its presentation.

The standard treatment of fifty features has been applied uniformly to all countries, regardless of their size, strength, position, or prominence on the world scene. This schema not only serves as a means for comparative study but also affords the reader balanced knowledge of the new and lesser known nations.

The editors have endeavored to transmit to the reader the realities of today's existence. To this end, specific details are related to other aspects of a particular country and to the world as a whole. Care has been taken to present these interrelationships not only in dealing with social, political, and historical aspects, but also in treating economic, statistical, and organizational material.

It was this supranational attitude that attracted the late Dr. Benjamin A. Cohen, former undersecretary of the United Nations, to assume the editorship-in-chief of the first edition. Ben Cohen's personal appeal and stature impelled hundreds of people, many with specialized talents and in positions usually not accessible to publishers, to contribute to this work. The *Worldmark Encyclopedia of the Nations* would not have had its wealth of resources but for him.

Thus, we had the unique opportunity of sending each article to an official authority for factual checking and general appraisal. The authority, either a representative of the country or a spokesman for an international organization, went over the material and made suggestions, which were evaluated for inclusion in the article. The practice of consulting such authorities was continued in the preparation of the second edition. Indeed, many of them assisted in bringing up to date the articles dealing with their countries or organizations.

The new material on individual nations and the updating of the information on the United Nations system required the physical enlargement of the encyclopedia. The second edition (1963) included 135 country articles, as compared with 119 in the first edition, as well as a glossary of intergovernmental organizations. The third edition (1967) included 141 country articles. The present edition contains 146 country articles. The addition of new country articles and new intergovernmental organizations reflects the progress made in the striving of peoples for independence and in the expanding realm of international cooperation.

The focal point in the concept of this encyclopedia is the hope imbued in the spirit of the Charter of the United Nations, an ideal heralded by the ancient Prophets.

Carved in stone, opposite the home of the United Nations, is an inscription taken from Isaiah: "... and they shall beat their swords into plowshares, and their spears into pruning hooks: nation shall not lift up sword against nation, neither shall they learn war any more." The Prophets' sense of moral justice, which was the foundation of their vision of peace as expressed in this inscription, is not yet the basis for current political thought. However, the effort to attain it continues, and the very force of man's aspiration to a just peace renews the momentum of the drive to achieve it.

The problems of peace preoccupy the minds of men everywhere. The ever intensifying complexities of our times, while serving to increase the responsibility of a larger number of persons, often also augment the individual's feeling of helplessness. Yet, knowledge of other lands and ability to see their people as fellow human beings can enable the individual to overcome this feeling of helplessness and to act for himself and others. In this spirit this work was conceived and is offered, with the hope that it may not only find many specific uses, but in so doing may bring into focus a broader world view for the reader, and thus contribute to international understanding.

MOSHE Y. SACHS
Editor and Publisher

Introduction
to the first edition

The swift course of domestic and world events, part of a hastened process of change, requires an enormous increase of basic understanding by peoples of the multiple factors influencing the tempo and direction of national developments. The pattern of intercultural penetration and cross-fertilizing exchanges of scientific and technological knowledge rests upon a concept of fundamental unity of diverse approaches to the central objective of all human endeavors: the creation of a better world, with general equality of opportunity to all individuals, everywhere.

Within a planet shrunk into community bounds by the progress of communications there are no substantial sectors of mankind still completely isolated from the main currents of 20th-century thought and action. A growing sense of identification among men is fostered by the adoption of certain basic standards of human rights and the slow growth of supranational law rooted in the fundamental principles that are common to all juridical systems.

No period in history has witnessed such accelerated search for adequate answers to the riddles that have so long beset humanity. Metaphysical explanations of the universe and of the individual's place within it vie with each other in the vast and only superficially explored realm of emotions; rationalized conceptions of economic and social philosophies contend in the market place of personal loyalties with a violence that frequently threatens to rend asunder the fabric of over-all unity; and the march forward of freedoms and improvements in the status of people throughout our earth is largely clouded by the supercharged treatment of political affairs in the media of mass communication.

At a time when people everywhere are truly eager for accurate, comprehensive, and timely information about themselves and their neighbors in the closely related various geographic areas, the vastness and multiplicity of the field to be covered promotes reporting that serves little the needs of the average person: it is either·too detailed in breadth and depth, so that only specialists can profit from its availability, or sketchy and fragmentary, to the point where it contributes more to confusion than enlightenment of the users.

Because such is the case also with practically all phases of activity, our times are characterized by the resort to all kinds of abstracts and digests which claim, not always rightly, to weed out the chaff of verbalism in order to set free the substantive contents in the overpowering flood of all kinds of informational and interpretive materials.

Encyclopedias and other sources of general information enjoy, at present, a significant vogue. They are the backbone of libraries everywhere, and enterprises in various countries and in many languages produce magnificent examples of high scholarship. I am personally much indebted to several of them because they have given me an insight into the wealth of diverse cultural attitudes which characterize their editorial patterns.

A specific reason has made necessary a new approach to analytical and basic data on each country, as a separate political unit, and as a member of the vast family of nations all constitute together: the universality of their interest in the maintenance of international peace and security through the joint exercise of agreed-upon powers to restrain violence, to police disturbed areas where peaceful relations are endangered; to promote the application of legal procedures to the adjudication of their differences, and to strike at the very sources of controversy, which are rooted in the deep chasms among their economic and social standards and their consequent basic inequalities of status.

While so-called realists may continue to voice their belief that conflict among nations is an outgrowth of their dynamic development, and that only practical arrangements which create "balances" of power can establish an equilibrium within the diverse segments of the world; and while theorists of the biological inevitability of war still proclaim the materialistic concept that only a concentration of authority in the hands of some overwhelmingly strong state can eliminate actual armed conflict and bring to subjected peoples the "benefits" of a freedomless "pax romana," others look longingly back to the days when, within the then small European world, monarchs ruled on disputes through the unilateral exercise of their moral or royal leadership.

But mankind has made great strides since the days of empires, the conquest of colonial dependencies, the plagues and misery that fixed the general expectation of human life under thirty years, and the spiritual darkness of illiteracy and isolation from the mainstreams of culture of variegated philosophical, religious, and scientific concepts; as the nations raced in competition to establish their dominance over peoples in other geographic areas, certain moral principles grounded on natural law stirred the conscience of religious and lay thinkers and brought about the formulation of modern international law—a tremendous advance over the Romans' "jus gentium"—by Francisco de Vitoria and the Spanish scholastics, and its systematization by Hugo Grotius and other learned scholars.

Under principles of ethics the peoples and the nations emerged as possessors of rights and bearers of responsibilities, and morality took its place in the councils of power. The advancement toward a universal rule of law has been too slow for the idealists and yet most encouraging to those who believe that peaceful evolutionary progress achieves more durable results than violent revolutionary change. Who can deny that there is more justice today than before in the relations among nations? The steady process of codification of generally recognized juridical principles and the formulation of new ones through general consensus constitute one of the most hopeful signs of this restless era of change. International compacts such as the covenant of the League of Nations and the Charter of the United Nations incorporate moral concepts side by side with legal standards. They recognize that there are both ethical and juridical duties and rights that must be observed by states in their reciprocal relations and in respect of their inhabitants, subjects, and citizens.

One particularly significant instance of such recognition is that of the high priority given to the protection and promotion of fundamental human rights and freedoms. In a world enriched by the variety of its cultural backgrounds and the diversity of its standards of civilization, there have developed differing concepts of individual rights and of the relationship between the political units and the human beings under their respective jurisdictions. A basic inequality—at both the national and the personal levels—has made voluntary and free cooperation for the common good extremely hard, when not impossible, to achieve.

Nevertheless, in the growing evolution from compulsion toward assent, man has conquered obstacles that previously seemed unsurmountable, and has overthrown barriers erected by sheer ignorance, to enter into a new stage of cooperation, made possible by greater opportunities to express himself freely, as endowed with an inner dignity that transcends racial, religious, economic, and social differences and disabilities of personal status.

Such cooperation is notable in the fields of economic development: through technical assistance, capital loans, exchanges of experts, administrative personnel; of social progress: UNICEF, rehabilitation of refugees, anti-discrimination, status of women, etc.; and of political freedom: the trusteeship system, control of conflicts arising out of former colonial status, etc., which result in an upward leveling of the peoples and in an ever-increasing equality of opportunity for all individuals, not as a matter of grace but as inherent personal right.

So far-reaching are the changes already wrought within the world community, particularly for its less developed segments, that the normal processes of history have lost considerable significance in the face of new realities recently created.

Feeling that none of the encyclopedias and specialized sources of information do sufficient justice to these accomplishments in political freedom, economic development, social progress, and the practice of international cooperation, Worldmark Press, Inc., decided to publish a basically new encyclopedia of the nations. It consists of two parts, the first devoted to information on each individual sovereign political unit, the second dealing with the machinery for international cooperation created by the governments.

The principal features of these two parts are set forth below:

After identifying the outward symbols of each state: the *capital*, a *map*, the *flag*, the *national anthem*, the *monetary unit*, the system of *weights and measures, holidays*, and *time*, each article proceeds to cover, as thoroughly as available data permit, 50 individual phases of the country's life, so as to furnish an over-all picture of its present as rooted in the past evolution of its institutions, customs, and traditions.

A precise definition of *location, size, and extent* of the individual territory is given, so that the reader can visualize, as a living reality, that which the map depicts graphically.

Topography, climate, and *flora and fauna* supplement the other natural physical features of the respective nation.

More than by any other factor, countries are what they are because of man's exertions to create his own environment, so *population, ethnic groups,* and *language* are the next items covered. Together with the section devoted to *religion*, they give a basic understanding of the demographic phenomena that determine the basic institutions, political, economic, and social, of each sovereign unit. It is impressive to notice how, notwithstanding centuries of effort to isolate certain communities in accordance with peculiar standards within restricted national boundaries, peoples have continued to live in a world of capillary communicating oases, through which the blood, the language, and varied concepts of religion, law, social organization, economic structure, and culture, have interpenetrated each other and reached that considerable degree of fundamental

xiii

cross-fertilized standard without which the present broad feeling of community could never have arisen.

Transportation and *communications* follow in the description of the positive factors working for the consolidation of each country's internal unity and of the reconstruction of the wider oneness of mankind.

Next there is a *historical survey*, in most cases kept brief because of the availability of comprehensive ones in other sources of general information.

As the result of individual national experience various *types of governmental authority* have been either adopted from the similar experience of other peoples or created to meet different requirements. In the operation of governments, there are diverse types of machinery which correspond to particular political philosophies and which the citizens control through *political parties*. Descriptions of the *local governmental structures* supplement the system of deliberative and executive authorities in charge of public interests.

Knowledge of the organizational pattern of the *judiciary* acquires considerable importance for all kinds of individual and corporate activities within a particular nation, so information is furnished thereon.

The internal stability of a country and its international security are made clear by adequate data on the organization and potential of the *armed forces*.

Because the pattern of *migrations* has undergone great changes, information on their effect upon demographic developments in each state is of deep significance for any evaluation of manpower prospects and consumer potentials.

No nation is an isolated unit unto itself. Problems formerly deemed of exclusive domestic concern have gradually acquired international significance, and are the object of intrastate cooperation in the search for adequate solutions through intergovernmental bodies. The extent to which each government engages in such *international cooperation* is a useful indicator of its concern with the peaceful handling of potential sources of tensions and conflicts. The second part of the encyclopedia covers the definition of the purposes and operations of such multinational bodies.

One of the phases of internal development with an international impact relates to the wide range of the economy. Outside of highly specialized handbooks, mostly regional in scope, and of yearly statistical reports frequently published after considerable delay, there are no accessible over-all sources of ready reference to which an individual can resort. In order to meet the demand of academic, financial, industrial, foreign trade, and other related activities, this encyclopedia deals comprehensively with *income, labor, agriculture, animal husbandry, fishing, forestry, mining, energy and power, industry, domestic trade, foreign trade, balance of payments, banking, insurance, securities, public finance, taxation, customs and duties, foreign investment,* and *economic policy*.

It also gives information on *health, social welfare,* and *housing,* important in the economically less developed nations as a mainspring of economic activity and financial investment for what is called the infrastructure, vital as a prerequisite of other actions to promote production, employment, higher standards of living and, in general, a broader enjoyment of basic human rights and fundamental freedoms by individuals and collectives.

While the domestic activities mentioned in the two previous paragraphs aim to ensure the availability of economic and financial means to fight the prevailing poverty and manpower shortages caused by health disabilities and social injustice, they also help in the struggle against illiteracy which, in even more advanced countries, reduces the number of citizens actively engaged in political life and is instrumental in the growth and maintenance of discriminatory practices and arbitrary stereotypes within each nation and between many nations. It is of the utmost importance to know the *educational* facilities available for supplying trained political leaders, administrators, economists, social workers, medical personnel, and technicians in industry, trade and commerce, agriculture, and livestock production required by ever more complex domestic structures and international cooperation. And to data on teaching establishments is added information on *libraries and museums* and on the *organizations* set up by the people of each country to promote their collective interests and welfare.

The *press* and other media of information and enlightenment constitute an important index of the cultural standing of the people; the degree of their freedom is the best evidence of the intellectual maturity of government and governed, and a significant indicator of the degree to which essential human rights in the field of opinion are truly respected.

Perhaps the most effective way to advance reciprocal understanding is by contacts among peoples of different countries and with each other's natural environment. The conditions which must be met for the purposes of *tourism* are fully explained.

Dependencies for which each individual state assumes international responsibilities are described in detail.

Finally a brief roll of *famous persons* is a biographical listing of national figures.

An up-to-date *bibliography*, for those who may wish to learn more about any of the states, closes each nation's description.

Such is the first part of our encyclopedia. But in our day and era nations are not islands unto themselves, busy solely with internal problems of varying magnitude. The field of exclusively domestic concern is shrinking under the tremendous impact of easy communications among nations.

Although political events, reported spectacularly by the mass media of information everywhere, may create serious doubts in the public mind as to the existence of other wide areas of common interest, the fact is that, where international cooperation is possible and essential to the smooth coexistence of diverse and even conflicting national interests, the machinery created by intergovernmental agreements to promote the peaceful working together and adjustment of relations has never been as abundant or covered such a broad variety of matters.

It is impossible in our day to understand the patterns of national development without reference to the impact of constant exchanges of governmental views on a broad range of individual problems or groups of problems within the multilateral agencies they have instituted for this very purpose of adjustment and reconcilement.

While the United Nations and the regional organizations of American states, directly or through their subsidiary or associated organs, may and do deal with practically every field of human interest, other organizations restrict their jurisdiction to the more specific areas of economic or social matters. They handle issues at the universal and at the close neighborhood levels and, large or small, they each play a part in the process of international cooperation to improve and give constructive meaning to the relations among peoples.

True, there are multilateral organizations set up primarily for collective defense and the promotion of closely knit specific national objectives, mostly of a political nature; but, significantly, even such military pacts have gradually broadened the scope of their concern as a result of the finding that merely negative aims do not afford by themselves the stability and coherence for which they were brought into being. Such enlargement of the area of original competence is effected through the direct adoption of additional responsibilities or the conclusion of collateral agreements for specific purposes.

Since the participants in all these organizations are, with a few exceptions of a primarily temporary nature, members of the United Nations, they are careful not to violate the charter of San Francisco and rather claim that they should be recognized as covered by Chapter VIII, or under the permissive provision of Article 51.

The Secretary-General of the United Nations, Mr. Dag Hammarskjöld, has repeatedly stated his views that any collective action conducted outside the United Nations, but consonant with the spirit of its charter, can be considered as cooperation toward the fundamental objectives of the world organization. Such is the specific case in regard to the Council of Foreign Ministers of the big powers, which deals with vital political issues at its meetings although it has no permanent international secretariat or services. Such are also meetings of responsible chiefs of state.

Because we live under the impact of global issues that affect every individual, for good or for ill, and because also of the advance of democratic processes domestically and internationally, more and more people are now actively concerned with the course of world affairs. The best channels to voice their hopes are the governments democratically elected and responsible to the wishes of the citizenry. When the people disagree with their authorities, whose judgment must necessarily take into account factors not always of public knowledge, the people then can use their nongovernmental bodies to express their prevailing views.

These international bodies are explained in the second part of the encyclopedia, so that individuals in all walks of life may know how to use them for the general welfare of all peoples and states.

The Worldmark Encyclopedia of the Nations is a pioneer effort. It is our earnest hope that this first edition may prove a truly useful tool to everyone.

BENJAMIN A. COHEN
Editor-in-Chief

Contents

Acknowledgments   vi

Foreword   vii

Preface   ix

Introduction to
the First Edition   xi

Index to Countries
and Territories   xix

Conversion Tables   xxii

Abbreviations   xxiii

Symbols   xxvi

THE UNITED NATIONS

Organizational Chart of
The United Nations System   2

Structure of the
United Nations System   3

Comparison with the
League of Nations   5

The Making of the
United Nations   8

Purposes and Principles   10

Membership   11

UN Headquarters and
Facilities   14

The United Nations Budget   17

The General Assembly   20

The Security Council   25

The Economic and Social
Council   30

The Trusteeship Council   33

International Court
of Justice   36

The Secretariat   41

The Political Role of the
Secretary General   44

Maintaining Peace and Security   49

Disarmament   58

Peaceful Uses of Outer Space   64

Preservation of the Seabed and
the Ocean Floor for Peaceful
Uses   66

UN Regional Economic
Commissions   67

Economic Commission
for Europe   68

Economic Commission for
Africa   70

Economic Commission for
Asia and the Far East   72

Economic Commission for
Latin America   74

Economic and Social
Development   77

The First Development
Decade   77

The Second Development
Decade   78

Technical Cooperation for
Development   81

Financing Development   84

United Nations Development
Program   91

Special Areas of Social
Progress   97

United Nations Children's
Fund   97

Narcotic Drugs Control   102

The Human Environment   108

Human Rights and the
United Nations   109

Assistance to Refugees   117

United Nations Relief and Works
Agency for Palestine
Refugees   119

Independence of Colonial
Peoples   123

The International Law
Commission   133

United Nations Bibliography   138

INTERNATIONAL LABOR
    ORGANIZATION (ILO)   139

FOOD AND AGRICULTURAL
    ORGANIZATION OF THE
    UNITED NATIONS (FAO)   153

WORLD HEALTH ORGANIZATION
    (WHO)   165

UNITED NATIONS EDUCATIONAL,
    SCIENTIFIC AND CULTURAL
    ORGANIZATION (UNESCO)   178

INTERNATIONAL MONETARY
    FUND (IMF)   192

INTERNATIONAL BANK FOR
    RECONSTRUCTION AND
    DEVELOPMENT (IBRD)   198

INTERNATIONAL FINANCE
    CORPORATION (IFC)   206

INTERNATIONAL DEVELOPMENT
    ASSOCIATION (IDA)   209

GENERAL AGREEMENT ON
    TARIFFS AND TRADE
    (GATT)   212

INTERNATIONAL ATOMIC
    ENERGY AGENCY (IAEA)   218

INTERNATIONAL CIVIL AVIATION
    ORGANIZATION (ICAO)   225

INTERNATIONAL
    TELECOMMUNICATION
    UNION (ITU)   232

UNIVERSAL POSTAL UNION
    (UPU)   236

INTER-GOVERNMENTAL
    MARITIME CONSULTATIVE
    ORGANIZATION (IMCO)   240

WORLD METEOROLOGICAL
    ORGANIZATION (WMO)   243

Glossary of
    Intergovernmental
    Organizations (IGO's)   247

    Table of IGO Membership   260

INDEX   271

Key to Subject Headings

All information contained in each of the articles on the United Nations specialized and related agencies is uniformly keyed by means of small superior numerals to the left of the subject headings, as follows:

1 Background
2 Creation
3 Purposes
4 Membership
5 Structure
6 Budget
7 Activities
8 Bibliography

Index to Countries and Territories

This alphabetical list includes countries and dependencies (colonies, protectorates, and other territories) described in the encyclopedia. It indicates in which continental volume (printed in *italics*) the article treating a particular country or dependency appears. Dependencies are listed here with the title of the volume in which they are treated, followed by the name of the article in which they are dealt with. The name of the volume *Asia and Australasia* was abbreviated in this list to *Asia*.

Adélie Land—*Asia*: French Southern and Antarctic Territories
Aden—*Asia*: Southern Yemen
Afars and the Issas, Territory of the—*Africa*: French African Dependencies
Afghanistan—*Asia*
Albania—*Europe*
Algeria—*Africa*
American Samoa—*Asia*: US Pacific Dependencies
Andaman Islands—*Asia*: India
Andorra—*Europe*
Angola—*Africa*: Portuguese African Dependencies
Anguilla—*Americas*: UK American Dependencies: Leeward Islands
Antigua—*Americas*: UK American Dependencies: Leeward Islands
Arabia, Federation of South—*Asia*: Southern Yemen
Arabia, Saʿudi—*Asia*: Saʿudi Arabia
Argentina—*Americas*
Aruba—*Americas*: Netherlands American Dependencies: Netherlands Antilles
Ashmore and Cartier Islands—*Asia*: Australia
Australia—*Asia*
Austria—*Europe*
Azores—*Europe*: Portugal

Bahama Islands—*Americas*: UK American Dependencies
Bahrayn—*Asia*: Persian Gulf Shaykhdoms
Barbados—*Americas*
Basutoland—*Africa*: Lesotho
Bechuanaland—*Africa*: Botswana
Belgium—*Europe*
Bermuda—*Americas*: UK American Dependencies
Bhutan—*Asia*
Bolivia—*Americas*
Bonin Islands—*Asia*: US Pacific Dependencies: Pacific Islands under Provisional US Administration
Borneo, North—*Asia*: Malaysia: Sabah
Botswana—*Africa*
Bouvet Island—*Europe*: Norway
Brazil—*Americas*
British Antarctic Territory—*Americas*: UK American Dependencies
British Honduras—*Americas*
British Virgin Islands—*Americas*: UK American Dependencies
Brunei—*Asia*: UK Asian and Pacific Dependencies
Bulgaria—*Europe*
Burma—*Asia*
Burundi—*Africa*

Caicos Islands—*Americas*: UK American Dependencies: Turks and Caicos Islands
Cambodia—*Asia*
Cameroon—*Africa*
Canada—*Americas*
Canal Zone—*Americas*: US
Canary Islands—*Europe*: Spain

Canton and Enderbury Islands—*Asia*: UK Asian and Pacific Dependencies: Gilbert and Ellice Islands; US Pacific Dependencies
Cape Verde Islands—*Africa*: Portuguese African Dependencies
Caroline Islands—*Asia*: US Pacific Dependencies: Trust Territory of the Pacific Islands
Cayman Islands—*Americas*: UK American Dependencies
Central African Republic—*Africa*
Ceuta—*Europe*: Spain
Ceylon—*Asia*
Chad—*Africa*
Chile—*Americas*
China (People's Republic of China)—*Asia*
China (Republic of China)—*Asia*: Taiwan
Christmas Island—*Asia*: Australia
Christmas Island—*Asia*: UK Asian and Pacific Dependencies: Gilbert and Ellice Islands
Cocos (Keeling) Islands—*Asia*: Australia
Colombia—*Americas*
Columbus Archipelago—*Americas*: Ecuador
Comoro Islands—*Africa*: French African Dependencies
Congo (Brazzaville)—*Africa*
Congo (Kinshasa)—*Africa*
Cook Islands—*Asia*: New Zealand
Corn Islands—*Americas*: US
Costa Rica—*Americas*
Cuba—*Americas*
Curaçao—*Americas*: Netherlands American Dependencies: Netherlands Antilles
Cyprus—*Asia*
Czechoslovakia—*Europe*

Dahomey—*Africa*
Denmark—*Europe*
Diego Ramirez Island—*Americas*: Chile
Dominica—*Americas*: UK American Dependencies: Windward Islands
Dominican Republic—*Americas*
Dutch Guiana—*Americas*: Netherlands American Dependencies: Surinam

East Germany—*Europe*: Germany, East
Easter Island—*Americas*: Chile
Ecuador—*Americas*
Egypt—*Africa*: UAR
El Salvador—*Americas*
England—*Europe*: UK
Equatorial Guinea—*Africa*
Estonia—*Europe*: USSR
Ethiopia—*Africa*

Falkland Islands—*Americas*: UK American Dependencies
Faeroe Islands—*Europe*: Denmark
Federation of Malaya—*Asia*: Malaysia
Fernando Póo—*Africa*: Equatorial Guinea

Index to Countries and Territories

Fiji—*Asia*
Finland—*Europe*
Formosa—*Asia*: Taiwan
France—*Europe*
French Guiana—*Americas*: French American Dependencies
French Polynesia—*Asia*: French Pacific Dependencies
French Somaliland—*Africa*: French African Dependencies
French Southern and Antarctic Territories—*Asia*: French Pacific Dependencies

Gabon—*Africa*
Galápagos Islands—*Americas*: Ecuador
Gambia—*Africa*
Germany, East—*Europe*
Germany, West—*Europe*
Ghana—*Africa*
Gibraltar—*Europe*: UK
Gilbert and Ellice Islands—*Asia*: UK Asian and Pacific Dependencies
Graham Land—*Americas*: UK American Dependencies: British Antarctic Territory
Great Britain—*Europe*: UK
Greece—*Europe*
Greenland—*Europe*: Denmark
Grenada—*Americas*: UK American Dependencies: Windward Islands
Guadeloupe—*Americas*: French American Dependencies
Guam—*Asia*: US Pacific Dependencies
Guatemala—*Americas*
Guiana, British—*Americas*: Guyana
Guiana, Dutch—*Americas*: Netherlands American Dependencies: Surinam
Guiana. French—*Americas*: French American Dependencies
Guinea—*Africa*
Guinea, Portuguese—*Africa*: Portuguese African Dependencies
Guinea, Spanish—*Africa*: Spanish African Dependencies: Spanish Equatorial Region
Guyana—*Americas*

Haiti—*Americas*
Heard and McDonald Islands—*Asia*: Australia
Honduras—*Americas*
Honduras, British—*Americas*
Hong Kong—*Asia*: UK Asian and Pacific Dependencies
Howland, Baker, and Jarvis Islands—*Asia*: US Pacific Dependencies
Hungary—*Europe*

Iceland—*Europe*
Ifni—*Africa*: Morocco
India—*Asia*
Indonesia—*Asia*
Inner Mongolia—*Asia*: China
Iran—*Asia*
Iraq—*Asia*
Ireland—*Europe*
Ireland, Northern—*Europe*: UK
Israel—*Asia*
Italy—*Europe*
Ivory Coast—*Africa*

Jamaica—*Americas*
Jan Mayen—*Europe*: Norway
Johnston Island—*Asia*: US Pacific Dependencies
Jordan—*Asia*
Juan Fernandez—*Americas*: Chile

Kenya—*Africa*
Korea, North—*Asia*
Korea, South—*Asia*
Kuwait—*Asia*

Laos—*Asia*
Lebanon—*Asia*
Leeward Islands—*Americas*: UK American Dependencies
Lesotho—*Africa*

Liberia—*Africa*
Libya—*Africa*
Liechtenstein—*Europe*
Lithuania—*Europe*: USSR
Luxembourg—*Europe*

Macao—*Asia*: Portuguese Asian Dependencies
Macquarie Island—*Asia*: Australia
Madagascar—*Africa*
Madeira—*Europe*: Portugal
Malagasy Republic—*Africa*: Madagascar
Malawi—*Africa*
Malaya—*Asia*: Malaysia
Malaysia—*Asia*
Maldive Islands—*Asia*: Maldives
Maldives—*Asia*
Mali—*Africa*
Malta—*Europe*
Mariana Islands—*Asia*: US Pacific Dependencies: Trust Territory of the Pacific Islands
Marquesas Islands—*Asia*: French Pacific Dependencies: French Polynesia
Marshall Islands—*Asia*: US Pacific Dependencies: Trust Territory of the Pacific Islands
Martinique—*Americas*: French American Dependencies
Matsu Islands—*Asia*: Taiwan
Mauritania—*Africa*
Mauritius—*Africa*
Melilla—*Europe*: Spain
Mexico—*Americas*
Midway—*Asia*: US Pacific Dependencies
Monaco—*Europe*
Mongolia—*Asia*
Montserrat—*Americas*: UK American Dependencies: Leeward Islands
Morocco—*Africa*
Mozambique—*Africa*: Portuguese African Dependencies
Muscat and Oman—*Asia*: Oman

Namibia—*Africa*: South Africa
Nauru—*Asia*
Nepal—*Asia*
Netherlands Antilles—*Americas*: Netherlands American Dependencies
Nevis—*Americas*: UK American Dependencies: Leeward Islands
New Caledonia—*Asia*: French Pacific Dependencies
New Guinea—*Asia*: Australia
New Guinea, West—*Asia*: Indonesia
New Hebrides—*Asia*: French Pacific Dependencies
New Zealand—*Asia*
Nicaragua—*Americas*
Niger—*Africa*
Nigeria—*Africa*
Niue—*Asia*: New Zealand
Norfolk Island—*Asia*: Australia
North Borneo—*Asia*: Malaysia: Sabah
North Korea—*Asia*: Korea, North
North Viet-Nam—*Asia*: Viet-Nam, North
Northern Rhodesia—*Africa*: Zambia
Norway—*Europe*
Nyasaland—*Africa*: Malawi

Oman—*Asia*
Oman, Trucial—*Asia*: Persian Gulf Shaykhdoms
Outer Mongolia—*Asia*: Mongolia

Pacific Islands, Trust Territory of the—*Asia*: US Pacific Dependencies
Pacific Islands under Provisional US Administration—*Asia*: US Pacific Dependencies
Pakistan—*Asia*
Palmyra Island—*Asia*: US Pacific Dependencies
Panama—*Americas*
Panama Canal Zone—*Americas*: US
Papua—*Asia*: Australia: New Guinea

Index to Countries and Territories

Paraguay—*Americas*
Persian Gulf Shaykhdoms—*Asia*
Peru—*Americas*
Peter I Island—*Europe*: Norway
Philippines—*Asia*
Pitcairn Island—*Asia*: UK Asian and Pacific Dependencies
Poland—*Europe*
Portugal—*Europe*
Portuguese East Africa—*Africa*: Portugal: Mozambique
Portuguese Guinea—*Africa*: Portuguese African Dependencies
Portuguese Timor—*Asia*: Portuguese Asian Dependencies
Portuguese West Africa—*Africa*: Portuguese African Dependencies: Angola
Puerto Rico—*Americas*: US

Qatar—*Asia*: Persian Gulf Shaykhdoms
Queen Maud Land—*Europe*: Norway
Quemoy Islands—*Asia*: Taiwan

Réunion—*Africa*: French African Dependencies
Rhodesia—*Africa*
Río de Oro—*Africa*: Spanish African Dependencies: Spanish Sahara
Río Muni—*Africa*: Equatorial Guinea
Romania—*Europe*
Ross Dependency—*Asia*: New Zealand
Ruanda-Urundi—*Africa*: Burundi; Rwanda
Rwanda—*Africa*
Ryukyu Islands—*Asia*: US Pacific Dependencies: Pacific Islands under Provisional US Administration

St. Christopher—*Americas*: UK American Dependencies: Leeward Islands
St. Helena—*Africa*: UK African Dependencies
St. Kitts—*Americas*: UK American Dependencies: Leeward Islands
St. Lucia—*Americas*: UK American Dependencies: Windward Islands
Saint Pierre and Miquelon—*Americas*: French American Dependencies
St. Vincent—*Americas*: UK American Dependencies: Windward Islands
Sala y Gómez Island—*Americas*: Chile
Samoa, American—*Asia*: US Pacific Dependencies
Samoa, Western—*Asia*: Western Samoa
San Ambrosio Island—*Americas*: Chile
San Félix Island—*Americas*: Chile
San Marino—*Europe*
São Tomé and Príncipe—*Africa*: Portuguese African Dependencies
Sarawak—*Asia*: Malaysia
Saʿudi Arabia—*Asia*
Scotland—*Europe*: UK
Senegal—*Africa*
Seychelles—*Africa*: UK African Dependencies
Sierra Leone—*Africa*
Sikkim—*Asia*: India
Singapore—*Asia*
Society Islands—*Asia*: French Pacific Dependencies: French Polynesia
Solomon Islands—*Asia*: UK Asian Dependencies
Somalia—*Africa*
Somaliland, French—*Africa*: French African Dependencies
South Africa—*Africa*
South Arabia, Federation of—*Asia*: Southern Yemen
South Georgia—*Americas*: UK American Dependencies: Falkland Islands
South Korea—*Asia*: Korea, South
South Viet-Nam—*Asia*: Viet-Nam, South
South West Africa—*Africa*: South Africa

Southern Rhodesia—*Africa*: Rhodesia
Southern Yemen—*Asia*
Spain—*Europe*
Spanish Guinea—*Africa*: Equatorial Guinea
Spanish Sahara—*Africa*: Spanish African Dependencies
Sudan—*Africa*
Surinam—*Americas*: Netherlands American Dependencies
Svalbard—*Europe*: Norway
Swan Islands—*Americas*: US
Swaziland—*Africa*
Sweden—*Europe*
Switzerland—*Europe*
Syria—*Asia*

Tahiti—*Asia*: French Pacific Dependencies: French Polynesia
Taiwan—*Asia*
Tanganyika—*Africa*: Tanzania
Tanzania—*Africa*
Thailand—*Asia*
Tibet—*Asia*: China
Timor, Portuguese—*Asia*: Portuguese Asian Dependencies
Tobago—*Americas*: Trinidad and Tobago
Togo—*Africa*
Tokelau Islands—*Asia*: New Zealand
Tonga—*Asia*
Trinidad and Tobago—*Americas*
Tristan da Cunha—*Africa*: UK African Dependencies: St. Helena
Trucial Oman—*Asia*: Persian Gulf Shaykhdoms
Trust Territory of the Pacific Islands—*Asia*: US Pacific Dependencies
Tuamotu Islands—*Asia*: French Asian Dependencies: French Polynesia
Tunisia—*Africa*
Turkey—*Asia*
Turks and Caicos Islands—*Americas*: UK American Dependencies

Uganda—*Africa*
USSR—*Europe*
UAR—*Asia*
UK—*Europe*
US—*Americas*
Upper Volta—*Africa*
Uruguay—*Americas*

Vatican City—*Europe*
Venezuela—*Americas*
Viet-Nam, North—*Asia*
Viet-Nam, South—*Asia*
Virgin Islands, British—*Americas*: UK American Dependencies
Virgin Islands of the US—*Americas*: US
Volcano Islands—*Asia*: US Pacific Dependencies: Pacific Islands under Provisional US Administration

Wake Island—*Asia*: US Pacific Dependencies
Wallis and Futuna Islands—*Asia*: French Asian Dependencies
West Germany—*Europe*: Germany, West
West Irian—*Asia*: Indonesia
Western Samoa—*Asia*
Windward Islands—*Americas*: UK American Dependencies

Yemen—*Asia*
Yugoslavia—*Europe*

Zambia—*Africa*
Zanzibar—*Africa*: Tanzania

Conversion Tables

LENGTH

1 centimeter	0.3937 inch
1 centimeter	0.03280833 foot
1 meter (100 centimeters)	3.280833 feet
1 meter	1.093611 US yards
1 kilometer (1,000 meters)	0.62137 statute mile
1 kilometer	0.539957 nautical mile
1 inch	2.540005 centimeters
1 foot (12 inches)	30.4801 centimeters
1 US yard (3 feet)	0.914402 meter
1 statute mile (5,280 feet; 1,760 yards)	1.609347 kilometers
1 British mile	1.609344 kilometers
1 nautical mile (1.1508 statute miles or 6,076.10333 feet)	1.852 kilometers
1 British nautical mile (6,080 feet)	1.85319 kilometers

AREA

1 sq. centimeter	0.154999 sq. inch
1 sq. meter (10,000 sq. centimeters)	10.76387 sq. feet
1 sq. meter	1.1959585 sq. yards
1 hectare (10,000 sq. meters)	2.47104 acres
1 sq. kilometer (100 hectares)	0.386101 sq. mile
1 sq. inch	6.451626 sq. centimeters
1 sq. foot (144 sq. inches)	0.092903 sq. meter
1 sq. yard (9 sq. feet)	0.836131 sq. meter
1 acre (4,840 sq. yards)	0.404687 hectare
1 sq. mile (640 acres)	2.589998 sq. kilometers

VOLUME

1 cubic centimeter	0.061023 cubic inch
1 cubic meter (1,000,000 cubic centimeters)	35.31445 cubic feet
1 cubic meter	1.307943 cubic yards
1 cubic inch	16.387162 cubic centimeters
1 cubic foot (1,728 cubic inches)	0.028317 cubic meter
1 cubic yard (27 cubic feet)	0.764559 cubic meter

LIQUID MEASURE

1 liter	0.8799 Imperial quart
1 liter	1.05671 US quarts
1 hectoliter	21.9975 Imperial gallons
1 hectoliter	26.4178 US gallons
1 Imperial quart	1.136491 liters
1 US quart	0.946333 liter
1 Imperial gallon	0.04546 hectoliter
1 US gallon	0.037853 hectoliter

WEIGHT

1 kilogram (1,000 grams)	35.27396 avoirdupois ounces
1 kilogram	32.15074 Troy ounces
1 kilogram	2.204622 avoirdupois pounds
1 quintal (100 kg)	220.4622 avoirdupois pounds
1 quintal	1.9684125 hundredweights
1 metric ton (1,000 kg)	1.1023x1 short tons
1 metric ton	0.984206 long ton
1 avoirdupois ounce	0.0283495 kilogram
1 troy ounce	0.0311035 kilogram
1 avoirdupois pound	0.453592 kilogram
1 avoirdupois pound	0.00453592 quintal
1 hundredweight (cwt., 112 lb.)	0.50802 quintal
1 short ton (2,000 lb.)	0.907185 metric ton
1 long ton (2,240 lb.)	1.016047 metric tons

ELECTRIC ENERGY

1 horsepower (hp)	0.7457 kilowatt
1 kilowatt (kw)	1.34102 horsepower

TEMPERATURE

Centigrade (C)	Fahrenheit − 32° × 5/9
Fahrenheit (F)	9/5 Centigrade + 32°

BUSHELS

	LB.	METRIC TON	BUSHELS PER METRIC TON
Barley (US)	48	0.021772	45.931
(UK)	50	0.02268	44.092
Corn (UK, US)	56	0.025401	39.368
Linseed (UK)	52	0.023587	42.396
(Australia, US)	56	0.025401	39.368
Oats (US)	32	0.014515	68.894
(Canada)	34	0.015422	64.842
	40	0.018144	55.115
Potatoes (UK, US)	60	0.027216	36.743
Rice (Australia)	42	0.019051	52.491
(US)	45	0.020412	48.991
Rye (UK, US)	56	0.025401	39.368
(Australia)	60	0.027216	36.743
Soybeans (US)	60	0.027216	36.743
Wheat (UK, US)	60	0.027216	36.743

BAGS OF COFFEE

	LB.	KG	BAGS PER METRIC TON
Brazil, Colombia, Mexico, Venezuela	132.28	60	16.667
El Salvador	152.12	69	14.493
Haiti	185.63	84.2	11.876

BALES OF COTTON

	LB.	METRIC TON	BALES PER METRIC TON
India	392	0.177808	5.624
Brazil	397	0.18	5.555
US (net)	480	0.217724	4.593
US (gross)	500	0.226796	4.409

PETROLEUM

Barrels of petroleum can be derived by dividing the number of metric tons by the average specific gravity indicated and multiplying the result by 2.898:

0.79 Netherlands, New Guinea
0.82 Chile, Cuba, Hungary, Italy, Qatar
0.83 Algeria, Ecuador
0.84 Brunei, Burma, India, Iran, Iraq, Pakistan, Peru, Romania, Sarawak
0.85 Canada, Indonesia, Morocco, Poland, Sa'udi Arabia, US
0.86 Bahrayn, Brazil, Israel, Kuwait, UK
0.87 Colombia
0.89 West Germany, Taiwan, Yugoslavia
0.90 Argentina, France, Japan, Kuwait Neutral Zone, Mexico, Netherlands, South Africa, Spain
0.91 Trinidad and Tobago, UAR
0.92 Venezuela
0.93 Austria, Czechoslovakia
0.94 Albania, Turkey
0.97 Sweden

One barrel = 42 US gallons = 34.97 Imperial gallons = 158.99 liters = 0.15899 cubic meters (or 1 cubic meter = 6.2898 barrels).

Abbreviations

AALCC—Asian African Legal Consultative Committee
AAPSO—Afro-Asian Rural Reconstruction Organization
AB—Balkan Alliance
ABA—A. B. Aerotransport (Swedish Air Lines)
a.c.—alternating current
ACC—Advisory Committee on Coordination
ACSSRB—Administrative Center of Social Security for Rhine Boatmen
A.D.—Anno Domini (in the year of our Lord)
AEF—French Equatorial Africa
Aeroflot—Soviet Airlines
AFL-CIO—American Federation of Labor–Congress of Industrial Organizations
AFPU—African Postal Union
AID—[US] Agency for International Development
AL—Arab League (League of Arab States)
Alitalia—Società Aerolinee Italiane Internazionali (Italian Airlines)
a.m.—morning
AM—amplitude modulation
AMSA—Aeronaves de México, S.A.
ANZUS—Security Treaty between Australia, New Zealand, and the United States of America
AOF—French West Africa
AOPU—Asian Oceanic Postal Union
APA—Aerovías Panamá
APFC—Asia Pacific Forestry Commission
APO—Asian Productivity Organization
APTU—African Postal and Telecommunications Union
ARPEL—Mutual Assistance of the Latin American Government Oil Companies
ASA—Association of Southeast Asia
ASFEC—Arab States Fundamental Education Center
ASPAC—Asian and Pacific Council
ASSR—Autonomous Soviet Socialist Republic
ATEC—Transequatorial Communications Agency
AUA—Austrian National Airlines
AVENSA—Aerovías Venezolanas, S.A.
Aviaco—Aviación y Comercio
Avianco—Aerovías Nacionales de Colombia

b.—born
B.C.—Before Christ
BCG—Bacillus Calmette-Guérin
BEA—British European Airways Corporation
BENELUX—Benelux Economic Union (Belgium-Netherlands-Luxembourg Economic Union)
Bibliog.—bibliography
BIE—International Bureau of Exhibitions
BIS—Bank for International Settlements
BIS—Inter-African Bureau for Soils
BLEU—Belgium-Luxembourg Economic Union
BOAC—British Overseas Airways Corporation
Braniff—Braniff International Airways
BTAO—UN Bureau of Technical Assistance Operations

c.—circa (about)
C—centigrade
C-Plan—Colombo Plan for Cooperative Economic Development
CAARC—Commonwealth Advisory Aeronautical Research Council
CAB—Commonwealth Agricultural Bureau
CACM—Central American Common Market
CAME—Conference of Allied Ministers of Education

CARE—Cooperative for American Remittances to Everywhere, Inc.
Caribair—Caribbean Atlantic Airlines
CARIFTA—Caribbean Free Trade Area
CAS—Commercial Air Services
CCC—Customs Cooperation Council
CCC—European Council for Cultural Cooperation
CCIR—International Radio Consultative Committee
CCITT—International Telegraph and Telephone Consultative Committee
CCP—Committee on Commodity Problems (of the FAO)
CCTA—Commission for Technical Cooperation in Africa
CD—Danube Commission
CDA—Compañía Dominicana de Aviación
CEC—Commonwealth Economic Committee
CECC—Commonwealth Economic Consultative Council
CELC—Commonwealth Education Liaison Committee
CEMA—Council for Mutual Economic Aid
CEMLA—Latin American Center for Monetary Studies
CENTO—Central Treaty Organization
CENTRO—Latin American Center for Social Sciences Research
CEPT—European Conference of Postal and Telecommunications Administration
CERN—European Organization for Nuclear Research
CFA—Communauté Financière Africaine
CFP—Colonies Françaises du Pacifique
CFP—Communauté Française du Pacifique
CGT—Confédération Générale du Travail
CGTA—Compagnie Générale du Transport Aérien
CIAP—Inter-American Committee on the Alliance for Progress
CIB—International Council for Building Research, Studies, and Documentation
CIDA—Inter-American Committee for Agricultural Development
CIDEM—Inter-American Music Council
CIEC—International Commission of Civil Status
CIEF—International Commission of Civil Status
CIESMM—International Commission for Scientific Exploration of the Mediterranean Sea
c.i.f.—cost, insurance, and freight
CIO—Congress of Industrial Organizations
CIOMS—Council of International Organizations of Medical Science
CIPSH—International Council for Philosophy and Humanistic Studies
CIS—International Occupational Safety and Health Information Center
CISS—Inter-American Conference on Social Security
CLAF—Latin American Center of Physics
CMA—Compañía Mexicana de Aviación
CO—Caribbean Organization
CODECA—Caribbean Economic Development Corporation
CODIP—Hague Conference on Private International Law
COJ—Court of Justice
COMECON—Council for Mutual Economic Aid
comp.—compiled, compiler
Cons.—Conservative
COPA—Compañía Panameña de Aviación
COSPAR—Committee on Space Research of the International Council of Scientific Unions
CPPS—Permanent Commission for the Conservation of the Maritime Resources of the South Pacific
CRC—Central Commission for the Navigation of the Rhine
CREFAL—Regional Fundamental Education Center for Latin America
CSA—Coal and Steel Authority
CTB—Commonwealth Telecommunications Board
cu.—cubic

CUBANA—Compañía Cubana de Aviación
cwt—hundredweight

d.—daily
d.—died
DCML—Diplomatic Conference of International Maritime Law
DDT—dichlorodiphenyltrichloroethane
Delta—Delta Air Lines
DF—Development Fund
DH—Hungarian Airlines
DLCOEA—Desert Locust Control Organization for Eastern Africa

e.—evening
E—east
EAAC—East African Airways Corporation
EAAFRO—East African Agricultural and Forestry Research Organization
EAEC—European Atomic Energy Community
Eagle—Luxembourg Airlines Company
EAMA—Association of the EEC and African and Malagasy States
ECA—Economic Commission for Africa
ECAC—European Civil Aviation Conference
ECAFE—Economic Commission for Asia and the Far East
ECCFD—European Commission for the Control of Foot-and-Mouth Disease
ECCP—European Committee on Crime Problems
ECE—Economic Commission for Europe
ECLA—Economic Commission for Latin America
ECMT—European Conference of Ministers of Transport
ECOSOC—Economic and Social Council [of the United Nations]
ECSC—European Coal and Steel Community
ed.—editor, edited, edition
EDF—European Development Fund
EEC—European Economic Council
EFC—European Forestry Commission
EFTA—European Free Trade Association
e.g.—exemplia gratia (for example)
EIB—European Investment Bank
EL AL—EL AL Israel Airlines
ELDO—European Launching Development Organization
ELMA—Empresa Líneas Maritimas Argentinas
EMA—European Monetary Agreement
ENEA—European Nuclear Energy Agency
EPPO—European and Mediterranean Plant Protection Organization
EPTA—Expanded Program of Technical Assistance
ESAPAC—Advanced School of Public Administration for Central America
ESC—Economic and Social Committee
ESF—European Social Fund
ESRO—European Space Research Association
est.—estimate(d)
et al.—et alii (and others)
EURATOM—European Atomic Energy Community
EUROCHEMIC—European Company for the Chemical Processing of Irradiated Fuels
EUROFIMA—European Company for the Financing of Railway Rolling Stock

f.—founded
F—Fahrenheit
FAC—Fonds d'Aide et de Coopération
FAO—Food and Agriculture Organization [of the United Nations]
FED—European Fund for Development
FIDES—Fonds d'Investissement pour le Développement Economique et Social
ff.—following
fl.—flourished
FLASCO—Latin American Social Science Faculty
FM—frequency modulation
f.o.b.—free on board
ft—foot, feet

GATT—General Agreement on Tariffs and Trade
GDP—gross domestic product

GFCM—General Fisheries Council for the Mediterranean
GHz—gigaherz
gm.—gram(s)
GMT—Greenwich Mean Time
GNP—gross national product
GRT—gross registered tons (tonnage)

HCFR—High Commissioner for Refugees
hp—horsepower

IACJ—Inter-American Council of Jurists
IACO—Inter-African Coffee Organization
IACW—Inter-American Commission of Women
IADB—Inter-American Defense Board
IAEA—International Atomic Energy Agency
IAIAS—Inter-American Institute of Agricultural Sciences of the OAS
IANEC—Inter-American Nuclear Energy Commission
IAPC—Inter-American Peace Committee
IAPSC—Inter-African Phytosanitary Commission
IATA—International Air Transport Association
IATTC—Inter-American Tropical Tuna Commission
IAU—International Association of Universities
IBAH—Inter-African Bureau for Animal Health
IBE—International Bureau of Education
IBEC—International Bank for Economic Cooperation
Iberia—Líneas Aéreas Españolas (Iberia)
IBRD—International Bank for Reconstruction and Development
IBWM—International Bureau of Weights and Measures
ICA—International Coffee Agreement
ICA—[US] International Cooperation Administration
ICAC—International Cotton Advisory Committee
ICAI—International Commission for Agricultural Industries
ICAITI—Central American Institute for Technological and Industrial Research
ICAITI—Central American Research Institute for Industry
ICAN—International Commission for Air Navigation
ICAO—International Civil Aviation Organization
ICAP—Inter-American Committee on the Alliance for Progress
ICC—International Children's Center
ICC—International Computation Center
ICC—International Control Commission
ICEM—Intergovernmental Committee for European Migration
ICES—International Council for the Exploration of the Sea
ICFTU—International Confederation of Free Trade Unions
ICI—Inter-American Children's Institute
ICJ—International Court of Justice
ICMMP—International Committee of Military Medicine and Pharmacy
ICNAF—International Commission for the Northwest Atlantic Fisheries
ICPB—Inter-Parliamentary Consultative Council of Benelux
ICPHS—International Council for Philosophy and Humanistic Studies
ICRP—International Commission on Radiological Protection
ICSU—International Council of Scientific Unions
ICTB—International Union for the Publication of Customs Tariffs
IDA—International Development Association
IDB—Inter-American Development Bank
i.e.—id est (that is)
IEFC—International Emergency Food Council
IFALPA—International Federation of Air Line Pilots Associations
IFAN—Institut Français d'Afrique Noire
IFC—International Finance Corporation
IFIPS—International Federation of Information Processing Societies
IFRB—International Frequency Registration Board
IGC—Intergovernmental Copyright Committee
IGO—Intergovernmental Organization
IGY—International Geophysical Year
IHB—International Hydrographic Bureau
IIA—International Institute of Agriculture
IIB—Internation Patent Institute
IIEP—International Institute for Educational Planning
III—Inter-American Indian Institute
IIR—International Institute of Refrigeration
ILC—International Law Commission
ILCE—Latin American Educational Film Institute

Abbreviations

ILI—Inter-African Labor Institute
ILO—International Labor Organization
ILZSC—International Lead and Zinc Study Group
IMCO—Inter-Governmental Maritime Consultative Organization
IMF—International Monetary Fund
IMO—International Meteorological Organization
in.—inch(es)
INCAP—Institute of Nutrition of Central America and Panama
Indep.—Independent
INPFC—International North Pacific Fisheries Commission
INTERPOL—International Criminal Police Organization
IOC—Intergovernmental Oceanographic Commission
IOLM—International Organization of Legal Metrology
IOOC—International Olive Oil Council
IPC—International Poplar Commission
IPFC—Indo-Pacific Fisheries Council
IRASA—International Air Radio Safety Association
IRC—International Rice Commission
IRLCS—International Red Locust Control Service
IRO—International Refugee Organization
IRSG—International Rubber Study Group
IRU—International Relief Union
ISC—International Sericultural Commission
ISC—International Sugar Council
ISSC—International Social Science Council
ITC—International Tea Committee
ITC—International Tin Council
ITC—International Tuberculosis Campaign
ITO—International Trade Organization
ITU—International Telecommunication Union
IUPLAW—International Union for the Protection of Literary and Artistic Works
IWC—International Wheat Council
IWO—International Vine and Wine Office
IWSG—International Wool Study Group

JAL—Japan Air Lines
JAT—Jugoslovenski Aero-Transport (Yugoslav Air Transport)
JINR—Joint Institute for Nuclear Research

kg—kilogram(s)
kHz—kilohertz
kl—kiloliter
KLM—Royal Dutch Airlines
km—kilometer(s)
kva—kilowatt = ampere
kw—kilowatt(s)
kwh—kilowatt-hour(s)

LAFC—Latin American Forestry Commission
LAFTA—Latin American Free Trade Association
LAI—See Alitalia.
LAN—Línea Aérea Nacional de Chile
LANICA—Líneas Aéreas de Nicaragua
LAV—Línea Aéropostal Venezolana (Venezuela Airlines)
lb.—pound(s)
Lufthansa—Deutsche Lufthansa (Lufthansa German Airlines)

m.—morning
MC—Monetary Committee
MEA—Middle East Airlines
MEDICO—Medical International Organization
MESA—Malaria Eradication Special Account
mg.—milligram(s)
MHz—megahertz
mi.—mile(s)
mm—millimeter(s)
MSC—Mediterranean Sub-Commission (Silva Mediterranea)
Mt.—Mount
MTS—machine and tractor stations
Mw—megawatt(s)

N—north
NATO—North Atlantic Treaty Organization

NC—Nordic Council
n.d.—no date
NGO—nongovernmental organization
NIB—Swedish Agency for International Assistance
n.i.e.—not included elsewhere
n.p.—no place
NPR—net material product
NWA—Northwest Orient Airlines

OAAPS—Organization for Afro-Asian Peoples Solidarity
OAMPI—African and Malagasy Industrial Property Office
OAS—Organization of American States
OAU—Organization of African Unity
OCAS—Organization of Central American States
OCAM—Organisation Commune Africaine et Malgache
OCCCE—Organization for Cooperation and Coordination of Epidemic Diseases
OCDN—Dahomey-Niger Common Organizations
OCLALAV—Joint Anti-Locust and Anti-Aviarian Organization
OCRS—Organisation Commune des Régions Sahariennes
OCTI—Central Office for International Railway Transport
ODECA—Organization of Central American States
OECD—Organization for Economic Cooperation and Development
OEEC—Organization for European Economic Cooperation
OEI—Ibero-American Bureau of Education
OEPT—Office Equatorial des Postes et Télécommunications
OIE—International Office of Epizootics
OIETA—African Inter-State Office for Tourism
OIHP—International Office of Public Health
OIRSA—Organismo Internacional Regional de Sanidad Agropecuaria
OLA—Common Organization for the Fight Against Birds
O.M.—Order of Merit
ONUC—UN Operation in the Congo
OPEC—Organization of Petroleum Exporting Countries
OPEX—Operational and Executive Personnel Program
ORIT—Inter-American Regional Organization
OSZhD—Organization for the Collaboration of Railways
OTC—Organization for Trade Cooperation
OUA—Union of African States

p.—page
PAB—Panair do Brasil
PAHO—Pan American Health Organization
PAIGH—Pan American Institute of Geography and History
PAL—Philippine Air Lines
Panagra—Pan American-Grace Airways
Pan Am—Pan American World Airways
PC of A—Permanent Court of Arbitration
PIA—Pakistan International Airlines
PIBAC—Permanent International Bureau of Analytical Chemistry of Human and Animal Food
PICAO—Provisional International Civil Aviation Organization
PL—Public Law
p.m.—afternoon or evening
pop.—population
pp.—pages
PPD—purified tuberculin
PSWO—Picture and Sound World Organization
PUAS—Postal Union of the Americas and Spain

Qantas—Qantas Empire Airways

r.—reigned

S—South
S.A.—Société Anonyme
SABENA—Société Anonyme d'Exploitation de la Navigation Aérienne (Belgian World Air Lines)
SAHSA—Servicios Aéreos Hondureños, S.A.
SAS—Scandinavian Airlines System
SEATO—Southeast Asia Treaty Organization
SIECA—General Treaty on Central American Economic Integration
SIM—International Moselle Company
SPC—South Pacific Commission

sq.—square
SSR—Soviet Socialist Republic
St.—Saint
SUNFED—Special United Nations Fund for Economic Development
SWAFAC—Southwest Atlantic Fisheries Advisory Commission
Swissair—Swiss Air Transport Co.

TAB—Technical Assistance Board
TABSO—Bulgarian Civil Airlines
TAC—Technical Assistance Committee
TACA—Taca International Airlines
TAD—Trade and Development Board
TAI—Compagnie des Transports Aériens Intercontinentaux
TAM—Transporte Aéreo Militar
TAN—Transportes Aéreos Nacionales de Honduras
TANU—Tanganyika African National Union
TAO—[United Nations] Bureau of Technical Assistance Operations
TAP—Transportes Aéreos Portuguéses
TAVA—Transportes Aéreos Centroamericanos
TB—tuberculosis
TCA—Trans-Canada Air Lines
TCRMG—Tripartite Commission for the Restitution of Monetary Gold
TEAL—Tasman Empire Airlines
TERLS—Thumba Equatorial Launching Stations
THY—Turk Hava Yollari Anonim Ortakligi (Turkish Airways Corporation)
Tunisair—Société Tunisienne de l'Air
TV—television
TWA—Trans World Airlines

UAMD—African and Malagasy Union Defense Pact
UAR—United Arab Republic
UDE—Equatorial Customs Union
UDEAC—Union Douanière et Economique de l'Afrique Centrale
UDOA—West African Customs Union
UEB—Union Economique Benelux
UHF—ultra high frequency
UIPPI—International Union for the Protection of Industrial Property
UK—United Kingdom of Great Britain and Northern Ireland
UN—United Nations
UNBTAO—UN Bureau of Technical Assistance Operations
UNCOK—UN Commission in Korea
UNCTAD—UN Conference on Trade and Development
UNCURK—UN Commission on the Unification and Rehabilitation of Korea
UNDP—United Nations Development Program
UNEF—United Nations Emergency Force

UNESCO—United Nations Educational, Scientific and Cultural Organization
UNFICYP—UN Force in Cyprus
UNICEF—United Nations Children's Fund
UNIDROIT—International Institute for the Unification of Private Law
UNHCR—United Nations High Commissioner for Refugees
UNITAR—UN Institute of Training and Research
UNKRA—United Nations Korean Reconstruction Agency
UNMOGIP—UN Military Observer Group for India and Pakistan
UNOC—UN Operation in the Congo
UNOID—UN Organization for Industrial Development
UNREF—United Nations Refugee Fund
UNRRA—United Nations Relief and Rehabilitation Administration
UNRWA—United Nations Relief and Works Agency for Palestine Refugees
UNSCEAR—UN Scientific Committee on the Effects of Atomic Radiation
UNTA—United Nations Technical Assistance
UNTAA—United Nations Technical Assistance Administration
UNTAO—United Nations Bureau of Technical Assistance Operations
UNTEA—UN Temporary Executive Authority
UNTSO—United Nations Truce Supervisory Organization
UPA—Arab Postal Union
UPU—Universal Postal Union
US—United States of America
USEP—United States Escapee Program
USIA—United States Information Agency
USSR—Union of Soviet Socialist Republics
UT—International Conference for Promoting Technical Uniformity of Railways
UTA—Union des Transports Aériens

VARIG—Empresa de Viacão Aérea Río Grandense
VASP—Viacão Aérea São Paulo
VHF—very high frequency
VIASA—Venezolana Internacional de Aviación, S.A.
vol., vols., Vol., Vols.—volume(s)
VOR—very high frequency omnirange [installations]

W—west
WEU—Western European Union
WFTU—World Federation of Trade Unions
WHO—World Health Organization
WMO—World Meteorological Organization
WRY—World Refugee Year
WTO—Warsaw Treaty Organization

EXPLANATION OF SYMBOLS

Data not available . . .
Nil (or negligible) —
Figures not included in totals and subtotals are given in parentheses ( ).
A fiscal or split year is indicated by a stroke (e.g., 1969/70).
The use of a hyphen (e.g., 1968–69) normally signifies the full period of calendar years covered (including the end year indicated).

THE UNITED NATIONS

SYSTEM

THE UNITED NATIONS SYSTEM

The United Nations

- United Nations Truce Supervision Organization in Palestine (UNTSO)
- United Nations Military Observer Group in India and Pakistan (UNMOGIP)
- United Nations Peace-keeping Force in Cyprus (UNFICYP)
- Main Committees
- Standing and Procedural Committees
- Other Subsidiary Organs of General Assembly
- United Nations Relief and Works Agency for Palestine Refugees in the Near East (UNRWA)
- United Nations Conference on Trade and Development (UNCTAD)
- Trade and Development Board
- United Nations Development Programme (UNDP)
- United Nations Capital Development Fund
- United Nations Industrial Development Organization (UNIDO)
- United Nations Institute for Training and Research (UNITAR)
- United Nations Children's Fund (UNICEF)
- United Nations High Commissioner for Refugees (UNHCR)
- Joint United Nations -FAO World Food Programme

Disarmament Commission
Military Staff Committee

- SECURITY COUNCIL
- INTER-NATIONAL COURT OF JUSTICE
- GENERAL ASSEMBLY
- TRUSTEESHIP COUNCIL
- ECONOMIC AND SOCIAL COUNCIL
- SECRETARIAT

- Regional Economic Commissions
- Functional Commissions
- Sessional, Standing and Ad Hoc Committees

The Specialized Agencies and IAEA

- **IAEA** International Atomic Energy Agency
- **ILO** International Labour Organisation
- **FAO** Food and Agriculture Organization of the United Nations
- **UNESCO** United Nations Educational, Scientific and Cultural Organization
- **WHO** World Health Organization
- **IMF** International Monetary Fund
- **IDA** International Development Association
- **IBRD** International Bank for Reconstruction and Development
- **IFC** International Finance Corporation
- **ICAO** International Civil Aviation Organization
- **UPU** Universal Postal Union
- **ITU** International Telecommunication Union
- **WMO** World Meteorological Organization
- **IMCO** Inter-Governmental Maritime Consultative Organization
- **GATT** General Agreement on Tariffs and Trade

STRUCTURE OF THE UNITED NATIONS SYSTEM

The UN System is often referred to as a "family" of organizations. The Charter of the UN, signed in San Francisco on 26 June 1945, defined only six main organs of the new world body, each with specific tasks and functions. However, because it was impossible to foresee all the demands that might be made on the organization, provision was made for extending its capacities as the need arose. Thus three of the main organs are specifically empowered to establish "such subsidiary organs" as may be considered necessary for the performance of their functions. In addition, Article 57 of the Charter provides that the various independent agencies, established by intergovernmental agreement, having international responsibilities in economic, social, cultural, educational, health, and related fields "shall be brought into relationship" with the UN. Since the signing of the Charter, the UN has founded numerous subsidiary organs and has entered into relationship with 14 independent organizations, known as "specialized agencies." Reproduced opposite is the official chart of the UN showing the various organs and bodies within the system as of July 1969.

For assistance in interpreting the chart, a brief survey of the UN's main organs, the different categories of subsidiary organs, and the related agencies is given below. A detailed description of the functioning of each of the main organs and an account of the work of selected subsidiary organs are contained in later chapters of the UN section of this volume. The constitution and work of the UN-related agencies are described in individual sections.

MAIN ORGANS OF THE UN

1. *The General Assembly,* composed of representatives of all member states, is the UN's central deliberative body, empowered to discuss and make recommendations on any subject falling within the scope of the Charter itself. It also decides the budget for the whole organization and determines—alone or with the Security Council—part of the composition of the other main organs, including the Security Council.

2. *The Security Council,* a 15-member body, has primary responsibility for maintaining international peace and security. In times of crisis it is empowered to act on behalf of all member states and to decide on a course of collective action that is mandatory for the entire membership. The Charter names five states as permanent members of the Council: China, France, UK, USSR, and US (those that were chiefly responsible for the defeat of the Axis powers in 1945). The remaining Council members are elected by the General Assembly for two-year terms.

3. *The Economic and Social Council (ECOSOC)* is assigned the task of organizing the UN's work on economic and social matters and the promotion of human rights. It consists of 27 members elected for 3-year terms by the General Assembly.

4. *The Trusteeship Council* operates the UN trusteeship system. It is composed of member nations administering trust territories, the permanent members of the Security Council, and a sufficient number of other members, elected by the Assembly for three-year terms, to ensure an equal division of administering and nonadministering powers.

5. *The International Court of Justice (ICJ)* is the principal judicial organ of the UN. It consists of 15 judges elected by the General Assembly and the Security Council voting independently.

6. *The Secretariat* is the administrative arm of the organi-zation. Its staff is headed by a secretary-general appointed by the General Assembly upon the recommendation of the Security Council.

SUBSIDIARY ORGANS OF THE UN

The UN Charter specifically confers the right to create subsidiary organs upon the General Assembly, the Security Council, and ECOSOC. The subsidiary bodies fluctuate in number from year to year, according to the changing requirements of the main organ concerned. Both the General Assembly and ECOSOC, for instance, continually create new bodies to assist them in their ever-expanding activities. In many cases, the newly established bodies are intended to take over the functions of several existing ones, which are then disbanded. Some of the subsidiary organs in turn set up their own subsidiary units—working groups and the like—and these are included in most of the official numerical surveys. A comprehensive listing for 1970 credited the Assembly with some 50 subsidiary organs (including subsubsidiary bodies), ECOSOC with over 40, and the Security Council with 18. The total of subsidiary organs within the UN, however, is far smaller than these figures suggest, since they do not account for many subsidiary organs that are established under a joint aegis—for example, the General Assembly and ECOSOC—and are therefore listed under both main organs.

Subsidiary Organs of the General Assembly

The Assembly's subsidiary organs range in complexity and status from temporary committees to highly organized, semiautonomous institutions that maintain their own secretariats or administrative departments. The names of the 10 semiautonomous bodies or institutions in existence in July 1969 (some of which were set up under the joint aegis of both the Assembly and ECOSOC) appear in the lower half of the left-hand column of the chart opposite. The remaining subsidiary organs are too numerous to list, so the chart merely indicates their principal types: main committees, standing and procedural committees, and what are called "other subsidiary organs." The committees comprise representatives of all member states and are formally reconstituted at each regular Assembly session to discuss the various items on the agenda for that year. (For further information on the work and constitution of these committees, see the chapter on the General Assembly.)

The standing committees are the Advisory Committee on Administrative and Budgetary Questions and the Committee on Contributions (see the chapter on the UN Budget). Both of these committees are maintained continuously, and their memberships are reelected on a staggered basis. Procedural committees include the 25-member General Committee, which is responsible for scrutinizing the Assembly's agenda prior to its adoption by the plenary (see the chapter on the General Assembly), and the 9-member Credentials Committee, which examines the credentials of delegations sent to the Assembly (see the chapter on Membership, under the heading "Representation of Nations in the UN"). Like the main committees, both of these procedural committees are constituted anew at every session. The category "other subsidiary bodies" encompasses the huge number of substantive committees set up ad hoc by a General Assembly resolution to study subjects of interest to the Assembly—for example, the peaceful uses of outer space, apartheid in South Africa, and independence for colonial territories. These committees, whose members are elected by the Assembly or appointed by the Assembly's president, usually meet several times a year. At each regular session of the Assembly, they report on their deliberations. They continue to exist for as long as is considered necessary. Even when their mandate seems completed, they are not necessarily formally disbanded, but may be adjourned indefinitely and reactivated when the need arises. It is through these committees that the Assembly accomplishes most of its work outside the spheres of responsibility that are specifically entrusted to ECOSOC, the Trusteeship Council, or the various semiautonomous bodies referred to above.

Subsidiary Organs of the Security Council

Five of the Security Council's subsidiary organs are shown on the chart. The two at the top center are permanent bodies. The Military Staff Committee, as provided for in the Charter, is to advise the Security Council on the military aspects of maintaining international peace. However the Military Staff Committee secretariat, though it holds regular formal meetings, has never been consulted on any of the UN's peacekeeping operations (see chapters on the Security Council and Maintaining Peace and Security). The Disarmament Commission, established jointly with the Assembly, consists of all member states and meets only on the request of the Council or a UN member (see chapter on Disarmament). The three other subsidiary bodies shown on the chart, at the top of the left-hand column, were set up, as their names suggest, to conduct the Council's peacekeeping operations in the areas specified. (For further information on the work of these bodies, see chapter on Maintaining Peace and Security under the heading "Some Case Histories of UN Action.")

In addition to the subsidiary organs shown on the chart, the Council maintains two permanently constituted committees of the whole: one to examine the provisional rules of the Council's procedure, the other to consider the admission of UN members.

In practice, however, it rarely convenes them, and the committee on admission of members has not met since 1949. From time to time, the Council also creates ad hoc committees or subcommittees—usually comprising all members—to consider special problems. This procedural device of establishing committees of the whole enables the Council to conduct informal discussions—in closed session, if desired—unencumbered by the elaborate and time-consuming ritual normally required for Council meetings. Among the Council's ad hoc subsidiary bodies are a committee to consider the question of admitting microstates to UN membership (see chapter on Membership) and a committee to study ways of implementing the Council's resolution on South Africa's continued control of Namibia, also known as South West Africa (see section B of the chapter on Independence of Colonial Peoples).

Subsidiary Organs of ECOSOC

As indicated on the chart, ECOSOC's subsidiary organs are of four types: (1) the semiautonomous bodies discussed above and shown in the left-hand column; (2) regional economic commissions; (3) functional commissions; and (4) sessional, standing, and ad hoc committees. A detailed survey of these organs is included in the chapter on the Economic and Social Council.

UN RELATED AGENCIES

The 14 intergovernmental agencies that have been brought into relationship with the UN—and which are named in the right-hand column of the chart—are separate autonomous organizations with their own policy-making and executive organs, secretariats, and financial arrangements. The precise nature of their relationship with the UN is defined by the terms of special agreements that were established with ECOSOC and subsequently approved by the General Assembly, as provided for in Article 63 of the Charter. Since Article 63 also empowers ECOSOC to coordinate the activities of the specialized agencies through consultation and recommendations, they are required to report annually to the Council.

Mention should be made here of the special status of the General Agreement on Tariffs and Trade (GATT). Although, for the sake of convenience, GATT is listed on the chart as one of the specialized agencies, it is, in fact a treaty establishing a code of conduct on international trade and providing machinery for reducing and stabilizing tariffs. The treaty was concluded pending the creation of a specialized agency to be known as the International Trade Organization, whose draft charter was completed in 1948 but was never ratified by the important trading powers (for further details, see the section in this volume on GATT). Nonetheless, GATT is regarded as part of the UN system and maintains a close working relationship with the world body.

The International Atomic Energy Agency (IAEA), which heads the right-hand column on the chart, is distinguished from the other agencies in that it was specifically established under the aegis of the UN and is therefore considered a category by itself. The IAEA reports annually to the General Assembly and only "as appropriate" to ECOSOC. Because of the nature of its work, IAEA also reports to the Security Council, again only "as appropriate."

COMPARISON WITH THE LEAGUE OF NATIONS

Since antiquity, individual thinkers and statesmen have dreamed of creating an institution wherein the peoples of the world would cooperate to solve common problems and settle their disputes. But the best that could be accomplished was the formation, from time to time, of alliances among particular groups of nations. All too frequently, these merely had the negative effect of producing counteralliances, which in turn led to new rivalries and conflicts. It was the catastrophe of World War I (1914–18) that finally brought home the need for a universal organization. Long before the war had ended, influential voices in Britain and France were urging statesmen to take steps toward creating a world body. In 1917 the project was debated both in the French Chamber of Deputies and in the British Imperial War Cabinet.

The most persuasive advocate, however, was US President Woodrow Wilson, who on 8 January 1918, declared as the last of his famous Fourteen Points that "a general association of nations must be formed under specific covenants for the purpose of affording mutual guarantees of political independence with territorial integrity to great and small nations alike." For Wilson and for millions throughout the world, the creation of the League of Nations was the most significant achievement to emerge from the 1919 Paris Peace Conference.

The League's failure to prevent the outbreak of World War II in 1939 did not erase the belief in the need for a universal organization. On the contrary, it bred a determination to learn from the mistakes of the past and to build a new world body more adequately equipped to maintain international peace in the future.

CREATION
The differences between the League of Nations and the UN begin with the circumstances of their creation. First, whereas the Covenant of the League was formulated after hostilities were ended, the main features of the UN were devised while war was still in progress. The more comprehensive powers assigned to the UN for the preservation of peace may well owe something to the urgent conditions in which it was conceived. Second, the Covenant was drawn up in an atmosphere of divided attention at the Paris Peace Conference and was incorporated as part of the peace treaty with Germany. Although countries were permitted to ratify the Covenant and the treaty separately, the link between them was not good psychology and contributed, for example, to the reluctance of the US Senate to ratify the Covenant. In contrast, the UN Charter was drafted as an independent legal instrument at a conference especially convened for the purpose. Third, the Covenant was hammered out behind closed doors, first by the five major powers of the era—France, Italy, Japan, UK, and US—and eventually in conjunction with nine other allied nations. The final text of the UN Charter, on the other hand, was the product of the combined efforts of 50 states represented at the 1945 San Francisco Conference and therefore took into account the views of the smaller nations, especially their concern to give the new organization far-reaching responsibilities in promoting economic and social cooperation and decolonization.

VOTING
Under the Covenant, decisions of the League could be taken only by unanimous vote. This rule applied both to the League's Council, which had special responsibilities for maintaining peace (the equivalent of the UN's Security Council), and to the all-member Assembly (the equivalent of the UN's General Assembly). In effect, each member state of the League had the power of the "veto," and, except for procedural matters and a few specified topics, a single "nay" killed any resolution. Learning from this mistake, the founders of the UN decided that all its organs and subsidiary bodies should make decisions by some type of majority vote (though, on occasion, committees dealing with a particularly controversial issue have been known to proceed by consensus). The rule of unanimity applies only to five major powers—France, China, UK, US, and USSR—and then only when they are acting in their capacity as permanent members of the Security Council. The Security Council also proceeds by majority vote, but on substantive (though not on procedural) matters it must include the concurring votes of all the permanent members.

CONSTITUTIONAL POWERS TO PREVENT WAR AND END AGGRESSION
The Charter was designed to remedy certain constitutional defects and omissions in the Covenant which the founders of the UN believed had been partly responsible for the League's inability to halt the drift toward a second world war in the 1930's. These defects and omissions included the absence of any provision imposing a total ban on war; the provision of a too rigid procedure for negotiating disputes between states; and the failure to vest the Council with sufficient powers to prevent the outbreak of hostilities or to terminate hostilities that had already begun.

Although, under the Covenant, military aggression was expressly forbidden, states still retained a limited right to start a war. The founders of the League sought to accommodate the traditional belief of nations in their right to wage a "just war" and at the same time to restrict the exercise of this right by making it dependent upon the outcome of negotiations. To this end, they established a complex system of rules for the peaceful settlement of disputes that was intended to delay appreciably the moment when a state could legally initiate hostilities against another.

Thus no member country was permitted to start a war without first having submitted the dispute at issue to arbitration, judicial decision, or to the Council of the League itself. If one of the parties in the dispute refused to accept or abide by the findings of the negotiating body concerned, the other party was permitted to go to war—provided that it had itself accepted the findings and only after waiting for three months following the judgment. In the case of disputes submitted to the League's Council, if that body could not reach a decision within six months, the parties were enjoined to observe an obligatory "cooling-off" period of an additional three months. The expectation was that the waiting periods would provide sufficient time for other countries to persuade the recalcitrant party to accept the international judgment and thus eliminate the need for war.

The link between the right to wage war and the failure of the negotiating process nowhere exists in the UN Charter, which does not recognize any circumstance when individual nations may legally start a war. (The inherent right of individual and collective self-defense guaranteed in Article 51 of the Charter is not the right to initiate armed hostilities; it is merely the right to answer an illegal armed attack.) In Article 2, which enumerates the UN's basic principles, all member states are unreservedly enjoined to settle their disputes by peaceful means "in such a manner that international peace and security are not endangered" and to refrain from "the threat or use of force against the territorial integrity or political independence of any state." Nor, in a later chapter of the Charter that elaborates various possible methods for the peaceful settlement of disputes, is there any provision for unilateral recourse to war should the disputing parties fail to resolve their differences. Moreover, the Charter stresses that states shall "first of all" seek to settle disputes by "peaceful means of their own choice," thereby leaving them greater latitude of action than they had under the Covenant.

In its capacity as the UN's chief guardian of the peace, the Security Council is empowered by the Charter to take certain preventive initiatives that were denied to the League's Council. The Covenant contained no provision enabling the Council of the League to intervene in a dispute unless the states directly involved brought the matter before it or until hostilities had actually broken out. Under the Charter, the Security Council need not wait for a request from the states concerned or for the outbreak of hostilities before taking action, but it may investigate any dispute or any ominous-seeming "situation" in order to determine whether it is likely to endanger peace and security. If the Council decides that a "threat to the peace" does exist, it is empowered to order collective enforcement measures—including both economic sanctions and military measures, at the discretion of the Council—which are mandatory upon the entire membership of the UN.

Although the League's Council could recommend collective military action once a member state had actually started an illegal war, no provision was made for placing armed forces at its disposal, and the degree of authority the Council was supposed to have over the League's membership in this regard was not clearly defined. (It should be noted that all League members were required by the Covenant to institute instant economic sanctions on an individual basis against an aggressor member state without waiting for a collective decision by the Council.) The UN Security Council, on the other hand, is empowered to initiate military action against any aggressor state, including those that are not UN members. The UN Charter provides for the conclusion of special agreements to determine the strength of the military contingents that member states are required to place at the disposal of the Security Council should the need for combined enforcement measures arise.

The UN Charter left no room for doubt concerning the primacy of the Security Council's role in directing all aspects of the UN's peacekeeping functions. The fact that the Council has proved unable to execute the Charter provisions to the full and that the General Assembly on occasion has deemed it essential to take over some of the Council's designated responsibilities suggests that the problem of adequately equipping a world organization for keeping the peace is less a matter of constitutional definition than a question of the determination of member states to make the relevant provisions in the constitution work in the manner intended.

MEMBERSHIP

The League never became the universal organization that had been envisaged. Moreover, it failed to secure or retain the membership of certain major powers whose participation and cooperation were essential to make it an effective instrument for preserving the peace. Despite President Wilson's advocacy, the US did not join, and the USSR joined only in 1934, when the League had already shown itself unable to contain the aggressive policies of Germany, Italy, and Japan. The three aggressor states themselves withdrew their membership during the 1930's to pursue their expansionist aims. Although the UN likewise has failed to achieve the goal of universality, only two major powers—Communist China and West Germany—and a handful of small countries are unrepresented, and no major power has withdrawn its membership.

PROMOTION OF HUMAN WELFARE

The UN Charter not only lays down specific injunctions for international economic and social cooperation, based on respect for the principle of equal rights and self-determination of peoples, but it establishes a special organ—the Economic and Social Council—to conduct the organization's activities in this sphere. Throughout its existence the UN, together with its specialized agencies, has gradually assumed primary responsibility for assisting the economic and social development of nonindustrialized member nations, most of them former colonial territories that joined the world body long after it was founded. The UN's many projects have become the cornerstone of the development policies adopted by almost all these countries. Since the Covenant of the League contained no provisions for a coordinated program of economic and social cooperation, there can be no comparison between the respective achievements of the two organizations in this respect. Nevertheless, the League performed valuable work in several fields—notably, in eliminating the illegal sale of women and children, or the "white slave" trade; providing assistance for refugees; reducing traffic in opium and other dangerous narcotics; and getting nations to lessen trade restrictions.

ADMINISTRATION OF COLONIAL TERRITORIES

Instead of sharing the colonial possessions of their defeated enemies as the traditional spoils of victory, the founding members of the League, with admirable foresight and restraint, regarded these territories as international mandates, and certain member states were designated to administer them on behalf of the world organization. This mandate system in a modified form was continued in the trusteeship system evolved by the founders of the UN. However, unlike the Covenant, the Charter expressly stipulates that the administering countries have an obligation to promote the progressive development of the territories placed in their charge toward self-government or independence (see chapter in this volume on the Trusteeship Council). In addition, the Charter embodies a declaration requiring the colonial powers to prepare the peoples in their dependencies for self-government. By 1960 when several newly independent territories joined the UN and began to influence the thinking in the world body, this declaration was superseded by one of the Assembly, which in effect proclaims the right of all colonial peoples to immediate independence (see chapter on Independence of Colonial Peoples).

BALANCE SHEET OF THE LEAGUE OF NATIONS

The League failed in its supreme test. It failed to contain the aggressive action of the Axis powers—Japan, Germany, and Italy—and thus halt the drift toward a new world war. From 1931, Japan, a permanent member of the League's Council, waged a war of aggression against China, in defiance of both the Council and the Assembly. Although the League did impose economic sanctions against Italy, another permanent member of the Council, when it wantonly invaded Ethiopia in 1935, support was half-hearted and the action unsuccessful. The League was unable to do anything against the illegal reoccupation of the Rhineland in 1936 by Germany, still another permanent member of the

Council, nor could it offer more than verbal protests against German and Italian intervention in the Spanish Civil War, the forcible incorporation of Austria into Germany in March 1938 and of Czechoslovakia into Germany a year later. The cumulative effect of these failures strengthened Hitler's belief in the impotence not only of the League itself but also of its principal remaining members. During the summer of 1939, when the world moved ever closer toward the abyss, and even when Hitler's armies marched into Poland on 1 September 1939, not a single member called for a meeting of the League's Council or Assembly.

The League's balance sheet in political matters was not wholly negative, however. It was able, for example, to settle the dispute between Finland and Sweden over the Åland Islands, strategically located in the Gulf of Bothnia; the frontier controversy between Albania, Greece, and Yugoslavia; the potentially explosive border situation between Greece and Bulgaria; and the dangerous conflicts between Poland and Germany over Upper Silesia and between Germany, Poland, and Lithuania over Memel. Through the League's Permanent Court of Justice, a border controversy between Czechoslovakia and Poland was straightened out, as were the disputes between Britain and Turkey over the Mosul area and between France and Britain over the nationality of Maltese residents in the French protectorates of Morocco and Tunisia. The League also stopped the incipient war between Peru and Colombia over territorial claims in the upper Amazon basin.

In addition to these successful peacekeeping activities, the League financially assisted the reconstruction of certain states, notably Austria, and was responsible for administering the Free City of Danzig and the Saar Territory. (The latter was transferred to Germany following a plebiscite in 1935.) It also carried out important humanitarian work. Some of its nonpolitical activities continued throughout World War II, and its secretariat did valuable preparatory work for the emerging UN. The League of Nations was not officially dissolved until April 1946, five months after the new world body came into being.

THE UN'S GREATER VITALITY

Like the League, the UN recorded several important successes in halting local armed conflicts and preventing the spread of disputes—for example, in the Congo, Kashmir, and Cyprus. However, it has proved unable to take effective action in any situation where the interests of either the US or the USSR are close-ly involved or where the two giant powers seem committed to opposite sides of disputes involving smaller nations. Thus it was unable to check the Soviet invasion of Hungary in 1956 and of Czechoslovakia in 1968; it has been unable to take the initiative in ending the civil war in Viet-Nam; and it has seemed unable to settle the prolonged crisis arising from the 1967 Arab-Israeli war in the Middle East, which has become a major arena in the US-USSR power struggle. The UN's ineffectuality in such situations has caused a loss of confidence in its relevance in international political relations. Nor is it a source of consolation that there is no discernible drift toward a world war, for in most cases where the US and the USSR have found themselves almost at the point of actual confrontation, as in the 1962 Cuban crisis, they have tended to resolve their differences bilaterally, outside the aegis of the UN.

On the other hand, if the two great powers do not always find it convenient to allow the UN to play too decisive a role in political matters, they find it equally impractical to bypass the world organization altogether. The truth is that, unlike the League, the UN is the center of a network of organizations whose activities reach into several aspects of the national life of every member state. As such, it has come to be regarded as an indispensable part of the machinery for conducting multiple-level international relations. Thus, despite its shortcomings—which, basically, are those of its member states—the UN has served to heighten the recognition of the essential interdependence of states and to give them a sense of participation in a defined community. Increased recognition of the interdependence of states and the new sense of community have, moreover, been underwritten by technological advances in communications and armaments that have made the world a much smaller and more obviously dangerous place in which to live. For this, if for no other reason, statesmen today are necessarily more acutely aware than their predecessors in the 1930's of urgent need to prevent the community from being torn apart by conflicting national interests and succumbing to global war. Possibly, as many have advocated, the format of the world organization may have to be modified to meet changing requirements. But so long as the recognition of the interdependence of states and the sense of community persist, buttressed by the fear of global war, the UN is likely to maintain a greater strength and vitality than the League of Nations could ever have hoped to possess.

THE MAKING OF THE UNITED NATIONS

The creation of the UN at the San Francisco Conference in June 1945 was the culmination of four years of preparatory work. During these years the idea of establishing a new world organization to replace the League of Nations was first debated and then fleshed out. Many of the important principles of the UN adopted at San Francisco were the fruits of earlier conferences.

DEVELOPMENTS LEADING TO THE SAN FRANCISCO CONFERENCE

1. *The Inter-Allied Declaration (London Declaration) of 12 June 1941*. By June 1941, World War II had been on almost two years, and most of Europe was under Nazi occupation. In that dark hour, representatives of the UK, Australia, Canada, New Zealand, and the Union of South Africa, of the governments-in-exile of Belgium, Czechoslovakia, Greece, Luxembourg, the Netherlands, Norway, Poland, and Yugoslavia, and of General Charles de Gaulle of France assembled at St. James's Palace in London to reaffirm their belief in a different world order. They pledged not to sign a separate peace and declared: "The only true basis of enduring peace is the willing cooperation of free peoples in a world in which, relieved of the menace of aggression, all may enjoy economic and social security. . . ."

Ten days later, Hitler launched his surprise attack against the Soviet Union.

2. *The Atlantic Charter of 14 August 1941*. As the German armies were sweeping eastward, US President Franklin D. Roosevelt and British Prime Minister Winston Churchill met on board the cruiser USS *Atlanta* off the coast of Newfoundland. On 12 August they signed a declaration that became known as the Atlantic Charter, released for security reasons on 14 August 1941 after both statesmen had left their secret rendezvous.

In that declaration, Roosevelt and Churchill announced "certain common principles . . . of their respective countries . . . for a better future for the world: the need for a secure peace; the abandonment by all nations of the use of force; the disarmament of aggressors; and the establishment of a wider and permanent system of general security." This was the first indication that the two powers would strive for the creation of a new world organization, once peace was restored.

3. *The United Nations Declaration of 1 January 1942*. With the Japanese attack on Pearl Harbor on 7 December 1941 and the entrance of the US into the war, the conflict assumed even more enormous dimensions. Japan's initial successes were staggering, and it was clear that the coalition against the Axis Powers (Germany, Italy, Japan, and their allies) would need to be strengthened and broadened.

On New Year's Day 1942 at Washington, D.C., representatives of 26 states signed a declaration whose preamble called for subscription "to a common program of purposes and principles embodied in the . . . Atlantic Charter" and also explicitly referred to the need for promoting respect for human rights on an international basis. In that declaration the phrase "united nations" made its first official appearance. It had been coined by President Roosevelt to express the unity of the signatory nations in their determination to withstand the onslaught of the Axis powers. The declaration subsequently was signed by the governments of 21 additional states.

4. *The Moscow Declaration of 30 October 1943*. By late 1943, victory for the Allies, or for the "united nations," seemed more closely in sight than at any time since the start of the war. In this hopeful atmosphere, US, British, and Soviet foreign ministers and a Chinese ambassador held a conference in Moscow. The resulting Declaration of Four Nations on General Security laid the foundation for the establishment of a new world body to replace the League of Nations. Article 4 of the declaration recognized "the necessity of establishing at the earliest practicable date a general international organization based on the principle of sovereign equality of all peace-loving States, and open to membership by all such States, large and small, for the maintenance of international peace and security."

5. *Dumbarton Oaks Conference, Washington, 21 August–7 October 1944*. The Dumbarton Oaks conference was the first big-power meeting specifically convoked to discuss the establishment of a new world organization. At the beginning of the conference, the delegations offered widely differing proposals. On some of these divergent views, they reached agreement. For example, the British and Soviet delegations accepted an American position that favored a strong role for the General Assembly as the organ in which all member states would be represented and which, therefore, would be the most "democratic" of the UN organs. There was agreement that a small Security Council should be "primarily responsible for the maintenance of international peace and security" and that the big powers should have the right of veto in that body. But a deadlock developed over whether a big power should abstain from voting (and therefore from using its veto) if a dispute involving that power itself was brought before the Security Council. The Americans and British refused to accept the Soviet proposal that the veto should also apply to such cases.

6. *Yalta Conference, February 1945*. This deadlock was resolved at a meeting in Yalta between Prime Minister Churchill, President Roosevelt, and Generalissimo Stalin. It was agreed that if one of the Big Five powers was involved in a dispute, that country would not have the right to veto Security Council recommendations for peaceful settlement, although it would be able to veto a Security Council decision to invoke sanctions against it. The "Yalta formula" was actually the compromise solution formerly proposed by the US at Dumbarton Oaks, which the USSR had then rejected.

After some initial objections from Churchill, the three leaders at Yalta also managed to agree on the basic principles of a trusteeship system for the administration of certain dependent territories under the aegis of the projected world body. The delicate colonial question had not been satisfactorily settled at the Dumbarton Oaks conference, owing to serious differences of opinion about the territories that should be placed under UN trusteeship and the extent to which nations should be answerable to the organization for the administration of their own colonies.

On 11 February 1945, the three leaders announced that a conference would be convened in San Francisco on 25 April 1945 for "the earliest possible establishment of a general international organization" along the lines proposed at Dumbarton Oaks.

THE SAN FRANCISCO CONFERENCE, 25 APRIL–26 JUNE 1945

Despite the sudden death of President Roosevelt in early April, the United Nations Conference on International Organization was opened as scheduled. (President Roosevelt had been working on his speech to the conference before he died. That never-delivered address contained the often-quoted words: "The work, my friends, is peace; more than an end of this war—an end to the beginning of all wars; . . . as we go forward toward the greatest contribution that any generation of human beings can make in this world—the contribution of lasting peace—I ask you to keep up your faith. . . .")

China, the USSR, the UK, and the US acted as the sponsoring powers, and 46 other states participated, comprising all those that had signed the Declaration of United Nations of 1 January 1942 or had declared war on the Axis powers by March 1945. The huge conference was attended by 282 delegates and 1,444 other officially accredited persons from those 50 countries, and by representatives of scores of private organizations interested in world affairs (50 from the US alone). The daily output of documents averaged half a million sheets and one day reached 1.7 million.

Major Modifications to the Dumbarton Oaks Draft for the UN Charter

After much debate, the smaller and medium-sized nations succeeded in restricting the Big Five's use of the veto in the Security Council. Herbert V. Evatt, then deputy prime minister of Australia, who was in the forefront of that fight, declared:

> In the end our persistence had some good effect. The Great Powers came to realize that the smaller powers would not accept a Charter unless certain minimum demands for restriction of the veto were accepted, viz., that there should be no veto upon the placing of items on the [Security Council] agenda and no veto on discussion [in the Security Council]. . . . If this vital concession had not been won, it is likely that discussion of matters in the open forum of the Security Council would have been rendered impossible: If so, the United Nations might well have broken up.

Another major change resulted from the desire of the smaller nations to give the world organization more responsibilities in social and economic matters and also in colonial problems. Accordingly, the Economic and Social Council and the Trusteeship Council were given wider authority than was provided for in the Dumbarton Oaks draft, and they were made principal organs of the UN.

Creation of a New World Court

The conference also unanimously adopted a constitution—called the Statute—for an International Court of Justice to be incorporated as a main organ of the UN and to succeed the Permanent Court of Justice established by the League of Nations. The Statute, which had originally been drafted by jurists from 44 nations meeting in Washington in April 1945, is included as part of the Charter of the UN.

Unanimous Acceptance of the Charter

The UN Charter touches on so many delicate and complex matters that its unanimous acceptance has often been ascribed to the particularly auspicious circumstances prevailing in the spring of 1945. In spite of some dissonance, the San Francisco Conference was imbued with a spirit of high mission. The Charter was worked out within two months. It was signed by 50 nations in its five official languages—Chinese, English, French, Russian, and Spanish—in an impressive ceremony on 27 June 1945.

ESTABLISHMENT OF THE UN, 24 OCTOBER 1945

The new world body officially came into being on 24 October 1945, when the Charter had been duly ratified by all permanent members of the Security Council and a majority of the other original signatory powers. This date is universally celebrated as United Nations Day.

SUBSEQUENT CHARTER AMENDMENT

Like other political constitutions, the UN Charter contains provisions for its own amendment. Amendments to the Charter come into force when they have been adopted by a vote of two thirds of the members of the General Assembly and ratified by two thirds of the UN member states, including all the permanent members of the Security Council.

The amendments that have come into force are essentially adjustments to take account of the huge increase in UN membership, which has more than doubled since 1945. As originally constituted, the 11-member Security Council and the 18-member Economic and Social Council were thought adequate to reflect the different interests of the various geographical groupings of states within the organization. However, the admission to the UN during the late 1950's and early 1960's of large numbers of newly decolonized African, Asian, and Caribbean countries, created additional groupings. To accommodate their interests without jeopardizing those of the older groups, the General Assembly at its 18th session in 1963 adopted amendments to Articles 23, 27, and 61 of the Charter. The first amendment enlarges the membership of the Security Council to 15; the second requires that decisions of the Security Council shall be made by an affirmative vote of 9 members (formerly, 7); the third enlarges the membership of the Economic and Social Council to 27. All three amendments officially came into force on 31 August 1965.

Charter Review. It is also established that a general conference of UN members "for the purpose of reviewing the Charter may be held at a date and place to be fixed by a two-thirds vote of the members of the General Assembly and a vote of any seven members (amended to nine, as of June 1968) of the Security Council." In addition, the Charter provided that if such a conference were not held by the tenth regular assembly session (in 1955), the proposal to call such a conference should be placed on the agenda. Accordingly, the 1955 Assembly duly considered the matter and decided that a general review conference should be held at an "appropriate" but unspecified date in the future. A committee consisting of the full UN membership was established to consider the time and place at which the conference should be held. The Security Council concurred in the Assembly's decision by a vote of 9 to 1, with 1 abstention. Since then, the committee has met every two years but has not yet recommended the holding of a conference.

PURPOSES AND PRINCIPLES

The UN has three chief aims. The first is to maintain international peace; or, in the words of the preamble to the Charter, "to save succeeding generations from the scourge of war, which twice in our lifetime has brought untold sorrow to mankind." The second aim is to establish effective machinery to ensure international security, thereby reducing the fear of war. To reduce the fear of war is to reduce the danger of war, for only when nations cease to feel threatened will they cease preparing for war. And only when they cease preparing for war will they be able to devote their energies to building the essential infrastructure for peace, by eliminating the underlying causes of conflict—poverty, ignorance, bigotry, and oppression.

To better the lot of humanity through improvement in economic and social conditions, raised standards of health and education, and promotion of respect for fundamental human rights and freedoms is therefore the third aim of the UN, assisted by its related agencies. Freedom from war and the fear of war is necessary for making the world a better place to live in. And conversely, making the world a better place to live in is necessary for preserving the peace. It is a reciprocal relation. The UN's peacekeeping functions and what Secretary-General U Thant has termed its "peacebuilding activities" are thus complementary and interdependent aspects of the total work of the organization.

The aims of the UN are embodied in a set of purposes and principles contained in the opening chapter of the Charter, which are summarized below.

PURPOSES

1. To maintain international peace and security, and to that end: to take effective collective measures for the prevention and removal of threats to the peace, and for suppression of acts of aggression or other breaches of the peace, and to bring about by peaceful means, and in conformity with the principles of justice and international law, adjustment or settlement of international disputes or situations which might lead to a breach of the peace.
2. To develop friendly relations among nations based on respect for the principles of equal rights and self-determination of peoples, and to take other appropriate measures to strengthen universal peace.
3. To achieve international cooperation in solving international economic, social, cultural, or humanitarian problems, and in promoting and encouraging respect for human rights and for fundamental freedoms for all without distinction as to race, sex, language, or religion.
4. To be a center for harmonizing the actions of nations in attaining these common ends.

PRINCIPLES

In pursuit of these purposes, the Charter stipulates that the UN and its members are to act in accordance with the following principles:

1. That the organization is based on the sovereign equality of all its members.
2. That all members are to fulfill in good faith their Charter obligations.
3. That they are to settle their international disputes by peaceful means and without endangering peace, security, and justice.
4. That they are to refrain in their international relations from the threat or use of force against other states.
5. That they are to give the UN every assistance in any action it takes in accordance with the Charter, and shall not assist states against which the UN is taking preventive or enforcement action.
6. That the UN shall also ensure that states which are not members act in accordance with these principles insofar as is necessary for the maintenance of international peace and security.
7. That nothing in the Charter is to authorize the UN to intervene in matters that are essentially within the domestic jurisdiction of any state, though this principle is not to prejudice the application of enforcement measures made necessary in the event of a threat to or breach of the peace.

MEMBERSHIP

As of 31 December 1970, the UN had 127 member states.

Afghanistan 19 November 1946
Albania 14 December 1955
Algeria 8 October 1962
*Argentina
*Australia
Austria 14 December 1955
Barbados 9 December 1966
*Belgium
*Bolivia
Botswana 17 October 1955
*Brazil
Bulgaria 14 December 1955
Burma 19 April 1948
Burundi 18 September 1962
Byelorussian Soviet Socialist
   Republic (SSR) 24 October
   1945
Cambodia 14 December 1955
Cameroon 20 September 1960
*Canada
Central African Republic
   20 September 1960
Ceylon 14 December 1955
Chad 20 September 1960
*Chile
*China (Taiwan)
*Colombia
Congo (Brazzaville)
   20 September 1960
Congo (Kinshasa)
   20 September 1960
*Costa Rica
*Cuba
Cyprus 20 September 1960
*Czechoslovakia
Dahomey 20 September 1960
*Denmark
*Dominican Republic
*Ecuador
*El Salvador
Equatorial Guinea
   12 November 1968
*Ethiopia
Fiji 13 October 1970
Finland 14 December 1955
*France
Gabon 20 September 1960
Gambia 21 September 1965
Ghana 8 March 1957
*Greece
*Guatemala
Guinea 12 December 1958
Guyana 21 September 1966
*Haiti
*Honduras
Hungary 14 December 1955

Iceland 19 November 1946
*India
Indonesia 28 September 1950
*Iran
*Iraq
Ireland 14 December 1955
Israel 11 May 1949
Italy 14 December 1955
Ivory Coast 20 September
   1960
Jamaica 18 September 1962
Japan 18 December 1955
Jordan 14 December 1955
Kenya 16 December 1965
Kuwait 14 May 1963
Laos 14 December 1955
*Lebanon
Lesotho 17 October 1966
*Liberia
Libya 14 December 1955
*Luxembourg
Madagascar
   20 September 1960
Malawi 1 December 1964
Malaysia 17 September 1957
Maldives 21 September 1965
Mali 28 September 1960
Malta 1 December 1964
Mauritania 27 October 1961
Mauritius 24 April 1968
*Mexico
Mongolia 27 October 1961
Morocco 12 November 1956
Nepal 14 December 1955
*Netherlands
*New Zealand
*Nicaragua
Niger 20 September 1960
Nigeria 7 October 1960
*Norway
Pakistan 30 December 1947
*Panama
*Paraguay
*Peru
*Philippines
*Poland
Portugal 14 December 1955
Romania 14 December 1955
Rwanda 18 September 1962
*Sa´udi Arabia
Senegal 28 September 1960
Sierra Leone
   27 September 1961
Singapore 21 September 1965
Somalia 20 September 1960
*South Africa

Southern Yemen
   14 December 1967
Spain 14 December 1955
Sudan 12 November 1956
Swaziland 24 September 1968
Sweden 19 November 1946
*Syria
Tanzania 14 December 1961
Thailand 16 December 1946
Togo 20 September 1960
Trinidad and Tobago
   18 September 1962
Tunisia 12 November 1956
*Turkey
Uganda 25 October 1962

*Ukrainian Soviet Socialist
   Republic (SSR)
*Union of Soviet Socialist
   Republics (USSR)
*United Arab Republic
   (UAR)
*United Kingdom (UK)
*United States (US)
Upper Volta
   20 September 1960
*Uruguay
*Venezuela
Yemen 30 September 1947
*Yugoslavia
Zambia 1 December 1964

The roster does not take account of the several federations or unions of states that were created or dissolved during membership. Thus Syria, an original member, ceased independent membership on joining with Egypt to form the United Arab Republic in 1958. On resuming its separate status in 1961, Syria also resumed separate membership, which is still officially dated from the country's original day of entry. By a contrary process, Tanganyika and Zanzibar joined the UN as separate states in 1961 and 1963, respectively, but in 1964 merged to form the United Republic of Tanzania with a single membership officially dated from Tanganyika's day of entry. Similarly, Malaya, which joined in 1957, merged with the British territories of Singapore, Sarawak, and Sabah to form the Federation of Malaysia with a single membership officially dated from Malaya's day of entry. When Singapore left the federation in 1965, it took up separate membership.

ADMISSION OF MEMBERS

In the words of Article 4 of the Charter, membership in the UN is open to all "peace-loving states which accept the obligations contained in the present Charter and, in the judgment of the Organization, are able and willing to carry out these obligations." The original members are the states that participated in the San Francisco Conference, or that had previously signed the United Nations Declaration of 1 January 1942, and subsequently signed and ratified the Charter.

The procedure of admission is as follows. A state wishing to join submits an application to the secretary-general, in which it formally states its acceptance of the Charter obligations. The application is forwarded to the Security Council. If the Council by a vote of at least nine members (formerly seven), including all the permanent members, recommends the application, membership becomes effective on the day it is approved by a two-thirds majority of the General Assembly. In other words, if any of the Council's permanent members vetoes it, or it fails to obtain a sufficient majority in the Council, the application does not reach the Assembly at all.

Up to 1955 there were bitter controversies and years of stalemate in the Security Council over the applications of some countries. Usually one or more of the Big Five was on bad terms with the applying state, or it would choose to withhold consent as a bargaining point against the other big powers. Finally, on 14 December 1955, by a compromise, 16 countries were admitted together. Nevertheless, four long-standing applications still await the recommendation of the Security Council: South Korea (which applied in January 1949), North Korea (February 1949), South Viet-Nam (December 1951), North Viet-Nam (December 1951). Admission of these four states involves complicated East-West issues.

Since the late 1950's, new applications have seldom raised any controversies. Most of the applicants have been newly independent states that have celebrated their freedom by applying for membership immediately. In almost all cases they have been admitted without delay and by unanimous vote.

The Problem of the "Microstates." Although there is general sympathy for the desire of former colonies to become members of the UN, some of the larger states have expressed concern at the continuing proliferation of new members with tiny populations and undeveloped economies that have the same voting power as other nations. In 1965 the secretary-general drew attention to the problems that might arise from the admission of a large number of very small states whose limited resources might not permit them to fulfill their financial obligations. In the Security Council's discussion of the application of the Maldive Islands (population 100,000), the US suggested that the Council's Committee on the Admission of Members, which has not met since 1949, should be reactivated. The suggestion was not taken up.

In July 1969 the US brought the question of the admission of "microstates," as they have come to be called, before the Council, which established a committee of experts comprising all the members of the Council to consider the problem. When the committee submitted its interim report in June 1970, the Council's discussion centered on the legal and other implications of the US proposal to create a special status of "associate membership" that would enable the microstates to enjoy some of the benefits and privileges of UN participation without the financial burden of full membership. The Committee was unable to formulate final recommendations, and the Council proposed that it should submit a further report, which is still pending. Although the application of Fiji (population 500,000) in October 1970 was endorsed unanimously by the Council, the US suggested reactivating the Committee on Admission of New Members, again without success.

WITHDRAWAL FROM MEMBERSHIP
While the Covenant of the League of Nations contained provisions for the legal withdrawal of members, the UN Charter deliberately omits all reference to the subject. The majority feeling at the San Francisco Conference was that provisions for withdrawal would be contrary to the principle of universality and might provide a loophole for members seeking to evade their obligations under the Charter.

Thus when the first—and so far the only—case of withdrawal arose, the procedure had to be improvised ad hoc. On 1 January 1965, Indonesia, which then was pursuing a policy of active confrontation against the newly formed Federation of Malaysia, announced that it would withdraw from the UN and its related agencies if Malaysia were to take its elected seat on the Security Council. Three weeks later, Indonesia's foreign minister officially confirmed withdrawal in a letter to the secretary-general who, after consultations with the Indonesian mission to the UN, merely noted the decision and expressed hope that Indonesia would in due time "resume full cooperation" with the world body. Following a coup later in 1965, Indonesia sent a telegram to the secretary-general just before the opening of the 1966 Assembly session announcing its decision to "resume full cooperation with the UN." Arrangements were made to ensure that Indonesia's reentry would take place with minimum formality. Hence it was decided that Indonesia need not make a formal reapplication via the Security Council, but that the matter could

be handled directly by the Assembly. Citing the telegram as evidence that Indonesia regarded its absence from the UN as a "cessation of cooperation" rather than an actual withdrawal, the Assembly's president recommended that the administrative procedure for reinstating Indonesia could be taken. No objections were raised, and Indonesia was immediately invited to resume its seat in the Assembly. In short, the problems raised by the first case of withdrawal from the UN were solved by treating it as if it had not been a matter of withdrawal at all. (Although South Africa withdrew from three of the UN's related agencies— UNESCO, FAO, ILO—because of the anti-apartheid sentiments of their members, it did not withdraw from the UN itself, despite numerous Assembly resolutions condemning apartheid and recommending stringent sanctions.)

SUSPENSION AND EXPULSION
The Charter provides that a member against which the Security Council has taken preventive or enforcement action may be suspended from the exercise of the rights and privileges of membership by the Assembly upon the recommendation of the Security Council. However, only the Security Council, not the Assembly, has the power to restore these rights. Any member that "has persistently violated the Principles" of the Charter may be expelled from the UN by the same procedure. By the end of 1970, no cases of suspension of rights or expulsion had been recommended or considered by the Council. Many states had called for the expulsion of South Africa because of its apartheid policies, but no formal proposal to this effect had been made. Perhaps this restraint was due to the foreknowledge that the Western permanent members of the Security Council would not agree to a recommendation for the expulsion of South Africa. However, during the 1968 Assembly session a number of African and other small states sponsored a draft resolution calling for South Africa's suspension from membership in the UN Conference on Trade and Development, a subsidiary body of the Assembly. The draft resolution failed to obtain the two-thirds majority required under Article 18 of the Charter for decisions on such "important" questions (for a list of important questions see the chapter on the General Assembly under "Voting Procedure"). The vote was 55 in favor with 33 against and 38 abstentions.

REPRESENTATION OF NATIONS IN THE UN
The members of the UN are nations, not governments. Whereas the UN may concern itself with the character of a government at the time a nation applies for admission and may occasionally defer admission on these grounds (Franco Spain, for example, applied for membership in 1945–46 but was not admitted until 1955), once a nation becomes a member any governmental changes thereafter do not affect continuance of membership— provided, of course, the nation continues to fulfill its Charter obligations. Nor, under the Charter, is the admission of a new nation dependent upon whether other nations individually recognize and have diplomatic relations with the government concerned. Though the relations of individual members with a nation applying for membership will affect the voting in the Security Council and the General Assembly, strictly speaking the only consideration enjoined by the Charter is the judgment by the members that the applying nation as represented by its government is "willing and able" to carry out its UN obligations. As a result, there are several nations in the UN that do not recognize or have diplomatic relations with each other.

Nations have to be represented at UN proceedings by delegations that are specifically authorized by their governments to speak on their behalf. Thus when a new ambassador appears, or when a new session of a UN organ convenes, it is necessary to examine the credentials of persons claiming to represent member states. The Credentials Committee must be satisfied that the person was duly appointed by his government, and that that government is the official government of the respective member nation. The matter can become controversial at the UN if, for example, two rival governments both claim to be the only legitimate government of a member state and each demands that its own representative be seated. An outstanding case in point is China; the unresolved issue of its representation in the UN has been one of the most important and controversial items on the Assembly's agenda.

The Question of the Representation of China

China was one of the sponsors of the San Francisco Conference and is therefore an original member of the UN. The issue is not a question of membership. It is, rather, which of two governments—that led by Chiang Kai-shek now located in Taiwan or the Communist regime based in Peking—should represent China in the world body. Each claims to be the only legitimate government of China, and each has pledged itself to gain control of the entire country. At the time of the San Francisco Conference, the Chiang Kai-shek government was the recognized government. Its representatives continued to sit in the UN without dispute until 1949 when the major hostilities in the Chinese civil war ended with the Peking government firmly established throughout the mainland. In that year the Peking government officially requested that the Assembly reject the credentials of the Chiang Kai-shek government's representatives. No action was taken. When, at the following Assembly session in 1950, India proposed that the representatives of Peking be seated, the proposal was rejected by a vote of 33 against and 16 for, with 10 abstentions. Thereafter, the supporters of Peking have brought the issue before each Assembly session, but, largely due to the efforts of the US, they have been unable to secure a sufficient majority to seat the representatives of Communist China in the UN, and to replace the Taiwan representatives.

From 1951 to 1960 the Assembly annually adopted a US-sponsored motion to exclude the question from the agenda, and hence not even to discuss it. In 1961, however, the US, bowing to pressure from member states to debate the proposal, refrained from tabling a deferment motion. Instead it drafted a resolution declaring that the issue falls within the scope of Article 18 of the

Charter requiring a two-thirds majority vote for decisions on all "important" questions. The US draft was duly adopted by the Assembly, but a proposal sponsored by Peking's supporters to replace the Taiwan representatives by Peking representatives won only 37 votes, far short of even a simple majority. At each Assembly session Peking's supporters continued to draft a resolution to seat Peking representatives and unseat the Taiwan representatives. Until 1969, the draft failed to command a simple majority, though in 1965 the vote was 47 to 47. But at the 1970 session the count was 51 in favor and 49 against with 25 abstentions. The draft would have passed had the Assembly not previously adopted the usual US-sponsored resolution reaffirming the issue as an "important" question requiring a two-thirds majority.

Following the close of the 1970 debate, the US government gave notice that it would "reexamine the new situation," though it did not specify how far it would go toward meeting the majority will of the UN membership on this matter. To most observers, the US would have no chance of pushing through a "two-China" solution, which had for several years been informally advocated by a number of members willing to seat Peking but reluctant to expel the Chiang Kai-shek government. The majority feeling has come to be that mainland China is the only China and should be represented as such in the UN. Another solution, which has been informally proposed, is to seat the Peking government as the representative government of China and the Chiang Kai-shek government as the representative government of Taiwan. But this would run counter to a growing feeling among the UN membership that the indigenous Taiwanese should be allowed the right of self-determination. Although the 1970 Assembly did not take up Tunisia's proposal that the secretary-general be requested to "explore the possibility of solving this problem," it seems evident that nations, especially the US, will do their own exploring. An increasing number of members have indicated their determination to find some way of enabling Communist China to be represented in the world body, even if it necessitates ousting the representatives of the Chiang Kai-shek government. Hence if no alternative is proposed, the standard draft resolution calling for the replacement of the Taiwan representatives by representatives of Communist China seems likely to win a two-thirds majority.

UN HEADQUARTERS AND FACILITIES

THE HEADQUARTERS BUILDING

When the UN came into being on 24 October 1945, it had no home. On 11 December 1945 the US Congress unanimously invited the UN to make its headquarters in the US. In February 1946 the General Assembly, meeting for its first session in London, voted for the general vicinity of Fairfield and Westchester counties, near New York City, but sites near Philadelphia, Boston, and San Francisco were also considered during 1946. Then came the dramatic offer by John D. Rockefeller, Jr., to donate $8.5 million toward the purchase of properties along the East River in midtown Manhattan. The City of New York rounded out the zone and granted rights along the river frontage. By November 1947 the Assembly approved the architectural plans, and nine months later the UN concluded a $65 million interest-free loan agreement with the US government. The director of planning for UN headquarters was Wallace K. Harrison of the US. The international board of design consultants included G. A. Soilleux, Australia; Gaston Brunfaut, Belgium; Oscar Niemeyer, Brazil; Ernest Cormier, Canada; Ssu-ch'eng Liang, China; Charles le Corbusier, Switzerland; Sven Markelius, Sweden; Nikolai D. Bassow, USSR; Howard Robertson, UK; and Julio Vilamajo, Uruguay.

The first structure to be completed, in the spring of 1951, was the 39-story marble and glass Secretariat building. The Conference building (which contains the three council halls designed by Scandinavian architects) and the General Assembly building were ready for use the following year.

Thus, it was five or six years before the UN was permanently housed. In the interim the Secretariat was established provisionally at Hunter College in the Bronx, New York, and in August 1946 the United Nations moved to the Sperry Gyroscope plant at Lake Success, Long Island. Several General Assembly sessions took place in the New York City Building at Flushing Meadow, and in 1948 and 1951 the Assembly met in Paris at the Palais de Chaillot.

A new library building at the Headquarters site, erected and equipped through a $6.2 million donation by the Ford Foundation, was dedicated in 1961 to the memory of former Secretary-General Dag Hammarskjöld.

Various equipment and works of art for the Conference and Assembly buildings have been donated by member governments. A unique feature of the Assembly building is the Meditation Room. The dimly lit "room of stillness" contains at its center a block of iron ore illuminated by a thin shaft of light from the ceiling. This block symbolizes, in the words of Dag Hammarskjöld, "an altar to the God of all." Since iron ore is basic material for plowshares as well as swords, the block is also intended to aid the meditator in making the proper choice between the two alternatives.

For a small fee, visitors may join one of the Secretariat's tours of the Headquarters building, which are conducted by a staff of 75 guides and are available in 36 languages. More than 100,000 people took advantage of this opportunity between June 1969 and May 1970.

Capacity

Despite the size of the buildings, continued expansion of UN membership and activities is creating a severe space problem. Since neither the Assembly Hall nor the various conference rooms were designed to accommodate representatives of more than 100 nations, some reconstruction has been required to increase the seating capacity.

In 1970 there were 5,213 regular staff personnel in the Secretariat building or in spaces in office buildings adjacent to the UN site. (This figure excludes staff appointed for short-term service during the Assembly sessions and personnel working for the various subsidiary organs of the UN that are housed at Headquarters.) Plans for constructing a new building adjoining the south side of the Secretariat were approved by the Assembly in 1969.

INTERNAL SERVICES

Library. The Dag Hammarskjöld Library contains 323,400 volumes, including 14,300 periodicals and sales publications, 350 newspapers, and 70,000 maps. About half the periodicals and almost all the maps were received as gifts in exchange for UN publications. The library is for the use of delegations and Secretariat staff, but it is also available to a limited extent to outside researchers.

Documents Services. Most of the UN documents are produced in mimeographed form for the use of members and the Secretariat. Headquarters houses one of the world's largest mimeographing and printing plants. Some of the mimeographed documents are later issued as UN publications for sale to the public. Sales in 1970 grossed over $1,400,000.

Conference Services. Headquarters, together with the UN's European office in Geneva and the secretariats of the four regional commissions, provides the interpreters, translators, précis writers, editors, and conference personnel required for all UN meetings throughout the world, as well as for other meetings held under UN auspices. The number of meetings at Headquarters is steadily increasing. From June 1968 to May 1969 there were 2,683, compared with 2,579 in the previous year. At Geneva there was a slight decline from 3,331 meetings in 1968 to 3,276 meetings in 1969.

Telecommunications System. The UN has its own telecommunications system. Headquarters is linked by radio with the European office in Geneva, which in turn provides liaison with UN organs and offices in different parts of the world. Only UN communications are accepted over this network.

United Nations Postal Administration

Under an agreement with the US postmaster general, a post office station is operated at UN Headquarters by the US Post Office Department. It provides at prevailing rates all the services offered by any comparable US post office. The UN, however, prints and issues its own stamps, which are the only ones sold or accepted as postage at the UN station. All states that are members of the Universal Postal Union recognize UN stamps as valid postage. Revenue from the sale of stamps at the UN post office is retained by the US Post Office Department, which is also reimbursed for all UN stamps used on official mail dispatched from UN Headquarters. The UN postal administration keeps only the revenue from philatelic stamp sales. The same rule applies to UN stamps sold to the general public in the visitors' lobby of the General Assembly Building. The UN's net income from the sale of stamps was about $5 million for 1970. Besides yielding revenue, UN stamps serve to make the organization better known. Various commemorative stamps are issued celebrating special occasions and projects, such as Human Rights Day, the Lower Mekong Basin Development, and the 25th anniversary of the UN. Since they can only be used as postage on items mailed at New York Headquarters, UN stamps can only be purchased elsewhere for philatelic purposes. They are sold to collectors by UN information centers, government agencies, and philatelic associations throughout the world.

PUBLIC INFORMATION SERVICES

Among the most important decisions taken by the General Assembly at its opening organizational session in January 1946 was to create a special Department (now called Office) of Public Information in the Secretariat. Recognizing that the UN's aims cannot be achieved unless the world is fully informed of its objectives and activities, the General Assembly directed that the department should work to promote the fullest possible informed understanding of UN affairs. Accordingly, OPI, which is based at Headquarters, provides a steady stream of official information on UN activities, covering virtually all media—press, publications, radio, television, films, photographs, and exhibitions.

Press, Publications, and Photographic Services

Press services provide information to news correspondents and facilitate their access to meetings, documents, and other news sources. Between June 1969 and May 1970 more than 3,600 press releases were issued at Headquarters, including accounts of meetings, texts of speeches, announcements of special programs, and background or reference papers on subjects of current interest. The OPI holds daily briefings, and helps to arrange press conferences for members of delegations and senior members of the Secretariat and the specialized agencies.

Booklets, pamphlets, and leaflets covering the work of the organization are published in some 50 languages. Among these publications is the *UN Monthly Chronicle*, published in English, French, and Spanish, which reports on all the proceedings and decisions of each of the main organs and their subsidiary bodies during the preceding month. In addition, the OPI puts out a *Yearbook of the United Nations*, which generally runs to over 1,000 pages.

Throughout the year, photo missions are undertaken to countries throughout the world to document UN economic and social programs in operation. Newspapers, periodicals, and book publishers, as well as government information agencies, make wide use of the UN photo library, both through the collection at Headquarters and through the facilities of the information centers and the regional visual information offices.

Radio, TV, and Film Services

UN radio assists national radio organizations, particularly in the developing areas, in their coverage of all aspects of the organization's work. This service includes the provision of shortwave broadcast and transcription facilities to radio correspondents at UN offices and meetings; direct shortwave broadcasts of the proceedings of the major organs; the supply of audio material from UN sound archives; and the production of complete radio programs in 33 languages. Particular attention has been devoted to radio material on the UN's activities relating to decolonization, economic and social development, and the problems of southern Africa. Between June 1969 and May 1970, the transcription service, with annual shipments via mail and pouch, provided approxi-

mately 40,000 tapes on request to broadcasting organizations. Shortwave broadcasts and transcriptions went to 142 countries and territories in the same period.

Practically every television organization makes use of UN programs and news material. In areas without television services, films are used for group showings by the UN information centers. Particularly in demand are informational films on the structure of the UN system. New productions have been started on support for the Second United Nations Development Decade, the 25th anniversary of the United Nations, and the United Nations Conference on the Human Environment, to be held in 1972. Like UN radio, UN television and film productions tend to lay heavy emphasis on economic and social development.

UN Information Centers

These centers, which are located in 51 countries, play an indispensable role in OPI's work of disseminating information on a worldwide basis. OPI material produced at Headquarters is sent to the centers for redistribution to the areas concerned. The centers work closely with government and private information agencies on the needs of information media, with educational authorities on programs for teaching about the UN, and with nongovernmental organizations on special programs. They also supply Headquarters with information on local UN activities, which in turn is redisseminated through the network.

PRIVILEGES AND IMMUNITIES

The Charter provides that the UN shall enjoy such privileges and immunities as are necessary for the fulfillment of its purposes, and that representatives of member nations and officials of the UN shall have a status allowing them an independent exercise of their functions. On 13 February 1946 the General Assembly adopted a Convention on the Privileges and Immunities of the United Nations, which had been drawn up by the Secretariat, and "proposed it for accession by each Member of the United Nations." As of June 1970, 102 nations, including the US, had acceded to this convention.

In the countries that have acceded to the convention, the salaries of UN officials are exempt from taxation; the UN itself is exempt from all direct taxes, including transportation tax for official travel, and from customs duties and export and import restrictions on articles for official use. Thus in such countries UNICEF, for example, can freely import and export medicines; equipment and supplies for UN special missions can be transported; and UN officials can leave and enter on travel papers, so-called *laissez-passer*, issued by the UN and are entitled to priority for speedy travel. Some governments have formally dispensed with visa requirements for UN staff traveling on official business.

Practically all member nations have established permanent missions to the UN in New York, and they enjoy privileges and immunities similar to those of diplomatic missions.

HEADQUARTERS AGREEMENT BETWEEN THE UN AND THE US

A special headquarters agreement, signed by Secretary-General Trygve Lie and US Secretary of State George C. Marshall at Lake Success on 26 June 1947, has been in force since 21 November 1947. It defines the 18 acres of land in New York City located between 42d and 48th Streets and First Avenue and the Franklin D. Roosevelt Drive as a Headquarters District. The Headquarters District is "under the control and authority of the United Nations as provided in this agreement." It is the seat of the UN, and the agreement stipulates that the district "shall be inviolable." Federal, state, and local personnel on official duty (for example, a policeman intent on making an arrest) may enter it only with the consent of the secretary-general. The UN may make regulations for the area; and US federal, state, and local law, insofar as it is inconsistent with UN regulations, does not apply here.

Otherwise, the US courts would have jurisdiction over actions and transactions taking place in the Headquarters District. The UN may expel persons from it for violations of regulations. In such cases, and generally for the preservation of law and order, US authorities have to provide a sufficient number of police if requested by the secretary-general. "No form of racial or religious discrimination shall be permitted within the Headquarters District." Other detailed provisions in the agreement between the UN and the US deal with the important matter of the accessibility of the seat of the UN to non-US citizens.

In principle, there is to be unimpeded transit to and from the district and protection for UN delegates, for UN officials, for correspondents accredited to UN headquarters (approximately 500 press, radio, and television correspondents from almost every country are permanently accredited, and an average of 50 others come to cover the General Assembly sessions) and for certain other categories of persons traveling on UN business, irrespective of the relations existing between the US government and their governments. Visas must be granted without charge and as promptly as possible. US laws regarding the residence of aliens are not to be applied in a manner that would interfere with such persons while they are on UN business. Of course, these rights are not to be abused. As soon as a person ceases to act on official UN business, US rules regarding the residence of aliens become effective.

EMBLEM AND FLAG OF THE UN

The General Assembly adopted an official seal and emblem for the organization, requesting member nations to prohibit the use of the emblem and the name and initials of the UN without the authorization of the secretary-general.

Emblem. The UN emblem depicts in silver against a light-blue background a map of the earth, projected from the North Pole, and encircled by two symmetrical olive branches. It is a slight modification of a design selected by the US Office of Strategic Services for buttons used at the San Francisco Conference in 1945. The shade of blue is now officially called United Nations blue.

Flag. The first UN flag was used in Greece in 1947, when it became necessary to identify and protect the members of a UN investigation committee who were moving about in a region where there was fighting. That first flag showed the UN emblem surrounded by the legend, "United Nations—Nations Unies." Subsequently these words were deleted. The emblem is white against a background of United Nations blue.

Display of UN Flag. The flag may be displayed not only by the UN and specialized agencies and by governments but also by "organizations and individuals to demonstrate support of the United Nations and to further its principles and purposes." It is considered "especially appropriate" to display the UN flag on national and official holidays, on UN Day, 24 October, and at official events in honor of the UN or related in some way to the UN.

Unless the laws of the country provide differently, the display of the UN flag is to be governed by the rules of *UN Flag Code and Regulations*. According to these rules, the flag may be displayed alone or with one or more other flags. In the latter case, all flags should be displayed on the same level and be of approximately equal size; hence no flag or flags displayed with the UN flag may be longer or be displayed on a higher level than the UN flag. If other flags are displayed in line, cluster, or semicircle together with the UN flag, they are to be arranged in the English alphabetical order of the countries represented by the flags, starting from the left and reading clockwise. The UN flag may either be displayed in the center of the line, cluster, or semicircle, or, if two UN flags are available, at either end. The national flag of the country where the display takes place may also be displayed twice, once at either side of the line.

Prohibition of Other Uses of the UN Flag. The replica of the UN flag may be manufactured in the form of a lapel button. Otherwise the *UN Flag Code and Regulations* forbids the use of the flag or the emblem on any article, and particularly "for commercial purposes."

THE UNITED NATIONS BUDGET

THE UN BUDGET

Under the Charter it is the task of the General Assembly to "consider and approve the budget of the Organization" and to apportion the expenses of the UN among the member nations. From an administrative standpoint, the expenditures of the UN may be said to fall into two categories: expenditures that are included in what is termed the "regular budgets," to which all members are obliged to contribute; and expenditures for certain high-cost items or programs, for which are established separate, or "extrabudgetary," accounts or funds, financed by special arrangements that do not necessarily involve obligatory payments by UN members.

Included in the regular budget are operating costs at UN Headquarters and all overseas UN offices; the expenses of the International Court of Justice; expenditures for certain technical programs, and for special missions, such as the UN Truce Supervision Organization in Palestine (UNTSO); expenses of the UN Field Service; special expenses, such as those for the UN Memorial Cemetery in Korea; and debt services charges, which are also listed as "special expenses."

Extrabudgetary accounts cover the work of the many subsidiary bodies of the UN that are financed either wholly or in part by voluntary contributions from government and other sources. These include the UN Children's Fund (UNICEF), the UN Development Program, and the UN Relief and Works Agency for Palestine Refugees (UNRWA). The administrative expenses of the Office of the High Commissioner for Refugees are included in the regular UN budget, but its actual programs are also financed through a special account. Special accounts have also been used to finance the costly UN peacekeeping operations along the borders of Israel, in the Congo, and in Cyprus. All told, these extrabudgetary accounts greatly exceed the regular UN budget in most years. The much publicized financial crisis of the UN, which came to a head in 1964 and was still unresolved at the end of 1970, arose chiefly over the financing of peacekeeping operations in the Middle East and in the Congo. (See the chapter on UN Peacekeeping Forces.)

SUBSIDIARY ORGANS ASSISTING THE ASSEMBLY IN FINANCIAL MATTERS

The General Assembly has established two permanent subsidiary organs concerned with administrative and budgetary affairs.

The Advisory Committee on Administrative and Budgetary Questions is responsible for expert examination of the UN budget and the administrative budgets of the specialized agencies. The committee's 12 members, elected by the Assembly for staggered 3-year terms, serve as individuals, not as government representatives.

The Committee on Contributions advises the Assembly on the apportionment of the expense of the UN among the member nations. Its 12 members are elected for 3-year terms and also serve as individuals.

PROCEDURE FOR DETERMINING THE REGULAR BUDGET

Each summer, the secretary-general presents detailed budget and appropriations estimates for the following calendar year. These estimates are reviewed by the Advisory Committee and are later debated in the Assembly. At the end of its debate, the Assembly approves the budget in the form of a three-part resolution, which states: (1) the total appropriations and the estimates for the major items of expenditures; (2) the estimates of anticipated income from sources other than assessments on member nations (see below, under Budget Estimates for 1971); and (3) the distribution scale for the financing of the appropriations for the year in question.

APPROPRIATIONS (GROSS) FOR THE REGULAR BUDGET OF THE UN, 1946–1971

YEAR	APPROPRIATION	YEAR	APPROPRIATION
1946	$ 19,390,000	1959	$ 61,657,100
1947	28,616,568	1960	63,149,700
1948	39,285,736	1961	72,969,300
1949	43,204,080	1962	82,144,740
1950	44,520,773	1963	93,911,050
1951	48,925,500	1964	101,327,600
1952	50,547,660	1965	108,472,800
1953	49,869,450	1966	121,567,420
1954	48,528,980	1967	130,314,230
1955	50,228,000	1968	140,430,950
1956	50,683,350	1969	156,917,300
1957	53,174,700	1970	168,956,950
1958	61,121,900	1971	192,149,300

Aside from the regular budget, the Assembly also allots a certain amount of money for unforeseen and extraordinary expenses and determines the level of the UN's working capital fund, to which member nations advance sums in proportion to their assessed contributions to the regular budget. The fund—$40 million—is used to finance appropriations pending receipt of contributions and may also be drawn upon by the secretary-general for other purposes determined by the Assembly.

Since the expenses of the organization can never be precisely predicted, the secretary-general reviews actual expenditures for the current year at each regular session of the Assembly and proposes adjustments in the original appropriations. Usually, a supplemental budget is voted, but on five occasions the Assembly voted reductions. During the 1970 session the Assembly voted for an increase of $586,950 in the budget it had adopted for the year 1970 at its previous session.

BUDGET ESTIMATES FOR 1971
A. Items of Expenditure

The amount of $192,149,300 was appropriated for gross estimated expenditures in 1971 as follows:

1. *Sessions of the General Assembly, the councils, commissions, and committees; special meetings and conferences* (including travel and other expenses of representatives): $4,704,900
2. *Staff costs and related expenses:* $108,501,300
3. *Premises, equipment, supplies, and services:* $24,783,800
4. *Special expenses* (including $8,556,200 in interest and

amortization on the $200 million UN bond issue floated in 1963): $10,647,500

　　5. *Technical programs* (including certain economic and social development activities, human rights advisory services, and narcotic drugs control): $6,908,000

　　6. *Special missions and related activities:* $8,133,100

　　7. *Office of the UN High Commissioner for Refugees:* $4,722,000

　　8. *International Court of Justice:* $1,453,900

　　9. *UN Conference on Trade and Development:* $10,072,300

　　10. *UN Industrial Development Organization:* $12,222,500

B. Income Estimates

It was estimated that gross expenditures would be offset to the amount of $31,777,000 in 1971 through certain accounting devices such as staff assessment and the prorating of certain expenses to the various extrabudgetary accounts and through income derived from interest on invested funds and from certain headquarters services. The estimates were as follows:

　　1. *Income from staff assessment:* $21,663,000

　　2. *Funds provided from extrabudgetary accounts:* $2,436,400

　　3. *General income:* $4,755,400

　　4. *Sale of UN postage stamps:* $2,137,000

　　5. *Sale of publications:* $255,000

　　6. *Services to visitors and catering services:* $530,200

UN Staff Assessment. Under UN regulations, a percentage of the earnings of the entire UN staff is deducted in lieu of taxes and credited to "income." In order to avoid double taxation of staff members of US nationality, who are the only ones taxed on their UN earnings by their own government, US nationals are then reimbursed by the UN for the taxes (federal, state, and city) levied on their UN earnings. The withholdings from the salaries of UN personnel of all other nationalities are credited to the member states' accounts against their assessed contributions.

C. Net Expenditures

After taking into account staff assessment and other items of income, the net estimated amount remaining to be raised through assessed contributions from member states for the year 1971 totaled $160,372,300.

ASSESSED CONTRIBUTION BY MEMBER STATES TO THE REGULAR BUDGET

The scale of contributions by individual countries is determined by the General Assembly on the recommendations of its Committee on Contributions. Originally, the major criteria for assessments were national income; per capita income; war-caused economic hardships; and countries' ability to acquire foreign currency. In this way, the US share was at first 39.89%. Gradually declining, it was set at 31.52% for 1971–73 and is to be lowered to 30%. The next highest share, until the mid-1950's that of the UK, has since then been paid by the USSR. For 1971–73, its share was 14.18%. For the same period, the third-highest share, that of France, was set at 6.00%, and the fourth-highest, that of the UK, at 5.90%. For the first time, the 1971–73 scale provides that a member state (Japan) which is not a member of the Security Council, will pay more (5.40%) than one of the permanent members of the Security Council (Taiwan, 4.00%). At the other end of the scale, 63 members pay the minimum of 0.04%.

In accordance with Rule 161 of the Assembly's rules of procedure, once the scale of assessments is fixed by the Assembly, it "shall not be subject to a general revision for at least three years, unless it is clear that there have been substantial changes in relative capacities to pay." At the 1970 Assembly session, a new scale of assessment was fixed for the three years 1971–73 as follows:

MEMBER STATE	PERCENT	MEMBER STATE	PERCENT
Afghanistan	0.04	Laos	0.04
Albania	0.04	Lebanon	0.05
Algeria	0.09	Lesotho	0.04
Argentina	0.85	Liberia	0.04
Australia	1.47	Libya	0.07
Austria	0.55	Luxembourg	0.05
Barbados	0.04	Madagascar	0.04
Belgium	1.05	Malawi	0.04
Bolivia	0.04	Malaysia	0.10
Botswana	0.04	Maldives	0.04
Brazil	0.80	Mali	0.04
Bulgaria	0.18	Malta	0.04
Burma	0.05	Mauritania	0.04
Burundi	0.04	Mauritius	0.04
Byelorussia	0.50	Mexico	0.88
Cambodia	0.04	Mongolia	0.04
Cameroon	0.04	Morocco	0.09
Canada	3.08	Nepal	0.04
Central African Republic	0.04	Netherlands	1.18
Ceylon	0.05	New Zealand	0.32
Chad	0.04	Nicaragua	0.04
Chile	0.20	Niger	0.04
China (Taiwan)	4.00	Nigeria	0.12
Colombia	0.19	Norway	0.43
Congo (Brazzaville)	0.04	Pakistan	0.34
Congo (Kinshasa)	0.04	Panama	0.04
Costa Rica	0.04	Paraguay	0.04
Cuba	0.16	Peru	0.10
Cyprus	0.04	Philippines	0.31
Czechoslovakia	0.90	Poland	1.41
Dahomey	0.04	Portugal	0.16
Denmark	0.62	Romania	0.36
Dominican Republic	0.04	Rwanda	0.04
Ecuador	0.04	Sa'udi Arabia	0.07
El Salvador	0.04	Senegal	0.04
Equatorial Guinea	0.04	Sierra Leone	0.04
Ethiopia	0.04	Singapore	0.05
Finland	0.45	Somalia	0.04
France	6.00	South Africa	0.54
Gabon	0.04	Southern Yemen	0.04
Gambia	0.04	Spain	1.04
Ghana	0.07	Sudan	0.04
Greece	0.29	Swaziland	0.04
Guatemala	0.05	Sweden	1.25
Guinea	0.04	Syria	0.04
Guyana	0.04	Tanzania	0.04
Haiti	0.04	Thailand	0.13
Honduras	0.04	Togo	0.04
Hungary	0.48	Trinidad and Tobago	0.04
Iceland	0.04	Tunisia	0.04
India	1.55	Turkey	0.35
Indonesia	0.28	Uganda	0.04
Iran	0.22	Ukraine	1.87
Iraq	0.07	USSR	14.18
Ireland	0.15	UAR	0.18
Israel	0.20	UK	5.90
Italy	3.54	US	31.52
Ivory Coast	0.04	Upper Volta	0.04
Jamaica	0.04	Uruguay	0.07
Japan	5.40	Venezuela	0.41
Jordan	0.04	Yemen	0.04
Kenya	0.04	Yugoslavia	0.38
Kuwait	0.08	Zambia	0.04
		TOTAL	100.00

(The assessment for Fiji, which became a member in 1970, will be made in 1971).

Contributions by Nonmember States

States that are not members of the UN but participate in certain of its activities (principally the International Court of Justice, the regional economic commissions, the UN Conference on

Trade and Development, the UN Industrial Development Organization, and the control of narcotic drugs) contribute toward expenses of such activities according to the following scale.

	PERCENT		PERCENT
Germany, West	6.90	San Marino	0.04
Korea, South	0.11	Switzerland	0.84
Liechtenstein	0.04	Vatican City	0.04
Monaco	0.04	Viet-Nam, South	0.07

PROPOSALS TO EASE THE UN'S FINANCIAL DIFFICULTIES

By and large the regular budget has never created major disputes among the member states, and most governments have usually paid their dues relatively punctually. However, since 1963 the USSR has refused as a matter of principle to contribute to certain items in the regular budget—the UN Commission for the Unification and Rehabilitation of Korea, the Memorial Cemetery in Korea, the US Truce Supervision Organization in Palestine, and the UN Field Service—or to those parts of the regular budget devoted to the redemption of UN bonds (a method of raising funds for certain UN peacekeeping operations). France has taken a similar stand in connection with the redemption of the bonds. Furthermore, a number of countries have refused to contribute to the special accounts for peacekeeping operations in the Congo and the Middle East. It was chiefly these controversial expenditures that caused the UN's financial crisis in the mid-1960's.

However, there has also been growing concern over the rapidly increasing expenditures on the noncontroversial items of the regular budget—meetings, staff costs, new development activities, and the like. In part, these increases reflect the continuing rise in the costs of operations and of expansion of the resources of the Secretariat to meet the requirements of an augmented membership and activities connected with disarmament, non-self-governing territories, and so on. Nevertheless, some member countries

have felt that there may be a serious element of costly wastage due to overproduction of documents, a plethora of meetings, conferences, and seminars, and inefficient administrative and budgetary procedures.

Accordingly, at the suggestion of France, the 1965 Assembly set up a 14-member Ad Hoc Committee of Experts to Examine the Finances of the UN and the Specialized Agencies. The committee was assigned two tasks: to comment on an analysis of the financial situation of the UN as of 30 September 1965, which the secretary-general was requested to prepare; and to submit proposals on ways to improve the use of available funds and ensure that any expansion of activities considers both needs and costs. The analysis prepared by the secretary-general showed that between January 1957 and September 1965 the organization had spent $193.9 million more than it received in income, chiefly due to costs of peacekeeping operations in the Middle East and the Congo. The Ad Hoc Committee estimated that between $31.9 million and $53.3 million in additional voluntary contributions was required as of September 1965 to meet the UN's deficit. With regard to the long-term financial outlook, the committee concluded that the future deficit in the regular UN budget would amount to about $3.2 million a year, if certain states continued to withhold contributions to cover the amortization of UN bonds and other items. Among its recommendations to improve budgetary and administrative procedures throughout the UN family, the committee suggested that all specialized agencies with an annual budget cycle should adopt a biennial cycle, and that efforts should be made to introduce medium and long-term planning. There have since been a number of moves in this direction. Several member states, including the US, have urged that the Ad Hoc Committee be reconstituted to examine (1) program budgeting in the UN and the specialized agencies; (2) the machinery for program and budget building, administrative control, inspection, and coordination; (3) evaluation arrangements; and (4) the financial, budgetary, and program relations between the UN and its related agencies.

BUDGET OF THE UN AND TEN AGENCIES OF THE UN SYSTEM

THIS TABLE SHOWS THE GROSS EXPENDITURES OR ESTIMATES OF GROSS EXPENDITURES OF THE UN AND THE TEN INTERGOVERNMENTAL AGENCIES WHOSE ADMINISTRATIVE BUDGETS ARE SUBMITTED FOR REVIEW TO THE GENERAL ASSEMBLY

	1966 ACTUAL EXPENSES $	1967 ACTUAL EXPENSES $	1968 ACTUAL EXPENSES $	1969 ACTUAL EXPENSES $	1970 APPROPRIATIONS $	1971 APPROPRIATIONS OR ESTIMATES $
United Nations	118,607,969	130,489,561	141,161,623	156,780,541	168,956,950	192,149,300
ILO	23,523,905	26,498,651	29,034,814	31,100,689	34,254,300	36,675,549
FAO	27,779,243	29,652,268	31,697,977	36,234,191	39,896,900	40,533,800
UNESCO	28,577,407	32,864,263	37,253,838	41,799,747	44,272,466	47,295,500
ICAO	7,537,852	6,984,326	7,604,971	7,734,365	8,169,554	8,514,359
UPU	1,308,093	1,486,251	1,539,632	2,050,497	2,012,083	2,162,917
WHO	48,204,153	56,328,664	61,071,643	68,824,146	75,768,176	81,774,465
ITU	7,015,409	6,830,607	7,248,006	7,708,819	8,991,111	9,290,037
WMO	1,978,496	2,378,532	2,628,470	3,113,610	3,803,224	4,018,944
IMCO	850,261	836,766	799,795	1,234,924	1,258,888	1,448,106
IAEA	9,970,804	10,432,979	11,969,130	13,521,456	14,837,000	17,029,000
TOTALS	275,353,590	304,782,868	332,009,899	370,102,985	402,220,652	440,891,977

THE GENERAL ASSEMBLY

First of the UN organs established by the Charter, the General Assembly is the pivot of the entire organization. All member states are represented in it. Each country, large or small, has one vote, and decides the way in which it chooses its own representatives.

FUNCTIONS AND POWERS

The central position of the Assembly within the organization is firmly established in a series of Charter provisions encompassing an extraordinarily wide range of functions and powers. First are the provisions setting forth the Assembly's powers as the major deliberative body of the UN. With two exceptions (described below), the Assembly has the right to discuss and make recommendations on any subject that falls within the scope of the Charter itself, including the function and powers of the other organs. Hence, it is in the Assembly that all of the UN's important projects (except for the Security Council's peacekeeping operations) originate: on political questions, disarmament, economic and social welfare, human rights, decolonization of dependent territories, and development of international law.

The second group of Charter provisions defining the pivotal position of the Assembly concerns the financing of the UN. The Assembly is empowered to "consider and approve" the budget of the organization (which includes that of the International Court of Justice at the Hague), and it also has the right to determine how the expenses shall be apportioned among the member nations.

Lastly, the Assembly's pivotal position is secured by provisions that give it specific powers in relation to the other organs. Thus both the Economic and Social Council and the Trusteeship Council are constituted under the direct authority of the Assembly to carry out designated tasks in their respective spheres. The administrative arm of the UN, the Secretariat, is also at the disposition of the Assembly. The Assembly's powers, however, are much more limited where the Security Council and International Court of Justice are concerned. Designed in some respects to be more powerful than the Assembly, the Security Council is in no way answerable to the Assembly for its activities—although it is required to make an annual report and, when necessary, special reports. Also, whereas the Assembly is empowered to make recommendations to the Council concerning the maintenance of international peace, it cannot give the Council instructions. In the case of the International Court of Justice, any attempt to render its activities answerable to the Assembly would have prejudiced the independent status that is normally accorded to judiciary bodies throughout the world. Nevertheless, inasmuch as the Assembly not only has budgetary power but also elects all the justices of the World Court and at least the nonpermanent members of the Security Council, it can be said to exercise an appreciable degree of indirect control over both these bodies.

Thus the one main UN organ on which all member states have the constitutional right to be represented is able to make its will felt throughout the organization, and indeed the entire UN system. Because its powers closely resemble those of a national parliament, the General Assembly has often been described as a "world parliament." Parliamentary powers are not to be confused, though, with governmental powers. Except insofar as the Economic and Social Council, the Trusteeship Council, and the Secretariat are bound to carry out its requests, the Assembly has no power to legislate and cannot enforce its decisions upon individual member nations. The only sanctions that the Assembly can wield against an uncooperative member are the suspension of the rights and privileges of membership and expulsion from the organization, but even these sanctions can be invoked only on the recommendation of the Security Council. In effect, then, all Assembly decisions are merely recommendations whose sole force is one of moral obligation. At the end of this chapter an attempt is made to assess their effectiveness on this score.

Charter Restrictions on the Assembly's Power to Discuss and Recommend

The Charter imposes two major restrictions on the Assembly's powers to discuss and make recommendations. The first is Principle No. 7 of the Charter, which states that "Nothing contained in the present Charter shall authorize the United Nations to intervene in matters which are essentially within the domestic jurisdiction of any state or shall require the Members to submit such matters to settlement. . . ." This principle is not so restrictive as it might seem, for whether a given issue is or is not of a domestic character is decided by the Assembly itself. The Assembly can and often does override by majority vote the attempt of a member nation to bar a particular topic from debate by invoking Principle No. 7 of the Charter. The most notable case in point is the annual discussions of South Africa's apartheid policy that take place at each regular session of the Assembly, despite South Africa's contention that the matter is essentially within its domestic jurisdiction and without international implications.

The second restriction is to be found in Article 12 of the Charter, which states that while the Security Council is exercising its functions in respect of any international dispute or crisis, "the General Assembly shall not make any recommendation with regard to that dispute . . . unless the Security Council so requests." This stipulation, then, clearly establishes the absolute primacy of the Security Council over the General Assembly in times of crisis. Here, the main object of the founders of the UN was to ensure against the possibility of the smaller nations forming a majority bloc to interfere with any decisions that might be taken by the Big Five acting in concert as permanent members of the Security Council, where each possesses the right of veto. (For a discussion on the conflict between the big and smaller powers over the veto right, see the chapter on the Security Council.)

Extension of the Assembly's Power to Discuss and Recommend through the Uniting for Peace Resolution

Designed to secure maximum unity of action in moments of acute danger, Article 12 in fact proved to be the chief obstacle to action of any kind during successive crises in the early postwar years. The effectiveness of the entire system presupposed a spirit of unanimity among the great powers in their determination to end a particular dispute that appeared to threaten international peace and security. But on each occasion the great powers might have been expected to display unanimity, the USSR and the other four permanent members of the Security Council took opposite sides in the dispute concerned. As a result, precisely because each of them possessed the veto right, all Council action was deadlocked. Meanwhile, the Assembly, prevented from taking action of its own accord because of Article 12, was forced to stand helplessly by.

It was the seriousness of the prolonged Korean crisis that finally impelled the Assembly to take steps to break through its constitutional straitjacket. Following a deadlock in the Council, when the USSR vetoed a US-sponsored resolution in connection with the entry of Red China into the Korean conflict on the side of North Korea, the Assembly convened an emergency special session to discuss the situation and adopted a resolution that enabled it to circumvent the restrictions imposed by Article 12. This resolution, which came to be known as the Uniting for Peace Resolution, provides that if the Security Council, because of lack of unanimity among its permanent members, fails to exercise its primary responsibility in the maintenance of peace, in a case where there appears to be a threat to the peace, breach of the peace, or act of aggression, the Assembly shall consider the matter immediately with a view to making recommendations to members for collective measures, including if necessary the use of armed force. Although the Uniting for Peace Resolution thus considerably extends the Assembly's powers with respect to maintenance of international peace and security, it in no way represents an attempt to usurp the Security Council's prerogatives when that body is functioning smoothly. Nor does it attempt to arrogate to the Assembly the enforcement powers that the Charter accorded to the Security Council and to the Council alone. Even under the Uniting for Peace Resolution, the Assembly can only recommend that members undertake collective peacekeeping measures; it cannot oblige them to do so. Nor can the Assembly impose peacekeeping action against the will of the parties to a dispute. It must obtain their explicit consent to the presence of UN personnel—observer commissions, mediators, troops—in their territories.

Since the Korean war, the Assembly has undertaken two other large-scale peacekeeping operations within the terms of the Uniting for Peace Resolution: in the Middle East and in the Congo. However, two permanent members of the Security Council, the USSR and France, have denied the legitimacy of these operations under the Charter, and both have refused on these grounds to contribute to their costs, thereby plunging the UN into financial and constitutional difficulties that have still to be resolved. (A discussion of the constitutional problems involved is included in the chapter Maintaining Peace and Security).

ORGANIZATION
Sessions
The General Assembly meets once a year in regular sessions that begin on the third Tuesday in September. Usually these sessions last about three months, ending before Christmas, but there is no fixed time limit, and several times the Assembly has adjourned to continue the session after the holidays. Special sessions on a particular topic may be held at the request of the Security Council, or of a majority of UN members, or of one member if the majority of members concur. To implement the terms of the Uniting for Peace Resolution, an emergency special session may be called within 24 hours at the request of the Security Council on the vote of any nine members, or

by a majority of UN members, or by one member if the majority concur.

Sessional Committees
Most of the Assembly's substantive work during its regular session is conducted through seven "Main Committees" which are reconstituted at every session. Each main committee is composed of representatives of all member nations.

Six of the main committees are officially designated by numbers. The *First Committee* deals with political and security issues, including the regulation of armaments. The *Second Committee* deals with economic and financial matters, including technical assistance and the work of the specialized agencies. The *Third Committee* reviews social problems and human rights issues, including the work of the appropriate specialized agencies. The *Fourth Committee* handles problems of granting independence to colonial and trust territories. The *Fifth Committee* deals with the administrative and budgetary matters of the organization. The *Sixth Committee* debates legal questions, including the general development and codification of international law. The seventh is the *Special Political Committee,* which was originally created in 1948 as an ad hoc committee of the whole to discuss the Palestine question. Never disbanded, it was subsequently retained as an additional main committee to assist the First Committee in dealing with political issues.

The Assembly maintains two other sessional committees, both of which deal with Assembly procedure. However, neither of these is a committee of the whole. The *General Committee,* composed of the Assembly president, the 17 vice-presidents, and the chairmen of the main committees, examines the provisional agenda of each session and makes recommendations to the Assembly on the inclusion or exclusion of items and on their assignment to the appropriate main committee. The *Credentials Committee* is a nine-member body appointed by the Assembly at the beginning of the session to examine the credentials of representatives and work out any problems that might arise in this connection.

Plenary Meetings
Since all the main committees are committees of the whole, the distinction between the Assembly meeting in committee and meeting in plenum is largely one of protocol. Always conducted by the president or a vice-president of the Assembly, plenary meetings are much more formal affairs. Normally, no one below the rank of head of delegation may actively participate in the proceedings, and no one is allowed to speak from his chair but must go to the speaker's rostrum. (None of the conference rooms in which the committees meet is provided with a speaker's rostrum.) The Assembly Hall itself—the only place in the Headquarters building where the delegates may not smoke—is reserved exclusively for plenary meetings and may not be used by the committees.

It is in plenary that all formal or ceremonial functions occur: the opening and closing of the Assembly session, election of officers and members of other organs, the final decision on all agenda items, and addresses by heads of state or government or by other high national officials who visit the UN while the Assembly is in session. Plenary meetings are also the forum for the statements of general policy that the head of each member delegation is entitled to make as part of what is known as the "general debate," which takes place during the first three weeks or so of the regular session.

Voting Procedure
Each member of the General Assembly and its committees has one vote. Article 18 of the Charter decrees that Assembly decisions on "important" questions shall be made by a two-thirds majority of the members present and voting. Among the important questions specified are recommendations with regard to main-

tenance of peace and security; election of the nonpermanent members of the Security Council and of the members of the Economic and Social Council and the Trusteeship Council; the admission of new UN members, suspension of rights and privileges of membership, and expulsion of members; questions relating to the operation of the trusteeship system; budgetary questions. Decisions on other questions, including the determination of additional categories of important questions requiring a two-thirds majority vote, are made by a simple majority of the members present and voting. The phrase "members present and voting" means members casting either affirmative or negative votes; members that abstain are considered as not voting. Thus, although the number of abstentions is usually listed for information purposes, it does not count in the final tally as to whether a resolution has received the requisite majority—provided that the rules of quorum have been observed. (A quorum is constituted by the presence of a majority of members.)

Voting may be by a show of hands, by roll call, or in certain instances, such as elections, by secret ballot. The normal method was intended to be by a show of hands, but any member can request a roll call. There has been an increasing tendency to do so, especially on the more contentious issues. Before a roll call vote is taken, a lot is drawn to determine the country that is to vote first. Starting with that country, voting proceeds according to the alphabetical order of the official names of states in English. Mechanical voting equipment has been installed in the Assembly Hall and was first used at the 1965 session. Similar equipment is to be installed in one conference room.

Seating Arrangements
Although the Charter permits each member nation to have only five representatives in the General Assembly, ten seats are assigned in the Assembly Hall to each delegation. Five of these are for the official delegates, and behind them are five seats for alternate representatives or advisers, most of whom actively participate in the meetings of the main committees. Both in the Assembly Hall and the committee rooms, delegations are seated in alphabetical order according to the official names in English of the countries. To ensure rotation of the advantageous seats (those near the rostrum or the chair), a lot is drawn prior to each session to determine the country with which the alphabetical seating starts. This sequence also determines the protocol position of each member for the session.

Election of Officers
At each regular session, the General Assembly constitutes itself anew. During the opening meetings, the main officers are elected, and they hold their positions until their successors are chosen at the next regular session. Thus, if a special or emergency special session is called, it is presided over by officers elected the previous September.

The first officer to be elected is the president of the Assembly. Delegates vote by secret ballot, and a simple majority suffices. In choosing the president, regard has to be paid to the equitable geographical rotation of the office among the following groups of states: African and Asian states, Eastern European states, Latin American states, Western European and other states. By tacit agreement, no representative of a permanent member of the Security Council is ever elected president of the Assembly.

PRESIDENTS OF THE GENERAL ASSEMBLY
First session, 1946–47, Paul-Henri Spaak, Belgium
Second session, 1947, Oswaldo Aranha, Brazil
Third session, 1948–49, Herbert V. Evatt, Australia
Fourth session, 1949, Carlos P. Romulo, Phillippines
Fifth session, 1950–51, Nasrollah Entezam, Iran
Sixth session, 1951–52, Luis Padilla Nervo, Mexico
Seventh session, 1952–53, Lester B. Pearson, Canada

Eighth session, 1953, Mrs. Vijaya Lakshmi Pandit, India
Ninth session, 1954, Eelco N. van Kleffens, Netherlands
Tenth session, 1955, José Maza, Chile
Eleventh session, 1956–57, Prince Wan Waithayakon, Thailand
Twelfth session, 1957, Sir Leslie Munro, New Zealand
Thirteenth session, 1958–59, Charles Malik, Lebanon
Fourteenth session, 1959, Victor Andrés Belaunde, Peru
Fifteenth session, 1960–61, Frederick H. Boland, Ireland
Sixteenth session, 1961–62, Mongi Slim, Tunisia
Seventeenth session, 1962, Muhammad Zafrulla Khan, Pakistan
Eighteenth session, 1963, Carlos Sosa Rodriguez, Venezuela
Nineteenth session, 1964–65, Alex Quaison-Sackey, Ghana
Twentieth session, 1965, Amintore Fanfani, Italy
Twenty-first session, 1966, Abdul Rahman Pazwak, Afghanistan
Twenty-second session, 1967–68, Corneliu Manescu, Romania
Twenty-third session, 1968, Emilio Arenales, Guatemala
Twenty-fourth session, 1969, Miss Angie E. Brooks, Liberia
Twenty-fifth session, 1970, Edvard Hambro, Norway

Following the election of the president, the main committees of the Assembly are officially constituted and retire to elect their own officers. Here again the matter of equitable geographical representation arises, and it is precisely regulated by a resolution adopted by the Assembly in 1963. Of the seven committee chairmen, three must be chosen from Africa and Asia and one each from Eastern Europe, Latin America, and Western Europe. The seventh chairmanship rotates in alternate years between representatives from Latin America and from Western Europe.

The final officers to be elected are the Assembly's 17 vice-presidents. Of these, 12 are elected in accordance with a geographical pattern: 7 from Africa and Asia, 1 from Eastern Europe, 3 from Latin America, and 2 from Western Europe and other areas. The remaining five represent the permanent members of the Security Council: China, France, USSR, UK, and US.

AGENDA OF THE ASSEMBLY
Under the Assembly's rules of procedure, the provisional agenda for a regular session must be issued no later than 60 days before the opening. However, up to 30 days before the opening, the secretary-general, any of the other principal organs of the UN, or any member of the UN, may request the inclusion of supplementary items. Additional items may also be included at a later stage, even after the session has formally started, if a majority of the Assembly agree.

Normally, the agenda includes about 100 items. The great majority of substantive (that is to say, nonprocedural) items arise out of decisions taken by previous sessions of the Assembly, and their inclusion on the agenda is automatic. Thus the Assembly frequently requests the secretary-general, a special committee, or another UN organ to submit a special report on a given topic. The report, at the time it is due, becomes an automatic agenda item. There also are several items that the Assembly is obliged to consider at each session under the Charter—for example, the annual report of the secretary-general on the work of the UN and the reports of the three councils. Moreover, certain items placed on the agenda by particular members of the UN come up at session after session because the sponsors are not satisfied with the Assembly's previous action on these matters.

Adoption of the Agenda
The adoption of the agenda is not a mere formality. The Assembly has to approve the entire agenda and may amend or delete any item by majority vote. A decision by the Assembly to reject a particular member's request to have an item placed on the agenda could have considerable political significance. It is the function of the 25-member General Committee (which could be described as the steering committee) to make recommendations to the Assembly on the inclusion of requested items in

the agenda. Most of the pros and cons of including a controversial item in the agenda are thrashed out in this committee rather than in the plenary, and the committee's proceedings sometimes afford a preview of the positions countries will take on certain questions when they come up for substantive debate.

Another important function of the General Committee is to recommend the routing of agenda items to the various main committees for debate. The General Committee may also recommend that an important item be debated in the plenary without being previously referred to a committee. Complicating this difficult task is the fact that member governments attach greatest prestige, first to debates conducted in the plenary and next to debates conducted in the First and Special Political committees. In all three, states are customarily represented by their highest-ranking delegates. Hence, when a new item is proposed for the agenda, its sponsor or sponsors always stress its political importance. Other members, to show their disapproval, may argue that the item has only technical significance and should be considered by one of the nonpolitical committees. Thus in 1965 the USSR strongly urged that the agenda item it had introduced on "Inadmissibility of Intervention in Domestic Affairs of States" be debated in the plenary. At the same time, the USSR strongly resisted the UK's wish to have the agenda item it had introduced on "Peaceful Settlement of Disputes" debated in the First Committee and suggested the Sixth Committee as the appropriate forum. In the end, the Soviet item was assigned to the First Committee, and the UK's item was debated in the Special Political Committee.

In hammering the agenda into manageable shape, the General Committee frequently recommends that certain proposed items be combined. For instance, a political item that has been proposed by one or more countries may logically be considered together with a report by some subsidiary UN body.

On many occasions, however, this procedure is adopted only after much dispute in the committee. Sponsoring members often feel that consideration of the item they have proposed might suffer in consequence. At other times they balk because the objectives of the items concerned appear to conflict with one another. For example, the USSR does not recognize the legitimacy of the UN Commission for the Unification and Rehabilitation of Korea and always formally opposes the inclusion of the commission's report on the agenda. It strongly objects to this item's being combined with two other items on Korea that have been sponsored by Eastern bloc countries and some Arab states—namely, the Withdrawal of US and Other Foreign Forces from South Korea and the Dissolution of the UN Commission for the Unification and Rehabilitation of Korea.

OUTCOME OF ASSEMBLY DEBATES

Depending on the nature of the question and on the views of the majority, Assembly debates may lead to one or a combination of the following: recommendations, phrased in varying degrees of urgency, to individual countries or to all countries; initiation of studies and reports; creation of new UN organs, committees of inquiry, and permanent special bodies assigned specific tasks; adoption of international covenants, treaties and agreements.

Significance of the Enlarged Membership and Changing Voting Patterns

Since 1960, when the impact of the number of newly independent African and Asian nations first began to make itself felt in the UN, the Assembly's voting patterns have been undergoing a marked alteration. Until then, the majority of controversial resolutions had tended essentially to reflect a simple East-West division of opinion. In the resulting lineup of votes, the Western view, marshaled under the leadership of the US, easily

attained comfortable majorities on most issues, since it was supported not only by the countries of Western Europe but by the Latin American states as well. The formation of what has come to be known as the "Afro-Asian group," coupled with the general detente in East-West relations, has introduced a new element into the voting equation.

Interested in wielding influence within the world body and preoccupied with the problems of development and decolonization rather than with cold war issues as such, African and Asian countries have sought to unite themselves into an independent or "nonaligned" voting bloc. On occasion, the unity of the group is split by divided interests. This occurs most frequently in major political issues of special importance to the big powers, when some small countries may find it expedient to associate themselves with the big power on which they are dependent for financial aid. At other times, notably on items connected with economic development, African and Asian nations may join the developing countries of the Latin American group, which now includes several Caribbean nations, to create a formidable voting bloc to force through requests to which the highly developed nations, from East and West alike, may be reluctant to accede.

Then again, the emergence of what is in effect a floating third voting force in the Assembly has resulted in the creation of special alliances as occasion demands. For example, the Soviet bloc and the nonaligned groups often combine to defeat or harry positions taken by the West on colonial issues. It has also opened up possibilities for striking voting bargains on individual draft resolutions. Accordingly, one group may support an initiative taken by a second group on a given item in exchange for support by the latter for an initiative taken by the first group on a different item.

The indiscriminate wielding of voting strength by small members that are without power as sovereign nations is subject to the law of diminishing returns. Indeed, many small nations have shown indications of growing restraint, realizing that there is little point in pushing through resolutions requiring, for example, increased expenditure on economic development, if the big powers, which have to foot most of the bill, are not prepared to implement them. Similarly, they have recognized that there is nothing to be gained from trying to compel the big powers to go beyond their own pace in agreeing upon measures for disarmament or for resolving their differences on peacekeeping issues. (The realization of their impotence on big power issues is one reason the small nations did not bring the US intervention in Viet-Nam or the Soviet invasion of Czechoslovakia before either the Assembly or the Security Council.)

One important outcome of the growing recognition by the small nations of the practical limitations of their voting strength, coupled with the complementary realization by the Western powers that they no longer can be certain of majority support, even on items of particular importance to them, has been a general recourse wherever possible to compromise resolutions that command unanimous or near unanimous support. However, notwithstanding this partial solution to the problems created by the emergence of a floating third voting force in the Assembly, the big powers, especially those from the West, have become increasingly dissatisfied with this situation, and some of its leaders have come to question the principle of one country one vote.

Effectiveness of Resolutions

In assessing the effectiveness of resolutions, one may easily overemphasize the significance of formal voting in the Assembly. As the secretary-general pointed out in his annual report to the Assembly in 1959: "Resolutions often reflect only part of what has, in effect, emerged from deliberations and what, therefore, is likely to remain as an active element in future developments." Hence, he continued, "it is natural for those who are not close to the UN sometimes to underestimate the results of the work of the General Assembly and the other organs, and equally to overestimate the significance of a formal voting victory or a voting defeat." (He added that this applies also to the work of the Security Council.) In other words, the fact that a resolution receives an overwhelming majority vote does not necessarily ensure its effectiveness. Nor does the fact that a resolution is adopted by the slenderest of margins necessarily mean that it will serve no purpose. For example, the Assembly in 1961 adopted a resolution by a vote of 55-0, but with 44 abstentions, declaring Africa a denuclearized zone. Almost everyone except the handful of African sponsors was skeptical of the value of the idea. Yet that resolution was among the initiative measures in a chain of resolutions that have since led to a crystallization of the "denuclearized zone" concept as an important part of the general UN drive to ensure nondissemination of nuclear weapons. Moreover, the effectiveness of the vast majority of Assembly resolutions is attested to by the existence of hundreds of UN projects that have materially benefited mankind. Even the Assembly's controversial peacekeeping operations in the Middle East and the Congo were successful in achieving their main objective of preventing the spread of violence.

In general it may be said that a resolution will be effective insofar as its adoption is not regarded by any country as inimical to its national interests. As long as a country feels that its interests are directly prejudiced by the terms of a resolution, that resolution is usually a dead letter. Hence, for example, the total ineffectiveness of two decades of resolutions calling upon the big powers to agree on measures for general and complete disarmament; upon Portugal to give up its colonial territories in Africa; upon South Africa to abandon its racially discriminatory system of apartheid.

The most effective resolutions, then, are those that concern matters on which all members are prepared to accept a degree of compromise (though this acceptance may not necessarily be reflected in the actual voting) and establish goals which all members are eager to achieve or to which they have no objection. For like the UN itself, resolutions can only be as effective as the membership wants them to be.

THE SECURITY COUNCIL

Under the Charter, the Security Council is assigned the primary responsibility for maintaining international peace and security. To facilitate its work as guardian of the peace and to ensure quick and effective action when required, the Council is vested with certain powers and attributes not accorded the other organs of the UN. Thus the Council is the only UN body with powers commensurate with those of a world government, since it is empowered by the Charter to enforce its decisions and prescribe them as a course of action legally binding upon all UN members. However, its governmental prerogatives can be invoked only in times of gravest crisis and under explicit conditions laid down in the Charter. Otherwise, the Council, like the General Assembly, can merely recommend and advise.

Another distinctive feature of the Council is the membership and voting privileges accorded to the five countries that were chiefly responsible for the defeat of the Axis nations and, at the time of the San Francisco Conference, were regarded as militarily the most powerful countries in the world. By the terms of these privileges, China, France, the USSR, the UK, and the US were each accorded permanent membership on the Council and the right to veto singlehandedly any substantive decision adopted by the majority of the other members. The underlying consideration here was the desire to preserve the unanimity of the Big Five; that is, to ensure that no peacekeeping action would be taken against the will of a country considered sufficiently powerful to oppose the Council's decision with military force and so open up the possibility of a third major international war. The fact that today only the US and the USSR are universally acknowledged as powerful in this sense has not altered the status of the other three permanent members of the Council. As all five countries were actually specified by name in the relevant Charter provisions, an amendment or revision of the Charter would be required if any change of status were contemplated by the rest of the UN membership. In turn, a Charter amendment requires ratification by all five permanent members of the Security Council before it can come into force.

COMPOSITION

To expedite decision and action, the membership of the Security Council was deliberately restricted to a small number. Originally an 11-member body, it was subsequently enlarged to 15 members by a Charter amendment that came into effect on 31 August 1965.

With five seats permanently assigned, the remaining ten are filled by other UN members elected by secret ballot in the General Assembly for two-year terms. At the very first election in January 1946, three seats were filled for one-year terms and three for two-year terms, so that afterward three seats on the Security Council would become vacant each year. Similarly, at the first election after the enlargement of the Council came into effect, two of the four additional nonpermanent seats were filled for one-year terms. Nonpermanent members of the Security Council are ineligible for immediate reelection upon retirement. In electing the nonpermanent members of the Security Council, the Assembly is required to pay due regard to the past and potential contribution of nations to the maintenance of international peace and security as well as to equitable geographic distribution. In view of the power of the Security Council, nations attach great importance to the choice of the nonpermanent members.

The problem of ensuring equitable geographical distribution of members elected to the Security Council has not been easy to resolve. Prior to the Council's enlargement, there had been a long-standing difference of views on a "gentlemen's agreement" reached in the early days of the UN that was intended to guarantee that the six nonpermanent seats would be so distributed that one of the seats would always be held by a Soviet bloc country. But until 1960 only Poland and the Ukrainian SSR were elected, and each served for only one two-year term. In the 1959 election, Poland and Turkey competed for the nonpermanent Council seat for the two-year term 1960–61. After 52 ballots, the Assembly gave the seat to Poland on the basis of the following compromise: though elected for two years, Poland would resign its seat at the end of the first year and Turkey would be the sole candidate to fill the unexpired term. Under a similar arrangement, Romania held a seat for 1962, resigning it for 1963 to the Philippines. To avoid the recurrence of such situations after the enlargement of the Council, the Assembly at its 18th session in 1963 adopted a resolution that established a fixed pattern for the geographical distribution of the 10 nonpermanent seats: 5 from African and Asian nations, 1 from East European nations, 2 from Latin American nations, and 2 from West European and other nations.

Composition of the Security Council for 1971: Permanent members: China, France, USSR, UK, and US. Nonpermanent members: Argentina, Belgium, Burundi, Italy, Japan, Nicaragua, Poland, Sierra Leone, Somalia, Syria.

GENERAL FUNCTIONS AND POWERS

The functions and powers assigned to the Security Council under the Charter relate to four categories of responsibilities: (1) maintenance of international peace and security; (2) formulation of plans for establishing a system for the regulation of armaments; (3) UN trusteeship responsibilities in trust territories designated as strategic areas; (4) organizational functions—namely, considering applications for UN membership, recommending and restoring suspension of a country's rights and privileges of membership, recommending the expulsion of a member state, electing (in conjunction with the Assembly) the judges of the International Court of Justice, recommending to the Assembly candidates for the office of secretary-general.

Of these four categories, only the first is discussed in this chapter. The Council's responsibility for formulating a system for the regulation of armaments is elaborated in the chapter on disarmament; its responsibilities in respect of strategic trust areas are described in the chapter on the Trusteeship Council; and its various organizational functions are considered in the chapters on Membership, the International Court of Justice, and the Secretariat.

MAINTAINING INTERNATIONAL PEACE AND SECURITY

By the very act of joining the world body, all members "confer on the Security Council primary responsibility for the maintenance of international peace and security, and agree that in carrying out its duties under this responsibility the Security Council *acts on their behalf*" (italics added). They also consent "to accept and carry out" the decisions of the Council on any peacekeeping action that may be required. Under Article 39 of the Charter, the Council's powers to take such enforceable decisions come into effect only when there has arisen a definite "threat to the peace," an actual "breach of the peace," or a particular "act of aggression." Only if the Council decides that one of these circumstances prevails may it invoke its power to take a course of enforcement action that constitutes a legally binding commitment on all other UN members. With regard to disputes between states that, in the opinion of the Council, have not yet led to a definite threat to the peace or do not constitute an actual breach of the peace or an act of aggression, it may merely recommend measures for a peaceful settlement.

The extreme caution with which the founders of the UN assigned governmental prerogatives to the Council is reflected in the fact that its powers with regard to its peacekeeping functions are set out in two quite separate chapters of the Charter. Chapter VI establishes its advisory functions in assisting the peaceful settlement of disputes. Chapter VII defines the kind of action it may take in the event of threats to the peace, breaches of the peace, and acts of aggression.

1. The Peaceful Settlement of Disputes

Under the Charter, the parties to any dispute "the continuance of which is likely to endanger the maintenance of international peace and security" are enjoined to seek a settlement of their own accord by peaceful means. These include "negotiation, enquiry, mediation, conciliation, arbitration, judicial settlement, resort to regional agencies or arrangements. . . ." When can the Security Council itself intervene? On this point, the Charter is as unrestrictive as possible. By no means does every "situation" of conflicting interests lead to an actual dispute. Yet the Security Council need not wait until a situation has given rise to friction before taking action. It may take the initiative of investigating any dispute, or any situation that might lead to international friction or give rise to a dispute, in order to determine whether the continuance of the dispute or situation is likely to endanger the maintenance of international peace and security. Moreover, any nation, whether a member of the UN or not, has the right to bring voluntarily any dispute or threatening situation before the Council (or before the General Assembly). Should the parties to a dispute fail to settle their differences by peaceful means of their own choice, they are bound under the terms of the Charter to refer the problem to the Council.

Once the Council has decided to intervene in a dispute, it can take several courses of action. It may recommend one of the methods of settlement listed in the Charter; or it may itself determine and recommend other "procedures or methods of adjustment" that it deems appropriate; or, if it considers that the continuance of the dispute is likely to endanger international peace and security, it can decide to recommend substantive terms of settlement.

What is an "appropriate" procedure or method of settlement? And what kind of specific, substantive recommendations can the Security Council make? Purposely, the Charter has left this to the Council's discretion.

An example of a major conflict during which the Security Council recommended both procedures and substantive terms for peaceful settlement was the struggle that eventually led to the independence of the Dutch East Indies. In that instance, the Security Council was unable to prevent bloodshed, but it forestalled the spread of the conflict, and it helped in the emergence of the new state of Indonesia.

On 1 August 1947 the Security Council called upon the Netherlands and Indonesia to cease hostilities and settle their dispute by arbitration or other peaceful means. It then offered, on 25 August 1947, to assist in the settlement through a Good Offices committee, with whose help a truce was signed. Later, negotiations for a final settlement ran into a snag, and eventually hostilities were resumed. On 28 January 1949 the Security Council called upon the Netherlands to discontinue all military operations and release political prisoners immediately and unconditionally. It also called upon Indonesia to cease guerrilla warfare. In addition, it recommended various measures, including the establishment of an interim federal government of Indonesia and the holding of elections within a certain period of time.

By way of contrast is the UK-Albania case of 1947, where a mere recommendation of method of settlement proved sufficient in a dispute that otherwise might have had serious repercussions. The conflict revolved around the shelling by Albanian coastal batteries of two British warships and the mining of the Corfu Channel by Albania, which caused damage to two British destroyers and loss of life. On 3 April 1947 the Council recommended that the case be immediately referred to the International Court of Justice. Both parties complied.

2. Threats to the Peace, Breach of the Peace, and Acts of Aggression

If in its opinion there is a threat to the peace, the Council has the duty to maintain peace and security by preventing the outbreak of actual hostilities. If there has been a breach of the peace or an act of aggression, its duty is to restore international peace and security.

In such cases, not even the principle of nonintervention in domestic jurisdiction of a state (Principle No. 7 of the Charter) is allowed to prejudice the application of enforcement measures. The Security Council is empowered by the Charter to call upon the parties to comply with any provisional measures it deems necessary or desirable. Such immediate instructions to the quarreling states are intended, without prejudice to the rights of the parties, to prevent an aggravation of the conflict. For example, the Council may demand the immediate cessation of hostilities and withdrawal of the forces from the invaded territory. If either or both parties do not comply with these demands, the Security Council "shall duly take account" of the failure to comply. In this event, the farthest-reaching prerogative of the Security Council can come into play—namely, the right to institute sanctions against the recalcitrant state or states.

Here again, the discretion of the Security Council is very wide. When the Council finds a threat to the peace, breach of the peace, or act of aggression to exist, it is authorized, though not compelled, by the Charter to invoke sanctions. Even if its first provisional demands are not heeded, it may continue to press for peaceful settlement or take various other actions, such as the dispatch of a commission of inquiry, short of sanctions. On the other hand, the Council is free to invoke whatever enforcement measures it may consider necessary under the circumstances. It need not begin with the mildest, but may, as in the Korean conflict, immediately start with the severest type of sanction—namely, the use of military force—if it considers that less drastic measures would be inadequate.

Types of Sanctions. The Charter does not provide an exhaustive list of sanctions that the Security Council may invoke, but it mentions two types: sanctions not involving the use of armed forces and military sanctions.

Sanctions not involving the use of armed forces may be of two kinds. One is the severance of diplomatic relations with one or more of the belligerent states. The other is economic sanctions, including partial or complete interruption of economic relations and communications—rail, sea, and air traffic, postal and telegraphic services, radio, and others. The purpose is to isolate physically, economically, and morally the country or countries against which they are directed. For example, a would-be aggressor that is denied certain strategic materials may be compelled to cease hostilities. If successful, such measures have great advantages over military sanctions. They impose fewer burdens on the participating countries and fewer hardships on the population of the areas of conflict. Moreover, they avoid the danger that once military action on behalf of the United Nations has been taken, the war may spread.

Military sanctions, the Charter stipulates, may include (1) demonstrations by air, sea, or land forces, (2) blockade, or (3) "other operations by air, sea, and land forces," the latter including actual military action against the offending country or countries.

Once the Security Council has decided on specific sanctions, all members of the United Nations are under legal obligation to carry them out. The Security Council may, however, at its discretion, decide that only certain member states shall take an active part. On the other hand, the Security Council may demand that even nonmember states participate in economic sanctions to make them effective. The Charter also stipulates that before any member state not represented on the Security Council is called upon to provide armed forces, that country must, upon its request, be invited to participate in the Council's deliberations with a right to vote on the employment of its own contingents.

SURVEY OF SECURITY COUNCIL PEACEKEEPING PRACTICE

To date, there has only been one case where the Council has invoked its powers to impose sanctions in a clear-cut decision taken under Chapter VII of the Charter. In December 1966 the Council imposed selective economic sanctions against the illegal Smith regime in Rhodesia. Two years later, in May 1968, it decided to make these sanctions extensive. (For an account of the Council's action, see the chapter on Independence of Colonial Peoples.) Apart from this case, the Council deliberately has refrained from designating a serious dispute as a threat to peace, a breach of the peace, or an act of aggression, precisely to avoid acting explicitly within the terms of Chapter VII.

The Council's reluctance to invoke its ultimate prerogatives is attributable to two main factors. The first is a genuine feeling that in most cases punitive measures are inappropriate and may be harmful to the chances for an eventual peaceful settlement. This attitude is in keeping with the spirit of the Charter itself. The very arrangement and wording of the provisions on the UN security system make it clear that peace is to be preserved whenever possible without recourse to force. The second major factor is that, in successive serious international disputes, the USSR and the four other permanent members have usually taken differing positions and on most occasions have sympathized with the opposing parties. Not only does division between the permanent members preclude punitive measures against one side, but it also seriously inhibits definitive action of any kind. For example, the initial action of sending a UN command into Korea was made possible only by the absence of the USSR from the Council at the time (in protest against the Council's decision on Chinese representation). Had the Soviet Union been there, it would be assumed to have vetoed the necessary resolutions. An example of the reverse situation is the issue of South Africa's apartheid policies. Since 1960 the African nations have appealed regularly to the Council to declare the situation in South Africa a threat to peace, so that mandatory economic sanctions could be instituted in the hope of forcing it to terminate the apartheid system. The Soviet Union has frequently expressed itself in favor of such a move, but the Western permanent members—in particular South Africa's major trading partners, the UK and the US—being reluctant to impose sanctions, have steadfastly refused to agree that the situation constitutes a threat to peace within the meaning of Chapter VII of the Charter.

Hence, though the Security Council in several serious crises—in Kashmir, the Middle East, Congo, and Cyprus—sent observer commissions or in some instances limited numbers of troops, such action has never been imposed by the Council against the will of the countries involved. On the contrary, with the exception of Korea, the formula has always been that the disputants themselves must expressly invite the Council to take these measures. By this formula, then, the Council has helped maintain peace and security, even though it may not have reconciled its own differences on recommending terms of settlement. On occasion, however, the Council has appointed a mediator to try to negotiate a settlement directly with the parties concerned.

Thus, in the majority of serious international crises, the peacekeeping operations undertaken by the Council have represented a kind of holding action. Such operations, involving, as has frequently been the case, the presence of UN troops and other personnel in a sovereign nation, yet performed under the formula of invitation by the disputing parties, do not, strictly speaking, fall within the provisions of either Chapter VI or Chapter VII of the Charter. Because of this, some UN members have urged that the Charter be amended to accommodate current practice. No move has been made in that direction, and the matter seems academic. The important issue at stake is not the legality of the Security Council's peacekeeping operations, but of those operations, referred to in the previous chapter, that have been carried out by the General Assembly under the Uniting for Peace Resolution. (Details of the Security Council's major peacekeeping operations and those undertaken by the Assembly are contained in the first chapter on Maintaining Peace and Security.)

ARMED FORCES FOR THE UNITED NATIONS

Although the Charter contains provisions to equip the Council with armed forces in case of need (the Covenant of the League of Nations contained no such provisions), these requirements have not been implemented. Under the Charter, all UN members "undertake to make available to the Security Council, on its call and in accordance with a special agreement or agreements, armed forces assistance, and facilities, including rights of passage, necessary for the purpose of maintaining international peace and security." These agreements were to determine the number and types of military forces to be provided by the nations, their degree of readiness, their location, and so on. And they were to come into effect only after ratification by the countries concerned according to their respective constitutional requirements. (With this in mind, the US Congress in December 1945 passed the "UN Participation Act," authorizing the President of the United States to negotiate a special agreement with the Security Council on the detailed provision of US forces, which agreement would then require approval by legislative enactment or joint resolution of the US Congress.) The troops and weapons would remain part of each country's national military establishments. They would not become international forces, but they would be pledged to the United Nations and at the request of the Security Council would be placed at its disposal.

However, the plan to place armed forces at the disposition of the Security Council required wide international agreement on a number of steps before it could be put into operation. The Charter provides for the establishment of a Military Staff Committee composed of the chiefs of staff (or their representatives) of the five permanent members to advise and assist the Council on all questions relating to its military requirements. The first task the Council assigned to the Military Staff Committee was to recommend the military arrangements that the Council should seek to negotiate with member states. After this was done, the Council itself would have to agree on these arrangements, and formal treaties to be concluded with the states concerned. Once the treaties had been properly ratified and armed forces placed at the Council's disposition, the Military Staff Committee would advise and assist the Council on all questions relating to their deployment and command and would be responsible to the Council for their strategic direction.

The hitch developed during the first step. On 30 April 1947 the Military Staff Committee submitted its recommendations on the arrangements the Council should seek to conclude with member states. The Committee agreed on 25 points but was deadlocked on 16. Among the points of disagreement were such crucial issues as the size of the forces to be provided by countries, the use by the country concerned of its forces earmarked for UN purposes, a general guarantee of free passage for UN-pledged troops, and the time limit for the withdrawal of UN forces after their mission was accomplished.

As these differences were never reconciled, the plan to earmark national forces for the UN has remained on paper, all military activities having been carried out on the basis of voluntary contributions of troops by member nations. In June 1964, in the midst of the furore over the financing of past UN peacekeeping operations, the Soviet Union issued a memorandum proposing the revival of the Military Staff Committee with a view to implementing the Charter provisions on armed forces. The US, the UK, and several other members were willing to consider this proposal in detail, but no attempt was made to do so. Meanwhile, certain medium and small countries, distressed by the inadequate arrangements for standby forces, held informal discussions on the problem. Eight of these countries—Canada, Denmark, Finland, Iran, Italy, the Netherlands, Norway, and Sweden—announced their intention of earmarking troops for possible UN use on a permanent basis.

ORGANIZATION OF THE SECURITY COUNCIL

The Security Council is organized to function continuously. It is not permanently in session, but it meets as often as necessary. Hence, a representative from each member country must always be available so that in an emergency the Council can convene at once. Chairmanship rotates among the Council's member states according to their English alphabetical order, a new president (as the chairman is called), presiding every month. It is up to the president to decide whether to preside during the discussion of a question that directly concerns his own country.

Council members normally are represented by the heads of their permanent missions to the UN, who have the status of ambassador. Any state that is not currently a Council member but is a party to a dispute under consideration by the Council must be invited to send representatives to participate in the proceedings, though without the right to vote. (In these circumstances the disputing states concerned usually send a high government official, very often the foreign minister.) When the Council is discussing a matter other than an actual dispute, the decision to invite the participation of any UN member states whose interests are directly affected is left to its discretion. The Council has usually acceded to requests for such invitations.

VOTING IN THE SECURITY COUNCIL

Each member of the Council has one vote. On questions of procedure, a motion is carried if it obtains an affirmative vote of any nine members. On substantive matters, a resolution requires the affirmative vote of nine members, including the concurring votes of the permanent members. However, any member, whether permanent or nonpermanent, must abstain from voting in any decision concerning the peaceful settlement of a dispute to which it is a party. (When the Council consisted of only 11 members, the number of affirmative votes required was 7.)

The Veto

The word "veto" does not appear in the Charter. Nonetheless, it is the common-usage term for the power to defeat a resolution that is conferred by the Charter on each of the Big Five while acting in their capacity as permanent members of the Security Council. By no means do all negative votes cast in the Council by its permanent members constitute an exercise of their veto power. This occurs only when the resolution would otherwise have obtained the requisite number of affirmative votes. Moreover, by long-standing practice, the Charter provision stipulating that all substantive resolutions must obtain the concurring votes of the permanent members has been interpreted to mean that, provided a permanent member does not actually vote "nay," a resolution may still be carried. So long as a resolution receives nine affirmative votes, the fact that a permanent member abstains from voting does not prevent it from being adopted.

Significance of the Veto

The veto power, then, is the constitutional instrument for giving expression to the requirement—discussed at the opening of this chapter—that, before the Council invokes its authority in peacekeeping action, the big powers should first resolve their differences on how a particular crisis should be handled. But though the principle of ensuring unanimity among the big powers was the major consideration underlying the institution of the veto, it was not the only one. A complementary consideration was the need of the major powers to ensure that their decisions would not be overriden by a majority vote of the smaller nations. In effect, conferring the right of veto upon a few powerful countries was a tacit acknowledgment of the natural conflict that exists between their interests and those of the less powerful nations. It was a recognition of the fact that, despite differing social systems and power rivalry, the large countries often share more interests with each other than they do with smaller nations having social systems and tenets similar to their own. And it was for exactly this reason that the smaller countries represented at the San Francisco Conference made strenuous efforts to prevent the institution of the veto power in the Charter.

Controversy over the Veto

In order to stem criticism of their demand for the veto right, the Big Five issued a *Joint Statement* at the San Francisco Conference setting out their "Reasons for the Need of the Veto in the Security Council." The following are the three principal points made in that statement:

1. Beyond the procedural stage, Security Council decisions and actions "may well have major political consequences and may even initiate a chain of events which might, in the end, require the Council to invoke measures of enforcement." Hence, even if no more is involved than deciding on an investigation (which implies calling for reports, hearing witnesses, dispatching a commission of inquiry), the big powers should be in agreement that this "might not further aggravate the situation."

2. The five big powers can never dominate the Security Council, for any decision in the Council requires at least two votes from among the six nonpermanent members (smaller states). "In other words, it would be possible for five (of the six) nonpermanent members as a group to exercise a 'veto.'" (In practice this has not yet occurred.)

3. However, "in view of the primary responsibilities of the permanent members, they could not be expected, in the present condition of the world, to assume the obligation to act in so serious a matter as the maintenance of international peace and

security in consequence of a decision in which they had not concurred."

Faced with the unanimity of the Big Five on their right of veto, the other nations at the San Francisco Conference had little choice but to give their consent to the inclusion of the appropriate voting procedure in the Charter. The signing of that document by no means ended the controversy over the issue, however. No sooner had the first General Assembly convened than the issue was raised with some force. During the second part of that session, held in the fall of 1946, no less than five draft resolutions were put forward by different delegations, all designed to curtail or restrict the veto power. In the end, a resolution was adopted that merely requested the permanent members to ensure that their use of the veto would not impede Security Council decisions and to take into consideration the views expressed in the Assembly. Due to the USSR's extensive use of the veto throughout 1946 and 1947, the issue was raised again at both the second and third sessions of the Assembly. But no decisive action was taken, and the matter was allowed to lapse until the eighth session, in 1953, when the Assembly began to discuss arrangements for a possible Charter review conference in 1955 (as prescribed in the Charter itself—see the chapter on the Making of the UN). The debate made it clear that many delegations viewed the conference primarily as an opportunity to consider revising the Charter provisions on the veto power. There is no doubt that the sharp division of opinion on the veto issue was the major reason the conference never took place, either at the appointed time or subsequently. Since the enlargement of the Security Council in 1965, the desire of the smaller nations to eliminate the right of veto seems to have lost much of its impetus, and the subject receives only occasional mention in the Assembly's general debate.

Number of Vetoes Cast

As of October 1970, the USSR had cast 105 vetoes, France 4, the UK 4, China 2, and the US 1. It can be noted that the USSR since the end of 1961 has exercised the veto only six times.

In assessing the significance of the actual use of the veto, it is important to remember that the number of vetoes cast cannot be correlated with the number of items discussed in the Security Council. Very often, several draft resolutions may be submitted on a single question. If none of these accommodate the views of a given permanent member, then it is forced to veto each one. Similarly, an application for UN membership that a permanent member may feel itself bound to reject may come before the Council several times within a relatively short time. Thus the USSR's 105 vetoes in no way represents a dissenting opinion on 105 items. For example, from 1946 to the end of 1947 the USSR exercised 23 vetoes, but these applied to only five substantive questions and to membership applications from five nations.

Some interpretive comment should be made on the use of the veto by individual permanent members. The few vetoes exercised respectively by China, France, and the UK have all applied to items that clearly related in some way to their own immediate concerns—for instance, the French and British vetoes in the Suez crises, the Chinese veto on the application of Mongolia for UN membership, the British vetoes on certain Security Council resolutions concerning Rhodesia. The single instance when the US exercised its veto right occurred, on 17 March 1970, on a resolution sponsored by African and Asian nations which among other things called for the severance of all diplomatic relations with the illegally proclaimed Republic of Rhodesia.

The USSR's extraordinarily heavy use of the veto in comparison with the US's almost total restraint is not so simple to explain. The answer properly lies in the realm of political speculation. Suffice to say that many commentators have attributed the contrasting Soviet-American veto records to the relative power positions of the two countries in the General Assembly. During the earliest and tensest years of the cold war, the US usually could count on majority support from Latin American and West European nations for most of its political objectives, whereas the USSR had the backing of only a handful of socialist states—hence its recourse to the veto in the Security Council, to thwart Western aims. The fact that the Soviet use of the veto has declined so sharply is probably as much due to the altered Assembly voting pattern as it is to the comparative détente in East-West relations. With the advent of some 50 African and Asian nations, which tend to act as an independent voting group, neither the US nor the USSR can count on automatic majority support, and the situation has thus been equalized.

THE ECONOMIC AND SOCIAL COUNCIL (ECOSOC)

One of the United Nations' outstanding accomplishments to date has been its success in promoting economic and social progress. The Charter contains a declaration on international economic and social cooperation wherein the UN pledges itself to promote:

"a) higher standards of living, full employment, and conditions of economic and social progress and development;

b) solutions of international economic, social, health, and related problems; and international cultural and educational cooperation;

c) universal respect for, and observance of, human rights and fundamental freedoms for all without distinctions as to race, sex, language, or religion."

The responsibility for discharging these functions is vested in the General Assembly and, under its authority, the Economic and Social Council (ECOSOC).

FIELDS OF ACTIVITY

The activities of ECOSOC, carried out through its subsidiary organs in cooperation with the specialized agencies, have reached into every aspect of human welfare, affecting the lives of people in every nation. The scope of the Council's work is illustrated in several chapters of the UN section. The activities described under Economic Development, Social Progress, Human Rights, and Assistance to Refugees all come within the direct purview of ECOSOC. For convenience, however, a list of the major spheres of activity supervised by the Council is given below.

Economic Development. Although this field encompasses the development of both industrialized and nonindustrialized nations, emphasis is focused on the problems of the latter group. Specific items dealt with include evaluating long-term projections for the world economy; fostering international trade, particularly in commodities, between industrialized and nonindustrialized countries; improving the international flow of private and public capital; promoting industrialization and the development of natural resources; resolving related political and legal issues, such as permanent sovereignty over natural resources and land reform; developing programs of technical assistance and cooperation for developing nations; applying the latest innovations of science and technology to improve the industrialization of nonindustrialized countries.

Social Progress. Among the social problems handled under the aegis of ECOSOC are housing, population, international traffic in narcotic drugs, the welfare of children in the developing countries, and the status of the world's refugees.

Human Rights. ECOSOC and its subsidiary organs have evaluated a series of important principles for the promotion of fundamental freedoms. Measures introduced include a Universal Declaration on Human Rights and a number of declarations and recommendations on specific rights—for example, the rights of women, freedom of information and the press, and racial equality.

Related Special Problems. An example of a special problem of interest to ECOSOC is the improvement of statistical techniques, since efficient statistics are essential to economic and social development. Work in this field includes techniques to improve world statistics on specific branches of economy such as industry and finance, the standard of national statistical services, and methods of comparing statistics from different countries.

Problems Dealt With by the UN-Related Agencies. Many of the specific problems connected with economic and social progress are not handled directly by ECOSOC or its subsidiary organs but by 15 independent agencies created within the UN system. However, since the activities of these agencies are coordinated by ECOSOC, insofar as they relate to the work of the UN, they may be said to fall within the Council's general sphere of interest. The respective fields of the various agencies are clearly denoted by the name of the organization. Among them they cover problems of labor relations, both national and international (ILO), food and agriculture (FAO), health (WHO), education and culture (UNESCO), international financing and development (IBRD, IDA, IFC, IMF), civil aviation (ICAO), telecommunications (ITU), postal services (UPU), maritime and shipping (IMCO), meteorology (WMO), trade (GATT), and the peaceful uses of atomic energy (IAEA).

FUNCTIONS AND POWERS

Under the Charter, ECOSOC is authorized to make or initiate studies, reports, and recommendations on economic, social, cultural, educational, health, and related matters; to make recommendations to promote respect for, and observance of, human rights; to prepare draft conventions for submission to the General Assembly on matters within its competence; to call international conferences on matters within its competence and in accordance with rules prescribed by the UN; to enter into agreements, subject to the approval of the General Assembly, with specialized agencies; to coordinate the activities of the specialized agencies; to obtain regular reports from the specialized agencies; to perform, with the approval of the Assembly, services at the request of member nations or the specialized agencies; to consult with nongovernmental agencies whose work is related to matters dealt with by the Council; to set up subsidiary organs to assist its work; and to perform any other functions that may be assigned to it by the Assembly.

COMPOSITION

Originally, ECOSOC consisted of 18 members, but the amendments to the Charter that came into force on 31 August 1965 raised the number to 27.

When ECOSOC was constituted on 12–14 January 1946, the General Assembly elected ECOSOC's first 18 members for staggered terms: 6 members each for one, two, and three years, respectively. Subsequently, all terms were for three years, so that each year one third of the membership is elected by the Assembly.

The resolution by which the Assembly adopted the amendment to the Charter enlarging the membership of ECOSOC also laid down a pattern for the equitable geographical distribution of the nine additional seats allocated. On the basis of this provision, the 27 members of the Council are now elected according to the following pattern: 12 from African and Asian nations, 3 from East European states, 5 from Latin American nations, and 7 from West European and other states. Elections are by a two-thirds majority vote on a secret ballot in the Assembly, and immediate reelection of members is permissible. Although the permanent members of the Security Council have no privileged position on ECOSOC and the Charter does not guarantee them membership in ECOSOC, it has been the custom to reelect them continuously—an unofficial privilege that has, however, ceased to be accorded to China. In general, the Assembly has less difficulty in agreeing on its ECOSOC selections than in filling Security Council vacancies. Moreover if, in the opinion of ECOSOC, a matter on its agenda is of particular concern to a UN member not represented on the Council, it may invite that state to participate in its discussions, but without a vote.

For 1971 the composition of ECOSOC was as follows: Brazil, Ceylon, Congo (Brazzaville), France, Ghana, Greece, Haiti, Hungary, Indonesia, Italy, Jamaica, Kenya, Lebanon, Madagascar, Malaysia, New Zealand, Niger, Norway, Pakistan, Peru, Sudan, Tunisia, USSR, UK, US, Uruguay, Yugoslavia.

PROCEDURE

ECOSOC normally meets for two sessions each year. The first session meets in the spring and generally lasts four to six weeks. A president and two vice-presidents are elected by the Council for each year. The second session meets in the summer, again for four to six weeks, and reconvenes briefly after the end of the General Assembly to plan ECOSOC's work for the following year in the light of the Assembly's pertinent resolutions.

Other ECOSOC sessions may be called at the request of a majority of its members, of the General Assembly, of the Security Council, of the president of the ECOSOC, with the approval of the two vice-presidents, of the Trusteeship Council, of any member of the UN, or of a specialized agency, if the president of the Council and the two vice-presidents agree.

Each of the 27 members in the Council has one vote. The big powers possess no veto or other special voting privilege. Any motion is carried by a simple majority of the members present and voting.

SUBSIDIARY ORGANS

As already indicated in the Structure of the UN System, ECOSOC accomplishes its substantive work through numerous subsidiary organs in the form of commissions, standing committees, ad hoc committees, and special bodies. In Article 68, the Charter specifically states that the Council "shall set up commissions in economic and social fields and for the promotion of human rights . . . ." Two types of commission have been set up within this provision: the regional economic commissions, to deal with economic problems in the different geographical areas of the world; and the functional commissions, to handle matters connected with social progress and human rights.

Regional Economic Commissions

There are four regional commissions: the Economic Commission for Europe (ECE); the Economic Commission for Asia and the Far East (ECAFE); the Economic Commission for Latin America (ECLA); and the Economic Commission for Africa (ECA). Each has its own staff members who are considered part of the regular staff of the UN. Regional commission expenditures come out of the regular UN budget. The organization and work of the regional commissions are considered in detail in a separate chapter.

Functional Commissions

The Council has six functional commissions and one subcommission:

Statistical Commission. Composed of 24 members elected by ECOSOC for staggered 4-year terms. Composition in 1971: Australia, Belgium, Brazil, Cuba, Czechoslovakia, Denmark, France, Ghana, India, Indonesia, Ireland, Libya, Morocco, Panama, Philippines, Poland, Thailand, Uganda, Ukrainian SSR, USSR, UAR, UK, US, Venezuela.

Population Commission. Composed of 27 members elected by ECOSOC for staggered 4-year terms. Composition in 1971: Barbados, Brazil, Central African Republic, Czechoslovakia, Denmark, France, Gabon, Ghana, Haiti, India, Indonesia, Iran, Jamaica, Japan, Kenya, New Zealand, Pakistan, Spain, Sweden, Tunisia, Ukrainian SSR, USSR, UAR, UK, US, Upper Volta, Venezuela.

Commission for Social Development. Composed of 32 members elected by ECOSOC for staggered 3-year terms. Composition in 1971: Byelorussian SSR, Cameroon, Canada, Chile, Costa Rica, Cuba, Cyprus, Czechoslovakia, France, Gabon, Guatemala, India, Italy, Jamaica, Japan, Lebanon, Mauritania, Netherlands, People's Republic of the Congo, Philippines, Sierra Leone, Somalia, Spain, Sweden, Thailand, Tunisia, USSR, UAR, UK, US, Venezuela, Yugoslavia.

Commission on Human Rights. Composed of 32 members elected by ECOSOC for staggered 3-year terms. Composition in 1971: Austria, Chile, Democratic Republic of the Congo, Finland, France, Ghana, Guatemala, India, Iran, Iraq, Lebanon, Mauritania, Mauritius, Mexico, Morocco, Netherlands, New Zealand, Pakistan, Peru, Philippines, Poland, Senegal, Tanzania, Turkey, Ukrainian SSR, USSR, UAR, UK, US, Uruguay, Venezuela, Yugoslavia.

Commission on the Status of Women. Composed of 32 members elected by ECOSOC for staggered 3-year terms. Composition in 1971: Austria, Belgium, Byelorussian SSR, Canada, Central African Republic, Chile, Colombia, Costa Rica, Democratic Republic of the Congo, Dominican Republic, Finland, France, Hungary, Indonesia, Iran, Iraq, Liberia, Malaysia, Mauritania, Morocco, Nicaragua, Nigeria, Norway, Philippines, Romania, Thailand, Tunisia, USSR, UAR, US, Uruguay.

Commission on Narcotic Drugs. Composed of 24 members elected for staggered 4-year terms from among members of the UN, members of the specialized agencies, and the parties to the 1961 Single Convention on Narcotic Drugs. Composition in 1971: Brazil, Canada, Dominican Republic, Federal Republic of Germany, France, Ghana, Hungary, India, Iran, Jamaica, Japan, Lebanon, Mexico, Pakistan, Peru, Sweden, Switzerland, Togo, Turkey, USSR, UAR, UK, US, Yugoslavia.

Subcommission on Prevention of Discrimination and Protection of Minorities. Composed of 26 persons elected for 3-year terms by the Commission on Human Rights from nominations of experts made by UN members.

The Statistical Commission, Population Commission, and the Commission on Narcotic Drugs meet biennially. The other commissions meet annually.

Other Subsidiary Organs

Article 68 of the Charter provides that in addition to the commissions specifically mentioned in the Charter, ECOSOC should establish "such other commissions as may be required for its functions." In fact, however, none of the other subsidiary organs created have been given the name "commission." Instead, ECOSOC has established committees and special bodies of varying kinds.

In 1970, ECOSOC had the following committees: Committee for Program and Coordination; Advisory Committee on the Application of Science and Technology to Development; Committee on Development Planning; Committee on Housing, Building, and Planning; Council Committee on Nongovernmental Organizations; Council Committee on Candidatures for Election to the International Narcotics Control Board Under the Single Convention on Narcotic Drugs, 1961. Special bodies assisting the work of ECOSOC are those listed on the left-hand column on the chart on the structure of the UN, which report to both ECOSOC and the General Assembly: Trade and Development Board; UN Development Program (UNDP); UN Capital Development Fund; UN Industrial Development Organization (UNIDO); UN Institute for Training and Research (UNITAR); UN Children's Fund (UNICEF); Office of the UN High Commissioner for Refugees (UNHCR); and Joint UN–FAO World Food Program (which reports only to ECOSOC).

RELATIONS WITH NONGOVERNMENTAL ORGANIZATIONS (NGO's)

Matters of concern to ECOSOC directly affect every aspect of people's lives—their incomes, their schools, their hospitals. Under the Charter, ECOSOC can grant consultative status to significant international organizations of private citizens or put them in a register for ad hoc consultations. By hearing their views, ECOSOC becomes acquainted with informed opinions other than those of governments and is able to draw on the special experience and technical knowledge of such groups. To underline their character as private citizens' organizations and to distinguish them from organizations formed by governments, they are known as nongovernmental organizations (or NGO's).

Applications for consultative status or for admission to the register for ad hoc consultations arrive continuously at the UN. Two types of consultative status are recognized by ECOSOC: Category I, which may be granted NGO's with a wide general interest in the work of ECOSOC; and Category II, for which organizations interested in some particular aspect of the ECOSOC's work, such as air transport or youth problems, are eligible. As of August 1970, ECOSOC had granted Category I consultative status to 16 NGO's and Category II status to 137, while another 263 are registered for consultation as occasion arises. All such officially recognized organizations may send observers to the public meetings of ECOSOC and its commissions and may submit memoranda for circulation. Representatives of Category I organizations are entitled to participate in ECOSOC debates and to propose items for the agenda. Representatives of Category II organizations may, with the permission of the chair, make oral statements.

The 16 international organizations in Category I are:
International Chamber of Commerce
International Confederation of Free Trade Unions
International Cooperative Alliance
International Council of Women
International Federation of Agricultural Producers
International Organization of Employers

International Union of Local Authorities
International Union of Official Travel Organizations
Inter-Parliamentary Union
League of Red Cross Societies
United Towns Organization
Women's International Democratic Federation
World Confederation of Labor
World Federation of Trade Unions
World Federation of United Nations Associations
World Veterans' Federation

Consultative status in Category II has been granted to nearly all important international businessmen's associations, cooperative societies, farmers' organizations, trade unions' and veterans' organizations; to leading professional groups, such as associations of architects, engineers, lawyers, newspaper publishers and editors, social welfare workers, tax experts, and many others; and to various women's and youth associations. Many associations formed along denominational lines—Greek Orthodox, Jewish, Muslim, Protestant, and Roman Catholic— also have consultative status. At least 15 NGO's have more than 5 million members each; others have a small but highly specialized membership. Most organizations that enjoy such official UN standing are international, in that they have members in more than one country. Organizations whose membership is restricted to one particular country may obtain consultative status only with the consent of its government.

ORGANIZATION OF INTERNATIONAL CONFERENCES

In accordance with a Charter provision, ECOSOC from time to time convokes international conferences on special world problems falling within its sphere of competence. Among the more important gatherings organized by ECOSOC was a World Population Conference held in Belgrade in August–September 1965 and attended by about 700 demographic experts from more than 100 countries. The purpose of the conference was not so much to make recommendations as to "improve understanding of populations problems," stimulate interest in pertinent scientific data, and enhance the effectiveness of work in this field. Data reviewed included fertility trends, mortality rates, and the movement of urban and rural populations.

In 1969, ECOSOC called an International Conference of Ministers Responsible for Social Welfare, attended by representatives of 97 countries. Despite the great diversity of experience among the participating countries, the conference produced a unanimous report, which identified promising developments in national social welfare policies and pointed to ways of achieving further progress at both national and international levels. The report also drew special attention to the preventive and development roles of social welfare programs within the broader framework of integrated development policies.

Scheduled conferences include a Conference of Plenipotentiaries for the Adoption of the Protocol on Psychotropic Substances (1971) and another World Population Conference in 1974. (For further details, see chapter on Special Areas of Social Progress.)

THE TRUSTEESHIP COUNCIL

Unlike the other main organs of the UN, the Trusteeship Council was established for the purpose of executing a closely defined system of operations. This is the trusteeship system, which was devised to adapt the League of Nations mandate system to meet the requirements of a new era and new ways of thinking on colonial matters and international relations. The composition and the functions of the Trusteeship Council, therefore, can best be understood by comparison of the main features and objectives of the two systems.

THE MANDATE SYSTEM OF THE LEAGUE OF NATIONS

The desire of nations to exercise power and enrich their own economic resources through the conquest of territories has always been a major cause of war. Through the centuries a succession of wars were fought by powerful states seeking first to establish colinies and then to retain them in the face of rebellion or efforts by other powerful states to seize the colonies for themselves. Indeed, in its political aspect, the history of the world may be read as the history of the creation and disintegration of successive empires, a chain of vicious cause and effect that brought much bloodshed and wretchedness. After World War I, however, a concerted effort was made for the first time, in a limited way, to break the chain. Recognizing that colonies are a source of friction and jealousy among wealthy nations, the victorious Allies decided not to appropriate for themselves the colonies of their defeated enemies. Instead, those territories belonging to Imperial Germany and the Ottoman Empire that were considered unable to function as independent states were placed under international administration supervised by the League of Nations.

In the view of the founders of the League, as stated in the Covenant, the former German colonies in Africa and the Far East were "inhabited by peoples not yet able to stand by themselves under the strenuous conditions of the modern world. . . ." Hence, their "well-being and development [should] form a sacred trust of civilization. . . ." The tutelage of such peoples should be entrusted to advanced nations, acting as "Mandatories of the League of Nations." Since the League's founders considered that certain communities of the former Ottoman Empire had achieved a higher stage of development, their existence as independent nations was to be provisionally recognized, but they were to be given "advice and assistance by a Mandatory [nation] until such time as they [were] able to stand alone."

According to these criteria, three types of mandates were created. Class A mandates covered territories that were considered to be ready to receive independence within a relatively short period of time; these territories were all in the Middle East—namely, Iraq, Palestine, and Transjordan, administered by the UK; and Lebanon and Syria, administered by France. Class B mandates covered territories for which the granting of independence was a distant prospect; these territories were all in Africa—the Cameroons and Togoland, each of which was divided between British and French administration; Tanganyika, under British administration; and Ruanda-Urundi, under Belgian administration. To the territories classified under Class C mandates virtually no prospect of self-government, let alone independence, was held out; these included South West Africa, administered by the Union of South Africa; New Guinea, administered by Australia; Western Samoa, administered by New Zealand; Nauru, administered by Australia under mandate of the British Empire; and certain Pacific islands, administered by Japan.

The terms of the mandate system implied an acknowledgment of the right of the peoples of the colonial territories belonging to states defeated in war to be granted independence if they were thought to have reached a sufficiently advanced stage of development. But no provision was made in the Covenant specifying that the countries designated to administer the mandated territories should take steps to prepare these peoples for eventual self-determination. In general the obligations that the administering countries were required to undertake were extremely modest, amounting to little more than a pledge to abolish the slave trade and liquor traffic and to refrain from using the indigenous populations for military purposes outside their own territories.

THE UN TRUSTEESHIP SYSTEM

Although the Covenant of the League forbade wars of aggression—that is, wars of conquest—the League's founding members did not see the need to underwrite this provision in a positive assertion of the principle of equal rights and self-determinations of peoples. This omission was corrected in the UN Charter. Among the 50 founding members of the new organization were many small states, including several that had only themselves just emerged from colonial rule. Their representatives were sympathetic to the colonial peoples' desire for independence, which had grown steadily in the years between the two world wars. Accordingly, the UN Charter embodies an implicit recognition of the belief that denial of equal rights and peoples' right to self-determination is a potential cause of war. Thus Article 1 of the Charter sets forth as a basic purpose of the UN "to develop friendly relations among nations based on respect for the principle of equal rights and self-determination of peoples, and to *take other appropriate measures to strengthen universal peace*." (Italics added.) Article 76, which sets out the main objectives of the international trusteeship system that was to replace the mandate system of the League, leaves no doubt of the value attached to its role as a means of assisting the UN, in the words of the Preamble to the Charter, "to save succeeding generations from the scourge of war." The article reads as follows:

The basic objectives of the trusteeship system, in accordance with the purposes of the UN laid down in Article 1 of the present Charter, shall be: (a) to further international peace and security; (b) to promote the political, economic, social, and educational advancement of the inhabitants of trust territories, and their progressive development towards self-government or independence as appropriate to the particular circumstances of each territory and its peoples and the freely expressed wishes of the peoples concerned, and as may be provided by the terms of each trusteeship agreement; (c) to encourage respect for human rights and for fundamental freedoms for all without distinction as to race, sex, language, or religion, and to encourage recognition of the interdependence of the peoples of the world; and (d) to ensure equal treatment in social, economic, and commercial matters for all members of the United Nations and their nationals, and also equal treatment for the latter in the administration of justice. . . .

As well as emphasizing the importance of the trusteeship system as an instrument for peace, Article 76 defines the framework for the elaboration of obligations that the countries designated to administer the territories placed under UN trusteeship must undertake toward the peoples concerned. In essence, these obligations amount to a pledge on the part of the administering authorities to work toward the liquidation of the trusteeship system itself by preparing the peoples in trust territories for independence, or at least self-government.

The Trust Territories and Their Administering Authorities

The Charter does not specify the actual territories to be placed under UN trusteeship. Article 77 merely states that the system shall apply to three categories: (1) territories still under mandate; (2) territories "detached from enemy states as a result of the Second World War"; and (3) territories voluntarily placed under the system by states responsible for their administration.

At the San Francisco Conference, several smaller states had wanted to vest the UN with the authority to place colonial territories under its own supervision. This demand was countered by the insistence of the colonial powers that the trusteeship system be confined, as the League of Nations mandate system had been, to territories belonging to defeated enemy states. The insertion of the third category of territory to which the trusteeship system can be applied was a compromise between the two positions, though it obviously worked in favor of the colonial powers since it left them free to ignore the invitation. And this is exactly what happened. Although West Irian, a former Dutch colony, was placed briefly under UN trusteeship in 1962, this was a special case. (See section B of the chapter on Independence of Colonial Peoples.)

On the question of designating the administrators of trust territories, the Charter is equally nonspecific. It states simply that the individual trusteeship agreements shall designate the authority in each case, which may be "one or more states or the Organization itself." The provision that the UN itself may serve as an administering authority is another compromise solution that was inserted when it was decided at the Charter conference to abandon an ambitious plan, originally proposed by China and initially supported by the US, to make the UN directly responsible for the administration of all trust territories.

In the event, it was decided that the powers that had administered mandates on behalf of the League of Nations were to conclude agreements with the new world organization and to administer the same territories that were still dependent. There was one exception. The Pacific islands, which after World War I had been given to Japan as Class C mandates, were, by a special arrangement embodied in the Charter, classified as strategic areas to be administered by the US under a modified trusteeship.

As a result of agreements worked out by the Assembly, 11 trust territories were placed under UN trusteeship, and 7 countries were designated as administering authorities. These figures exclude the former German colony of South West Africa, which after World War I had been mandated to the Union of South Africa because South Africa refused to place the territory under UN trusteeship (see section B of the chapter on Independence of Colonial Peoples). The distribution of the territories and their respective administering authorities was as follows.

In East Africa: Ruanda-Urundi administered by Belgium; Somaliland by Italy; Tanganyika by the UK.

In West Africa: Cameroons administered by the UK; Cameroons by France; Togoland by the UK; Togoland by France.

In the Pacific: Nauru, administered by Australia and on behalf of New Zealand and the UK; New Guinea by Australia; Western Samoa by New Zealand; the Pacific islands of the Marianas, Marshalls, and Carolines by the US.

As of December 1970, only New Guinea and the Pacific islands remain within the trusteeship system. The other nine territories have either achieved separate independence or else, on being granted self-determination, have chosen to unite themselves with other independent states (see section B of the chapter on Independence of Colonial Peoples).

THE TRUSTEESHIP COUNCIL

The fact that the Trusteeship Council was made a main organ of the UN is evidence of the importance attached to the role of the trusteeship system. The Council's functions, however, are decidedly more limited than those of the other main organs. Like the Economic and Social Council, it acts under the direct authority of the General Assembly, but whereas ECOSOC is empowered by the Charter to share the "responsibility" for the discharge of the UN's prescribed tasks in economic and social matters, the Trusteeship Council may only "assist" the Assembly in implementing the trusteeship system. The Charter provisions make it clear that the Council has a purely executive capacity in supervising the day-to-day operations of the trusteeship system. Policy decisions originate in the General Assembly, which concluded the individual trusteeship agreements with the administering authorities.

Composition

The Charter provides that the Council is to be composed of three groups of members: the countries administering trust territories; permanent members of the Security Council that do not administer trust territories; and a number of other UN members elected for three-year terms by the General Assembly to ensure an equal division between administering and nonadministering countries in the Council.

Until 1960, the Council consisted of 14 members: the 7 administering countries, Australia, Belgium, France, Italy, New Zealand, UK, and US; 2 permanent nonadministering members: China (Taiwan) and USSR; and 5 other nonadministering countries, elected by the General Assembly.

As the various trust territories gained independence, the size and composition of the Council changed accordingly. France ceased to be an administering country in April 1960 when French-administered Togoland became independent; Italy, when Somaliland became independent on 1 July 1960; and Belgium, when Ruanda-Urundi became independent in 1962. Both the UK and New Zealand ceased to be administering countries when Nauru became independent in 1968. Thus at the time of Nauru's accession to independence, the Council consisted of two administering countries—Australia and the US; four nonadministering permanent members of the Security Council—China, France, UK, USSR; and one member, Liberia, elected by the Assembly. The General Assembly decided that when Liberia's term of office expired in December 1968, the Council thereafter would be composed only of administering powers and the nonadministering permanent members of the Security Council.

Procedure

Each member of the Trusteeship Council has one vote. Decisions are made by a simple majority vote. The permanent members of the Security Council have no veto or other special voting privileges. Since administering and nonadministering countries originally were evenly balanced there was some apprehension that the Council would be chronically deadlocked. This, however, has not been the case, although the Council's discussions have been frequently contentious.

Now that the Council has only two territories under its purview, it holds annual sessions in the summer. Until 1968 it met twice a year, in January and June. The meetings normally are public. If the Council so decides, or if a majority of its members, the General Assembly, or the Security Council so request, special sessions are held. The president and the vice-president of the Trusteeship Council are elected for one year at the beginning of the regular summer session.

Powers

In carrying out its supervisory and administrative functions, the Council is specifically authorized to consider reports submitted by the administering authority; to accept petitions and examine them in consultation with the administering authority; to provide for periodic visits to the trust territories at times agreeable to the respective administering authorities; and to formulate a questionnaire on the political, economic, social, and educational progress in each trust territory, which the administering authorities are required to answer.

OPERATION OF THE TRUSTEESHIP SYSTEM

Trusteeship and Strategic Area Agreements

Since trusteeship territories are merely entrusted to the administering authorities, the precise terms of the agreement had to be carefully prescribed for each territory and approved by a two-thirds vote of the General Assembly. In general, the trusteeship agreements were quickly concluded with few difficulties.

Article 82 of the Charter provides that there may be designated in any trusteeship agreement a strategic area or areas, which may include part or all of the trust territory concerned. In such cases, all trusteeship functions of the UN, including approval of the terms of the trusteeship agreement, are to be exercised by the Security Council, not the General Assembly. The objectives of the trusteeship system are also applicable to the people of strategic areas.

In fact, there exists only one strategic area agreement—that concluded between the UN and the US government on the Pacific islands mandated to Japan after World War I. Most of the general provisions of the other trusteeship agreements are included in it, but the right of accessibility to the area is curtailed, and supervision by the UN is made dependent on US security requirements. The US is also authorized to close certain areas for security reasons, as in connection with nuclear fission experiments.

The Role of the Administering Authorities

Administering countries have full legislative, administrative, and judicial powers over the territories entrusted to them. If they so desire, they may administer the trust territory in conjunction with one of their own colonies. Thus, the trust territory of Ruanda-Urundi was united administratively with the Belgian Congo, and Australia has established an administrative union between the trust territory of New Guinea and its own dependency, Papua. However, the UN trusteeship territories are not under the sovereignty of the administering authorities, which govern them only on behalf of the UN.

The obligations of the administering authority elaborated on the basis of the objectives of the UN trusteeship system, as described in Article 76 of the Charter, include: to be responsible for the peace, order, and good government of the area; to develop free political institutions and to give the inhabitants an increasing share in the government; to protect land rights of the indigenous population; to develop education; to guarantee freedom of religion, worship, speech, press, assembly, and petition, subject only to requirements of public order; to ensure that the territory

plays its part in maintaining international peace and security, which implies that the territory must not be built up as a base for potential military aggression; and not to discriminate in social, economic, industrial, and commercial matters against any UN member or its nationals.

The Work of the Trusteeship Council

In essence, the work of the Council consists in the exercise of the powers specifically granted to it by the Charter for the purpose of supervising the operation of the trusteeship system and ensuring that the administering authorities are carrying out their obligations as laid down by the trusteeship agreements.

Examination of Petitions. Any inhabitant or group of inhabitants of a trust territory and anyone else, regardless of his place of residence, has the privilege of petitioning the Trusteeship Council. The peoples of the trust territories have made frequent use of the privilege. Between July 1958 and August 1959, when several trust territories moved closer toward independence, 6,278 communications were handled. Petitions cover a wide range of topics. Many are strictly personal, and some, whether a plea for financial assistance or a request by the women of a Pacific island that the UN do something about their husbands' overindulgence in alcohol, reveal naïve ideas about the UN's powers. Other petitions, such as those asking for redress of legal and economic grievances, deal with matters legitimately of concern to the UN.

The inhabitants of a trust territory may also request the Trusteeship Council to grant them an oral hearing. In all but exceptional cases, the Council grants such a hearing only in support of a written petition.

Visiting Missions. Through its visiting missions the Trusteeship Council examines conditions in the trust territories. Each trust territory is visited once every three years. The four members of each mission are appointed by the Council: two must be citizens of administering countries and two of nonadministering countries.

Examination of Annual Reports. The administering authorities are required to submit annual reports to the Trusteeship Council. These reports must be specific and are based on a questionnaire drawn up by the Council itself. The questions relate to such topics as details about the territory's government; the training and salaries of indigenous teachers; imports and exports; taxation; the development of political parties; the use of corporal punishment in the territory's penal system; measures taken against contagious diseases of cattle; and the frequency of polygamy. Formal examination of each report in the Trusteeship Council starts with an opening statement by a special representative of the administering authority. The Council then holds a general discussion of the report, during which any member may question the special representative on political, economic, social, and educational conditions in the territory. In examining the reports, the Council takes into consideration the petitions it has received, and it may also decide to grant petitioners a hearing. Reports by UN visiting missions to the territories, along with the administering authorities' observations on such reports, and the observations of specialized agencies on conditions in various territories, are also taken into account. After examining and discussing each report, the Council finally edits a lengthy statement of its own on each trust territory. All of these reports are then transmitted to the General Assembly, where the Fourth Committee uses them as a starting point for its own scrutiny of conditions in the trust territories.

INTERNATIONAL COURT OF JUSTICE (ICJ)

The International Court of Justice, known also as the World Court, was established at the San Francisco Conference in 1945. It is a successor to and resembles the Permanent Court of Justice created under the League of Nations. Its competence is wider, however, because membership in the League did not automatically require a nation to join the Permanent Court. Since the Statute of the World Court is an integral part of the Charter of the UN, all UN members automatically become parties to the Court's Statute. By joining the UN, each country binds itself, in the words of the Charter, "to comply with the decision of the International Court of Justice in any case to which it is a party." If any party to a case violates this obligation, the other party "may have recourse to the Security Council, which may, if it deems it necessary, make recommendations or decide upon measures to be taken to give effect to the judgment."

The Charter further provides that nonmembers of the UN may also become parties to the Statute of the International Court of Justice "on conditions to be determined in each case by the General Assembly upon recommendations of the Security Council." After agreeing to accept the Court's decisions and to recognize the right of the Security Council to enforce them, three countries not members of the UN—Liechtenstein, San Marino, and Switzerland—joined the Court. Japan also became a party to the Statute of the Court in this manner two years before its admission to the UN.

The rules under which the Court is constituted and by which it functions are laid down in the Statute. The seat of the Court is the Peace Palace at The Hague in the Netherlands, but it can meet elsewhere if it so desires. Due to the unsuitability of the Peace Palace, plans are now afoot for the construction of a new house for the court at The Hague. The Court is "permanently in session, except during the judicial vacations," and the judges are bound "to hold themselves permanently at the disposal of the Court."

JUDGES OF THE COURT

The Court consists of 15 independent judges, known as "members" of the Court. They are elected "from among persons of high moral character" without consideration of nationality, except that no two judges of the same nationality may serve concurrently. The judges must be persons possessing the qualifications required in their respective countries for appointment to the highest judicial offices or be jurists of recognized competence in international law. No judge of the International Court of Justice may exercise any political or administrative function or engage in any professional occupation. "When engaged on the business of the Court," judges enjoy diplomatic privileges and immunities. A newly elected judge "must make a solemn declaration in open court that he will exercise his powers impartially and conscientiously." A judge cannot be dismissed except by a unanimous decision of the other judges that "he has ceased to fulfil the required conditions."

As in any court, a judge may disqualify himself from sitting on a particular case. The Statute enumerates certain conditions under which this is obligatory—for example, if a judge was previously involved in the case as a member of a commission of inquiry.

Significance of Nationality of Judges

The Statute declares specifically that a judge has the right to sit on a case in which his own country is a party. Furthermore, any country that is a party to a case before the Court may add "a person to sit as judge" on that case if there is not already a judge of its nationality on the Court. If there are "several parties in the same interest," they may add only one judge to the bench. Such ad hoc judges are chosen by the respective states themselves and may, or may not, be nationals of the states choosing them. They must preferably be chosen from the list of candidates from which the Security Council and the General Assembly elected the regular judges.

Nomination and Election of Judges

Two international conferences at The Hague, in 1899 and 1907, attempted to set up a permanent international court. The conferees were unable to agree on a system for electing judges, and the endeavors failed. They did agree, however, on a convention establishing a Permanent Court of Arbitration. That convention provides that each country party to it name four jurists as arbitrators who would be available to consider a concrete matter for international arbitration. When the Permanent Court of International Justice was established after World War I, a solution was found for the difficult problem of electing judges. The legal experts named as potential arbitrators under the Hague convention were given the right to nominate candidates for judgeships on the Court, and the League of Nations then elected the judges from among these nominees. To ensure that the judges of the World Court would not be merely nominees of the governments of their countries, the judges are nominated not by governments, but by national groups of jurists: either the groups already established in the Permanent Court of Arbitration or, in countries not belonging to this court, by specially constituted groups. No national group may nominate more than four persons, and only two of these candidates can be of the same nationality as that group.

The list of candidates so nominated then goes to the UN. To be elected to a judgeship on the Court, a candidate must obtain an absolute majority in the Security Council and the General Assembly, both bodies voting independently and simultaneously. If more than one candidate of the same nationality obtains the required votes, the eldest is elected. On these occasions, Liechtenstein, San Marino, and Switzerland, the three nonmembers of the UN that are parties to the Statute of the Court, vote in the Assembly. In electing judges to the Court, delegates are requested to bear in mind that "the main forms of civilization" and "the principal legal systems of the world" should be represented at all times on the international tribunal.

Terms of Judgeships

Judges are elected for nine years. To stagger the expiration of terms, the terms of five of the judges named in the first election (1946) expired at the end of three years, and the terms of five others at the end of six years, as determined by lot. Hence, five judges are now elected every three years. Reelection is permissible and frequently occurs. Every three years, the Court elects its president and vice-president from among the judges.

As of March 1970 the 15 judges of the Court were as follows, in order of precedence. Terms of office expire on February 5 of the year given in parentheses.

Sir Muhammad Zafrulla Khan, Pakistan (1973), president
Fouad Ammoun, Lebanon (1976), vice-president
Sir Gerald Fitzmaurice, United Kingdom (1973)
Luis Padilla Nervo, Mexico (1973)
Isaac Forster, Senegal (1973)
André Gros, France (1973)
Cesar Bengzon, Philippines (1976)
Sture Petren, Sweden (1976)
Manfred Lachs, Poland (1976)
Charles D. Onyeama, Nigeria (1976)
Hardy C. Dillard, United States (1979)
Louis Ignacio-Pinto, Dahomey (1979)
Federico de Castro, Spain (1979)
Platon D. Morozov, USSR (1979)
Eduardo Jiménez de Aréchaga, Uruguay (1979)
Registrar of the Court: Stanislas Aquarone, Australia

PROCEDURE OF THE COURT

Normally, all 15 judges sit to hear a case, but 9 judges constitute a quorum. The Court, however, may form chambers composed of three or more judges, to hear particular categories of cases—for example, labor, transit, communications. The Court may also form a chamber to deal with a particular case, the number of judges being determined by the Court with the approval of the parties concerned. Moreover, with a view to speedy dispatch of business, the Court is required by its Statute to form annually a chamber, composed of five judges, which at the request of parties may hear cases by summary procedure. A judgment given by any of the chambers is considered a judgment of the Court as a whole.

All questions are decided by a majority vote of the judges present. If the votes are equal, the president has the casting, or deciding, vote. The judgments have to be read in open court and are required to state the reason on which they are based and the names of the judges responsible for the decision. If a judgment does not represent the unanimous opinion of the judges, any judge is entitled to deliver a separate opinion. All hearings are public unless the Court decides otherwise or the parties demand that the public not be admitted.

Judgments are final and without appeal. An application for revision of a judgment will be considered by the Court only if it is based on the discovery of some decisive fact that was unknown to both the Court and the party seeking revision when the judgment was made. Should a dispute arise concerning the meaning or scope of a judgment, the Court shall construe it on the request of any party.

COMPETENCE AND JURISDICTION OF THE COURT

Only states can be parties in cases before the World Court. Hence, proceedings may not be instigated by or against an individual, corporation, or other entity that is not a state under international law. However, if certain rules are satisfied, a state may take up a case involving one of its nationals. Many cases that have come before the Court are of this kind. The *Ambatielos Case—Greece* vs. *United Kingdom*—judgment of 19 May 1953, involved three Anglo-Greek agreements and concerned claims of a Greek shipowner, N. E. Ambatielos. The *Nottebohm Case—Liechtenstein* vs. *Guatemala*—judgment of 6 April 1955, involved a claim by the former state in respect of injuries sustained by a German-born, naturalized citizen of Liechtenstein as a result of certain measures Guatemala had taken during World War II. Among the case histories cited below are several that concerned the interests of private corporations or groups of bondholders.

All countries that are parties to the Statute have automatic access to the Court and can refer to it any case they wish. In addition, the Security Council may recommend that a legal dispute be referred to the Court. Under the Charter, nations are not automatically obliged to submit their legal disputes for judgment. At the San Francisco Conference it had been argued by some that the Court should be given compulsory jurisdiction and that UN members should bind themselves to accept the Court's right to consider legal disputes between them. This would have meant that if one member filed a case against another member, the Court would automatically, and without reference to the second member concerned, have the right to try the case. The proposal was rejected because some delegates feared that such a provision might make the Statute unacceptable to their countries. Moreover, it was generally felt that since the disputants in an international court are sovereign states, they should not be summoned against their will to submit to the Court's jurisdiction. Thus the World Court cannot proceed to adjudicate a case unless all parties to a dispute agree to submit it for judgment.

The consent by states to the Court's right to take up a case comes about in one of three main ways:

1. *Through specific agreement between the parties to submit a dispute to the Court.* This is the simplest method, but experience has shown that once a dispute has arisen there is little likelihood, in the prevailing atmosphere of controversy, that the parties will come to a specific agreement to submit the matter for judgment. Since the creation of the World Court, only six cases have been brought before it in this way.

2. *Through specific clauses contained in treaties and conventions.* Many treaties and conventions expressly stipulate that disputes that may arise under them, such as a claim by one country that a treaty has been violated by another country, will be submitted to the World Court for decision. More than 430 treaties and conventions, including peace treaties concluded after World War II, contain clauses to this effect, which attests to the readiness of countries to agree in advance to accept judicial settlement.

3. *Through voluntary recognition in advance of the compulsory jurisdiction of the Court in specified types of disputes.* Article 36 of the Statute states that all parties to the Statute

may at any time declare that they recognize as compulsory *ipso facto* and without special agreement, in relation to any other state accepting the same obligation, the jurisdiction of the Court in all legal disputes concerning: (a) the interpretation of a treaty; (b) any question of international law; (c) the existence of any fact which, if established, would constitute a breach of international obligation; (d) the nature or extent of the reparation to be made for the breach of an international obligation.

Such declarations may be made for only a limited period if desired, and with or without any conditions; or they may state that they will become operative only when a particular country or number of countries accept the same obligation. The most far-reaching reservation that has been attached to a declaration is the condition that the Court must not adjudicate any dispute that the country itself determines to be an essentially domestic matter. In effect, this leaves the country free to deny the Court's jurisdiction in most cases in which it might become involved; and in general, the practical significance of many of the declarations is severely limited by the right to make conditions. As of March 1970, declarations recognizing the compulsory jurisdiction of the Court were in force for 46 states.

The jurisdiction of the Court therefore comprises all legal disputes which the parties to the Statute refer to it and all matters specially provided for in the UN Charter or in treaties and conventions in force. In the event of a dispute as to whether the Court has jurisdiction, the Statute provides that the matter shall be decided by the Court. Article 38 of the Statute requires that in deciding the disputes submitted to it, the Court shall apply: (a) international conventions establishing rules recognized by the contesting states; (b) international custom as evidence of a general practice accepted as law; (c) the general principles of law recognized by civilized nations; (d) judicial decisions and teachings of the most highly qualified publicists of the various nations as a subsidiary means for determining the rules of law. In certain cases, however, if the parties concerned agree, the Court may decide a case *ex aequo et bono*—that is, by a judgment in equity taken simply on the basis of what the Court considers is right and good.

Advisory Opinions

The Charter provides that the General Assembly and the Security Council may request the Court to give an advisory opinion on any legal question and that other UN organs and specialized agencies, when authorized by the General Assembly, may also request advisory opinions on legal questions arising within the scope of their activities. In such cases the Court does not render a judgment but merely provides guidance for the international body concerned. Thus advisory opinions by their nature are not enforceable, and, though the bodies may receive them with respect, they may not necessarily find it politic to act on them.

Extrajudicial Functions of the Court

Many international conventions, treaties, and other instruments confer upon the International Court of Justice or its president the function of appointing umpires or arbitrators in certain eventualities. Furthermore, even when no treaty provision to this effect exists, the Court or individual judges may be requested to carry out functions of this nature. For example, at the French government's request, the Court's vice-president nominated neutral observers for the referendum to determine the status of the French settlements in India: Pondicherry, Karikal, Yanaon, Mahé, and Chandernagor.

SURVEY OF ICJ PRACTICE

Since the ICJ's inauguration in 1946, some 38 legal disputes have been submitted to it and 13 advisory opinions have been requested by international organizations.

Legal Disputes. Of the 38 cases submitted by states, 6 were withdrawn by the parties before a decision was reached, and in 12 the Court found that it had no jurisdiction under its Statute to determine the merits of the disputes involved. The remaining cases on which the Court has rendered judgment encompassed a wide range of topics, including: sovereignty over disputed territory or territorial possessions; the international law of the sea; commercial interests or property rights either of states or of private corporations and persons (examples of these types of disputes are given in the case histories below).

Many of the cases, including some that fall into the three categories just described, involve differences in interpretations of specific bilateral or multilateral treaties and other legal instruments. Thus, in the case of the rights of US citizens in Morocco—*France* vs. *US*—the Court found, on 27 August 1952, that the prohibiting of certain imports into Morocco had violated US treaty rights. But it rejected the US claim that its citizens in principle were not subject to the application of Moroccan laws unless they had received the US's prior assent. Another case involving the interpretation of legal obligations was one concerning the arbitral award made by the king of Spain on 23 December 1906, *Honduras* vs. *Nicaragua*. The Court ruled, on 18 November 1960, that Nicaragua had failed to give effect to the 1906 arbitral award delineating certain portions of the boundary between the two countries.

Probably the most famous case of interpretation of legal obligations to come before the Court involved the claims by Ethiopia and Liberia that South Africa had violated its obligations

under a League of Nations mandate for the territory of South West Africa. After six years of deliberations the Court decided, on 18 July 1966, that Ethiopia and Liberia had failed to validate any legal rights or interests in their claims and dismissed them without ruling on their substantive merits. (For further details, see under section B of the chapter on Independence of Colonial Peoples.)

Advisory Opinions. The 13 advisory opinions requested by the General Assembly, Security Council, or authorized specialized agencies likewise have dealt with a variety of matters. Two opinions were concerned with admission to UN membership. One concerned reparation for injuries suffered in the service of the UN, requested by the Assembly after the assassination of the UN mediator in Palestine in 1948. In this, the Court found that the UN had the capacity to maintain a claim in international law against a state for injuries to an agent of the organization. Another opinion concerned the question of whether the costs of the peacekeeping operations in the Middle East and the Congo could, within the scope of Article 17 of the Charter, be regarded as expenses of the organization to be financed by contributions of member states, as assessed by the General Assembly. (For further details of the Court's opinion, see the final section of the chapter on Maintaining Peace and Security.) Four requests for advisory opinions have been concerned with legal questions relating to the territory of South West Africa, the last being made by the Security Council in July 1970. (For details of the circumstances leading to the requests and of the three earlier opinions handed down by the Court, see under section B of the chapter on Independence of Colonial Peoples.)

SOME CASE HISTORIES OF DISPUTES SUBMITTED TO THE COURT

For convenience, the following sample case histories have been drawn from the three categories of legal disputes indicated above.

Disputes over Territorial Claims and Territorial Possessions

In the *Case Concerning Sovereignty over Certain Frontier Land—Belgium* vs. *Netherlands*—the Court traced developments that had begun before the 1839 separation of the Netherlands from Belgium, and in its judgment, 20 June 1959, decided that sovereignty over the disputed plots belonged to Belgium.

In the dispute regarding sovereignty over certain islets and rocks lying between the British Channel island of Jersey and the French coast—the *Minquier and Ecrehos Islands Case*—the UK and France invoked historical facts going back to the 11th century. The UK started its argument by claiming title from the conquest of England in 1066 by William, Duke of Normandy. France started its argument by pointing out that the dukes of Normandy were vassals of the king of France and that the kings of England after 1066, in their capacity as dukes of Normandy, held the duchy in fee from the French kings. The Court decided, on 17 November 1953, that "the sovereignty over the islets and rocks of the Ecrehos and Minquier groups, insofar as these islets and rocks are capable of appropriation, belongs to the United Kingdom."

In the two *Antarctica Cases*, instituted by the UK against Argentina and Chile, respectively, the Court was asked to recognize British sovereignty over certain Antarctica territories, and to declare the pretensions of Argentina and Chile, and their alleged encroachments in those territories, contrary to international law. Since Argentina and Chile had not accepted the Court's jurisdiction, the Court, on 16 March 1956, ordered the cases removed from the docket.

The first case involving two Asian countries, *Cambodia* vs. *Thailand,* was filed with the Court, in October 1959, as the *Case Concerning the Temple of Preah Vihear.* It concerned, as stated by Cambodia, "a sacred place of pilgrimage and worship for the

Cambodian population." On 15 June 1962, the Court found, 9 to 3, that the temple was in Cambodian territory and that therefore Thailand must withdraw any military or police forces or other guards it had stationed there; it further held, by 7 to 5, that Thailand must restore to Cambodia any works of art that might, since Thailand's occupation of the temple area in 1954, have been removed.

Disputes Relating to the Law of the Sea

The Corfu Channel Case (UK vs. Albania), the first case decided by the Court, was brought before it at the suggestion of the Security Council. The facts were as follows: On 22 October 1946 two UK destroyers passing through the Corfu Channel off the Albanian coast struck mines whose explosion caused the death of 46 seamen and damage to the ships. The British thereupon mine-swept the Channel. Albania claimed that it had not laid the mines. The Court found Albania "responsible under international law for the explosions . . . and for the damage and loss of human life that resulted therefrom" and determined the compensation due to the UK at £843,947, equivalent to approximately $2.4 million. The Court also found that the British mine-sweeping activities in Albanian territorial waters had violated international law. The unanimous rejection by the Court of the British claim that the action was justified under the principle of "self-protection" constituted the first judicial finding that the use of force for self-help is in certain circumstances contrary to international law.

The Anglo-Norwegian Fisheries Case settled a long-standing difference between the UK and Norway concerning fishing rights off the Norwegian coast. The UK argued that a Norwegian decree of 1935 closed considerable areas off the Norwegian coast that, under international law, were high seas and open to the fishing vessels of all nations. The UK also demanded damages for the seizure of British trawlers. The Court, on 18 December 1951 ruled that the Norwegian delimitation of the zones was not contrary to international law. The two *North Sea Continental Shelf Cases* were concerned with the delineation of the continental shelf boundaries between West Germany and Denmark and West Germany and the Netherlands. In two special agreements of February 1967, the parties agreed to ask the Court to rule on the applicable principles of international law in fixing the appropriate boundary lines. The Court was not asked actually to fix the boundaries. The parties agreed to settle these themselves on the basis of the Court's decision. In its judgment, on 20 February 1969, the Court rejected Denmark's and the Netherlands' contention that West Germany was bound to observe the equidistance principle defined in the 1958 Geneva Convention on the Continental Shelf. It ruled that agreement should be reached in accordance with "equitable principles" in such a way as to leave to each party as much as possible of those parts of the continental shelf that constituted a natural prolongation of its respective land territory, and that where such delineation produced overlapping areas, these areas were to be divided in agreed proportions.

Disputes Involving Commercial Interests and Property Rights

The background of the *Monetary Gold Case—Italy* vs. *France, UK, and US*—was extremely complicated. In 1943, during World War II, Germany seized in Rome a certain amount of monetary gold that was the property of the National Bank of Albania and transported it to Germany. After the war, when US forces found substantial amounts of monetary gold in a salt mine near Merker, Germany, the Allies concluded a "gold pool" agreement under which monetary gold found in Germany was to be distributed among countries in proportion to their gold losses as a result of German looting. Pending restitution, the Bank of England became the custodian of the gold. Regarding the gold due to the

Bank of Albania, the governments of France, the UK, and the US, which were responsible for carrying out restitution from the "gold pool," were confronted with conflicting claims by Albania on the one hand and Italy on the other. Italy claimed that the assets of the National Bank of Albania had been largely owned by the Italian government and that, in partial satisfaction for damages caused to Italy by a 1945 Albanian law confiscating these assets, Italy was entitled to any gold that might be due to Albania. France, the UK, and the US decided to put the matter before an arbiter, but with the proviso that if the arbiter were to decide in favor of Albania, the gold would be delivered (subject to the right by Albania and Italy to contest this before the World Court) to the UK in partial satisfaction of the indemnity payable by Albania to the UK under the Court's decision in the Corfu Channel Case (see above). The arbiter, who was designated at the request of the three governments by the president of the International Court of Justice, decided in 1953 in favor of Albania.

At this juncture, Italy asked the Court to direct France, the UK, and the US to deliver the gold to Italy. The Court found, on 18 November 1953, that to decide the merits of Italy's case it would first have to determine whether the 1945 Albanian law confiscating Italian assets was contrary to international law. The Court found it could not make such decision without the consent of Albania. As long as this question was not decided, it could not allow the gold to either Italy or the UK.

The Anglo-Iranian Oil Company Case. Iran on 1 May 1951 passed a law terminating the concessions of the Anglo-Iranian Oil Company and expropriating the company's refinery at Abadan, the largest in the world. On 26 May the UK instituted proceedings against Iran before the International Court. On 5 July, the Court ordered important "interim measures" enjoining the two governments to refrain from any action that might aggravate the dispute or hinder the operation of the company. The company was to continue under the same management as before nationalization, subject to such modification as agreed to by a special supervisory board, which the Court requested the two governments to set up. A year later, however, on 22 July 1952, the Court in its final judgment ruled that it lacked jurisdiction and lifted the "interim measures." On 22 July 1952 the Court found that the 1933 agreement, which gave the Iranian concession to the Anglo-Iranian Oil Company and which the UK claimed had been violated by the act of nationalization, was merely a concessionary contract between Iran and a foreign corporation. The Court ruled that the interpretation of such a contract was not one of the matters regarding which Iran had accepted the compulsory jurisdiction of the Court. The controversy was settled by negotiations in 1953, after the Mossadegh regime in Iran had been replaced by another government.

The Barcelona Traction Case—Belgium vs. *Spain*—arose out of a 1948 adjudication by a provincial Spanish law court of bankruptcy of a company incorporated in Canada with subsidiaries operating in Barcelona. Belgium was seeking reparation for damages alleged to have been sustained by Belgian shareholders in the company as a result of the Spanish court's adjudication, which Belgium claimed was contrary to international law. The Belgian government filed its first application with the ICJ in 1958 and then discontinued it, renewing the case in 1962. The Court, on 5 February 1970, found that the Belgian government lacked standing to exercise diplomatic protection of Belgian shareholders in a Canadian company with respect to measures taken against that company in Spain.

REVIEW OF THE ROLE OF THE ICJ BY THE GENERAL ASSEMBLY

Since 1967 the Court has had only three legal disputes before it, the *North Sea Continental Shelf Cases*, on which it passed judgment in 1969, and the *Barcelona Traction Case*, on which it passed judgment in February 1970. As of January 1971, its only judicial business was a consideration of the Security Council's request, submitted in July 1970, for an advisory opinion on the legal consequences for states of the continued presence of South Africa in the territory of South West Africa. By the end of 1970, only 38 disputes were submitted to ICJ, of which 6 were withdrawn before a decision was awarded, and many UN members have come to question the usefulness of the Court.

At the 1970 Assembly session, nine states—Argentina, Canada, Finland, Italy, Japan, Liberia, Mexico, US, and Uruguay—sponsored an agenda item on a review of the role of the ICJ. In an explanatory memorandum, they cited the "lack of business currently before the Court" as evidence of the need for a review, observing that "this situation is not commensurate with either the distinction of the judges or the needs of the international community." The memorandum suggested that a study be undertaken "of obstacles to the satisfactory functioning" of the Court and ways of overcoming them. During the general debate on the item in the Assembly's Sixth (Legal) Committee, members listed a variety of reasons for the reluctance to use the Court: high costs in submitting disputes; the Court's cumbersome and time-consuming rules of procedure; its limited field of competence; and its unresponsiveness to contemporary legal and moral needs. (The last point was given particular stress by African states, who were outraged at the Court's failure to rule on the merits of Ethiopia's and Liberia's claims against South Africa in regard to South West Africa. They charged, in addition, that the Court functions predominantly on the basis of traditional Western modes of legal thought.)

Proposals for remedying the situation included a revision of the Court's Statute and rules of procedure; the appointment of younger judges and or shorter terms of office; and wider acceptance of the Court's compulsory jurisdiction. Some states (notably the USSR and its allies, which fear that a revision of the ICJ's Statute might open the way for a review and revision of the entire UN Charter, an idea they have always opposed) suggested that what is required is not so much a revision of the Statute as a reform of individual state practice.

In the discussion of measures that the Assembly might take to investigate the problem, controversy centered on a proposal by 22 Western, Latin American, and Western-orientated African states to establish an ad hoc committee to study the issues. Delegates unsympathetic to the idea of a full-scale review of the ICJ's functioning opposed the proposal on the ground that it was premature to establish a committee before the views of governments and the Court itself were known. After protracted in camera negotiations, the Sixth Committee reached a consensus decision to have the Assembly invite UN members and parties to the Statute to submit their views on the role of the Court on the basis of a questionnaire to be prepared by the secretary-general, invite the Court to give its own views "should it so desire," and request the secretary-general to prepare a comprehensive report on the question for the 1971 Assembly session in the light of the opinions expressed.

THE SECRETARIAT

CHARTER REQUIREMENTS

The Charter lays down very few requirements governing the establishment of the sixth main organ of the world body. Such requirements as are specified may be conveniently listed under the following headings.

Composition. The Charter states simply: "The Secretariat shall comprise a Secretary-General and such staff as the Organization may require."

Appointment of Staff. With regard to the secretary-general, the Charter merely stipulates that he "shall be appointed by the General Assembly upon the recommendation of the Security Council." In other words, the Security Council first must agree on a candidate, who then must be endorsed by a majority vote in the General Assembly. The other members of the Secretariat are to be appointed by the secretary-general "under regulations established by the General Assembly." The Charter stipulates that the "paramount consideration" in the employment of staff "shall be the necessity of securing the highest standards of efficiency, competence, and integrity." However, to this consideration is added an important rider—namely, that "due regard shall be paid to the importance of recruiting the staff on as wide a geographical basis as possible." This requirement presumably was included to allay the fears of smaller nations that the Secretariat might be dominated by nationals from the larger, more developed countries, where a high percentage of the population normally receives advanced education.

Functions of the Secretariat. The duties of the general staff are not specified beyond an instruction that an appropriate number shall be permanently assigned to ECOSOC and the Trusteeship Council, and "as required, to the other organs of the United Nations." With respect to the functions of the secretary-general, the Charter states only that he shall be "the chief administrative officer of the Organization," and that he shall "act in that capacity" at all meetings of the Assembly and the three councils, and that he shall also perform "such other functions as are entrusted to him by these organs." Apart from these general requirements, the Charter accords the secretary-general one specific duty and one specific power: he must make an annual report to the Assembly on the work of the organization, and he has the right to bring to the attention of the Security Council any matter that "in his opinion may threaten the maintenance of international peace and security."

The single restriction on the Secretariat is that "in the performance of their duties the Secretary-General and the staff shall not seek nor receive instructions from any government or from any authority external to the Organization," and that "they shall refrain from any action which might reflect on their position as international officials responsible only to the Organization." As a corollary to this injunction, the Charter puts member nations under the obligation to "respect the exclusively international character of the responsibilities of the Secretary-General and the staff and not to seek to influence them in the discharge of their reponsibilities."

APPOINTMENT OF THE SECRETARY-GENERAL

Since the Charter is silent on the qualifications for secretary-general and on his term of office, these decisions had to be taken by the first Assembly, in January 1946. It was agreed that, in making its recommendations to the Assembly, the Security Council should conduct its discussions in private and vote in secret, for the dignity of the office required avoidance of open debate on the character of the candidate. The Assembly also decided that the term of office would be five years (the League of Nations' secretary-general was elected for ten years), and that the secretary-general would be eligible for reappointment.

The appointment of a person to fill this pivotal office in international affairs is a delicate task. Except for a tacit agreement that the secretary-general should not be a national of one of their own countries, the permanent members of the Security Council have been divided in their views as to the suitability of a candidate and have reached settlements only after protracted negotiation. The issues involved in the appointment or reappointment of each secretary-general are described in the next chapter.

As of December 1970, only three men had held the post of secretary-general. The first, Trygve Lie of Norway, was appointed for a five-year term on 1 February 1946. On 1 November 1950 he was reappointed for three years. He resigned on 10 November 1952 and was succeeded by Dag Hammarskjöld of Sweden on 10 April 1953. On 26 September 1957, Hammarskjöld was appointed for a further five-year term beginning 10 April 1958. After Hammarskjöld's death in a plane crash in Africa on 17 September 1961, U Thant, of Burma, was appointed acting secretary-general on 3 November 1961, to complete the unexpired term. In November 1962, U Thant was appointed secretary-general for a five-year term beginning with his assumption of office on 3 November 1961. On 2 December 1966 his mandate was unanimously renewed for another five years.

Brief Biographies of the Secretaries-General Prior to Their Appointment

Trygve Lie. Born in Oslo, 1896. Law degree from Oslo University. Active in his country's trade union movement from the age of 15, when he joined the Norwegian Trade Union Youth Organization. At 23, became assistant to the secretary of the Norwegian Labor Party. Legal adviser to the Norwegian Trade Union Federation (1922–35). Elected to the Norwegian parliament (1935). Minister of justice (1935–39). Minister of trade, industry, shipping, and fishing (1939–40). After the German occupation of Norway in 1940 and until the liberation of Norway in 1945, he was, successively, acting foreign minister and foreign minister of the Norwegian government in exile in London. A prominent anti-Nazi, he rendered many services in the Allied cause during the war. For example, he was instrumental in preventing the Norwegian merchant marine, one of the world's largest, from falling into German hands. Reelected to parliament in 1945. He headed the Norwegian delegation to the San Francisco Conference.

Dag Hjalmar Agne Carl Hammarskjöld. Born in Jönköpirg,

Sweden, 1905. Studied at Uppsala and Stockholm universities; Ph.D., Stockholm, 1934. Secretary of Commission on Unemployment (1930–34). Assistant professor of political economy, Stockholm University (1933). Secretary of the Sveriges Riksband (Bank of Sweden, 1935–36); chairman of the board (1941–45). Undersecretary of state in the Swedish ministry of finance (1936–45). Envoy extraordinary and financial adviser to the ministry of foreign affairs (1946–49). Undersecretary of state (1949). Deputy foreign minister (1951–53). Delegate to the Organization for European Economic Cooperation (OEEC; 1948–53). Vice-chairman of Executive Committee of the OEEC (1948–49). Swedish delegate to the Commission of Ministers of the Council of Europe (1951–52). Hammarskjöld was a member of the Swedish Academy, which grants the Nobel prizes, and vice-president of the Swedish Tourist and Mountaineers' Association.

U Thant. Born in Pantanaw near Rangoon, Burma, 1909. Educated at University College, Rangoon. Started career as teacher of English and modern history at Pantanaw High School; later became senior and headmaster. Active in development and modernization of Burma's educational system. Author and free-lance journalist. Books include a work on the League of Nations (1932), *Democracy in Schools* (1952), and *History of Post-War Burma* (1961). After Burma's independence, became Burma's press director (1947), director of broadcasting (1948), secretary in the ministry of information (1949–53). Chief adviser to his government in many international conferences. Member of Burma's delegation to the 1952 General Assembly. In 1957, moved to New York as head of Burma's permanent delegation to the UN. Vice-president of the 1959 Assembly session. U Thant is a Buddhist. Like many Burmese, he has only one name (Thant). The "U" is a Burmese title of respect, for which the English language has no exact equivalent.

CURRENT STRUCTURE AND COMPOSITION OF THE SECRETARIAT

In 1970 the Secretariat was organized into the following major units: (1) offices of the secretary-general, comprising the executive office of the secretary-general and the office of General Assembly affairs (headed by an undersecretary-general); (2) offices of the two undersecretaries-general for special political affairs; (3) office of legal affairs; (4) office of the undersecretary-general for administration and management; (5) office of the controller; (6) office of personnel; (7) office for inter-agency affairs; (8) department of political and Security Council affairs; (9) department of economic and social affairs; (10) department of Trusteeship and non-self-governing territories; (11) office of public information; (12) office of conference services; (13) office of general services; (14) UN office at Geneva.

Each of these units is headed by an undersecretary-general or an assistant secretary-general, who is responsible to the secretary-general and acts as his principal adviser on matters within his competence. In addition to the assistant or undersecretaries-general directing the units listed above, there are the heads of the special bodies (for example, UNICEF) who also have the rank of assistant or undersecretary-general.

Immediately below the rank of undersecretary are what the office of personnel refers to as "D-level" staff: directors of main subdepartments and chiefs of specific bureaus within the major organizational units. Below them is the stratum of "P-level" staff: personnel with professional qualifications as administrators, specialists, technical experts, statisticians, translators, editors, interpreters, and so on. And below them is the army of general services, or "G-level," personnel, which includes administrative assistants, clerical workers, secretaries, typists, and the like. Manual workers, such as building maintenance staff, are separately classified.

P-level personnel and above are recruited in the various member countries of the UN and, when serving outside their own country, are entitled to home-leave travel, repatriation allowances, and other special benefits. General service personnel include a variety of nationalities, but they are recruited locally and are not selected according to any principle of geographical representation. The majority of G-level staff at Headquarters are Americans.

Organizational Distribution of Staff, 1970

As of 31 May 1970 the Secretariat consisted of 10,577 staff members holding permanent or temporary appointments of a year or more. Of this total, 8,518 were in the regular Secretariat financed by the annual budget of the UN, and 2,059 were serving with five subsidiary organs which were wholly or largely financed by voluntary contributions.

By organ and location, the staff members of the regular Secretariat were distributed as follows: Headquarters—4,122; Office at Geneva (except the Economic Commission for Europe)—978; Economic Commission for Europe—210; Economic Commission for Asia and the Far East—390; Economic Commission for Latin America—454; Economic Commission for Africa—345; Economic and Social Office in Beirut—39; information centers—258; special missions—529; International Court of Justice—34; Conference on Trade and Development—434; Industrial Development Organization—725.

The staff members serving with subsidiary organs were distributed as follows: Children's Fund—876; Development Program (excluding local staff)—760; High Commissioner for Refugees—289; Institute for Training and Research—50; Relief and Works Agency for Palestine Refugees in the Middle East (excluding local staff)—84.

By category, the staff of the regular Secretariat consisted of 2,908 in the professional and higher categories; 5,314 in the general service and related categories; and 296 in the field service category. Those specifically serving with subsidiary organs consisted of 783 in the professional and higher categories and 1,276 in the general service and related categories.

In its report to the Assembly on the budget estimates for 1969, the Advisory Committee on Administrative and Budgetary Questions suggested that the available manpower in the Secretariat was not being utilized fully and that savings might be achieved by a reorganization of work or a redeployment of staff. In response to the committee's recommendation for a manpower survey, the secretary-general in 1969 established an Administrative Management Service (AMS) responsible to the undersecretary-general for Administration and Management. AMS's initial survey on the deployment and utilization of staff is expected to be completed by 1971.

Problems of Staff Appointment According to Equitable Geographical Distribution

All UN staff members are appointed by the secretary-general under regulations established by the Assembly. Some of the appointments, such as the high commissioner for refugees, are subject to confirmation by the General Assembly. Staff recruitment, in general, is handled by the Office of Personnel, salary scales and other conditions of employment being determined by the General Assembly.

Although the Charter stipulates that staff members are to be regarded as international civil servants, who are barred from representing the interests of their own countries, UN member governments attach great importance to having a fair proportion of their nationals employed in the Secretariat. However, a genuinely equitable representation of nationalities has proved almost impossible to achieve. Budgetary considerations limit the extent to which the demands of new member countries can be met by the creation of new Secretariat posts. Another difficulty is reconciling equitable geographic representation with the need to secure "the highest standards of efficiency, competence, and integrity," as prescribed in the Charter.

With the influx of many new UN members, the problem of achieving equitable geographical distribution has become acute, as evidenced by the frequency of General Assembly resolutions on the subject. The most far-reaching of these resolutions was adopted in 1962. While appreciating that some improvements had been made in the geographical distribution of the staff, the resolution noted that "significant imbalances . . . continue to exist." It recommended that in applying the principle of equitable geographical distribution the secretary-general should take into account the fact of membership, members' financial contributions to the UN, the respective populations of the member countries, the relative importance of posts at different levels, and the need for a more balanced regional composition of the staff at D-level. It further recommended that in confirming permanent contracts (UN staff are initially hired on the basis of two-year contracts), particular account should be taken of the need to reduce underrepresentation. In addition, the resolution requested the secretary-general to report annually to the Assembly on the situation.

Since 1962, successive Assemblies have noted that progress has been made but have continued to request further improvement. A report by the secretary-general showed that as of 31 August 1969 the Secretariat included nationals of 116 member states and of 4 states that are not UN members but participate in the work of its subsidiary organs. The report also stated that only two regions, Eastern Europe and the Caribbean, remain substantially underrepresented in the Secretariat.

THE EVOLVING ROLE OF THE SECRETARIAT

The UN's administrative arm has developed largely in accordance with the demands made upon it. In the process, it has evolved a distinctive character of its own, in keeping with the dignity of its status as a constitutionally defined organ of the world body.

The secretary-general has played the most significant part in shaping the character of the Secretariat. As chief administrative officer the secretary-general has wide discretionary powers and latitude to administer as he thinks fit. As Mrs. Eleanor Roosevelt, a former chairman of the UN Commission on Human Rights noted in 1953, the secretary-general, "partly because of the relative permanence of his position (unlike the president of the General Assembly who changes every year) and partly because of his widely ramified authority over the whole UN organization, tends to become its chief personality, its embodiment and its spokesman to the world."

The first three secretaries-general strove to develop and maintain the positive functions of the Secretariat. Although each had his own views on the role of the office, all shared the belief that the Secretariat is the backbone of the UN system. The most eloquent statement of that belief was probably made by Dag Hammarskjöld in an address at the University of California in 1955: ". . . the United Nations is what Member nations made it, [but] within the limits set by government action and government cooperation, much depends on what the Secretariat makes it." He went on to say that in addition to the Secretariat's function of providing services and facilities for governments in their capacity as members of the UN, the Secretariat also "has creative capacity. It can introduce new ideas. It can, in proper forms, take initiatives. It can put before Member Governments findings which will influence their actions." Stressing the fact that members of the Secretariat serve as international officials rather than as government representatives, Hammarskjöld concluded that "the Secretariat in its independence represents an organ, not only necessary for the life and proper functioning of the body, but of importance also for its growth. . . ."

Thus few people whose work brings them into association with the world organization regard the Secretariat as a mere handmaiden of the other UN bodies. On the contrary, the Assembly and the three Councils frequently look to the Secretariat to provide solutions to the more intractable world problems that come to their attention.

THE POLITICAL ROLE OF THE SECRETARY-GENERAL

From the outset, the secretary-general has played a crucial part in helping to settle crises that have troubled nations since the end of World War II. In practice, the role has gone far beyond what might be anticipated from a reading of the terse Charter provisions for the office. Yet the role has been developed precisely through a skillful exploitation of the potentialities inherent in these provisions.

As early as 1945, the preparatory commission on the establishment of the UN predicted that the secretary-general would have "an important part to play as a mediator and as an informal advisor to many governments." The commission pointed out that his right under the Charter to bring to the attention of the Security Council any matter that in his opinion may threaten the maintenance of international peace and security was "a quite special right which goes beyond any power previously accorded to the head of an international organization," requiring "the exercise of the highest qualities of political judgment, tact and integrity." Another means by which the secretary-general can bring his views to the attention of the world's governments is the Charter requirement that he submit an annual report to the Assembly on the work of the organization. By long-standing custom, such reports are usually prefaced by an introduction containing the secretary-general's personal comments, criticisms, and suggestions. The secretary-general's role has been enhanced through exploiting the Charter provision that he shall perform "such other functions" as are entrusted to him by the main organs of the UN. Perhaps the greatest tribute to the caliber of the first three secretaries-general is that both the Assembly and the Security Council depended on them to find solutions to many difficult political problems.

The role of the secretary-general in international affairs has varied with the individuality of the incumbent, the political crisis involved, and the limitations imposed on his freedom of action by the big powers. The history of the part played by the secretary-general is essentially the history of the responses made by three men to a specific set of circumstances. Below is an outline account of the initiatives taken by the three secretaries-general, and of the reactions these provoked among the big powers, in successive crises.

DEVELOPMENTS UNDER TRYGVE LIE
Appointment of Trygve Lie

Trygve Lie was sponsored originally by the US for the presidency of the first session of the General Assembly, held in London, rather than for the post of secretary-general. The USSR concurred in the suggestion and nominated him for the presidency. The first choice for secretary-general among the Western delegations was Lester B. Pearson, former Canadian ambassador to the US. The USSR at first suggested Stanoje Simic, then foreign minister of Yugoslavia. As a compromise, the Security Council in private session on 30 January 1946 recommended Trygve Lie to the General Assembly for the post. The Assembly appointed him, by a vote of 46 to 3, on 1 February 1946.

First Term, 1946–51

Trygve Lie had not yet been in office three months when he assumed the initiative of advising the Security Council on the Secretariat's interpretation of the Charter. The Council was considering its first case, the Iranian complaint against the USSR. The Secretary-General delivered a legal opinion that differed sharply from that of the Security Council. The Council did not accept his interpretation, but it upheld his right to present his views. After setting this precedent, Lie submitted legal opinions on other matters.

During Lie's first term as secretary-general, East-West tension distinctly colored the UN atmosphere. As the world situation became increasingly threatening, the political role of the secretary-general expanded. Lie took a definite stand on three issues. His position on seating the representatives of the People's Republic of China in the UN, his plan for a general settlement of the cold war, and his attitude after the outbreak of the Korean War each earned him the dislike of some of the permanent members of the Security Council.

Chinese Representation. By the end of 1949 a number of states, including the USSR and the UK—permanent members of the Security Council—had recognized the mainland government, the People's Republic of China. In January 1950 the USSR representatives, having failed to obtain the seating of the representatives of the People's Republic, began boycotting UN meetings at which China was represented by delegates of the Republic of China, based on Taiwan. In private meetings with delegations, Lie tried to solve the impasse. He indicated that he favored the seating of the Peking delegates. He adduced various reasons, including a ruling of the International Court of Justice, for the thesis that nonrecognition of a government by other governments should not determine its representation in the UN.

Trygve Lie's 20-Year Peace Plan. Lie developed extraordinary initiative during the first half of 1950. He "wanted to find out," as he put it at a press conference on 26 May 1950, "if the cold war was just going to go on month after month with no end but ultimate disaster in sight, or whether there was a basis for the renewal of general negotiations between the two sides on at least some of the outstanding issues of the so-called cold war." In a letter to the Security Council dated 6 June 1950, approximately two weeks before the outbreak of the Korean War, he said, "I felt it my duty to suggest a fresh start to be made towards eventual peaceful solution of outstanding problems." In his *Twenty Year Program for Achieving Peace through the United Nations,* Lie proposed new international machinery to control atomic energy and to check the competitive production of armaments, and the establishment of a UN force to prevent or stop localized outbreaks.

Armed with these proposals and other memoranda, including the one on Chinese representation, Lie journeyed first to Washington, then to London, to Paris, and finally to Moscow. He held conversations not only with foreign ministers and high-ranking diplomats, but with US President Harry S Truman; British Prime Minister Clement Attlee; French President Vincent Auriol; and Soviet Premier Joseph Stalin. Lie's reception was most cordial in Moscow, warm in Paris and friendly in London, but cool in Washington.

The international picture changed abruptly, however, with the outbreak of the Korean War and the attitude of a number of governments toward Lie changed dramatically as well.

The Korean War. An outstanding example of the Secretary-General's taking a stand on an issue was Lie's intervention in the emergency meeting of the Security Council on 24 June 1950. He unequivocally labeled the North Korean forces aggressors because they had crossed the 38th parallel; declared that the conflict constituted a threat to international peace; and urged that the Security Council had the "clear duty" to act. After the Security Council (in the absence of the Soviet delegate) had set in motion military sanctions against North Korea, Lie endorsed that course for the UN and rallied support from member governments for the UN military action in Korea. This brought him into sharp conflict with the USSR, which accused him of "slavish obedience to Western imperialism" and to the "aggression" which, in the Soviet view, the US had committed in Korea.

As the Korean conflict grew more ominous with the intervention of the People's Republic of China, Lie played an active role in getting cease-fire negotiations under way in the field. At the same time, he fully identified himself with the military intervention in Korea on behalf of the UN.

Extension of Lie's Term as Secretary-General
Lie's five-year term of office was due to expire on 1 February 1951, and in the fall of 1950 the question of reappointing him to a second term was raised in the Security Council. The USSR on 12 October cast the only negative vote in the Council against nominating Lie for a second term, but this was sufficient to block the nomination. Thereupon, the Council informed the General Assembly that it was unable to recommend a candidate for the office of secretary-general, a situation unforeseen in the Charter.

A few days later, the Council split three ways: supporters of Lie's candidacy; opponents (the USSR and, later, China); and those who had voted for Lie on 12 October but would have preferred a candidate who could obtain a unanimous vote of the Council. On 23 October 1950, Andrei Vishinsky of the USSR stated that his government would back any candidate except Lie who would be agreeable to the other permanent members. On 25 October, Warren Austin, speaking for the US, declared he would veto anybody except Lie. This, however, did not prove necessary because in that meeting the compromise candidate, Carlos P. Romulo of the Philippines (nominated by China), received only four votes (China, Egypt, India, USSR), and the Soviet compromise nominee, Dr. Charles H. Malik of Lebanon, received the same number of votes.

In the General Assembly, discussion was opened on a motion to extend Lie's term of office for three years. Supporters of Lie argued that since the Security Council was unable to recommend a candidate and the UN could not be left without an administrative head, the Assembly was within its rights to interpret the Charter in a way that would make the organization effective and to extend the secretary-general's term of office on its own initiative. Lie's opponents, on the other hand, argued that, procedurally speaking, a recommendation by the Security Council was necessary and that it was of utmost importance for the secretary-general to enjoy the confidence of all camps in the UN. Hence, the extension was not only illegal but politically unwise. The resolution to extend Lie's term for three years, beginning 1 February 1951, was carried 46 to 5, with 8 abstentions. The negative votes were cast by the Soviet bloc. The abstaining nations included China, Australia, and the Arab states.

The USSR maintained normal relations with Lie until the expiration of his original term, 31 January 1951. Thereafter, it stood by its previous announcement that the extension of the term was illegal and that it would "not consider him as Secretary-General." By the fall of 1951, however, its nonrecognition policy toward Lie subsided.

Lie's Resignation
Other complications were facing Lie, and on 10 November 1952 he tendered his resignation to the General Assembly.

Subsequently, Lie again became active in the public affairs of his native Norway. But he allowed some time to elapse in deference to a resolution adopted by the General Assembly in 1946 which states that "because a Secretary-General is a confidant of many governments," no member government "should offer him . . . immediately upon retirement, any governmental position in which his confidential information might be a source of embarrassment to other Members, and on his part a [retired] Secretary-General should refrain from accepting any such position."

DEVELOPMENTS UNDER DAG HAMMARSKJÖLD
Appointment of Dag Hammarskjöld
Four months after Lie's resignation, on 11 March 1953, the Security Council held its first of a series of private meetings to consider a successor to Lie. In the early balloting, which began on 13 March, neither Carlos P. Romulo of the Philippines (proposed by the US), Stanislaus Skrzeszewski of Poland (proposed by the USSR), nor Lester B. Pearson of Canada (proposed by Denmark) received the required majority. There followed fruitless discussions among the permanent members. The USSR nominated Mrs. Vijaya Lakshmi Pandit (the sister of Prime Minister Nehru of India, and the first woman president of a UN General Assembly), but she received only two votes.

A stalemate seemed unavoidable. But on 31 March 1953 the Council adopted a French motion to recommend Dag Hammarskjöld of Sweden. The vote was 10 to 0, with China abstaining, possibly because Sweden had recognized the People's Republic of China. On 7 April 1953, the Assembly accepted Lie's resignation and appointed Hammarskjöld by secret ballot, 57 to 1 with 1 abstention.

First Term, 1953–58
Hammarskjöld's activities in the political field were more numerous and far-reaching than Lie's had been. Both the General Assembly and the Security Council repeatedly relied on his initiative and advice, and entrusted important tasks to him.

The 1954 General Assembly set a precedent when it asked the Secretary-General to seek the release of 11 US fliers who were held prisoners by mainland China. The resolution left the course of action entirely to his judgment. After various preparations, Hammarskjöld flew to Peking for personal negotiations with that government, and the 11 were released. This success greatly increased the readiness of the Assembly to rely on the Secretary-General as a troubleshooter.

The Suez Crisis. Grave responsibilities were entrusted to the Secretary-General by the Council and Assembly in connection with the establishment and operation of the UN Emergency Force (UNEF). On 4 November 1956, at the height of the crisis resulting from British, French, and Israeli intervention in Egypt, the Secretary-General was requested to submit a plan within 48 hours for the establishment of a force "to secure and supervise the cessation of hostilities." The Assembly approved his plan and, at his suggestion, appointed Major-General E. L. M. Burns, Chief of Staff of the UN Truce Supervisory Organization (UNTSO), as the chief of UNEF. The Assembly authorized the Secretary-General to take appropriate measures to carry out his plan, and an advisory committee of seven UN members was appointed to assist him. Hammarskjöld flew to Egypt to arrange for the Egyptian government's consent for UNEF to be stationed and to operate in Egyptian territory. He was given the task of arranging with Egypt, France, Israel, and the UK the implementation of the cease-fire and the halt of troops and arms into the area, and was authorized to issue all regulations and instructions essential to the effective functioning of UNEF.

Second Term, 1958–61

On 26 September 1957, after endorsement by the Security Council, the General Assembly reelected Hammarskjöld for a new five-year term, until 10 April 1963.

Hammarskjöld's Views on Developing the Role of Secretary-General. Even before the Middle East crisis of 1956, Hammarskjöld had pointed to the need for the secretary-general to assume a new role in world affairs. On his reelection, Hammarskjöld told the Assembly that he considered it to be the duty of the secretary-general, guided by the Charter and the decisions of the main UN organs, to use his office and the machinery of the organization to the full extent permitted at each stage by practical circumstances. But he then declared: "I believe it is in keeping with the philosophy of the Charter that the Secretary-General be expected to act also *without such guidance*, should this appear to him necessary in order to help in *filling a vacuum* that may appear in the systems which the Charter and traditional diplomacy provide for the safeguarding of peace and security." (Italics added.) In other words, inaction or stalemate either at the UN or outside of it may be the justification for the secretary-general to act on his own.

Thus in 1958, Hammarskjöld took an active hand in the Jordan-Lebanon crisis. After a resolution for stronger UN action failed to be carried in the Security Council, he announced that he would nevertheless strengthen UN action in Lebanon and "accept the consequences" if members of the Security Council were to disapprove; but none did. In the fall of 1959 the USSR made it known that it did not favor a visit by the Secretary-General to Laos and, in particular, the assignment of a special temporary "UN ambassador" there. Yet Hammarskjöld did go to Laos to orient himself on the situation in that corner of Southeast Asia and assigned a high UN official as the head of a special mission to Laos. In March 1959, Hammarskjöld sent a special representative to help Thailand and Cambodia settle a border dispute. He did this at their invitation, without specific authorization by the Security Council or the General Assembly. The dispute was settled.

In the introduction to his report to the 1959 General Assembly, the Secretary-General commented on this "quiet diplomacy" and the considerable degree of discretion available to him when entrusted with special diplomatic and operational functions:

> The main significance of the evolution of the Office of the Secretary-General . . . lies in the fact that it has provided means for smooth and fast action which might otherwise not have been open to the Organization. This is of special value in situations in which prior public debate on a proposed course of action might increase the difficulties . . . or in which . . . members may prove hesitant, without fuller knowledge of the facts or for other reasons, to give explicit prior support in detail to an action which, however, they approve in general terms or are willing should be tried without formal commitment.

The Congo Crisis. By far the greatest responsibilities Hammarskjöld had to shoulder were in connection with the UN Operation in the Congo (designated by its French initials, ONUC). This is described more fully in the chapter on UN Peacekeeping Operations.

On 12 and 13 July 1960, respectively, President Joseph Kasavubu and Premier Patrice Lumumba of the newly independent country each cabled the Secretary-General asking for UN military assistance in view of the arrival of Belgian troops and the impending secession of Katanga. At Hammarskjöld's request, the Security Council met on the night of 13 July. He gave his full support to the Congo's appeal and recommended that the Council authorize him to "take the necessary steps" to set up a UN military assistance force for the Congo, in consultation with the Congolese government and on the basis of the experience gained in connection with the UN Emergency Force in the Middle East. The Security Council so decided.

Since the Congo operation thus initiated was of much greater dimensions than the UNEF operation, the responsibilities imposed upon the Secretary-General were correspondingly heavier. For though the Security Council and the General Assembly guided Hammarskjöld, he himself had to make extraordinarily difficult decisions almost daily, often on highly explosive matters. That arose as a result of serious rifts within the Congo government and many other factors.

Various member governments, including certain African countries, the USSR, and certain Western countries, criticized Hammarskjöld for some actions the UN took or failed to take in the Congo. At times, he had to face the possibility that some country that had contributed military contingents to the UN force would withdraw them.

When it became known in February 1961 that Lumumba, who had been deposed by Kasavubu early in September 1960 and thereafter lived in a house in Léopoldville protected by UN guards, had been handed over to Katanga authorities, and subsequently murdered, Hammarskjöld declared that the UN was blameless for the "revolting crime." But several delegates claimed that he should have taken stronger measures to protect Lumumba, and some smaller countries demanded his resignation.

The "Troika" Proposal. The USSR had asked for Hammarskjöld's dismissal long before the assassination of Lumumba. Premier Khruschchev as head of the Soviet delegation to the 1960 General Assembly criticized Hammarskjöld for lacking impartiality and for violating instructions of the Security Council in his conduct of the UN Operation in the Congo. He also proposed a basic change in the very institution of the secretary-general. Since the secretary-general had become "the interpreter and executor of decisions of the General Assembly and the Security Council," this one-man office should be replaced by a "collective executive organ consisting of three persons each of whom would represent a certain group of states"—namely, the West, the socialist states, and the neutralist countries. The institution of a "troika" would guarantee that the UN executive organ would not act to the detriment of any of these groups of states.

Hammarskjöld rejected the accusations against his impartiality; declared he would not resign unless the member states for which the organization was of decisive importance or the uncommitted nations wished him to do so; and received an ovation from the overwhelming majority of the delegations. He also stated that to replace the one-man secretary-general by a three-man body would greatly alter the character and limit the scope of the UN.

Outside the Soviet bloc there had been little support for a troika proposal. However, during the 1960 General Assembly, some "subtroika" proposals were made. President Nkrumah of Ghana suggested that there be three deputy secretaries-general, one each from the Western, Eastern, and neutralist camps, and that they be assigned a degree of authority that would make them more than mere assistants to the secretary-general. President Sékou Touré submitted a similar scheme. Hammarskjöld, in turn, proposed that five of his top aides—one US citizen, one Soviet citizen, and three from countries outside any power bloc—be made responsible for advising the secretary-general on political problems. Discussions on these and similar plans were interrupted by Hammarskjöld's death.

Death of Dag Hammarskjöld

In view of dangerous developments in the Congo, Hammarskjöld flew there in September 1961. On the 17th, the plane carrying him from Léopoldville to a meeting with the Katanga secessionist leader at Ndola, Northern Rhodesia, crashed in a wooded area about 10 miles west of Ndola airport. Hammarskjöld and all 15 UN civilian and military personnel traveling with him, including the crew, were killed. The exact cause of the tragedy has not been determined. An investigation commission appointed by the General Assembly reported several possibilities: inadequate technical and security preparations for the flight; an attack on the plane from the air or the ground; sabotage; or human failure by the pilot.

DEVELOPMENTS UNDER U THANT
Appointment of U Thant

For a few weeks after Hammarskjöld's death, UN activities were guided under an informal arrangement by some of the top UN officials. The problem was not only finding a successor but also resolving the controversial question of the number and responsibilities of his top collaborators. Eventually, the Security Council accepted U Thant's proposal that, if elected, he would decide about the top posts in the Secretariat. On 3 November 1961 following the Security Council's unanimous recommendation, the General Assembly unanimously appointed U Thant as acting secretary-general until 10 April 1963 (when Hammarskjöld's term would have expired). On 30 November 1962, the General Assembly, again on recommendation by the Security Council, unanimously appointed U Thant secretary-general for a term ending 3 November 1966.

First Term, 1961–66

In his acceptance speech on 30 November 1962, U Thant said:

> I believe that I may play a role, however humble, in the easing of tensions and in bridging the gulf between the major powers . . . [the world's] difficult problems can be solved only by goodwill and a spirit of 'give and take.' When the future of mankind itself is at stake, no country or interest-group can afford to take a rigid stand or claim that its position is the only right one and that others may take it or leave it. No difficult problem can be solved to the complete satisfaction of all sides. We live in an imperfect world and have to accept imperfect solutions, which become more acceptable as we learn to live with them and as time passes by. In solving these complex problems, I myself and the Secretariat . . . are at the service not only of all member governments but of [alluding to the openings words of the UN Charter] 'the peoples of the United Nations.'

Because Hammarskjöld's dynamic concept of the secretary-general's political role had aroused such opposition in the Soviet bloc, U Thant could not take the same initiatives as his predecessor. However, U Thant consistently sought to use the prestige of his office to engage in quiet personal diplomacy to help settle disputes. Moreover, the Assembly frequently assigned him to mediate in extremely delicate situations. Also, through the medium of the introduction to the secretary-general's annual report on the work of the UN, U Thant put forth numerous proposals on basic issues continually under consideration at the UN—for example, disarmament and economic and social cooperation—and many of his suggestions have been adopted.

An early example of a successful initiative taken by U Thant was in connection with the long-standing dispute between Indonesia and the Netherlands over the status of West Irian. The territory, formerly known as West New Guinea, had belonged to the Dutch East Indies, and Indonesia now claimed it as its own. In December 1961 fighting broke out between Dutch and Indonesian troops. Appealing to both governments to seek a peaceful solution, the Secretary-General helped them arrive at a settlement. That settlement, moreover, brought new responsibilities to the office of the secretary-general: for the first time in UN history a non-self-governing territory was, for a limited period, administered directly by the world organization (see under section B of the chapter on Independence of Colonial Peoples).

The Cuban Crisis. Shortly after that dispute was resolved, the world came to the brink of nuclear disaster during the crisis over the Soviet missile bases in Cuba and the US blockade in the Caribbean. At the request of many delegations, U Thant cabled identical messages to President Kennedy and Premier Khrushchev urging the voluntary suspension "of all arms shipments to Cuba" and "of the quarantine measures involving the searching of ships bound for Cuba." On 23 September 1962 he made an impassioned appeal in the Security Council for "moderation, self-restraint, and good sense." His proposal that he fly to Cuba for direct consultation with Premier Fidel Castro was approved by the Security Council without a formal vote. After his return from Cuba, U Thant also participated in the delicate "quiet diplomacy" negotiations between the US and the USSR that led to the dismantling of the Soviet missile bases in Cuba, the removal of the missiles from Cuba, and the lifting of the blockade.

US Intervention in the Dominican Republic. Three years after the Cuban crisis, another Latin American country became the arena of potential major conflict. In April 1965 the US informed the Security Council that, due to civil strife in the Dominican Republic, it had ordered its troops to enter the country to protect US citizens and that it had also brought the matter before the Organization of American States (OAS). The USSR thereupon requested a meeting of the Security Council to consider the "armed interference by the United States in the internal affairs of the Dominican Republic." Calling for a cease-fire among the opposing Dominican factions, the Council invited the Secretary-General to send a representative to the republic and report back to the Council.

For the next 15 months the Secretary-General kept the Council informed on the UN mission's efforts to help bring about a cease-fire and on the general situation in the country as negotiations for a political settlement, under the auspices of the OAS, proceeded. The UN mission was withdrawn in October 1966, following the election of a new Dominican government and the departure of the Inter-American Peace Force that had been established by the OAS. U Thant stated that, while the mandate of his representative had been limited, he felt that the presence of the UN mission undoubtedly had been "a moderating factor in a difficult and dangerous situation."

U Thant's Stand on the Viet-Nam War. Throughout his tenure U Thant was deeply involved in the problem of Viet-Nam. By tacit consent this issue was never debated formally in the Assembly, and was only cursorily touched upon in the Security Council. The general feeling was that because three of the parties in the conflict—the two Viet-Nams and Communist China—were not UN members, and because of Peking's generally hostile attitude toward the world body, direct UN intervention would be useless or even harmful. For this reason, prior to the opening of the Paris peace talks in 1968, the Secretary-General was unremitting in his efforts to persuade the parties in the conflict to initiate peace negotiations on their own. In an effort to ease tensions as a necessary preliminary for fruitful discussion, U

Thant tried privately to get Washington and Hanoi to hold secret exploratory meetings on conditions for a cease-fire and the withdrawal of troops. He also sought to overcome Washington's resistance to Hanoi's demand that the National Liberation Front, the political arm of the Vietcong guerrillas in South Viet-Nam, be represented as a separate party in any peace negotiations.

But his labors were to no avail, and the situation deteriorated further when the US started bombing North Viet-Nam in February 1965. U Thant publicly deplored these attacks, fearing that continued escalation of hostilities might lead to a major war. In the summer of 1966 he put forth a three-stage proposal for creating a suitable atmosphere for discussions: cessation of the bombing of North-Vietnam; scaling down by all parties of all military operations; and a willingness of all parties engaged in actual fighting to enter into discussions. This proposal was ignored by the US. Since a halt to the bombing was the essential first step in the three-stage plan, U Thant's proposal could not be implemented.

Another two years passed before the US yielded to international opinion, and to urgent pressure at home, by halting its bombing raids on North Viet-Nam and consenting to engage in peace talks that included representatives of the National Liberation Front as well as of the Hanoi government. After these talks were begun, U Thant deliberately refrained from making any public statements on Viet-Nam "in order to avoid creating unnecessary difficulties" for the parties. He broke this silence only once, when on 5 May 1970 he expressed his deep concern "regarding the recent involvement of Cambodia in the war."

Second Term, 1966–71

Many observers believe that U Thant's disappointment at the US's negative response toward his plan for Viet-Nam peace talks was largely responsible for his initial decision, announced early in September 1966, that he would not "be available" for reappointment when his term of office expired on 3 November of that year. Dismayed by this development, and having no other candidate in mind, all factions among the UN membership made a concerted effort to persuade U Thant to change his mind. The Security Council even went so far as to issue, on 29 September 1966, a consensus asking him to reconsider his decision. By 3 November 1966 he still had not reached a decision but offered to remain in office until the end of the regular Assembly session in December, to ensure continuity of administration during that period. U Thant later consented to accept another term, and on

2 December 1966 the Security Council's unanimous recommendation for his reappointment was unanimously endorsed by the Assembly.

U Thant's second term of office was dominated by the protracted Middle East crisis that arose in the aftermath of the Six-Day War in 1967. His quick action in removing UNEF troops from the Suez area at the request of the UAR just before that war began occasioned much criticism and some misunderstanding (see the appropriate section of the chapter on Maintaining Peace and Security).

Of the two other major political conflicts during the period 1967–70, the savage civil war in Nigeria and the Soviet invasion of Czechoslovakia on 20 August 1968, only the latter was debated at the UN. The political aspects of the Nigerian situation were never raised in either the Assembly or the Security Council out of deference to the African countries themselves, whose main object was to keep external intervention to a minimum. However, as the troops of the federal government of Nigeria began to penetrate more deeply into the eastern region (which had announced its secession from the Federation and proclaimed itself an independent state under the name of Biafra), the various humanitarian organs of the UN became increasingly concerned about the plight of the people there. Accordingly, in August 1968 the Secretary-General took the initiative of sending a personal representative to Nigeria to help facilitate the distribution of food and medicine.

At the request of its six Western members, the Security Council decided to debate the situation in Czechoslovakia, despite the protests of the USSR. On 23 August 1968, ten members voted for a resolution condemning the Soviet action, which the USSR vetoed. Another resolution requesting the Secretary-General to send a representative to Prague to seek the release of Czechoslovak leaders under detention was not put to a vote. In view—as one UN text puts it—of the "agreement reached on the substance of the problem during the Soviet-Czechoslovak talks held in Moscow from August 23 to 26," no further action was taken by the Council. However, it is worth noting that U Thant was among the first world figures publicly to denounce the invasion. At a press briefing on 21 August at UN Headquarters, he expressed unequivocal dismay, characterizing the invasion as "yet another serious blow to the concepts of international order and morality which form the basis of the Charter of the United Nations . . . and a grave setback to the East-West détente which seemed to be re-emerging in recent months."

MAINTAINING PEACE AND SECURITY

The first purpose of the UN, as stated in Article 1 of its Charter, is the maintenance of international peace and security. To this end, the organization is required "to take collective measures for the prevention and removal of threats to the peace, and for the suppression of acts of aggression or other breaches of the peace, and, to bring about by peaceful means . . . adjustment or settlement of international disputes or situations which might lead to a breach of the peace."

Since the Security Council was established as the UN's main organ with "primary responsibility" in this sphere, the present chapter closely relates to the chapter on the Council. Although some duplication of material has been unavoidable for the sake of completeness, the two chapters are designed to be essentially complementary. Thus a good deal of the material in the chapter on the Council will take on full significance only in the light of the present chapter, while much of the discussion below assumes a knowledge of the workings of the Council as already described.

BASIC CHARTER PROVISIONS

1. *Relative Powers of the Security Council and the General Assembly.* (This topic has already been discussed in general terms in the chapters on the Security Council and the Assembly. But as the relevant Charter provisions are the key terms of reference in the long-standing constitutional controversy on the financing of certain Assembly-sponsored peacekeeping operations, which is reviewed below, their main features are summarized here.) As the UN's chief guardian of the peace, the Security Council has been equipped with special powers enabling it to decide, on behalf of the entire UN membership, to take collective action when peace is threatened (Articles 39–42). The Council is further empowered to negotiate agreements with individual members of the UN for the provision of armed forces necessary to maintain international security, and to determine how many members shall participate in any collective action undertaken (Articles 43–48).

The General Assembly, on the other hand, is empowered merely to consider and make recommendations, either to the Security Council or to particular states, on matters pertaining to peace and security. Moreover, it may discuss but may not make actual recommendations on any special dispute between nations that is currently under consideration by the Council (Articles 11, 12). However, if the Assembly is not expressly empowered to take action, neither is it expressly prohibited from doing so. In the only Charter provision touching on the subject, paragraph 2 of Article 11—which is the focus of conflicting interpretation in the current constitutional controversy—the actual wording is as follows: "Any such questions [of peace and security] on which action is necessary shall be referred to the Security Council by the General Assembly either before or after discussion."

2. *Bringing a Dispute or Serious Situation Before the UN.* Although the Charter firmly establishes the primacy of the Security Council over the Assembly in matters of peace and security, it does not stipulate that disputes or serious situations must be discussed in the Council before they are discussed by the Assembly. A dispute may be brought before the UN in a variety of ways specified in the Charter without order of preference. One or more of the disputing parties voluntarily may bring the matter before the Security Council; or the Security Council itself may choose to exercise its constitutional right to investigate a dispute at its own discretion; or any UN member, whether or not it is involved in the dispute, may propose the matter for discussion by the Assembly; or a non-UN member that is a party to the dispute may—under certain conditions—bring it to the attention of the Assembly; or the Security Council may ask the Assembly to discuss the matter.

Despite these liberal provisions, the Charter does not intend that all political disputes should be brought before the UN. Article 33, for example, enjoins UN members "first of all" to seek a solution to their differences on their own initiative (though if they fail to take this initiative, the Security Council is empowered to call upon them to do so). Only after their efforts to achieve a peaceful settlement have proved fruitless are the disputing parties obliged by the Charter to refer the matter to the Security Council. Again, the UN was never intended by its founders to be regarded as the sole international agency for dealing with political disputes. Thus Article 52 states: "Nothing in the present Charter precludes the existence of regional arrangements or agencies for dealing with such matters relating to the maintenance of international peace and security as are appropriate for regional action . . . ." Members participating in such regional arrangements or agencies "shall make every effort to achieve pacific settlement of local disputes through such regional arrangements or by such regional agencies before referring them to the Security Council." Accordingly, several border disputes between the new African states are currently under consideration by the Organization for African Unity (OAU) instead of the UN. Likewise, the Organization of American States (OAS) has been given the task of settling a number of disputes that have arisen between nations in its region.

However, it cannot be claimed that Charter obligations are necessarily the chief reason that a number of disputes have failed to make their appearance before the UN. The postwar era has seen many cases of important disputes that were not before any international agency during the crucial moment and were subsequently allowed to linger on, quiescent though unresolved, without any serious attempt at even bilateral negotiation. The question of the future status of Berlin is the most outstanding case of this type—the situation in Viet-Nam being an example of a dispute that did not remain quiescent. The reasons for the failure of the UN to discuss these two major issues are fairly self-evident. In the absence of any will on the part of either the US or the USSR to negotiate on them through UN machinery, consideration could only jeopardize the survival of the organization itself. With respect to the numerous unresolved disputes between smaller nations, the reasons for UN inaction obviously vary with the individual circumstances and are too diverse to be discussed here with any sense of relevance.

POLITICAL BACKGROUND TO THE UN'S PEACEKEEPING ACTION

The UN's efforts to preserve peace and security are the most contentious aspect of its entire work. This is due to the inherently political nature of its role and to the fact that both the Security Council and the Assembly are essentially political bodies. They are not intended to function like a court of law, apportioning blame and impartially handing down judgments drawn from a set of established legal codes. On the contrary, when a dispute between nations is brought before either the Council or the Assembly, theirs is the much more difficult task of finding a compromise solution satisfactory to all parties which is at once consistent with the principles of the Charter and yet based on the political realities of the world situation. In this way, each local dispute brought before the UN automatically becomes a dispute involving the entire membership, as nations express differing views on the appropriate course of action to be taken.

The involvement of the general membership in all disputes is precisely what the founders of the UN intended—as a means of ensuring collective international responsibility for political solutions that are both just and realistic. But in order to provide a counterweight to the unavoidable taking of sides, they established the principle of unanimity among the great powers by bestowing the right of veto on the permanent members of the Security Council. The workability of this principle in practice presupposed a basic measure of cooperation among the great powers. As events turned out, however, unanimity among the great powers proved to be a chimera. Within a year of the signing of the Charter, the world was in the throes of the cold war, and the US and USSR were engaged in a violent power struggle. The effects of this unexpected political development on the UN's work in maintaining peace and security were immediate and devastating. Each dispute between the smaller nations that came before the UN was subsumed under the developing power struggle between the giants. As a result, not only was the Security Council deadlocked again and again by the Soviet veto but the Charter requirements for agreements on the provision of armed forces for the UN also could not be implemented.

Where the USSR looked to the Security Council and the veto as its power instrument in the UN, the US looked to the support of the majority vote in the Assembly. To circumvent the Soviet stranglehold on the Council, and being at that time confident of majority support for most of its substantive policy objectives, the US spearheaded a drive to turn the Assembly into a body for action in periods of international crisis. This drive culminated in the adoption in 1950 of the Uniting for Peace resolution, which empowered the Assembly to undertake collective measures for maintaining or restoring peace when the Security Council found itself unable to act in times of emergency (for the terms of the resolution, see the chapter on the Assembly). It was the US, represented by Secretary of State Dean Acheson, that originated the proposal for the resolution. Although some of the small nations expressed reservations about certain clauses, most of them were eager to participate more fully in the UN's peace and security responsibilities. Only India and Argentina abstained in the vote, and only the Soviet bloc voted against, branding the move as illegal and contrary to the Charter.

The Uniting for Peace resolution has been invoked in three major crises: the Korean War, the Suez crisis, and the Congo crisis (for details, see below under Case Histories). In all three instances the Security Council found itself deadlocked, and Assembly action was deemed essential by the majority of members. Nevertheless, despite its proven usefulness as an instrument for restoring peace in these instances, the resolution seems unlikely to be invoked in future disputes. Certain countries questioned the legality of the resolution and of the Assembly's action taken thereunder, and they felt justified on these grounds in refusing to contribute to the costs of the Suez and Congo peacekeeping operations. This opened the way for a major constitutional controversy, which came to a head in 1964-65, and brought the

UN to a virtual standstill and threatened to split the entire organization. The controversy has remained quiescent since that date because the main countries concerned, in order to preserve the UN, tacitly agreed not to make an issue of their differences. Nevertheless, the controversy is still unresolved, and its continued existence has subtly influenced the nature of subsequent UN peacekeeping operations. (An outline of the constitutional controversy and its financial repercussions is given in a separate section at the end of the present chapter.)

Not surprisingly, the various quarrels associated with the UN's work in peace and security have attracted considerable publicity. Each deadlock in the Security Council is liberally reported on and the inability of the UN to do anything in crucial trouble areas like Viet-Nam is also highlighted. As a result, the UN has acquired in some quarters a reputation for ineffectualness. Such a view, however, completely ignores the UN's very real achievements in the field of peace and security. What is encouraging about the UN, despite the quarreling, is the remarkable resourcefulness and persistence with which the membership has managed to overcome inner conflicts and dissensions in order to discharge its responsibilities in several major political disputes.

TYPES OF ACTION TAKEN BY THE UN

The UN has two main responsibilities with respect to the political disputes that are brought before it: helping the parties concerned to arrive at a pacific settlement of the issue that caused the dispute; and maintaining the peace if animosities threaten to erupt into violence or restoring the peace if hostilities have already broken out.

Depending on the nature of the issue—and on the extent of agreement between the great powers on the course of action to be taken—the UN may either discuss the matter and make recommendations or it may actually intervene. On occasion the mere public airing of disputes has been followed by a rapid settlement. Two early cases in point were the requests lodged with the Security Council during 1946 by Iran for the withdrawal of USSR troops and by Lebanon and Jordan for the withdrawal of UK and French troops from their territories. In both instances, despite some great-power altercation in the Council, the offending troops were withdrawn within the year. On other occasions when the UN has confined its efforts to discussion and recommendation, the dispute has either been resolved outside the UN or it has simply been allowed to lapse unresolved. An example of the former was the 1953 Anglo-Egyptian agreement on the evacuation of UK troops from the Sudan and the termination of UK administration of the area, which followed an Egyptian complaint to the Security Council in 1947. An example of a dispute being allowed to lapse occurred when the UN failed to take action on the charge, brought by Ireland and Malaya to the Assembly in 1959, that Communist China had violated the human rights and fundamental freedoms of the people of Tibet.

In keeping with the dual nature of its responsibilities, action by the UN may take two forms: peacemaking or peacekeeping. Although the two kinds of intervention may be undertaken simultaneously in reaction to a single dispute, they are usually applied as separate aspects of the work in hand and kept quite distinct from each other. In its efforts to assist the parties to reach a substantive settlement of the issue under dispute, the UN may dispatch to the scene investigation or conciliation bodies (special committees or commissions consisting of selected UN members); the secretary-general may send his representatives or take on the mission himself. There is no set formula. Peacekeeping action, on the other hand, generally falls into one of two categories, depending on the seriousness of the situation. In cases where the dispute is still relatively under control, the UN may undertake observer operations involving the stationing of UN personnel in the area on a quasi-permanent basis to supervise cease-fire and truce lines and to conduct immediate investigations of any complaints of violations. If full-scale hostilities have broken out, military operations may be necessary to bring the fighting to a halt and to maintain the peace until a final settlement has been reached.

Since the inception of the UN, peacemaking missions have been undertaken in over 30 different cases of dispute. These efforts have not always proved successful, but in those cases where the dispute has finally been resolved, the settlement usually has been due to the labors of the UN's teams. An example of failure was the attempt to negotiate compliance by South Africa with the World Court's 1950 opinion on its obligations in South West Africa (see chapter on Independence of Colonial Peoples, Section B). An example of success was the establishment of Indonesia as an independent state in 1949 (for the UN's work in that case, see the chapter on the Security Council).

In contrast to its extensive peacemaking activities, the UN, as of October 1970, had mounted peacekeeping operations in only 10 cases: (1) the Balkan boundary disputes—observer group in Greece from 1952 to 1954; (2) the Arab-Jewish conflict over the establishment of Israel—observer group patrolling borders since 1948; (3) the India-Pakistan dispute over Kashmir—observer group patrolling borders since 1949; (4) the Suez crisis—UN peace forces on borders since 1956; (5) simultaneous allegations by Jordan and Lebanon of UAR intervention in their internal affairs—an observation group in Lebanon during 1958 and a special representative in Jordan since 1958; (6) the Congo crisis—UN forces in Congo from 1960 to 1964, civilian operations still continuing; (7) Indonesia-Netherlands dispute over future status of West New Guinea—a temporary administrative authority in the territory in 1962–63 (see chapter on Independence of Colonial Peoples, section B); (8) the overthrow of the royalist regime in Yemen—observation mission, 1963–64; (9) outbreak of hostilities between Greek and Turkish communities in Cyprus—UN forces on island since 1964; (10) outbreak of civil strife in the Dominican Republic (plus US dispatch of troops and USSR charge of US interference)—representative of the secretary-general sent May 1965 to help negotiate cease-fire, remaining until October 1966 to report to the Security Council on the general situation. In addition, the UN undertook an enforcement operation in Korea, 1950–53.

SOME CASE HISTORIES OF UN ACTION
The following descriptions are of actions taken—both peacemaking and peacekeeping—in cases where the situation remains unstable or where at least part of the original peacemaking or peacekeeping machinery has had to continue in operation. The special case of Korea is also included. The cases are arranged in order of the dates when disputes in the areas indicated were first brought before the UN.

The Middle East
1. *Establishment of Israel.* In April 1947 the General Assembly at a special session established a Special Committee on Palestine to make recommendations for the future status of the British mandate. The resulting partition plan, which divided Palestine into an Arab and a Jewish state, with an international regime for the city of Jerusalem, was adopted by the Assembly in November of the same year. A UN Palestine Commission was established to carry out the recommendations, and the Security Council was requested to implement the plan. The date for termination of the British mandate and withdrawal of British troops was 1 August 1948. However, violent fighting broke out between the Arab nations and the Jewish community in Palestine. The Security Council thereupon established a Truce Commission consisting of Belgium, France, and the US, while the Assembly authorized a UN Mediator for Palestine to replace the Palestine Commission. On 14 May 1948 the Jewish state of Israel was pro-

claimed. Almost immediately, the Arab nations instituted full-scale armed action. Following a four-week truce at the request of the Security Council, hostilities were renewed on 8 July. This time the Security Council, invoking Chapter VII of the Charter, ordered the governments concerned to desist from further military action and proclaimed a cease-fire. (Until the case of Rhodesia in December 1966, that was the only occasion on which the Council had expressly invoked Chapter VII in deciding upon a course of action, though it did not at the time make use of the Chapter VII provisions for instituting sanctions or military action.)

Through the UN mediator, the Council then established a UN Truce Supervision Organization (UNTSO) of military observers from different countries, with a headquarters in Jerusalem, and assigned it the task of patrolling the frontiers. Fighting continued, however, and the mediator was assassinated in September 1948. During its regular session in the fall of 1948 the General Assembly established a three-member Conciliation Commission (France, Turkey, and the US) to negotiate a settlement and the UN Relief for Palestine Refugees (later replaced by UNRWA; see chapter on Assistance to Refugees). Following negotiations with the acting UN mediator in the first half of 1949, Israel, Egypt, Jordan, Lebanon, and Syria signed armistice agreements. The agreements provided for mixed armistice commissions to check on their implementation. UNTSO was continued in operation to observe the cease-fire. As of this writing, it is still in existence, investigating complaints of armistice violations and reporting as the need arises to the Security Council. Likewise, the Conciliation Commission continues to function, still trying to fulfill its mandate from the Assembly to assist the parties concerned to negotiate a final settlement of all issues.

2. *The Suez Crisis.* In July 1956, Egypt nationalized the Suez Canal. Upon Egypt's rejection of the subsequent London Conference plan for international control of the canal, France and the UK informed the Security Council in September that Egypt's attitude was endangering peace. The Council adopted six principles as a basis for negotiation, but in October Israel invaded Egypt's Gaza Strip. Since the Security Council resolution calling for an immediate cease-fire and withdrawal of Israeli troops was vetoed by both France and the UK, the Council convened an emergency meeting of the Assembly under the terms of the Uniting for Peace Resolution. (These terms provide that a requisite majority of the Council may convene an emergency session of the Assembly even if all the permanent members do not consent.) Thereafter, the situation was handled exclusively by the Assembly. Even before the Assembly met, France and the UK had begun armed intervention against Egypt. After calling for a cease-fire, withdrawal of troops, and restoration of freedom of navigation in the canal, the Assembly established the UN Emergency Force (UNEF) to secure and supervise cessation of hostilities. Since Israel would not permit UNEF contingents in its territory, it was agreed by a special arrangement between the secretary-general and President Nasser that the UN forces would be stationed on the UAR's side of the armistice demarcation line. Within 48 hours UNEF troops, comprising contingents from several small nations, began patrolling the armistice demarcation line and the international frontier to the south of the Gaza Strip. (At its peak strength, in February 1957, UNEF numbered nearly 6,000 officers and men.) At Egypt's request, the secretary-general was authorized to make arrangements for clearing the canal, which had been blocked by ships sunk during the hostilities. Withdrawal of British and French forces was completed by December 1956 and of Israeli forces by March 1957. The canal was cleared by April of the same year, and Egypt declared it open to international traffic (Israeli ships were barred, however).

The Suez crisis was over, save for its enormous repercussions. Because of the continuing tension in the area, UNEF has had to maintain its operations at considerable expense to the UN.

3. *The Six-Day War.* By the mid-1960's the tension between Israel and the Arab countries had begun to manifest itself in frequent and sometimes major hostilities across the various armistice borders. On 18 May 1967 the UAR, which two days previously had begun deploying troops to the armistice demarcation line in the Sinai peninsula, officially requested Secretary-General U Thant to withdraw all UNEF units from the area. After consultations with the UNEF Advisory Committee the secretary-general ordered the withdrawal of the force that evening.

U Thant's prompt compliance with the UAR's request aroused severe criticism in Israel and other quarters. In subsequent reports on the matter, however, U Thant made it clear that he believed he was bound both by legal and practical considerations to act without delay. He pointed out that UNEF was not an enforcement operation ordered by the Security Council but a peacekeeping operation dependent upon the consent of the host country, whose sovereignty over its own territory could not be challenged. He argued that since Israel refused to allow UNEF on its side of the armistice line even after the UAR had demanded the withdrawal of UNEF, the force's usefulness had already ended with the deployment by the UAR of troops to the line, as it could no longer serve as a buffer between the two sides. Moreover, in his consultations with the UNEF Advisory Committee, two of the four countries supplying UNEF units—India and Yugoslavia—had declared that they would in any case pull out their contingents if the UAR's request was not heeded.

In reply to criticism that the Assembly should have been consulted before such an important decision was taken, U Thant observed that he was obliged to consult the Assembly only if requested by the Advisory Committee, which had not done so. Nor could he have called an emergency session under the Uniting for Peace Resolution, since the necessary precondition of lack of unanimity among the veto powers did not exist, as the issue was not then under debate in the Security Council. U Thant's unilateral decision to disband UNEF remains perhaps the most controversial action of his career as secretary-general. Though none of his critics challenged the validity of his stand, many believed that he could have used his office to try to persuade the UAR at least to agree to a postponement of its request for UNEF's withdrawal, which they felt only helped pave the way for the crisis that followed.

Two days after UNEF's formal disbandment (total withdrawal was not completed until 17 June), UAR troops occupied the fortress of Sharm el-Sheikh overlooking the Strait of Tiran on the mouth of the Gulf of Aqaba, which constitutes Israel's only direct outlet to the Red Sea. On 22 May the UAR declared the gulf closed to Israeli ships and to other ships carrying strategic goods to Israel. Various high-level negotiations between governments, including the US, and in the Security Council, which had been called into session by Canada and Denmark to discuss the new situation, proved unable to avert the impending war. Feeling that it had not received sufficient assurance of help from Western governments and that the UAR's blockade of the Gulf of Aqaba —together with the military agreement the UAR had recently signed with Jordan—was a justified *casus belli*, Israel simultaneously attacked the UAR, Jordan, and Syria on 5 June and within three days had penetrated deep into the territory of each country. Called into immediate emergency session on the outbreak of hostilities, the Security Council on 6 June demanded a cease-fire.

Israel announced that it would accept a cease-fire provided the other parties accepted. Jordan announced acceptance on

7 June, the UAR on 8 June, and Syria on 9 June. UNTSO, whose Jerusalem headquarters had been temporarily taken over by Israeli forces, was detailed to assist in implementing the cease-fire. Violations of the cease-fire, especially along the Israel-Syria border, continued until 13 June, when the secretary-general was able to report the "virtual cessation" of all military activity. By this time Israel had voluntarily withdrawn its forces from much of the territory it had occupied but had retained control of several areas regarded as essential to its security—namely, the whole of the UAR's Sinai peninsula up to the Suez Canal, including Sharm el-Sheikh and the Gaza Strip; the Jordanian part of the city of Jerusalem and the West Bank area of the Jordan River; and the Golan Heights in Syrian territory overlooking the Sea of Galilee. On 14 June the Security Council adopted a resolution calling upon Israel to ensure the "safety, welfare and security" of the inhabitants of the occupied areas and upon the "Governments concerned" to scrupulously respect the humanitarian principles governing the treatment of prisoners of war contained in the 1949 Geneva Conventions. The Council failed, however, to adopt a USSR draft resolution, supported by Bulgaria, India, and Mali, vigorously condemning Israeli aggression and demanding withdrawal of Israeli troops behind the 1949 armistice lines.

At the emergency special session of the General Assembly, convened on 19 June at the request of the USSR, which lasted until 21 July, tempers waxed hot as delegates struggled to forge a substantive resolution that would command an adequate majority. Such a resolution would have had to reconcile the position taken by the Arab countries and its supporters (the Soviet bloc and some African and Asian states) that the Assembly should condemn Israeli aggression and demand Israel's unconditional withdrawal with the Israeli position (supported mainly by the US and several other Western nations) that withdrawal terms could only be negotiated in the context of a full treaty that formally ended the "state of belligerency" in the area and established "secure and agreed" boundaries between the various nations. The division of opinion proved too deep to be overcome, and the Assembly failed to adopt any resolutions on the substance of the issue. It did, however, adopt a resolution on the safety of prisoners of war and civilians in the area of hostilities, which prompted the secretary-general to dispatch a special representative to obtain information on these matters. It also adopted a resolution declaring invalid Israel's proclamation on 28 June that Jerusalem would henceforth be a unified city under Israeli administration. By that single action, Israel almost succeeded in uniting the Assembly against it. The vote was 99 in favor, with only 20 abstentions from among Israel's staunchest supporters.

Meanwhile, in the Security Council, a consensus was reached in early July to implement the secretary-general's suggestion that UNTSO observers be stationed along the Suez Canal, where intermittent fighting had again broken out. It was decided to prohibit all movement of ships along the canal. But the Council, like the Assembly, was unable to draft an acceptable formula for establishing permanent peace in the area. Finally in November 1967, after weeks of secret negotiations, the Council adopted a resolution based on a British draft, establishing certain principles for a peaceful settlement without going into contentious specifics or prescribing priorities. The principles include withdrawal of Israeli forces from occupied areas (the text deliberately avoided requesting withdrawal from "all" occupied areas, in view of Israel's declaration that it would not give up certain strategic places, including Jordanian Jerusalem); an end to states of belligerency; respect for the rights of all states in the area to peaceful existence; and an affirmation of the need to guarantee free navigation through international waterways, settle the long-standing Palestine refugee problem, and guarantee the territorial integrity and political independence of the countries involved. All parties—except, initially, Syria—accepted the formula, and at the Council's request the secretary-general appointed a special representative—the Swedish ambassador to Moscow, Gunnar Jarring—to help conduct the negotiations. Jarring established a UN Middle East Mission on Cyprus in December 1967, but was unable to initiate effective substantive negotiations owing to the Arabs' refusal to participate in direct discussions with Israel and Israel's insistence on direct negotiations. In an attempt to strengthen Jarring's efforts, the ambassadors to the UN of four permanent members of the Security Council, have regularly held informal private meetings on the Middle East situation in New York since the middle of 1969. By the end of 1970, however, concrete progress toward the opening of substantive negotiations between the parties remained uncertain, and the fragile truce between Israel and its neighbors was subjected to a growing number of violations, as tensions in the area seemed once again to be reaching a new boiling point.

Korea

At the end of World War II, the Allied powers agreed that Soviet troops would accept the Japanese surrender north of the 38th parallel in Korea and that US forces would accept it south of that line. The two occupying powers established a joint commission to set up a provisional government for the country. The commission could not come to an agreement, and the US brought the matter to the General Assembly in September 1947. In November the Assembly created a Temporary Commission on Korea to facilitate nationwide elections. However, since the commission was denied access to North Korea, it was able only to supervise elections in the southern half of the country. These elections took place in May 1948, and in August the US transferred governmental and military functions to the duly elected South Korean government. A separate government meanwhile was established in North Korea. In December 1948 the Assembly, over the objection of the USSR, established a seven-member Commission on Korea (UNCOK) to replace the Temporary Commission and to seek reunification.

On 25 June 1950 both UNCOK and the US informed the Security Council that North Korea had attacked South Korea that morning. The Council met the same day and (the USSR being absent at the time in protest against a Council decision on Chinese representation) declared the attack to be a breach of the peace. The Council called for a cease-fire, withdrawal of North Korean forces to the 38th parallel, and the assistance of member states to South Korea. As fighting continued, the Council on 27 June recommended that UN members furnish assistance to South Korea to repel the attack and restore peace and security. On the same day, the US announced that it had ordered its own air and sea forces to give cover and support to the South Korean troops. On July 7 the Council voted to recommend that states make forces available to a UN Unified Command under the US. (It should be noted that though the Council had used the language of Chapter VII of the Charter—"breach of the peace," etc.— it did not specifically invoke the chapter itself or use its constitutional power thereunder to order all states to comply with its decision.) In all, 16 nations supplied troops—Australia, Belgium, Canada, Colombia, Ethiopia, France, Greece, Luxembourg, Netherlands, New Zealand, Philippines, Thailand, Turkey, South Africa, the UK, and the US; South Korea also placed its troops under the UN Command.

On 1 August the USSR returned to the Council (having by then been absent for six months) and declared that all the actions and decisions that had previously been taken by the Council were illegal. On 6 November the USSR vetoed a resolution proposed by the US. As a result of the ensuing deadlock, the Assembly virtually took over the handling of the entire situation (the Security Council even agreeing unanimously, on 31 January 1951, to remove the item from its agenda). The legalistic device by which the Assembly voted itself competent to continue with collective measures that under the Charter are the preserve exclusively of the Security Council was the Uniting for Peace Resolution.

Even before the Council became deadlocked, the Assembly had considered an agenda item entitled "The Problem of the Independence of Korea." Under this item, it established the Commission for Unification and Rehabilitation of Korea (UNCURK) to replace UNCOK. Then, on 6 November 1950, events were given a new twist of intensity when Communist China entered the war on the side of North Korea. The Assembly promptly added the agenda item entitled "Intervention of the Central People's Government of the People's Republic of China in Korea." Under this item, the Assembly in December established the Korean Reconstruction Agency for Relief and Rehabilitation (UNKRA), and a three-member Cease-fire Group that included the president of the Assembly to determine a basis for ending hostilities. Following Communist China's refusal to cooperate, the Assembly in February 1951 adopted a resolution that that government had engaged in aggression. It also established a Good Offices and Additional Measures Committees to supplement the Cease-fire Group. Truce negotiations began in July 1951, but fighting continued until 1953, when an armistice agreement was signed on 27 July. A year later, the Assembly called for the political conference that had been provided for in the armistice agreement. The conference was held between April and June 1954, but it failed to resolve problems and negotiate reunification of the country. Though UNKRA ceased operations in 1960, UNCURK has continued to function. It reports annually to the Assembly, beginning each year what has become a routine debate on the obstacles in the way of a unified independent Korea.

Kashmir

The state of Kashmir (officially, Jammu and Kashmir) was originally one of the princely states of British India. Under the partition plan and the Indian Independence Act of 1947, it became free to accede to either India or Pakistan. The maharajah requested accession to India, and India accepted the accession. The dispute between India and Pakistan began in January 1948 when India complained that tribesmen were invading Kashmir with the active assistance of Pakistan. Pakistan countered by declaring that Kashmir's accession to India was illegal. The Security Council, after asking the parties to mediate, called for withdrawal of Pakistan nationals, reduction of Indian forces, and arrangement of a plebiscite on Kashmir's accession to India. A UN commission was sent to mediate in July 1948. By 1949 the commission had effected a cease-fire and was able to state that principles on a plebiscite has been accepted by both governments. In July 1949 agreement was reached on a cease-fire line, and the commission appointed a group of military observers to watch for violations. However, the commission was unable to reach agreement on terms for the demilitarization of Kashmir prior to the plebiscite.

In March 1951, after several attempts at further negotiation failed, the Council decided to continue the observer group—now called the UN Military Observer Group for India and Pakistan (UNMOGIP)—to supervise the cease-fire within Kashmir itself. Despite continued mediation, the differences between the parties remained. The Council repeatedly considered the matter without achieving appreciable progress. In August 1965, however, there was a sudden outbreak of serious hostilities. UNMOGIP reported clashes between the regular armed forces of both India and Pakistan, and fighting continued into September, although the Security Council had twice called for a cease-fire. Following a report that fighting had spread to the international border between India and West Pakistan, the Council on September 20 requested that both sides issue orders for a cease-fire within two days and withdraw their forces to originally held positions. The cease-fire was accepted by both states, but continuous complaints of violations were made by each side. Accordingly, the Council requested the secretary-general to increase the size of the military observer group in Kashmir and to establish a separate group on the border between India and West Pakistan. On 5 November the Council urged that a meeting between the parties be held as soon as possible and that a plan for withdrawal containing a time limit for execution be developed. The secretary-general appointed a representative to meet with authorities of both countries on the question. On 17 February 1966 the secretary-general informed the Council that a plan and rules for withdrawals had been worked out. He also stated that on 10 January the prime minister of India and the president of Pakistan had agreed at Tashkent, where they had met at the initiative of the USSR, that their respective forces would be withdrawn to their original positions by 25 February. Thus, though the crisis remains quiescent, the conflict itself is unresolved, and UNMOGIP is still in operation.

The Congo

One week after the Democratic Republic of the Congo, a former Belgian colony, had become independent on 30 June 1960, troops of the Force Publique mutinied against the Belgian officers, demanding higher pay and promotions. As violence and general disorder spread rapidly throughout the country, Belgium rushed troops to the area to protect its extensive mining interests. On 11 July, Katanga, the richest province of the country by virtue of its Belgian-controlled copper mines, proclaimed its secession from the new state. The following day, President Kasavubu and Prime Minister Patrice Lumumba appealed for UN military assistance "to protect the national territory against acts of aggression committed by Belgian metropolitan troops."

Secretary-General Dag Hammarskjöld brought this request to the Security Council, and in the series of meetings that ensued the Council called for the withdrawal of Belgian troops and authorized the secretary-general to provide such military and technical assistance as might be necessary. In less than two days, the first contingents of UN troops—again supplied by small states—began to arrive in the Congo, together with UN civilian personnel who had been dispatched to help maintain operation of essential public services. In August the Security Council called upon Belgium to withdraw from Katanga and announced that it would be necessary for UN forces to enter that province, since the secessionist president, Moise Tshombe, refused to dismiss Belgian troops. At the same time, the Council reaffirmed the aim of the UN force not to intervene in or influence the outcome of the internal conflict. That conflict was growing daily more disruptive and complex. A serious dispute over tactics began to alienate the president of the Congo from his prime minister, and this rapidly degenerated into a struggle for power. At the same time, Prime Minister Lumumba began to clash with the secretary-general over the role of UN forces, demanding that they subdue Katanga. These conflicts were faithfully reflected in the discussions of the Security Council, with the West supporting Kasavubu and Secretary-General Hammarskjöld, and the USSR supporting Lumumba and severely criticizing the secretary-general.

In September 1960, Kasavubu and Lumumba each "dismissed" the other from office, and in New York, the Security Council was deadlocked. As a result, it once again invoked the Uniting for Peace Resolution and called an emergency session of the Assembly. Meeting in response to that call, the Assembly authorized the secretary-general to continue assisting in the restoration of law and order in the Congo. Toward the end of the month, a new caretaker government was installed in the Congo by Colonel Mobutu, with the approval of the President Kasavubu, and the country sought admission to the UN. Both Kasavubu and Lumumba sent delegations to New York, but in the end the Assembly accepted the credentials of the Kasavubu representatives.

Subsequent Assembly missions attempted to reconcile the various factions within the country, and in June 1961 an accord was reached to end Katanga's secession. But strife in the Congo continued with bewildering twists and turns for four years. Finally, in February 1964, Secretary-General U Thant announced that the objective of the UN operation—the removal of foreign troops, particularly the foreign mercenaries in Katanga—had been largely completed. In June the UN Operation in the Congo (ONUC), which at its peak strength had totaled more than 20,000 officers and men, was disbanded.

Civilian aid continues, however. By early 1970 there were still some 270 experts at work in what has been the largest single program of assistance ever undertaken by the UN (peak manpower strength was approximately 2,000). These experts participate in many sectors of the nation's life—including public health, education, medicine, and agriculture. The US has financed a substantial portion of the assistance program through bilateral aid projects under UN auspices. Other sources of financing are the special Congo Fund, established on the basis of voluntary contributions from governments, and the UN Development Program.

Cyprus

Cyprus was granted independence from British rule in 1960 through agreements signed by the UK, Greece, and Turkey. Under these agreements, Cyprus was given a constitution containing certain unamendable provisions guaranteeing specified political rights to the Turkish minority community. The three signatory powers were constituted guarantors of Cyprus's independence, each with the right to station troops permanently on the island.

The granting of independence had been preceded by a prolonged conflict between the Greek and Turkish communities on the future status of Cyprus. The Greek Cypriots, who form the majority community, originally had wanted some form of union with Greece, thereby provoking a hostile reaction among the Turkish Cypriots, who countered by demanding partition. Each side was supported in its aims by the country of its ethnic origin. Independence did nothing to alleviate dissension on the island. Both sides were dissatisfied with the constitution that had been granted them, but their aims were diametrically opposed. The Turks wanted partition or a type of federal government, whereas the Greeks wanted a constitution free of outside controls and of provisions perpetuating the division between the two communities.

After three years of continuous tension, culminating in a major incident on 21 December 1963, the Cyprus government (under Greek Cypriot President Makarios) complained to the Security Council on 27 December 1963 that Turkey was interfering in its internal affairs and committing acts of aggression. Against a background of mounting violence on the island, the Council considered the matter but did not immediately take any peacekeeping action. With the consent of Cyprus, British troops had been trying to restore order during the crisis. However, in mid-February 1964, the UK informed the Security Council that its efforts to keep the peace would have to be augmented. Accordingly, on 4 March 1964, the Council unanimously authorized the establishment of the UN Force in Cyprus (UNFICYP) for a three-month period and at the same time requested the secretary-general to designate a UN mediator to promote a substantive settlement. UNFICYP became operational on 27 March 1964 and eventually consisted of 7,000 officers and men from Austria, Canada, Denmark, Finland, Ireland, Sweden, and the UK. On 20 June the Council extended its mandate for a further three months. From 1964 until mid-1966, no appreciable progress having been made toward a substantive settlement, the Council extended UNFICYP's mandate for successive three-month periods. On 16 June 1966 the mandate was extended for a six-month term and has since continued to be extended on a six-monthly basis. On each occasion, however, various members of the Council have expressed a growing reluctance to extend the mandate, emphasizing with increasing firmness the need for sufficient progress toward a final solution to make possible "a withdrawal or substantial reduction of the Force."

Secretary General's Appraisal

As this survey shows, the UN has been far more successful at peacekeeping than at peacemaking. So much so indeed that the secretary-general in his Introduction to the 1966 Report on the Work of the Organization warned that there is a danger of forgetting that peacekeeping is only a means and not an end. He pointed to the paradox that whereas the object of peacekeeping is to provide "time and quiet" for a solution of the issue that caused the outbreak of hostilities, in effect the continued presence of the UN on the scene may tend to free the disputing parties from feeling obliged to exert a really serious effort toward a settlement of their differences—hence, the fact that a number of peacekeeping operations have come to assume a semipermanent character. In practical terms the paradox poses a considerable dilemma for the UN: while the peacekeeping effort is costly, "the continuation of that effort will be much less costly in every respect and for all concerned than a resumption of hostilities." The secretary-general's remarks are as valid today as they were in 1966. And, as was indicated in the case history of Cyprus, member states have become increasingly aware of the need to find solutions to the more persistent of the world's political disputes in order to terminate costly peacekeeping operations that impose a severe financial strain on the UN. Whether or not this awareness will produce concrete results is a matter of, possibly skeptical, conjecture.

Methods of Financing

These have varied widely. The costs of almost all the various negotiating or investigation committees on peacemaking missions were incorporated into the UN's regular budget. So too were the two observer peacekeeping operations: UNTSO in Jerusalem and UNMOGIP in Kashmir. With regard to the other UN observer operations: the observation mission sent to Lebanon for six months during 1958 was financed out of the regular budget; costs for the observer group sent to Yemen in 1963 were divided between Saʿudi Arabia and the UAR (both interested parties in the future status of Yemen); similarly, costs for the UN Temporary Executive Authority stationed in West New Guinea from October 1962 to May 1963 to supervise the transfer of the territory from the Netherlands to Indonesia were divided equally between those two nations.

The four operations involving military forces (except possibly for some minor associated expenses) were financed outside the regular budget. The UN Command in Korea was paid for exclusively by those countries contributing forces under arrangements negotiated outside the UN. (Indeed, the whole administration of this command was only nominally a UN affair.) Both UNEF and ONUC were financed through special accounts by a combination of assessments levied on all UN members and voluntary contributions. The Cyprus crisis, however, flared up in the midst of mounting tension in the prolonged controversy over the financing of UNEF and ONUC through levied assessments. To avoid giving the controversy a new twist, the Security Council decided

that the UN force in Cyprus would be financed entirely through voluntary contributions. Although this decision solved the political problem, the secretary-general several times complained that voluntary contributions were unsatisfactory as a practical method of financing major peacekeeping operations. In his introduction to the 1970 Report on the Work of the Organization, he estimated that even if all the contributions pledged to the UNFYCYP account as of 31 August 1970 were paid in full, there would still be a shortage of some $8.4 million required to meet past commitments and keep the force in Cyprus up to 15 December 1970.

CONSTITUTIONAL AND FINANCIAL ISSUES: THE UNRESOLVED CONTROVERSY

The USSR's objections to the Uniting for Peace Resolution did not have any repercussions on payment for the costs of the UN Command in Korea because the operation was paid for exclusively by the nations contributing troops. It was the decision of the Assembly to apply the principle of collective responsibility to the financing of UNEF in the Middle East and ONUC in the Congo that unwittingly gave the USSR a lever by which to give effective expression to its constitutional confrontation with the US over the latter's persistent attempts, in the Soviet view, to have the Assembly usurp the authority of the Security Council for its own purposes (see above). It would be wrong, however, to assume that the constitutional controversy is a simple confrontation between the two superpowers. Indeed, there are many who maintain that the USSR-US deadlock on the peacekeeping issue results rather from a tacit collusion on their part to agree to disagree, in order to remind the small nations, especially the numerous Afro-Asian voting bloc, that without the cooperation of the giant states little can be achieved in the UN. The issue, moreover, is a multifaceted one. In the years that have elapsed since the establishment of UNEF, new aspects of the central controversy have constantly developed, and these have provoked different responses among the various geographical groupings of nations within the membership.

First Phase of Developments: Disputes over the Methods of Financing UNEF and ONUC, 1956–61

In order to secure funds for UNEF with minimum delay, Secretary-General Hammarskjöld proposed to the 1956 Assembly that a special fund be set up outside the regular budget. He further proposed that the major portion of UNEF expenses be paid for by the same method as that used in the regular budget—through assessments on all members according to an agreed scale of contributions—the balance of the force's expenses to be paid through voluntary contributions. Normally, accounts outside the regular budget, such as the major development programs, are financed by voluntary contributions, and the principle of collective responsibility of all members is not applied. Hence, the secretary-general's proposal was from the outset a controversial one and, though supported by the West, was not enthusiastically received in general. The Soviet bloc objected that it was the obligation of the "aggressors" in the Suez crisis, who had caused the need for UNEF in the first place, to pay for its costs. At that time, the USSR (which had voted in favor of invoking the Uniting for Peace Resolution in the Suez crisis) did not make an issue of the constitutional aspect of the proposal. This aspect was raised instead by the Latin American states: they questioned whether UNEF costs ought to be treated as ordinary "expenses of the Organization" under Article 17 of the Charter, by which members are obliged to accept the apportionment of costs decided by the Assembly. Once expenses are apportioned under Article 17, a default in payment becomes subject to the penalty of loss of vote, as provided for in Article 19, if the arrears exceed two years of assessments. The Latin American states did not feel that contributions to the special expenses incurred by UNEF should be subject to Article 19. Nevertheless, the secretary-general's proposal was adopted by the Assembly, and it was agreed that for the first year $10 million would be appropriated for the special account, assessed according to the regular budget scale (many of the smaller nations wanted a special scale, giving them lighter assessments). In each succeeding year, the major portions of costs also were paid for by assessments—$15 million in 1957, $25 million in 1958, $15 million in 1959—but each year arrears and defaults accounted for one third of the total assessments. Voluntary contributions met about 20% of the total costs.

When the time came to discuss the financing of ONUC on a similar basis, division of opinion became far more acute because of the much greater sums involved (about $10 million per month). On this occasion, the USSR presented a full-scale "legal" argument against the idea of treating ONUC expenses as ordinary expenses of the organization: The creation of ONUC had been a Security Council decision; therefore, under Article 48 (see earlier in this chapter) it was for the Council to decide how the operation should be financed; the Assembly was exceeding its powers in seeking to assess the costs under Article 17; and since Belgium was the aggressor in the Congo, Belgium should pay the greatest share of the costs, and the balance should be made up by voluntary contributions. The concept of collective responsibility was again supported by the majority of the West, including the US. Some of the Latin American states suggested that the costs be treated as special and emergency expenses, with the permanent members of the Security Council paying 70% of them. In the final outcome, an ad hoc account was opened for ONUC (again outside the regular budget), and $100 million was appropriated for the period 1 January to 31 October 1961, to be paid for chiefly by assessed contributions. The Soviet bloc, Mexico, and Belgium voted against the resolution.

Second Phase: Crisis over Application of ICJ's Advisory Opinion, 1962–65

By the summer of 1961, cumulative arrears in the UNEF account totaled some $35 million, while of the $100 million appropriated for the ONUC action the UN had received only about $41 million. The USSR had announced during the previous session that it would not pay its assessments for either operation, and France had announced the same decision in April 1961 (though it continued to make voluntary contributions to UNEF). By the time the 16th Assembly convened in September that year, the UN was confronted with a full-scale financial crisis. As a stopgap measure, it was decided to authorize the secretary-general to issue $200 million worth of UN bonds, with interest and amortization payable from the regular budget. (By December 1964, when the issue was finally closed, 64 countries had purchased $169.9 million worth.) Lastly, in an attempt to settle the legal dispute over whether these expenses constituted ordinary expenses within the meaning of Article 17, it was decided—by a bare majority—to seek an advisory opinion from the ICJ on the matter.

The ICJ handed down its opinion on 20 July 1962, advising by 9-5 majority that the unqualified word "expenses" occurring in Article 17 should be taken to mean all expenses and not just certain types of expenses. On this basis, it considered that the expenses of both UNEF and ONUC could be regarded as expenses of the organization within the meaning of Article 17. (Dissenting judges were from USSR, Poland, Argentina, France, and Peru.) When the 1962 Assembly came to debate this opinion, the main point of controversy was whether to "accept" it or merely "take note" of it. The US, which had been one of the chief sponsors of the move to seek the opinion, fought hard for acceptance. And the Assembly accepted the opinion, despite the reluctance of many nations to take on the commitment that

this implied. However, acceptance had no practical effect on the situation. Neither the USSR nor France altered its basic position, and the arrears continued to mount.

What the acceptance of the opinion did achieve was to strengthen the resolve of the US to press for the application of Article 19 as soon as nations fell subject to the penalty of loss of vote for being more than two years in arrears in their contributions. By September 1964 a number of states, including the USSR and France, came within this category with respect to their assessments for UNEF and ONUC. But since the penalty had never before been applied, there was no precedent for the appropriate procedure. The US took the view that it was automatically applicable and that on the first vote taken during the 1964 session the president of the Assembly was bound to announce names of the delinquent states and formally deprive them of their vote. The USSR, on the other hand, held the opinion that the suspension of vote was an important matter under Article 18, requiring a two-thirds majority decision by the Assembly. The majority of the smaller nations, meanwhile, desperately wished to avoid a head-on confrontation in the UN between its two major powers and the opening of the 19th session was postponed again and again as behind-the-scene negotiations continued. When the session finally did begin in November, it was agreed to conduct proceedings entirely on the basis of consensus without formal voting. Needless to say only the minimum of the most essential decisions (such as the regular budget) could be adopted in this way, and virtually no substantive work could be done.

In August 1965 the US reluctantly acknowledged that the majority of the membership evidently was not prepared to apply Article 19 in the prevailing situation and announced that it would not raise the question of the applicability of the penalty in connection with the ONUC and UNEF accounts. Thus the 20th Assembly was able to convene the following month without the inhibiting atmosphere of crisis. But the organization's financial difficulties were not easily dispelled. In the words of the secretary-general, the situation regarding the UNEF and ONUC accounts remains "a matter for serious concern." As of September 1970 unpaid assessed contributions to UNEF totaled $49.6 million and to ONUC $82.1 million, while amounts the UN owed to governments that had provided contingents for the two operations totaled $21 and $10.2 million, respectively.

Third Phase: The Quiet Debate Continues

One of the few substantive measures adopted during the Assembly's 19th session had been establishment, by consensus, of a Special Committee of 33 members (four permanent members of the Security Council and a representative number of countries from the main geopolitical groupings of nations) to undertake a comprehensive review of peacekeeping questions in all their aspects, including ways of overcoming the UN's financial difficulties. Since that time all serious discussion of peacekeeping matters has been handled by the committee, with the full membership playing a largely formal role during the Assembly's consideration of the committee's annual reports. The small nations have come to recognize that as long as the US and the USSR are unwilling to come to an agreement, there is little point in pressing for a solution. Also, it is generally felt that the informal forum of debate provided by the committee offers the best chance of encouraging the superpowers eventually to adopt compromise positions.

For three years, the committee was unable to report any progress toward agreement, due to an insurmountable and fundamental division of opinion concerning Charter interpretation. The USSR, together with France, maintains that under the Charter the Security Council is the sole body empowered to authorize the use of armed forces in the name of the organization and to determine the method of financing such operations (though

France concedes the right of the Assembly to establish observer missions). The US, the UK, and most Western powers, on the other hand, argue that while the Security Council has been accorded by the Charter the primary role in peacekeeping action, it does not have exclusive authority. To help the committee find a way out of its prolonged deadlock, the 1967 Assembly gave it a more specific mandate, requesting the committee to report on progress toward agreement on matters relating to facilities, services, and personnel that UN members might provide for peacekeeping operations consistent with the Charter. Accordingly, the committee decided to concentrate on areas of agreement instead of disagreement and in 1968 set up a small working group, comprising four permanent members of the Security Council and the four officers of the committee, to prepare as a "first model" a study of UN military observer missions established

or authorized by the Security Council. By the following year, the working group had completed five chapters of a projected eight-chapter scheme for Model 1 operations. The five chapters deal with the authorization of missions; their organization, development, and functioning; operating procedures; equipment, facilities, and services; and administrative matters. But by 1970, the Committee had still been unable to complete the texts for the remaining three chapters: command, direction, and control of observer missions; legal arrangements; and financial arrangements. Nor had it been able even to begin substantive discussion of the more complex Model 2 operations, those involving military contingents. The 1970 Assembly instructed the committee to intensify its efforts, with a view to completing its report on observer missions by May 1971, or failing this to suggest whether alternative methods of procedure were advisable.

DISARMAMENT

The UN Charter is emphatic in denouncing the "scourge of war," and it lists the maintenance of international peace and security as the first of the UN's basic "purposes." To the Security Council the Charter assigns the task of formulating plans for the "regulation of armaments" to be submitted to UN members with a view to establishing an appropriate system of controls. The General Assembly is explicitly authorized by the Charter to consider "principles governing disarmament and the regulation of armaments." Since—aside from a brief attempt in the early years—the Security Council has not initiated disarmament plans, UN concern with disarmament has been expressed almost exclusively by the General Assembly. However, the Assembly has no power to conduct actual negotiations, but only to make recommendations. The basic disagreements were concerned with which aspects of disarmament should have priority.

On the issue of whether nuclear or conventional disarmament should come first, the Western powers chose conventional disarmament, whereas the Eastern powers gave priority to nuclear disarmament. Each side accused the other of seeking to retain the arms in which it had superiority, and at the same time aiming at disarming the other side of weapons in which the latter had more strength. Eventually it was agreed that conventional and nuclear disarmament must be carried out in a balanced manner, although there has been no agreement as to what such a balance constitutes.

Eastern European powers wanted priority for concrete disarmament measures, while the West preferred effective control. The view has been accepted that disarmament and control must go hand in hand. The USSR complained that the Western powers wanted arms control as a means of collecting military intelligence, and the West countered that an inspection system was necessary to ensure that there were no evasions of disarmament agreements.

Discussion has centered also on the question of whether political settlements should precede disarmament. The West sought priority for political settlement, while the USSR and its allies insisted on agreement on disarmament measures first. Participants in disarmament talks have also been concerned with the problem of whether security should come before disarmament or after. The emphasis has been on the establishment of an international peace force as part of the quest for political settlement and international confidence. The majority of states now take the view that the two questions should be dealt with simultaneously.

International discussion has also taken place on whether disarmament efforts should begin with first steps and partial measures or whether immediate general and complete disarmament should be the goal. The USSR has maintained that disarmament plans should be contained in a single treaty, whereas the West's view is that general and complete disarmament should be started with initial measures. This difference of view has been partially settled in this way: while negotiations proceed for a single treaty, other disarmament measures might be undertaken in the hope that this would create confidence.

Another subject of discussion has been the question whether technical studies on the specific details of disarmament measures and their control should have priority over agreements in principle. Western powers have given priority to technical studies, the USSR to agreements in principle. Progress has been slow but real. The world has a clearer understanding of the problems that have to be solved before there can be realistic disarmament.

CHRONOLOGY OF DEVELOPMENTS, 1946–1962

First Approach: Separate Consideration of Atomic and Conventional Armaments, 1946–50

In its very first resolution, adopted unanimously on 24 January 1946, the General Assembly established a UN Atomic Energy Commission to work out a plan to put the production of atomic energy under international control and inspection and to eliminate atomic weapons and other weapons of mass destruction. No agreement could be reached in the atmosphere of distrust among the big powers.

On the initiative of the US, at that time the only power possessing atomic weapons, the Commission concentrated its study on the so-called Baruch Plan for an International Atomic Development Authority. The proposed authority was to have a worldwide monopoly "on all phases of the development and use of atomic energy, starting with the raw material." It was to control "all atomic energy activities potentially dangerous to world security" and to "control, inspect, and license all other atomic activities" in all countries. The USSR rejected the plan, arguing that it could not submit to an agency that might refuse the USSR the necessary permission to carry out work it regarded as essential to advance its peaceful atomic energy program. The Soviet counterproposal called for immediate prohibition of the production, stockpiling, and use of atomic weapons and for the destruction of all existing stocks.

Thus the main lines of disagreement were drawn. In particular, it was impossible to obtain West-East agreement on three essential questions: (1) whether establishment of effective controls or the outlawing of nuclear weapons should come first; (2) whether control functions should be exercised by a powerful international system, as proposed by the Baruch Plan, or by individual governments, with international control limited to period inspections, as proposed by the USSR; (3) whether decisions in the atomic field should require a simple majority vote or Big Five unanimity. By the spring of 1948, the Atomic Energy Commission was hopelessly deadlocked.

In the meantime, on 13 February 1947, the Security Council had created a Commission for Conventional Armaments, composed of the 11 nations then seated on the Council. This Commission's debates ended when, on 27 April 1950, a USSR proposal to exclude from its membership the representative of the Republic of China was rejected, and the USSR representative left the Commission.

A New Approach: UN Disarmament Commission, 1952

After the two separate Commissions were dissolved, a new start was made in January 1952 when a single UN Disarmament Commission was formed under the Security Council. The new body was to prepare proposals for the regulation, limitation, and balanced reduction of all armed forces and all armaments, nuclear and conventional alike, and it was to propose an effective system of international control of atomic energy to ensure that atomic energy would be used only for peaceful purposes. The debates in the full 11-member Disarmament Commission ended inconclusively in October 1952. In November the first hydrogen bomb, whose force dwarfed that of the Hiroshima-type atomic bomb, was tested by the US at Eniwetok. In August 1953 a hydrogen bomb was exploded by the USSR.

Five-Power Negotiations on a Comprehensive Agreement, 1953–55

On 28 November 1953 the Assembly adopted a resolution suggesting that the Disarmament Commission should establish "a subcommittee consisting of representatives of the Powers principally involved which should seek in private an acceptable solution." Accordingly, the representatives of Canada, France, UK, US, and USSR met as a subcommittee of the Commission at Lancaster House in London from 13 May to 22 June 1954. France and the UK submitted a joint plan on 11 June. It provided that the five big powers should consider themselves prohibited, in accordance with the UN Charter, from using nuclear weapons except in defense against aggression. (The wording is important, because it does not say except in defense against *nuclear* aggression.) It called for the establishment of an international control organ endowed with adequate powers to guarantee the effective observance of a comprehensive disarmament plan. Disarmament would begin as soon as the control organ certified that it was able effectively to enforce the first phase of disarmament. Nuclear and certain other weapons of mass destruction eventually would be prohibited altogether, and conventional armaments and forces would be cut back to agreed levels.

The Anglo-French plan was the first Western proposal specifying the eventual prohibition and abolition of nuclear weapons. At first the USSR rejected it, claiming that in reality it would indefinitely postpone the abolition of such weapons. But later in the 1954 General Assembly the USSR accepted the plan as a basis for further negotiation. The long deadlock seemed to be broken.

New five-power discussions (London, 25 February to 18 March 1955) reached the most encouraging stage they had ever attained, and in July 1955 the heads of government of France, USSR, UK, and US met in Geneva for a "summit conference." The US suggested "open sky supervision" through aerial photography. The UK proposed a reduction of forces and the establishment of a trial inspection zone in central Europe where NATO and Warsaw-Pact forces faced each other. The USSR recommended a solemn declaration by the atomic powers that none of them would be the first to use nuclear weapons. It also recommended that the armed forces of all countries except China, France, UK, USSR, and US be limited to 150,000 to 200,000 effectives, a proposal obviously aimed against German rearmament.

All these proposals were forwarded to the subcommittee, which held another round of meetings in New York from 29 August to 7 October 1955, but the progress toward a general agreement which had seemed to be taking place in London and Geneva proved illusory. The meetings of the five powers in New York ended in recriminations, the Western delegations berating the USSR for its rigidity, the USSR charging the Western powers with reneging on their previous agreement to certain amendments to the comprehensive Anglo-French plan. Thereafter, the subcommittee limited itself to considering partial, rather than comprehensive, disarmament plans.

Efforts to Agree on a Partial Disarmament Plan, 1957

The longest series of five-power meetings behind closed doors took place in London from 18 March to 6 September 1957. Numerous proposals and counterproposals were made, all for partial disarmament, dealing with such matters as the cessation of nuclear tests, the control of a nuclear test ban, foreign bases, and the reduction of conventional armed forces. The Western powers found it impossible to agree beforehand to specific target dates as the USSR demanded because, in their view, the success of each step in actual disarmament would depend on the confidence created by a fully working inspection and control system. The USSR held that the Western proposals would result in an indefinite period of "inspection without disarmament."

Enlargement of Disarmament Commission, 1957–58

On 19 November 1957 the General Assembly resolved (60 to 9, with 11 abstentions) to enlarge the Disarmament Commission from 11 to 25 nations. This decision was taken over strenuous opposition by the USSR, which unsuccessfully proposed that all UN members should sit on the Disarmament Commission. The USSR declared that it would not take part in the work of the 25-member body because it was still heavily weighted in favor of nations belonging to Western military alliances. The stalemate over the composition of the Disarmament Commission was broken a year later when, on 4 November 1958, "reaffirming the responsibilities of the UN for seeking a solution of the disarmament problem," the Assembly (75 to 0, with 3 abstentions) enlarged the Disarmament Commission for 1959 to comprise all UN members.

Geneva Conference on Nuclear Testing, 1958

In 1958 some significant developments began to take place outside the UN. Nuclear weapons tests were discontinued by the USSR in the spring of 1958 and by the UK and US as of 31 October 1958. As a result of direct correspondence between the heads of government of the USSR and the US, a conference of experts met in July-August 1958 to study methods of detecting violations of a possible ban on nuclear tests. The conference was held at the European headquarters of the UN in Geneva.

These experts, from four Western countries and four Eastern European countries, unanimously reported that violation of an agreement concerning nuclear weapons tests within certain specific limits could be detected. Although the role of the UN was limited to that of host, the secretary-general was represented by a personal representative and the conference reported to the UN on its work. After 1958 the conference was organized on a more or less continuous basis, remaining in being until March 1962.

New 10-Nation Committee with East-West Parity, 1959

In the summer of 1959 the foreign ministers of France, UK, USSR, and US agreed that disarmament negotiations would "most efficiently advance" if held outside the UN framework in a 10-nation disarmament committee, based on equal East-West representation. The committee was composed of five Western countries—Canada, France, Italy, UK, US—and five Soviet-bloc countries—Bulgaria, Czechoslovakia, Poland, Romania, USSR.

This became the first group to discuss "general and complete" disarmament.

The committee was quickly deadlocked on the issue whether to begin with plans for general and complete disarmament, as the USSR proposed, or to start with partial measures, as the US and its allies suggested.

Assembly Emphasis on General and Complete Disarmament, 1959

A feeling of great urgency, but also a spirit of unprecedented initiative and unity, characterized the disarmament debates in the 1959 General Assembly. Two major new plans were submitted to the Assembly: a UK plan, avowedly "pragmatic," and a Soviet plan, avowedly "radical." Many delegates emphasized that the two plans were not too dissimilar. Both would abolish the ability of all states to wage war and reduce all military forces and armaments to the requirements of internal security.

The British plan envisaged three phases of disarmament, but without specific time targets. Phase one would involve solution of the question of nuclear tests, great power agreement on maximum forces, and the establishment of an international body to consider armament reduction. Phase two would start after agreement was reached on the nature and functions of the international control organ. During this phase, major reductions in conventional armaments and forces would be carried out, and the production of nuclear weapons would be curbed. Under phase three, the international arms control organ would assume its final form, and under its effective control final disarmament could be realized. This would include a universal ban on the production and use of nuclear and other weapons of mass destruction; the reduction of military forces and equipment to the levels required for internal security; and international approval of military budgets.

The USSR plan envisaged three phases of disarmament, to be accomplished in four years. During phase one the military forces of the USSR, the US, and the People's Republic of China would be reduced to 1.7 million each, and of those of the UK and France to 650,000. The forces of other states would be reduced to levels agreed upon by the General Assembly or a special non-UN world conference. Armaments would be reduced in the same proportion as armed forces. During phase two, the remaining military forces would be completely disbanded and all military bases in foreign countries abolished. Phase three would involve the destruction of all nuclear and other weapons of mass destruction, missiles, and air force equipment. Appropriations for military purposes in any form would be barred from national and other budgets. War ministries, general staffs, and all military and paramilitary establishments and organizations would be abolished, all military training terminated, and the military education of young people prohibited by law. The size of the "strictly limited" contingents of police or militia that states would be allowed to maintain would be agreed upon for each country. The USSR added that if "at present" general and complete disarmament was not acceptable, it would agree to certain partial measures.

In the three-week debate that followed in the Assembly's Political and Security Committee, many proposals and suggestions were brought forward and discussed, virtually without acrimony or mutual recrimination. Finally, on 20 November 1959, the Assembly adopted unanimously and without a formal vote the first resolution ever to be sponsored by all member nations. In it the Assembly declared that it was "striving to put an end completely and forever to the armaments race," and stated "that the question of general and complete disarmament is the most important one facing the world today." The resolution transmitted to the Disarmament Commission and to the 10-nation disarmament committee "for thorough consideration" the UK and USSR disarmament declarations and all other proposals and suggestions made during the Assembly debate.

Total Collapse of Negotiations, 1960–61

The shooting down of a US airplane on photo reconnaissance over the Soviet Union (the "U-2 incident"), and the subsequent breakup of the summit meeting between the leaders of France, UK, USSR, and US in early May 1960, greatly worsened the international climate. Revised versions of the Soviet and Western plans were thereafter submitted to the East-West 10-nation committee in Geneva. But at the end of June, the five Eastern delegates walked out of the committee, and no talks on disarmament were held for almost a year.

US-USSR Agreement on Eight Principles of Negotiation, 1961

In the spring of 1961 the US and USSR began top-level discussions to reopen formal disarmament talks. On 20 September 1961, they submitted to the Assembly at the opening of its 16th regular session a Joint Statement of Agreed Principles for Disarmament Negotiations. Eight principles were set forth, dealing with (1) the stated goal of negotiations—a program ensuring that disarmament was to be "general and complete" and was to be accompanied by reliable procedures for the maintenance of peace; (2) the reduction of nonnuclear weapons and facilities to such levels as might be agreed to be necessary for the maintenance of internal order and provision of agreed manpower for a UN peace force; (3) the main elements of the disarmament program; (4) implementation of the disarmament program in an agreed sequence of stages within specified time limits; (5) the balance of armaments to be maintained throughout the disarmament process; (6) the need for international control under an International Disarmament Organization to be created within the framework of the UN; (7) the need during and after disarmament to strengthen institutions for maintaining world peace; (8) the need for speedy and continuous negotiations to achieve these objectives.

These principles were endorsed unanimously by the 1961 Assembly and have served as the basic terms of reference for all subsequent discussions on general and complete disarmament. But differences remained on how the principles should be applied.

Addition of Nonaligned Nations to the East-West Disarmament Body: A New Phase in Negotiations Begins. The experience of the 10-nation disarmament committee suggested that disarmament negotiations involving only the two great power blocs would almost inevitably be deadlocked. When in 1961 the Assembly found itself in the position of being able to endorse the joint US-USSR agreement on basic disarmament principles, it immediately urged the two powers to agree to replace the moribund 10-nation disarmament committee, with its equal East-West representation, with a larger committee, including a number of "nonaligned" nations which might be able to bridge the differences between the two factions. By the end of the 1961 session, the USSR and the US were able to agree that the new body should be composed of the original 10 members of the former committee plus the 8 nonaligned nations: Brazil, Burma, Ethiopia, India, Mexico, Nigeria, Sweden, UAR. Unanimously endorsing this decision, the Assembly requested the new body to start work "as a matter of the utmost urgency" and not to stop until it had accomplished the tasks set forth in the Joint Statement of Agreed Principles.

In accordance with this mandate, the Conference of the Eighteen Nation Disarmament Committee (ENDC) has been in intermittent session since it began activities in March 1962. Although ENDC was not strictly speaking a UN body or a UN subsidiary organ, it nevertheless reported annually to the Assembly and used the Assembly's resolutions and debates as starting points for its own discussions. Similarly, the Assembly used the material in the ENDC reports to provide the substance of most of its debates on disarmament items. Indeed, the ENDC was the world's chief forum for informed discussion on all issues connected with disarmament. Since the representatives were all specialists in their field, the committee was able to concentrate on technical aspects of disarmament matters and examine them in detail that neither the Assembly nor the Disarmament Commission—both primarily "political" bodies—could hope to achieve.

ENDC was based in Geneva and organized under the cochairmanship of the US and USSR. France did not take its seat on the committee, claiming that disarmament negotiations were useless without a substantial improvement in the general political climate. Nevertheless, a chair was reserved for the French delegation. Negotiations have developed on the lines of general and complete disarmament, a nuclear weapons test ban, and collateral measures of disarmament.

In 1969, following agreement between the cochairmen of the conference (USSR and US) the name of the ENDC was changed to the Conference of the Committee on Disarmament, and its membership was increased from 18 to 26. The new members were Argentina, Hungary, Japan, Mongolia, Morocco, Netherlands, Pakistan, and Yugoslavia.

STATUS OF NEGOTIATIONS ON MAJOR DISARMAMENT ISSUES SINCE 1962
1. Developments Concerning General and Complete Disarmament

Due to generally improved international relations, the atmosphere of disarmament negotiations from 1962 until the beginning of 1964 was markedly more cooperative than in previous years. Both the US and the USSR submitted plans for phased general and complete disarmament, and both agreed to discuss a number of "collateral measures," designed to lessen international tension, that could be implemented prior to an overall disarmament treaty. US proposals included a verified freeze on the number of nuclear delivery vehicles and a verified cessation of the production of fissionable material for nuclear weapons. Soviet proposals included a nonaggression pact between NATO and the Warsaw Pact countries and a reduction in military budgets. In April 1964 the US and USSR made a simultaneous announcement of respective cutbacks in their production of fissionable material. From May to September 1964 the committee was deadlocked over the question of which of the numerous "collateral measures" proposed should be given priority of debate. The committee adjourned in September 1964 and did not reconvene until July 1965, in response to a request of the Disarmament Commission, which had met a month earlier. Since then, it has concentrated on underground nuclear testing and nonproliferation of nuclear weapons.

Basic Differences Between the US and USSR Disarmament Plans. Both plans are similar in that they are intended to be an embodiment of the principles agreed to in 1961. Both envisage disarmament as a three-stage process, and both provide for establishment of peacekeeping machinery and an International Disarmament Organization to implement controls. The crucial difference between the two plans lies in the proposed sequence of disarmament moves. The USSR wishes to give priority to the elimination of overseas military bases and all but a limited number of nuclear missiles. The US maintains that these measures should be reserved for stage two of the disarmament program and that priority should be given to a reduction of conventional standing forces. Each power sees the other's plan as an attempt to gain a military advantage and hence as a threat to its own security. Other differences between the US and the USSR concern the inspection powers of the proposed International Disarmament Organization. As has frequently been the case, US anxiety that violations might go undetected has been matched by Soviet fear of what it terms "legalized espionage."

Proposal by the Secretary-General. In the introduction to his

1966 report on the work of the UN, Secretary-General U Thant expressed profound anxiety at the lack of progress in disarmament negotiations. Since the results of negotiations were so "meager," he thought it natural "to question to what extent Governments and people really understand the effects of the nuclear arms race." Pointing out that the UN had never carried out a comprehensive study of the consequences of nuclear weapons, he suggested that an appropriate body should "explore and weigh the impact and implications of all aspects of nuclear weapons," adding that "to know the true nature of the danger we face may be a most important first step towards averting it." In its resolution under the agenda item on general and complete disarmament, the Assembly responded to this suggestion by requesting the Secretary-General himself, assisted by experts, to prepare a concise report to be transmitted to member nations before the 1967 session on "the effects of the possible use of nuclear weapons and on the security and economic implications for States of the acquisition and further development of these weapons."

The experts reported that the problem of ensuring security for a particular state could not be solved by increasing that state's nuclear weapons, or by increasing the number of states possessing nuclear weapons, or by the retention of nuclear weapons by states that now possessed them. An agreement to prevent the spread of nuclear weapons and one on the reduction of existing nuclear weapons would be powerful steps in the right direction, the experts added.

In 1969 the General Assembly discussed general and complete disarmament more extensively than at any previous session. It expressed satisfaction that the US and the USSR had initiated at Helsinki, on 17 November 1969, bilateral talks on strategic arms limitation (SALT).

In 1968 the Assembly had urged the US and the USSR to initiate such talks. Subsequent talks were held in 1970 in Vienna, and they are to be resumed in Helsinki. The Assembly also appealed to the US and the USSR to agree on a moratorium on further testing and deployment of new offensive and defensive strategic nuclear weapon systems; invited the Disarmament Committee to consider effective control measures against radiological warfare and the implications of the possible military applications of laser technology; declared the 1970's a disarmament decade; called on governments to take measures relating to cessation of the nuclear arms race and nuclear disarmament; urged the Disarmament Committee to work toward a comprehensive program of disarmament; and recommended that the resources freed by disarmament be channeled into economic development of poorer countries.

The General Assembly in 1969 adopted a resolution stating that chemical and biological methods of warfare had always been viewed with horror and condemned by the international community. It called for adherence to an existing convention banning the use of these weapons, the Protocol for the Prohibition of the Use in War of Asphyxiating, Poisonous or Other Gases, and of Bacteriological Methods of Warfare, signed in Geneva on 17 June 1925.

A group of 14 experts appointed by the secretary-general reported in 1969 that were chemical and bacteriological weapons ever to be used on a large scale in war, no one could predict how enduring the effects would be and how they would affect the structure of society and the environment.

Socialist and most nonaligned states favored a convention banning the development of all chemical and bacteriological weapons jointly. Western powers believe it is more practical to ban biological weapons first because of the complexities of a ban on chemical weapons.

The Disarmament Committee met in Geneva from 17 February to 30 April 1970 and again from 16 June to 3 September 1970. It submitted to the General Assembly the text of a draft treaty to prohibit the emplacement of weapons of mass destruction on the seabed.

In 1970 the Assembly also adopted a resolution banning weapons of mass destruction from the seabed. The US and the USSR supported the resolution.

When discussions opened on the subject in 1968 these two countries had widely diverging positions on the seabed question. By 1969 they had resolved their own differences and accepted amendments to a draft they jointly presented to the Assembly. This failed to be adopted because the smaller powers believed their vital interests were being ignored.

Following compromises acceptable to many states, large and small, the Assembly finally accepted the draft treaty. It allows for an inspection system with UN participation, refers to a 12-mile territorial sea, and contains a commitment that the seabed pact will be followed up with an agreement on a ban against all military activity beyond the 12-mile limit.

In 1970 the General Assembly called on all nuclear-armed states to halt the nuclear arms race and to cease all testing and deployment of nuclear weapons. The resolution was passed by a vote of 80 to 9 with 14 abstentions; among the abstentions were the US, UK, and France.

The General Assembly urged the Conference of the Committee on Disarmament to intensify its efforts toward a more rapid achievement of disarmament measures. The resolution was adopted by a vote of 91 in favor, none against, with 11 abstentions.

The Assembly also asked the Conference to take into account a comprehensive program of disarmament submitted by Ireland, Mexico, Morocco, Pakistan, Sweden, and Yugoslavia. This program deals with the prevention and limitation of armaments, the reduction of all armaments, armed forces, and military expenditures, and the elimination of armaments.

2. Negotiations for a Comprehensive Nuclear Test-Ban Treaty

The problem of nuclear testing has been discussed annually in the Assembly since 1954, when the US began experiments in its Pacific proving grounds in March 1954. In 1958 the nuclear powers (then the UK, US, and the USSR) made the first responsive move toward placating the anxiety of the world over the harmful radiation effects of continued testing, by establishing the three-power Geneva conference to negotiate a test-ban treaty (see above, under the Chronology). Although the conference accomplished nothing appreciable, private negotiations among the three powers led in 1963 to a partial test-ban treaty prohibiting tests in the atmosphere, in outer space, and under water. The treaty was signed in August by the representatives of the UK, US, and USSR meeting in Moscow. It was subsequently signed or adhered to by more than 100 countries. These countries do not as yet include either France or Mainland China. At the time the treaty was drafted, France was already a nuclear power and China was well on the way to becoming one, and both countries have conducted atmospheric tests since the treaty came into force.

During its 1963 session the Assembly, and in particular the nonaligned nations, made strenuous efforts to persuade the US and USSR to extend the Moscow Treaty to include a ban on underground tests. Pending such an agreement, the nonaligned powers urged that the nuclear countries accept an informal "interim arrangement" for banning underground tests. This the nuclear powers steadfastly refused to do. Nor did they accept any of the numerous compromise proposals put forward by the eight nonaligned members of the Eighteen Nation Disarmament Committee to reconcile the technical differences between the US and Soviet positions on an underground test ban.

Basic Differences Between the US and USSR on an Underground Test Ban. The obstacle that long prevented the conclusion of even a partial test-ban treaty was the difficulty of establishing adequate methods of control and verification. The US has always insisted in every sphere of its disarmament plans on the need for strict international control, backed by appropriate verification procedures. The USSR, on the other hand, tends to believe that these stringent US demands, if implemented, would constitute an infringement on national sovereignty. The Moscow Treaty largely owes its existence to the fact that technical progress by 1963 had made it possible for each nuclear power to ascertain exclusively from observations conducted in its own territory whether another nuclear power was conducting tests in any of three environments—the atmosphere, outer space, or under water. The failure to develop similar methods for distinguishing underground tests—below a certain threshold of magnitude—from natural seismic activity was responsible for the deadlock on an underground test ban. At least it is stated to be so by the US, which contends that, for adequate verification, observation posts and on-site inspection are required in the territory of each nuclear power. The USSR, for its part, declares that it is possible for any nuclear power to identify underground tests conducted anywhere in the world by systems of detection and verification based in its own national territory. Hence it maintains that the US demand for international control methods is tantamount to an attempt at legalized espionage.

Compromise Proposals by the Nonaligned Powers on the Disarmament Committee. The eight nonaligned powers of the Eighteen Nation Disarmament Committee produced several proposals to bridge the gap between the US and USSR positions on underground testing. Among the various suggestions put forward are: (1) a "threshold" treaty whereby all tests above a certain seismic magnitude—and therefore detectable by national, as opposed to international, networks of observation stations—would be banned; (2) a moratorium on underground tests below an agreed threshold, together with an exchange of scientific and technical information by the nuclear powers and a progressive lowering of the threshold as national detection methods improve; (3) a temporary trial suspension of all underground tests, with or without a threshold treaty, accompanied by a system of "verification by challenge"— meaning that a nation suspected of having conducted an underground test could be challenged to prove its innocence by inviting outside impartial observers to make an on-the-spot inspection; (4) a "detection club" whereby a number of countries would agree to develop their seismic detection systems and cooperate in an exchange of appropriate information and data; (5) an impartial body of scientists, recruited on a personal basis from nonaligned countries, to give their opinion on the general problem of identification of underground tests.

General Attitude in the Assembly. The majority of members see the conclusion of a comprehensive test-ban as a first substantial move toward general disarmament and even more importantly as a prerequisite to the prevention of the proliferation of nuclear weapons among other powers. As each of the proposals listed above seems to contain promising avenues of negotiation, the fact that none of them has been seriously explored by the nuclear powers is a cause of great concern. Most members deeply suspect that the real reason for the failure of the US and USSR to conclude a treaty banning underground tests is a tacit understanding between them that it is in their best interests, at least for the moment, to agree to disagree. For as the secretary-general has frankly stated: "It is difficult to conceive of any other reason for these underground tests than that they are intended to produce more sophisticated nuclear weapons or, perhaps, to develop antiballistic missile systems." And he went on to warn that "if there should be a unilateral technological breakthrough by one of these Powers in either offensive or defensive nuclear weapon capability, it could upset the existing uneasy balance of terror and lead at once to a new and greatly accelerated nuclear arms race."

3. Prevention of Nuclear Proliferation

In the early years of the atomic era, it had been assumed that only a very few highly industrialized nations would be able to afford to manufacture nuclear weapons. Owing to the unexpected simplification of nuclear production processes, however, by the mid-1960's some 20 nations, including relatively small countries, were recognized as possessing nuclear capability. In the absence of a nonproliferation treaty and a comprehensive test ban, international conflicts sorely tempt some of these countries to consider developing nuclear weapons. Although the General Assembly had already discussed the problem of nuclear proliferation at earlier sessions, during 1965 and 1966 it devoted the greater part of its disarmament debates to this matter. The discussions were lent a special note of urgency by Mainland China's sudden emergence as a proven nuclear power. The concern felt at Peking's nuclear bomb explosions of October 1964 and May 1965 deepened into real alarm when its first nuclear missile was tested in October 1966.

At the 1965 Assembly session, prospects for early agreement seemed remote. Both the US and USSR submitted draft treaties that combined a nondissemination undertaking on the part of the nuclear powers with a statement of renunciation of the use of nuclear weapons by the nonnuclear powers. But the US draft stressed the need for international safeguards on peaceful nuclear activities, which the USSR repudiated. The USSR draft included provisions designed to forestall "loopholes" for indirect proliferation through military alliances (that is, to prevent West Germany from becoming a nuclear power by virtue of its membership in NATO), which the US found unacceptable. In addition, there was an important difference of view between the two major nuclear powers and the nonaligned nations. The latter felt that if they were to undertake not to acquire nuclear weapons, then the nuclear powers in turn should pledge not to use nuclear weapons or the threat of nuclear weapons against nonnuclear countries and also take "tangible steps" to halt the nuclear arms race. While both the US and USSR have offered the nonnuclear powers general assurances along these lines, neither has consented to embody such assurances in the text of a nonproliferation treaty.

During 1966, however, the US and USSR made definite attempts to reconcile their differences (at least with each other, if not with the nonaligned powers). The 1966 General Assembly adopted a resolution urgently requesting all nations to "refrain from any actions conducive to the proliferation of nuclear weapons or which might hamper the conclusion of an agreement on the nonproliferation of nuclear weapons." In another 1966 resolution, by a vote of 48 to 1 with 59 abstentions, the Assembly

also decided to convene a conference of nuclear-weapon states not later than July 1968 to consider how the security of such states could best be assured and how they could cooperate among themselves to prevent nuclear proliferation.

Following years of negotiations, an agreement was reached in 1968 to prevent the spread of nuclear weapons. The Treaty on the Nonproliferation of Nuclear Weapons was signed by more than 80 states. It prohibits the spread of nuclear weapons under international safeguards, contains provisions for promoting peaceful uses of nuclear energy, makes nuclear material available for peaceful purposes to nonnuclear weapon states, and provides for negotiations for an early end to the arms race. The treaty came into force on 5 March 1970, after three nuclear powers (UK, US, and USSR) and 40 nonnuclear states had ratified or acceded to it.

In September 1968 a conference of nonnuclear weapon states, meeting in Geneva, had asked for greater commitments and assistance to nonnuclear weapon states.

The Establishment of Nuclear-Free Zones was one of the measures considered at that conference. The idea of establishing "nonnuclear clubs" among regional groupings of nations has had a long history of discussion in the Assembly. Indeed, two specific declarations have already been adopted: the Declaration on the Denuclearization of Latin America (1963) and the Declaration on the Denuclearization of Africa (1965). The regional organizations in both areas worked on the texts of appropriate draft treaties, and in February 1967 a Treaty for the Prohibition of Nuclear Weapons in Latin America (Treaty of Tlatelolco) was signed. The treaty prohibits the stationing, manufacture, acquisition, or use of nuclear weapons in Latin America.

Convention on the Prohibition of the Use of Nuclear Weapons. This too is a measure that is likely to be discussed both at the nonnuclear power conferences and at the forthcoming World Disarmament Conferences. The idea of a convention totally outlawing the use of nuclear weapons was first sponsored as a proposal to the 1961 Assembly by a group of nonaligned nations. Although it has remained on the Assembly agenda and is under consideration by the Eighteen Nation Disarmament Committee, the idea has never been explored thoroughly as a practical likelihood, largely because of opposition on the part of the Western powers.

PROPOSALS FOR A WORLD DISARMAMENT CONFERENCE

The Cairo Conference of Nonaligned Nations, held in October 1964, adopted a resolution proposing a world disarmament conference that could be attended by representatives of all nations, including non-UN members. The proposal was debated during the 1965 summer session of the Disarmament Commission and by the 1965 Assembly. While the Western powers were generally unenthusiastic, they nevertheless voted for the decision to hold the conference in 1967. The primary aim of the nonaligned powers was to bring Mainland China into general disarmament negotiations. However, the very day following the Assembly's decision to convene the conference, Peking announced that it would have nothing to do with it.

PEACEFUL USES OF OUTER SPACE

In October 1957 the USSR launched the first sputnik into orbit round the earth. The following year, the General Assembly for the first time debated the question of outer space. Two items were proposed for inclusion on the agenda: "The Banning of the Use of Cosmic Space for Military Purposes, the Elimination of Foreign Bases on the Territories of Other Countries, and International Cooperation on the Study of Cosmic Space," proposed by the USSR; and a "Program for International Cooperation in the Field of Outer Space," proposed by the US. The very titles of these items indicate the differences that initially existed between the two powers in regard to an international accord on the uses of outer space. The USSR proposed that the first order of business should be a ban on armaments in space but wished to link this with the dismantling of US overseas military bases. The US preferred to avoid the disarmament issue altogether in this connection and wished merely to emphasize that it was the common aim of mankind to ensure the use of outer space for peaceful purposes. This disagreement provoked a series of disputes over the composition and terms of reference of the special UN body that should be established to deal with outer space problems. The USSR wanted a body with East-West parity, while the US preferred a body more broadly geographic in representation.

CREATION OF A COMMITTEE ON THE PEACEFUL USES OF OUTER SPACE

Due to these differences, the 1958 Assembly contented itself with merely setting up an ad hoc committee to consider technical programs in the use of outer space, related legal problems, and future organizational arrangements. The committee consisted of 18 nations, including only 3 members of the Soviet bloc—Czechoslovakia, Poland, and the USSR itself. The three nations declared that they would not participate in the committee because its composition did not reflect fairly the USSR's advanced position in outer space research. Two other countries named to the committee, India and the UAR, subsequently decided not to participate, basing their decision on the assumption that without the USSR the committee could not carry out its assigned functions. Reduced to 13 participants, the committee nevertheless went ahead with its work.

After intensive negotiations, the 1959 Assembly set up a permanent 24-nation Committee on the Peaceful Uses of Outer Space. The 1961 Assembly enlarged the committee to 28 members: Albania, Argentina, Australia, Austria, Belgium, Brazil, Bulgaria, Canada, Chad, Czechoslovakia, France, Hungary, India, Iran, Italy, Japan, Lebanon, Mexico, Mongolia, Morocco, Poland, Romania, Sierra Leone, Sweden, USSR, UAR, UK, and US.

In 1962 the committee constituted itself into two subcommittees of the whole—one to deal with scientific and technical cooperation, the other with the task of evolving outer space law.

DEVELOPMENTS IN SCIENTIFIC AND TECHNICAL COOPERATION

The recommendations of the scientific and technical subcommittee, transmitted through its parent body to the Assembly, are arranged under seven heads.

Exchange of Information. In response to Assembly requests in 1961 and 1962, a number of countries have provided the committee with information on their space activities and programs. The UN Secretariat produces annual reports on national and cooperative international programs.

Encouragement of International Programs. In its report to the 1966 Assembly, the committee called attention to several possible outer space programs of particular international interest. A satellite-based world civil navigation system would, the committee noted, be a "very useful practical consequence of the exploration of outer space." The committee also noted the work being done by certain member countries and specialized agencies on the application of space technology to television communications and meteorology.

International Sounding Rocket Launching Facilities. At its 1962 session the Assembly endorsed the committee's proposal that the UN sponsor a sounding rocket facility on the geomagnetic equator in time for the International Year of the Quiet Sun. India, through which the magnetic equator passes, offered itself as a host state for the facility. Located at a site near Thumba, the project is called Thumba Equatorial Launching Station (TERLS).

Education and Training. From the outset, the Assembly has been keenly aware of the need to train personnel from countries not yet advanced in space activities if true international cooperation in outer space is to be achieved. Accordingly, the committee has recommended that the material in UN documents on national and international space programs and on availability of space-training facilities and fellowships be compiled periodically in a printed directory and to be distributed on the basis of a mailing list supplied by each member nation.

Special Cooperation with WMO and ITU. By the terms of its 1961 resolution on outer space, the Assembly requested the World Meteorological Organization to submit reports to the UN committee on the international cooperation required in weather research. The following year it endorsed the efforts that had been taken under WMO auspices to establish a World Weather Watch. The same resolution also requested the International Telecommunication Union to submit reports on cooperation required to develop effective space communications.

Public Registry of Launchings of Space Vehicles. An essential requirement for international cooperation in outer space development is that launchings of space vehicles, together with scientific data on the results of such launchings, should be made public. In 1961 the Assembly decided unanimously that the UN "should provide a focal point" for such information and requested the secretary-general to open a public registry for this purpose. The information is transmitted to the outer space committee for review and is then placed in the registry. Both the US and USSR regularly supply appropriate data.

1967 International Conference

Beginning in 1965, the outer space committee started work on the organization of an international conference on the exploration and peaceful uses of outer space. The arrangements recommended by the committee were approved by the General Assembly in 1966, and it was decided that the conference should be held in early September 1967. The object of the conference was to be twofold: (1) to examine the practical benefits to be derived from space research and exploration and the extent to which nonspace powers, particularly the developing countries, could enjoy these benefits; and (2) to study the opportunities available to nonspace powers for participating in international space cooperation. Participants were invited to submit papers on the following topics: general appraisal of contributions that have been or may be made in the application of outer space research to such fields as biology, medicine, communications, meteorology, and navigation; implications of space exploration for education; other implications of expanding space exploration and research; opportunities for participation in space exploration and research.

DEVELOPMENT OF INTERNATIONAL LAW ON OUTER SPACE

The early work of the legal subcommittee was marked by disputes that delayed progress on the development of outer space law. The majority of members stressed the dangers of spectacular scientific advances without corresponding legal obligations and safeguards.

In originally proposing the formulation of an international legal code on outer space, the Assembly had recommended that such a code be based, insofar as possible, on the existing body of international law (including the UN Charter) and the principle of freedom of space exploration for all states. At the beginning of the legal subcommittee's discussions, in 1962, a major source of Soviet-US divergence of view was the relation between prevention of armaments in space to disarmament on earth. But whereas in 1959, when the Assembly first debated outer space, it had been the USSR that had linked the two questions, in 1962 the position was reversed and it was the US that saw the two problems as being inseparable. The USSR, supported by the majority of the nonaligned smaller powers, now maintained that the two matters could and ought to be treated separately. On the strength of this view, the USSR pressed for adoption of its own draft of basic principles governing the use of outer space and for their early incorporation into a legal declaration with binding force. The US, besides rejecting certain clauses in the Soviet draft, contended that with the outstanding disarmament issues still unsolved it was too early to adopt or even consider in detail a general declaration of basic principles. Instead, the US advocated that priority should be given to two specific agreements, for which both space powers had submitted drafts: an agreement on liability for damages caused by launching of objects into outer space, and an agreement on assistance to and return of astronauts and space vehicles in the event of forced landing outside their national territories.

The breakthrough in this quasi-procedural deadlock came a year later, as part of the general East-West détente that followed the partial nuclear test-ban treaty signed in August 1963. During its 1963 autumn session, the Assembly was able to adopt by acclamation two important measures relating to restricting the use of outer space to peaceful purposes. The first was a resolution calling upon all states to refrain from placing in orbit objects carrying nuclear weapons or other weapons of mass destruction. The second was a resolution embodying a Declaration of Legal Principles Governing the Activities of States in the Exploration and Use of Outer Space. Though not an agreement with binding force, as the USSR had wished, it was regarded as being the forerunner to a full legal treaty to be drawn up in the future.

The 1966 Treaty of Principles. Based on drafts submitted individually by both the US and the USSR, the 17 articles of the treaty state that the exploration and use of outer space shall be carried out for the benefit of all countries and shall be the province of all mankind; that outer space and celestial bodies are not subject to national appropriation by claim of sovereignty or any other means; and that exploration will be carried on in accordance with international law. Parties to the treaty undertake not to place in orbit any objects carrying nuclear weapons, install such weapons on celestial bodies, or otherwise station them in outer space. The moon and other celestial bodies shall be used by all parties exclusively for peaceful purposes, and military bases or maneuvers on celestial bodies shall be forbidden. States shall regard astronauts as envoys of mankind in outer space and shall render them all possible assistance in case of accident, distress, or emergency landing. Parties launching objects into outer space are internationally liable for damages caused by such objects or their component parts. The principle of cooperation and mutual assistance shall be followed in space exploration. Harmful contamination of the moon and other celestial bodies shall be avoided. All stations, installations, equipment and space vehicles on the moon and other celestial bodies shall be open for inspection to representatives of other states on a reciprocal basis. The treaty, which contains provisions for withdrawal, was to come into force after ratification by five governments, including those that are designated as depositary governments under its terms—namely the governments of the UK, US, and USSR.

UN members regarded the treaty with unqualified approval as a historic achievement, possibly the most outstanding one of the UN during its 1966 session. The treaty entered into force on 10 October 1967.

The Agreement on the Rescue of Astronauts, the Return of Astronauts, and the Return of Objects Launched into Outer Space, under which contracting parties agreed to procedures for assistance to spacecraft personnel in the event of accident or emergency landing, and for the return of space objects, came into force on 3 December 1968.

In 1969 the Assembly asked the outer space committee to continue to study questions relating to the definition and utilization of outer space: and welcomed the committee's decision to promote the application of space technology. It invited member states with experience in remote earth-resources surveying (by satellite) to make such experience available to others and to join in exploring the various aspects involved in the analysis and application of data obtained through such techniques.

In 1970 the Assembly drew the attention of member states, specialized agencies, and other interested international organizations to the potential benefits to be derived from direct broadcast satellite services, especially in developing countries, for improving their telecommunications infrastructure, thereby contributing to general economic and social development.

The Assembly also urged the drafting of a convention on liability for damage caused by space objects. Expressing its concern over the devastating effects of typhoons, the Assembly called on member states to exert efforts within their means to implement fully the World Weather Watch Plan of the WMO.

PRESERVATION OF THE SEABED AND THE OCEAN FLOOR FOR PEACEFUL USES

World concern about the exploration and exploitation of the seabed was first expressed in the UN in 1967. The General Assembly declared that exploitation of the seabed beyond the limits of national jurisdiction should be carried on for the benefit of all mankind.

For centuries the sea has been a source of food. In the 20th century, technology has shown that it is also an abundant source of mineral wealth, and that with proper conservation the sea could produce much needed food.

There is general agreement that the ocean floor should be regarded as the common heritage of mankind, but the distribution among states of the benefits that will accrue from this exploitation has raised complex and interlocking problems. They involve such matters as the extent of national jurisdiction over waters off a coast and the seabed beneath them, the possible functions and powers of international bodies that might be given authority over the area beyond national jurisdiction, and the laws that should govern the exploitation of resources of the seabed.

The law regarding the continental shelf has never been clearly defined. The width of coastal waters that a state can declare to be its territorial waters may be fixed arbitrarily by each state. Some claim a 3-mile limit, others as much as 200 miles.

The extraction of certain minerals from the sea could cause serious hardships to those countries whose economy depends on the extraction of such minerals on land. The need for clarity and review of these problems is widely recognized.

STUDIES AND REPORTS

The General Assembly's 42-member Committee on the Peaceful Use of the Seabed and the Ocean Floor Beyond the Limits of National Jurisdiction, appointed in 1968, reported on many of the seabed issues in 1969 and 1970.

The committee's functions were to study legal principles that would promote international cooperation in the exploration and use of the seabed; to study ways and means of promoting the exploitation and use of its resources; to encourage the exchange of scientific knowledge; to study measures for the prevention of marine pollution; and to study the reservation of the seabed for peaceful uses.

Following a review of the committee's first report, the Assembly in 1969 assigned it three specific tasks: to expedite the preparation of principles to promote the exploitation and use of the seabed and its resources for the benefit of all mankind; to report on the question of international legal machinery that would have jurisdiction over this environment; and to recommend the economic and technical conditions and the rules of exploitation of seabed resources, in the context of an international regime to be set up in the area.

Besides calling for studies on the subject, the Assembly declared that, pending the establishment of an international regime, states and persons, physical or juridical, should refrain from all activities of exploitation of the resources of the area and that no claim to any part of that area or its resources should be recognized. A resolution to this effect was adopted by 62 votes to 28, with 28 abstentions. Opponents argued that the resolution sought to retard the exploitation of seabed resources,

that it would encourage states to extend claims over large areas, and that it prejudged questions relating to the establishment of international legal machinery. In 1970 the Assembly adopted a draft treaty prohibiting the placement of weapons of mass destruction on the seabed.

In 1970 the committee held two substantive sessions, one in Geneva in March and the other in New York in August. The committee reported that states had become increasingly aware of the complexity and range of all the issues involved in the question of the seabed. A significant proportion of the preparatory work had been completed, and the extent of agreement had increased since 1968. However, progress had been slower than the committee had expected, and many differences remained.

LAW OF THE SEA CONFERENCE PROPOSED

At its August 1970 session, the committee had before it a statement by the president of the US giving details of plans for an international regime for the seabed and ocean floor. Reports on international legal machinery were also submitted by France, UK, and US.

At its 1970 session the Assembly had comments from governments on the desirability of convening at an early date a conference on the law of the sea, particularly in order to arrive at a clear and internationally accepted definition of the area of the seabed and ocean floor that lies beyond the limits of national jurisdiction. The majority of governments favored the convening of such a conference. Some Eastern European countries, France, and Japan saw no need to hold such a conference at that time. Still others suggested that the conference should be held only after thorough preparation. The UK's view was that the outstanding issues of the law of the sea should be settled separately. The US suggested that some of the outstanding questions might be solved at a future conference and that the committee should continue its consideration of a regime for the seabed.

A report to the Assembly in 1970 outlined the various causes of marine pollution, and labeled gas and oil exploitation as potentially the most likely cause of serious pollution. Legal regulation of the problem, according to the report, would have to deal with such issues as the definition of pollution, measures to prevent it, and a system to provide indemnities for the financial losses of pollution victims.

On 17 December 1970 the General Assembly enlarged the seabed committee from 42 to 86 and charged it with the task of planning a world Law of the Sea Conference in 1973 to consider rules for an international regime to govern the peaceful exploitation of the ocean floor.

During the discussions many members wanted a committee of the whole, reflecting the greater interest of states in the benefits that could come from the seabed. Eastern European countries opposed the arrangements for the 1973 conference on the ground that they had been inadequately planned. Another view was that several conferences on the law of the sea may have to be held to solve related questions in the following order: limits of territorial waters and the continental shelf; a convention on fishing on the high seas in the contiguous zone; and a regime for the seabed. The vote on the resolution was 108 in favor, 7 against, with 6 abstentions.

UN REGIONAL ECONOMIC COMMISSIONS

The four economic commissions form an outstanding feature of the UN system. Each covers a different part of the world and is an important instrument for economic cooperation within its own region.

Three of these regional economic parliaments, as they have been called, were established early in the history of the UN: the Economic Commission for Europe (ECE) and the Economic Commission for Asia and the Far East (ECAFE), on 28 March 1947, and the Economic Commission for Latin America (ECLA), on 25 February 1948. The Economic Commission for Africa (ECA) was established on 29 April 1958 and began work in 1959. Originally, an Economic Commission for the Middle East was planned, but the plan was abandoned because of political tension between the Arab states and Israel. Governments in this area are assisted instead by a small UN Economic and Social Office at Beirut, Lebanon.

ECOSOC is the parent body of the four commissions. While the commissions owe their existence to the recognition that certain problems are best approached on a regional basis, they must take into account the possible repercussions of regional measures on world economy as a whole and are enjoined to act "within the framework of the policies of the United Nations."

COMPOSITION

Membership in the regional commissions is not necessarily limited to states that are members of the UN. Thus, though they are not members of the UN, West Germany is a full member of the ECE, and South Korea and South Viet-Nam are full members of ECAFE. Furthermore, membership in a particular regional commission is not strictly limited to countries located in the region but may include any outside countries that ECOSOC decides have a special interest in the region's economic development. Thus the US is a member of ECE, ECAFE, and ECLA; France and the UK are not only members of the ECE but belong to the three other regional commissions as well; and the USSR is represented on ECE and ECAFE.

Consultative Participation and Associate Membership

Countries not belonging to a particular regional commission may be invited to participate in its work in a consultative capacity. These countries do not have the right to vote, but since formal vote-taking is rare, particularly in the committees and other subsidiary bodies where most of the continuous work goes on, their de facto position is not too different from that of a regular commission member. Switzerland participates as a consultant in the work of all four commissions, while West Germany, a full member of ECE, participates in the work of the other three.

Dependent or non-self-governing territories in any of the regions covered by the work of the commissions may become associate members until such time as they become independent states.

MEMBERSHIP IN THE REGIONAL ECONOMIC
COMMISSIONS, AUGUST 1970

ECONOMIC COMMISSION FOR EUROPE (*ECE*)

Albania	Belgium
Austria	Bulgaria
Byelorussia	Netherlands
Cyprus	Norway
Czechoslovakia	Poland
Denmark	Portugal
Finland	Romania
France	Spain
Germany, West	Sweden
Greece	Turkey
Hungary	Ukraine
Iceland	USSR
Ireland	UK
Italy	US
Luxembourg	Yugoslavia
Malta	

ECONOMIC COMMISSION FOR ASIA AND THE FAR EAST (*ECAFE*)

Afghanistan	Pakistan
Australia	Philippines
Burma	Singapore
Cambodia	Taiwan
Ceylon	Thailand
France	USSR
India	UK
Indonesia	US
Iran	Viet-Nam, South
Japan	Western Samoa
Korea, South	
Laos	**Associate Members**
Malaysia	Brunei
Mongolia	Fiji
Nepal	Hong Kong
Netherlands	Territory of Papua and
New Zealand	New Guinea

ECONOMIC COMMISSION FOR LATIN AMERICA (*ECLA*)

Argentina	Mexico
Barbados	Netherlands
Bolivia	Nicaragua
Brazil	Panama
Canada	Paraguay
Chile	Peru
Colombia	Trinidad and Tobago
Costa Rica	UK
Cuba	US
Dominican Republic	Uruguay
Ecuador	Venezuela
El Salvador	
France	**Associate Members**
Guatemala	British Honduras or Belize
Guyana	Associated States of Antigua,
Haiti	Dominica, Grenada, St.
Honduras	Kitts-Nevis-Anguilla, and
Jamaica	St. Lucia

ECONOMIC COMMISSION FOR AFRICA (*ECA*)

Algeria	Burundi
Botswana	Cameroon

Central African Republic
Chad
Congo (Brazzaville)
Congo (Kinshasa)
Dahomey
Equatorial Guinea
Ethiopia
Gabon
Ghana
Guinea
Ivory Coast
Kenya
Lesotho
Liberia
Libya
Madagascar
Malawi
Mali
Mauritania
Morocco
Niger
Nigeria

Portugal
Rwanda
Senegal
Sierra Leone
Somalia
South Africa
Sudan
Swaziland
Tanzania
Togo
Tunisia
Uganda
UAR
Upper Volta
Zambia

Associate Members
Nonself-governing territories
   in Africa
France
Spain
UK

ORGANIZATION

Although their budgets form part of the regular UN budget and their personnel part of the regular UN staff, the economic commissions in most respects resemble full-fledged, permanent international agencies. Each commission has its own secretariat, headed by an executive secretary. As decided by the participating governments, the commissions organize their work through various subsidiary bodies: committees, subcommittees, working groups, and special conferences.

ECE headquarters are in Geneva, at the European office of the UN, where its annual sessions also take place.

ECAFE headquarters were established originally in Shanghai. Early in 1949, after a short stay in Singapore, the commission moved to Bangkok, Thailand, where it is still located. However, the annual sessions of the commission are held in different countries of the region.

ECLA headquarters are in Santiago, Chile, with local offices in Mexico City, Rio de Janeiro, and Washington. ECLA sessions take place normally at intervals of two years, each time in a different Latin American country. In alternate years, the committee of the whole, composed of all ECLA members, meets at headquarters in Santiago to review the commission's work.

ECA has its headquarters in Addis Ababa, Ethiopia, and it holds biennial sessions. Owing to the difficulty of communications within the African continent, the commission has divided its area of activity into four subregions, each served by an outpost of its secretariat. North Africa is served by a subregional office at Tangier; East Africa by an office at Lusaka, Zambia; Central Africa by an office in Kinshasa, Congo; and West Africa by an office in Niamey, Nigeria.

FUNCTIONS

Each commission serves as a regional forum where governments consult one another, exchange experiences, and endeavor to coordinate their policies and devise measures to solve common economic problems. For each commission ECOSOC has established a set of "term of reference" that serve as its statute or constitution. The prescribed objective of all the commissions is to "facilitate concerted action" to raise the level of economic activity in the region, and to maintain and strengthen the economic relations of the countries of the region both among themselves and with other countries of the world.

The specific functions of the commissions are the pooling and exchange of information and experience, discussion, harmonization and coordination of economic policies, and general cooperative stimulation of regional economic growth—all these with due consideration for the social implications of economic measures, especially in the less developed regions, where such implications may be particularly far-reaching. The four commissions are also important forums for the discussion of technical assistance programs in the region. The secretariats and subsidiary organs of the commissions play a major role in initiating and implementing regional technical assistance projects.

Cooperation with Other Organizations

The regional commissions maintain close contact with UN headquarters and the specialized agencies. Cooperation between the regional commissions is also extensive. Whenever one commission has acquired a body of knowledge and experience that can be of help to another, it makes this available through exchange of information, and mutual consultations.

Since the end of World War II, a number of regional institutions and agencies have been set up outside the UN structure, especially in Europe. The ECE, for instance, has made working arrangements with intergovernmental bodies such as the Council of Europe, the High Authority of the European Coal and Steel Community, the European Economic Community, and the Danube Commission. Regional organizations with whose work ECLA is closely associated include the Organization of American States (OAS) and the Inter-American Development Bank (IDB). Similarly, ECA maintains close liaison with the Organization for African Unity (OAU), which was established in 1963.

The work of the UN economic commissions also involves the participation of professional and other nongovernmental organizations. In view of the highly technical character of many of the commissions' tasks, specialized advice is often required, and outside contribution is fully acknowledged.

Publications

A significant aspect of the work of the three older commissions is the preparation and publication of their comprehensive annual economic surveys: *The Economic Survey of Europe,* published in Geneva; *The Economic Survey of Asia and the Far East,* published in Bangkok; *and The Economic Survey of Latin America,* published in Santiago. These annual surveys are supplemented by the quarterly *Economic Bulletin for Europe,* the quarterly *Economic Bulletin for Asia and the Far East,* and the semiannual *Economic Bulletin for Latin America.* These publications are widely used as authoritative sources of information by other UN bodies, governments, business and industry, educational institutions, and the press.

ECONOMIC COMMISSION FOR EUROPE (ECE)

Established in the spring of 1947, when Europe's post-World War II reconstruction had only just begun, ECE was given heavy initial responsibilities in continuing the work of the Emergency Economic Committee for Europe, the European

Coal Organization, and the European Central Inland Transportation Organization that had been set up by the Allies in 1945. In the subsequent period of East-West tension, ECE survived as one of the few European institutions with common membership, providing almost the only forum for regular meetings to consider the economic problems of Europe as a whole.

Each spring, the member governments meet to review the economic situation in the region, consider the work accomplished by the various ECE subsidiary bodies, and chart the course of the commission's future activities. Policies formulated under ECE auspices have found increasingly wide acceptance among member countries.

ECE's substantive work is conducted by its subsidiary bodies, some of which meet several times a year. Between them, they cover most of the major fields of economic activity. Each topic reviewed below is in the hands of a permanently constituted, principal subsidiary body or committee. ECE publishes statistical bulletins and studies in connection with these subjects, and it organizes periodic conferences or seminars on particular aspects.

Coal

The postwar coal shortage was one of the most critical problems that ECE initially had to deal with. Between April 1948 and September 1950, the ECE Coal Committee allocated 60 million tons of European-mined coal and lignite among the various countries of the region.

The committee meets every three months to examine coal import requirements and export availabilities for all countries of the region over the following quarter. It balances European requirements against the tonnages available from regional sources and calculates the amount of coal that must be imported from overseas. The committee also assists governments in solving specific coal problems and coping with the cycles of acute shortage, such as resulted from the 1956 Suez crisis, and serious glut. Currently, the committee is considering projects for developing new coal resources, increasing the output of existing mines, and upgrading coal into secondary forms of energy more adaptable to modern needs, such as gas, coke, and thermal electricity.

Electric Power

European electric power consumption continues to double every ten years without any sign of saturation. Hence, one of the principal concerns of the ECE's Electric Power Committee is a systematic continuous analysis of the regional electric power situation, including such aspects as the determination of Europe's hydroelectric resources, rural electrification, and the integration of nuclear energy into the European electric power system.

The building of new power stations in Europe in the 15 years following the war led to a progressive exhaustion of natural power resources in many countries. The export of electric power from countries with large unexploited hydropower sources to other European countries is an attractive solution. The ECE has worked out recommendations for simplifying and standardizing the complex and diverse national regulations involved in international exchanges of electric power.

Agriculture

ECE's program in agriculture is developed and carried out jointly with FAO. The committee, which includes both government representatives and agricultural experts, meets every year to review the agricultural situation in the region as a whole. It devotes special attention to the relationship between prices paid to and by farmers, and publishes periodic reports on *Output, Expenses and Income of Agriculture in European Countries.* Each year it examines the production, consumption, and trade outlook for the coming 12 months; 5-year and 10-year trends are also systematically studied. Attention is given to the establishment of quality standards for perishable foodstuffs. A protocol accepted by a majority of ECE governments prescribes standard rules for grading the quality of certain types of fruit and vegetables. The committee also promotes the exchange of experience and information on different aspects of agricultural mechanization. Technical studies cover such diverse subjects as the control of weeds and plant diseases by chemical means, new methods of planting vineyards, and the conservation and improvement of soil fertility.

Timber

Responsibility for consideration of Europe's timber problems has been divided between the ECE and the FAO. After Europe's timber production recovered from the immediate consequences of World War II, the principal efforts of the ECE Timber Committee were directed toward establishing and maintaining a reasonable balance between supply and demand through stabilization of the market and rational utilization of forest resources. The committee conducts an annual review and appraisal of the timber situation in Europe and forecasts the prospective supply and demand for the coming 12 months. The joint ECE-FAO committee on forest working techniques and the training of forest workers, with the collaboration of ILO, endeavors through conferences, study tours, and other means to increase the productivity of forest work in the region. In 1962 the ECE Timber Committee started new projects on the economic aspects and productivity in the wood-processing industries and on the utilization of fiberboard.

Gas

International problems relating to the production, transport, and utilization of natural and manufactured gas are handled by the Gas Committee. Through its subsidiary bodies, the committee considers such topics as the economic aspects of the use of gas by different branches of industry, the economics of long-distance transport by pipeline and by sea in liquefied form, and storage problems. Other aspects of its work include the forecasting of demand, evaluation and exploitation of natural gas reserves, gas statistics, and preparation of maps on natural gas deposits and transport networks. Efforts are made to solve, through technical and legal measures, and through price policies, the problems caused by the fluctuations of demand at different hours of the day and times of the year.

Water

The ECE established its Committee on Water Problems as a principal subsidiary body in 1969. The committee is responsible for preparing a manual on the balances of water resources and needs of individual ECE countries to ensure that future demands can be met. Other important subjects under study are water pollution control and the management of river basins. The committee, in formulating its program of activities, is requested to bear in mind that its work is an integral part of broad environmental issues that ECE has made a priority area.

Steel

Through its continuing analysis of trends in the steel-producing and steel-consuming industries, the ECE Steel Committee assists the governments of the region to formulate their national steel policies. The ECE Steel Committee is the only body in which all European countries as well as the US are represented. The committee conducts an annual review of the European steel situation and world market trends. A 1949 study, *European Steel Trends in the Setting of the World Market,* prepared by the committee, helped pave the way for the creation of the European Coal and Steel Community, comprising Belgium, West Germany, France, Italy, Luxembourg, and the Netherlands. The committee examines methods of expanding output of steel and steel products, and investment policies affecting the industry. Its studies relate to such problems as air and water pollution arising from the iron and steel industry; distribution of steel products; and long-term prospects for steel production and consumption.

Chemical Industry

At its 1970 session the ECE reconstituted the Working Party on the Chemical Industry, created in 1968, as a principal subsidiary committee. The committee has published a study on market trends and prospects for chemical products, and it issues an annual review of the industry. Its current program relates to such problems as transportation and storage, effects of technological progress on the long-term development of the industry, its place in the national economy, the production of synthetics, and patterns of use of plastic materials.

Trade

The ECE Committee on the Development of Trade is primarily concerned with intra-European trade. The following have evolved as the committee's principal regular functions:

1. *East-West trade consultations,* to provide a forum for the consideration of questions of policy and for practical commercial negotiations.

2. *Annual review of European trade questions,* which covers such questions as methods of expanding intra-European trade; economic, administrative, and other obstacles hampering such expansion; and the results of long-term trade arrangements.

3. *Arrangements for settling international accounts.* To eliminate the need for a strict balancing of bilateral trading accounts and to improve intra-European payment facilities, the committee is developing a system of multilateral transfers of trade credits and debits. The ECE secretariat acts as a central clearinghouse for the participating governments.

4. *Special problems and activities for promoting trade.* The committee has dealt with such special problems as commercial arbitration, international patent rights, and standardization of general conditions of sale. It also promotes international trade fairs and technical shows in the region.

Housing, Building, and Planning

World War II left Europe with a staggering housing shortage. Even today this remains a pressing problem in many European countries. ECE's Housing, Building, and Planning Committee conducts an annual review of the housing situation in Europe, based on surveys prepared by the ECE secretariat. It studies the housing policies of various countries and drafts recommendations. The committee fosters coordinated research and international technical exchanges. Partly as a result of its efforts, a nongovernmental organization, the International Council for Building Research, Studies, and Documentation (CIB), was created in 1953, with ECE consultative status, to serve as a link between building research organizations in different countries.

Transport

Created in 1947, ECE's Inland Transport Committee was given the initial task of reorganizing the rolling stock pools of the European railway systems, which had been left in complete disorder by the war. After this problem had been solved, the committee became the principal organ for the formulation and coordination of European transport policy.

Because of the rapid postwar growth of highway traffic in Europe, the committee has focused its attention primarily on problems of road safety and transport. Over the years it has formulated and revised several important European agreements in this area—for example, the 1968 Agreement on the Adoption of Uniform Conditions of Approval and Reciprocal Recognition of Approval for Motor Vehicle Equipment and Parts; a revised text for the European Agreement on the Work of Crews of Vehicles engaged in International Road Transport; two European agreements to supplement the 1968 Conventions on Road Traffic and Road Signs and Signals; a revised text of the 1962 Agreement on the International Carriage of Perishable Foodstuffs; and a Declaration on the Construction of Main International Traffic Arteries. The committee has also promoted the simplification or abolition of the papers required for the temporary admission of foreign privately owned motor vehicles into European countries.

Statistics

Although not a committee as such, the Conference of European Statisticians is a principal subsidiary body of the ECE and holds regular sessions to develop statistical methodology, improve statistical standards in numerous fields, and promote coordination of the statistical work of European organizations. Its current program accords high priority to studies on electronic data processing, further extension of systems of national accounts and balances, the development of an integrated system of demographic and social statistics, and the use of computers.

Other Topics

In addition to the topics handled by ECE's principal subsidiary bodies, several other subjects are studied by specially constituted research or working groups. These include problems of air pollution, mechanical and electrial engineering, productivity of labor, applied economics, exchange of scientific abstracts, and tourism.

ECONOMIC COMMISSION FOR AFRICA (ECA)

At the opening of the first session of the ECA in Addis Ababa on 29 December 1958, UN Secretary-General Dag Hammarskjöld said: "One day we may look back to the establishment of the commission as marking the moment when Africa began to assume its full role in the world community."

Economic and social conditions in the various parts of Africa differ widely, but as a whole the continent is perhaps the poorest region of the world. Many obstacles stand in the way of economic development in areas needing it most. Some of these are a shortage of investment capital, lack of trained personnel, and outmoded commercial and industrial legislation. Many political units in Africa are small in size, and depend for their economic progress on cooperative regional and subregional efforts. The ECA, embracing "the whole continent of Africa, Madagascar, and other African islands," is the only intergovernmental organization established to promote economic and social progress through cooperation in the entire region, including territories that are still non-self-governing. Since 1963, however, South Africa has been barred from participating in ECA's activities because of its apartheid policies.

INITIAL PROGRAM

It was decided that in its initial phase ECA would concentrate its efforts on a limited number of objectives. It would promote and facilitate concerted action on the part of various countries and territories to solve common economic and social problems; and it would carry out a program of research and investigation to include studies on economic development programming, surveys of resources, and work in the field of statistics.

ECA's research and investigation program was designed to deal with urgent practical problems involved in economic development, and to be closely linked with advisory services that ECA provides to member governments on request.

Regarding the social aspects of economic development,

ECA decided to concentrate at first on promoting community development programs. One of the first ECA-sponsored conferences was a meeting of experts in September 1959 to consider the role of community development in Africa.

EXPANDING SCOPE OF ECA

When the ECA met for the first time, there were only 10 independent countries in Africa; by July 1970 there were 41 (excluding South Africa). The work of ECA has been marked by a sense of urgency and a determination to match the rapid pace of African political progress with economic and social progress.

The member countries aim to achieve this in several coordinated ways: by actions taken on the country level; by concerted policies, based on closer ties between them at both subregional and the continent-wide levels; through advice and assistance from the UN and the specialized agencies; and by drawing on the know-how and the financial and technical resources of industrialized countries outside Africa. ECA has played an increasingly significant role in promoting, guiding, and coordinating the efforts of its member countries in these directions.

The general directions taken by the work of the ECA are indicated by the major decisions of its seventh session, held in Nairobi in February 1965. At this session, a general reorganization of the commission's structure was carried out to enable it to play a more active role in African development. The original standing committees, modeled on those of the older economic commissions, were replaced by seven working parties dealing with the following problems: (1) intra-African trade (the ECA Working Party cooperates closely with the OAU Committee on Trade and Development); (2) monetary management and intra-African payments; (3) industry and natural resources; (4) transport and telecommunications; (5) agriculture; (6) manpower and training; and (7) economic integration. Each working party consists of ten members and is assisted by a member of the ECA secretariat and a staff member of the Organization of African Unity. The first six working parties function primarily at the subregional level of operations within each of the four ECA subregions: North Africa, East Africa, Central Africa, and West Africa. The seventh working party, the one on economic integration, coordinates the activities of the other working parties and concerns itself with the economic and social development of Africa as a whole. So that its maximum resources could be devoted to these seven working parties, the commission also decided in 1965 that it would meet only once every two years instead of once a year, as formerly. At its 1969 session the commission further decided that these regular biennial sessions should be at ministerial level and be known as the Conference of Ministers.

Members of ECA have made it clear that their emphasis on tackling economic problems at the subregional level does not mean that they had abandoned the goal of pan-African economic integration, but that the subregional approach is regarded as a necessary first step.

THE WORK OF THE SECRETARIAT

As ECA has steadily expanded its membership and work programs, its secretariat has had to undergo several reorganizations to enable it to keep pace with growing demands. As of February 1970, the secretariat consisted of 8 substantive divisions, each comprising several subsections that between them cover 13 work fields.

Economic Development Planning

In late 1969 the secretariat brought out its first survey of economic conditions in Africa, covering the period 1960–67, and work is under way on a survey covering the remainder of the 1960's. In the future, annual surveys will consist of two parts: a review of the general economic situation in the region and an in-depth analysis of specific economic and social problems in the various countries. In connection with preparations for the second UN Development Decade, the secretariat has identified for each member country the industrial projects most readily capable of modification in their economic and social structure. It is also continuing work on a comparative study of national development plans with the object of promoting greater uniformity of concepts and policies.

Economic Cooperation. A Center for Economic Cooperation has been set up within the secretariat. It is responsible for providing member countries with advisory services in establishing or developing economic cooperation bodies; assisting countries and institutions in preparing and implementing multinational projects; and following up regional activities. The center also directs the work of the secretariat's four subregional offices in the Democratic Republic of the Congo (Central Africa), Zambia (East Africa), Morocco (North Africa), and Niger (West Africa).

Trade. The secretariat's main activities in this sphere are studying possibilities for developing and expanding intra-African trade and strengthening the position of African countries generally in their negotiations to secure a more adequate consideration of their development needs as part of the process of the rationalizations of the world trade system. In its efforts to promote intra-African trade, the secretariat has established within its administrative structure an African Trade Center; it has undertaken joint missions with the Center for Development Planning, Projections, and Policies to strengthen economic cooperation in the West and East African subregions; and it has prepared papers on trade development within the continent.

Fiscal and Monetary Affairs. The secretariat carried out a three-part study on the harmonization of fiscal and budgetary procedures with development, which was used in special budget plan courses held in 1970. The purpose of the courses and of the study was to emphasize the role of fiscal policy in development and to demonstrate that improved budgetary and fiscal systems enable governments to mobilize more effectively their internal resources for development. To encourage actual measures of budgetary reform, the secretariat circulated to member states a questionnaire on problems arising in their field, preparatory to recommending practical steps that might be taken. In the monetary sphere, the secretariat's first concern has been to render assistance to the Association of African Central Banks, inaugurated in December 1969, to ensure its smooth operation.

Industry. Studies on the strategy of harmonized industrial development have been carried out in the four subregions as a basis for meetings of experts to discuss measures for appropriate harmonization programs in each area. To strengthen national and multinational industrial promotion institutions, the secretariat circulated a questionnaire on governmental policies designed to encourage indigenous enterprises. It also organizes frequent round-table conferences at both the national and multinational subregional levels with experts and industrial organizations from outside Africa to debate specific problems and projects. In the field of small-scale industries, it has obtained from governments a list of projects in which they are interested and on this basis prepared six model schemes for small-scale industry manufacture. The secretariat also provides advisory services to governments on the development or establishment of specific industries. Using prefeasibility studies prepared by the secretariat, some 50 new projects were formulated in 1969, 22 of them of a multinational character.

Natural Resources. The secretariat's natural resources section is directing its work to three main areas of development: energy sources, with special emphasis on electric and hydroelectric power; water resources, including a study of the major deficiencies in African hydrological data and a program, undertaken jointly with WMO, for the establishment of hydrometerological networks on the continent; and mineral resources, including a comparative study of laws and agreements on the exploration and exploitation of minerals, petroleum, and natural gas, and a plan to establish a special institute for the development of mineral resources in East Africa.

Agriculture. The activities of ECA and FAO have been combined under a single program for agricultural development in Africa. ECA's main task is a comprehensive three-phase study on intraregional cooperation and trade in the field of agriculture. This study, which is subdivided according to the four subregions, is closely coordinated with FAO's Indicative World Plan for Agricultural Development. In addition, the ECA secretariat has actively helped set up the Association for the Advancement of Agricultural Sciences in Africa, providing secretarial and technical services to the Interim Executive Committee, which met in 1969 to discuss the association. As with industry, the secretariat also provides to individual governments advisory or consultative services on launching or improving specific projects.

Transport and Communications. The secretariat prepares studies and surveys of various transport systems in the four subregions and across the continent generally and assists various groups of countries in their efforts to develop integrated transport networks. Thus it has begun a study for an integrated system in the Maghreb countries of North Africa, and has prepared papers for a meeting of East and Central African states on transport. It has also given assistance to the newly created African Civil Aviation Commission and Association of African Airlines. In telecommunications, the secretariat maintains a special ECA-ITU Joint Unit, which has completed the preliminary survey for a Pan-African telecommunications network financed by UNDP.

Human Resources. The secretariat's Human Resources Development Division is divided into three sections: the Social Development Section, which gives particular attention to the formulation of an integrated approach to the problems of rural development in the region; the Manpower and Training Section, which prepares training courses for officials responsible for manpower planning and the coordination of national training programs; and the Public Administration Section, which, in conjunction with the specialized agencies and with bilateral financial assis-

tance, organizes meetings and seminars on the adminstration of public enterprises.

Population Programs. The secretariat established its own Population Program Center in January 1970. Its task is threefold: to call the attention of member governments to the population situation in the region; to help governments set up national population program services; and to ensure the training of personnel for such services. At government request, the center will also help in the establishment of national population policies.

Housing, Building, and Physical Planning. Working with the specialized agencies, the ECA secretariat assists member states to accelerate improvement of their housing situations, mobilize financial and technical resources from the industrialized countries and financial organizations, and promote training at all levels in building techniques, including cooperative housing and aided self-help. In addition, it provides individual advisory services to member states. In January 1969 the secretariat organized a regional meeting on Technical and Social Problems of Urbanization, which recommended the establishment of a housing cooperative pilot project in an African country. Tanzania was chosen as the country with the appropriate housing policy and institutions to support the project.

Statistical Services. The secretariat helps member states improve the quality of normal statistical returns, extend the scope of available data, increase the size of statistical staff, standardize concepts and methods throughout the region, obtain exchange of information among countries, and prepare more exhaustive studies to assist the production of better economic and social development plans. The Conference of African Statisticians, a subsidiary body of ECA, meets biennially.

Science and Technology. A major program in this sphere is the preparation of regional proposals as a contribution to the World Plan of Action for the Application of Science and Technology to Development. The ECA secretariat conducted on-the-spot surveys in 39 of the 41 independent member countries to determine needs and priorities in this area, and these surveys will form the basis of the African regional programs for the World Plan. A 1968 UNESCO-OAU Conference on Education and Scientific and Technical Training in Relation to Development in Africa discussed the need for creating centers for advanced studies in applied science and technology, and the ECA secretariat undertook to examine the appropriate form that such a center might take if it were established in the region of Africa.

ECONOMIC COMMISION FOR ASIA AND THE FAR EAST (ECAFE)

The ECAFE region is vaster than those with which the other regional commissions deal, and its economic, social, religious, and cultural conditions are more diverse. ECAFE's work has evolved from fact-finding in support of reconstruction activities to systematic analysis of economic and technical problems relating to industry, trade, natural resources, transport, and allied matters. The commission has concentrated its attention largely on economic development, with special emphasis on projects of regional or subregional significance. ECAFE's primary interest is the formulation and application of policy. Its current program covers 12 subject fields: economic development and

planning, statistics, industrial development, mineral resource development, water resource development, agricultural development, transport, communications, social development, population, public administration, and promotion of trade.

To facilitate intraregional cooperation, ECAFE has helped establish a number of specialized institutions. The Asian Development Bank, for example, grew out of an ECAFE decision in the early 1960's on the need for a source of additional capital. Most of the other regional institutions have been established in connection with ECAFE's work in special fields. ECAFE has also pursued a policy of convening periodic ministerial conferences among its member countries. The 1968 conference, held in Bangkok, promulgated a "strategy for integrated regional cooperation." Follow-up action has included the appointment by governments of high-level "national units" and the creation within the ECAFE secretariat, where the continuing work of the commission is carried out, of a special task force to work toward specific goals in connection with the strategy. ECAFE also gives attention to ways of achieving regional growth within the framework of the second UN Development Decade (1971–1980) along guidelines adopted at the commission's 25th session in 1969.

DEVELOPMENT RESEARCH, PLANNING, AND STATISTICS

As a foundation for action programs, ECAFE's secretariat publishes an annual *Economic Survey of Asia and the Far East,* studies problems of development planning and plan harmonization, and aids national planning projects. In 1964 the Asian Institute for Economic Development and Planning was established as an autonomous body under ECAFE to provide training for regional personnel engaged in economic and social development programs in Asia. By the end of 1969 the institute had trained more than 1,000 fellows. A particularly striking example of regional cooperation and plan harmonization in a specified field has been the establishment of the Asian Coconut Community, which was formally inaugurated under ECAFE auspices in September 1969 and is the first association of Asian producers organized on a commodity basis. The community promotes, coordinates, and harmonizes all activities of the coconut industry throughout the region.

The preparation of the annual *Economic Survey* and other analytical studies required for effective planning emphasized the dearth of reliable data and data-gathering techniques in many Asian countries. To assist the improvement of national statistical services in the region, ECAFE in 1966 established a statistics division in its own secretariat. Its first issue of the *Statistical Yearbook for Asia and the Far East* was published in 1969. That same year the Asian Statistical Institute was set up in Tokyo as an outgrowth of an ECAFE resolution adopted in 1967. The institute is a joint undertaking of Asian governments and the UNDP, and its main function is to train official statisticians in the region. ECAFE is assisting countries in planning for the forthcoming round of population and housing censuses, in which nearly all member countries are expected to participate.

INDUSTRIAL DEVELOPMENT

The desire of less-developed countries to industrialize has increased their awareness of the complexities of industrialization. In the ECAFE Committee on Industry and Natural Resources, representatives of governments, business, and other interests annually review their industrial programs and measures for promoting industrialization. These measures may consist of improving programming techniques, feasibility surveys, investment promotion, industrial research and training, standardization and the establishment of joint enterprises among the countries. Particular attention is paid to the need for coordinating industrialization planning with development programs in other fields such as agriculture, home industry, transportation, communication, and education.

Recommendations for joint-venture petrochemical plants in several Asian countries were drawn up in July 1969. An Iron and Steel Institute for Southeast Asia, initiated by ECAFE, was inaugurated late in 1970. Located in Singapore, it is designed to foster regional cooperation in the development of these industries. Besides its work in the promotion of heavy industry, ECAFE also gives much attention to the modernization of cottage and small handicraft industries—textiles, ceramics, bamboo, lacquerware, leather goods—that continue to occupy an important place in the economies of many Asian states.

MINERAL RESOURCE DEVELOPMENT

ECAFE promotes regional geological surveys by developing various forms of cooperative action, such as study tours and joint use of modern laboratory and research facilities. A major ECAFE-sponsored project, completed in 1959, was the preparation of the first geological map ever made of Asia and the Far East. Since then, work has proceeded on a tectonic map for the entire region and on individual mineral maps to show both potential and known mineral-bearing areas. In addition, the ECAFE-sponsored Committee for Coordination of Joint Prospecting for Mineral Resources in Asian Offshore Areas (CCOP) promotes and coordinates explorations for undersea resources of mineral wealth adjacent to countries in the western Pacific region. Through a partnership involving 13 governments, specially equipped vessels, aircraft, and other facilities have been provided by industrialized countries to aid in offshore prospecting by developing nations. The fourth Symposium on the Development of the Petroleum Resources of Asia and the Far East was held in October 1969 to consider the utilization of these resources and methods of exploration and progress in the search for new deposits.

WATER RESOURCE DEVELOPMENT AND FLOOD CONTROL

Throughout history, the disastrous floods of Asia's great rivers have brought famine and death to the inhabitants of many areas of the continent. The initial task assigned to ECAFE's Bureau of Flood Control and Water Resources Development, on its establishment in 1949, was to study methods of flood control and related operations. But it soon became evident that flood control could best be approached in the context of multipurpose river basin development. The bureau therefore has emphasized the importance of unified river-basin development projects aiming not only at flood control but at hydroelectric power development, irrigation, inland navigation, and industrialization. To advance large-scale land reclamation, a Symposium on Development of Deltaic Areas was held in November 1969. And under the auspices of ECAFE's Water Resources Consulting Group, organized in 1967, experts from donor countries provide advisory services on water conservation and development. In 1968, ECAFE and WMO set up a Joint Unit on Typhoons to help in the task of minimizing the damage caused by typhoons and associated floods, which cost the region an estimated $500 million a year.

By far the largest water resources development project actively promoted by ECAFE is the Lower Mekong River Project. The Mekong is one of the world's great rivers. Its lower basin drains an area of 609,000 sq. km in four countries—Cambodia, Laos, Thailand, and Viet-Nam—and is inhabited by about 17 million people. Multipurpose development of the lower Mekong for flood control, power, improved navigation, and related purposes is directed by a committee of the four countries of the lower basin under the joint auspices of ECAFE and the UNDP. Resources equivalent to $200 million have come from the four countries, from 26 countries outside the region, and from several other UN bodies. Two major "tributary" projects were completed in Thailand and one in Laos by 1970, and work continues on plans for harnessing the Mekong River itself.

AGRICULTURAL DEVELOPMENT

Problems of agriculture in the region are dealt with by a Joint ECAFE-FAO Agriculture Division, whose activities include studies, meetings of expert groups, and advisory aid to ECAFE member governments. In October 1969, for example, an ECAFE-FAO expert group met in Bangkok to consider forecasts for the 1975 production of rice and other cereals, and possibilities for coping with an anticipated surplus of milled rice in the region.

TRANSPORT AND COMMUNICATIONS

ECAFE's Inland Transport and Communications Committee

and its subcommittees on railways, highways and inland waterways provide a forum for experts from within and outside the region for the exchange of knowledge and experience and the planning of relevant construction projects. One of ECAFE's most ambitious undertakings, the Asian Highway Project, launched in 1959, envisages a network of 60,000 km of highway covering 14 Asian countries. The project is being carried out in stages, by improving existing roads and connecting them with new ones. By late 1969, 83% of the network was judged motorable in all weathers, and 93% of the first through-route from west to east, Route A–1 from Iran to South Viet-Nam (10,000 km), had been completed. Work on the project is guided by the Asian Highway Coordinating Committee, composed of representatives of ministerial level from member countries, and its recommendations are carried out by the Asian Highway Transport Technical Bureau, based at ECAFE headquarters.

Another ambitious project, now under study, is a Trans-Asian Rail Network to provide greater uniformity of rail services in the region and permit links with Europe and Africa. The proposed network would run from Istanbul to Singapore and cover about 14,000 km. A joint unit of ECAFE and ITU is also laying the groundwork for establishing an integrated regional network of telecommunications services.

SOCIAL DEVELOPMENT, POPULATION, AND PUBLIC ADMINISTRATION

In keeping with the principle of the UN Development Decade that development is an integrated, balanced process in which economic and social factors interact, ECAFE is expanding its social programs. In 1969 the commission set up a Working Party on Social Development, which will meet every two years to review social trends in the region. The secretariat now provides advisory missions in social development planning and community development training.

Also in 1969, ECAFE established a Population Division in its secretariat to assist an expanded Asian Population Program, which gives high priority to improving the effectiveness of evaluation and training procedures in national family planning projects. Advisory services are available on request to governments of the region.

Public administration is likewise a relatively new field of ECAFE activity and includes surveys, regional advisory services, and seminars on such topics as national personnel systems, administrative reforms, and civil service training. In November 1969 a panel of experts drew up plans for a proposed Regional Center for Development Administration, designed to carry out high-level training and research to help meet the needs of Asian countries in this sphere.

PROMOTION OF TRADE

Through easing of customs formalities, promotional efforts, and improved regional payments arrangements, ECAFE seeks to help its members to expand both regional and worldwide trade. ECAFE's Trade Promotion Center, established in 1968, organizes training courses, offers advisory services to governments, and aids in national and international exhibitions designed to stimulate commerce. The First and Second International Trade Fairs, held respectively in Bangkok in 1966 and in Tehran in 1969, were arranged with the commission's support. ECAFE's Center for Shipping Information and Advisory Services, established in 1968, offers governments aid with such problems as freight rates, creation of shippers' councils, and development of merchant marines. To speed the flow of international trade, the commission has evolved a Code of Recommended Customs Procedures and fosters cooperation among customs officials to prevent fraud and smuggling. It also provides training facilities for customs officials in member countries. Since its inception in 1962, ECAFE's Center for Commercial Arbitration has drawn up standards and conducted research for improving arbitral facilities and practices in the region.

ECONOMIC COMMISSION FOR LATIN AMERICA (ECLA)

Since its inception, ECLA has recognized that Latin America's two most basic needs are to accelerate its rate of economic growth and to strengthen economic relations among the countries of the region and between the region and the rest of the world. The first is particularly urgent inasmuch as Latin America's rate of population increase is among the world's highest. By 1975, it is estimated, the region's population will reach 295 million, a 50% increase over its estimated population in 1959. In order for the standard of living, as measured by per capita income, to rise by 2% per year through that period, the gross product of the region would have to expand by 150% between 1959 and 1975, agricultural production by 90%, and industrial production (assuming a moderate growth in exports) by 200%. An annual per capita income growth of 2.7% would require a 300% increase in industrial production over the period 1959–1975. During the 1960's a more or less steady improvement in the rate of economic growth was sustained.

OVERALL ECONOMIC DEVELOPMENT AND PLANNING

Even at the earliest ECLA meetings, the participating governments realized that a vigorous development policy was necessary if economic growth was to be accelerated. At first, ECLA concentrated on fact finding and the preparation of comprehensive analytical studies, until then nonexistent, on long-term economic trends and development problems. This work has continued and been expanded. Topics have ranged from a study of Latin America's transportation to an inventory of its industrial activities, the development of which would best promote the expansion of trade and regional integration.

The industrial development division of the ECLA secretariat prepares industrial studies dealing with individual countries or particular industries. Recent studies, for example, of the chemical industries, pulp and paper, textiles, and heavy industrial equipment, stress the development possibilities offered by growing economic integration.

A series of studies on the role of agricultural commodities in the regional economy and in the Latin American common market has been carried out jointly by ECLA and FAO. In view of the great importance of coffee in the hemisphere's economy, coffee production, sales problems, and prospects receive much attention in these studies. A joint ECLA-FAO agricultural program has been under way since 1954. The fact that agriculture in Latin America develops too slowly to keep pace with the demands of a rapidly growing population has been of much concern to ECLA, which frequently has emphasized the need to do away with the outmoded agricultural institutions still existing in some countries and to improve the system of land tenure. In 1961 the Inter-American Committee for Agricultural Development (known by its Spanish initials CIDA) was established by the Organization of American States, the UN Food and Agriculture Organization (FAO), ECLA, the Inter-American Development Bank, and the Inter-American Institute of Agricultural Sciences. The work program drawn up by CIDA for the Joint ECLA-FAO Agricultural Division consists of two phases: basic studies on specific agricultural problems in Latin America, and assistance to governments, at their request, in the formulation and implementation of agricultural development and land reform plans.

The ECLA secretariat, in cooperation with other UN bodies and the specialized agencies, has for years assisted the governments of the region in economic development planning. Intensive economic development training courses for economists from Latin American countries have been organized and economic advisory groups have been set up to work with government economists and planners. Economic problems common to various countries of the region are discussed at ECLA-sponsored conferences. The problem of labor supply is closely related to development programming. This and other population questions are among those studies by the Latin American Demographic Center for Research and Training in Santiago, Chile. ECLA collaborates in the work of the center, which inaugurated regular training courses in 1958.

The growing attention that the member governments pay to development planning was shown in the establishment by ECLA in 1962 of the Latin American Institute for Economic and Social Planning (ILPES), with its headquarters at Santiago, Chile. Its function is, under the aegis of ECLA, to provide governments at their request with "training and advisory services" for the following purposes: (1) to raise the technical competence of government officials and specialists in development planning; (2) to assist governments in establishing the institutions required for the more efficient programming of their economic and social development policies; and (3) to assist governments, "at a purely technical level," in preparing their economic and social development programs. Another function of the institute is to undertake "the theoretical studies required for the improvement of planning techniques in Latin America." The head of the institute is appointed by the secretary-general of the UN after consultation with the institute's governing council.

ECONOMIC INTEGRATION
Although the common cultural heritage of the Latin American countries gives the continent a greater homogeneity than perhaps any other extensive region, economic relations between the various Latin American countries were extremely limited. Prior to the creation of ECLA and the Inter-American Economic and Social Council of the Organization of American States in 1948, no serious attempt to organize a cooperative program for trade and economic development for the region had been made. The two organizations have cooperated closely, maintaining close liaison to avoid duplication of effort. To facilitate economic liaison with the US, ECLA has a branch office in Washington.

During the 1950's and 1960's, a number of subregional organizations were set up to integrate economic development, especially intracontinental trade, throughout Latin America. Though these organizations are independent government bodies that function outside the aegis of the UN, they were established with the active partipation of ECLA, which continues to maintain a close liaison with each of them through its various branch offices and performs advisory services for them on request.

Economic Intergration of Central America. ECLA took the first steps toward the economic integration of the five small Central American republics, Costa Rica, El Salvador, Honduras, Guatemala, and Nicaragua, in 1951. In the following year, the ministers of economy of the five countries met at Tegucigalpa,

Honduras, and established the permanent Central American Economic Cooperation Committee. This committee, ECLA's first subsidiary organ, was to advise the Central American governments on measures for the gradual integration of their economies and the coordination of their national economic development programs. Three objectives were drawn up: the establishment of a Central American common market; the integrated industrial development of the five countries; and the coordination of fundamental aspects of agriculture and other basic economic sectors of the five countries.

A milestone on the road to Central American economic integration was reached in June 1958 when the five governments signed at Tegucigalpa the Multilateral Treaty on Free Trade and Economic Integration. This basic instrument was supplemented by three other treaties, also signed on that occasion: the Agreement on Central American Integration Industries; the Central American Agreement on Road Traffic; and the Central American Agreement on Uniform Road Signs and Signals. In the summer of 1959 the ministers of economy of the five republics signed a convention and protocol regarding equalization of tariffs on imports into the region. The protocol provided for an immediate 20% preferential tariff reduction on all goods imported from one of the five Central American states into another.

By 1962 the basic legal framework for the Central American Common Market was completed, and the countries turned their attention to the task of developing a regional economic policy. To this end, the Central American Bank for Economic Integration plays an important role, and the bank's special integration fund is used to finance basic projects of importance to the whole area. The continuing work of integration is conducted by the Permanent Secretariat or the General Treaty on Central American Economic Integration (known by its Spanish initials SIECA).

Latin American Free Trade Area. ECLA has given the highest priority to the preparatory work for a much more ambitious project, the gradual formation of a common market throughout Latin America. When the Central American Economic Cooperation Committee was first established, ECLA governments asked the commission to undertake a thorough study of the problems of inter-Latin American trade as a whole and measures that might be taken to expand it. Agreement was reached by 1955 that the creation of a regional Latin American common market was a desirable goal, but the free trade area so far established covers only the South American states and Mexico.

There followed another five years of studies and negotiations, with the active participation of the ECLA, regarding the structure and guiding principles of the scheme. Proposals often differed widely. The number of ECLA countries showing active interest fluctuated. The long-drawn-out preparations culminated in the Latin American Free Trade Area Treaty (LAFTA or, in its Spanish initials, ALALC), signed at Montevideo, Uruguay, on 18 February 1960. The original members were Argentina, Brazil, Chile, Mexico, Paraguay, Peru, and Uruguay. Bolivia, Colombia, Ecuador, and Venezuela joined at a later date. Hence, the free trade area now covers almost four-fifths of the territory of Latin America and is inhabited by approximately three fourths of Latin America's population. In production and trade of goods, the share of the LAFTA area is even higher.

The treaty obligates member countries to "make every effort . . . to reconcile their import and export regimes, as well as the treatment they accord to capital, goods, and services from outside the Area. . . ." They are to promote "progressively closer coordination of corresponding industrialization policies" and to persevere in establishing "gradually and progressively, a Latin American common market."

The timetable for this gradual and progressive abolition of

obstacles to trade between the participating countries is as follows. Each year, each member is to reduce the weighted average of its duties and charges against the other members by at least 8% of those applicable against nonmember countries. Concessions can be rescinded as long as the cumulative annual minimum average of 8% is maintained. Hence, for this major proportion of reciprocal trade, all restrictions are to be eliminated by 1973. Regarding the remaining goods, the members also "collectively agree to eliminate duties, charges, and other restrictions completely" by 1973. But for those goods the 8% annual reduction rule does not apply. Instead, concerning them, "common schedules" are to be negotiated every three years. Each common schedule lists the goods for which reductions have been agreed upon and the reductions granted. Goods put on the list cannot be withdrawn from it, nor can the specific concession be decreased. Special provisions regarding agricultural products permit continued trade restrictions where necessary.

The ECLA secretariat assists LAFTA in the establishment of norms and regulations, in the procedures for tariff negotiations, and in other ways. LAFTA has no formal relations with the Central American Common Market.

Formation of the Andean Subgroup. The high hopes that inspired the establishment of LAFTA have not been fully realized. Certain member countries were reluctant to relinquish part of their control over decisions on development and investment policy in favor of concerted action, while a majority of the other members wished to amend the Montevideo Treaty and expand its scope with a view to establishing a common market. Because of difficulties in reconciling these opposing positions, other courses of action were sought. The formation of subgroup treaties was proposed as a feasible solution. After lengthy negotiations, the Andean Subregional Integration Agreement was concluded in 1968 and subsequently declared to be compatible with the Montevideo Treaty. Parties to the agreement are Bolivia, Chile, Colombia, Ecuador, and Peru. At their meeting in October 1969, these countries requested the secretariats of ECLA and the Latin American Institute for Economic and Social Planning to prepare a preliminary study on joint programming approaches and methods, the area's industrial possibilities, and requirements for its balanced development.

Establishment of the Caribbean Free Trade Association and the East Caribbean Common Market. The decolonization during the 1960's of several of the UK's territories in the Caribbean created a new subregion within the Latin America area. Recognizing that these Caribbean countries form a homogeneous group whose economic patterns, as well as cultural traditions, are quite distinct from those of the other Latin American countries, the Caribbean Free Trade Association (CARIFTA) was established in 1968. In addition to the independent nations of Jamaica, Guyana, Barbados, and Trinidad and Tobago, CARIFTA's membership includes the several tiny associated island states that are still in part British-administered—Antigua, Dominica, Grenada, St. Kitts-Nevis-Anguilla, St. Lucia, Montserrat, and St. Vincent—and that have established an East Caribbean Common Market within its area. The aims of CARIFTA are expansion and diversification of trade, development of intra-Caribbean trade, balanced and progressive development of national economies, and equitable distribution of the benefits of free trade.

ECONOMIC AND SOCIAL DEVELOPMENT

The Charter Declaration on International Economic and Social Cooperation enjoins UN members to cooperate in promoting higher standards of living, full employment, and conditions of economic and social progress and development. The fostering of economic and social development, however, was only one of several objectives specified in the Charter, and no special emphasis was accorded to it. Yet in his *Five-Year Perspective,* published in 1960, Secretary-General Dag Hammarskjöld said that the most clearly marked trend in the work of the United Nations organizations in the economic, social, and human rights fields was the shift in emphasis to development. The League of Nations and the early International Labor Organization were concerned primarily with defensive or protective action—the protection of countries against diseases that might cross international frontiers; prevention of international traffic in women and children and in illicit drugs; protection of workers against unfair and inhumane conditions of labor. Such early action in the economic and social fields was taken in a climate of thought that hardly recognized the concept of economic development.

Toward the middle of this century, however, the idea of development as a major objective of international cooperation took root in the international scene, and the major goal of the United Nations and the specialized agencies in the economic and social fields came to be promoting the development of the less developed countries.

THE RICH AND THE POOR NATIONS

The UN's preoccupation with development is rooted in the sharp division of its membership between rich nations and poor nations: a division that the secretary-general has frequently characterized as a leading long-term threat to world peace and security.

In 1945, when the UN was established, this sharp dichotomy could not be drawn between its members. The wealth of Europe had been wasted by the ravages of war. Only the US could claim to be rich, and even the US, with the depression of the 1930's still a fresh memory, could not be confident of lasting prosperity. What made the challenge of development central to the thinking of every aspiring country was the rapidity with which the countries of Western Europe recovered their prosperity and went on to attain higher levels of economic and social well-being than they had ever experienced before. Meanwhile, economic expansion continued apace in the more prosperous countries that had not been hurt by the war—the US, Canada, Australia, and New Zealand. And within a few years, in Asia, the miracle of Japan's recovery and growth was matching Europe's postwar record.

Nothing comparable occurred among the colonial peoples and former colonial peoples. Tropical Asia, Africa, and Latin America had been cultivated in preceding generations largely as appendages to industrial Europe and North America—on the one hand supplying essential primary commodities not commonly found in the temperate regions and on the other hand serving as profitable markets for consumer goods produced in the temperate regions. The peoples of these economically underdeveloped areas made rapid political progress in the postwar era. Significant economic progress was also recorded in a number of these countries, so that by the late 1950's it was considered not only tactful but proper to refer to them as "developing" rather than "underdeveloped" nations. As a group, however, the developing countries were far outdistanced in economic growth by the temperate zone industrialized countries, which were finding the postwar era the most propitious in history for their development. Before the UN had completed its first 15 years, it was abundantly evident that a very disturbing gap had opened up between the industrialized and the developing nations and that, despite very substantial foreign aid efforts, the gap was growing broader year by year.

SCOPE OF THE UN'S WORK AND OF THE PRESENT CHAPTER

The international community was not slow to recognize the political and economic dangers inherent in such an imbalance of national wealth. As early as 1946, when "recovery" rather than "development" dominated UN thinking on economic matters, the General Assembly requested ECOSOC to study ways and means of furnishing advice to nations desiring help in developing their resources. As a result the UN, in cooperation with the specialized agencies of the UN system, began its first programs of technical assistance. The numerous economic and social subsidiary bodies of ECOSOC have undertaken exhaustive studies of particular aspects and techniques of development, and the UN has become the world's leading publisher of information in this field.

In its programs of aid to development, the UN has drawn on almost every field of economic, social, and administrative expertise. Its activities have ranged from assigning junior international officials to national posts to helping governments in the establishment of long-range national development targets.

The UN's activities in the sphere of development are too diverse and numerous to detail here. This chapter therefore confines itself to the principles and goals of the UN development effort, the technological scope of the UN's work, the problem of financing development (through external aid and the expansion of trade), and the major programs undertaken by the UN to assist countries in specific demonstration and preinvestment projects.

The principles and goals of the UN development effort are best considered in connection with the first UN Development Decade, which was launched in 1961 as a framework for coordinated international action, and the international development strategy for the second Development Decade adopted by the General Assembly in 1970.

THE FIRST DEVELOPMENT DECADE

The terms of reference for international cooperation during the first Development Decade were as follows:

(1) *Statement of the Overall Objectives.* Member states will intensify their efforts to mobilize support for measures required to accelerate progress toward self-sustaining growth of the economy of the individual nations and their social advancement so as to attain in each developing country an increase in the rate of growth, with each country setting its own target, taking as the objective a minimum rate of growth of aggregate national income of 5% at the end of the decade.

(2) *Principles for Action on Financial Aspects.* All member states should pursue policies designed to enable the developing countries to sell more of their products at stable and remunerative prices in expanding markets so as to enable them to finance more of their economic development. Member states should follow policies designed to ensure developing countries an equitable share of earnings from extraction and marketing of their natural resources by foreign capital. Member states should pursue policies that will lead to an increase in the flow of developmental resources to developing countries on mutually acceptable terms, and adopt policies that will stimulate the flow of private capital to developing countries on mutually satisfactory terms. In a resolution adopted in 1960, the Assembly had recommended that the flow of international capital and assistance to developing countries should be about 1% of the combined national incomes of the economically advanced countries.

(3) *Concrete Proposals for Action.* The secretary-general will submit action proposals with particular reference to industrialization and agricultural development; formulation of development plans; improved use of international institutions for economic and social development; elimination of hunger and disease; promotion of all forms of education; promotion of trade; review of facilities for the provision of basic statistical data; and utilization of resources released by disarmament.

SECRETARY-GENERAL'S PROPOSALS

The secretary-general's report *The United Nations Development Decade Proposals for Action* dealt with development planning, mobilization of human resources, sectoral development, international trade, development financing and technical cooperation.

Having elaborated the basic concepts of the Development Decade, the secretary-general observed that a number of unsolved problems carried over from the previous decade seemed to call for urgent attention. He specified seven of these problems: improvement in development planning within countries; instability of commodity prices; assurance of continuing and increased flow of foreign capital to developing countries; increase in agricultural and industrial output; development and application of science and technology; social reform.

Referring to the attainment of a 5% growth rate, the secretary-general estimated that if the flow of capital from the wealthier countries to the developing countries reached the target level of 1% of the former's combined national incomes, this would double net capital formation in the developing countries and would raise the rate of growth of their aggregate incomes by about half the amount required. It was estimated that the difference could be picked up if the developing countries' terms of trade could be improved by 10% and their exports increased by about 5% a year throughout the decade.

ASSESSMENT OF PROGRESS AT MIDPOINT IN THE DECADE

In his appraisal of the decade at midpoint (1965), the secretary-general noted the harsh fact that many of the poorest economies had continued to grow most slowly. The growth in developing countries as a whole slowed down from an average annual rate of 4.5% in 1955–60 to 4% in 1960–63. At the same time the growth rate in the economically advanced market economies had accelerated from 3.4% in the earlier period to 4.4% in 1960–63. The gap between the per capita incomes of the developing countries and those of the developed countries had also widened. Between 1960 and 1962 the average annual per capita income in the developed market economies increased by almost $100, while that in the developing countries increased by barely $5. Two thirds of the world's population living in the less developed regions of the world still had less than one sixth of the world's income. In 1962 annual per capita income in these regions averaged $136 while that of the population of the economically advanced market economies in North America and Western Europe averaged $2,845 and $1,033, respectively.

The secretary-general reported in 1969 that the slower progress in development had been accompanied by the emergence or aggravation of major imbalances which imperiled future growth. Without greater progress in food production and the more effective control of communicable diseases, the necessary conditions for steady economic and social development could hardly be said to have been laid. Further, compared with the 1950's, the constraint on domestic growth imposed by persistent scarcity of foreign exchange had been experienced by many more developing countries. Although the strong upward thrust of economic activity exhibited by some major developed countries had been transmitted in some measure to the export earnings of the developing world, this had been accompanied neither by a steady improvement in the terms of trade of developing countries nor by any comparable extension in the flow of external assistance. The terms of trade had, if anything, weakened since 1960, and the total flow of external assistance to the developing countries in 1964 was still below the peak recorded in the second year of the decade. The prospects for attaining the objectives for the decade had dimmed with the passage of time.

However, the secretary-general pointed out that the experience of a few countries had undoubtedly demonstrated that "given a favorable constellation of circumstances and policies, an adequate and sustained pace of development can be achieved." The secretary-general also said that acceptance of development as a fundamental objective had gradually wrought a desirable change in attitudes and modes of action on the part of developing countries. Public decisions were no longer made solely in response to immediate expediency, and policies and programs previously decided in relative isolation were gradually being integrated and harnessed to a common purpose. At an international level, the secretary-general noted that the institutional machinery for the review and advancement of international policies had been considerably strengthened by the creation of such bodies as the UN Conference on Trade and Development (UNCTAD), the Advisory Committee on Science and Technology, and the Committee for Development Planning.

The first UN Development Decade ended in December 1970 with one of its major goals, the attainment of a 5% growth rate, unattained in the developing countries. During the period 1960–67 these countries achieved an annual rate of increase in their total domestic product of about 4.6%; but in view of the population increase, the increase in their per capita gross product reached only about 2%. The Assembly concluded that one of the reasons for the slow progress was the absence of a framework of international development strategy.

THE SECOND DEVELOPMENT DECADE

At its 25th session, in 1970, the General Assembly adopted a resolution outlining international development strategy for the second UN Development Decade for the 1970's.

The main objective of the plan is to promote sustained economic growth, particularly in the developing countries, to ensure a higher standard of living, and to facilitate the process of narrowing the gap between the developed and developing countries.

The Assembly declared that the developing countries bore primary responsibility for their development but that their efforts would be insufficient without increased financial assistance and more favorable economic and commercial policies on the part of the developed countries.

Under goals and objectives of the second decade, the Assembly stated that the average annual rate of growth in the gross product of the developing countries as a whole should be at least 6%, with the possibility of attaining a higher rate in the second half of the decade. Each developing country should set its own target for growth according to its own circumstances.

The average annual rate of growth of gross product per capita in developing countries as a whole during the decade should be about 3.5%, with the possibility of accelerating it during the second half of the decade.

Such a growth rate will represent a doubling of average income per capita in the course of two decades. The target for growth in average income per head is calculated on the basis of an average annual increase of 2.5% in the population of developing countries, which is less than the average rate forecast for the 1970's.

An average annual rate of growth of at least 6% in the gross product of developing countries during the decade will imply an average annual expansion of 4% in agricultural output and 8% in manufacturing output.

For attaining the overall growth target of at least 6% per year, there should be an average annual expansion of 0.5% in the ratio of gross domestic saving to the gross product, so that this ratio would rise to around 20% by 1980, and somewhat less than 7% in imports and somewhat higher than 7% in exports. The Assembly stated that it is essential to bring about a more equitable distribution of income and wealth for promoting social justice and efficiency of production; to raise substantially the level of employment; to achieve a greater degree of income security; to expand and improve facilities for education, health, nutrition, housing, and social welfare; and to safeguard the environment. Thus qualitative and structural changes in society must go hand in hand with rapid economic growth, and existing disparities—regional, sectoral, and social—should be substantially reduced. These objectives are both determining factors and end results of development and should therefore be viewed as integrated parts of the same dynamic process.

POLICY MEASURES

Under policy measures the Assembly stated that the goals and objectives call for a continuing effort by all peoples and governments to promote economic and social progress in developing countries by the formulation and implementation of a coherent set of policy measures. The Assembly called on all governments to solemnly resolve to adopt and implement the following policy measures.

International Trade

All efforts will be made to secure international action before 31 December 1972, including, where appropriate, the conclusion of international agreements or arrangements on commodities specified by UNCTAD. Commodities already covered by international agreements or arrangements should be kept under review.

All possible resources for the prefinancing of buffer stocks, when necessary, will be considered when concluding or reviewing commodity agreements incorporating buffer stock mechanisms.

Efforts will be made to reach agreement, before the third UNCTAD session, on a set of general principles on pricing policy to serve as guidelines for consultations and actions on individual commodities.

No new tariff and nontariff barriers will be raised nor will the existing ones be increased by developed countries against imports of primary products of particular interest to developing countries.

Developed countries will accord priority to reducing or eliminating duties and other barriers to imports of primary products by the end of 1972.

Developed countries will give increased attention within the framework of bilateral and multilateral programs to supplement the resources of the developing countries in their endeavor to accelerate the diversification of their economies. Specific funds for diversification will be one of the features of commodity arrangements wherever considered necessary.

Appropriate action, including the provision of finance, will be taken, as far as practicable, to initiate intensive research and development efforts designed to improve market conditions and cost efficiency and to diversify the end uses of natural products facing competition from synthetics and substitutes.

The machinery for consultation on surplus disposal that existed during the 1960's will be widened and reinforced in order to avoid or minimize possible adverse effects of disposals of production surpluses or strategic reserves, including those of minerals, on normal commercial trade and to take account of the interest of both surplus and deficit countries.

Arrangements concerning the establishment of generalized, nondiscriminatory, nonreciprocal preferential treatment to exports of developing countries in the markets of developed countries have been drawn up by UNCTAD and considered mutually acceptable to developed and developing countries. Preference-giving countries are determined to seek as rapidly as possible the necessary legislative or other sanction with the aim of implementing the preferential arrangements as early as possible.

Developed countries will not, ordinarily, raise existing tariff or nontariff barriers to exports from developing countries nor establish new tariff or nontariff barriers or any discriminatory measures, where such action has the effect of rendering less favorable the conditions of access to the markets of manufactured and semimanufactured products of export interest to developing countries.

Intergovernmental consultations will be continued and intensified with a view to giving effect to measures for the relaxation and progressive elimination of nontariff barriers affecting trade in manufactures and semimanufactures of interest to developing countries. Efforts will be made with a view to implementing such measures before 31 December 1972.

Developed countries will consider adopting measures and, where possible, evolving a program for assisting the adaptation and adjustment of industries and workers in situations where they are, or may be threatened to be, adversely affected by increased imports of manufactures and semimanufactures from developing countries.

Developing countries will intensify their efforts to make greater use of trade promotion as effective international assistance will be provided.

Restrictive business practices particularly affecting the trade and development of the developing countries will be identified by 31 December 1972 with a view to the consideration of appropriate remedial measures.

The Socialist countries of Eastern Europe will take into consideration the trade needs of the developing countries and in particular their production and export potential. They will promote the diversification of the structure and geographical basis of their trade with developing countries in order that the largest number of developing countries derive the maximum benefit from this trade.

Trade Expansion
The developing countries will continue their efforts to negotiate and put into effect further commitments for instituting the schemes for regional and subregional integration or measures of trade expansion among themselves.

The developed market economy countries will, through the extension of financial and technical assistance or through action in the field of commercial policy, support initiatives in regional and subregional cooperation of developing countries. The Socialist countries of Eastern Europe will extend their full support within the framework of their socioeconomic system.

Financial Resources for Development
Developing countries must bear the main responsibility for financing their development. To this end, they will pursue sound fiscal and monetary policies and, as required, remove institutional obstacles through the adoption of appropriate legislative and administrative reforms. They will keep the increase in their current public expenditure under close scrutiny with a view to releasing maximum resources for investment.

Each economically advanced country should endeavor to provide by 1972 annually to developing countries financial resource transfers of a minimum net amount of 1% of its gross national product at market prices in terms of actual disbursements, having regard to the special position of those countries which are net importers of capital.

In recognition of the special importance of the role that can be fulfilled only by official development assistance, a major part of financial resource transfers to the developing countries should be provided in the form of official development assistance.

Developed countries will consider measures aimed at the further softening of the terms of assistance and will endeavor to arrive at a more precise assessment of the circumstances of the individual developing countries and at a greater harmonization of terms given by developed countries to developing countries.

Financial assistance, in principle, will be untied. While this may not be possible in all cases, developed countries will take what measures they can to reduce the tying of assistance and to mitigate any harmful effects. Where loans are tied essentially to particular sources, developed countries will make such loans available for utilization by the recipient countries for the purchase of goods and services from other developing countries.

Financial and technical assistance should be aimed exclusively at promoting the economic and social progress of developing countries and should not be used by the developed countries to the detriment of the national sovereignty of recipient countries.

Developed countries will provide an increased flow of aid on a long-term and continuing basis and simplify the procedure for the granting and expeditious disbursement of aid.

Arrangements for forecasting and, if possible, forestalling debt crises will be improved.

The volume of resources made available through multilateral institutions for financial and technical assistance will be increased to the fullest extent possible, and techniques will be evolved to enable them to fulfill their role in the most effective manner.

Developing countries will adopt appropriate measures for inviting, stimulating, and making effective use of foreign private capital.

Invisibles, Including Shipping
The objective is to promote, by national and international action, the earnings of developing countries from invisible trade and to minimize the net outflow of foreign exchange from those countries arising from invisible transactions, including shipping.

The terms and conditions on which bilateral aid and commercial credit are available for the purchase of ships by developing countries should be kept under review in the light of relevant resolutions of UNCTAD.

Developing countries will expand their tourist industry through the building of tourist infrastructure, adoption of promotional measures, and relaxation of travel restrictions. Developed countries will assist in this endeavor.

Special Measures for Least Developed Countries
While it is the objective of the decade to achieve the rapid economic and social progress of all developing countries, special measures will be taken to enable the least developed among them to overcome their particular disabilities. Wherever necessary, supplementary measures will be devised and implemented at the national, subregional, regional, and international levels.

National and international financial institutions will accord appropriate attention to the special needs of landlocked developing countries by extending financial and technical assistance to projects for the development and improvement of their transport and communications systems.

Science and Technology
Concerted efforts will be made by the developing countries, with appropriate assistance from the rest of the world community, to expand their science and technology capability for development so as to significantly reduce the technological gap.

Developing countries will continue to increase their expenditure for research and development and will endeavor to attain, by the end of the decade, a minimum average level equivalent to 0.5% of their gross product. Full international cooperation will be extended for the establishment, strengthening, and promotion of scientific research and technological activities that have a bearing on the expansion and modernization of the economies of developing countries. Within the framework of their individual aid and technical assistance programs, developed countries will substantially increase their aid for the direct support of science and technology in developing countries during the decade.

Developed and developing countries and competent international organizations will draw up and implement a program for promoting the transfer of technology to developing countries.

Human Development
Those developing countries which consider that their rate of population growth hampers their development will adopt measures that they deem necessary in accordance with their concept of development. Developed countries, consistent with their national policies, will upon request provide support through the supply of means for family planning and further research. International organizations concerned will continue to provide the assistance that may be requested by interested governments.

Developing countries will formulate and implement educational programs taking into account their development needs. Educational and training programs will be so designed as to increase productivity substantially in the short run and to reduce waste.

Developing countries will establish at least a minimum program of health facilities comprising an infrastructure of institutions, including those for medical training and research for bringing basic medical services within the reach of a specified proportion of their population by the end of the decade.

Developing countries will adopt policies consistent with their agricultural and health programs in an effort toward meeting their nutritional requirements.

Developing countries will adopt suitable national policies for involving children and youth in the development process and for ensuring that their needs are met in an integrated manner.

Developing countries will take steps to provide improved housing and related community facilities in both urban and rural areas, especially for low-income groups.

Governments will intensify national and international efforts to arrest the deterioration of the human environment and to take measures toward its improvement, and to promote activities that will help to maintain the ecological balance on which human survival depends.

Expansion and Diversification of Production

Developing countries will take specific steps to augment production and improve productivity in order to provide goods and services necessary for raising levels of living and improving economic viability. They will take steps to develop the full potential of their natural resources. Concerted efforts will be made, particularly through international assistance, to enable them to prepare an inventory of natural resources for their more rational utilization in all productive activities.

Developing countries will formulate appropriate strategies for agriculture including animal husbandry, fisheries, and forestry designed to secure a more adequate food supply, to expand rural employment, and to increase export earnings. They will undertake, as appropriate, reform of land tenure systems for promoting both social justice and farm efficiency. International organizations will also provide appropriate support.

Developing countries will take parallel steps to promote industry in order to achieve rapid expansion, modernization, and diversification of their economies. They will seek to prevent emergence of unutilized capacity in industries, especially through regional groupings wherever possible. Developed countries and international organizations will assist in this task.

Developing countries will enlarge their transport and communication facilities, and their supplies of energy. They will seek, where appropriate, to achieve this purpose through regional and subregional groupings. International financial and technical assistance will support their endeavors.

Plan Formulation and Implementation

Developing countries will establish or strengthen their planning mechanisms, including statistical services, for formulating and implementing their national development plans during the decade.

Review and Appraisal of Objectives and Policies

Appropriate arrangements are necessary to keep under systematic scrutiny the progress toward achieving the goals and objectives of the decade—to identify shortfalls in their achievement and the factors that account for them and to recommend positive measures, including new goals and policies as needed.

At the national level, each developing country will, where appropriate, establish evaluation machinery or strengthen the existing one and, whenever necessary, seek international assistance for this purpose. Particular attention will be devoted to improving and strengthening national programming and statistical services.

An overall appraisal of the progress in implementing the international development strategy will be made by the General Assembly, through the Economic and Social Council.

MOBILIZATION OF PUBLIC OPINION

An essential part of the work during the decade will consist of the mobilization of world public opinion in support of the objectives and policies for the decade. Governments of the more advanced countries will continue and intensify their endeavor to deepen public understanding of the interdependent nature of the development efforts during the decade—in particular of the benefits accruing to them from international cooperation for development—and of the need to assist the developing countries in accelerating their economic and social progress. The efforts of developing countries themselves to meet the requirements of their economic and social progress need to be more clearly and more generally made known in developed countries. Similarly, governments of the developing countries will continue to make people at all levels aware of the benefits and sacrifices involved and to enlist their full participation in achieving the objectives of the decade.

TECHNICAL COOPERATION FOR DEVELOPMENT

In the secretary-general's *Appraisal of the UN Development Decade at Mid-point,* development is described as "the process whereby, at different times and at different speeds but with complete irreversibility, the whole human race is adapting to its use of the modern instruments of science and technology. This process involves all mankind—from the commuter in modern Megalopolis to the herdsman on the Saharan fringe." The appraisal remarks that "one forgets how much in earlier technological advance was based on uncertain experiment and lucky guess. Above all, one forgets the mystery in which the whole process of modernization was shrouded. The early entrepreneurs tried out new processes, tested the market, made a profit—or perhaps were ruined—and all the time they were unwittingly changing the face of the earth." Today, however, development is no longer left to the chance occurrence of haphazard inventions. Instead, it has become a conscious objective of endeavor. The connotation of development has broadened into an overall concept of "growth plus change" in all spheres of economic and social life. In developed and developing countries alike, development has become a process that is rationalized, fostered, and planned for.

The problems of development confronting today's rich and poor are scarcely comparable. Whereas the developed countries seek to build upon what has already been achieved, most of the developing countries are only just embarking on the modern, technological phase of their development. For them, development is essentially a process of "catching-up."

Through the UN and the specialized agencies, nations cooperate in mounting a multi-pronged attack on the technological problems of development.

DEVELOPMENT PLANNING

One natural outcome of the rationalization of the development process has been an emphasis on planning. National economic planning has guided for some time the development efforts of several industrialized countries. The concept of development planning is not a new one, but its successful application to the developing countries poses peculiar difficulties.

Almost all the organizations in the UN family contribute in one way or another to development planning—by helping to evolve and introduce new planning methods, by assisting governments in establishing realistic growth targets, and by trying to ensure that overall plans take account of the needs of the different sectors of society.

Development planning is reviewed by the Committee for Development Planning. A subsidiary body of ECOSOC, the committee is composed of 18 experts representing different planning systems. At its first session, in May 1966, the committee adopted as its terms of reference four major functions: the consideration and evaluation of planning and projections within the UN family of organizations (including the specialized agencies); consideration and evaluation of progress in the transfer of knowledge to the developing countries and in the training of personnel in development planning and projections; the analysis of major world trends in planning problems and solutions; and the study of such individual planning and programming questions as might be referred to its consideration.

PROVISION OF BASIC STATISTICAL DATA

The Statistical Office of the UN Secretariat provides a substantial portion of the essential data used by the various organizations within the UN system that are concerned with economic and social development. The office puts out the following periodical data publications: *Statistical Yearbook, Demographic Yearbook, Yearbook of National Accounts Statistics, Yearbook of International Trade Statistics, World Energy Supplies, Commodity Trade Statistics, Population and Vital Statistics Report,* and *Monthly Bulletin of Statistics.*

The Statistical Commission (a functional commission of ECOSOC), in October 1966, discussed three major topics: the extension and revision of the UN system of national accounts to provide more adequate data for economic and social analysis and a framework for developing and coordinating basic statistics; recommendations for the world population and housing censuses held in 1970; and the coordination of an integrated five-year program of international statistics undertaken in conjunction with the principal agencies working in the statistical field.

APPLICATION OF SCIENCE AND TECHNOLOGY TO DEVELOPMENT

In his *Appraisal of the UN Development Decade at Mid-point,* the secretary-general pointed out that in one respect the developing nations are better situated than the industrial pioneers of earlier centuries, since they have at their disposal the vast body of scientific and technical knowledge accumulated by the industrialized countries. On the other hand, the secretary-general observed, much of the knowledge pertains to other societies and other times and does not always fit in with the needs of emergent countries. For example, modern industrial technology largely is geared to societies where labor is scarce and capital abundant, whereas in the developing countries just the opposite conditions obtain.

Recognizing that the developing countries have special requirements in regard to the application of science and technology, ECOSOC in 1964 established an Advisory Committee on the Application of Science and Technology to Development, composed of 18 experts. In 1966 the committee adopted a comprehensive World Plan of Action for the Application of Science and Technology to Development. The plan, which carries science and technology into all spheres of development, has these principal elements: (1) a five-year plan for the development of basic structures in science and technology in developing countries; (2) a series of objectives to be implemented over a five-year period for science education in developing countries; (3) a program aimed at improving documentation and tech-

nology transfer processes in developing countries; (4) an intensified attack on specific problems of concern to developing countries, through the application of existing knowledge and the acquisition of new knowledge; (5) a program to encourage scientific efforts in developed countries to assist the developing countries in their problems.

In 1970 the Assembly called on governments to give due attention to the promotion of science and technology in their national policies. It noted the recommendations and the world plan of action formulated by the Advisory Committee on the Application of Science and Technology to Development.

The Assembly requested the secretary-general to prepare a study, in consultation with member states and competent organizations within the UN system, which would evaluate the main implications of modern science and technology, particularly for development; appraise the results achieved by the UN system and the difficulties encountered; suggest ways and means of implementing various recommendations and measures agreed upon, and of removing difficulties that have been identified; and suggest practical ways and means of strengthening international cooperation in new applications of science and technology in the economic and social fields.

The secretary-general's study is to be submitted to member states and competent UN organizations for analysis and discussion. It will then be examined by the ECOSOC and the Assembly.

TRAINING OF SKILLED PERSONNEL

All the specialized agencies and many UN subsidiary bodies promote the training of personnel in their respective fields of activity. Training schemes are not usually integrated with plans in such fields as production, investment, finance, and trade. The responsibility for organizing training is often divided.

The UN itself has initiated research and operational programs in industrial training at three levels: for public officials who deal with the process of industrial development; for engineers and technicians in specific branches of industry; and for higher level technical personnel in specialized fields of management. UN technical assistance programs provide large numbers of experts, part of whose work is to train local personnel in social development and public administration. The UN's services in the field of training were enhanced by the establishment in 1964 of the UN Institute of Training and Research (UNITAR). This is an autonomous body within the UN, financed entirely by voluntary contributions, whose chief function is to train personnel (particularly from developing countries) for administrative and operational assignments with the UN and the specialized agencies. The Institute of Training also offers a small number of UNITAR–Adlai E. Stevenson Memorial Fellowships (sponsored by the US) to enable a select group of men and women to improve their competence for public, national, or international service related to the objectives of the UN. As of June 1970, UNITAR had received $6,560,941 in voluntary contributions. Of this amount, $5,424,129 was paid by governments and $774,612 by nongovernmental sources, with $362,200 constituting special purpose grants.

Among the new training activities undertaken in 1970 are the holding of UNITAR weekends for diplomats and scholars and a study concerning the feasibility of a United Nations staff college. In the field of research, UNITAR has completed studies on questions relating to the use by mass media of public information on the United Nations; the comparative effectiveness of measures against racial discrimination; the "brain drain"; the verification of international treaties—for example, IAEA safeguards machinery; relations between the United Nations and intergovernmental organizations; and problems of the human environment.

In the introduction to his annual report, the secretary-general in 1969 put forward the idea for an international university. The Assembly welcomed the secretary-general's initiative and asked for a feasibility study. This study, submitted to the Assembly in 1970, deals with such subjects as possible curricula, selection of sites and recruitment of faculty and method of financing. It proposed a fund with an initial target of $100 million.

PROMOTING POPULAR PARTICIPATION IN DEVELOPMENT

Without the wholehearted participation of peoples in their own development, no plan, however well conceived, is likely to succeed. One of the most important factors contributing to the disappointing results in development progress is its failure to command popular support. A UN study reports that unfavorable social conditions, such as unemployment, low wages, inadequate diet, poor housing, lack of education, and "institutional short-comings" are in themselves a deterrent to popular participation in development. The study concludes that such measures as land reform, tax reform, and a partial redistribution of wealth may be essential prerequisites for popular participation in development in many countries.

Drawing on the opinion of some 400 national experts who have worked on local development projects, the UN study discusses problems in enlisting citizen cooperation. Issues considered include the choice of population groups to be used for introducing innovations; criteria for priorities; channels and methods of information; the education process as an instrument of social change; various incentives and other kinds of appeal; and prerequisites of local planning. The study also notes that "very substantial improvements in living conditions could be achieved if local populations would adopt certain changes or innovations derived from modern science and technology in their methods of production, their food habits, health practices, ways of building houses, etc.—which do not require particular skills or education or expensive equipment."

THE POPULATION PROBLEM

The ever-expanding population of the developing countries is a major problem adversely affecting the development process. The rapid population growth is resulting in an increase in the proportion of peoples in the dependent age groups; in a heavy influx of people to urban areas, thereby causing serious disruptions in economic and social patterns; and in a steady decline of food output per person. In many developing countries the rate of population growth amounts to 3% or more a year—sufficient to double the population in less than 25 years. Demographic projections, based on anticipated fertility trends, show world population rising from approximately 3 billion in 1960 to 4.3 billion by 1980 and to over 6 billion by the end of the century.

The problems attendant upon the population growth received a thorough airing at the second World Population Conference held in Belgrade in 1965, and a nontechnical summary of the deliberations was published in a booklet entitled *World Population: Challenge to Development*. However, no formal resolutions or specific recommendations were adopted by the conference, which had as its purpose the improvement in understanding of population problems, particularly with respect to development. Moreover, the matter of birth control raises delicate moral issues that prevent the UN from giving any blanket endorsement to measures of family planning. However, during ECOSOC discussions of population questions, a number of delegates expressed the view that the UN should undertake generally to assist governments, upon request, in the planning and implementation of "action programs." The UN Advisory Mission on Family Planning to India was cited as an example

of the kind of practical assistance that the UN could make available to developing countries if they so desired. During a 1965 session, ECOSOC endorsed the recommendations of its Population Commission for a long-range work program aimed at increasing the supply of technically trained demographers in developing countries, expanding and intensifying research and technical work, improving the collection of basic data and statistics, and enlarging the program of conferences. ECOSOC also requested the secretary-general to provide advisory services and training on action programs at the request of governments. It was agreed, however, that the UN and the specialized agencies should not recommend any particular population policies to governments.

ECOSOC, in its report for 1969–70, suggested that 1974, the year of the third Population Conference, be World Population Year to help focus world opinion on the various aspects of population problems and on the need to stimulate efforts to cope with them.

SPECIFIC AREAS OF DEVELOPMENT

A number of specific fields of development—education, health, agriculture, labor relations, postal communications, telecommunications—are the concern of the specialized agencies described in Part II of this volume. Although the UN, through the Assembly and ECOSOC, generally oversees the aggregate of development activities carried out within the UN system, its immediate concern is with four sectors: administrative and social reform; housing, building, and physical planning; industrial development; and development of nonagricultural natural resources.

ADMINISTRATIVE AND SOCIAL REFORM

Proper administrative and institutional machinery is essential for mobilizing people in the cause of development. In particular, there is a need for land tenure and tax reform. Outdated land tenure systems hinder efforts to develop agriculture and modernize farming communities. Together with the FAO, the UN organized a World Land Reform Conference at Rome in June 1966, with the object of identifying basic problems and thereby encouraging governments to take action. It is recognized that research into methods for improving the basic administrative machinery for development should be accelerated. Toward this end, it has been proposed that the UN draw up a draft inventory of practical research needs and convene a conference to review proposals for research and explore means of financing.

HOUSING, BUILDING, AND PHYSICAL PLANNING

The target for housing construction set in the secretary-general's 1962 Proposals for Action was a ratio of 10 dwelling units for each 1,000 of population in the developing countries, at a combined cost for dwelling plus facilities of $1,000 per unit in urban areas and $200 in rural areas. However, in his *Appraisal of the Development Decade at Mid-point*, the secretary-general reported that the average rate of construction was only 2 new dwellings per 1,000 inhabitants and that the cost of housing units for low-income families was about three times as high as the original targets. In 1970, the General Assembly recommended that member states, with the assistance of UN bodies, should formulate definite and long-term housing, building, and planning policies and programs for the improvement of human settlements. To this end, it should devote particular attention to the problem of rapid and uncontrolled urbanization; the application of comprehensive planning; and the development of the building industry and building technology.

The Assembly declared that a Center for Housing, Building, and Planning should play a major role in the formulation, coordination, and implementation of UN programs and projects relating to housing and human settlements. In addition, the work of the center should be given high priority, aided by a greater allocation of resources and additional personnel.

INDUSTRIAL DEVELOPMENT

The scope of UN activities in industrial development underwent considerable expansion during the first Development Decade. This expansion was in direct response to urgent need. Industrial output in the developing countries grew by 7% to 8% annually, but industry in these countries started from such a small base that even at these not unsatisfactory growth rates it was estimated that several generations would elapse before developing countries began to approach the per capita industrial production of the developed countries. Development of industry is a major objective of the World Bank and affiliated agencies. During the first half of the decade, the World Bank Group committed about $1 billion for industrial development and placed increasing emphasis on technical and financial assistance to development finance companies serving industries.

The groundwork for a new spurt of effort in industrialization was laid by an International Symposium on Industrial Development, convened in Athens in December 1967. Another impetus to development activity in the industrial sector was provided by the establishment in 1966 of the United Nations Industrial Development Organization (UNIDO) as an organ of the General Assembly to promote industrial development and, in particular, to help accelerate the industrialization of the developing countries. A 45-member Industrial Development Board was set up to serve as the principal organ of UNIDO. UNIDO has its headquarters in Vienna.

Technical cooperation activities of UNIDO are financed from a number of established programs available to the UN system of organizations, including the UNDP, the regular program of technical assistance, and certain other financing arrangements such as funds-in-trust.

Highlights of UNIDO activities in 1969 and 1970 included further expansion of operational activities financed by UNDP and other sources; arrangements for continuation of the Special Industrial Services (SIS) program, financed under the UNDP Revolving Fund; expansion of the program of industrial development field advisers; and development of promotion activities and strengthening of training programs.

At its 24th session, the General Assembly requested UNIDO, in cooperation with other organizations of the United Nations system, to intensify efforts in the training of national technical personnel for the accelerated industrialization of the developing countries. At its 25th session, in 1970, the Assembly stressed the need to provide UNIDO with adequate manpower and resources to enable it to give greater substantive support for the implementation of a larger number of projects for the industrial development of developing countries. It requested the UNDP governing council to take all necessary steps to ensure the continuity of the SIS program. The Assembly also arranged to convene a special international conference of UNIDO at the

highest possible level of governmental representation in Vienna in June 1971. It drew attention to the proclamation of the second UN Development Decade, with special reference to the goals and policy measures related to industrial development.

DEVELOPMENT OF NONAGRICULTURAL NATURAL RESOURCES

As with industrial development, the UN family has increased its activities in the field of natural resources and is stepping up its effort to apply technology to resources development.

Mineral Resources. The UN has held regional and interregional seminars on geochemical techniques in mineral exploration and concentration of ores in water-short areas.

Energy Resources (Nonnuclear). Significant changes are taking place that have begun to alter the character of energy problems faced by developing countries. Technological advances have greatly improved the prospects for economic exploitation of energy sources such as oil shales and tar sands, which, if extracted at a cost competitive to petroleum, could increase the world's reserves of hydrocarbon fuels tenfold.

Water Resources. With the demand for water steadily rising all over the world, UN aid to water development projects has sharply increased. These projects involve reconnaissance of river basins, groundwater inventories, and study of specific problems such as desalinization, development of hydroelectric power, river navigation, water for industry, and related legal and administrative issues.

Survey and Mapping Aids. Continuing expansion in surveying and mapping is a prerequisite for the success of many natural resource projects. Modern scientific instruments and techniques, including aerial surveys, have enabled numerous countries to gain information for natural resource development previously hard to obtain because of rugged terrain.

Five-Year Natural Resources Survey Program. In 1966 the secretary-general planned a five-year survey program designed as a major practical contribution in the field of natural resources development during the second half of the Development Decade. The program comprises nine global surveys: (1) world iron ore resources; (2) important nonferrous metals; (3) selected mines in developing countries; (4) offshore mineral potential in developing areas; (5) water needs and water resources in potentially water-short developing countries; (6) development potential of international rivers; (7) potential geothermal energy resources in developing countries; (8) oil shale resources; (9) needs for small-scale power generating plants in developing countries. Each survey has two objectives: to provide significant new information; to provide data for a worldwide perspective of the long-term potentials and needs in selected areas.

FINANCING DEVELOPMENT

Because of the overwhelming economic power of the developed nations, their cooperation is essential if the developing nations are to reach the ultimate goal of self-sustaining economic growth. This is particularly true in regard to trade. But finance and trade by their very nature are activities in which countries tend to look out for their own interests first. It is not surprising, therefore, that in these fields the ideal of partnership between the developed

and the developing nations that was proclaimed at the beginning of the first UN Development Decade has been very imperfectly realized. The first part of this chapter reviews the progress that has been attained in overcoming the conflicting claims of self-interest in regard to the provision of external aid for development. The second part deals with progress that has been attained in improving the trading position of the developing countries.

A. EXTERNAL FINANCE AS AN AID TO DEVELOPMENT

The UN keeps under constant review the matter of the external financing of economic development in the low-income countries. The following analysis of the financial difficulties of the developing nations is a synthesis of information abstracted from three official documents: *World Economic Survey 1965* (Part I of which is devoted to "The Financing of Economic Development"); *International Flow of Long-Term Capital and Official Donations 1961–1965*; and the UNCTAD *Review of International Trade and Development 1966.*

THE NEED FOR EXTERNAL AID

All countries are concerned with maintaining continuing economic growth. Each nation is in constant economic competition with other nations, the competition itself producing a steady increase in world economic growth. A serious imbalance exists in the distribution of national wealth, largely because more than half the nations are not industrialized. Even among industrialized nations there are considerable disparities of wealth, but at least these compete with each other on the basis of similar standards of economic and social development. The problem for the developing countries is to catch up with these standards. Hence their ultimate goal of achieving "self-sustaining" growth essentially means self-sustaining at the level of development already achieved by the industrialized portion of the world.

In order to grow economically, a country must increase its productive capacity and expand the volume of goods and services available to its people. This requires capital formation for investment purposes, which is usually supplied by domestic savings. However, where the degree of industrialization is low, as in the developing countries, the problem of increasing productivity is compounded by the need to import much of the necessary plant and equipment, and in most cases human skills as well. Thus, for such countries, increasing the rate of growth requires an increase not only in the level of domestic savings but also in export earnings to provide foreign exchange. In practice, all this is virtually impossible for very poor countries to accomplish unaided. The lower the level of personal income, the greater the proportion that must be spent merely for basic living expenses, leaving relatively little margin for savings. Similarly, export earnings cannot be substantially increased without a prior increase in productive capacity. To break this vicious circle, the developing countries clearly require external financial resources provided by the developed nations. Only with help from the international community at large will they be able to mobilize their own resources in order to attain a "takeoff point" for self-sustaining growth at a world competitive level.

Economic Classification of Countries

For the purpose of compiling and comparing statistical data, countries are classified usually into three groups: developing countries, developed market economies, and centrally planned economies. The developing countries are generally those of Africa (excluding South Africa), Latin America, and Asia (exclusive of Japan and the Communist bloc). The developed market economies comprise Western Europe, the US, Canada, Australia, New Zealand, Japan, and South Africa. The centrally planned economies are the Eastern bloc of Socialist countries, including mainland China.

The UN Conference on Trade and Development employs a somewhat more complicated system of classification. Under this system countries are grouped as follows:

Group A: the industrial exporting countries, comprising the US, the European Economic Community, the European Free Trade Association (except Portugal), and Japan;

Group B: the primary exporting countries, which comprise two subgroups—Group I, consisting of Canada, Australia, New Zealand, South Africa, Finland, Ireland, Iceland, Spain, Greece, Turkey, Yugoslavia, and Portugal; and Group II, consisting of all other primary exporting countries (a separate subdivision has also been introduced as part of Group II to designate petroleum-exporting countries, comprising Bahrein, Iran, Iraq, Kuwait, Libya, Oman, Neutral Zone, Qatar, Sa'udi Arabia, Trucial States; Netherlands Antilles, Trinidad and Tobago, Venezuela, Brunei, Sabah, and Sarawak);

Group C: Eastern Europe and mainland China.

Types of Resources Transferred to the Developing Countries

Transfers to the developing nations are grouped under the following heads: (1) official bilateral transactions; (2) transactions with multilateral agencies; (3) private long-term investment.

Official bilateral transactions may consist of government grants, both in cash and kind; sales of commodities against local currencies; government long-term loans (for periods exceeding one year), net of repayments of principal—in recipients' currencies or convertible currencies, as specified.

Transactions with multilateral agencies include grants and other contributions, capital subscription, and net purchases of bonds, loans, and participations from those agencies. The transactions may be conducted through government or private portfolio investment.

Direct private long-term investment is net of repatriation of principal, disinvestment, and retirement, but it is not net of reverse flows of capital originating with residents of developing countries or of investment income.

International Agencies Disbursing Multilateral Aid

The *World Economic Survey* lists 17 bodies that disburse multilateral aid. These include the various subsidiary bodies of the UN that disburse resources chiefly in the form of technical assistance, program supplies, and other direct aid; the UN Development Program, the World Food Program, the UN Industrial Development Organization, UNICEF, and the several relief and refugee agencies. (The World Food Program, a joint UN-FAO venture, is described in the chapter on FAO in Part II of this volume. The UN itself finances certain technical assistance activities under its regular budget.)

Multilateral financial aid is disbursed largely through the financial collective foreign aid associations. The work of the International Monetary Fund, the World Bank, and the Bank's two affiliates—the International Finance Corporation and the International Development Association—are discussed in Part II of this volume. The oldest of the regional banks is the Inter-American Bank, which has been in operation since 1960 making long-term loans to member governments and private enterprises at the rate of about $63 million a year. Neither the African Development Bank, established in 1963, nor the Asian Development Bank, established in 1965, has begun lending operations, but the latter is expected to provide an important channel for the flow of development financing. Multilateral foreign aid programs include the Colombo Plan, involving 17 Asian countries and 6 developed market-economy countries outside the region, and the European Development Fund, which provides an average of $55 million a year from appropriations by member governments of the European Economic Community.

RESOURCES AVAILABLE FOR DEVELOPMENT, 1960–65
1. Domestic Savings in the Developing Nations

It has been estimated that the domestic savings rate should be about 15%–20% of the gross domestic product in order to sustain an annual rate of economic growth at 5% on the basis of the average incremental capital-output ratios recorded from 1955 to 1965. In general, domestic savings rose by almost 6% a year to just under 14% of the gross domestic product in 1964. However, a UN study covering 36 countries showed that in 1962–64 there were as many developing countries saving less than 13% of the gross national product as there were countries with higher savings rates. Of the countries reviewed, 13 reached or exceeded the average level of 15% of GNP during 1961–63.

2. Outflow from Developed Market Economies to Developing Nations

In the aggregate, the new outflow of long-term capital and official transfers to multilateral institutions declined significantly between 1961 and 1963, and though recovering in 1964 remained below the peak 1961 figure of approximately $8 billion. However, between 1964 and 1965 most of the principal types of resources registered an increase—with the exception of official bilateral grants, which had remained around $3.7 billion since 1962. Accounting for 60% of the total increment in 1964–65 was the expansion in private investment, which exceeded $2.6 billion. About one fourth of the total increment in 1964–65 was in the form of official bilateral loans—up to a new record of about $1.7 billion.

The increase in the flow of resources in 1964–65 was fairly general among the major providers of capital, the principal exceptions being France and Portugal. The French contribution declined to about one eighth (or 13%) of the total flow, compared with an average of one sixth (16%–17%) between 1956 and 1963. The contributions of the UK and West Germany remained more or less at their 1962–64 proportions of 8% and 6%, respectively, but there was a sharp increase in the contribution of Japan (from 2% to 4% of the total flow) and a partial recovery (from 1% to 2%) in that of the Netherlands. It was a rise of $0.7 billion in the outflow from the US, however, that provided the bulk of the overall increment. This kept the US share of the total flow at about 57% ($5.040 billion). Total outflow for 1965 was $8.8 billion, against $7.7 billion in 1964.

3. Inflow of Resources to Developing Countries

Total inflow increased from $7.7 billion in 1963 to $7.9 billion in 1964 and to $8.9 billion in 1965. The disbursements of the multilateral agencies in or on behalf of the developing countries increased considerably over the period 1961–65, from twofold to threefold between 1961 and 1963. Though disbursements increased in 1964 and 1965, the increase was smaller than in the previous three years.

4. Flow of Resources from the Centrally Planned Economies

The resources provided to the developing countries by the centrally planned economies are credits almost exclusively in the form of machinery, equipment, and skills. The credits are based on bilateral agreements covering cost of prospecting and exploration, preparation of blueprints, and training of personnel, as well as the cost of the actual equipment and machinery required and of technical assistance personnel. Commitments to transfer resources to the developing countries were at an initial peak of $1 billion in 1961 but fell away sharply the following year to about one third of that figure. A slight rise in 1963 was followed in 1964 by an upsurge to a new record level of $1.2 billion. In 1965, however, the amount dropped back again to about half the 1964 figure.

The USSR, on the average, accounts for between one half and two thirds of the yearly total amounts committed—$618 million in 1964 and $369 million in 1965. The next most important lender is generally mainland China ($305 million in 1964, $77 million in 1965), although East Germany in 1965 suddenly swung into second position with $132 million. Previously, in 1964, it had been in fourth position, tying with Romania at

around $70 million. Czechoslovakia provided $118 million in 1964 but only $43 million in 1965. All in all, the commitments of the centrally planned economies have fluctuated widely, in some years one or two countries (notably Bulgaria) not even registering $1 million.

MAJOR PROBLEMS CONNECTED WITH EXTERNAL FINANCE

1. The "Debt Explosion"

One of the consequences of this heavy borrowing by the developing countries is that they have gradually accumulated an external debt that is extremely burdensome both in absolute terms and in their capacity to meet debt service payments. In 1964 the total debt had reached almost $40 billion, substantially more than the developing countries' total export earnings for that year, and the outflow of interest and amortization payments reached about $5 billion—or half the total net inflow of new long-term external capital and donations and 9% to 12% of export earnings. Between 1956 and 1964, the average rate of increase in service payments was approximately 17%, compared with an average rate of increase in external transfers from the developed market economies of only 8%. About three fourths of the debt is public debt guaranteed by governments.

This high rate of increase in debt service payments has led in some cases to acute balance-of-payments problems. Although a heavy debt burden is unavoidable in view of the need for continual heavy borrowing, the developing countries maintain that the developed nations could take several obvious steps to ease their balance-of-payments position. One way would be to increase the total flow of resources so as to ensure that the gross transfer was large enough to provide adequate net inflow of new resources each year. Another method would be to make debt service charges payable in goods or in nonconvertible currencies. A third method, which has been practiced to some extent, is the rescheduling of previously incurred obligations so as to reduce their current impact on the debtor country's external balance. Yet another method would be to ease the terms on which loans are made. Loans gradually tended to replace outright cash in the aid programs of countries like the US. In the aggregate, for all the industrial countries combined, loans carrying an annual interest rate of 3% or less declined from 83% to 78%. Similarly, the proportion of loans carrying a maturity of 25 years or more declined from 83% to 75%, and even the average grace period granted before commencement of debt servicing was appreciably reduced—from just under seven years to just over five.

2. Concentration of the Flow of Resources

Another unsatisfactory feature of the present flow of official external resources, from the point of view of the developing nations, has been its high degree of concentration on a few recipient nations. In the 1961–64 period, almost half the total movement of resources from the developed market economies into Latin America went to three countries: Brazil, Chile, and Colombia. In Africa nearly half the regional total was received by four countries: Algeria, Congo (Kinshasa), Morocco, and the UAR. In Asia about two thirds of the total went to four countries: India, South Korea, Pakistan, and South Viet-Nam.

There is also a similar concentration of aid provided by the centrally planned economies. Although they have supplied aid to over 30 developing countries, the bulk of it has been heavily concentrated on a limited number. Thus 67% of the total credits allocated to Asia went to three countries: Afghanistan, India, and Indonesia. In Africa more than half the total went to the UAR. In Latin America over two thirds of the total has gone to Brazil.

3. Tied Loans

The third major problem associated with external finance is the practice of tying loans either to the purchase of goods from the lending countries or to specific development projects in the recipient countries. This is done by all lenders—bilateral, multilateral, and private. The developing countries claim that this practice reduces the flexibility and effectiveness of aid. They would like to see a much higher proportion of resources lent for general use at their own discretion.

4. Possible Solutions

Ultimately, the inadequate flow of resources from the developed to the developing nations, and the unfavorable loan terms that aggravate the latter's difficulties, have their roots in the complexities of the financial situation within the donor countries. For example, donor countries may be obliged to tie loans to the purchase of their own goods because they are experiencing balance-of-payments difficulties. Interest rates may be high because of the need to fight internal inflationary pressures.

The 1966 Geneva Assembly adopted a resolution urging the developed nations to try to provide "not later than by 1968, at least 80% of their assistance in the form of grants or loans at interest rates of 3% or less with a repayment period of twenty-five years or more." The resolution also affirmed the target of 1% of individual income of the developed nations as the target to be reached in the flow of external resources.

ESTABLISHMENT OF THE UN CAPITAL DEVELOPMENT FUND

It was largely to circumvent the difficulties associated with conventional loan terms that the developing countries first began in the early 1950's to agitate for the creation of a special UN fund for grants-in-aid and low-interest, long-term loans. Owing chiefly to the determined resistance of the developed nations, the proposed fund, which came to be known as the Special United Nations Fund for Economic Development (SUNFED), never materialized. As a compromise, a UN Special Fund was established in 1958 to channel external aid, financed through voluntary government contributions, into "preinvestment" channels. The Special Fund, now incorporated into the UN Development Program (see below), was quite successful in its own right, but it did not satisfy the developing nations' demand for a UN fund to provide investment capital proper. In 1960 the developing countries managed to persuade the Assembly to adopt a resolution by which it decided "in principle" to establish a UN capital development fund. After six years of intense canvassing by the developing countries, the fund was finally established by Assembly resolution on 13 December 1966.

The object of the developing nations was to bring a greater share of multilaterally disbursed funds under the control of the General Assembly, in which they could muster a majority of the votes. The General Assembly invited the governing council of the UNDP to act as the fund's executive board.

In 1969 the governing council approved plans for limited operations of the fund. Under these plans, countries contributing to the fund would fulfill their pledges in kind. The General Assembly requested the governing council to undertake a study aimed at broadening the functions of the fund to enable all member states to support it.

In January 1970 the UNDP administrator reported that resources amounted to the equivalent of $3.4 million, most of it in nonconvertible currencies.

In 1970, at its 25th session, the General Assembly requested the UNDP governing council to consider all possibilities for reaching the objectives of the United Nations Capital Development Fund. Deciding to preserve the original functions of the fund until 31 December 1971, the Assembly invited member states at the same pledging conference to contribute separately to the UNDP and the fund.

UTILIZATION OF RESOURCES RELEASED BY DISARMAMENT

A consultative group appointed by the secretary-general reported in 1962 that the "world is spending roughly $120 billion annually on military account at the present time . . . equivalent to about 8–9% of the world's annual output of all goods and services . . . [and] at least two-thirds of the entire national income of all the under-developed countries." It was also estimated that the total number of persons in the armed forces or in productive activities resulting from military expenditures probably amounted to well over 50 million. The report went on to analyze the peaceful uses to which the released resources could be put, the technical problems involved in conversion, and the impact that disarmament would have in various spheres of national and international life. The 1962 Assembly expressed its unanimous conviction that disarmament and the conversion of military resources would open up vast opportunities for peaceful cooperation and trade, ensure the growth of production, and provide new jobs for millions of people. Member countries have been requested to conduct, and transmit to the secretary-general, the results of national studies on conversion problems and on the economic and social consequences of disarmament. Since 1962, the secretary-general has been reporting annually to the Assembly on the status of studies in this field. At its 1970 session the General Assembly requested the secretary-general to prepare with the assistance of consultants a report on the economic and social consequences of the arms race and of military expenditure. The Assembly expects to consider the report at its 1971 session.

B. TRADE AS AN INSTRUMENT FOR DEVELOPMENT

The preceding review of the problems of external finance makes it clear that developing countries urgently need to expand their trade so as to reduce their reliance on foreign financial aid. As is pointed out in the *World Economic Survey,* "In the long run, measures to raise the debt-servicing capacity of a developing country are likely to prove more important than the softening of the terms of a particular loan." However, the success of developing countries in expanding their external trade is largely dependent upon cooperative policies on the part of the developed nations, since the latter, to quote the *Survey,* "play a key role in determining the magnitude of the developing countries' export receipts . . . ." Moreover, there is the added disadvantage that "the pattern of goods that most developing countries have available for export is quite unsuitable for providing the steady expansion in earnings necessary for financing the imports required . . . ."

MAJOR TRADING DIFFICULTIES OF THE DEVELOPING NATIONS

Over 90% of the developing countries' exports are primary commodities. Due to a number of factors, there has been a steady decline in the long-term demand for the primary commodities exported by developing nations. The demand for manufactured goods outstrips that for primary commodities. As a result of technological advances in the developed countries, industrially produced synthetics increasingly are replacing natural materials. The developed nations wish to increase their own production of many natural commodities. Consequently, they not only export these goods to compete with those of developing countries but also impose restrictive quotas on imports in order to protect domestic production.

In addition to this lag in long-term demand for their prod-

ucts, the developing nations are confronted with the problem
of short-term price fluctuations. When a country relies, as do
so many developing nations, upon the export of only one or
two basic commodities to provide the bulk of its foreign-
exchange earnings, the effects of these short-term fluctuations
can be disastrous.

Therefore, the developing countries try to diversify their economies and augment their export of manufactured goods. But
not only is output of manufactures hampered by possible under-
industrialization, but their export is often frustrated by the
high tariff barriers introduced by the developed nations. Yet
access to foreign markets is essential if industry in the developing nations is to expand. Hence, the tariff policies of developed
nations affect both the volume of export receipts of foreign
exchange and the actual expansion of industry, which is the key
to further development. The predicament in which the developing countries constantly find themselves takes on a new dimension when problems of trade are considered.

1964 UN CONFERENCE ON TRADE AND DEVELOPMENT

Between 1950 and 1960, the share of the developing countries
in world exports steadily declined. What seemed to be required
was the establishment of entirely new patterns of international
production and trade. The developing countries urged that a
UN conference on trade be convened to discuss trade problems,
with particular reference to their effect on development.

The UN Conference on Trade and Development (UNCTAD)
was convened in Geneva on 23 March 1964. It lasted for 12
weeks and was attended by representatives of 120 nations.
Determined to make the most of their opportunity, the developing nations organized themselves into a formidable working Caucus of Seventy-Five. Within this caucus, they established
regional caucuses, a coordinating group, a steering committee,
and an informal contact group for conducting compromise
negotiations with the developed nations, both East and West.

The Final Act of the conference contains 35 general and
special principles and 57 recommendations. Taken together,
the principles express the theme that economic development
and social progress should "be the common concern of the
whole international community." To this end, since "international trade is one of the most important factors in economic
development . . . all countries should cooperate in creating
conditions of international trade conducive, in particular, to
the achievement of a rapid increase in the export earnings of
developing countries and, in general, to the promotion of an
expansion and diversification of trade between all countries,
whether at similar levels of development, at different levels
of development, or having different economic and social systems."
Developed countries are progressively to reduce and eliminate
barriers against the trade of developing countries and are to
take positive measures to increase markets for exporting countries. They are also to grant concessions to the developing
countries without expecting any return concessions, and they
are to eliminate the practice of granting special preferences to
selected developing countries. These and other principles are
related to specific aspects of trade and development in the 57
recommendations.

ESTABLISHMENT OF UNCTAD AS AN ORGAN OF THE GENERAL ASSEMBLY

The compromise that finally materialized represented an almost total victory for the developing nations. The recommendation contained in the Final Act provided for the establishment
of the conference as an organ of the Assembly to be convened at
intervals of not more than three years. It was to be given wide
powers, including the power to formulate principles and policies
and make proposals for their implementation; generally, to review

the facilities for the coordination of activities of other bodies in
the UN system with regard to international trade and related
problems of development; and to initiate action, where appropriate in cooperation with the competent UN organs, for negotiating multilateral legal instruments in the field of trade.
To carry out the functions of the conference when it is not in
session, a permanent 55-member Trade and Development Board
was to be established, consisting of representatives elected at
each regular session of the conference from 22 African and Asian
nations, 18 developed market nations, 9 Latin American nations,
and 6 Socialist nations. Arrangements were also to be made
for the establishment of an adequate full-time secretariat headed
by a secretary-general to be appointed by the secretary-general
of the UN and confirmed by the Assembly. The expenses of the
conference, all its subsidiary bodies, and its secretariat were
to be carried in the regular UN budget.

The chief compromise concessions to the West were in the
wording of certain provisions on the functions of the conference
and the board. Thus in facilitating coordination of work in
the field of trade within the UN system, the conference is enjoined to cooperate with both the Assembly and ECOSOC.
In initiating action for negotiating legal instruments, the conference must pay "due regard to the adequacy of existing organs
of negotiation" and must not duplicate their activities. Similarly,
it is stipulated that the board shall "act in conformity with the
responsibilities of ECOSOC under the United Nations Charter,"
and report annually to the Assembly "through the Economic
and Social Council," which may "transmit such comments
on the reports as it deems necessary." Most important of all
was a provision requesting the secretary-general of the UN to
appoint a special committee to prepare proposals on conciliation procedures to be employed by the conference and all
subsidiary bodies when discussing matters "substantially affecting the economic or financial interests of particular countries."

Action Taken by the 1964 Assembly

The special committee appointed by the secretary-general presented an elaborate set of provisions that were intended to form
part of the basic rules of procedure written into the constitution
of the conference and all its subsidiary bodies. The committee
recommended that requests for conciliation should be made
after the conclusion of debate but prior to voting on a proposal. In order to initiate the actual procedures, however,
there would have to be a minimum number of members requesting conciliation on a given issue: 10 members in the conference, 5 in the Trade and Development Board, and 3
in committees established by the board. The procedures themselves would consist of the nomination, by the president of the
conference or chairman of the board or a committee, of a small
conciliation committee (to include countries especially interested in the matter); the conciliation committee would reach
its conclusions without voting and then report back to the
body concerned, but if necessary its mandate could be extended
beyond the session at which it was required.

These proposals were generally hailed as a constructive step
toward fostering goodwill and cooperation among the members
of the conference. The conciliation procedures were duly incorporated into the text of the original recommendation of
the 1964 conference, which the Assembly then adopted—by
consensus—on 30 December 1964.

MAIN DEVELOPMENTS, 1965–66

The original recommendation for the establishment of UNCTAD
had provided for the election of the members of the Trade and
Development Board by the 1964 conference. Thus the board
was fully constituted before the Assembly adopted the resolution
that formally brought UNCTAD into being. The 55-man board

held its first session in New York in April 1965. It decided to establish the UNCTAD secretariat in Geneva and also set up four permanent functional committees. They are the committees on commodities (55 members), manufactures (45 members), invisibles and financing related to trade (45 members), and shipping (45 members). The board itself normally meets twice a year, in the spring and in the fall, but may be called in special session when required. In 1966 the Assembly decided to convene the second session of the conference at New Delhi from 1 February to 25 March 1968.

The following is a brief review of the major developments in each of the four main areas of trade covered by the board's committees.

Primary Commodity Trade

In the latter half of 1964 and in 1965 many developed nations adopted decisions that are difficult to reconcile with the standstill on protection measures recommended by the conference. Several examples were cited. It was estimated that for each dollar spent on imports of agricultural commodities from the developing nations, the consumer or taxpayer in the developed countries spends another dollar to protect domestic production.

Such protectionist policies accelerate the natural trend to the self-sufficiency of developed market economies in the supply of primary commodities, made possible by technological advances. The share in the consumption of oils, fats, sugar, and cotton accounted for by domestic products in the developed areas showed significant increases. Similarly, the share of synthetic fibers in the total consumption of apparel fibers grew to 38% in 1963–64, while synthetic rubber accounted for more than three fifths of all rubber consumption by 1963–65. These trends created a rapidly deteriorating situation for the traditional exporters of primary commodities. Thus the share of developing countries in total world exports of primary commodities dropped from 44% in 1953–55 to less than 40% in 1963–64.

Intergovernmental Commodity Agreements. One of the methods used to combat short-term price fluctuations of commodities has been through agreements between the leading producer and consumer countries on machinery to stabilize prices within stated maximum and minimum levels. Prior to the creation of UNCTAD, such agreements had been established for sugar (1958), tin (1960), wheat (1962), coffee (1963), and olive oil (1963). Since the inception of UNCTAD, only one commodity agreement has been successfully negotiated—the third international tin agreement in 1965—though it was not signed by several leading consumer countries. The international wheat agreement, which expired in July 1965, was also extended until 1967.

Trade in Manufactures and Semimanufactures

Manufacturing industries of the developing countries accounted for only 6.3% of the world output in 1964, much the same as at the beginning of the decade. The developing countries' share of world exports of manufactures was even smaller—less than 5% in 1964. It was also noted that intratrade in manufactures among the developing countries was still at a very low level. An exception was trade among the members of the Central American Common Market, which had more than tripled between 1960 and 1964, with its share of intraregional exports in total exports increasing from 7.4% to 15.8%. Efforts were made to intensify cooperation for intratrade in other underdeveloped regions. In Africa the Central African Customs and Economic Union was successfully established, but the East African Common Market (Kenya, Tanzania, and Uganda) encountered difficulties, and the common currency arrangements were terminated in 1966. The Arab Common Market

and the Asian trade liberalization plan (prepared under the auspices of ECAFE) were still in the formative stages. One of the most favorable trends noted by the UNCTAD report was the increase in the imports of manufactures and semimanufactures from developing countries by the Socialist nations. These imports amounted to $185 million in 1963 and increased to $299 million in 1964.

With regard to the implementation of the conference's recommendations concerning the tariff policies of the developed market economies, an UNCTAD survey pointed out:

(1) that the European Common Market countries had decided to raise their tariffs with regard to 860 tariff items in which the developing countries have an important export interest;

(2) that although some developed countries had reduced a few tariffs on manufactured and semimanufactured products (e.g., grapefruit juice, "horticultural" glass, instant coffee, sacks and bags for packing, pineapple and citrus fruits in containers), for the most part it appeared that tariff schedules remained unchanged;

(3) that tariffs are so graduated that they afford higher protection against the more sophisticated manufactures, a circumstance that particularly affects the development of export-based industrialization in the developing countries;

(4) that despite measures to remove certain items from quantitative or quota restrictions, a significant number of products of major export interest to the developing nations are still under quota; and

(5) that the idea of general preference to be granted by all developed countries to manufactures from all developing countries has not yet been accepted, although there had been "considerable progress in the evolution of ideas and political will" and that governments of certain developed countries had advanced useful concrete suggestions to this end.

Invisibles and Financing Related to Trade

(1) *Invisibles.* These items account for a very large share of the balance of payments of developing countries. In 1963 invisible transactions other than financial items accounted for 26% of the value of all receipts of merchandise trade and 18% of both merchandise and nonmerchandise trade. Annual world expenditure on international travel (excluding transport costs) now amounts to between $8,000 million and $10,000 million, representing a rise of about 75% from 1958 to 1963, with the rise in 1964 continuing at a rate of 15%. International tourism accounts for a sizable proportion of the national income in several countries. However, the benefits of this spectacular rise in world tourism have largely bypassed the countries of Asia and Africa.

In 1963, ECOSOC convened in Rome a UN Conference on International Travel and Tourism, which was attended by representatives of 87 countries. Besides making general recommendations for promoting tourism, the Rome conference established guidelines for simplifying governmental travel formalities, and it recommended that the UN give high priority to requests for assistance in this field.

(2) *Finance.* As a result of a recommendation of the 1964 Conference on Trade and Development, the International Bank (IBRD) prepared a study on "supplementary financial measures" aimed to meet the difficulties created by unexpected shortfalls in the exports of the developing countries. The bank estimated the eventual yearly requirements of the projected scheme to be about $300 million to $400 million. The 1966 UNCTAD report commented that the bank's proposal represents an instance whereby the discussion on problems of principle with UNCTAD may lead to the creation of suitable instruments for practical action.

In 1966 the question of international monetary reform was being considered by the International Monetary Fund's "Group of Ten"—the main financial powers—but the developing countries have strongly deplored the tendency of these nations to try to reach a settlement of vital liquidity issues without their participation. In a memorandum on international liquidity, the developing countries point out that they too have major liquidity problems and that monetary management affecting all nations should be the result of truly international decisions. The expert group, whose report was before the UNCTAD committee on invisibles and financing during 1966, submitted to the International Monetary Fund a proposal to establish the IMF as a central agent in a scheme for establishing "fund units" as accepted reserves in international payments. Member states would deposit their own currencies with the IMF and be credited with the fund units accordingly.

Shipping

The share of the developing countries in total seaborne world exports amounts at present to 57.2%, while their share of the world fleet is only about 7%. The 1964 Conference on Trade and Development had expressed concern about the impact of rising freight rates on the competitive position of developing countries in overseas markets. Prices for the type of charter most commonly used for the transport of developing countries' exports increased by some 30% during the first half of the 1960's and by almost 20% from 1964 to 1965. As a result, in 1965 a given quantity of primary commodities could buy only two thirds of the ocean mileage it could have bought in 1958. One of the special principles adopted by the conference stated that all countries should help developing nations to build up their own shipping lines, but this was opposed by seven leading developed market countries.

The committee formulated a work program for the development of consultation machinery on shipping matters, improvement of port operations, and establishment or expansion of merchant marines in developing countries. It also approved a program of studies on the level and structure of freight rates, practices at liner conferences, and adequacy of shipping services. According to the 1966 UNCTAD report, the 1964 conference had stimulated a new interest in the idea of establishing shippers' councils in the developing countries.

Transit Trade of Landlocked Countries. Countries without access to the sea have added transport problems, and 16 of the world's 25 landlocked countries are developing nations. The conference adopted without dissent eight special principles designed to help them overcome the effects of their landlocked position on their trade. The 1964 Assembly then convened a conference of plenipotentiaries to draw up a convention on the subject. The Convention on Transit Trade of Landlocked States was adopted in July 1965. It affirms the eight principles adopted by the conference and defines the conditions under which freedom of transit is to be granted. Also included are provisions for special transit dues, the use of a transit country's transport facilities, and the creation of free zones.

Summary

(1) *Some Overall Trade Trends.* Between 1960 and 1965, world exports increased in value from $127 billion to $186 billion. Of the total world exports in 1965, developed market economies accounted for $128 billion, or over two thirds; developing countries accounted for $37 billion, or less than one fifth; Socialist countries accounted for $22 billion, or 11%. The share of the developing countries declined from over 25% in 1955 to less than 20% in 1965. Petroleum, whose proceeds accrue only to a very few nations, is the fastest-growing export commodity, accounting for almost one third of the total exports of develop-

ing countries. Imports by the developed countries from the developing countries declined from 29% in 1955 to 21% in 1965. On the other hand, imports by the Socialist countries from the developing countries rose from $0.6 billion in 1955 to $2.3 billion in 1965. Intratrade between the developing countries declined from 26% in 1955 to 20% in 1965. Nevertheless, the boom in the developed market economies produced an overall expansion of world trade that was also reflected in the exports of the developing countries. In value terms, these grew from an annual rate of about 3% in the second half of the 1950's to about 6% in the first half of the 1960's. The annual compound rate of growth for imports was about 4% throughout. While this reflected favorably on their trade deficit, it also indicated that (because of financial factors discussed in part A above) the urgent need for imports could not be translated into effective demand.

(2) *Views of the Three Main Groups of Countries Expressed at the Fourth Session of the Trade and Development Board in September 1966.* In a joint memorandum, the developing countries declared that the recommendations of the 1964 conference "have not been implemented either adequately or in a concentrated manner and have so far resulted only in isolated and limited measures by individual countries." Setting forth a "short-term program of implementation," they urged the developed countries to take action, before the opening of the second conference in 1968, to conclude international commodity agreements on cocoa and sugar; to observe the standstill on protective policies adverse to developing countries; to institute a scheme of general and nondiscriminatory preferences; to increase the flow of financial assistance to developing countries to the 1% target; to alleviate the latter's debt burden by appropriate rescheduling of debts; to improve loan conditions; and to cooperate on a practical scheme for supplementary finance.

The representatives of the developed market economies for their part indicated that they shared the deep concern over the situation of the developing countries and wished to contribute to its improvement. They could not; however, subscribe to the memorandum. In their view, it did not state the problem in a sufficiently balanced manner, and they could not agree to the way in which the demands were formulated.

The representatives of the Socialist countries stressed the importance of the dynamic growth in their trade with the developing countries. They believed that the general normalization of trade would also help to increase the trade of developing countries.

MAIN DEVELOPMENTS, 1966–70

A declaration on trade expansion, economic cooperation, and regional integration among developing countries was adopted at the second session of the UN Conference on Trade and Development held in New Delhi in 1968. A key decision of the session was the recommendation that each advanced country should provide to developing countries financial resources amounting to 1% of its gross national product.

The conference also approved new approaches to trade relations between countries with different economic and social systems; adopted a program of international action on commodities; and recognized unanimously the need for a system of nondiscriminatory preferences to be granted by developed countries to increase the flow of exports from developing countries. A special committee on preferences was set up to seek agreed arrangements for such a system.

At its 1969 session the Assembly expressed concern that most issues referred to UNCTAD's continuing machinery still were outstanding and requested the Trade and Development Board to attempt to resolve those issues and to accelerate in particular its work relating to preparations for the second UN Development Decade.

The Assembly urged states to engage in constructive consultations in the special committee on preferences. Early implementation of the system of preferences would be a concrete example of effective international action for trade expansion and development.

The Assembly welcomed the agreement reached by the Trade and Development Board whereby specific measures in favor of landlocked developing countries would be elaborated within the context of UNCTAD's contribution to the international development strategy, and it requested the board to consider adoption of practical measures related to landlocked countries. The Assembly also urged action by members to bring into effect the 1965 Convention on Transit Trade of Landlocked States.

Meeting in Geneva in February 1970, the board adopted by consensus a text on UNCTAD's contribution to the preparatory work for the second Development Decade. The document outlined policy measures to be taken by governments during the 1970's in many fields related to trade.

Priority objectives listed by the board included increasing the net foreign exchange export earnings of developing countries, supplementing the resources available to those countries through financial and technical assistance from the developed countries, and increasing the flow of modern technology to meet development needs. The board also included in its contribution to the decade provisions regarding mobilization of world opinion in support of international development efforts.

The board was unable to reach agreement on some important issues—notably, target dates for carrying out measures, as in regard to elimination of tariff barriers; conclusion of commodity agreements; and the transfer of financial resources from developed to developing countries.

Developing countries maintained that the 1% target for transfer of resources should be achieved by 1972, and that developed countries should provide a minimum of 0.75% of their gross national product by way of net official financial resource transfers. Developed countries held differing views.

The board agreed that continued efforts would be made to seek agreements before the launching of the decade. It decided that UNCTAD's contribution to the decade should be seen in a dynamic context and would require continuing review within the machinery of UNCTAD.

At the meeting of the special committee on preferences, 31 March to 17 April 1970, developing countries expressed appreciation for the political will and for the efforts leading to the submission of provisional offers by the prospective preference-giving countries according to an agreed time schedule. They welcomed the submissions as a major step toward implementation of the generalized scheme of preferences and called for assurances that countries at different levels of development would benefit from the scheme.

As a step toward reconvening the United Nations cocoa conference, as urged by the Assembly, representatives of 41 countries, including the major cocoa producers and consumers, met in Geneva from 1 to 11 June 1970 to consider outstanding issues in the preparation of a draft international cocoa agreement. They were not able to complete their task and recognized the need for further consultations at a later stage.

The tin conference, held in Geneva from 14 April to 15 May 1970 under UNCTAD auspices, successfully negotiated a fourth international tin agreement to replace the agreement due to expire on 31 June 1971.

The board provisionally decided that the third session of UNCTAD should be held in Geneva.

Taking into account its 1970 resolution on the international development strategy for the second UN Development Decade, the Assembly decided that the third session of UNCTAD will be held in April–May 1972. The Trade and Development Board will recommend the location of the third session.

The Assembly invited the Trade and Development Board to draw the attention of UNCTAD, when implementing the second Development Decade, to the importance of reviewing the progress made and seeking implementation of the policy measures agreed upon within the context of the strategy for the second decade; reaching agreement on issues that have not been resolved fully in the strategy; seeking new areas of agreement and the widening of existing ones; and evolving new concepts and seeking agreement on additional measures.

The Assembly recommended that the institutional machinery of UNCTAD should be fully oriented toward the implementation of the relevant provisions of the international development strategy, and particularly for enabling countries that have difficulty in accepting certain provisions in the policy measures of the strategy to make a fuller and more effective contribution to the goals of the second Development Decade.

The Assembly also asked the board to consider such reforms that would promote further evolution in UNCTAD'S institutional arrangements.

(See also section on second Development Decade.)

UNITED NATIONS DEVELOPMENT PROGRAM (UNDP)

The technical assistance activities carried out by the various UN organizations in individual countries have had a direct impact on the lives of hundreds of millions and have probably won the UN more acclaim than anything else it has done.

The pivot of the technical assistance programs is an institution known as the United Nations Development Program (UNDP), a subsidiary body of the General Assembly and ECOSOC that allocates funds to assistance projects administered by the various UN organizations. Although the specialized agencies and the UN itself have carried out projects under their regular budgets, the greater part of their project assistance is financed, coordinated, and administered through the UNDP.

EVOLUTION OF THE UNDP
Although the UNDP came into formal existence in January 1966, it had a considerable history, for it grew out of two long-established UN institutions.

In 1948 the General Assembly had decided to appropriate funds under its regular budget to enable the secretary-general to supply teams of experts, offer fellowships, and organize seminars to assist national development projects at the request of governments. About the same time, many of the specialized agencies had also begun to undertake similar projects. However, no sooner had the Regular Programs of Technical Assistance, as they were called, begun to operate, than it became apparent that the money that could be spared from the regular budget would not suffice to meet demand. In 1949 the Assembly set up a separate account for voluntary contributions toward technical assistance and decided to make this a central account to finance the activities not only of the UN itself but also of the specialized agencies as well. Machinery was established for distributing the financial resources and coordinating the projects, and the whole enterprise was called the Expanded Program of Technical Assistance (EPTA), to distinguish it from the UN's regular technical assistance program financed under the regular budget. The venture proved remarkably successful. Ten years after it had begun operations, EPTA was financing technical assistance programs in some 140 countries and territories. Between 1950 and 1960 the number of governments contributing funds had grown from 54 to 85, while the total annual contributions had correspondingly risen from $10 million to $33.8 million.

In 1958 the Assembly felt that it would be desirable to broaden the scope of UN technical assistance to include vital large-scale preinvestment surveys and feasibility studies on major national development projects, which would lay the groundwork for subsequent investment of capital. These surveys and studies necessarily involved a much greater financial outlay than the kind of technical assistance programs then being undertaken, and the Assembly decided to set up a new institution, which would be run along similar lines to EPTA. Thus the Special Fund was established to act as a multilateral channel for voluntary contributions toward preinvestment projects and as a coordinating center for the work of the various UN agencies. The Special Fund began operations in 1959 and within three years 86 governments had pledged a total of $110,836,585.

In January 1964 the secretary-general formally proposed to ECOSOC that EPTA and the Special Fund be merged into a single enterprise. The advantages to be derived from the merger were a pooling of resources, simplification of procedures, improvement in overall planning, elimination of duplication, reduction in overhead administrative costs, and a general strengthening of UN development aid. By August 1964, ECOSOC had adopted recommendations for the merger. But due to the political situation at the 1964 Assembly, no action could be taken until the following year. On 22 November 1965 the Assembly unanimously voted to consolidate the two operations, effective 1 January 1966. At the time of its inception, UNDP inherited from its two predecessors a combined commitment of some 2,000 projects with a total price tag of over $1.5 billion. By 1970 the agency was spending about $230 million annually in supporting 1,234 large projects and some 2,500 smaller projects. On 16 November 1970, UNDP's administrator stated that it was "not a case of wishful thinking" to project a $1,000 million program for the year 1975.

FUNCTIONS AND GUIDING PRINCIPLES OF UNDP

UNDP is a global partnership between governments of developed and developing countries working through the UN family of organizations. UNDP-assisted projects originate in special government requests for project assistance on the part of the international community. UNDP's role is essentially that of management. Its functions are to evaluate requests and make a selection of projects; to allocate the available funds to the projects selected; and generally to oversee the total program. UNDP itself does not normally implement the actual projects, nor does it provide expert technical personnel or procure equipment. Functional aspects of the projects are left largely to the executing agencies (see below).

The General Assembly has established criteria for guiding the work of UNDP. All projects assisted by UNDP must be selected on the basis of the requesting government's priority needs; capable of contributing directly to economic and social progress; integrated into overall national or regional development efforts; coordinated, as closely as possible, with other development aid; designed, whenever appropriate, for progressive transfer to the participating government; and free from political interference of any kind.

Obligations of Participating Governments

A government whose development projects are assisted by UNDP funds is required to undertake considerable obligations. It is expected to contribute to the living costs of experts working in its territory, to pay internal travel costs, and to provide interpreters and secretarial help. These local costs are assessed against participating countries in their currencies. More significant, additional expenditures are required on the part of a participating country to make technical assistance and preinvestment aid really meaningful. For example, the government must assign local counterpart personnel to work with the international experts and must establish its own coordination machinery so that UNDP projects may function within the framework of national development plans and be coordinated with assistance received from other sources. Every participating government, furthermore, is obligated to give full and prompt consideration to the advice provided and to publicize the program within its own borders. It must publish the results of any technical assistance it receives or provide the organization furnishing the assistance with material for its own study and analysis of the results. Finally, it must assume full responsibility for the necessary follow-up operations once the UNDP-aided phase is completed.

ORGANIZATION OF UNDP

Policy Control. Ultimate responsibility for approving projects, overseeing UNDP operations, and allocating funds rests with a 37-member Governing Council, which meets twice a year and reports to ECOSOC. The members are representatives of governments elected by ECOSOC for three-year terms. Distribution of seats was laid down by Assembly resolution as follows: 19 seats to developing countries, 17 to developed countries, and 1 seat to rotate among the various geographical groupings. Geographical distribution of seats was likewise established by the Assembly: of the 19 seats allocated to developing countries, 7 must go to representatives of African nations, 6 to Asian nations, and 6 to Latin American nations or Yugoslavia; of the 17 seats allocated to developed countries, 3 must go to East European nations and 14 to West European and other countries. Retiring members are eligible for reelection.

By January 1971 the Governing Council consisted of Australia, Belgium, Brazil, Cameroon, Canada, Central African Republic, Chile, Congo (Brazzaville), Cuba, Czechoslovakia, Denmark, France, West Germany, India, Indonesia, Italy, Ivory Coast, Japan, Kuwait, Libya, Mauritania, Mexico, Netherlands, Norway, Pakistan, Panama, Peru, Philippines, Romania, Sweden, Switzerland, Syria, Tanzania, Uganda, USSR, UK, and US. (Participation in UNDP is not confined to UN members, since both West Germany and Switzerland are included in the Governing Council.)

Central Administration. UNDP personnel are part of UN Headquarters staff, but, due to limitations of space, they are not lodged in the Headquarters building but across 48th Street at 866 UN Plaza. The chief executive officers are the administrator and the coadministrator. In 1970 these posts were filled respectively by Paul Hoffman of the US (formerly the managing director of the Special Fund) and E. V. Narasimhan of India. To advise on coordination of the overall program and on selection of projects, the Assembly has established an Inter-Agency Consultative Board comprising the executive heads of all the UN agencies participating in UNDP activities. The board meets as required, under the chairmanship of the administrator or coadministrator.

The administrator is also responsible for the administration of certain special trust funds including, as of November 1970, the UN Population Trust Fund with total pledges of $22.5 million and the Fund for the Development of West Irian, whose resources total about $30 million.

Field Administration. UNDP maintains field offices in 93 countries. These are headed by resident directors, who perform several important duties on behalf of UNDP. They also act as country agents of the World Food Program (see under FAO in this volume) and may directly represent various other UN agencies, depending on the country concerned.

Resident directors assist governments in formulating their requests for UNDP aid and frequently become key advisers to governments. Working closely with government officials and in consultation with the executing agencies, the resident director tries to ensure that the limited international resources available are used to meet a country's most urgent needs. He also plays an essential role in coordinating the work of the different agencies executing UNDP-assisted projects within a country and of these projects with other assistance programs. Lastly, it is his job to help speed implementation of UNDP-assisted projects and to ensure effective follow-up action by the government when the projects are completed.

The Executing Agencies
As of January 1971 the executing agencies for UNDP-assisted projects included 11 specialized agencies, the UN itself, and 2 subsidiary bodies—the Industrial Development Organization and the Conference for Trade and Development. The specialized agencies participating in the work of UNDP are the International Labor Organization (ILO), Food and Agriculture Organization (FAO), United Nations Educational, Scientific and Cultural Organization (UNESCO), International Civil Aviation Organization (ICAO), World Health Organization (WHO), International Bank for Reconstruction and Development (IBRD), International Telecommunication Union (ITU), World Meteorological Organization (WMO), International Atomic Energy Agency (IAEA), Universal Postal Union (UPU), and Intergovernmental Maritime Consultative Organization (IMCO). The services of regional development banks are also resorted to, including the African Development Bank, the Asian Development Bank and the Inter-American Development Bank (IADB). Four large agencies account for a major part of expenditures: FAO 30%, UN 16%, UNESCO 12.8%, and ILO 10.6%.

FINANCING
As indicated, the governments of countries where UNDP projects are executed contribute substantially to their costs. Roughly, the ratio of UNDP expenditure to government expenditure is 60:40. However, depending on the circumstances and nature of the work involved, either the governments or UNDP may pay considerably more than half the total costs. There is no fixed rule, and each case is assessed individually. In principle, the richer countries pay proportionately more and the poorer countries less.

Annual voluntary contributions to UNDP funds are made by almost every member of the UN and by several nonmembers as well. As may be expected, the biggest contributions come from the richest nations. But since UNDP is designed for the benefit of developing countries, these nations also try to contribute as generously as their resources permit. A notable case in point is India, which is one of the countries that has received the most UNDP aid and is also among the biggest contributors (see below). Also, some of the smaller countries, both developed and developing, have consistently tried to increase their annual pledges. On the combined EPTA and Special Fund accounts, contributions rose by about 134% between 1960 and 1966.

Contributions to UNDP for 1971 pledged by 129 countries as of November 1970 totaled $238,887,455. Of the 129 countries that had made pledges for the 1971 program, 20 pledged contributions of $1 million or more. The countries and the sums pledged in descending order are as follows: US—$86,267,500*; Sweden—$23,000,000; Denmark—$16,933,333; Canada—$16,000,000; UK—$14,400,000; West Germany—$13,114,754; Netherlands—$11,111,011; Norway—$6,579,868; France—$5,009,009; Japan—$4,800,000*; India—$3,750,000; Switzerland—$3,750,000; Italy—$3,500,000; USSR—$3,000,000; Finland—$3,000,000; Belgium—$2,800,000; Australia—$2,000,000; Austria—$1,600,000; Pakistan—$1,067,000; Brazil—$1,050,000.

FORMS OF ASSISTANCE OFFERED THROUGH UNDP
Technical and preinvestment assistance offered through UNDP includes the services of experts, the provision of equipment, the award of fellowships for further education and training abroad, and the organization of local or regional seminars or training courses. The following is a description of the main features of the most important forms of assistance offered.

Provision of Experts
Experts may be sent out individually or in teams, depending on their assignments. Teams often include experts recruited by two or more of the participating agencies. An expert in a particular field may follow up the work begun by a specialist in another field. The length of an expert's stay in the country to which he is assigned may vary from a few weeks to several years. His assignment may require him to work in government offices, survey factories, conduct research in scientific institutions, or teach in universities. His work may involve travel by horseback or on foot to remote villages and may take him into disease-ridden areas. Fields of assignment cover the whole range of economic and social development. The technical assistance assignments approved for the biennium 1967–68 included experts to examine the medical application of radioactive isotopes in Burma; a team of specialists to advise Chile on ways of increasing exports of manufactured goods and boosting industrial productivity; an expert in public administration to advise on pension plans in Algeria.

In the 15 years of EPTA's existence, prior to the establishment of UNDP, some 13,000 qualified specialists were thus assigned to advise, assist, and train nationals of the less developed countries. All told, more than 150,000 persons were trained in that period. Between 1960 and 1970 the UNDP trained more than 500,000 persons.

Selection of Experts. Experts are chosen by the executing agencies responsible for the projects involved. The selection of the best-qualified persons to carry out these assignments is essential to the success of the entire program of expert assistance, and an intricate system of intelligence has been built up to recruit the thousands of specialists whose services are required. Professional associations, universities, and government departments are indispensable contacts, and many expert assignments are filled from their ranks. Some experts are chosen from the staffs of the UN and the specialized agencies themselves. An expert is sent on a technical assistance mission only after his candidacy has been approved by the participating government. The outstanding characteristic of this corps of experts is its multinationality. By no means do all or even the majority of experts chosen come from the more highly developed countries. The 8,000 UNDP experts who were carrying out field

---

* Pledge not yet announced. Amount shown represents 1970 pledge.

assignments in 1969 had been recruited by executing agencies from 90 nations. Indeed, among the less-developed countries the flow of experts may be said to be a thoroughly two-way process. All told, about one in five experts comes from a developing country and can put his experience at the service of other developing countries.

Equipment

Each expert, or team of experts, is provided by the executing agency with the necessary equipment for carrying out an assignment. For example, an expert assigned to promote the use of films in adult education will be provided with a projector and films for demonstration purposes, or drilling equipment may be furnished to a team of specialists on a water resources project. The demand for equipment and supplies has grown steadily. In the 1969 program, expenditures for equipment cost $30 million.

Fellowships

Fellowships are awarded to nationals of the less-developed countries by the executing agencies. During the EPTA period, from 1950 to the end of 1965, more than 30,000 men and women profited from these fellowship programs.

The following illustrates how arrangements typically are carried out. A national bank of a Latin American country is being modernized under UNDP, part of the assistance consisting of two fellowships. After consulting with the government, the UN (the agency executing the project) grants the fellowships to two employees of the bank who have worked closely with the UN expert assigned to give advice on improving the bank's operations. The UN arranges for the two fellowship holders to study banking methods in three European countries, paying their travel expenses and a daily living allowance. If they attend foreign educational institutions, the UN will pay their tuition. Their home government continues to pay their regular salaries and may, in addition, contribute toward their travel expenses. More than 5,000 fellowships were financed by the UNDP in 1969.

Large-Scale Preinvestment Surveys and Feasibility Studies

These projects are of three principal types. First, there are the the large-scale surveys of natural resources and feasibility studies of their economic potential for future development—for example, a four-year investigation of potash deposits in the Khemisset Basin in Morocco, and a five-year pilot agricultural study conducted by FAO to develop the natural resources of the Jebel Marra in the Sudan. Projects of the second type provide for the establishment of centers for advanced education and training in the productive use of natural resources. In Somalia, for example, the Rural Tanning Training Center is being substantially expanded by FAO to develop the country's hides, skins, and leather industries. The third principal type of preinvestment project is the establishment or strengthening of applied research institutes for bringing modern technology to bear on development needs. Two regional projects of this type have been carried out by the UN. The first is a five-year plan to establish a regional Transport Technical Bureau to support research, training, and planning activities of governments participating in the Asian Highway Program. The second is a four-year project to develop the activities of the Latin American Institute for Economic and Social Planning in Santiago, originally established with the aid of a Special Fund project approved in 1962.

An important part of UNDP's preinvestment work is to stimulate the necessary follow-up capital investment. (The capital may be provided by many sources—private or public, domestic or foreign—but the UNDP itself does not offer funds for capital investment.) One measure instituted by UNDP to stimulate investment has been to bring regional and national

financing institutions into the projects at the initial planning stages. When projects show sufficient promise, these institutions may then request additional studies in depth. By June 1970 reported investment commitments coming as follow-up to UNDP projects totaled about $4 billion.

MAJOR FIELDS OF UNDP ACTIVITY

The scope of UNDP-assisted projects covers the entire range of economic and social development requirements. The major fields of activity may be classified as follows.

Development Planning—including assistance in drawing up and implementing regional, national, and local development schemes; high-level training in development planning principles and practices, together with administrative and technical support services.

Industry—including mining, manufacturing, and light industry techniques; product development and trade promotion; establishment of cooperatives, pilot plants, and industrial estates; training of entrepreneurs, plant managers, supervisors, and industrial instructors.

Agriculture—including land and water use; crop protection and improvement; animal health and husbandry; forest conservation and management; fisheries development; land reclamation and resettlement; agricultural economics, marketing, and technology (including application of nuclear sciences); pilot farm establishment; training, demonstration, and extension work.

Public Utilities—including hydroelectric, geothermal, and atomic energy production; civil aviation, ports, and waterways, roads and railways, regional and national telecommunications networks.

Education—including training of teachers for primary and secondary schools and for technical and scientific education, of professional engineers, and of middle-level technicians; establishment and strengthening of educational institutions; educational administration and research.

Health—including communicable disease control and eradication; family and child health services; medical and nursing training; environmental sanitation; public health administration.

Major Social Services—including town planning and urban renewal; building and housing; community development; industrial and labor relations; social welfare legislation.

Projects undertaken in any of these sectors may be national, regional, or even interregional in application. Within a single country, several agencies may be executing different UNDP-assisted projects that between them cover the entire range of national development activity.

COUNTRY PROGRAMMING

Country programming is used as a means of achieving the most rational and efficient utilization of resources at the disposal of UNDP for its activities in order to have the maximum impact on the economic and social development of the recipient country. Country programming is based on individual national development plans, or, where these do not exist, on national development priorities or objectives. The government of the country concerned has the exclusive responsibility for formulating its national development plans or priorities and objectives.

The programming of UNDP assistance is carried out in each country within the framework of planning figures indicating the magnitude of the resources expected to be available from

UNDP during the program period. The UNDP country program is formulated by the government of the recipient country in cooperation, at an appropriate stage, with representatives of the system, under the leadership of the UNDP resident director. The formulation of the country program normally involves (1) a broad identification of the needs that arise out of the country's objectives in particular sectors, within the framework of its overall development objectives, and that might appropriately be met by UNDP assistance; (2) as precise an indication as possible of the internal inputs, UNDP inputs, and, wherever possible, other UN inputs to meet these needs; (3) a preliminary list of projects to be subsequently worked out for financing by the UNDP to implement the country program.

ALLOCATION OF FUNDS TO SMALL-SCALE TECHNICAL ASSISTANCE PROJECTS

For the 1969–70 program under UNDP's technical assistance component, more than 2,000 small projects were assisted at a total cost of $44.5 million. Distribution of funds in millions of dollars was as follows.

REGION	AMOUNT	PERCENT
Africa	17.1	38.6
The Americas	8.2	18.6
Asia and the Far East	13.0	29.4
Europe	1.4	3.0
Middle East	2.7	6.0
Interregional	2.1	4.4
TOTALS	44.5	100.0

EXECUTIVE AGENCY	AMOUNT	PERCENT
United Nations	7.7	17.4
ILO	4.6	10.4
FAO	9.8	22.0
UNESCO	7.6	17.2
ICAO	2.1	4.7
WHO	5.5	12.3
ITU	1.8	4.1
WMO	1.5	3.4
IAEA	1.1	2.5
UPU	0.5	1.0
IMCO	0.2	0.4
UNIDO	2.0	4.5
UNCTAD	0.1	0.1
TOTALS	44.5	100.0

TYPES OF ASSISTANCE	PERCENT
Experts	84.7
Fellowships	11.4
Equipment	3.9
TOTAL	100.0

FIELDS OF ACTIVITY	PERCENT
Agriculture	23.4
Industry	12.2
Transport, communications, other public utilities	13.3
Housing, building, physical planning	1.7
Multisector	6.0
Public health	11.9
Education	16.7
Social welfare	3.9
Public administration	10.9
TOTAL	100.0

ALLOCATION OF FUNDS TO PREINVESTMENT PROJECTS

In 1970 the Governing Council approved the allocation of funds for 161 new preinvestment projects, bringing the total number of such projects approved since the inception of the Special Fund to 1,234. The 161 projects were scheduled to involve a total cost of $361.3 million, of which UNDP was to provide $139.3 million and participating governments $222.0 million. Allocation of UNDP funds was as follows.

REGION	NUMBER OF PROJECTS	COST (MILLIONS OF $US)
Africa	58	46.7
The Americas	32	27.1
Asia and the Far East	43	43.6
Europe	12	9.8
Middle East	12	8.5
Interregional	3	2.0
Global	1	1.6

TYPES OF ASSISTANCE	COST (MILLIONS OF $US)
Experts	67.0
Equipment	23.8
Subcontracts	18.9
Fellowships	10.7

(remainder used for overhead costs of UNDP and executing agencies)

TYPES OF PROJECTS	NUMBER OF PROJECTS	COST (MILLIONS OF $US)
Resource surveys	53	44.4
Research	41	33.2
Training	60	56.1
Economic development and planning	7	5.6

FIELDS OF ACTIVITY	NUMBER OF PROJECTS	COST (MILLIONS OF $US)
Agriculture	44	42.4
Industry	45	28.3
Public utilities	27	26.8
Housing, building, etc.	1	0.9
Education	15	16.7
Social welfare, public administration, etc.	18	15.7
Multisector (e.g., river basin development)	11	8.5

Allocation of projects to the executive agencies: FAO 43, UN 24, ILO 17, UNESCO 19, ITU 5, IBRD 8, WMO 3, WHO 11, ICAO 6, UPU 4, IAEA 2, UNIDO 17, ASDB 1, UNDP 1.

THE WORK OF THE UN AS EXECUTING AGENCY

The UN carries out projects of technical assistance both under its regular budget and as part of the UNDP aid complex. All technical cooperation activities of the UN are under the direction of the UN commissioner for technical cooperation. The task of supervising the UN's activities—whether carried out under the regular budget or through UNDP—is exercised by the Governing Council of UNDP.

For the year 1965, the total financial value of the assistance executed by the UN (including regular and UNDP programs and certain activities financed under funds-in-trust arrangements) was $66 million, compared with $32.9 million in 1964 and $23.2 million in 1963. The rise was due mainly to the steadily increasing role of the UN as an executing agency for

UNDP (Special Fund) preinvestment projects—for 109 preinvestment surveys and studies.

A program deserving special mention is OPEX (Operational and Executive Personnel Program), for providing executive and administrative personnel to work in the employ (paid at local salary rates) of governments faced with a serious shortage of trained top-echelon civil servants. This program, which was initiated by the Assembly in 1958 under the UN regular budget, is now largely financed through UNDP funds, and the majority of OPEX personnel are now provided by the specialized agencies.

Technical Programs Financed under the UN Regular Budget

The annual appropriations set aside for the UN's regular programs of technical assistance and cooperation now stand at $6.4 million. The operational programs financed with this sum are officially classified under three main categories: economic development, social development, and public administration; human rights advisory services; and narcotic drugs control.

Activities under the first category are varied. They include natural resource surveys, the entire gamut of industrial development and productivity projects; advisory services to governments on organization and improvement of their administrative operations, particularly in the field of taxation; advisory services in social welfare; and statistical services.

UN assistance in the field of human rights consists chiefly of organizing local or regional seminars on the various aspects of the subject. The UN's program on narcotics control is designed to help countries in which the problem is a major concern.

SPECIAL AREAS OF SOCIAL PROGRESS

UNITED NATIONS CHILDREN'S FUND (UNICEF)

This organization, originally known as the UN International Children's Emergency Fund, was established by the General Assembly in December 1946 to provide emergency relief in the form of milk, drugs, soap, blankets, shoes, and other sorely needed items for children in war-ravaged countries. By the end of 1949, UNICEF had allocated almost $77 million to these projects. In December 1950, with its crash relief program successfully completed, UNICEF received a fresh mandate from the Assembly which extended the Fund's life for three years. The Assembly, in addition, directed UNICEF to shift its emphasis from emergency aid to long-term programs for improving the health and nutrition of children in underdeveloped countries. In 1953 the Assembly decided to maintain UNICEF as a permanent body and changed its name to the UN Children's Fund (the old acronym was retained, for it had by then become world famous).

In 1961, in response to a heightened realization of the importance of preparing children and young people to contribute to the growth of their countries, UNICEF broadened the scope of its assistance to include projects that promote the role of children as an invaluable "human resource" in national development. This approach emphasized increased aid to education. In 1965, UNICEF was awarded the Nobel Peace Prize.

PURPOSES

The Assembly's resolutions of 1950, 1953, and 1961 were based on the belief that the time was ripe to take action against a different kind of emergency from that produced by civil strife or natural disaster—the continuing emergency occasioned by the perennial threat of hunger, sickness, and severely limited opportunities among millions of children in the developing nations. Today, a major function of UNICEF's field staff is to help governments to plan the most effective use of UNICEF aid within the context of national development programs. While continuing to assist health, educational, and nutrition projects, it is putting increasing emphasis on the training of local staff. Moreover, because the rapid pace of social and economic change in many countries has magnified family problems, UNICEF also provides training grants for welfare personnel and gives special attention to the problem of preparing women and girls to take an active, responsible part in community life. In addition, it continues to respond to children's needs arising out of emergency situations occasioned by civil strife and natural disaster. In fulfilling its mandate, UNICEF has brought the UN directly into the lives of millions of persons in remote parts of the world. It has also brought them hope in ways that no other international enterprise has done and has given them a stake in the modern world. As UNICEF's executive director stated in his Nobel Prize acceptance speech in December 1965:

In more than one hundred developing countries of the world, the odds that confront the average child today—not to say a sickly one—are still overwhelming. They are 4 to 1 against his receiving any medical attention, at birth or afterwards. Even if he survives until school age, the chances are 2 to 1 that he will get no education at all; if he does get into school, the chances are about 3 to 1 that he will not complete the elementary grades. Almost certainly he will have to work for a living by the time he is twelve. He will work to eat—to eat badly and not enough. And his life will, on the average, end in about 40 years.

Such statistics make us face the staggering waste of human talent which drains, year in, year out, the very nations which need them the most. The developing countries are making a courageous effort to catch up with the industrial ones. But development means, above all, people—not numbers of people but quality of people. One of the crucial factors in the progress of a country is the development of the child, the adult of tomorrow—tomorrow's engineers, doctors, progressive farmers, teachers, scientists, social leaders. That is the great task in which UNICEF is taking a share.

As the UN began its second Development Decade, the work of UNICEF assumed a new significance. Addressing a meeting of the UNICEF Executive Board in May 1970, the secretary-general of the UN pointed up the importance of UNICEF's special task of cooperating with developing countries for the benefit of their children: "In the less-developed regions of the world where poverty, illiteracy, and disease are greatest, children and youth under 15 years of age account for more than 40 per cent of the total population. There are over 1,000 million children in these countries today, and this overwhelming number will rise to 1,300 million by 1980. If today's children are to assume a useful and responsible role in the society of tomorrow the promotion of their welfare is of paramount concern to an organization dedicated to furthering human well-being."

With the aims of the second Development Decade in mind, UNICEF is placing increasing emphasis on projects designed to improve the quality of children's lives. But its on-going, overall concern is to stimulate the efforts of governments, voluntary agencies, and private citizens to mobilize local resources on behalf of children. UNICEF aid, which is provided only at the request of governments, is given without regard to race, sex, creed, nationality, or political belief.

ORGANIZATION

UNICEF is a part of the UN, but it has a semiautonomous status. It is governed by a 30-nation Executive Board that meets regularly to set policy, consider requests, allocate aid, evaluate results, and establish the annual administrative budget of the Fund.

The members of the Executive Board are elected for terms of three years by ECOSOC from among members of the UN or of the specialized agencies. In 1970 the following states were members of the Executive Board:

Belgium, Brazil, Bulgaria, Canada, Chile, China, Costa Rica, Czechoslovakia, France, Gabon, West Germany, India, Indonesia, Italy, Malawi, Nigeria, Pakistan, Philippines, Poland, Sierra Leone, Sweden, Switzerland, Thailand, Tunisia, Turkey, USSR, United Arab Republic, United Kingdom, United States, and Venezuela.

The day-to-day operation of UNICEF is the responsibility

of the executive director, who is appointed by the secretary-general of the UN in consultation with the Executive Board. UNICEF's first executive director, who served continuously until his death in January 1965, was Maurice Pate, an American who had been closely associated with Herbert Hoover in European war relief. He was succeeded by Henry R. Labouisse, former head of the UN Relief and Works Agency for Palestine Refugees and former US ambassador to Greece.

UNICEF has a staff of approximately 885 persons stationed either at its central offices at UN Headquarters in New York or in some 36 regional and field offices throughout the world.

UNICEF cooperates closely with several other subsidiary bodies of the UN—notably, the UN Bureau of Economic and Social Affairs, the UN Development Program (UNDP), and the UN Fund for Population Activities—and with certain specialized agencies, such as WHO, FAO, UNESCO, and ILO. Through the cooperative use of their expertise and resources, all the agencies can together render more effective assistance than any of them could alone, and duplication or fragmentation of effort is avoided.

UNICEF and Voluntary Organizations

Eighty international nongovernmental organizations (NGOs), representing a wide range of interests and activities, have consultative status with the UNICEF Executive Board, and representatives of these organizations have formed a NGO Committee on UNICEF. In many countries receiving UNICEF aid, the role of voluntary organizations is very important, and in a number of instances governments accepting the responsibility for carrying out UNICEF-aided projects rely on such voluntary organizations to handle part of the operations. These voluntary organizations also provide important services beyond the scope of government activities. The work of voluntary organizations, for example, is involved to a considerable degree in the new programs of assistance to social services for children that UNICEF is inaugurating.

In addition, national committees for UNICEF had, by the end of 1970, been organized in 27 countries and were planned in a number of other countries. The object of these national committees is to foster broad popular interest and participation in UNICEF programs. A number of these committees have been active in fund-raising and in promoting the sale of UNICEF greeting cards. Particularly successful has been the "Trick or Treat" Halloween program in the US and Canada, which collects over $4 million a year for UNICEF.

FINANCES

UNICEF depends entirely on voluntary contributions from governments, private organizations and individuals.

Income for 1969 came to over $47 million, of which about two thirds was contributed by governments. As awareness of UNICEF's importance has grown, the number of contributing governments has increased: 30 governments contributed to UNICEF in 1950, 61 in 1954, 102 in 1962, 128 in 1969.

GOVERNMENT CONTRIBUTIONS TO UNICEF
AMOUNTING TO $200,000 OR MORE IN 1969

COUNTRY	CONTRIBUTION
US	$13,000,000
Sweden	2,906,977
West Germany	1,750,000
France	1,398,988
UK	1,200,000
Canada	1,112,400
India	800,000
Norway	721,044
USSR	675,000
Australia	616,039
Japan	584,672
Denmark	533,333
Mexico	500,000
Italy	319,317
Iran	300,000
Belgium	240,000
Thailand	223,750
Netherlands	222,222
Turkey	222,222
Finland	220,000
Poland	200,000
Yugoslavia	200,000

Included in UNICEF income from governments (though not in the individual figures cited above) are special funds that certain governments may designate for use in "specific-purpose" projects. In 1969 about $3.8 million was donated, for example, for health and family projects in India and Pakistan, rehabilitation projects in Nigeria, social welfare projects in South Viet-Nam.

Private contributions accounted for $7.7 million of UNICEF's total income for 1969, while $3.9 million was provided by the sale of some 60 million greeting cards as part of UNICEF's 1968 greeting card campaign. These cards are designed by outstanding contemporary artists, and their world-wide sale is a unique method of raising money for aid to children.

As UNICEF's scope of activity and the world of children continue to grow, so does the need for funds. As UNICEF's executive director put it, there is "an effective demand for at least twice the volume of aid now being provided by UNICEF." In 1970, UNICEF's Executive Board set an annual income target of $100 million, to be reached by 1975.

Allocation of Funds

The UNICEF Executive Board meets once a year to allocate funds for program aid and for administrative costs. Program assistance requests, which are considered on a project-by-project basis, originate in the field. Officially, they are government requests, but each is based on a "project plan of operations" drawn up among government officials, UNICEF representatives, and representatives of the other UN agencies concerned. The requests are reviewed at headquarters, and those that are recommended by the executive director as conforming to UNICEF's assistance policies and financial capabilities are submitted to the Executive Board's program committee. Projects recommended by the program committee are submitted to the Executive Board itself for allocation of funds.

AVERAGE ANNUAL UNICEF ALLOCATIONS, 1968–1970
IN MILLIONS OF US DOLLARS

	AFRICA	ASIA	EAST MED.	EU-ROPE	AMER-ICAS	INTER-REG'L	TOTAL
Health	3.3	9.5	1.9	0.0	3.3	0.1	18.1
Educational & Pre-vocational Training	3.8	4.9	0.8	—	1.2	0.1	10.8
Nutrition	1.3	2.5	0.5	0.0	0.4	0.2	4.9
Family & Child Welfare	0.5	0.7	0.2	—	0.3	—	1.7
Other Long-Range Aid	0.0	0.2	0.1	0.0	0.5	1.1	1.9
Emergency Aid	1.3	0.0	0.2	—	—	0.1	1.6
Subtotal, Program Aid							39.0
Operational Services							6.7
TOTAL ASSISTANCE							45.7

Administration	3.8
GRAND TOTAL	
ALLOCATIONS	49.5

SCOPE AND METHODS OF WORK

Improvement of maternal and child welfare is the final end of every aid program provided by UNICEF, and these programs are grafted onto, and are an integral part of, overall national development programs. Between 1947 and 1969, 137 countries and territories received UNICEF assistance. UNICEF aid reaches 112 developing countries with a total child population of more than 1,000 million. It is estimated that by 1980 the number of children in UNICEF aided countries will increase to 1,300 million.

During the 1960's there was an important change of emphasis in UNICEF's work, away from individual projects conceived as essentially separate entities and toward the evolution of comprehensive programs that encompass all children's welfare projects within a given country and are related to its own national development priorities. Another important change in UNICEF's work methods has been an increasing selectivity in projects aided with a growing number of projects being planned on a long-term basis and special attention paid to the most vulnerable age groups—preschool children and adolescents.

Arranging for the Provision of "Matching-Funds"

A major function of UNICEF's field staff is to help governments plan the most effective use of UNICEF aid within the context of the country's total development programs. It is the assisted governments concerned, not UNICEF, that are responsible for the administration of UNICEF-aided projects. Furthermore, all governments requesting UNICEF aid are required to supply and pay for the buildings, basic equipment, and labor needed in the projects. In UNICEF terminology, the local resources thus made available by governments are known as "matching funds." Governments have provided an average of $2.50 for every dollar allocated by UNICEF for a given project. (These funds are supplied over and above the contributions that the assisted governments may make to UNICEF itself as part of its annual income.) "Matching" is a dynamic device for ensuring that children's needs are given a high priority in the national development plans and that the programs launched will be continued by the assisted governments in the future.

Division of Responsibility between UNICEF and Other Agencies

UNICEF provides supplies and technical equipment that are not available for a given project in the countries concerned. It also provides material help for training national personnel and engineering assistance for food conservation projects, and it offers general help in project planning, patterns of budgetary support, and organization and staffing for expansion of permanent services. The other agencies give technical advice both to governments and to UNICEF, and in many instances supply qualified personnel to assist in the execution of the projects. In the health field, for example, a joint UNICEF–WHO committee on health policy decides the types of health programs that UNICEF will assist, and UNICEF's Executive Board approves a project only after it has received the approval of WHO. WHO is also responsible for setting the technical specifications for UNICEF-provided equipment and supplies for all health projects.

MAIN TYPES OF UNICEF-ASSISTED PROJECTS

In helping governments to provide assistance for children, UNICEF supports specific projects in the fields of health, nutrition, education, vocational training, and social welfare. As of April 1970, UNICEF was providing assistance to 37 countries in Africa, 27 in Asia, 13 in the Eastern Mediterranean, 1 in Europe, and 34 in the Americas. Financial allocations approved at the April 1970 session of the Executive Board were distributed as follows: $13,129,650 for Africa; $10,484,700 for East Asia and Pakistan; $9,660,000 for South Central Asia; $4,878,000 for the Americas; $3,013,475 for the Eastern Mediterranean; $1,416,086 for interregional projects; $90,692 for Europe; and $1,005,399 for emergency aid.

Basic Mother and Child Health

A primary long-term interest of UNICEF is to help countries establish networks of basic health services for mothers and children. In 1970, maternal and child health projects in 112 countries and territories were receiving UNICEF assistance. In all, UNICEF had approved aid for basic equipment (and in many cases drugs, milk powder, vitamins, and soap) for more than 50,000 health centers and subcenters. Aid also had been approved for more than 2,000 district and urban health centers, maternity and pediatric wards, and kindred services, and for more than 1,700 training institutions.

The safe delivery of babies was the objective first emphasized in this part of UNICEF's work. The present objective is to extend basic health services to include broader prenatal care and care for young children in the especially vulnerable period between weaning and school age. To implement these objectives, UNICEF, through a variety of forms of assistance, and with the close technical cooperation of WHO, encourages the development of networks of maternal and child health services that are integrated into the local, provincial, and national general health services.

Aid to maternal and child health services at first was confined to basic technical equipment, supplies, drugs, and diet supplements. In later years, UNICEF has steadily increased its emphasis on aid for training health service personnel. Since an important function of maternal and child health centers should be to provide education, especially to mothers, in child rearing and better health and nutrition practices, training in health education is also stressed. UNICEF provides training equipment for schools, hospitals, and centers where doctors, public health nurses, midwives, health visitors, and auxiliary workers are trained for work in the field of maternal and child care. Under certain conditions, UNICEF provides stipends for trainees and in some cases pays part of the salaries of training instructors. A start has also been made in helping selected schools of medicine and public health to strengthen their teaching of pediatrics and preventive medicine and to establish graduate training programs for medical officers serving in health centers.

Environmental Sanitation. Gastrointestinal and parasitic diseases, which are responsible for much sickness in young children and many deaths, can be controlled through effective environmental sanitation. In the majority of the 112 countries where UNICEF works, environmental sanitation, especially safe water, is associated with maternal and child health services. In Upper Volta, for example, through self-help by local communities, 415 wells were dug and equipped with pumps and 42 new community water plans were installed in 1970 (bringing the total number of such plans to 225), serving some 300,000 people. Besides providing the necessary equipment for these projects, UNICEF furnishes education materials and stipends for training experts in this field.

Family Planning. In 1967, UNICEF decided to move into this field, and since that time a growing number of countries have begun to link family planning with their basic maternal and child health services. Aid for the family planning aspects of these services has been approved for India, Malaysia, Pakistan, South Korea, Singapore, Thailand, and the UAR. Similar projects for

Indonesia and the Philippines have been "noted" for assistance when additional funds become available. The aid provided includes facilities for the transport and training of workers, equipment for health centers, and special drugs. In addition, UNICEF's Executive Board decided at its 1970 session that it would supply contraceptives on the request of governments and with the technical approval of WHO.

Mass Disease Control Campaigns

No health service can hope to build up a permanent program of preventive health benefits for mothers and children if its resources are constantly being drained to treat widespread chronic sickness. In most of the countries aided by UNICEF, mass campaigns to control or eradicate the endemic diseases affecting children, and large numbers of adults as well, are a necessary prerequisite to any effective maternal and child welfare program. Moreover, the large-scale disease control programs aided by UNICEF and WHO arouse general interest in modern concepts of health, prepare the way in the public mind for other health programs, and strengthen permanent health services.

About 25% of UNICEF aid goes for the control of serious communicable diseases common among children that can be prevented or treated on a mass scale at a low cost per capita. Mass campaigns against these diseases are conducted in parts of the world where the countries concerned will be able to consolidate the gains made on a permanent basis. Often the first step in such a campaign in a particular country is a pilot project for experience and training. In the 1960's there was a progressive integration of these campaigns into basic health services.

The overall achievements of UNICEF-aided campaigns against communicable diseases are impressive. Over 300 million children have been vaccinated against tuberculosis with UNICEF-supplied vaccine, about 180 million of them in 1960–69. More than 40 million children have been treated for trachoma and related eye diseases, about 36 million in 1960–69. Also in 1960–69, 10 million children were cured of yaws by treatment with penicillin. Over 453,000 children have been treated for leprosy with the new sulfone drugs, about 400,000 of them since 1960. In 1955, UNICEF began participating in WHO's worldwide campaign to eradicate malaria, which has stultified development in vast areas and has had devastating effects on children. Although more than half the population of the malaria-afflicted areas have been freed of the disease, total eradication has not yet been accomplished. Nevertheless, in 1969 alone, some 32 million children were protected against this scourge with UNICEF-supplied materials.

Nutrition

In the underdeveloped areas of the world, malnutrition is a major cause of infant and child mortality, stunted growth, mental apathy, and lowered resistance to infectious disease. One of the most serious problems is protein deficiency in the diet of children during the critical postweaning and preschool years. It has been estimated that in many countries as many as 70% of the children under five years of age are malnourished and have no chance of developing to their full potential.

Milk Distribution and Dairy Development. The shipment of skim milk powder donated by the US, Canada, and other dairy-surplus countries was a prominent feature of UNICEF's early relief activities in Europe. Almost all of UNICEF's early programs in the developing countries also featured the distribution of surplus skim milk, and in the mid-1950's UNICEF was shipping about 100 million pounds of milk powder a year to beneficiary countries. Shipments fell off sharply in the early 1960's, however, as dairy surpluses in the donor countries dwindled. Hence, UNICEF has concentrated on stimulating local production of safe milk and increasing its availability to children in low-income groups. To this end, it has helped to equip some 235 milk-processing plants, to establish 16 related training institutes, and, with FAO-recruited experts, to improve milk collection and distribution services.

Applied Nutrition. UNICEF, with technical cooperation from FAO and WHO, has concentrated on what are called "applied nutrition projects" to stimulate greater production and use of eggs, fish, garden vegetables, and other nutritious products at the village and community level. In 1970, 13% of UNICEF allocations went to improved nutrition. UNICEF provides 70 countries with tools and seeds for school and community gardens; nets and other equipment for village fish ponds; incubators, brooders, and the like for poultry raising; and training stipends for nutrition workers. The basic object of all these applied nutrition schemes is to teach people the importance of high-protein and other protective foods in their children's diet and to show them how to produce these foods. Special attention has been given to nutrition training for extension workers, schoolteachers, community leaders, and village auxiliaries.

New High Protein Foods. The primary object of UNICEF's work in developing new high-protein foods is to alleviate malnutrition among the children of poorer urban families who must choose their foods from among the cheaper products available in shops and markets. Recognizing the difficulty of expanding production of milk and other conventional animal foods in many tropical and subtropical areas, UNICEF embarked in 1956 on a cooperative venture with FAO, WHO, and other agencies aimed at the development of low-cost children's foods based on such products as soya, cottonseed, and fish flours.

The most economical products developed are cereal-based mixtures that include vegetable protein concentrates. A corn-sorghum-cottonseed flour mixture, named Incaparina in honor of the Institute of Nutrition of Central America and Panama (INCAP), where it was developed, has been widely marketed in Central America. By 1970 some 94 million pounds of a high-protein blended food made of corn, soya, and milk powder called CSM had been shipped to developing countries, with a major portion going for emergency relief and rehabilitation in Nigeria. In response to the urgency of the situation in that country, UNICEF nutritionists also developed an effective product for the short-term crash-feeding of children suffering from severe and prolonged protein-calorie malnutrition. Named K-Mix-II, the food is essentially a premix that can be fed either by nasogastric tube or by cup. It consists of three parts casein, five parts skim milk powder, and ten parts sucrose. With peanut oil, iron, vitamins, and water added, it produced dramatically successful results in Nigeria. After a week of K-Mix-II feeding, many children were able to be transferred gradually to a more substantial mixed diet to aid their recuperation.

Family and Child Welfare Services

Rapid social and economic changes associated with industrialization, urbanization, and the growth of populations are leading to a disruption of traditional patterns of family and community life in many parts of the developing world. Children are the chief sufferers, for whom there is an acute need for basic social services in almost all the developing countries. Primarily, UNICEF supports programs designed to keep the family together and improve the care given children in their own homes. In some countries, women's clubs have been organized, as part of a broader community development movement, to teach mothers and young women better ways of raising children. Day-care centers are stressed as one of the most practical ways of helping the family meet its responsibilities to the child when both parents must work. UNICEF assists training projects for family and child welfare workers at all levels, from professional supervisors to village volunteers. UNICEF aid in this field was inaugurated in 1958 and since that time has helped to equip some 1,800 day-care centers, over 3,300 women's clubs, 600 training institutions for welfare workers, and about 2,700 community centers, youth clubs, and orphanages.

Education and Training

In developing countries only one child in five finishes primary school. Yet more and better schooling is recognized as the chief requisite for economic and social progress. The physical obstacles to an expansion of the educational systems of most developing countries are a limited capacity for teacher training, a shortage of buildings and equipment, and a shortage of texts and other teaching materials.

To overcome these obstacles, UNICEF allocates roughly one third of its annual budget to projects in education and training, helping to equip 1,400 teacher-training schools and more than 47,000 associated primary schools. It has also assisted in the establishment of some 900 prevocational training schools to enhance the employment opportunities of older children who are unable because of lack of available facilities to attend secondary schools or universities.

Training of Local Staff for UNICEF-aided Projects

This is an extremely important aspect of UNICEF's work. Over the years equipment, stipends, and other aid have been provided for the training of some 570,000 persons serving children—pediatricians, nurses, midwives, child-care workers, community leaders, nutritionists, and schoolteachers. In 1969 alone, approximately 132,000 persons received special training.

Integrated Services

Since 1966, UNICEF has aided a number of projects that provide integrated services for children and their families in specific communities. Each project encompasses virtually all the types of services normally covered by UNICEF aid—basic mother and child health services, nutrition work, day-care for the young, the equipment of primary and vocational schools. One of the most ambitious of these projects focuses on the UAR government's program for establishing villages of migrant workers for reclaiming land in the area of the Aswan Dam.

Emergency Aid

Prior to 1951 more than three fourths of UNICEF's budget went to emergency aid. In later years, however, emergency aid has played a relatively small role. In times of disaster—floods, hurricanes, or hardships due to war—countries are encouraged to turn first to the League of Red Cross Societies and other organizations specializing in emergency rather than long-term assistance. Whenever possible, UNICEF prefers to help in the restoration, or "postdisaster" stage. Of the several instances of natural disasters and military strife during 1969, the destruction and deprivation in the aftermath of the Nigerian civil war stood out as the most serious situation requiring UNICEF aid. At its April 1970 session, the Executive Board allocated $7,391,000 to assist the Nigerian government in rehabilitating and expanding nationwide services for children.

NARCOTIC DRUGS CONTROL

In the first issue of the *United Nations Bulletin on Narcotics* (October 1949), Trygve Lie, then secretary-general of the UN, summarized the importance of international narcotics control:

The problem of narcotic drugs is in no sense a problem confined to one continent or civilization.

In themselves narcotic drugs are neither dangerous nor harmful. Indispensable to modern medicine, they are used the world over to alleviate pain and restore health. Thus used they bring a great benefit to mankind. But abused they cause havoc and misery. The social dangers of drug addiction are well known.

This dual nature of narcotic drugs has made it necessary to submit them to the most stringent international control. . . . This control, functioning now under the auspices of the United Nations and expanding rapidly to the field of newly discovered synthetic drugs, ensures the limitation of their manufacture, trade and consumption to legitimate needs only.

Until the end of the 19th century, the question of narcotic drugs was not regarded as an international problem calling for international action. Trade in narcotics was considered a legitimate business. Misuse of addiction-producing substances—opium, coca leaf, Indian hemp—was considered the result of ingrained habits in particular areas of the world.

Early in the 19th century, a number of bilateral treaties curbed the import of narcotics into some Asian countries. The problem was considered a domestic one. However, modern technology and the expansion of transport and world trade introduced a new dimension. An increasing number of alkaloids and derivatives were being produced from opium and coca leaves and easily distributed. What was once considered a local problem soon became a world problem.

The UN exercises functions and powers relating to the worldwide control of narcotic drugs in accordance with 10 international treaties concluded between 1912 and 1961. By 1970 over 100 countries were parties to one or more of the treaties. The international control system is based on the cooperation of the states that are bound by these treaties in controlling the manufacture and sale of narcotic drugs within the limits of their jurisdiction. The treaties stipulate that these states are bound to adopt appropriate legislation, introduce necessary administrative and enforcement measures, and cooperate with international control organs as well as with each other.

NARCOTICS CONTROL UNDER THE LEAGUE OF NATIONS

The League of Nations Covenant provided that League members should "entrust the League with the general supervision over agreements with regard. . . to the traffic in opium and other dangerous drugs." The first League Assembly created an Advisory Committee on Traffic in Opium and Other Dangerous Drugs to assist the League's Council in its supervisory tasks in the field. The International Permanent Central Opium Board was composed at first of eight independent experts, to which League members were required to submit annual statistics on the production of opium and coca leaves, the manufacture, consumption, and stocks of narcotic drugs, and quarterly reports on the import and export of narcotic drugs. The convention also required specific governmental authorization for every import

and export of narcotic drugs. The Convention for Limiting the Manufacture and Regulating the Distribution of [Narcotic] Drugs, signed at Geneva in 1931, created a new technical organ composed of independent experts, the Drug Supervisory Body. The aim of the 1931 convention was to limit world manufacture of drugs to the amount actually needed for medical and scientific purposes.

The last pre-World War II treaty on narcotics was the Convention for the Suppression of Illicit Traffic in Dangerous Drugs, signed at Geneva in 1936. This convention called for severe punishment of illicit traffickers in narcotics. The parties to the convention undertook to enact measures to prevent offenders from escaping prosecution by taking advantage of technical loopholes in the law and to facilitate extradition for drug offenses. Thus by the outbreak of World War II, a worldwide narcotics control was in operation.

DEVELOPMENT UNDER THE UNITED NATIONS

A protocol signed 11 December 1946 transferred to the UN the functions previously exercised by the League of Nations under the pre-World War II narcotics treaties.

As the post-World War II system of international control has been worked out, the UN shares responsibility with the World Health Organization in the field of narcotic drugs. There were, as of 1966, four organs within the UN system exclusively concerned with the problems of narcotics: the Commission on Narcotic Drugs, a policy-making organ, and the specialized administrative organs, the Permanent Central Narcotics Board, the Drug Supervisory Body, and the WHO Expert Committee on Addiction-Producing Drugs. The first three of these organs are subsidiary bodies of the UN's Economic and Social Council (ECOSOC).

A new body, the International Narcotics Control Board (INCB), replaced the Central Narcotics Board and the Drug Supervisory Body under the Single Convention on Narcotic Drugs of 1961.

The Commission on Narcotic Drugs is composed of 24 members appointed by ECOSOC for rotating 4-year terms. The countries chosen to serve on the commission are important producers of narcotic raw materials such as coca leaf and opium, important drug manufacturers, or countries in which the illicit traffic in narcotics presents a serious problem.

The commission is the general organ of control, exercising policy-making and quasi-legislative functions. In addition, the commission assists and advises ECOSOC in exercising policy-making and quasi-legislative functions. The commission also assists and advises ECOSOC in exercising its powers of supervision over the application of international conventions and agreements dealing with narcotic drugs, recommends changes that may be required in the existing machinery for international control of narcotics, and performs any other functions relating to narcotic drugs that ECOSOC directs it to carry out. The commission meets biennially to review the status of narcotics control in all countries. Observers from countries not represented on the commission and from countries not even represented in the UN are invited to attend its meetings whenever an item is to be discussed that is of particular interest to them.

The WHO Expert Committee on Addiction-Producing Drugs, composed of technical experts, evaluates the dangerous properties of new drugs to determine whether they should be placed under international control. The International Narcotics Control Board has its own secretariat in the Palais des Nations, Geneva. Secretariat services for the ECOSOC Commission on Narcotic Drugs are provided by the UN secretariat's Division of Narcotic Drugs, which is also located in Geneva.

The Division of Narcotic Drugs maintains its own research laboratory in the Palais des Nations in Geneva.

SCOPE OF INTERNATIONAL CONTROL

Because the International Narcotics Control Board is authorized to estimate the legitimate narcotic drug needs of all countries not furnishing such estimates, whether or not they are parties to the treaties, and because the board has the power to embargo imports in excess of these estimated requirements, the system of quantitative controls over the international trade in narcotics has nearly universal application. The number of countries and territories complying with their obligations under the narcotics treaties to supply information and reports exceeds the number of UN members. There is now practically universal cooperation of governments, whether or not they were parties to the conventions. The system of control instituted by the conventions of 1925 and 1931 and continued after World War II under UN auspices is aimed at eliminating the risk of diversion of narcotic drugs from legitimate channels to the illicit market. However, the problem of illicit production and trafficking in narcotic drugs, as distinct from that of the diversion of legitimately produced narcotics, remains unsolved.

PERFECTING THE TREATY SYSTEM

One of the tasks of the UN in the field of narcotic drugs control is to adapt the international treaty machinery to changing conditions. Three narcotics agreements—the Paris protocol of 1948, the opium protocol of 1953, and the Single Convention on Narcotic Drugs—have been drawn up under UN auspices.

The Paris Protocol of 1948. The prewar international conventions on narcotics applied to all addictive products of three plants, the opium poppy, the coca bush, and the cannabis plant, and to products belonging to certain chemical groups known to have addictive properties. By the end of the war, however, a number of synthetic narcotics not belonging to the defined chemical groups had been developed. A protocol signed in Paris on 19 November 1948 authorized the WHO to place under full international control any new drug not covered by previous conventions that was found to be addictive or could be converted into an addictive drug. The Paris protocol came into force on 1 December 1949 and by the end of 1964 had been accepted by 80 countries. The protocol aimed at preventing any large-scale abuse of the new addictive drugs that have come into medical use since 1939.

The Opium Protocol of 1953. Although the existing system of international control aimed to limit to medical and scientific needs the manufacture and use of all narcotic drugs, including opium and its derivatives, an overproduction of opium continued in certain countries that found its way into illicit channels. To remedy this situation, the Commission on Narcotic Drugs first proposed an international opium monopoly, complete with production quotas and a system of international inspection. It was impossible, however, to obtain the agreement of all the principal opium-producing countries on such important questions as the price of opium and inspection rights.

A compromise, first proposed by France, was worked out by the UN Opium Conference held in New York in May–June 1953 and embodied in a Protocol for Limiting and Regulating the Cultivation of the Poppy Plant, the Production of, International

Trade in, and Use of Opium. Under this protocol only seven states—Bulgaria, Greece, India, Iran, Turkey, the USSR, and Yugoslavia—are authorized to produce opium for export. Producing states are required to set up a government agency to license opium poppy cultivators and designate the areas to be cultivated. Cultivators are to deliver all opium immediately after harvesting to this agency, which is the only body with a legal right to engage in the country's internal or international trade in opium. The Permanent Central Narcotics Board, under the protocol, was empowered to employ certain supervisory and enforcement measures and, with the consent of the government concerned, to carry out local inquiries. The protocol came into force in December 1964, when it was ratified by 49 states, including, as required, 3 of the 7 principal opium-producing countries—India, Iran, and Greece.

THE 1961 SINGLE CONVENTION ON NARCOTIC DRUGS

After more than a decade of studies, inquiries, and meetings, a special conference held at the UN with 73 countries participating (24 January to 25 March 1961) adopted the Single Convention on Narcotic Drugs. The convention updates, broadens, and tightens the provisions contained in the treaty network above described, incorporating them in a single instrument. All countries bound by it are required to license the cultivation of opium poppy, coca leaves, and cannabis plants for the production of cannabis resin and immediately to buy and take possession of each crop. Production must be reduced when necessary, and illegally cultivated plants must be destroyed. The countries are also required to tighten export and licensing and control over manufacture and trade of drugs and to cooperate more closely in combating illicit traffic. According to the degree of danger to public health, all substances declared to be addiction producing are to be listed in four categories ("schedules"), and strict national and UN control measures are prescribed for each category.

The convention came into force on 14 December 1964 with the deposit of the fortieth instrument of ratification. As of September 1970, the convention had been acceded to by 79 states: Afghanistan, Algeria, Argentina, Australia, Belgium, Brazil, Bulgaria, Burma, Byelorussia, Cameroon, Canada, Ceylon, Chad, Chile, China, Costa Rica, Cuba, Cyprus, Czechoslovakia, Dahomey, Denmark, Ecuador, Ethiopia, Finland, France, Gabon, Ghana, Guatemala, Guinea, Holy See, Hungary, India, Iraq, Israel, Ivory Coast, Jamaica, Japan, Jordan, Kenya, Kuwait, Lebanon, Malawi, Malaysia, Mali, Mauritius, Mexico, Monaco, Morocco, Netherlands, New Zealand, Niger, Nigeria, Norway, Pakistan, Panama, Peru, Philippines, Poland, South Korea, South Viet-Nam, Senegal, Spain, Sweden, Switzerland, Syria, Thailand, Togo, Trinidad and Tobago, Tunisia, Turkey, Ukraine, the USSR, the UAR, the UK, the US, Upper Volta, Venezuela, Yugoslavia, and Zambia.

Implementation of the Single Convention. The Commission on Narcotic Drugs has adopted an administrative guide for the use of governments, as well as several questionnaires and a model form of import certificate for submission of information to the UN secretary-general.

To implement its provisions, the convention provided for the establishment of an International Narcotics Control Board, replacing the Permanent Central Narcotics Board and the Drug Supervisory Body.

The 11 members of the board are elected by ECOSOC for three-year periods.

NARCOTIC DRUGS UNDER INTERNATIONAL CONTROL
Opium and Its Derivatives

Opium, the coagulated juice of the poppy plant *Papaver somni-*

ferum Linnaeus, was known to the Sumerians living in Lower Mesopotamia in 5000 B.C. It was used by the Greeks and Arabs for medicinal purposes and was probably introduced to China by the Arabs in the 9th or 10th century. The opium poppy can be grown in most of the habitable parts of the world and is often cultivated for its beautiful flowers or its seeds, which are a valuable food. As an addictive drug, opium was originally eaten or drunk as an infusion. The practice of smoking opium is only a few hundred years old.

The best-known derivatives of opium are morphine, codeine, and diacetylmorphine, more commonly called heroin. While morphine and codeine have valuable medicinal properties, heroin has no medical uses for which less dangerous analgesics cannot be substituted, and upon the recommendation of the Commission on Narcotic Drugs its manufacture has been banned in most countries. A number of drugs are derived from morphine, or are compounded with it, including ethylmorphine and benzylmorphine. Some morphine derivatives, such as apomorphine, are not addictive in themselves.

The most important drugs in national and international illicit traffic are still opium and its derivatives, in particular morphine and heroin. As a result of effective international controls, there has been little diversion of opium or opiates from legitimate channels into the illicit trade. The supplies for the illicit traffic come from areas in the Middle and Far East where poppies are grown in huge fields and where local control is inadequate to prevent the smuggling of large quantities of raw opium, which eventually falls into the hands of international criminal syndicates. Clandestine factories use the raw opium for the manufacture of morphine, which in turn is often converted into heroin. Morphine and particularly heroin are much more potent than raw opium and, being much less bulky, are easier to smuggle. There is a great illicit demand for these drugs in such countries as Canada and the US.

An effective way of eradicating the illicit traffic in opium and its derivatives would be to cut off the supply of illicitly sold raw opium at its source. This is the intent of the 1953 opium protocol. Furthermore, the UN has been working to develop methods of scientific analysis to determine the geographical origin of different opium samples. If the origin of all raw opium seized in illicit traffic could be determined, the UN would be able to call the attention of the governments concerned to the need for improving their control and could offer to assist them in so doing. This scientific research program is being carried out by the UN secretariat's Division of Narcotic Drugs in its Geneva laboratory. National laboratories and individual scientists in a number of countries also participate in the program.

Coca Leaf and Cocaine
Coca leaves are leaves of an evergreen shrub, *Erythroxylon coca,* which grows in western South America and some regions of the Far East. The leaves are the raw material for the manufacture of the drug cocaine. In addition, the leaves themselves for centuries have been chewed by some of the Andean peoples. In 1949, at the request of Peru and Bolivia, the UN dispatched a commission of inquiry to those countries to determine whether the chewing of coca leaf was harmful. It was frequently claimed that coca-leaf chewing acts in some way as a substitute for food. The commission found that this is untrue. When the leaves are chewed, cocaine enters the bloodstream. This has a stimulating effect on the user, but it leads to physical exhaustion and reduces appetite. If practiced habitually, it may lead to malnutrition.

The commission concluded that coca-leaf chewing is a dangerous habit and constitutes a form of addiction. In 1954, ECOSOC recommended that the countries concerned should gradually limit the cultivation and export of coca leaf to medical, scientific, and other legitimate purposes and should progres-sively abolish the habit of coca-leaf chewing. At the same time it was recognized that there was little chance of eliminating coca-leaf addiction unless the living conditions of the economic classes among whom the habit was widespread could be improved and that the problem must be attacked on this front as well.

In 1959 the Commission on Narcotic Drugs noted that Argentina had decided to limit gradually imports of coca leaves for chewing and that Chile had prohibited them completely. Colombia had continued its policy of prohibition with good results, but in two provinces the problem remained a serious one. In Bolivia and Peru, however, the main producers and consumers of coca leaves, the number of chewers was still considerable.

The commission has also expressed concern over what appears to be a well-organized and growing traffic in clandestinely manufactured cocaine affecting a number of South American countries. It was "particularly disturbed" by indications that the national authorities responsible for combating this illicit traffic were not fully cooperating.

Cannabis (Marijuana)
The plant *Cannabis sativa,* or the crude drug derived from it, is known under almost 200 different names—marijuana, hashish, Indian hemp, charas, ganji, kif, bhang, and maconha, to name a few. Widely used as an intoxicant by millions of people for at least 4,000 or 5,000 years, the plant can be grown successfully in almost all parts of the inhabited world. Depending on the soil and the degree of cultivation, the plant grows to a height of 1 to 20 feet. The narcotic resin is found in the flowering tops, particularly of the female plant.

Cannabis is used as a narcotic drug in many countries, its use being particularly widespread in great parts of Africa, the Middle East, and South America. Because the plant grows wild in many regions and is easy to cultivate illicitly in out-of-the-way areas, traffickers have little difficulty in obtaining cannabis. Aggregate statistics on the number of habitual users of cannabis are not available, but, judging from police seizures and information contained in official reports, their number must run well in the millions.

Although the medical use of cannabis is regarded as obsolete and its discontinuation has been recommended, possible medical properties of certain derivatives have been under study by several countries and WHO.

Synthetic Drugs
The widespread development of new synthetic drugs, which can be made from materials widely used in industry, has raised new and serious control problems. The 1948 protocol provides for new drugs that are found to have addictive qualities to be placed under full international control, but drugs not fully tested sometimes appear on the market under the unproved claim that they do not produce addiction. The Narcotics Control Commission has repeatedly warned governments to apply immediate control measures to these substances pending the definite establishment of their effects by WHO. In such cases, in the commission's view, commercial interests must yield to overriding public health considerations. The commission has also recommended that misleading publicity and advertising concerning these new drugs should be prohibited and that they should be clearly identified under nonproprietary names. Since 1953 a joint ECOSOC–WHO research program on the basic problems arising from the development of the synthetic narcotics has been carried out. The results are published in a series of reports entitled *Synthetic Substances with Morphine-like Effects.*

CONTROL OF PSYCHOTROPIC SUBSTANCES
In January 1970 the Commission on Narcotic Drugs drafted the Protocol on Psychotropic Substances for adoption by a Conference of Plenipotentiaries in Vienna in February 1971.

The way is now open for effective controls to be imposed on psychotropic substances—the hallucinogens like LSD and mescaline, the amphetamine-type "pep pills," sleeping pills of barbiturate type, and a large number of "tranquillizers," which are increasingly used and abused throughout the world. One of the perplexing problems that has beset any consideration of psychotropic substances is the identification of those substances that ought to be controlled by treaty. A solution was found when a group of WHO experts proposed a preliminary listing of 38 substances in four schedules.

The names printed in the left-hand column are the International Non-Proprietary Names (INN). With one exception ((+)-Lysergide), other non-proprietary or trivial names are given only where no INN has yet been proposed.

LIST OF SUBSTANCES IN SCHEDULE I

INN	Other non-proprietary or trivial names	Chemical name
1.	DET	N,N-diethyltryptamine
2.	DMHP	3-(1,2-dimethylheptyl)-7,8,9,10-tetrahydro-6,6,9-trimethyl-6H-dibenzo [b,d] pyran-1-ol
3.	DMT	N,N-dimethyltryptamine
4. (+)-Lysergide	LSD, LSD-25	(+)-N,N-diethyllysergamide (d-lysergic acid diethylamide)
5.	mescaline	3,4,5-trimethoxyphenethylamine
6.	parahexyl	3-hexyl-7,8,9,10-tetrahydro-6,6,9-trimethyl-6H-dibenzo [b,d] pyran-1-ol
7.	psilocine, psilotsin	3-(2-dimethylaminoethyl)indol-4-ol
8. Psilocybine		3-(2-dimethylaminoethyl)indol-4-yl dihydrogen phosphate
9.	STP, DOM	2,5-dimethoxy-4-methyl-phenethylamine
10.	tetra-hydro-cannabi-nols, all isomers	3-pentyl-6a,7,10,10a-tetrahydro-6,6,9-trimethyl-6H-dibenzo [b,d] pyran-1-ol

LIST OF SUBSTANCES IN SCHEDULE II

1. Amphetamine	(±)-α-methylphenethylamine
2. Dexamphetamine	(+)-α-methylphenethylamine
3. Methamphetamine	(±)-N-α-dimethylphenethylamine
4. Methylphenidate	α-phenyl-2-piperidineacetic acid methyl ester
5. Phenmetrazine	3-methyl-2-phenylmorpholine

LIST OF SUBSTANCES IN SCHEDULE III

1. Amobarbital	5-ethyl-5-isopenthylbarbituric acid
2. Cyclobarbital	5-(1-cyclohexen-1-yl)-5-ethylbarbituric acid
3. Glutethimide	2-ethyl-2-phenylglutarimide
4. Pentobarbital	5-ethyl-5-(1-methylbutyl)barbituric acid
5. Secobarbital	5-allyl-5-(1-methylbutyl)barbituric acid

LIST OF SUBSTANCES IN SCHEDULE IV

1. Aminorex		2-amino-5-phenyl-2-oxazoline
2. Amfepramone		2-(diethylamino)-propiophenone
3. Barbital		5,5-diethylbarbituric acid
4.	chloral hydrate	trichloro-2,2,2-ethanediol-1,1
5. Chlordiazepoxide		7-chloro-2-methylamino-5-phenyl-3H-1,4-benzodiazepine-4-oxide
6. Diazepam		7-chloro-1,3-dihydro-1-methyl-5-phenyl-2H-1,4-benzodiazepin-2-one
7.	ethchlor-vynol	ethyl-β-chlorovinylethinylcarbinol
8. Ethinamate		1-ethynylcyclohexanolcarbamate
9. Meprobamate		2-methyl-2-propyl-1,3-propanediol dicarbamate
10. Methaqualone		2-methyl-3-o-tolyl-4(3H)-quinazolinone
11. Methohexital		(±)-5-allyl-1-methyl-5-(1-methyl-2-pentynyl) barbituric acid
12. Methylpheno-barbital		5-ethyl-N-methyl-5-phenyl-barbituric acid
13. Methyprylon		3,3-diethyl-5-methyl-2,4-piperidine-dione
14.	paral-dehyde	cyclic ether of acetaldehyde
15. Phencyclidine		1-(1-phenylcyclohexyl)-piperidine
16. Phenobarbital		5-ethyl-5-phenylbarbituric acid
17. Pipradrol		α,α-diphenyl-2-piperidinemethanol
18.	SPA	(−)-1-dimethylamino-1,2-diphenylethane

These listings are not final and will be subject to further study under the protocol. When new substances are proposed for control after the protocol has entered into force, a machinery and a procedure are provided for to determine whether such new substances should be controlled and under which regime of control they should be placed.

Parties to the protocol have the right not to apply the full scheme of controls to all substances in schedules III and IV provided they apply certain minimal controls and scrupulously abide by the controls on international trade set down in the protocol. This right is not granted to a party insofar as substances in schedules I and II are concerned and to substances already placed in schedule III and IV when the protocol comes into force.

A very difficult problem the commission had to resolve was to decide which preparations of psychotropic substances could be exempted from protocol regime. The commission decided that no exemption would be allowed for preparations containing substances in schedule I. However, a state may decide, with respect to substances contained in schedules II, III, and IV, that there is no public health or social problem and the risk of abuse is nil or negligible. A state may exempt a preparation from all control, except certain controls from the international point of view.

Schedule I substances, such as LSD and mescaline, are controlled in a way that is more stringent than the controls for morphine under narcotics treaties. Such substances can be moved in international trade only by government authorities and institutions.

Schedule II substances, such as amphetamines, are to be traded only by export-import authorization.

In the case of schedule III and IV substances, importers are required to declare imports to their governments, indicating the importer and the quantity and date of shipment. The exporting government passes on this information to the importing government.

States have the right to prohibit the imports of one or more substances in schedules II, III, and IV. Other states receiving this information must respect these prohibitions under the treaty.

TECHNICAL ASSISTANCE IN THE FIELD OF NARCOTICS

At its 1968 session the UN General Assembly called on the

secretary-general to submit to the 1970 session plans for ending illegal and uncontrolled production of narcotic raw materials. The Assembly also recommended that the governments concerned seek assistance from the UN and from bilateral sources in their efforts to develop alternative economic programs and activities as a means of ending illegal and uncontrolled cultivation of narcotic raw materials. It cited crop substitution as one such activity.

Dealing with the broader question of narcotics control, ECOSOC in July 1970 decided to convene a special session of the Commission on Narcotic Drugs to consider short-term and long-term policy recommendations for integrated action against drug abuse.

Commission Recommendations taken by States

As the Commission on Narcotic Drugs opened its special session in Geneva in September 1970, it received a message from Secretary-General U Thant stating that the abuse of narcotic drugs had reached epidemic proportions and that it had become a universal menace from which no country was immune. Furthermore, any delay in adopting strong measures to eliminate illegal narcotics production and illicit drug traffic would make a solution to the problem "beyond our grasp."

The commission decided that the concept of drug abuse should always be understood to include narcotic drugs as well as psychotropic substances. It urged the vigorous execution of national and international controls of narcotic drugs, including cannabis, and that governments should adopt national controls of psychotropic substances such as those of the hallucinogen, amphetamine, and barbiturate type and adhere to international instruments as soon as they come into force.

In the commission's view, the phenomenon of drug abuse was actually a series of epidemics in different countries arising in relation to different drugs. The scope of the problem differed from drug to drug. For example, the abuse of cannabis in the forms of marijuana and hashish was more widespread and had increased more rapidly than that of heroin, though the latter had also risen. The abuse of coca leaf remained widespread but was a static problem, confined to a well-defined area. Cocaine as a drug of abuse seemed to be less prominent than cannabis or the opiates. The abuse of the amphetamines had swept certain countries in sudden waves, had abated in one country, and in others had become a grave problem. The hallucinogens, in particular LSD, remained mainly a problem of certain developed countries but constituted a very serious danger. Barbiturate-type drugs also presented a serious and growing problem.

The commission observed that increasing drug abuse was based on the interdependence of supply and demand, which were bridged by illicit traffic. A number of factors underlay the abuse of dangerous drugs, among which economic and social stress remained significant. Therapeutic addiction was negligible, but restraint in medical dispensing practices was necessary to prevent other forms of drug dependence. The phenomenon of drug abuse had spread to many countries. It was no longer confined to economically depressed classes or to emotionally disturbed persons.

The commission noted that with the spread of drug abuse had also come a wider recognition of its grave implications. The factor of drug abuse provided the "demand" aspect of the drug problem. The "supply" side of the problem was based in the illicit, uncontrolled or inadequately controlled production of narcotic raw materials. The commission said that to impinge upon the supply component of the narcotics problem required a broadly based program of economic and social advancement in the areas where illicit or uncontrolled production took place. The problem of psychotropic substances was more the result of

indiscriminate and irresponsible practices of manufacturers. Illicit traffic, as a criminal activity, might be contained by immediate measures of improved enforcement, together with better national administration and international collaboration.

Turning to the problem of the nonmedical supply of psychotropic substances, the commission expressed the hope that the promulgation of the Protocol on Psychotropic Substances at the Conference of Plenipotentiaries in Vienna in January–February 1971, would contribute toward stemming the supplies that had been channeled into criminal organizations.

The commission recommended, as an initial measure and as a matter of urgency, the establishment of a UN Fund for Drug Control. The proposed fund, to be made up of voluntary contributions from government and nongovernment sources, would provide resources for the following activities: (1) expanding UN research and information facilities, to gather data on all aspects of drug abuse in order to supply timely information to governments and the public and for the preparation of educational materials; (2) planning and implementation of programs of technical assistance to countries for the establishment and improvement of national drug control administrations and enforcement machinery, and the training of personnel, including assistance in the setting up or expansion of research and training centers that could serve national or regional needs; and (3) enlarging the capabilities and extending the operation of the secretariats of UN drug control bodies by providing additional personnel as required.

The commission asked the secretary-general to prepare a plan for concerted long-term action against drug abuse. Such a plan, it said, should: (1) limit the supply of drugs to legitimate requirements by putting an end to their illegal or uncontrolled production, processing, and manufacture, making use of crop substitution or other methods as appropriate; (2) improve the administrative and technical capabilities of existing bodies concerned with the elimination of the illicit traffic in drugs; (3) develop measures to prevent drug abuse through programs of education and special campaigns, including the use of mass media; (4) provide facilities and develop methods for the treatment, rehabilitation, and social reintegration of drug-dependent persons.

The following countries are represented on the commission: Brazil, Cananda, Dominican Republic, West Germany, France, Ghana, Hungary, India, Iran, Jamaica, Japan, Lebanon, Mexico, Pakistan, Peru, Sweden, Switzerland, Togo, Turkey, USSR, United Arab Republic, United Kingdom, United States, and Yugoslavia. In December 1970 the UN General Assembly in a resolution declared that addiction to narcotic drugs had become an alarming problem in many countries and that the measures taken against illicit trade and traffic in narcotic drugs had not been successful in arresting widespread addiction. The Assembly noted that the term "narcotic drugs" had been defined by the Commission on Narcotic Drugs to include psychotropic substances. The Assembly called on all member and nonmember states to consider seriously the possibility of enacting adequate legislation providing severe penalties for those engaged in illicit trade and trafficking in narcotic drugs.

DRUG ADDICTION AND SUPPRESSION OF ILLICIT TRAFFIC

The basic purpose of the international treaties on narcotics control supervised by the UN is to reduce, and if possible eliminate, drug addiction. Addiction is detrimental both to the individual and to society. There are, however, millions of addicts in countries where no social opprobrium is attached to drug addiction, and many of these display no antisocial character traits. Many governments have become increasingly aware of the far-reaching social and economic consequences of drug addiction and concerned with the problem of treating and curing addicts.

The Commission on Narcotic Drugs reviews the problem of illicit trade in individual drugs and the situation regarding all narcotic drugs on a country-by-country basis. This review is based on information supplied by governments and other sources as the International Criminal Police Organization. Reports furnished by governments have indicated a decrease in the quantities of drugs seized in the illicit traffic, but commission surveys indicate that the illicit trade continues at a high level and is well organized.

The high degree of organization, the considerable financial backing apparent in a number of cases, and the ease with which traffickers move from country to country indicate that the international drug smuggling is a top-drawer criminal operation. The top organizers do not, in most cases, handle any illegal shipments themselves. Instead, they instigate, finance, and direct operations carried out by less important criminals, who engage in smuggling as a sideline to their legitimate work. Merchant ships and their crews, the commission has found, are most frequently involved in the international traffic, and there is a growing use of aircraft by smugglers.

Many countries have tightened their narcotics laws and increased the penalties for convicted traffickers. The adoption of uniform penal sanctions and extradition procedures for narcotics offenders is very difficult to obtain, however, because of widely differing legal and cultural traditions.

Valuable aid is rendered by the International Criminal Police Organization in combating the criminal activities of drug traffickers. INTERPOL, with headquarters in Paris, acts as a clearinghouse for government law-enforcement agencies and provides important information to UN narcotics control organs, as well as to national agencies.

THE HUMAN ENVIRONMENT

The UN General Assembly at its 1968 session took up the question of the human environment. In a resolution adopted that year it referred to the increasing impairment of the environment through air and water pollution, erosion and other forms of soil deterioration, waste, noise and secondary effects of biocides. The rapidly increasing population and the quickening pace of urbanization accentuated these problems, it said.

The Assembly decided that a conference on the human environment should be held in Stockholm in June 1972. Proposals for such a conference had been made by Sweden at a meeting of ECOSOC earlier in 1968.

In response to an Assembly request, the secretary-general submitted a report in May 1969. The report, prepared in consultation with the advisory committee on the application of science and technology to development, outlined the main problems of the human environment and contained various proposals relating to the conference.

At its 1969 session, the Assembly affirmed that the conference's main aim should be to encourage and provide guidelines for action by nations and international organizations to protect and improve the human environment. It established a 27-nation preparatory committee to advise the secretary-general. The preparatory committee held its first session in March 1970, including in its agenda a definition of the program contents for the conference, documentation, and measures to encourage national participation. The committee stressed the need for an action-oriented conference and identified a number of areas for national and international action. The committee also emphasized the importance of ensuring in the conference program a proper balance between the environmental problems of the developing countries and those of the developed countries.

The preparatory committee also recommended that discussion topics be grouped in three main categories: environmental aspects of human settlements, such as accelerated urbanization; rational management of natural resources, such as soil and water; and environmental degradation due to pollution and nuisances. National reports, the committee recommended, should serve as background material for conference preparations.

In a progress report to ECOSOC at its 1970 July session, the secretary-general reported that a conference secretariat had been set up at UN Headquarters and that a unit especially concerned with preparing substantive conference documents would be located in Geneva. An ad hoc interagency working group had been formed to harness the talent already at work on environmental problems in specialized agencies and regional economic commissions. This group met in June/July in Geneva and prepared a detailed tentative program outline for the 1972 Stockholm conference, based on the preparatory committee's proposals.

Valuable suggestions for the conference on human environment had already been obtained from a number of intergovernmental and nongovernmental organizations. The secretary-general of the UN reported that the continuing support of these organizations was essential, both from a technical point of view and for the purpose of ensuring wide public support for the conference.

ECOSOC also endorsed the proposal that the 1972 Stockholm conference should be action-oriented and that areas for immediate action should be identified prior to the convening of the conference. In taking into account the needs of developing countries, ECOSOC discussed the possibility of providing assistance to those countries for the preparation of national reports and case studies for the conference.

GENERAL ASSEMBLY ACTION

At its 25th session, in 1970, the Assembly noted that the international development strategy for the second UN Development Decade called for intensified national and international efforts to arrest the deterioration of the human environment, measures toward its improvement, and the promotion of activities that will help maintain the ecological balance on which human survival depends.

The Assembly declared that environmental policies should be considered in the context of economic and social development, taking into account the special needs of development in developing countries.

It recommended that the preparatory committee, in its global and comprehensive preparations for the UN conference on the human environment in 1972, consider, among other things, the financing of possible action in this field with a view to ensuring that additional resources are provided to developing countries for the protection of the environment. The General Assembly requested the secretary-general to submit a comprehensive report on the progress of the preparatory work for the conference to the 26th session in 1971.

The report was to include information on the work of the second session of the preparatory committee in February 1971 and the comments, suggestions, and recommendations of ECOSOC made at its meeting in 1971.

Following the Assembly's debate in 1969 on the subject of the human environment, the secretary-general revised the estimated conference budget downward from $1,918,000 to $1,564,000. However, in his progress report in 1970, the secretary-general said that a number of significant developments, both at the national and international level, resulting primarily from mounting public concern about environmental problems, necessitated an addition of $444,600 to the approved budget estimates.

HUMAN RIGHTS
AND THE UNITED NATIONS

THE CHARTER OF THE UNITED NATIONS, SAN FRANCISCO, 1945

In the Preamble to the Charter of the United Nations, "the peoples of the United Nations" express their determination "to reaffirm faith in fundamental human rights, in the dignity and worth of the human person, in the equal rights of men and women and of nations large and small." One of the purposes of the United Nations is that of "promoting and encouraging respect for human rights and for fundamental freedoms for all without distinction as to race, sex, language, or religion" (Article 1). In Articles 55 and 56, "all Members pledge themselves to take joint and separate action in cooperation with the Organization for the achievement" of this purpose. The Charter vests responsibility for assisting in the realization of human rights and fundamental freedoms in the General Assembly, on which all member states are represented; under the authority of the General Assembly, in the Economic and Social Council, a body of 27 member states; and in the Trusteeship Council, another principal organ the importance of which, however, has declined as almost all former trust territories have become independent. The Charter also provides for the establishment of commissions for the promotion of human rights as subsidiary bodies of the Economic and Social Council. Early in the history of the Organization two such commissions were created: the Commission on Human Rights and the Commission on the Status of Women.

The San Francisco Charter did not define the human rights and fundamental freedoms to the promotion of which the UN is devoted. The Charter, however, has made it abundantly clear that one particular activity at least is repugnant to it: discrimination on the grounds of race, sex, language, or religion.

THE INTERNATIONAL BILL OF RIGHTS

At the San Francisco Conference a proposal to embody an international bill of rights in the Charter itself was put forward but not proceeded with for the reason that it required more detailed consideration. The idea of establishing an international bill of rights, however, was regarded as inherent in the Charter. Even before the Charter was ratified and before it entered into force and before the United Nations as an organization was established, steps were taken toward this goal. The Preparatory Commission of the United Nations and its Executive Committee, meeting in the fall of 1945, both recommended that the work of the Commission on Human Rights should be directed, in the first place, toward the "formulation of an international bill of rights." The General Assembly agreed with these recommendations in January 1946. Accordingly, when the terms of reference of the Commission on Human Rights were laid down in February 1946, "an international bill of rights" was the first item on its work program. When the Commission and the drafting committee started their work on this ambitious project, it turned out that there was doubt and disagreement among the members about the form that the draft bill of rights should take. Some members thought the bill should be a "declaration" or "manifesto" that would be proclaimed by a resolution of the General Assembly. Others urged that it should take the form of an international treaty, which, in addition to being approved by the General Assembly, would have to be opened for signature, ratification, and accession by governments and would be binding only on those governments which had ratified it or acceded to it. The relevant report of the drafting committee records that it was agreed by those who favored the declaration form that the declaration should be accompanied or followed by one or more conventions. It was also agreed by those who favored the convention form that the General Assembly in recommending a convention to Member Nations might make a declaration wider in content or more general in expression. As a consequence, drafts of a "declaration" and of a "convention" were prepared, and studies were undertaken for the creation of international supervisory and enforcement machinery, usually styled "measures of implementation."

Eventually the decision emerged that the international bill of rights should not be produced by one single, comprehensive and final act but that it should consist of two or more international instruments, namely a declaration, a convention (covenant), and measures of implementation. Later it was decided that there should be not one but two covenants and that the provisions on the measures of implementation should be embodied in the texts of the covenants. The latter decision was modified somewhat in 1966, when the provisions regulating one specific aspect of the implementation arrangements, the right of petition (communication), were included in a separate optional protocol.

The first part of this International Bill of Human Rights was adopted by the General Assembly in the form of a resolution as the Universal Declaration of Human Rights, on 10 December 1948. The remaining parts—namely, the International Covenant on Economic, Social and Cultural Rights, the International Covenant on Civil and Political Rights, and the Optional Protocol to the International Covenant on Civil and Political Rights—were adopted and opened for signature, ratification, and accession on 16 December 1966, the two Covenants unanimously, the Optional Protocol by majority vote.

THE UNIVERSAL DECLARATION OF HUMAN RIGHTS

The Universal Declaration was prepared by the Commission on Human Rights in 1947 and 1948 and adopted and proclaimed by the General Assembly by a vote of 48 for, none against, with 6 abstentions. Two representatives were absent. One of them stated later that, if he had been present, he would have voted in favor.

The Universal Declaration proclaims—and in this regard it differs from the traditional catalogues of the rights of man that are contained in various constitutions and fundamental laws of the 18th and 19th centuries and of the first decades of the 20th century—not only civil and political rights but deals also with the rights which were eventually regulated in the International Covenant on Economic, Social and Cultural Rights.

The Declaration proclaims that all human beings are born free and equal in dignity and rights (Article 1). It states further that "everyone is entitled to the rights and freedoms set forth in this Declaration, without distinction of any kind, such as race, color, sex, language, religion, political or other opinion, national or social origin, property, birth or other status" (Article 2, paragraph 1). The authors of the Declaration, recognizing the problem that was destined to become decisive in the decades following upon its proclamation, provided that "no distinction shall be made on the basis of the political jurisdictional or international status of the country or territory to which a person belongs, whether it be independent, trust, non-self-governing or under any other limitation of sovereignty" (Article 2, paragraph 2).

In Articles 3 to 21 the Declaration deals with the traditional civil and political rights: the right to life, liberty, and security of person; freedom from slavery and servitude; freedom from torture and from cruel, inhuman, or degrading treatment or punishment; equality before the law and equal protection of the law; freedom from arbitrary arrest, detention, and exile; the right to be presumed innocent until proved guilty; inviolability of the home and secrecy of correspondence; the right to protection against arbitrary interference with one's privacy, family, home or correspondence and to protection against attacks upon one's honor and reputation; freedom of movement and residence; everyone's right to leave any country, including his own; the right to seek and enjoy in other countries asylum from persecution (but not the right to be granted asylum); the right to a nationality and to change one's nationality; the right of men and women of full age to marry, without any limitation due to race, nationality, or religion; freedom of thought, conscience, and religion; the right to own property and not to be arbitrarily deprived of it; freedom of opinion and expression; the right to peaceful assembly and association; the right to vote and to take part in the government of one's country, and to equal access to public service.

The economic, social, and cultural rights (Articles 22 to 27) are introduced by Article 22, which states generally that "everyone, as a member of society, has the right to social security" and is entitled to the realization of "economic, social and cultural rights indispensable for his dignity and the free development of his personality." The article implies, however, that those economic, social, and cultural rights are not everywhere and immediately achievable. It states that the "realization" of these rights is to be brought about "through national effort and international co-operation and in accordance with the organization and resources of each State."

The Declaration affirms everyone's right to work, to free choice of employment, to just and favorable conditions of work, and to protection against unemployment. It affirms the right of everyone to equal pay for equal work; to "just and favorable remuneration"; to form and join trade unions; to "a standard of living adequate for the health and well-being of himself and of his family"; and to "rest and leisure, including reasonable limitation of working hours and periodic holidays with pay." It also proclaims "the right to security in the event of unemployment, sickness, disability, widowhood, old age or other lack of livelihood in circumstances beyond (one's) control." Everyone has the right to education, which shall be free "at least in the elementary and fundamental stages" and be compulsory on the elementary level. The Declaration affirms everyone's right "freely to participate in the cultural life of the community, to enjoy the arts and to share in scientific advancement and its benefits."

Article 28 asserts that "everyone is entitled to a social and international order in which the rights and freedoms set forth in this Declaration can be fully realized." In the exercise of his rights and freedoms everyone shall be subject only to such limitations as are determined by law. The law must provide for limitations solely for the purpose of securing due recognition and respect for the rights and freedoms of others and of meeting the just requirements of morality, public order and the general welfare in a democratic society (Article 29). In order to protect a democratic society against totalitarian movements, Article 30 states that nothing in the Declaration may be interpreted as implying for any State, group or person any right to engage in

any activity or to perform any act aimed at the destruction of any of the rights and freedoms set forth in the Declaration.

The Universal Declaration of Human Rights was adopted, not in the form of an international convention which, when ratified, is legally binding on the States that are parties to it, but in the form of a resolution of the General Assembly. It claims to be "a common understanding" of the rights and freedoms to the respect for and observance of which Member States have pledged themselves and was proclaimed as "a common standard of achievement for all peoples and all nations." In the view of most of those who were instrumental in its preparation and adoption, the Universal Declaration of Human Rights was not meant to be a "binding" instrument. However, as soon as the Declaration was adopted, it began to be used as a code of conduct and as a yardstick to measure the compliance by governments with the international standards of human rights.

The first instance occurred in April 1949, when a complaint had been brought before the General Assembly that the Soviet Union had violated fundamental human rights by preventing Soviet wives of citizens of other nationalities from leaving their country with their husbands or in order to join them abroad. The General Assembly invoked the articles of the Declaration which provide that everyone has the right to leave any country including his own and that men and women of full age have the right to marry without any limitation due to race, nationality or religion. The General Assembly declared that measures taken by the Soviet Union were not in conformity with the UN Charter and it called upon the USSR government to withdraw them.

Another human rights conflict that came before the General Assembly early in its history was the treatment of people of Indian and Pakistani origin in South Africa. In repeated resolutions the General Assembly exhorted the parties to solve the dispute on the basis of the provisions of the Charter and of the Declaration. On the question of the racial situation in southern Africa, a perennial issue before the United Nations, the Assembly repeatedly invoked the Declaration in its endeavor to have South Africa and the other authorities in southern Africa abandon the policy of racial discrimination.

In countless other disputes and controversies that it was called upon to examine, the United Nations and its various organs had recourse to the Declaration, whether they were dealing with allegations of forced labor, discrimination in non-self-governing and trust territories, with the situation in Tibet, with customs and practices inconsistent with the physical integrity and dignity of women, or with other blemishes on our civilization. The Universal Declaration has played a great role also in the activities of specialized agencies such as the International Labor Organization, UNESCO, and the International Telecommunication Union, in regional organizations such as the Organization of American States, the Council of Europe, and the Organization of African Unity. The All African Charter of Unity of 1963, which is the constitution of the Organization of African Unity, lists among the purposes of the organization "to promote international cooperation, with due regard for the United Nations Charter and the Universal Declaration of Human Rights."

From these examples alone it is clear that the Universal Declaration of Human Rights has acquired a purpose different from that which was contemplated by many of the governments that brought it into being in 1948. The international community, the states that had been instrumental in its creation as well as those that later acceded to independence, used the Declaration for the purpose of fulfilling an assignment greater and more far-reaching than that which had been originally carved out for it. In the decades following upon 1948, the process of creating a comprehensive international law of human rights by the traditional method of concluding international treaties, by establishing and putting into force the worldwide International Covenants on Human Rights, slowed down. As a consequence the Declaration has, temporarily at least, filled the void. It took over the function originally contemplated for the International Bill of Rights as a whole. Only in 1966 were the two International Covenants on Human Rights adopted and opened for signature and ratification. By the beginning of 1971 they had not yet entered into force. The Universal Declaration continues therefore to perform the comprehensive function that it had to assume in the interval between 1948 and the entry into force of the International Covenants on Human Rights.

THE INTERNATIONAL COVENANTS ON HUMAN RIGHTS

The United Nations Commission on Human Rights, the Economic and Social Council and the General Assembly devoted 19 years (1947–1966) to the preparation and adoption of the Covenants. One problem created a considerable amount of controversy particularly in the first years. This was whether the treaty that would give effect in law to the rights and freedoms set forth in the Universal Declaration of Human Rights should regulate only those rights that traditionally had been guaranteed in national constitutions or catalogues of rights, and are known in UN parlance as "civil and political rights," or whether the treaty should set forth also what have become known as "economic, social and cultural rights."

As already indicated, it was eventually decided that there should be two covenants dealing with the two sets of provisions, respectively. The principal reason for having two separate instruments regulating the two groups of rights has been the fundamentally different character of the rights concerned, which lead some even to question whether the "economic, social and cultural rights" are, technically, rights at all, rights in the sense of subjective, enforceable, and justiciable rights. The different character of these rights made it necessary to provide for a difference in the type of international obligations to be undertaken by states parties that accept one or the other of the two covenants. Another reason for establishing two different covenants was thought to be the necessity to adjust the arrangements for international supervision—the "measures of implementation"—to the different character of the rights.

The Difference in the Type of Obligation Undertaken by States in the Two Covenants

In the International Covenant on Civil and Political Rights, each State Party undertakes to *respect* and to *ensure* to all individuals within its territory and subject to its jurisdiction the rights recognized in that covenant. In the International Covenant on Economic, Social and Cultural Rights, each State Party only undertakes to *take steps,* individually and through international assistance and cooperation to the maximum of its available resources, *with a view to achieving progressively* the full realization of the rights recognized in that covenant by all appropriate means. Subject to certain exceptions and modifications, into which this article cannot enter in detail, the Civil and Political Rights Covenant imposes upon States Parties the obligation to maintain defined standards. The States Parties to the International Covenant on Economic, Social and Cultural Rights assume the obligation to promote an objective.

By and large the two Covenants between them cover the rights proclaimed in the Universal Declaration of Human Rights as they have been described above. However, there are considerable differences between the Universal Declaration on the one side and the International Covenants on the other in regard to the coverage of rights.

The provisions of the Universal Declaration proclaiming that everyone has a right to own property and that everyone has the right to seek and to enjoy in other countries asylum from perse-

cution have no counterpart in the Covenants. On the other hand, the International Covenants deal with a number of questions in regard to which the Universal Declaration of Human Rights contains no provision. Examples are the provisions of both Covenants that all peoples have the right to self-determination by virtue of which they freely determine their political status and freely pursue their economic, social and cultural development. The International Covenant on Civil and Political Rights, but not the Declaration, protects aliens against expulsion, entitles everyone not to be compelled to testify against himself or to confess guilt, provides for a right to compensation for miscarriage of justice, and also that no one shall be liable to be tried or punished again for an offense for which he has already been finally convicted or acquitted. The Covenant on Civil and Political Rights prohibits any propaganda for war and any advocacy of national racial or religious hatred. It provides for the protection of ethnic, religious or linguistic minorities. The Declaration does not contain corresponding provisions. While the Declaration proclaims *everyone's* right to a nationality, the Civil and Political Rights Covenant provides that *every child* has the right to acquire a nationality. The International Covenant on Economic, Social and Cultural Rights sets forth the right to work, including the right of everyone to the opportunity to gain his living by work that he freely chooses or accepts; the right of everyone to the enjoyment of just and favorable conditions of work; the right of everyone to form and to join trade unions and, subject to the law of the land, the right to strike; the right of everyone to social security, including social insurance and the protection of the family; the right to an adequate standard of living and freedom from hunger; the right to the enjoyment of the highest attainable standards of physical and mental health, the right to education and the right to take part in cultural life.

The "International Measures of Implementation" of the Two Covenants

Both covenants contain provisions instituting a certain amount of international supervision of the fulfillment by the States Parties of the obligations they undertake in becoming parties to them. The International Covenant on Civil and Political Rights will establish an international organ called the Human Rights Committee, consisting of 18 persons of high moral character and recognized competence who will be elected by the states parties and will serve in their personal capacity. The states parties undertake to submit reports on the measures they have adopted that give effect to the rights recognized in the Covenant and on the progress made in the enjoyment of those rights. These reports are to be studied by the Human Rights Committee, which on its part shall submit its reports and such general comments as it may consider appropriate to the States Parties. These comments of the committee may also be submitted to the Economic and Social Council of the United Nations.

The Covenant together with the Optional Protocol provides for two additional methods and procedures of international supervision. These additional measures, however, are applicable only to such states parties to the Covenant as have expressly accepted them. Among states that have recognized the Committee's jurisdiction to this effect, a state party that considers that another state party is not giving effect to the provisions of the Covenant may bring the matter before the Human Rights Committee. The Committee shall make available its good offices with a view to a friendly solution of the matter on the basis of respect for human rights and fundamental freedoms. If no friendly solution is reached, an *ad hoc* Conciliation Commission may be established, which shall also aim at an amicable solution. If this commission does not reach such a solution, it shall embody in its report its findings on all questions of fact relevant to the issues between the parties and its views on the possibilities of an amicable solution of the matter. The Covenant does not provide for adjudication of such differences by an international court or tribunal.

In regard to states parties that become parties to the Optional Protocol, the Human Rights Committee has also the right to receive and consider communications from individuals who claim to be victims of a violation by the state concerned of any of the rights set forth in the covenant. As a result of the proceedings, the Committee eventually forwards its views to the state party concerned and to the individual.

The state parties to the Covenant on Economic, Social and Cultural Rights undertake to submit to the Economic and Social Council reports on the measures they have adopted and the progress made in achieving the observance of the rights recognized in that Covenant. These reports are to be studied by the Council and, if the Council so decides, by the Commission on Human Rights. Both are expected to make recommendations of a general nature.

OTHER INTERNATIONAL CONVENTIONS IN THE FIELD OF HUMAN RIGHTS

Pending the elaboration and adoption of the International Covenants on Human Rights, the United Nations and two of the specialized agencies, the International Labor Organization and UNESCO, have prepared and put into force a number of conventions in the human rights field which, while not as comprehensive as the International Bill of Human Rights, deal with a number of important specific rights. These conventions on special subjects, most of which implement various provisions of the Universal Declaration of Human Rights, will now be considered.

The Genocide Convention

In 1948 the General Assembly adopted the Convention on the Prevention and Punishment of the Crime of Genocide. Genocide means any of the following acts committed with intent to destroy in whole or in part a national, ethnical, racial or religious group as such: (a) killing members of the group; (b) causing serious bodily or mental harm to members of the group; (c) deliberately inflicting on the group conditions of life calculated to bring about its physical destruction in whole or in part; (d) imposing measures intended to prevent births within the group; (e) forcibly transferring children of the group to another group. One result of this convention, which entered into force in 1951, is that the states parties place it beyond doubt that genocide (and conspiracy, incitement, and attempt to commit it, and complicity in it), even if perpetrated by a government in its own territory against its own citizens, is not a matter essentially within the domestic jurisdiction of states but one of international concern. States parties confirm that genocide whether committed in time of peace or in time of war is a crime under international law which they undertake to prevent and to punish. Any contracting party can call upon United Nations organs to intervene.

Conventions on the Rights of Women

The Convention on the Political Rights of Women, adopted in 1952 and in force since 1954, represents the culmination of the endeavors of generations of fighters for women's rights. It provides that women shall be entitled to vote in all elections, that they shall be eligible for election to all publicly elected bodies, and that they shall be entitled to hold public office and to exercise all public functions on equal terms with men and without any discrimination.

The Convention on the Nationality of Married Women of 1957 (in force since 1958) provides that neither the celebration nor the dissolution of marriage between a national and an alien, nor the change of nationality by the husband during marriage, shall automatically affect the nationality of the wife.

The Convention on Consent to Marriage, Minimum Age for Marriage, and Registration of Marriages of 1962 (in force since 1964), the substance of which is of particular relevance to the developing countries, provides that no marriage shall be legally entered into without the full and free consent of both parties, such consent to be expressed by them in person after due publicity and in the presence of the authority competent to solemnize the marriage. States parties to the convention are committed to take legislative action to specify a minimum age for marriage. All marriages shall be registered in an appropriate official register by a competent authority.

In a recommendation on the same subjects as those of this convention, adopted in 1965, the General Assembly stated that the minimum age shall be not less than 15 years.

Statelessness and Refugees

In the *Convention Relating to the Status of Refugees* of 1951 (in force since 1954, with a Protocol of 1967) and by the *Convention Relating to the Status of Stateless Persons* of 1954 (in force since 1960), far-reaching provisions for the protection of refugees and stateless persons have been enacted. Two principles are the basis of both conventions: (1) there shall be as little discrimination as possible between nationals on the one hand and refugees or stateless persons on the other; (2) there shall be no discrimination based on race, religion, or country of origin at all among refugees and among stateless persons.

Slavery, Servitude, Forced Labor, and Similar Institutions and Practices

The fight against slavery has been an international concern since the beginning of the 19th century. In more recent times, under the auspices of the League of Nations, the Slavery Convention of 1926 was enacted by which the contracting parties undertook to prevent and suppress the slave trade and to bring about "progressively and as soon as possible" the complete abolition of slavery in all its forms. Under United Nations auspices, *the Supplementary Convention on the Abolition of Slavery, the Slave Trade and Institutions and Practices Similar to Slavery* was adopted in 1956 (in force since 1957), by which the states parties undertook to bring about, also only "progressively and as soon as possible," the complete abolition or abandonment of other objectionable practices such as debt bondage and serfdom. In addition to these are prohibited: any institution or practice whereby a woman without the right to refuse is promised or given in marriage on payment of a consideration to her parents, guardian, or family; whereby the husband of a woman, his family, or his clan has the right to transfer her to another person for value received or otherwise; whereby a woman on the death of her husband is liable to be inherited by another person; whereby a child or a young person is delivered by either or both of his natural parents or by his guardian to another person with a view to the exploitation of the child or the young person or of his labor.

By the Convention Concerning the Abolition of Forced Labor, adopted by the International Labor Conference in 1957 and in force since 1959, states parties undertake to suppress and not to make use of any form of forced or compulsory labor, *inter alia,* as a means of political coercion or education or as a punishment for holding or expressing political views or views ideologically opposed to the established political, social, or economic system; as a punishment for having participated in strikes; or as a means of racial, social, national, or religious discrimination.

Freedom of Association

The Freedom of Association Convention of 1948 (in force since 1950) was the first great achievement of the joint efforts of the United Nations and of the International Labor Organization in the field of international legislation on human rights problems. By this convention, states parties undertake to give effect to the right of workers and employers, without distinction whatsoever, to establish and join organizations of their own choosing without previous authorization. In exercising the rights provided for in the convention, workers and employers and their respective organizations, like other persons or organized collectivities, shall respect the law of the land. However, the law of the land shall not be such as to impair, nor shall it be so applied as to impair, the guarantees provided in the convention. Under the Right to Organize and Collective Bargaining Convention of 1949 (in force since 1951), workers shall enjoy adequate protection against acts of anti-union discrimination in respect of their employment, particularly in respect of acts calculated to make the employment of a worker subject to the condition that he shall not join a union or shall relinquish trade union membership.

INTERNATIONAL CONVENTIONS AGAINST DISCRIMINATION

Three important international treaties prohibiting discrimination were adopted in 1958, 1960, and 1965, respectively.

The Discrimination (Employment and Occupation) Convention, 1958

By the *Discrimination (Employment and Occupation) Convention, 1958* adopted by the International Labor Conference in 1958 (in force since 1960), each state party undertakes to declare and pursue a national policy designed to promote, by methods appropriate to national conditions and practices, equality of opportunity and treatment in respect of employment and occupation, with a view to eliminating any discrimination in respect thereof. The fulfillment of the obligations undertaken by this convention are subject to the supervisory arrangements that apply under the Constitution of the International Labor Organization.

The Convention Against Discrimination in Education, 1960

In 1960 the General Conference of the United Nations Educational, Scientific and Cultural Organization (UNESCO) adopted the *Convention against Discrimination in Education,* which has been in force since 1962. Like the Discrimination (Employment and Occupation) Convention of 1958, the Convention against Discrimination in Education prohibits any distinction, exclusion, limitation, or preference based on race, color, sex, language, religion, political or other opinion, national or social origin, or economic condition or birth having the purpose or effect of impairing equality of treatment in education. The establishment or maintenance of separate educational systems or institutions for pupils of the two sexes is not prohibited, provided that these systems or institutions offer equivalent access to education and provide a teaching staff meeting the same standard of qualification. A special Protocol adopted in 1962 institutes a Conciliation and Good Offices Commission to be responsible for seeking a settlement of any disputes that may arise between the states parties to the Convention against Discrimination in Education.

The International Convention on the Elimination of All Forms of Racial Discrimination

In 1965 the General Assembly adopted the International Convention on the Elimination of All Forms of Racial Discrimination (in force since 1969). States parties undertake not only to condemn racial discrimination, and to pursue a policy of eliminating it in all its forms, but also to prohibit and bring to an end, by all appropriate means including legislation as required by circumstances, racial discrimination by any persons, group or organization. States parties undertake to declare an offense punishable by law all dissemination of ideas based on racial superiority or hatred and incitement to racial discrimination. They also commit themselves to declare illegal and prohibit organizations which promote and incite racial discrimination and to recognize participation in such an organization as an offense punishable by law. The convention provides for the establishment of international supervisory machinery similar to that laid down in the International Covenant on Civil and Political Rights but contains tighter provisions.

Under the convention, a Committee on the Elimination of Racial Discrimination has been established, which, like the Human Rights Committee provided for in the Covenant, has the function of considering reports by states and allegations by a state party that another state party is not giving effect to the provisions of the convention. States parties to the convention may also recognize the competence of the Committee on the Elimination of Racial Discrimination to receive and to consider petitions (communications) from individuals or groups of individuals. In the last instance the International Court of Justice can be seised of disputes between states parties with respect to the interpretation and application of the convention.

For several years the General Assembly has also been seised of a draft International Convention on the Elimination of All Forms of Intolerance and of Discrimination Based on Religion or Belief. The Assembly's work on this project had not been completed by the beginning of 1971.

Freedom of Information

Out of the very ambitious legislative program of the United Nations and of the specialized agencies to guarantee through international instruments the right set forth in Article 19 of the Universal Declaration of Human Rights to seek, receive, and impart information and ideas through any medium and regardless of frontiers, only the Convention on the International Right of Correction was opened for signature in 1952. At a UN Conference on Freedom of Information held in 1948, two additional conventions in this field were drafted—namely, a general Convention on Freedom of Information and a Convention on the International Transmission of News—but these have not yet received the final approval of the General Assembly and have not been opened for signature and ratification. Two agreements concerned with the international circulation and the importation of educational, scientific and cultural materials were concluded under the auspices of UNESCO in 1948 and 1950, respectively.

The idea underlying the Convention on the International Right of Correction (in force since 1962) is the attempt to transfer to the international level an institution that has been part of national law in a great number of countries. Its philosophy is that embodied in the maxim *audiatur et altera pars,* i.e., that the other party must also be heard. A right of reply or correction has not, apart from isolated exceptions, been provided in the common law jurisdictions. The rule that both parties must be heard is, however, a fundamental principle of natural justice as conceived by English and American law. In the convention of 1952 the contracting states agree that in cases where a contracting state contends that a news dispatch capable of injuring its relations with other states, or its national prestige or dignity, transmitted from one country to another by correspondents or information agencies and published or disseminated abroad, is false or distorted, it may submit its version of the facts (called *communiqué*) to the contracting states within whose territories such dispatch has been published or disseminated. The receiving state has the obligation to release the *communiqué* to the correspondents and information agencies operating in its territory through the channels customarily used for the release of news concerning international affairs for publication.

The Convention affords no remedy against articles in newspapers or statements over the radio if there is no proof that a "news dispatch" has been transmitted "from one country to another" by correspondents or information agencies. Nor does the Convention impose a legal obligation on the press or other media of information to publish the *communiqué*. The obligation of the receiving state to release a *communiqué* arises, however, whatever be its opinion of the facts dealt with in the news dispatch or in the *communiqué* that purports to correct it. In the event that the receiving state does not discharge its obligation, the complaining state has, among others, the right to seek relief through the Secretary-General of the United Nations, who through the information channels at his disposal shall give appropriate publicity to the *communiqué* together with the original dispatch and the comment, if any, submitted to him by the state complained against.

In 1949 the General Assembly adopted a Draft Convention on the International Transmission of News and the Right of Correction. The part of it that deals with the right of correction was opened for signature and ratification separately in 1952. The provisions on the international transmission of news, though approved, have not yet been opened for signature. The General Assembly resolved that this should not take place until it has taken definite action on the draft Convention on Freedom of Information. The subject matter of the latter convention, however, has been found to be so controversial that by the beginning of 1971 the draft had not yet been approved by the General Assembly.

War Crimes and Crimes Against Humanity

In 1968 the General Assembly adopted and opened for signature, ratification, and accession the Convention on the Non-Applicability of Statutory Limitations to War Crimes and Crimes Against Humanity. The convention provides that no statutory limitation shall apply to war crimes and crimes against humanity irrespective of the date of their commission. It also revises and extends the concepts of war crimes and crimes against humanity as they were defined in 1945 in the Charter of the International Military Tribunal and were applied and interpreted by the tribunal. The states parties to the 1968 Convention have undertaken to adopt all necessary domestic measures with a view to making possible the extradition of persons who have committed such crimes.

REGIONAL HUMAN RIGHTS INSTRUMENTS

The work in the human rights field, for which the provisions of the United Nations Charter cited above have been the point of departure, has inspired important developments for the protection of human rights also on the regional level by the Council of Europe and by the Organization of American States.

The European Convention on Human Rights, 1950

Under the auspices of the Council of Europe, the European Convention on Human Rights was signed in 1950 and entered into force in 1953. The convention is based on an early draft of what is now the International Covenant on Civil and Political Rights. It was concluded by the governments of European countries "to take the first steps for the collective enforcement of certain of the Rights stated in the Universal Declaration" of Human Rights. It was subsequently supplemented by five additional Protocols. As far as the substantive provisions are concerned, the European Convention and the International Covenant on Civil and Political Rights cover, more or less, the same ground, although there are a number of important differences between the two instruments.

The European Convention has established two international organs "to ensure the observance of the engagements undertaken by the High Contracting Parties in the present Convention"— that is, the European Commission on Human Rights and the European Court of Human Rights. Any party to the Convention has the right to refer to the Commission any alleged breach of the Convention by another party. The European Commission may also receive petitions from any person, non-governmental organization, or group of individuals claiming to be the victim of a violation by one of the parties of the rights set forth in Convention and in the relevant Protocols. The exercise of this power by the Commission is subject to the condition that the state against which the complaint is directed has recognized this competence of the Commission. Of the 15 states that were parties to the Convention at the end of 1970, 11 have accepted the right of petition.

If the Commission does not succeed in securing a friendly settlement on the basis of respect for human rights as defined in the Convention, it draws up a report on the facts and states its opinion as to whether the facts found disclose a breach by the state concerned of its obligations under the Convention. The final decision is taken either by the Committee of Ministers of the Council of Europe, a political organ, or, if it has jurisdiction and the matter is referred to it, by the European Court of Human Rights. Of the 15 parties to the Convention, 11 have accepted the compulsory jurisdiction of the court. Only states and the Commission can bring a case before the court.

The European Social Charter, 1961

The European Social Charter is the European counterpart to the International Covenant on Economic, Social and Cultural Rights. The provisions of the European Social Charter, however, are more specific and detailed. The European Social Charter has established a reporting procedure. The reports are examined by a committee of independent experts, which submits its conclusions to a governmental social subcommittee. The Consultative Assembly of the Council of Europe is consulted. In the final stage the Committee of Ministers may make to any contracting party any recommendation it considers necessary.

The American Convention on Human Rights

In 1948, several months before the adoption by the United Nations General Assembly of the Universal Declaration of Human Rights, the Ninth International Conference of American States adopted at Bogotá the American Declaration of the Rights and Duties of Man. In 1969 this Declaration was followed by the signing of the "Pact of San José, Costa Rica," the American Convention on Human Rights. This is a very comprehensive instrument, similar both to the European Convention on Human Rights and to the International Covenant on Civil and Political Rights. The organs of implementation of the Pact of San José are the Inter-American Commission on Human Rights (corresponding to the European Commission and to the Human Rights Committee under the United Nations Covenant) and the Inter-American Court of Human Rights. While under the European Convention and under the International Covenant on Civil and Political Rights and the Optional Protocol thereto, the right of petition of individuals is optional, in the Inter-American system every state party accepts the right of petition automatically. The provisions of the American Convention are progressive also in other respects. The Convention is not yet in force.

ACTION TAKEN BY UNITED NATIONS ORGANS ON THE BASIS OF AUTHORITY VESTED IN THEM UNDER THE CHARTER OF THE UNITED NATIONS

So far, apart from the Universal Declaration of Human Rights, we have dealt with that part of the work of the United Nations in the human rights field which has consisted in the effort to persuade states to accept through the conclusion of treaties legal obligations in human rights matters additional to those which they had undertaken by becoming parties to the Charter and Members of the United Nations. The Economic and Social Council in 1946 stated that "the purpose of the United Nations with the regard to the promotion and observance of human rights . . . can only be fulfilled if provisions are made for the implementation of human rights and of an International Bill of Rights." The expression "implementation of human rights," as used here, refers to the human rights as set forth in the Charter. The expression "implemention of an International Bill of Rights" denotes the implementation of an instrument or a series of instruments by which states would undertake obligations additional to those contained in the Charter and establish supervisory machinery. The two Covenants, the Optional Protocol, and the many treaties and draft treaties that have been described above belong within the category of instruments by which governments assume additional obligations.

The activities of the United Nations in trying to make as great use as possible of the opportunities that the Charter alone offers have also been very comprehensive. The beginnings, however, were not promising. The Commission on Human Rights, which was established by virtue of an express provision of the Charter and which was given comprehensive terms of reference in 1946, passed at its first session in 1947 a self-denying ordinance stating that it "recognizes that it has no power to take any action in regard to any complaints concerning human rights," a statement that was promptly approved by the Economic and Social Council. Since that time, repeated attempts have been made to reverse or modify this ruling—by the Secretary-General in 1949, by Egypt in 1952, by Greece in 1956–57, and by Israel in 1958–59—without success. However, inroads into the principle have repeatedly been made by organs other than the Commission on Human Rights—for example, when the Economic and Social Council, jointly with the International Labor Organization, established international machinery to deal with allegations of the infringement of trade union rights; when the Council initiated investigations concerning the existence of forced labor in Eastern Europe and other parts of the world; when the General Assembly, in 1963, sent a commission to South Viet-Nam to make an on-the-spot investigation of the allegations made against the then government of South Viet-Nam concerning the treatment of the Buddhist community. The best-known case of UN action undertaken directly under the Charter in matters of human rights has been the organization's concern with racial discrimination and segregation, the policy of *apartheid* of the government of South Africa which has occupied the United Nations practically from its beginning to this day.

In the years since 1966 important inroads have also been made into the ruling that the Commission on Human Rights has no power to take action on claims that human rights have been violated. After protracted negotiations, the Economic and Social Council decided in 1970 that a subsidiary organ of the Commission on Human Rights, the Subcommission on the Prevention of Discrimination and Protection of Minorities, shall be authorized to initiate investigations of situations that appear to reveal a consistent pattern of gross and reliably attested violations of human rights and fundamental freedoms. Proceedings thus initiated may lead to the appointment of an *ad hoc* committee to undertake an investigation which shall, however, be undertaken only with the express consent of the state concerned and conducted in constant cooperation with that state and under conditions agreed with it. Apart from these general arrangements the Commission on Human Rights has also established working groups of experts to investigate various charges relating to southern Africa and to the territory occupied by Israel in the 1967 war.

Three more items should be mentioned under the heading of human rights activities based directly on the Charter without the intervention of an additional treaty. They have been known under the collective title of Program of Practical Action and were proposed by the United States when, in 1953, the administration of President Eisenhower, reversing the policy of Presidents Roosevelt and Truman, stated that it did not believe in "treaty coercion" and did not favor "formal undertakings" as the proper way to spread throughout the world the goals of human liberty. As a substitute, the United States government proposed: (1) that worldwide studies of particular rights or groups of rights should

be undertaken; (2) that states should periodically submit reports on developments in human rights; and (3) that a system of advisory services in human rights should be instituted. The advisory services in the human rights field consist of convening international or regional conferences, called "seminars," of making available the services of experts, and of granting fellowships and scholarships. These lines of action were accepted by the United Nations not as substitutes for the drafting of treaties in the human rights field, but as additions to it. These three branches of the program of practical action have been in effect since the mid-1950's. The regional and international seminars have been particularly successful and have had a considerable impact on developments in many parts of the world.

DECLARATIONS IN THE HUMAN RIGHTS FIELD

Between the field of action taken on the basis of the authority vested in United Nations organs by the Charter and the preparation, opening for signature, and putting into force of international conventions adding to the obligations deriving from the Charter, there is a twilight zone of acts and developments that do not fully belong within either of these two categories. As a consequence of the political and technical obstacles that have been in the way of concluding international multilateral treaties on human rights and making them operative, the international community has had recourse to the proclamation of declarations that emanate from United Nations organs, are not subject to ratification by states, and do not intend to create obligations in the strict legal sense, but that nevertheless have had a great impact on developments. The first and best-known example is the Universal Declaration of Human Rights described and analyzed above.

The Universal Declaration was followed in 1960 by the adoption of the Declaration on the Granting of Independence to Colonial Countries and Peoples, in which the General Assembly declared that the subjection of peoples to alien subjugation, domination, and exploitation constitutes a denial of fundamental human rights, is contrary to the Charter of the United Nations and is an impediment to the promotion of world peace and cooperation. The 1960 Declaration proclaims that all peoples have the right to self-determination. It declares that all states shall observe faithfully and strictly the provisions of the Charter, of the Universal Declaration of Human Rights, and of the 1960 Declaration itself. In 1961 the General Assembly established comprehensive machinery for supervising the implementation of this anticolonial Declaration. The 1960 Declaration has had a great impact upon contemporary international affairs.

In 1959 the General Assembly adopted the Declaration of the Rights of the Child. This Declaration proclaims that every child, without distinction or discrimination on account of race, color, sex, language, religion, political or other opinion, national or social origin, property, birth or other status, whether of himself or of his family, shall enjoy special protection and be given opportunities and facilities to enable him to develop physically, mentally, morally, spiritually, and socially in a healthy and normal manner and in conditions of freedom and dignity. Every child shall be entitled from birth to a name and nationality and shall enjoy the benefits of social security. The child who is physically, mentally, or socially handicapped shall be given the special treatment, education, and care required by his particular condition. Every child is entitled to receive education that shall be free and compulsory, at least in the elementary stages. Every child shall be protected against all forms of neglect, cruelty, and exploitation and from practices that may foster racial, religious, and any other form of discrimination.

In 1963 the General Assembly proclaimed the United Nations Declaration on the Elimination of All Forms of Racial Discrimination which, two years later, was followed by the International

Convention on the Elimination of All Forms of Racial Discrimination, which has already been described.

In 1967 the General Assembly adopted and proclaimed the Declaration on Territorial Asylum. This Declaration supplements the relevant provisions of the Universal Declaration of Human Rights and provides that asylum granted by a state in the exercise of its sovereignty to persons entitled to invoke Article 14 of the Universal Declaration, including persons struggling against colonialism, shall be respected by all other states. The right to seek and to enjoy asylum may not be invoked by any person with respect to whom there are serious reasons for considering that he has committed a crime against peace, a war crime, or a crime against humanity. It rests with the state granting asylum to evaluate the grounds for asylum. Where a state finds difficulty in granting or continuing to grant asylum, states individually or jointly or through the United Nations shall consider, in a spirit of international solidarity, appropriate measures to lighten the burden on that state. No person entitled to invoke Article 14 of the Universal Declaration shall be subjected to measures such as retention at the frontier or, if he has already entered the territory in which he seeks asylum, expulsion or compulsory return to any state where he may be subjected to persecution. States granting asylum shall not permit persons who have received asylum to engage in activities contrary to the purposes and principles of the United Nations.

Also in 1967 the General Assembly solemnly proclaimed the Declaration on the Elimination of Discrimination against Women. The Declaration states that discrimination against women, denying or limiting as it does their equality of rights with men, is fundamentally unjust and constitutes an offense against human dignity. All appropriate measures shall be taken to abolish existing laws, customs, regulations, and practices that are discriminatory against women and to establish adequate legal protection for equal rights for men and women. All appropriate measures shall be taken to educate public opinion and to direct national aspirations toward the eradication of prejudice and the abolition of customary and other practices that are based on the idea of the inferiority of women. The Declaration of 1967 again proclaims the political rights of women as defined in the Convention of 1952, and it also proclaims the independent status of women in regard to the acquisition, change, or retention of their nationality on the lines of the Convention of 1957. The Declaration of 1967 contains detailed provisions about the status of the woman in the family; the right of women to acquire, administer, enjoy, dispose of, and inherit property; and the right to equality in legal capacity. The Declaration proclaims that all appropriate measures shall be taken to ensure the principle of equality of status of the husband and the wife. All provisions of penal codes that constitute discrimination against women shall be repealed. All appropriate measures shall be taken to combat all forms of traffic in women and exploitation of prostitution of women. Women shall enjoy equal rights with men in education at all levels. The Declaration lists in detail the measures to be taken to ensure to women equal rights with men in economic and social life. Measures shall be taken to prevent the dismissal of women in the event of marriage or maternity and to provide paid maternity leave and the necessary social services including child-care facilities. Measures taken to protect women in certain types of work for reasons inherent in their physical nature shall not be regarded as discriminatory.

On 24 October 1970, which was the 25th anniversary of the entry into force of the Charter of the United Nations, the General Assembly adopted the Declaration on Principles of International Law concerning Friendly Relations and Co-operation among States in accordance with the Charter of the United Nations. One of the principles thus proclaimed reads as follows:

"States shall co-operate in the promotion of universal respect for, and observance of, human rights, and fundamental freedoms for all, and in the elimination of all forms of racial discrimination and all forms of religious intolerance."

ASSISTANCE TO REFUGEES

The problem of refugees existed before the UN was formed. World War II created millions of refugees, the Arab-Israeli War of 1948 added almost a million more, and later developments in Asia, Europe, and Africa have swept great numbers of persons from their homes and their homelands. This chapter deals with the two United Nations agencies that provide aid to refugees: the Office of the High Commissioner for Refugees and the UN Relief and Works Agency for Palestine Refugees.

OFFICE OF THE UN HIGH COMMISSIONER FOR REFUGEES (UNHCR)

BACKGROUND

The United Nations Relief and Rehabilitation Administration (UNRRA) was established on 9 November 1943. Through its services, some 7 million refugees were fed and repatriated or resettled. The UN approved the constitution of a second agency, the International Refugee Organization (IRO), on 15 December 1946. The functions previously performed by UNRRA were taken over by IRO's Preparatory Commission on 1 July 1947. IRO resettled more than 3 million refugees, repatriated 310,000 others, and gave assistance in some form to masses of displaced persons and refugees before its liquidation in December 1951.

Recognizing that the refugee problem was still nowhere near solution, the General Assembly in December 1949 appointed a High Commissioner for Refugees to provide certain limited services after the expiration of IRO. The Office of the UN High Commissioner for Refugees was established for a period of three years, beginning January 1951. Since new refugee problems continued to arise, the life of the agency has been extended by the Assembly three times. The 1962 Assembly decided to extend its mandate for another five years, beginning January 1964. The mandate was extended again in 1969.

The office was awarded the Nobel Peace Prize in 1954.

HIGH COMMISSIONER

The high commissioner is elected by the UN General Assembly on the nomination of the secretary-general and is responsible to the Assembly. The first high commissioner was G. J. van Heuven Goedhart of the Netherlands, who died in office in 1956. The second was Auguste R. Lindt of Switzerland, who resigned in November 1960. He was succeeded by another Swiss, Felix Schnyder, who served unitl the end of 1965. The Assembly then elected Prince Sadruddin Aga Khan, who had been deputy high commissioner since 1962, for a three-year term. He was reelected in 1969.

HEADQUARTERS AND OFFICES

UNHCR's headquarters are in Geneva, Switzerland. There are European branch offices in Austria, Belgium-Luxembourg, France, West Germany, Greece, Italy, the Netherlands, and the UK. Its Middle East branch office is in Cairo, and its African regional office is in Addis Ababa. There is a branch office in Latin America and in the US. An office jointly operated by UNHCR and the Intergovernmental Committee for European Migration (ICEM) is located in Hong Kong.

FINANCES

The financial arrangements made at the creation of UNHCR reflected the fundamental difference between that office and the International Refugee Organization. IRO's budget was separate from that of the UN and ran into millions. IRO had a staff of several thousand and carried out huge relief and transportation activities, including the operation of a fleet of some 30 ocean vessels for the movement of refugees overseas.

The high commissioner's budget is part of the regular UN budget. It was only $300,000 for the first year, and UNHCR's statute expressly forbade him to appeal to governments for funds or make a general appeal without the prior approval of the General Assembly.

The 1954 General Assembly authorized the high commissioner to appeal for $16 million in voluntary contributions for an intensified four-year program. When the drive for donations terminated at the end of 1958, nearly $14.5 million had been contributed by governments and over $2 million by private organizations.

In 1959–60, the most extensive drive to date was made to obtain funds for UNHCR and, above all, to dramatize the urgent need for greater efforts to improve the lot of the world's refugees, then estimated at no fewer than 15 million. Called the World Refugee Year, the drive had a beneficial impact, financially and otherwise, well beyond the formal end of the campaign.

UNHCR expenditures in 1969 from voluntary funds totaled $8,685,437. Contributions and other income amounted to $8,209,545. The programs included $3,089,000 for Africa, $531,000 for Asia, $803,000 for Europe, and $303,000 for Latin America. In 1969, 73 states contributed $4,986,580, and private donations totaled $759,537. Administrative expenditures paid out of the UN regular budget came to $3,922,797.

TASKS OF THE COMMISSIONER

The tasks assigned the Office of the High Commissioner are, in general, to find permanent solutions for the refugees under the commissioner's mandate and to deal as quickly as possible with new emergencies as they arise. The UNHCR's work is humanitarian and entirely nonpolitical.

Three permanent solutions are recognized for refugees, and individuals are given complete freedom to accept or reject any of them. They are voluntary repatriation, emigration to a new country, and integration in the life of the country where the refugee has found asylum.

Repatriation

UNHCR tries to ensure that any refugee wishing to repatriate is allowed to do so. Not being an operative agency, UNHCR normally does not provide transportation to refugees who wish to return to their countries of origin, but in exceptional cases the office may cover the costs of repatriation.

Integration: Emigration for Resettlement

Much of UNHCR's work consists in promoting resettlement opportunities. In Europe this is done in close cooperation with the Intergovernmental Committee for European Migration (ICEM) and other organizations interested in refugee work. In 1952–60, ICEM moved some 360,000 refugees who were under the UNHCR's mandate.

The Problem of Ensuring International Protection

The high commissioner seeks to persuade governments to accede to relevant international agreements or introduce national legislation to guarantee refugees a measure of security.

The 1951 Convention Relating to the Status of Refugees

As of May 1970 this convention was in force in 59 countries. A number of other countries that have not acceded to it generally apply its principles. The 1967 protocol relating to the status of refugees, which entered into force in October 1967, has been ratified by 40 countries. These instruments have been supplemented by the Organization of African Unity (OAU) Convention Governing the Specific Aspect of Refugee Problems in Africa of 1969.

The convention does not guarantee the right of immigration or of permanent settlement. It does guarantee to refugees the same treatment as nationals in such matters as the right to work (although some countries with employment problems of their own that ratified the convention made reservations on this point), and on the right to obtain travel documents, social security benefits, elementary education, and access to law courts.

Whether a person is recognized as a refugee within the convention and thus comes under the mandate of the high commissioner is for the authorities of the country of residence to decide. But the high commissioner participates in the decision. However, in this regard, since the terms of the convention apply only to persons who became refugees as a result of events occurring before 1 January 1951, the commissioner's chief object is to promote intergovernmental action to extend the personal scope of the convention. A recommendation to this effect was made by a Colloquium on Legal Aspects of Refugee Problems, held at Bellagio, Italy, in April 1965.

Agreement Relating to Refugee Seamen. The situation of refugees serving as seamen is particularly difficult. Normal regulations regarding landing permits and similar matters do not apply to them, so that some could not even leave their ships. An Agreement Relating to Refugee Seamen, signed at The Hague in 1957, allows refugee seamen to acquire permanent residence in the country with which they have the closest association. The agreement, which came into force in December 1961, was ratified by 16 states as of 31 March 1970.

The Right of Asylum. The right of asylum is the cornerstone of the work of protecting refugees. But the legal aspects remain undefined. One step toward solving this problem is the drafting of a Declaration on the Right of Asylum, which has been before the Assembly since the 17th session (1962). Another step is the recommendation adopted by the Consultative Assembly of the Council of Europe calling upon the Committee of Ministers to speed up the elaboration of an instrument designed to give full legal recognition to the practice of granting asylum in the Council's member states.

National Legislation. The high commissioner actively encourages governments to introduce measures of benefit to refugees or to insert clauses in existing laws taking the interests of refugees into account with regard to terms of employment, naturalization, freedom of movement, and the like.

REFUGEES UNDER THE MANDATE OF THE HIGH COMMISSIONER

Refugees under the high commissioner's mandate are defined in UNHCR's Statute as persons who, owing to well-founded fear of persecution for reason of race, religion, nationality, or political opinion, are living outside their country of origin or former habitual residence and who cannot or, because of such fear, do not wish to seek the protection of their country of origin. The high commissioner's office does not concern itself with refugees who receive protection or assistance from other UN organs or agencies, such as the Arab refugees from Palestine, or with refugees who, like those in India and Pakistan, enjoy the same rights in the country of asylum as do its own citizens. By 1970 the major part of UNHCR's refugee problems were to be found in Africa.

When the office began operations in 1951 some 2 million refugees were under its mandate. In 1970 the number was about 1,900,000, more than 1 million of whom were in Africa. Unsettled refugees, in the terminology of the office, are persons who live under precarious conditions, in refugee camps or not, in a country of asylum. Their situation is regarded as provisional, even though it may have been unchanged for years. Settled refugees are those who are in the process of becoming integrated into their country of asylum or into a new country to which they have emigrated.

European Refugees

"Old" Refugee Problems. When the agency came into existence in 1951, it inherited some 120,000 persons still living precariously, and often in squalor, in refugee and displaced persons' camps, mainly in West Germany, Austria, Italy, and Greece. The great majority of these persons had been uprooted during World War II, primarily through the Nazi policies of removing people from occupied territories for forced labor and forcibly shifting populations for racial reasons. Particularly deplorable was the situation of the children born in the camps. Clearance of those camps was long delayed, mainly for lack of funds. Thanks largely to UNHCR assistance programs, more than 90% of their inhabitants were able to leave the camps between 1954 and 1962.

In 1960 the Office of the High Commissioner concluded an agreement with West Germany on indemnification of refugees under UNHCR mandate who had suffered permanent injury to body or health as a result of persecution on the grounds of their nationality. West Germany set up a fund of DM45 million ($4,250,000) for that purpose. By the deadline of 31 March 1962, 40,000 applications had been received from over 50 countries. The indemnification fund was closed on 30 September 1964, but a small reserve was maintained to enable the high commissioner to make payments in cases where appeals lodged by the applicants proved successful. By 31 March 1970 a total of 36,556 applications had been received by West Germany. Under the indemnification agreement of 1960, 25,512 of those had been settled, 2,717 favorable decisions were taken, and payments amounting to DM 123.5 million were made. There was also a tendency toward a more liberal application of criteria. Whereas in 1968 the monthly average of positive decisions was 31, in 1969 it rose to 53.

Altogether, some 150,000 "old" European refugees were assisted under major aid programs between 1955 and 1965. Of the 18,000 assisted during 1965, about 7,500 were permanently settled. As of 31 December 1965, assistance was still required for 1,200 "old" European refugees in the Far East; for some 1,500, mostly handicapped, in France; 2,800 in Greece; and some 1,200 in the Middle East and Morocco. The major aid programs to these "old" refugees have been terminated.

"New" Refugee Problems. Although the problem of the European refugees created by the upheavals consequent upon World War II were almost at an end, movements of "new" refugees have continued to arise.

One of the biggest of these "new" refugee problems, now resolved, was the result of the Hungarian crisis in 1956. The high commissioner was called on, in October 1956, to coordinate the activities of governments and voluntary organizations on behalf of the 200,000 Hungarians who sought refuge in Austria and Yugoslavia. From October 1956 until the end of December 1959, 179,000 Hungarian refugees arrived in Austria, 19,000 in Yugoslavia, and 1,000 in other countries. The total movement involved 203,100 persons. Of these, 18,000 eventually chose to return to

Hungary. Of the remainder, 9,600 elected to remain in Austria; 65,400 went to other European countries; 107,400 emigrated overseas; and the whereabouts of 2,700 are not known. Over $11.6 million was contributed to the UNHCR to assist these refugees.

In 1969 there were over 31,000 officially recognized "new" European refugees, compared with 22,500 in 1968. Much of the increase was offset by resettlement and naturalization, while a number of refugees returned voluntarily to their country of origin. The number of refugees within UNHCR's competence in Europe was about 650,000 in 1969.

African Refugees

The first serious refugee problem to arise in Africa was the result of Algeria's struggle for independence from France. From 1957 until the end of the war in 1962, large numbers of Algerians (200,000 of them by 1959) fled to neighboring Tunisia and Morocco. Working in cooperation with the League of the Red Cross, Red Crescent, Red Lion and Sun Societies, UNHCR organized and mounted substantial material aid programs. Following the signing of the Algerian-French cease-fire agreement, similar aid programs were extended to repatriates for as long as was required. Elsewhere in Africa the refugee problem has steadily intensified. By 1970 the number of refugees within the competence of UNHCR was about 1 million. As a consequence, almost half of UNHCR's 1966 operating budget was earmarked for Africa, and a new regional office was opened in Addis Ababa. To facilitate the work of moving, feeding, and retraining refugees for jobs that will not displace local inhabitants, two specialized agencies have been drawn into the operations: the Food and Agricultural Organization (FAO) and the International Labor Organization (ILO).

Rwandese Refugees. A serious African refugee problem is the plight of some 160,000 refugees from Rwanda. The exodus of these refugees began in the fall of 1961, on the eve of the division of the Belgian-administered trust territory of Ruanda-Urundi into two independent states, Rwanda and Burundi. Tensions between Rwanda's two main tribes, the Watutsi and the Bahutu, erupted into mutual persecution. Since independence, the number of Rwandese refugees has continued to rise. By the end of 1965 about 69,000 had fled to Uganda; 52,000 to Burundi; 25,000 to the Congo (Kinshasa); and 14,000 to Tanzania. UNHCR allocated about $1.1 million for resettlement projects for these refugees in 1965. At the end of 1969 the number of Rwandese in Burundi was

estimated at 36,000. In Uganda, where the largest number had sought sanctuary, about half the refugees were being helped by friends and relatives, while the other half were receiving international assistance toward settlement in agriculture and stock raising.

Sudanese Refugees. The Sudan has two major ethnic and cultural groups, the "African" Sudanese, who mainly inhabit the southern part of the country, and the "Arab" Sudanese, in the north, who largely control the government. Considerable conflict has arisen between the two groups, and a serious refugee problem has been created by the growing number of African Sudanese who fled in 1969. There were 23,000 of these refugees in Uganda, 60,000 in the Congo (Kinshasa), 20,000 in the Central African Republic, and 20,000 in Ethiopia.

Refugees from Portuguese Colonial Territories

In 1969 there were about 400,000 refugees from Angola in the Congo (Kinshasa)—most of whom had already been settled there for a number of years—60,000 refugees from Portuguese Guinea in Senegal, some 40,000 refugees from Mozambique in Tanzania, and a further 12,700 from this territory and Angola in Zambia.

Asian Refugees

The UNHCR has also had to concern itself with the continuing refugee problem in the Far East created by the flight of thousands of Chinese and Tibetans from their homelands. By the end of 1969 there were 65,000 refugees from Mainland China in Macao. UNHCR contributed $65,162 for their assistance in that year.

Of the 56,000 Tibetan refugees who had accumulated by the end of 1969, 50,000 were living in India and 8,000 in Nepal. Both groups are being assisted by several voluntary organizations as well as by UNHCR, which contributed about $340,000 to projects for their social welfare in that year.

Latin American Refugees

Between 20,000 and 30,000 refugees from Cuba were estimated to have fled to Latin America by 1965. Nearly 1,000 of these were settled under UNHCR programs. There were some 12,000 Cuban refugees in Spain in 1965. Assistance was provided by a network of governmental and voluntary organizations, with UNHCR contributing more than $150,000 that year to resettlement projects and supplementary aid for the newly arrived.

The number of refugees within UNHCR's mandate in Latin America was 110,000 in 1969. UNHCR contributed $316,250 to facilitate their resettlement.

UNITED NATIONS RELIEF AND WORKS AGENCY FOR PALESTINE REFUGEES

The problem of the Palestine refugees is one of the most tragic consequences of the Arab-Israeli War of 1948. When a cease-fire came into effect early in 1949, hundreds of thousands of Arabs—men, women, and children—who had lived within the territory of what is now Israel were stranded on the other side of the armistice line from their homes. The Arab states claim that the refugees were driven out by the Israelis or fled in fear of reprisals. Israel, on the other hand, asserts that the Arab states ordered the Arab population to evacuate the area temporarily so that their armies could more easily drive the Israelis into the sea. The plight of these refugees has been a serious concern to the UN ever since. By 1966, 1.3 million persons living in Syria, Jordan, Lebanon, and Gaza were registered as Palestine refugees, and over 90% of

them were largely dependent on UN relief. The total in 1969/70 had risen to 1,425,219.

CREATION AND EXTENSION OF UNRWA

Stopgap relief was given the refugees at first by the International Committee of the Red Cross, the League of Red Cross Societies, and the American Friends Service Committee, using money and supplies provided by the temporary United Nations Relief for Palestine Refugees, established in December 1948. In December 1949 the General Assembly created a special agency, UNRWA, to provide relief and works projects in collaboration with the local governments. In the following year, the Assembly extended UNRWA's mandate to June 1952 and instructed it to carry out development projects that would enable the refugees to be absorbed into the economy of the region. As originally conceived, UNRWA was a large-scale but definitely temporary operation to be terminated by the end of 1952. The Assembly accordingly asked Israel and its neighbors to secure "the permanent re-establishment of the refugees and their removal from relief." In carrying out programs of resettlement, however, all parties concerned, including UNRWA, were to act without prejudice to the rights of those refugees who "wished to return to their homes and live in peace with their neighbors." These were to "be permitted to do so at the earliest practicable date."

In 1952, however, the Assembly recognized that the immediate realization of UNRWA's goals had not proved possible. It approved a new program for large-scale development projects designed to induce the refugees to leave the temporary camps where they were living and to enable them to become self-supporting and an asset to their host countries. The Assembly hoped that the new program would enable UNRWA to complete its task by 1954. The two most widely discussed development projects were the Jordan River Valley Project and a plan to irrigate a region in the Sinai desert where some of the refugees could be settled. Water for the Sinai project was to be brought from the Nile via a canal and a siphon under the Suez Canal. Neither of these projects materialized, and the 1954 General Assembly extended the life of UNRWA through mid-1960. Again, in December 1959, the Assembly noted "with deep regret . . . that no substantial progress [has] been made in the program . . . for the reintegration of refugees either by repatriation or resettlement" and decided to extend the mandate of UNRWA for another three years, through mid-1963. UNRWA's mandate was extended for a further three years in 1962 and again in 1965 and 1968.

ORGANIZATION OF UNRWA
UNRWA extends its activities over an area of more than 100,000 sq. mi., and it deals with four host governments, Jordan, Lebanon, Syria, and the UAR.

UNRWA is a special body within the UN, and its policy and functions are determined by the General Assembly. UNRWA is headed by a commissioner-general, who is assisted by a nine-nation advisory commission composed of Belgium, France, Jordan, Lebanon, Syria, Turkey, UAR, UK, and US. The commissioner-general is appointed by the secretary-general in consultation with the nine governments of the advisory committee. As of December 1970, the commissioner-general was Laurence Michelmore, who took office in January 1964.

Headquarters are in Beirut, and field offices are located in Cairo, Gaza, Amman, Beirut, and Damascus. UNRWA liaison offices are located in Geneva and at UN Headquarters in New York. Each field office is headed by a representative of the director, who is responsible for UNRWA activities in his area. The UNRWA staff consists of some 120 international officials and over 1,000 locally recruited persons, virtually all refugees.

FINANCES
UNRWA depends entirely on voluntary contributions. Total expenditure for 1966 was estimated at $37.8 million; requirements for 1967 exceeded $39 million. Estimates for 1971 totaled $47,545,000.

About 90% of UNRWA's annual income is contributed by four governments—Canada, France, the UK, and the US. But the leading donor, the US, reduced its 1965/66 contribution by $1.8 million. Numerous private organizations, as well as individuals, throughout the world also contribute to UNRWA's income. In his annual report for 1969/70, the commissioner-general of UNRWA stated that a decision concerning the method of future financing could no longer be delayed. The human problem persisted and had become more complicated. The refugees regarded themselves as temporary wards of the the international community whom they held responsible for their plight. In addition, the

persisting effects of the 1967 hostilities, including military occupation; the continuing displacement of hundreds of thousands of persons who fled in 1967; and the growing impact of the policies and activities of the various *fedayeen* movements on the situation in some host countries and on the attitudes of the refugees in all of them combined to intensify the difficulties.

In 1970, for the first time in UNRWA history, education became the main item of expenditure (45%) surpassing the relief programs (42%) that for many years had been the major preoccupation of the agency. This was achieved by not putting into effect all of the significant curtailments in the agency's program that had been planned for 1969/70. As a consequence, the agency was virtually insolvent by the end of 1970. Inasmuch as UNRWA in the 20 years of its activity had become a de facto element of stability in some of the host countries, any major diminution of its role could only serve to worsen an already inflammatory situation, the commissioner-general reported.

At the beginning of 1970, the agency's financial position was so critical that the commissioner-general considered there was no alternative to substantial reduction in the agency's program unless he could be assured of an increase in income sufficient to cover a deficit estimated at nearly $5 million. If income in 1971 did not exceed the estimate for 1970 (approximately $41 million), the agency would face a deficit of about $6 million and be likely to run out of funds by September 1971.

In the commissioner-general's view, a prerequisite for continuation was the balancing of the agency's budget for 1971, either by the assurance of adequate income to maintain existing services or by a radical review of the agency's role and program. He asked the Assembly for an unequivocal decision. On 15 December 1970 the Assembly renewed its appeal to all governments to join in a collective effort to solve UNRWA's financial crisis. It appointed a working group to assist the secretary-general and the commissioner-general in reaching solutions to UNRWA's financial problems. Members of the group are France, Ghana, Japan, Lebanon, Norway, Turkey, Trinidad, UK, and US.

Change in Environment
The agency's financial situation has to be viewed against the background of a marked change in its environment, due primarily to a transformation in the political role of the Palestine refugee community and the acceptance by the refugee community and the host governments of a representative and negotiating role for the Palestine politico-military organizations. The commissioner-general pointed out that unless some progress is made toward settling the refugee problem, a radical reconsideration of UNRWA's role, methods, and program may be required.

In 1969 and 1970 the agency faced operational problems on the West Bank and Gaza involving curfews, screenings, detention of staff, demolition of shelters, damage to installations and movement of supplies.

In Syria the government authorized the agency in 1970 to replace tents with concrete block shelters. The agency's training center in Homs, Syria, which had been occupied by Syrian displaced persons since 1967, was returned to the agency. Problems concerning visas and posting of staff were not solved by 1970.

In Lebanon and east Jordan, the power and influence of the Palestine politico-military organizations raised basic questions of authority and identification and of the attitude of the agency's locally recruited staff. As regards refugee camps in Lebanon, negotiations took place in 1969 and 1970 between Lebanese authorities and representatives of Palestine organizations for the return of police or other government officials to the camps and the release of occupied installations, with no appreciable results.

In east Jordan the successive confrontations between the government and Palestine organizations have had repercussions on the work of the UNRWA and its staff.

NUMBER AND GEOGRAPHIC DISTRIBUTION OF THE REFUGEES

As of 30 June 1970, 1,425,219 refugees were registered with UNRWA, compared with 1,395,074 on 30 June 1969. Because the natural growth of the refugee population—by 1962 the number of babies born annually to refugee parents passed the 42,000 mark— far exceeds the rate at which refugees have become self-supporting, the number of persons registered with UNRWA has increased constantly. In the period 1950–70 births totaled 723,258.

About 307,000 of the refugees are crowded into the narrow Gaza Strip along the Mediterranean. More than 700,000 are in Jordan, the majority in the region west of the Jordan River that was formerly part of Palestine, particularly the Jerusalem-Bethlehem-Hebron area, the Jericho area, and the Nablus area. Most of the other refugees in Jordan are found near Amman, the capital. Some 164,000 refugees are in Lebanon and over 140,000 in Syria, particularly in the Damascus area but also in the south of the country and in the Aleppo area to the northwest near the Turkish border.

The gravity of the situation can be seen from the fact that the refugees in the Gaza Strip outnumber two to one the long-time inhabitants of that small area, where the economic situation was so unfavorable that the majority of the local inhabitants themselves were receiving relief from the UAR up to June 1970. In Jordan, a relatively large but economically weak country, registered refugees constitute more than 40% of the population.

For the agency's purposes, a person is a refugee if he normally resided in Palestine for at least two years prior to the 1948 conflict and if, as a result of this conflict, he lost both his home and his means of livelihood. This rule would make ineligible for UNRWA services all children born after 1946, or more than half of the persons registered as refugees by 1966. For children born up to 1951, the rule has not been applied. For those born since then, the budget provides special medical care, a daily milk ration and supplementary feeding, and education. But these children receive basic food rations only insofar as the UNRWA budget permits.

The problem is closely tied to what UNRWA has constantly referred to as the "sensitive and complicated" problem of rectifying the "large inaccuracies" in its registers. The agency, in cooperation with the host governments, has been "striving to remove false and duplicated registration and the names of the dead, and for each name so eliminated, the name of a needy eligible refugee [usually that of a child] is being added." In this way, and by also excluding persons who have become self-supporting, UNRWA was able to make 34,200 such changes between mid-1961 and mid-1962 alone. In response to urgent requests from the General Assembly, UNRWA has continued its efforts to rectify the ration rolls. During 1965 the names of 33,607 persons were removed from the register, including 30,192 recipients of rations. These rectifications made it possible to issue 7,984 rations during that year to children on the waiting list and 8,749 rations to needy refugees. However, as the agency maintains a limit on the maximum number of ration recipients in each host country—with no allowance for population increase—the number of children over the age of one year for whom no rations are available continues to grow. By June 1966 these children totaled 257,099, of whom 205,247 were in Jordan, 5,153 in Lebanon, 19,235 in Syria, and 27,464 in the Gaza Strip.

Altogether, of the total number of refugees now registered with the agency, 861,122 were registered for rations at the end of June 1966, compared with 874,594 in June 1965, while the number of persons registered for agency services other than rations increased from 406,229 to 456,627.

SERVICES PROVIDED BY UNRWA
Relief Services

Food. The basic food ration provided by UNRWA consists of flour, pulses, sugar, rice, oil, and fats. Dates are added in winter. The ration provides a total of approximately 1,600 calories in winter and 1,500 calories the rest of the year. Since November 1969 additional flour has been substituted for part of the pulses and rice components of the ration in order to utilize donations of flour.

It is generally agreed that the ration fails to provide a balanced diet and is inadequate, but refugees barter some of it for fresh foods, such as meat and vegetables, and most families manage to earn a little money through casual labor to buy extra food. Moreover, under a supplementary feeding program, UNRWA provides milk for all pregnant women and nursing mothers and for all infants and children up to the age of 15. A supplementary dry ration of 500 to 600 calories is provided for women from the 5th month of pregnancy to the 12th month after delivery. A hot midday meal is given six days a week to persons (mainly young children) who require one on medical grounds, and vitamins are provided for infants and schoolchildren.

During 1961–62 the UN Interdepartmental Committee on Nutrition carried out full-scale nutrition surveys of both the refugee and nonrefugee populations in Jordan and Lebanon. The commissioner-general reported to the General Assembly in 1962 that "the nutritional status of the refugee population has been found to be approximate to the standard of nutrition of other sections of the local population."

Other Basic Subsistence Rations. Persons eligible for the basic food ration also receive 150 grams of soap per month. During the five winter months, those in the Gaza Strip receive one liter of kerosene per month and those in Jordan, Lebanon, and Syria 1.5 liters per month. More than 400,000 blankets are distributed yearly.

Shelter

When the agency first began its work, some 30,000 tents provided the principal shelter for the 30% of the refugees living in the camps. As funds and the availability of suitable sites permitted, the agency gradually replaced the tents with huts. At first, many refugees objected to using a shelter that they regarded as permanent, but this objection was gradually overcome. By the end of 1959 all the tents in UNRWA camps had been replaced by huts. These camps now accommodate some 39% of the greatly increased refugee population, one hut being normally provided to a family, and the construction program has continued. The camps still cannot accommodate all the refugees who wish to live in them, however, and many squatters are living in makeshift shelters near the camps. But all those living outside the camps, if otherwise eligible, are covered by UNRWA's food, health, education, and other services.

Special Hardship Assistance—Clothing. Because of UNRWA's limited means, it has had to rely for clothing on donations by voluntary agencies. During 1965, 675 tons of donated clothing were distributed to needy families. Some $50,000 was spent by UNRWA to meet inland transport and freight costs for clothing shipped from countries other than the US. As of 30 June 1970 there were 440,259 officially registered persons in 53 camps. The number actually living in the camps was 496,973. In addition the population of 10 emergency camps totaled 119,169. These persons were displaced in 1967 and 1969. The total number of persons in established and emergency camps was 616,142.

Health Services

Under an agreement with UNRWA, the World Health Organization has been responsible since 1949 for the technical direction of the agency's health services. WHO also provides certain senior medical staff, including the agency's chief medical officer. The preventive and curative health services, as well as the health education and environmental sanitation programs, are very extensive. In 1966, 105 health centers were operated directly by the agency. It also subsidizes clinics and outpatient facilities of hospitals in the host countries. Some 7 million visits were paid to clinics in the year ending at mid-1969. A total of 1,706 hospital beds were maintained or reserved by the agency in 1970.

Preventive medicine campaigns have paid remarkable dividends. Malaria, which used to be rampant and was the principal incapacitating disease among the refugees, has been virtually wiped out, as have smallpox, cholera, and other pestilential diseases. Only 2 cases of diphtheria and 273 of tuberculosis were counted in 1969–70. The infectious eye diseases common in the Middle East have been greatly reduced: 1,393 cases of trachoma (4,384 in 1965–66) and 27,423 of conjunctivitis (55,797 in 1965–66). Special emphasis has been placed on prenatal and postnatal care through maternity clinics and infant health centers, which, in addition to their other services, issue layettes and supplementary food rations. Two school health teams operate in Jordan and one each in Syria, Lebanon, and Gaza.

Educational and Vocational Services

UNRWA–UNESCO schools for refugee children have been in operation in Jordan, Lebanon, Syria, and the Gaza Strip since 1951. In 1953, UNRWA, in cooperation with UNESCO, introduced the policy of making elementary education available to all children whose parents wished to enroll them, and in that year some 31,000 pupils entered the first grade. Eventually UNRWA, after building hundreds of schools and fostering teacher training, was able to offer six years of elementary education to all refugee children and three years of preparatory education to all elementary school graduates. As UNRWA has reported, "the refugee child today has considerably greater educational opportunities than his parents had."

In 1969/70, 219,378 pupils were enrolled in UNRWA–UNESCO elementary schools, and the agency paid subsidies for another 64,359 who attended state and private elementary and secondary schools.

Noteworthy is the increase in attendance by girls in UNRWA–UNESCO schools on the elementary level, which rose from 11,676 in 1951 to 64,657 in 1966. Teacher training for men and women and other vocational training have been increasingly stressed. The total number of refugee teachers under training in 1969/70 was 3,656.

An increasing number of scholarships (1,101 in 1966) to various universities in the Middle East have been awarded by UNRWA, financed partly through special donations. In addition, 115 were abroad on training-in-industry programs, for the most part in West Germany.

Placement Assistance. UNRWA constantly endeavors to place job-seeking refugees, particularly those graduating from its various vocational and training centers. Contacts with potential employers have opened up new possibilities, and a number of employers have given contracts to whole classes even before the students have completed their training. Close consultation with employers has also made it possible to adjust courses to requirements.

Social Welfare. Over the years, UNRWA, assisted by various international organizations, has found increasingly effective ways to combat the idleness, lethargy, and low morale, especially among the youth, which are unavoidable in refugee camps. It has organized special community development projects, fostered small cooperatives, and systematically developed sports programs, mutual-help projects, tree-planting projects, sewing circles for women, and similar activities.

Allocation of the Budget

	1971 BUDGET ESTIMATES	1970 ADJUSTED BUDGET ESTIMATES	1969 ACTUAL EXPENDITURE
	(in thousands of US dollars)		
PART I: RELIEF SERVICES			
Basic rations	12,487	12,461	13,546
Supplementary feeding	2,204	2,111	2,165
Shelter	261	348	1,390
Special hardship assistance	534	529	524
Share of common costs from part IV	3,539	3,585	3,509
TOTALS, PART I	19,025	19,034	21,134
PART II: HEALTH SERVICES			
Medical services	3,799	3,662	3,523
Environmental sanitation	1,522	1,369	1,101
Share of common costs from part IV	1,136	1,139	1,093
TOTALS, PART II	6,457	6,170	5,717
PART III: EDUCATION SERVICES			
General education	15,335	14,452	12,589
Vocational and professional training	3,911	3,679	4,050
Share of common costs from part IV	2,817	2,810	2,671
TOTALS, PART III	22,063	20,941	19,310
PART IV: COMMON COSTS			
Supply and transport services	3,429	3,539	3,587
Other internal services	2,617	2,556	2,321
General administration	1,446	1,439	1,365
TOTALS, PART IV	7,492	7,534	7,273
Costs allocated to operations	(7,492)	(7,534)	(7,273)
GRAND TOTALS	47,545	46,145	46,161

INDEPENDENCE OF COLONIAL PEOPLES

During the decades of the 1950's and 1960's, nearly 50 territories that were formerly under foreign rule have become sovereign states and members of the UN. In this radical transformation of the world's political map, the UN has played a significant role that stems from the basic precepts of its Charter as laid down in Article 1, which states that one of the purposes of the UN is to "develop friendly relations among nations based on respect for the principle of equal rights and self-determination of peoples. . . ." And chapters XI, XII, and XIII of the Charter are devoted specifically to measures designed to promote the welfare of dependent peoples.

In its efforts to implement these measures, the UN has dealt with two types of territories: (1) non-self-governing dependents or colonies of UN member states, and (2) former colonial territories administered by designated member states as UN Trust Territories pending independence. Since the UN's powers and responsibilities differ considerably in regard to the two categories of territories, this chapter has been divided into two sections.

A. NON-SELF-GOVERNING TERRITORIES

Delegates attending the 1945 San Francisco Conference, at which the UN was founded, included many spokesmen for anticolonialist sentiment. Due to their efforts and to generous proposals by Australia and the UK (which possessed the world's largest colonial empire at the time), the Charter incorporates a pledge on the part of the colonial powers to assume certain obligations toward the peoples of their dependencies.

CHARTER DECLARATION ON NON-SELF-GOVERNING TERRITORIES

The pledge takes the form of a declaration that is embodied in Article 73, Chapter XI. Under Article 73, all UN members "which have or assume responsibilities for the administration of territories whose peoples have not yet attained a full measure of self-government recognize the principle that the interests of these territories are paramount, and accept as a sacred trust the obligation to promote to the utmost, within the system of international peace and security established by the present Charter, the well-being of the inhabitants of these territories. . . ." This general obligation is then broken down into five specific obligations: (a) to "ensure, with due respect for the culture of the peoples concerned, their political, economic, social, and educational advancement, their just treatment, and their protection against abuses"; (b) to "develop self-government, to take due account of the political aspirations of the peoples, and to assist them in the progressive development of their free political institutions, according to the particular circumstances of each territory and its peoples. . ."; (c) to "further international peace and security"; (d) to "promote constructive measures of development. . ."; and (e) to "transmit regularly to the Secretary-General for information purposes, subject to such limitations as security and constitutional considerations may require, statistical and other information of a technical nature relating to economic, social, and educational conditions in the territories for which they are respectively responsible. . ."

Today, when so many of these dependent peoples have claimed and won their independence, the obligations contained in the declaration may not seem very far-reaching. For example, nothing is said about preparing non-self-governing territories for actual independence—indeed, the word "independence" nowhere appears in the declaration. Although due account is to be taken of the "political aspirations of the people," all that is explicitly acknowledged is the obligation to prepare the people for "self-government," which does not necessarily imply independence. But the validity of the declaration must be considered in the context of its era. Few people at the San Francisco Conference foresaw how intense or universal the desire of colonial peoples for full political sovereignty would be. All told, the obligations included in the declaration probably represented the maximum that reasonably could be expected from colonial countries at that time. Moreover, in the circumstances then prevailing, the colonial nations' agreement, under paragraph (e) of Article 73, to submit information to an international body concerning their own territories—in effect to yield up a degree of their sovereignty—was a considerable concession.

Territories Covered by the Declaration

The somewhat unwieldy term "non-self-governing territory" was chosen primarily because it was broad enough to include the various constitutional designations given by administering powers to their dependencies—colony, protectorate, and so on—as well as all stages of political development short of actual self-government or independence. The declaration covers all territories "whose people have not yet attained a full measure of self-government." But the precise meaning of "a full measure of self-government" is not specified, thus leaving the door open for subsequent dispute and controversy.

At the outset it was considered the responsibility of the eight colonial powers that were UN members to identify the dependencies they regarded as non-self-governing within the meaning of Article 73 of the Charter. At its first working session, in 1946, the General Assembly adopted a resolution enumerating 74 non-self-governing territories that the administering countries had identified as falling within the provisions of the declaration. The eight colonial countries were Australia, Belgium, Denmark, France, the Netherlands, New Zealand, the UK, and the US. The combined population of their dependencies, which ranged from tiny Pitcairn Island with a population of a mere 100 persons to the Netherlands Indies with 73 million, was estimated at 215 million. (The dependencies of Spain and Portugal could not be included in the 1946 list, since these two colonial powers were not UN members at the time.)

THE WORK OF THE UN

The Charter does not assign any particular task to the UN with respect to non-self-governing territories. It does not even specify what should be done with the information transmitted to the secretary-general. Hence, the General Assembly has considered itself free to define its own functions.

Since even in the very beginning the majority of UN members were vehemently anticolonial, the immediate task the Assembly set for itself was to induce the colonial countries by every means in its power to fulfill their obligations under the declaration. Judging from the disputes and controversies that arose even as early as 1946, it seems safe to assume that this development was totally unforeseen by the colonial countries as the time of the San Francisco Conference.

Although the Assembly lacks the power to enforce its recommendations, the colonial powers had no wish to see themselves recorded as being in constant opposition in majority decisions. Consequently, they fought from the start to maintain the right initiative in affairs concerning their own territories and to prevent the UN from expanding its role in colonial matters. However, they were fighting a losing battle against an irreversible trend of world opinion; in effect, the story of the UN's role essentially has been one of increasing involvement in the process of decolonization.

DISPUTES WITH THE COLONIAL POWERS OVER THE TRANSMISSION OF INFORMATION ON NON-SELF-GOVERNING TERRITORIES

The first dispute that arose between the colonial powers and the other UN members concerned the Assembly's desire to discuss the reports that had been submitted on the various territories. Some of the colonial governments, particularly Belgium, contended that the mere submission of reports fulfilled the Charter's requirements under paragraph (e) of Article 73. Disregarding these protests, the 1947 Assembly set up a special committee to report on the information received. In 1949 this committee was established on a quasi-permanent basis as the Committee on Information from Non-Self-Governing Territories, composed of an equal number of administering and nonadministering countries. In that same year the Assembly adopted a comprehensive standard questionnaire, which the administering powers were expected to answer in annual reports. The questionnaire covered virtually every aspect of the social, economic, and educational conditions in the territories. However, due to the controversies discussed below, the committee received reports on only 56 of the territories originally enumerated.

Cessation of Information

By 1949 some of the administering powers had unilaterally interpreted Article 73 paragraph (e) as meaning that when they themselves considered that a territory had attained self-government, they need no longer submit reports on it to the UN. On this basis, the UK had ceased sending information on Malta after its first report in 1946. Likewise France, after 1946, stopped sending reports on certain of its territories that it regarded as overseas departments of France with rights equal to the metropolitan departments of France or as having reached a requisite stage of "internal autonomy." Nor had the US sent reports on the Panama Canal Zone after 1946 (though this was possibly because Panama itself contested classification of the Zone as a non-self-governing territory). Concerned at these developments, the 1949 Assembly, over the opposition of the colonial powers (the US abstaining), decided that it was "within the responsibility of the General Assembly to express its opinion on the principles which have guided or which may in future guide the members concerned in enumerating the territories for which the obligation exists to transmit information under Article 73 (e) of the Charter."

The Assembly in 1952 established a special committee to draw up a list of criteria of self-government and at its next session voted itself competent to decide on the basis of this list whether reports were due on a given territory. Since that time the Assembly has formally approved the cessation of reports on a number of territories, finding that they had "attained a full measure of self-government." However. in each case the administering power in question had already announced, prior to the Assembly action, that it would no longer transmit information on these territories. These territories and the dates of Assembly approval were: from 1953 to 1955, Puerto Rico (US), Greenland (Denmark), Surinam and Curaçao (Netherlands); in 1959, Alaska and Hawaii (US); and in 1965, the Cook Islands (New Zealand). (It should be noted, however, that so long as a territory is not actually independent, the Assembly considers it has the right to reopen the question of the territory's status whenever it feels circumstances warrant.) In 1967 the UK announced that as a number of its small Caribbean dependencies—namely, Antigua, Dominica, Grenada, St. Kitts-Nevis-Anguilla, and St. Lucia—had achieved the status of Associated States with a "full measure of self-government," it would no longer submit reports on these territories. To date, however, the Assembly has failed to approve the territories' new status as constituting self-government and has continued to request, in vain, that the UK resume the transmission of information.

Refusal to Transmit Information: The Problem of Spain and Portugal

When Spain and Portugal became UN members in 1955, they maintained that they were not colonial powers but were countries with "overseas provinces"; and on these grounds they refused to transmit information on their overseas possessions. Spain retreated from this position in 1960, to the "satisfaction" of the Assembly, and began to submit reports. But Portugal has never altered its stand and has continued to argue that UN attempts to extract information amount to interference in its "domestic affairs." Exasperated by the Portuguese position, the 1960 Assembly adopted a resolution that unequivocally defined "a full measure of self-government" to mean one of three specific conditions: (a) emergence of the territory as a sovereign independent state; (b) free association with an independent state; or (c) integration with an independent state—both "b" and "c" to be the result of a free and voluntary choice of the people concerned and the people themselves to possess certain specified rights and safeguards in their new status. Unless one of these three conditions pertained, the Assembly asserted, the administering power had an obligation to transmit information on any territory that is geographically separate and ethnically and culturally distinct from itself. On the strength of this resolution all the territories under Portuguese administration were designated as non-self-governing in the Charter sense, and Portugal has since been requested repeatedly to submit information on them—to no avail. (As is described later in this chapter, a similar situation has existed since 1962 with regard to the UK and Southern Rhodesia.)

THE 1960 ASSEMBLY DECLARATION ON THE ENDING OF COLONIALISM

Throughout the 1950's, the various disputes with colonial powers over the transmission of information on non-self-governing territories took place against a background of steady decolonization. Whether gracefully granted or bitterly fought for, sovereignty was achieved by a growing number of former colonial dependencies. In 1946, at the first working session in the Assembly, only a handful of members had memories of recent foreign rule: India, the Philippines, and the four Arab countries that had been League of Nations mandate territories (Iraq, Jordan, Lebanon, Syria). By 1959, eight Asian countries (Burma, Cambodia, Ceylon, Indonesia, Laos, Malaya, Nepal, Pakistan) and two

African countries (Ghana and Guinea) had become sovereign independent states. As these nations joined the UN, many of them after years of struggle against their former masters or with humiliating memories of the indignities of foreign rule, anticolonialist sentiment became increasingly bitter and significantly influenced the tone of the debates in the Assembly. Wholeheartedly supported by the Soviet-bloc nations, the newly independent nations began a drive to put a speedy end to colonialism altogether, thus going far beyond anything specifically spelled out in the Charter.

The 1960 Assembly proved to be decisive for the triumph of the anticolonialist forces in the UN. At the opening of that session, 16 new African states and Cyprus became members, thereby bringing the total number of African and Asian nations to 44 out of a total UN membership of 100. In addition, the Afro-Asian Group, as it is called, knew they could count on the support of the Soviet bloc, many Latin American countries, and the Scandinavian countries. By the end of the session, they had drafted the text of a Declaration on the Granting of Independence to Colonial Territories and Peoples that was designed, to all intents, to replace the Charter declaration as the UN's basic terms of reference for its work in colonial matters.

Main Provisions of the Declaration

Whereas the Charter declaration had been a gentlemanly agreement among masters to look after the welfare of their subjects, the Assembly declaration in effect was an assertion of the right of these subject peoples to be subjects no longer. Written entirely from the viewpoint of the colonial peoples themselves, the declaration in its preamble unequivocally recognizes "the passionate yearning for freedom in all dependent peoples"; the existence of "increasing conflicts resulting from the denial . . . of the freedom of such peoples, which constitute a serious threat to world peace"; and "the important role of the United Nations in assisting the movement for independence in Trust and Non-Self-Governing Territories." In tones of military command, the declaration proper then raps out seven provisions: (1) the subjection of peoples to alien domination "is contrary to the Charter of the United Nations and an impediment to the promotion of world peace and cooperation"; (2) "all peoples have the right to self-determination"; (3) inadequacy of preparedness "should never serve as a pretext for delaying independence"; (4) all armed action or repressive measures against dependent peoples "shall cease in order to enable them to exercise peacefully and freely their right to complete independence"; (5) "immediate steps shall be taken . . . to transfer all powers to the peoples of dependent territories, without any conditions or reservations"; (6) any attempt to disrupt the national unity and territorial integrity of a country "is incompatible with the purposes and principles of the Charter"; (7) all states "shall observe faithfully and strictly" the provisions of the Charter, the Universal Declaration of Human Rights, and "the present Declaration" on the basis of equality, noninterference in the internal affairs of states, and respect for the sovereign rights of all peoples.

Although the phrase "colonial powers" does not appear, the declaration was clearly a declaration of war against those countries. Nevertheless, such was the force of anticolonial sentiment that no colonial power cared to record a negative vote. Accordingly, on 14 December 1960 the Declaration on the Granting of Independence to Colonial Territories and Peoples was adopted 89–0, with only 9 abstentions (Australia, Belgium, Dominican Republic, France, Portugal, South Africa, Spain, the UK, the US).

Establishment of the Committee of 24 to Assist in Implementing the Declaration

A year after the adoption of the Assembly declaration, the USSR took the initiative by asking the Assembly to discuss the problem of implementing the declaration. The ensuing debate led to the creation of a 17-member Special Committee on the Situation with regard to the implementation of the Declaration on the Granting of Independence to Colonial Territories and Peoples. Due to the importance attached to its work, seven additional members were added the following year. Since that time, the composition of the Committee of 24—as it came to be known—has changed slightly when certain countries have withdrawn their services for various reasons, to be replaced by countries representing the same geopolitical grouping as the outgoing members. Originally, the committee included three colonial or administering powers—Australia along with the UK and the US—but France, Spain, and the two most recalcitrant administering countries, Portugal and South Africa, have never been members. Thus the committee's deliberations have always been predominantly, not to say violently, anticolonialist in tone.

In 1963 the committee's functions were expanded to include the work of the 1947 Committee on Information, which was promptly dissolved. At the same time, the Assembly gave the Committee of 24 the right to apprise the Security Council of any developments in any territory that it examines that might threaten international peace and security. (Normally, subsidiary bodies do not have this right, but must act through the Assembly.) In addition, the Assembly empowered the committee to examine information on the trust territories as well as on non-self-governing territories—though the Trusteeship Council continues to exercise its normal functions. The committee is also empowered to send visiting missions to dependent territories. Hence, since 1963, the Committee of 24 has been the Assembly's chief executive arm in colonial matters.

Besides considering problems connected with individual colonial territories, the committee, which is in session for about nine months of every year, debates topics of a more general nature assigned to it by the Assembly; for example, the role played by foreign economic and military interests in preventing the granting of independence or exploiting the natural resources of the territories that rightfully belong to the indigenous inhabitants. Another important topic is the provision of funds for scholarships to assist colonial peoples, especially those from southern Africa, to obtain advanced education and training.

The 1970 Program for Implementing the Declaration

In the 10 years following the adoption of the declaration on the ending of colonialism, 27 territories (with a total population of over 53 million) attained independence. Some 44 territories (population approximately 28 million) remain under foreign rule or control, however, and the Assembly's work in hastening the process of decolonization is far from completed. As the 1970 Assembly's commemorative session celebrating the UN's 25th anniversary happened to coincide with the 10th anniversary of the declaration, the leaders of the drive to end colonialism deemed this an appropriate occasion to reaffirm the aims of the declaration and set forth a program for its implementation. Actually, the 9-point program ceremonially adopted on 12 October 1970 consists for the most part of measures that had been recommended in several Assembly resolutions adopted throughout the 1960's.

The purpose of the program was chiefly to reorganize and rearticulate these measures in the form of a comprehensive plan of action that could then be used as a new frame of reference governing the UN's future work in decolonization. Many of the measures contained in the program are highly controversial, and the aggressive tone of the entire document is set in the opening operative paragraph denouncing the continuation of colonialism as "a crime which constitutes a violation of the Charter of the United Nations, the Declaration on the Granting of Independence to Colonial Territories and Peoples and the principles of international law." Among the more controversial measures recommended are requests to member states "to render all necessary moral and material assistance" to colonial peoples "in their struggle to attain freedom and independence" and "to wage a vigorous and sustained campaign" against foreign economic and financial interests operating in colonial territories for the benefit of colonial Powers and their allies, as well as against "all military activities and arrangements by colonial Powers in Territories under their administration." The program also further widens the powers of the Committee of 24, directing it to assist the Assembly in making arrangements, in cooperation with the administering powers, for securing a UN presence in the colonial territories to help elaborate procedural measures for implementing the 1960 declaration and observing the final stages of the process of decolonization.

Because some of the program's provisions amount to an open invitation to the UN membership to take hostile action against the colonial or administering powers, the latter group of countries, together with their supporters, strongly opposed its formulation. And though the majority view, led by the Afro-Asian Group, finally won out, the program was adopted by only 86 votes in favor—three less than the number of votes that had been cast in favor of the 1960 declaration when the Assembly had a considerably smaller membership. Moreover, whereas no country had cared to vote against the declaration, five countries—Australia, New Zealand, South Africa, the UK, and the US—felt compelled to vote against the 1970 program, thereby giving expression to the growing irritation at the attempts by the Afro-Asian Group to use its voting power to bully them into taking action they did not desire to take. Fifteen countries abstained in the vote on the program; nine abstained on the declaration. Although the determination of the African and Asian nations to bring a speedy end to colonialism undoubtedly helped accelerate the decolonization process in the 1960's, there are signs that their uncompromising and somewhat doctrinaire attitude on specific colonial questions has reached the point of diminishing returns.

OUTSTANDING COLONIAL ISSUES AS OF DECEMBER 1970

Some 26 of the remaining dependent territories are small islands scattered across the globe. Their tiny populations (under 100,000) and minimal economic resources render it almost impossible for them to survive as viable, fully independent states. Most of these small territories belong to the UK, the remainder to the US and other Western nations. Although the administering powers join with the rest of the UN membership in asserting that the peoples of these small territories have an inalienable right to the exercise of self-determination, the leaders of the drive to end colonialism have doubted the genuineness of the preparations for achieving this goal. As evidence to justify their skepticism, the African and Asian nations point out that military bases have been established in many of the small territories, which they declare "is incompatible with the purposes and principles of the Charter." Moreover, in the case of territories which the administering powers have declared their intention of preparing for self-governing status rather than for full independence, the majority of UN members feel that the Assembly should be granted an active role in ascertaining the wishes of the inhabitants and furnished with more comprehensive information on conditions prevailing in the territories. The refusal of most of the administering powers to supply this information or to permit visiting UN missions has tended to reinforce the skepticism of the anticolonialist nations. It is largely on account of the UK's refusal to allow visiting missions to enter the small Caribbean dependencies, for instance, that the Assembly

has so far failed to approve the 1967 Associated Statehood agreements drawn up with Antigua, Dominica, Grenada, St. Kitts-Nevis-Anguilla, and St. Lucia (referred to above) as constituting a "full measure of self-government."

Other small or sparsely populated territories that have been brought under the Assembly's surveillance through the Committee of 24 include the Australian territory of Papua, the Spanish Sahara and territory of Ifni, and three UK possessions where the issue of decolonization is complicated by conflicting claims of sovereignty by other nations—the Falkland Islands claimed by Argentina, British Honduras claimed by Guatemala, and Gibraltar claimed by Spain. (In the last case, the Assembly rejected a 1967 UK-sponsored referendum in which the Gibraltarians voted to retain their link with Britain. The majority of the Assembly seems to support Spain's claim to the territory.) The Committee of 24 has also brought under surveillance the Sultanate of Muscat and Oman in southern Arabia, despite protests by the UK. Britain contends that the Sultanate is fully independent and that British troops have been sent there only at the request of the Sultan, in order to preserve his authority against the claims of the Imam of Oman, who is supported by the League of Arab States.

The dominant colonial issue before the Assembly, especially its African members, however, is the fate of territories in southern Africa: Portuguese Angola, Guinea, and Mozambique; Southern Rhodesia, which is legally still a British possession; and the old League of Nations mandate territory of South West Africa (now officially renamed by the UN as Namibia) controlled by the Republic of South Africa. These three sets of territories together account for roughly 18 of the 28 million people still living under alien rule.

In each case the paramount concern is to bring to an end a repressive regime of white minority rule, but only the case of the Portuguese territories constitutes a straightforward colonial question as such. In Southern Rhodesia, on the other hand, the problem is not the UK's desire to maintain a colonial presence in the territory but rather its inability (or, as the Africans would have it, its reluctance) to use its residual constitutional powers in the territory to topple the rebel and illegal Ian Smith government or else force it to make provision for instituting majority (that is, black) government. In Namibia the problem is South Africa's gradual extension of its own racially discriminatory system of apartheid to, and the virtual annexation of, a territory that it was originally designated to administer as a "sacred trust" on behalf of the international community. Yet despite the essential differences of these problems, the Assembly—partly in response to a growing collaboration between South Africa, Portugal, and the Ian Smith government—has come to view them as aspects of a single consuming issue of white minority rule versus black majority rights, an issue which many delegates fear could touch off a bloody race war engulfing the whole of Africa.

The strategy advocated by the Afro-Asian Group, supported by the Communist countries, for rectifying the situation in these territories is essentially the application through a Security Council decision taken under Chapter VII of the Charter of mandatory enforcement measures, including full economic sanctions and military force as circumstances warrant. And in each case—except partially in the case of Southern Rhodesia—the use of mandatory enforcement measures has been decisively resisted by two permanent members of the Security Council, the UK and the US, which together with several other Western nations feel they cannot afford to embark on a concerted policy of economic confrontation, let alone military confrontation, against the wealthy white minority regimes of southern Africa.

Thus year after year, as the African and Asian nations have brought one or another of these cases before the Security Council in the hope of achieving effective action, the Assembly has adopted by substantial majorities militant resolutions that have no chance of being implemented. As a result, the anger and frustration of the Afro-Asian Group at the defiant posture assumed by South Africa, Portugal, and the Ian Smith government has been steadily transferred to the UK and the US and their allies.

The history of the UN's involvement in Portugal's African territories and Southern Rhodesia is outlined below, and its involvement in the question of Namibia is described at the end of the section on Trust Territories.

The Problem of the Portuguese-Administered African Territories

Since 1961 the question of the Portuguese territories has several times been brought before the Security Council by African nations seeking punitive action by the Council under Chapter VII of the Charter. Though the Council has found that the situation is seriously disturbing international peace, though it has condemned Portuguese repressive measures and sharply requested Portugal to implement measures leading to independence, it has declined to initiate punitive action. In 1965 the Assembly adopted a resolution that for the first time urged members to take specific measures against Portugal (to break off diplomatic relations, to boycott all trade, or to close ports to Portuguese ships). Moreover, the Assembly specifically called upon members of the North Atlantic Treaty—Portugal's military allies—to stop the sale of arms to Portugal and refrain from giving any assistance that might be used by Portugal in furtherance of its repressive policies. The Assembly also requested all the specialized agencies—in particular the World Bank and the International Monetary Fund—to refrain from granting Portugal any assistance. These requests were repeated in sharper terms at the 1966 session.

In response to the Assembly's recommendations, arms sales to Portugal have dwindled but not stopped, but investment has if anything increased. Portugal, even after a change in government, when Marcello Caetano succeeded Antonio Salazar as premier in 1968—a development that caused the Assembly briefly to adopt a relatively conciliatory tone in the hope that the new government would prove more cooperative—has remained firm. It still refuses to transmit information to the UN on the territories and persists in its attempt to integrate its "overseas provinces" into a "multiracial, multicontinental" Portugal. Meanwhile, the Assembly has continued to condemn Portugal for its refusal to implement the 1960 declaration on the ending of colonialism, for waging war against the peoples of the territories under its domination, and for its collaboration with South Africa and the illegal Smith regime in Southern Rhodesia to perpetuate colonialism and oppression in southern Africa. In its 1970 resolution the Assembly called on Portugal to cease forthwith all repressive and military activities against the peoples of the territories, proclaim an unconditional military amnesty, restore democratic political rights, and apply the 1949 Geneva Conventions on the treatment of prisoners of war.

Since 1966 several independent African states bordering on the Portuguese territories, where Portugal maintains an estimated 150,000 troops to combat dogged and well-organized guerrilla resistance, have filed complaints with the Security Council charging that Portuguese troops have violated their sovereignty. The latest of these complaints was brought by Guinea on 22 November 1970, charging that Portugal had launched a full-scale attack on its country. After sending out a mission of inquiry to investigate Guinea's charges, the Security Council censured Portugal for its invasion of that country which was quickly quelled by the Guineans and requested that it pay reparations for damages and loss of life.

The Problem of Southern Rhodesia

According to 1964 estimates, Southern Rhodesia had a population of about 4.2 million, of which 3,970,000 were Africans. White European settlers numbered about 217,000, "coloreds" 12,400, and Asians 7,900. Southern Rhodesia in 1923 was given full internal self-government—though under a constitution that vested political power exclusively in the hands of the white settlers. Hence, the UK did not include this dependency in its original 1946 list of non-self-governing territories and has never transmitted information on it to the UN. Although by the terms of the 1923 constitution the UK retained residual power to veto any legislation contrary to African interests, this power was never used, and no attempt was made to interfere with the white settlers' domination of the territorial government.

Substantial UN involvement in the question of Southern Rhodesia began in 1961, when African and Asian members tried, without success, to bring pressure to bear upon the UK not to permit a new territorial constitution, adopted at a Southern Rhodesian constitutional conference in 1960 and affirmed by a referendum in 1961, to come into effect. While giving Africans their first representation in the Southern Rhodesian parliament, the 1961 constitution restricted their franchise through a two-role electoral system heavily weighted in favor of the European community. What alarmed the Afro-Asian countries was the UK's agreement to give up its residual veto in Southern Rhodesian legislation (the only legal check on the power of the white settlers) in return for certain clauses in the new constitution providing for majority rule and for a promise by the Southern Rhodesian government to introduce no new discriminatory legislation contrary to African interests.

In June 1962, acting on the recommendation of its special committee on the ending of colonialism, the General Assembly adopted a resolution declaring Southern Rhodesia to be a non-self-governing territory in the sense of Article 73 of the UN Charter, on the grounds that the vast majority of the African population had no voting rights and had exercised no voice in drawing up the new constitution. The Assembly also requested the UK to submit information on the territory and to convene a conference of all political parties in Rhodesia for the purpose of drawing up a new constitution that would ensure the rights of the majority on the basis of "one-man-one-vote." However, the UK continued to maintain that it could not provide information since Southern Rhodesia, being self-governing, did not supply it, and further asserted that it could not interfere in Rhodesia's domestic affairs. The new constitution duly came into effect in November 1962.

The next burst of Assembly activity concerned the terms of disposal of the military assets of the Central African Federation following its dissolution in 1963. The federation, formed ten years earlier at the instance of the UK, embraced Southern Rhodesia; Northern Rhodesia, now the independent state of Zambia; and Nyasaland, now the independent state of Malawi. The Africans of Northern Rhodesia and Nyasaland had achieved a relatively decisive voice in internal political affairs and had insisted on severing their federal ties with the white-dominated territory of Southern Rhodesia. The African nations asked the Security Council to prevent transfer of some of the forces of the federation, especially the jet-bomber-equipped air force, to Southern Rhodesia. The UK contended that since these forces had belonged to Southern Rhodesia prior to formation of the federation, it could not prevent their return to Southern Rhodesia. Such was the extent of anticolonial feeling in the UN at the time, however, that the UK was compelled to use its veto in order to defeat a Security Council resolution requesting it not to transfer these forces to Rhodesia. Whereupon, the African states took the identical resolution to the 1963 Assembly, which overwhelmingly adopted it, together with a second resolution again calling for a constitutional conference of all political parties in Rhodesia.

The third and most recent phase of UN involvement has centered on the measures to be taken in response to Southern Rhodesia's unilateral declaration of independence on 11 November 1965. The UK, after branding the declaration an "illegal act" and an "act of treason," brought the matter to the Security Council the following day, and a resolution was immediately adopted condemning the declaration and calling upon all states to refrain from recognition and from giving assistance to the "rebel" regime. In further debate in the Council, the African powers demanded application of enforcement measures under Chapter VII of the Charter to bring the illicit regime to an immediate end. The UK, however, took the position that because Southern Rhodesia was a British possession, it had the sole responsibility for dealing with the situation, and it did not consider the application of force to be appropriate. On 20 November the Security Council adopted a resolution condemning the "usurpation of power," calling upon the UK to bring the regime to an immediate end, and requesting all states, among other things, to sever economic relations and institute an embargo on oil and petroleum products. In April 1966, following the appearance of two oil tankers near the port of Beira in Portuguese Mozambique, the Council—meeting at the urgent request of the UK—called upon the UK to prevent, by force if necessary, the two ships from docking at Beira, since they could reasonably be believed to be transporting oil destined for Southern Rhodesia.

In November 1966 the Assembly adopted a resolution deploring the failure of the UK to put an end to the "illegal racist minority regime" in Southern Rhodesia and condemning Portugal and South Africa for supporting this regime. Acknowledging that voluntary economic sanctions had failed to achieve the desired effect of toppling the Ian Smith government, the UK made one more attempt to negotiate with Smith an acceptable basis for legal independence founded on "unimpeded progress" to majority rule. Following the failure of these negotiations, the UK again brought the issue of Southern Rhodesia before the Security Council in mid-December 1966, this time with a request that the Council initiate selective mandatory sanctions to be applied to a specified list of "critical commodities." These, however, did not include the most critical commodity of all—oil—and the encensed African nations immediately drafted an amendment to ban the supply of all petroleum and petroleum products to Southern Rhodesia. In the end, on 16 December 1966, the Council adopted its first resolution ever to be based explicitly on the terms of Chapter VII of the Charter. Describing the situation as "a threat to international peace and security," the Council directed that member states should halt all imports of asbestos, iron ore, chrome, pig iron, sugar, tobacco, copper, meat and meat products, hides, skins, and leather originating in Southern Rhodesia. In addition, members were instructed to halt all petroleum and petroleum-product shipments to Southern Rhodesia involving their territories, facilities, nationals, or vessels. A similar embargo was imposed on the sale or shipment to Southern Rhodesia of arms, ammunition, aircraft, and equipment and materials for manufacturing or assembling these items.

After another 18 months had elapsed, with the Ian Smith government still firmly in power, it became clear that more stringent measures were required. Accordingly, in May 1968 the Security Council unanimously decided to extend the sanctions to include all exports and imports save for certain humanitarian and related goods. The resolution also required member states to cease to make financial or economic resources available to the territory, and it established a committee composed of Algeria, France, Pakistan, Paraguay, the USSR, the UK, and the US to examine reports submitted by nations on their implementation of the resolution. In its second report, on June 1969, the sanctions committee stated that while the majority of states had reported compliance with the Council's decisions, certain states had not complied or had failed to comply fully. South Africa and Portugal were maintaining close economic, trade, and other relations with the regime. In its third report, the following year, the committee noted a considerable increase in Rhodesian exports, stating that while the greatest portion of Rhodesian trade was with South Africa and Portugal, over a third of its exports went to countries outside Africa "presumably under false declarations of origin."

On 1 March 1970 the Smith government took the final step in its defiance of the UK by proclaiming the territory a republic, pursuant to a decision taken by Rhodesia's white voters in a referendum held the previous year. The Security Council, on 18 March at the request of the UK, met to consider the new twist in the situation. Once again the sharp division of opinion made itself apparent. The UK submitted a draft resolution that merely made it clear that the regime would not be recognized or permitted to enter the family of nations. The African and Asian members of the Council considered the resolution inadequate and submitted a draft of their own condemning the UK's failure to use force against the Smith government and calling for the extension of sanctions to South Africa and Portugal for their rejection of the Security Council's decisions. The UK draft did not receive sufficient votes for adoption (there were 10 abstentions), but the other draft failed to be adopted only because the UK and the US exercised their right of veto. (This was the first occasion in which the US had ever applied the veto, and its gesture may be interpreted, in part, as an expression of its increasing annoyance at the belligerent stand taken by the Afro-Asian Group on all colonial issues.) In the end the Council adopted a compromise resolution, drafted by Finland, condemning the illegal proclamation of republican status, reaffirming the previous measures adopted by the Council under Chapter VII of the Charter, and imposing a ban on all foreign representation, even at the consular level, in Rhodesia and on all transportation to and from the territory. At its 1970 regular session the Assembly adopted on 3 December a resolution that among other recommendations drew the attention of the Security Council to the "urgent necessity" of widening the scope of the sanctions to include all the measures provided for in Article 41 of the Charter (notably, severance of rail, sea, air, postal, telegraphic, radio, and other means of communications) and of imposing sanctions against South Africa and Portugal. However, the likelihood of the Council's adopting a decision embodying these recommendations seems remote, especially since it has failed to ensure full compliance with the decisions it has already taken. Meanwhile it appears that the illegal republic of Rhodesia will continue to survive, assisted by its two white minority allies in southern Africa, and will persist in its course of establishing an apartheid state similar to that of the Republic of South Africa.

B. TRUST TERRITORIES

The main features of the trusteeship system are outlined in the earlier chapter on the Trusteeship Council. What follows here is a brief description of the current status of the territories originally placed under UN trusteeship in 1946, together with an account of the proceedings related to two other territories, West Irian and Namibia, that were subsequently placed under the direct responsibility of the UN.

TRUST TERRITORIES THAT HAVE ACHIEVED INDEPENDENCE

Of the 11 territories that were placed under the trusteeship system in 1946, 9 have since achieved the goals of the Charter, either as independent states or as parts of independent states.

Togoland under UK Administration. To ascertain the freely expressed wishes of the people as to their political future, the UN, in agreement with the UK, conducted a plebiscite in 1956. As a result of the plebiscite, the territory united in March 1957 with the former Gold Coast as part of the independent state of Ghana.

Togoland under French Administration. In 1958, with the agreement of France, the UN supervised elections, and the territory became the independent state of Togo on 24 April 1960.

Cameroons under French Administration. Following a notification in 1958 by its legislative assembly of the desire of the territory to become independent, and acting upon the recommendation of the Trusteeship Council, the Assembly in agreement with France, resolved that on 1 January 1960 trusteeship status would end and the territory would become independent as Cameroon.

Cameroons under UK Administration. Both the northern and southern sectors of the territory were administered as part of the federation of Nigeria, a British dependency. Following a plebisicite held under UN supervision in March 1961, the northern sector became part of newly independent Nigeria on 1 June 1961. Following a similar plebiscite, the peoples of the southern sector joined the newly independent state of Cameroon on 1 October 1961.

Somaliland under Italian Administration. In union with the dependency of British Somaliland, the territory became the sovereign state of Somalia on 1 July 1960.

Tanganyika under UK Administration. Following negotiations between the UK and African leaders, the territory attained independence on 9 December 1961.

Ruanda-Urundi under Belgian Administration. In a special session convened in June 1962, the General Assembly approved separate independence for the two sectors, which were established on 1 July 1962 as the Republic of Rwanda and the Kingdom of Burundi.

Western Samoa under New Zealand Administration. In agreement with the administering authority, the UN conducted a plebiscite in May 1961, as a result of which the territory attained independence on 1 January 1962. It has decided, chiefly on economic grounds, not to apply for UN membership.

Nauru Administered by Australia on Behalf of a Joint Administering Authority Comprising Australia, New Zealand, and the UK.

The territory became independent on 31 January 1968, in accordance with an Assembly resolution adopted in 1965 setting this date as the outside target for accession to independence. Like Western Samoa, and for similar reasons, Nauru has not applied for UN membership.

TERRITORIES STILL UNDER UN TRUSTEESHIP

As of December 1970, two territories remain under the direct purview of the Trusteeship Council (now assisted, as described in Section A above, by the deliberations of the Committee of 24): New Guinea under Australian administration; and the Pacific Islands, collectively known as Micronesia, which are administered by the US under a special strategic area agreement (see the chapter on the Trusteeship Council), which brings the area under the ultimate authority of the Security Council, not of the Assembly. Early in 1970 a UN visiting mission to Micronesia, consisting of Australia, China, France, and the UK, concluded that the inhabitants of the territory would be better able to deal with the problems resulting from economic underdevelopment and from the effects of US use of the land area for strategic purposes if the government were "in their own hands." Negotiations between the US and a delegation of Micronesians on the future status of the territory were initiated in May 1970. With regard to the trust territory of New Guinea, the Assembly at its 1965 session requested Australia to fix an early date for independence. However, as yet no date has been fixed, and the 1970 Assembly called upon the administering power "to prescribe, in consultation with freely elected representatives of the prople, a specific timetable" for the exercise of the right of self-determination in the territory of New Guinea and also in Australia's own dependency of Papua (Australia administers the two territories as a joint unit) and "to report to the Trusteeship Council and the Special Committee [the Committee of 24] on the action taken in that regard."

UN ADMINISTRATION OF WEST NEW GUINEA (WEST IRIAN)

When Indonesia gained its independence from the Netherlands in 1949, its national boundaries were defined as including the former Dutch possessions in the archipelago then known as the Dutch East Indies. One issue, however, remained unsettled—the future of West New Guinea (or West Irian, as it is called by the Indonesians, and which has become the official name). The Netherlands maintained that the Papuans who inhabit the territory are not Indonesians and should therefore be allowed to decide their own future political status in due course. Indonesia, claiming that West Irian was part of its rightful territory, brought the issue to the UN in 1954. The matter was hotly debated in several Assembly sessions but remained unresolved. Emotions ran high in both countries, and in 1961 fighting broke out between Dutch and Indonesian forces stationed in West New Guinea. U Thant, then acting secretary-general, appealed to both governments to seek a peaceful solution of their differences. Negotiations followed with UN assistance, and on 15 August 1962 the two nations signed an agreement, which was endorsed by the General Assembly a month later. By the terms of this agreement, the UN was to take over administration of the area for an interim period, after which, on 1 May 1963, the territory was to be transferred to Indonesian administration pending an act of self-determination of the Papuans by the end of 1969.

Accordingly, on 1 October 1962 the UN took over administration of West New Guinea, establishing a UN Temporary Executive Authority. On 1 May 1963, as scheduled, administration was transferred to Indonesia. The agreement had provided for the UN to reenter the picture at a later stage and participate in the arrangements for the act of self-determination to be exercised by the 700,000 Papuans living in the territory. When President Sukarno withdrew Indonesia from membership in the UN in January 1965, there were some doubts as to whether the agreement would be honored. However, with the fall of Sukarno and the return of Indonesia to the UN in September 1966, the secretary-general was able, when the appropriate moment came, to consult with the Indonesian government on measures to implement the provision for the projected act of self-determination in the territory. Thus in August 1968 the secretary-general dispatched a personal representative to assist Indonesia's preparations for this event, which took place between 14 July and 2 August 1969. During this period, eight elected representative councils of the people were consulted as to whether West Irian should remain with Indonesia or not. The councils, which comprised a total of 1,026 members, decided without dissent in favor of the territory remaining with Indonesia. Final reports on the decision were then submitted by the secretary-general to the Assembly, which "took note" of them on 19 November 1969.

In addition to its role in facilitating the peaceful solution of the political future of the territory, the UN also took important measures to promote its economic welfare by launching in 1963 the Fund of the UN for the Development of West Irian (FUNDWI) with major contributions provided by both the Netherlands and Indonesia. FUNDWI has continued in existence under the administration of the UNDP and is the largest single Funds-in-Trust program operated by the UNDP.

THE PROBLEM OF NAMIBIA (SOUTH WEST AFRICA)

The status of South West Africa (officially designated as Namibia by the Assembly in June 1968), a pre-World War I German colony that since 1920 has been administered by South Africa under a League of Nations mandate, has preoccupied the General Assembly almost from the first moment of the UN's existence. In 1946, South Africa proposed that the Assembly approve its annexation of the territory. Fearing that the South African government would seek to extend its apartheid system to South West Africa, the Assembly did not approve the proposal and recommended instead that the territory be placed under the UN trusteeship system. The following year, South Africa informed the Assembly that while it agreed not to annex the territory, it would not place it under trusteeship. Although South Africa had reported to the Assembly on conditions in the territory in 1946, it declined to submit further reports, despite repeated requests from the Assembly.

During its 1947 and 1948 sessions, the Assembly continued to urge trusteeship, but without success. In 1949, however, when a South African law established a closer association with the territory, the General Assembly sought an advisory opinion from the International Court of Justice on South Africa's legal rights and obligations with respect to its mandate. The World Court handed down its opinion on 11 July 1950. It found unanimously that South West Africa was still a territory under the international mandate assumed in 1920, and that South Africa was not legally competent to change the status of the territory without the consent of the UN. By a majority of 12 to 2, the Court further advised that South Africa had the obligation to transmit to the UN petitions from the indigenous inhabitants and to submit annual reports on conditions in the territory. By a vote of 8 to 6, the Court also found that South Africa did not have a legal obligation to bring the territory within the UN trusteeship system. The 1950 Assembly accepted this opinion and established a special committee to confer with South Africa

on its implementation. South Africa declined, however, to accept the Court's opinion or to confer with the UN committee. Between 1954 and 1962, two further committees were successively established by the Assembly to examine conditions in the territory, but South Africa refused to allow them entry.

In 1964, the Committee of 24 called upon South Africa to refrain from implementing the recommendations of its Odendaal Commission. This body, appointed by South Africa in 1962, had recommended the partitioning of the territory into separate homelands based on ethnic groupings, closer integration of the territory's administrative structure into that of South Africa, and a program of three five-year development plans. Under the circumstances, the Assembly began to seek means of preventing South Africa from pursuing its declared course and of alleviating the situation of the territory's inhabitants. Thus the 1965 Assembly adopted (by 85 votes to 2, with 19 abstentions) a resolution declaring that "any attempt to partition the Territory or to take any unilateral action, directly or indirectly, preparatory thereto constitutes a violation of the Mandate" and warning that "any attempt to annex part or the whole of the Territory of South West Africa constitutes an act of aggression." On 9 June 1966 the Committee of 24 recommended that the Security Council take steps to ensure the withdrawal of all military bases and installations from South West Africa. It also appealed to all states to give moral and material support to the African population and asked the secretary-general to approach the specialized agencies with a view to extending the assistance already being given to refugees by the UN high commissioner. Finally, it appointed a subcommittee to examine the whole situation and, among other things, to recommend an early date for the territory's independence.

Meanwhile, the International Court of Justice since 1960 had been considering two claims that had been brought by Liberia and Ethiopia against South Africa for its conduct in the mandated territory. On 18 July 1966, after almost six years of deliberation, the Court finally handed down an opinion dismissing the claims of Liberia and Ethiopia without ruling on the merits of the case. In an 8–7 decision (an original 7–7 tie was resolved by the casting vote of the Court president, Sir Percy Spender of Australia), the Court held that the applicants had no legal right or interest in the subject matter of their claims and that this therefore made it "unnecessary" to rule on the substance of the dispute itself. The Court's opinion provoked worldwide protest.

Confronted with this unexpected turn of events, the African members, when the Assembly met for its regular session in the fall of 1966, requested urgent priority for discussion of the South West Africa agenda item. In the ensuing resolution, adopted by the Assembly on 27 October 1966 by 114 votes to 2 (Portugal, South Africa) with 3 abstentions (France, Malawi, UK), the Assembly decided to terminate South Africa's mandate and to bring South West Africa henceforth "under the direct responsibility of the United Nations." The delicate problem of precisely how the Assembly would be able to implement its decision in the face of almost certain opposition from South Africa was postponed by establishing an ad hoc committee to "recommend practical means by which South West Africa should be administered, so as to enable the people of the Territory to exercise the right of self-determination and to achieve independence. . . ." The committee was asked to report to the General Assembly at a special session scheduled for April 1967. At that session, the militant Afro-Asian Group, overriding the more cautious members in the Assembly who were anxious to avoid putting the UN in a position of ridicule, drove through a resolution establishing a UN Council for South West Africa to be based in the territory until independence. The Council was requested to "enter immediately into contact" with the South African government to formulate procedures for the transfer of the territory to UN authority. In addition, the Assembly actually set a target date for independence—June 1968.

As was expected, South Africa refused to allow the Council for South West Africa to enter the territory. Meeting in a resumed session in June 1968, the Assembly announced that the territory would henceforth be known as Namibia and recommended that the Security Council take measures to end the South African presence in Namibia and facilitate the territory's accession to independence. On 20 March 1969 the Security Council, which in September 1967 and again in March 1968 had severely censured South Africa regarding its treatment of 37 South West African political prisoners, for the first time joined with the Assembly in calling for the immediate withdrawal of South Africa from Namibia. In January 1970 the Council took its first concrete action in connection with this call—which had gone unheeded—by establishing, with France and the UK abstaining in the vote, an ad hoc subcommittee to study ways for implementing the relevant resolutions of the Council.

After studying the subcommittee's report, the Council adopted two important resolutions on 25 July 1970. In the first resolution it requested all states to refrain from any relations with South Africa that would imply recognition of its authority over Namibia, to withdraw diplomatic or consular personnel from Namibia, to cease commercial relations in respect of Namibia, and to refrain from further investment in the territory. In addition, the resolution requested the Assembly to set up a UN Fund for Namibia and to finance an education and training program for Namibians. In its second resolution the Council took the

unexpected step of asking the International Court to give an advisory opinion on the legal consequences for states of the continued presence of South Africa in Namibia despite the Security Council's resolutions categorically calling for its withdrawal. This was the first occasion the Council had ever sought an opinion from the ICJ, and the step was all the more surprising in view of the Court's refusal to pronounce on the merits of the case brought by Ethiopia and Liberia against South Africa in 1960.

At its 1970 session the Assembly decided to act on the Security Council request that it establish a UN Fund for Namibia. The secretary-general was asked to make a study of the requirements for a comprehensive assistance program for Namibians. As an interim measure the secretary-general, in consultation with the heads of various bodies, was authorized to make available, as necessary, grants from the UN's regular budget for 1971 to increase by a maximum of $50,000 the resources of the existing UN programs for assisting Namibians. In another positive measure, the Assembly also endorsed the measures taken by the UN Council for Namibia concerning the issuance of internationally acceptable identity certificates and travel documents to Namibians fleeing the territory. And, as it had done in previous years, the Assembly censured South Africa for its defiance of the UN and recommended to the Council that it take enforcement measures provided for under Chapter VII of the Charter. However, although the Council seems to be moving slowly in the direction of initiating minimal punitive measures, it is questionable whether the US or the UK, or France for that matter, will give up their commercial interests in South Africa to permit the kind of stringent enforcement action that the Afro-Asian nations have in mind.

STATUS OF NON-SELF-GOVERNING TERRITORIES 1946–1970

Note: The material in the parentheses includes the year of the territory's accession to independence or other change of status approved by the Assembly, as a result of which information on it is no longer required to be sent to the secretary-general. Territories acquiring self-governing status approved by the Assembly are indicated by a † following the parentheses. (No dates are given for the year in which a territory is said by the administering power to have become self-governing if the Assembly has not approved the new status and still asks for information to be submitted.) In the case of territories acquiring independence the parentheses include any change of name subsequently adopted. Asterisks indicate that the newly independent state also became a UN member.

Territories Enumerated by the General Assembly in 1946

Australia
    Cocos (Keeling) Islands[1]
    Papua

Belgium
    Belgian Congo (Kinshasa—1960)*

Denmark
    Greenland (1954)

France
    French Equatorial Africa:
        Chad (1960)*
        Gabon (1960)*
        Middle Congo (Congo, Brazzaville—1960)*
        Ubangi Shari (Central African Republic—1960)*

French establishments in India (1947)
French establishments in Oceania (1947)
French Guiana (1947)
French Somaliland (1957)
French West Africa:
    Dahomey (1960)*
    French Guinea (Guinea—1958)*
    French Sudan (Mali—1960)*
    Ivory Coast (1960)*
    Mauritania (1960)*
    Niger (1960)*
    Senegal (1960)*
    Upper Volta (1960)*
Guadaloupe and dependencies (1947)
Indo-China (1947)[2]
Madagascar and dependencies (including Comoro Archipelago) (Malagasy Republic—1960)*
Martinique (1947)
Morocco (1956)*
New Caledonia and dependencies (1947)
New Hebrides under Anglo-French Condominium
Réunion (1947)
St. Pierre and Miquelon (1947)
Tunisia (1956)*

Netherlands
    Netherlands Indies (Indonesia—1949)*
    Netherlands New Guinea (West Irian) (1969)
    Netherlands Antilles (Curaçao) (1951)†
    Surinam (1955)†

New Zealand
    Cook Islands (1965)†

Niue Island
Tokelau Islands

United Kingdom
Aden Colony and Protectorate (Southern Yemen—1967)*
Bahamas
Barbados (1966)*
Basutoland (Lesotho—1966)*
Bechuanaland Protectorate (Botswana—1966)*
Bermuda
British Guiana (Guyana—1966)*
British Honduras
British Somaliland (Somalia—1960)
Brunei
Cayman Islands[3]
Cyprus (1960)*
Falkland Islands
Fiji (1970)*
Gambia (1965)*
Gibraltar
Gilbert and Ellice Islands Colony
Gold Coast Colony and Protectorate (Ghana—1957)*
Hong Kong
Jamaica (1962)*
Kenya (1963)*
Leeward Islands:[4]
   Antigua
   St. Kitts-Nevis-Anguilla
   Montserrat
   British Virgin Islands
Malayan Union (Malaya—1957)*
Malta (1964)*
Mauritius (1968)*
Nigeria (1960)*
North Borneo (1963)[5]
Northern Rhodesia (Zambia—1964)*
Nyasaland (Malawi—1964)*
Pitcairn Island
St. Helena and dependencies
Sarawak (1963)[5]
Seychelles
Sierra Leone (1961)*
Singapore (1963)*
Solomon Islands Protectorate
Swaziland (1966)*
Trinidad and Tobago (1962)*
Turks and Caicos Islands*[3]
Uganda (1962)*

Windward Islands:
   Dominica
   Grenada
   St. Lucia
   St. Vincent
Zanzibar (1963)*[6]

United States
Alaska (1959)†
American Samoa
Guam
Hawaii (1959)†
Panama Canal Zone (1947)†
Puerto Rico (1952)†
Virgin Islands of the United States

Territories Listed by the General Assembly Since 1960

Portugal
Angola, including the enclave of Cabinda
Cape Verde Archipelago
Goa and dependencies (1961)[7]
Guinea (called Portuguese Guinea)
Macao and dependencies
Mozambique
São João Batista d'Ajuda (1961)[8]
São Tomé and Príncipe
Timor and dependencies

Spain
Fernando Póo (1968)[9]
Ifni (1968)[10]
Rio Muni (1968)[9]
Spanish Sahara

United Kingdom
Southern Rhodesia

1. Originally administered as part of Singapore.
2. Became Cambodia, Laos, and Viet-Nam.
3. Originally administered as part of Jamaica.
4. The group of islands was listed in 1946 as one territory.
5. United with Malaya in the Federation of Malaysia.
6. Subsequently joined Tanganyika to form Tanzania.
7. Nationally united with India in December 1961.
8. Nationally united with Dahomey in August 1961.
9. In 1963, Fernando Póo and Río Muni merged and were named Equatorial Guinea, which became independent in 1968.*
10. Transferred to Morocco in 1968.

THE INTERNATIONAL LAW COMMISSION

Article 13 of the UN Charter requires the General Assembly to "initiate studies and make recommendations for the purpose of . . . encouraging the progressive development of international law and its codification." To help it fulfill this mandate, the Assembly in 1947 set up the International Law Commission as a permanent subsidiary organ with its own separate Statute. The Commission began meeting in 1949 and over the years has completed an impressive body of work. Many of its individual studies have gained the special plaudits of the Assembly. On the occasion of the 25th anniversary of the UN, the 1970 Assembly took the opportunity to express "profound gratitude" to the Commission for "its outstanding contribution to the work of the Organization during this period."

COMPOSITION AND PROCEDURE

Like the judges of the International Court of Justice, the members of the International Law Commission, 25 (originally 15), are not representatives of governments. Instead, they are chosen in their individual capacity "as persons of recognized competence in international law" and with due consideration to representation of "the main forms of civilization" and "the principal legal systems of the world." No two members of the Commission may be nationals of the same country. They are elected for five-year terms by the General Assembly, from a list of candidates nominated by UN member states. Each state may nominate up to four candidates, but only two may be of its own nationality.

Unlike the judges of the World Court, the legal experts do not serve in a full-time capacity on the International Law Commission and need not give up their other professional activities. Many of them are law school professors. They meet each year, normally in Geneva, for a session of approximately 12 weeks. The various topics under consideration are usually assigned to individual members, who then serve as special rapporteurs on the item concerned, carry out the necessary studies between sessions, and submit reports to the Commission at its annual sessions.

FUNCTIONS

Development of New International Law

The Charter does not lay down any principles for determining a desirable "progressive development" of international law. Nevertheless, from the outset the discussions in the Commission and the Assembly have made very clear the main considerations involved. Because the development of international law is a continuous process, the traditional legal norms prevailing at the time of the San Francisco Conference were inherited from an era when world politics was dominated by a handful of Western European nations. As a consequence, international law itself reflected the values and interests of these nations. In essence, therefore, what has been required is an adjustment of the entire international legal order so as to take account of the interests and traditions of a much broader community of nations.

As prescribed by the decision of the 1947 Assembly, the International Law Commission is to give effect to the Charter provision for the progressive development of international law by preparing "draft conventions on subjects which have not yet been regulated by international law or in regard to which the law has not yet been sufficiently developed in the practice of States."

Since the filling of any gap in international law directly affects the behavior and obligations of states, it is for the UN member nations acting through the Assembly to decide the subjects on which the Commission may prepare draft conventions.

Preparing an international convention is a complex and often lengthy business. After appointing a rapporteur, the Commission formulates a plan of work and circulates a questionnaire to governments, inviting them to supply relevant information. It may also consult with scientific institutions and individual experts in law and other fields. If the rapporteur's draft is satisfactory to the Commission, it is sent by the secretary-general of the UN to governments for comment. The draft is then reconsidered by the Commission in the light of these comments, and the final version is submitted to the General Assembly. When the Assembly has discussed and approved the draft—which may not occur until the Commission has responded to requests for further modifications—it usually convokes a special international conference of plenipotentiaries for the purpose of adopting the actual convention, which subsequently has to be ratified by a given number of states (as specified in the articles of the convention itself) before it can come into force as a legal instrument.

Codification of Existing International Law. To give effect to the Charter request for the codification of law, the 1949 Assembly charged the Commission with providing "more precise formulation and systematization of [existing] rules of international law in fields where there already has been extensive State practice, precedent and doctrine."

In this respect, the Commission may act on its own initiative, and it is authorized to "survey the whole field of international law with a view to selecting topics for codification."

SCOPE OF THE COMMISSION'S WORK

The Assembly does not assign all legal issues with which it is concerned to the International Law Commission. Thus the legal aspect of an agenda item that relates to another sphere of the Assembly's work is often handled by a subcommittee of the special committee that was set up to study that particular subject. This is the case, for example, with the legal aspects of the peaceful uses of outer space and the peaceful uses of the seabed (see above under the appropriate chapters) and with many items on matters of human rights and economic and social development. On occasion, too, the Assembly has established a special committee to consider certain legal topics that directly affect the conduct of nations in international peace and security and are therefore highly political. Thus the agenda item on the Consideration of Principles of International Law Concerning Friendly Relations and Cooperation Among States in Accordance with the Charter of the United Nations was assigned to a special 31-member committee.

After 8 years of contentious discussion, the committee completed a draft declaration, as requested, in time for the commemorative session to celebrate the UN's 25th anniversary. The declaration embodies seven principles: the nonuse of force; peaceful settlement of disputes; nonintervention; sovereign equality; duty to cooperate; equal rights and self-determination; and fulfillment of obligations under the charter. Another example of a legal topic having a strongly political character is the definition of aggression. The International Law Commission originally was asked to draw up a definition of aggression. The task was taken over by the Assembly only after the Commission had failed to reach agreement (see below, under the next head). The Commission was requested also to consider two other topics relating to peace and security—namely, the draft Declaration on the Rights and Duties of States and the Draft Code of Offenses against the Peace and Security of Mankind (see below). But for the most part, the Commission's work has been confined to topics that affect the day-to-day relationship of nations, such as the conclusion and observance of treaties, exchange of envoys at various levels, definition of nationality, codification of the law of the sea, and so forth.

At its first session in 1949 the Commission drew up a provisional list of 14 topics for consideration. Although this list has remained the basis of its program, the Commission frequently has had to defer its own studies in order to take up specific requests from the Assembly. As a consequence, work on several topics remains incomplete. In the following survey of the individual topics handled by the Commission since its inception, the items are grouped according to whether the Commission has completed its work and submitted a final draft or report to the General Assembly.

TOPICS ON WHICH THE COMMISSION HAS COMPLETED ITS WORK

By 1970 the Commission had submitted final drafts or reports on 15 topics, which are discussed below in order of completion. The Commission's drafts on the last eight topics subsequently became the basis for the adoption of conventions.

Draft Declaration on Rights and Duties of States

The preparation of this draft, undertaken in response to an Assembly request, was completed at the Commission's first session in 1949.

Basic Rights of Every State

1. The right to independence, and hence to exercise freely, without dictation by any other state, all its legal powers, including the choice of its own form of government.

2. The right to exercise jurisdiction over its territory and over all persons and things therein, subject to the immunities recognized by international law.

3. The right to equality in law with every other state.

4. The right of individual or collective self-defense against armed attack.

Basic Duties of Every State

1. The duty to refrain from intervention in the internal or external affairs of any other state.

2. The duty to refrain from fomenting civil strife in the territory of another state, and to prevent the organization within its territory of activities calculated to foment such civil strife.

3. The duty to ensure that conditions prevailing in its territory do not menace international peace and order.

4. The duty to refrain from resorting to war as an instrument of national policy, and to refrain from the threat or use of force against the territorial integrity or political independence of another state, or in any other manner inconsistent with international law and order.

5. The duty to carry out in good faith its obligations arising from treaties and other sources of international law; no state may invoke provisions in its constitution or its laws as an excuse for failure to perform this duty.

The 1949 General Assembly commended the draft "to the continuing attention of Member States and of jurists of all nations."

Availability of Evidence of Customary International Law

In accordance with an article of its own Statute, the Commission, at its 1950 session, considered ways and means of making the evidence of customary international law more readily available and submitted a report recommending that the secretary-general issue certain publications. Since that time, the secretary-general has been authorized to issue most of the publications suggested.

Formulation of the Nuremberg Principles

The Commission was requested by the Assembly to draw up a formulation of the principles of international law recognized in the charter of the Nuremberg International Military Tribunal and in its judgment passed on the major German war criminals. It completed this task at the 1950 session. The principles formulated declare that, under international law, the perpetrator of a crime, irrespective of whether the act is punishable under the law of any particular country, is personally responsible for the crime and, provided a moral choice was open to him, is not relieved from such responsibility either because he acted as head of state or under superior orders. The Commission also gave a general definition of of "crimes against peace," which includes the planning of aggressive war; "war crimes," that is, violations of the laws of war regarding the treatment of prisoners of war or conduct in occupied territories; and "crimes against humanity," crimes committed under certain conditions against civilian populations.

International Criminal Jurisdiction

Should there be an international court which, under given circumstances, would have the authority to punish individuals for international crimes? A decision to establish an International Criminal Court was made in 1937 under League of Nations auspices, after the king of Yugoslavia and French Premier Barthou were assassinated on French soil by foreign terrorists. But the 1937 Convention for the Creation of an International Criminal Court did not obtain the required number of ratifications to come into force. The 1949 session of the General Assembly invited the Commission "to study the desirability and possibility of establishing an international judicial organ for the trial of persons charged with genocide or other crimes over which jurisdiction will be conferred upon that organ by international conventions." At its 1950 session the Commission decided, by a vote of 8 to 1, with 2 abstentions, that the establishment of such an international judicial organ is desirable, and by a vote of 7 to 3, with 1 abstention, that it is possible. After creating two committees to consider the various implications establishing such a court, the Assembly decided, in 1954 and 1957, to defer further consideration pending agreement on a definition of aggression.

Reservations to Multilateral Conventions

In response to an Assembly request, the Commission in 1951 submitted a report on the question of a state's right to attach reservations to a treaty to which it is a party. The subject was also considered again as part of the Commission's work of preparing the Law of Treaties (see below).

Question of Defining Aggression

When the 1950 General Assembly received a USSR proposal recommending an enumerative definition of acts of aggression, it referred the problem to the International Law Commission. Although the Commission did not draw up a definition, it included "any act of aggression" or threat of aggression among the offenses enumerated in its Draft Code of Offenses against Peace and Security (see next topic).

Since 1952 the question of defining aggression has been under consideration by a series of special committees of the General Assembly. Between 1952 and 1957 discussion centered on the preliminary issue of whether a definition of aggression is either desirable or possible. Some delegates thought that a definition would reduce international tension, serve as a warning to a potential aggressor, and promote the cause of peace. Other members, particularly the Western nations, were doubtful of such beneficial results and did not consider it advisable or feasible to try to arrive at a definition. They warned that a definition could restrict the flexibility of action of the Security Council and the General Assembly in maintaining peace and security. Others emphasized that a definition of aggression, to be really useful, would have to be accepted by an overwhelming majority of UN member nations, including all the major powers.

In 1957 the controversy was still unresolved, and a committee was established to determine "when it shall be appropriate for the Assembly again to consider the question of defining aggression." The committee met in 1959, 1962, 1965, and 1967 but was unable to reach a decision. However, as the result of a Soviet initiative, the 1967 Assembly established a 35-member committee for the purpose of formulating an acceptable draft definition. The committee had held three sessions by 1970, but was unable to agree on a definition.

In view of the fact that various international bodies have been trying without success to define aggression since the inception of the League of Nations, the prospects for achieving a satisfactory definition are not encouraging. Fundamental disagreement begins with the very concept of the definition. Three types of definition have been advanced: (1) a broad statement of general principles, which commands the reluctant support of the West; (2) a list of specific acts formally declared to constitute aggression, which is the proposal of the Eastern nations; (3) a mixed definition, to include both a generalized concept of aggression and a nonexhaustive list of specific aggressive acts. Even if the third type of definition were to become the basis for an acceptable compromise, countries would still have to settle another controversial issue—namely, the degree of the binding force of the definition, whether it should be written into a formal legal instrument (the Soviet view) or merely embodied in an Assembly resolution. Another controversial point is whether aggression should be restricted to the use of armed force, as the West desires, or whether, as the Eastern nations and some African and Asian countries insist, it should include indirect aggression through economic and political pressure. And in addition to these major areas of disagreement, there are also serious differences on a number of technical issues, such as whether the principle of "first use" of armed force should be included in the definition.

Draft Code of Offenses Against the Peace and Security of Mankind

The Law Commission completed a draft for this code in 1951, but in the light of comments by governments, it made certain important modifications and in 1954 produced a revised version.

Under the revised draft code, as under the Nuremberg principles, the fact that a person responsible for one of the enumerated crimes acted as head of a state or a responsible government official would not exonerate him. A person who had committed such a crime under the direct orders of his government or of a superior, including a military superior, would be responsible only if, under the circumstances at the time, it was possible for him not to comply with the order.

The following are included as offenses punishable as crimes against the peace and security of mankind:

1. Any act of aggression.
2. Any threat to resort to an act of aggression.
3. Preparation by the authorities of any state for the employment of armed forces against another state for any purpose other than national or collective self-defense or in pursuance of a decision or recommendation by a competent organ of the UN.
4. Incursion into the territory of another state by armed bands acting for a political purpose.

5. The undertaking, encouragement, or toleration by the authorities of a state of activities calculated to foment civil strife or terrorist activities in another state.
6. Violation by the authorities of a state of treaty obligations regarding limitation of armaments, military training, fortifications, or similar restrictions.
7. Annexation of a territory in violation of international law.
8. Intervention by the authorities of a state in the internal or external affairs of another state by coercive measures.
9. Genocide, whether committed by the authorities of a state or by private persons.
10. Inhuman acts by the authorities of a state or by private individuals against any civilian population, such as murder, extermination, enslavement, deportation, or persecution on political, racial, religious, or cultural grounds.
11. Acts in violation of the laws of war.
12. Conspiracy, direct incitement, or attempt to commit any of the foregoing offenses as well as complicity in committing them.

In its 1954 session and again in 1957, the General Assembly took the position that the draft code raised problems closely related to the problem of defining aggression. Accordingly, the Assembly decided to postpone consideration of the draft code until it had made more headway with the latter subject.

Reduction or Elimination of Future Statelessness

The difficulties in arriving at an international convention on a topic on which the laws and practices of nations differ widely are illustrated by the fate of the Commission's drafts regarding statelessness of persons. In 1954 the Commission prepared two drafts, one for a convention on the elimination of future statelessness, and another, which would impose fewer obligations on states, on the reduction of future statelessness. General Assembly discussions showed that the first and more sweeping draft had no chance of acceptance. Even the measures on which countries would have to agree in order to reduce the number of stateless persons raised so many problems that it eventually required two special conferences, one in 1959 and one in 1961, to arrive at a Convention on the Reduction of Statelessness (28 August 1961). The convention, which is to come into force two years after six countries have ratified or acceded to it, was still not in force by the end of 1970.

The Law of the Sea

In accordance with its 1949 program, the commission worked for a number of years on the codification of the law of the sea, frequently revising draft articles in the light of comments received from governments. Following a request of the 1954 Assembly, the Commission grouped together the articles it had previously adopted and submitted a final draft on the law of the sea in 1956. The Assembly called a special conference on the law of the sea at Geneva in February–April, 1958. At that conference, which was attended by 86 countries, four conventions were adopted: (1) the Convention on the High Seas, which came into force on 30 September 1962; (2) the Convention on the Continental Shelf, on 24 April 1964; (3) the Convention on the Territorial Sea and Contiguous Zone, on 10 September 1964; and (4) the Convention on Fishing and Conservation of Living Resources of the High Seas, on 20 March 1966.

Arbitral Procedure

Arbitration is one of the most useful methods of settling international disputes, but a more precise formulation or clarification of the rules governing arbitral procedure would greatly add to its effectiveness. For several years the Commission drafted and redrafted a convention on the subject. In 1958 it reshaped its proposals in the form of a model set of rules. This device obviated the need for an international convention on the subject. The 1958 Assembly decided to commend the text of the Model Rules on Arbitral Procedure to the attention of the member states.

Diplomatic Relations

In 1959 the International Law Commission adopted final draft articles on Diplomatic Intercourse and Immunities. After discussion in the General Assembly and scrutiny by governments, that draft formed the basis for a conference of 81 governments held in the Imperial Palace in Vienna on 2 March 1961. On 18 April 1961 this "Second Congress of Vienna" adopted the Vienna Convention on Diplomatic Relations. It adapts to 20th-century requirements the rules for diplomatic intercourse formulated by the 1815 Congress of Vienna which since that time have essentially governed diplomatic relations. The new convention, which came into force on 24 April 1964, covers establishment of diplomatic relations and missions; functions of a diplomatic mission; persons declared persona non grata; size of the staff of a diplomatic mission; use of flags and emblems; inviolability of the premises of missions; personal inviolability; immunity; and freedom of communication, including the diplomatic pouch.

Consular Relations

Final draft articles on consular relations were submitted by the Commission to the Assembly in 1961. On the basis of this draft the UN Conference on Consular Relations, held at Vienna in March–April 1963 and attended by representatives of 92 states, adopted the following conventions and protocols: the Vienna Convention on Consular Relations; Optional Protocol Covering Acquisition of Nationality; Optional Protocol Covering Compulsory Settlement of Disputes. The convention and the protocols all came into force on 19 March 1967.

Extended Participation in Multilateral Treaties Concluded Under the Auspices of the League of Nations

The Commission's conclusions on this question were submitted to the Assembly in 1963. On the basis of these conclusions, the Assembly decided, in Resolution 1903 (XVIII), that it was the appropriate organ of the UN to exercise the functions of the League Council in respect of 21 general multilateral treaties of a technical and nonpolitical character concluded under the auspices of the former world body.

Law of Treaties

By far the most far-reaching task undertaken by the International Law Commission has been its work on the Law of Treaties—the laws governing the way in which treaties are to be negotiated, adopted, altered, and abrogated. The Commission, which began work on this project in 1949, finally completed it in 1966, after 18 sessions. Throughout this period, the Commission regularly submitted provisional draft articles to the Assembly's Sixth Committee and to individual governments for comment. Accordingly, the final draft of 75 articles adopted by the Commission and submitted to the Assembly's 1966 session included many revisions.

Because of the complexity of the subject, the Assembly convoked a two-stage conference, the first in 1968 and the second in 1969. Both sessions were held at Vienna. The first was attended by representatives of 103 states and the second by representatives of 110 states. The Vienna Convention on the Law of Treaties, consisting of 85 articles and an annex, was adopted on 22 May 1969 and is due to come into force 30 days after the 35th state has ratified or acceded to it.

The convention combines a codification of existing law with the development of new law. In many respects, the final text hammered out at the two conferences was a compromise solution, and several of the articles included were controversial. The convention was adopted by a vote of 79 in favor, 1 against, and 19 abstentions. Precisely because of its controversial character, the convention does not attempt to be comprehensive. It does not include, for instance, as the International Law Commission had originally intended it should, any provisions for treaties concluded between states and international organizations. Thus, while its preamble stresses "the ever increasing importance of treaties as a source of international law and as a means of developing peaceful cooperation among nations," the convention expressly stipulates that the rules of customary international law will continue to govern questions not regulated by its provisions: these apply only to treaties between states. The term "treaty" is defined in Article 2 as "an international agreement concluded between states in written form and govered by international law . . . whatever its particular designation," and therefore includes any treaty adopted within an international organization. Articles 19–21 allow states to formulate reservations to treaties, provided they are not contrary to the actual provisions of a treaty or incompatible with its object and purpose.

Among the more controversial provisions are those that establish peremptory norms of international law. A norm, as defined in Article 53, is a standard that is "accepted and recognized by the international community of States as a whole," and that can be modified only by a subsequent norm having the same character. This principle is applied, for instance, in Article 52, which declares a treaty void if it is concluded "by the threat or use of force in violations of the principles of international law embodied in the Charter of the United Nations." Even more controversial were the provisions for establishing a conciliation commission to assist the settlement of disputes arising out of an attempt by a party to a treaty to impeach its validity, terminate or withdraw from it, or suspend its operation. The commission is to be set up under the auspices of and financed by the UN. Yet another controversial issue was the delicate question of whether the convention should be opened to states which are not members of the UN. The conference solved this problem by adopting a declaration that multilateral treaties of interest to the international community as a whole should be open for universal participation, and it asked the Assembly to consider inviting nonmember states to become parties. The matter was placed on the agenda of the 1969 regular session, but the Assembly deferred consideration until the 1970 session, when the item was again deferred.

Special Missions

Arising out of its work on diplomatic relations, the International Law Commission prepared a brief draft on questions concerning the dispatch of temporary envoys and submitted it to the 1961 UN Conference on Diplomatic Intercourse and Immunity (see above), recommending that it be given further study. Following a request of the 1961 Assembly, the Commission submitted a final draft on the subject in 1968. Contrary to usual practice the Assembly decided not to convoke a special conference to adopt a convention but to have its Sixth Committee sit in this capacity. (The Sixth Committee, the main committee of the Assembly, is responsible for examining the legal items on the agenda for the regular sessions; see the chapter on the General Assembly.) The Sixth Committee completed the draft for the Convention on Special Missions in 1969, when it was formally adopted by the Assembly in Resolution 2530 (XXIV) of 8 December 1969. It is due to come into force after 22 countries have ratified or acceded to it.

TOPICS ON WHICH THE COMMISSION HAS NOT COMPLETED ITS WORK

These include four topics currently under study and five topics from the 1949 program, on which work has been temporarily suspended: (1) recognition of states and governments; (2) jurisdictional immunities of states and their property; (3) jurisdiction with regard to crimes committed outside national territory; (4) treatment of aliens; and (5) right of asylum.

The four topics currently under study are:

Succession of States and Governments, which dates from the 1949 program and deals with the question of succession in respect both to treaties and to other spheres of international relations. Work is still far from complete.

Relations Between States and International Organizations, a topic requested by the 1958 Assembly, on which work is nearing its final stage, the Commission having provisionally adopted parts I and II of its draft articles and circulated them for comment both to agencies and governments (including the Swiss government, since Switzerland acts as host country of the UN's European office, although it is not itself a UN member).

State Responsibility, dating from the 1949 list, which concerns the question of responsibility for damages caused to one state by another. The 1969 Assembly asked the Commission to expedite its work on this topic, which intermittently has been under consideration by the Commission since 1955.

Most-Favored-Nation Clause, a topic requested by the 1967 Assembly that relates to trade law.

The Commission is to review its future program of work with a view to jettisoning from its original 1949 list topics that are no longer relevant. New topics that the 1970 Assembly is likely to request the Commission to study include protection of diplomats (during 1970 several foreign diplomats were kidnapped and held for ransom by members of national liberation movements seeking to pressure their governments into yielding to their demands), hijacking of aircraft, and a draft for a convention on the law of international waterways.

UNITED NATIONS BIBLIOGRAPHY

General

Charter of the United Nations and Statute of the International Court of Justice. 85 pp. $0.50

Annual Report of the Secretary-General on the Work of the Organization. $4.00

Yearbook of the United Nations. Comprehensive annual account of the activities of the UN and related agencies. Contains full texts of important resolutions, etc. Yearbook for 1967. 1,110 pp. $25.00

Everyman's United Nations. Published at intervals of 3 or 4 years; describes the structure and activities of the organizations within the UN system. 8th edition, 1967. 634 pp. $2.50

Basic Facts about the United Nations. 25th anniversary edition. 1970. 89 pp. $0.75

UN Monthly Chronicle. The official UN magazine, covering the full range of UN activities. Illus. One year, $9.50; single copies, $1.00.

United Nations Documents Index. Eleven issues a year and cumulative checklist and cumulative index. One year, $25.00

The United Nations and Disarmament 1945–1970. 1970. 515 pp. $5.00

Portfolio for Peace. Excerpts from the Writings and Speeches of U Thant, Secretary-General of the United Nations on Major World Issues 1961–1970. 1970. 140 pp. $1.50

Atomic Energy and Radiation

Report of the UN Committee on the Effects of Atomic Radiation. 1969 report to General Assembly. 165 pp. $4.00

Economics, and Economic and Social Development

World Economic Survey. Annual comprehensive review and analysis of world economic conditions and trends. The *Survey* for 1968, published in 1969, is divided into two parts: Part I: Financing of Economic Development; Part II: Current Economic Developments. 118 pp. $2.00

Economic Bulletin for Africa.

Economic Bulletin for Asia and the Far East.

Economic Bulletin for Europe.

Economic Bulletin for Latin America.

Prepared by the respective UN regional economic commissions and published at irregular intervals; prices vary from $1.50 to $4.00

Industrialization and Productivity Bulletin. Published at irregular intervals. No. 14. 1969. 124 pp. $2.00

The External Financing of Economic Development: International Flow of Long-term Capital and Official Donations, 1964–1968. 1970. 102 pp. $1.50

Toward Accelerated Development Proposals for the Second United Nations Development Decade. 1970. 46 pp. $0.75

Economic and Trade Statistics

Statistical Yearbook. 1969 ed. 770 pp. $13.50

Monthly Bulletin of Statistics. Statistics on more than 70 subjects from over 200 countries. One year, $25.00

Yearbook of National Accounts Statistics. 1969 ed. 2 vols. I: *Individual Country Data.* $12.50. II: *International Tables.* $3.50

The Growth of World Industry. 1968 edition. 2 vols.: I: *General Industrial Statistics 1958–1967.* $8.00. II: *Commodity Production Data 1958–1967.* $5.00

Commodity Trade Statistics. Issued in fascicles as quarterly data become available. One year, $30.00

Yearbook of International Trade Statistics. 1968 ed. 941 pp. $12.50

World Energy Supplies. An annual publication covering a four-year period. 1970 ed. contains statistics for years 1965–1968 on production, trade, and consumption of solid fuel, liquid fuel, electricity, and gas in about 180 countries. 108 pp. $2.00

Demography

Demographic Yearbook, 1969 ed. 694 pp. $13.50

Population and Vital Statistics Report. Quarterly. $1.00

General Social Questions (including Human Rights)

1967 Report on the World Social Situation. 1969. 208 pp. $3.00

Compendium of Social Statistics: 1967. 1968. 662 pp. $8.75

International Social Development Review. Published at irregular intervals. No. 2. 1970. 43 pp. $1.00

Rural Housing: A Review of World Conditions. 1969. 186 pp. $3.00

Progress in Land Reform. Fifth Report. 1970. 367 pp. $2.00

International Review of Criminal Policy. Published at irregular intervals. No. 28. 1970. 131 pp. $2.00

Yearbook on Human Rights for 1966. 1969. 482 pp. $4.75

The United Nations and Human Rights. 1968. 93 pp. $1.25

Narcotic Drugs

Bulletin on Narcotics. Quarterly. Information on traffic in narcotics and on national and international control measures. One year, $6.00

Statistics on Narcotic Drugs for 1968. 1969. 80 pp. $1.50

International Law

Yearbook of the International Commission. Vol. I of each yearbook contains the sessional summary records of the Commission, and vol. II its documents and annual report. Prices vary $3.50–$5.00

Report of the United Nations Commission on International Trade Law. Annual. $1.00

United Nations Juridical Yearbook, 1968. 299 pp. $4.00

Reports of International Arbitral Awards. Vols. in series published at irregular intervals. Vol. XVI. 1969. 336 pp. $4.00

Multilateral Treaties in Respect of Which the Secretary-General Performs Depositary Functions. List of Signatures, Ratifications, Accessions, etc. as at 31 December 1969. 421 pp. $5.75. *Annex: Final Clauses.* Loose-leaf ed. 1968. $5.00. Annual supplements. $0.75 each

Treaty Series. Over 600 vols.; 7 cumulative index vols. $6.00 per vol.

ICJ Publications

Yearbook of the International Court of Justice 1969–1970. 145 pp. $1.50

Reports of Judgments, Advisory Opinions and Orders. Published in fascicles following each decision, and in annual clothbound vol. Prices vary for both forms.

INTERNATIONAL LABOR ORGANIZATION (ILO)

¹BACKGROUND : The ILO is the only major organization originally part of the League of Nations system that has existed from the founding of the League in 1919 down to the present day. Its name is actually too narrow, for it is an organization neither of nor for labor alone. As the late James T. Shotwell, president emeritus of the Carnegie Endowment for International Peace, pointed out long ago, the ILO might more accurately have been termed an International Organization for Social Justice. Furthermore, as the organization's responsibilities have widened, it has given increasing attention to measures designed to help raise general standards of living, and its work now includes activities as remote from the traditional field of labor relations as training courses for management personnel and high government officials in modern methods to improve productivity and efficiency.

²CREATION

The ILO was created by the 1919 Peace Conference that followed World War I. Its original constitution, which formed part of the Treaty of Versailles, established it as an autonomous organization associated with the League of Nations.

The statement in the constitution's preamble, "Conditions of labor exist involving such injustice, hardship, and privation to large numbers of people as to produce unrest so great that the peace and harmony of the world are imperilled," was not mere rhetoric. The World War had shaken many countries to their foundations. The revolution had succeeded in Russia. All over the world there was labor unrest, and the conviction of the need to improve the workingman's lot was by no means limited to labor itself. Organized labor, however, had been especially active during the war in demanding that the peace treaty include a recognition of the rights of labor and that labor be given a voice in international matters. The American Federation of Labor (AFL) and other powerful trade union bodies demanded in particular an international organization of labor that would wield "tremendous authority."

At the 1919 Paris Peace Conference, the president of the AFL, Samuel Gompers, was the chairman of the conference's Commission on Labor Legislation. The Peace Conference, instead of establishing an international organization of labor, created an organization in which labor, employers, and governments were to be represented on an equal footing. As so constituted the ILO was, and still is, unique among international governmental organizations, inasmuch as it is the only one in which private citizens, namely, representatives of labor and of employers, have the same voting and other rights as possessed by government delegates.

The ILO's principal function was to be the establishment of international labor and social standards through the drafting and adoption of international labor conventions. Prior to the existence of the ILO, only two international labor conventions had been adopted; one, designed to protect the health of workers in match factories, prohibited the use of white phosphorus, a poisonous compound, in the manufacture of matches; the other prescribed modest restrictions on night work by women. Neither of these had been widely ratified. By way of contrast, 130 international labor conventions were adopted by the ILO between 1919 and 1969, many of which were widely ratified.

³PURPOSES

The aims and objectives of the ILO were originally set forth in the preamble to its constitution, written in 1919. The preamble declares that "universal and lasting peace can be established only if it is based upon social justice." Hence, the basic objective of the organization is to help improve social conditions throughout the world. The following examples of concrete measures "urgently required" are specifically mentioned in the preamble:

Regulation of the hours of work, including the establishment of a maximum working day and week.

Regulation of the labor supply.

Prevention of unemployment.

Provision of an adequate living wage.

Protection of the worker against sickness, disease, and injury arising out of his employment.

Protection of children, young persons, and women.

Provision for old age and injury.

Protection of the interests of workers when employed in countries other than their own.

Recognition of the principle of equal remuneration for work of equal value.

Recognition of the principle of freedom of association.

The organization of vocational and technical education, and other measures.

International action in these matters is required, the preamble makes clear, because "the failure of any nation to adopt humane conditions of labor is an obstacle in the way of other nations which desire to improve the conditions in their own countries." Finally, in agreeing to the ILO constitution, the member governments declare in the preamble that they are "moved by sentiments of justice and humanity as well as by the desire to secure the permanent peace of the world."

The Declaration of Philadelphia, adopted by the 1944 International Labor Conference, rephrased and broadened the "aims and purposes" of the ILO and "the principles which should inspire the policy of its members." President Roosevelt stated that the declaration summed up the aspirations of an epoch that had known two world wars and that it might well acquire a historical significance comparable to that of the US Declaration of Independence. The declaration, which was incorporated into the amended constitution of the ILO, affirms that labor is not a commodity; that freedom of expression and association are essential to sustained progress: that poverty anywhere constitutes a danger to prosperity everywhere; and that the war against want must be carried on, not only with unrelenting vigor within each nation, but also by "continuous and concerted international effort in which the representatives of workers and employers, enjoying equal status with those of Governments, join with them in free discussion and democratic decision with a view to the promotion of the common welfare."

The Declaration of Philadelphia recognizes the "solemn obligation" of the ILO to further among nations of the world programs that will achieve:

a. Full employment and the raising of standards of living.

b. Employment of workers in the occupations for which they are best suited and where they can make their greatest contribution to the common well-being.

c. Facilities for training and the transfer of labor, including migration for employment and settlement.

d. Policies in regard to wages and earnings, hours, and other conditions of work calculated to ensure a just share of the fruits of progress to all, and a minimum living wage to all employed and in need of such protection.

e. Effective recognition of the right of collective bargaining, the cooperation of management and labor in the continuous improvement of productive efficiency, and the collaboration of workers and employers in the preparation and application of social and economic measures.

f. Extension of social security measures to provide a basic income to all in need of such protection and comprehensive medical care.

g. Adequate protection for the life and health of workers in all occupations.

h. Child welfare and maternity protection.

i. Adequate nutrition, housing, and facilities for recreation and culture.

j. Assurance of equality of educational and vocational opportunity.

4 MEMBERSHIP

Originally, ILO membership was identical with League of Nations membership, since adherence to the League carried with it participation in ILO. However, several countries not members of the League were admitted to ILO, notably the US, which joined in 1934. The constitution of the ILO now provides that any nation that is a member of the UN can become a member of the ILO by unilaterally notifying the Director-General that it accepts the obligations of the ILO constitution. Other nations may be admitted to ILO membership by a two-thirds vote of the International Labor Conference.

The ILO constitution originally made no provision for the expulsion of a member. However, a pair of amendments adopted by the International Labor Conference in 1964 and now open for ratification would empower the ILO membership, by a two-thirds vote, to expel or suspend any member that had been expelled or suspended by the United Nations or that had been found by the United Nations to be flagrantly and persistently pursuing by its legislation a policy of racial discrimination. The amendments were adopted in response to South Africa's policy of racial apartheid. They will take effect when they have been ratified or accepted by two-thirds of the member nations, including five of the ten that are represented on the Governing Body as "members of chief industrial importance."

A state may withdraw from the ILO by formal notification of its intent to do so, such withdrawal to be effective two years after ILO receives the notification. South Africa notified the organization of its intent to withdraw even before the amendments that could have led to its expulsion were adopted and its withdrawal became effective on 11 March 1966. Albania withdrew in 1967. Germany, which was one of the original members, withdrew in 1935. Fourteen other countries withdrew their membership at various times (11 of them during the World War II period), but all sooner or later rejoined the organization. Readmission is governed by the same rules that govern original admission to membership. On 1 May 1970 there were 121 member states:

Afghanistan 1934–	Lebanon 1948–
Albania 1920–1967	Lesotho 1967–
Algeria 1962–	Liberia 1919–
Argentina 1919–	Libya 1952–
Australia 1919–	Luxembourg 1920–
Austria 1919–38, 1947–	Malagasy Republic 1960–
Barbados 1967–	Malawi 1965–
Belgium 1919–	Malaysia 1957–
Bolivia 1919–	Mali 1960–
Brazil 1919–	Malta 1965–
Bulgaria 1920–	Mauritania 1961–
Burma 1948–	Mauritius 1969–
Burundi 1963–	Mexico 1931–
Byelorussia 1954–	Mongolia 1968–
Cambodia 1969–	Morocco 1956–
Cameroon 1960–	Nepal 1966–
Canada 1919–	Netherlands 1919–
Central African Republic 1960–	New Zealand 1919–
Ceylon 1948–	Nicaragua 1919–38, 1957
Chad 1960–	Niger 1961–
Chile 1919–	Nigeria 1960–
Colombia 1919–	Norway 1919–
Congo (Brazzaville) 1960–	Pakistan 1947–
Congo (Kinshasa) 1960–	Panama 1919–
Costa Rica 1920–27, 1944–	Paraguay 1919–37, 1956–
Cuba 1919–	Peru 1919–
Cyprus 1960–	Philippines 1948–
Czechoslovakia 1919–	Poland 1919–
Dahomey 1960–	Portugal 1919–
Denmark 1919–	Romania 1919–42, 1956–
Dominican Republic 1924–	Rwanda 1962–
Ecuador 1934–	Senegal 1960–
El Salvador 1919–39, 1948–	Sierra Leone 1961–
Ethiopia 1923–	Singapore 1965–
Finland 1920–	Somalia 1960–
France 1919–	Southern Yemen 1969–
Gabon 1960–	Spain 1919–41, 1956–
Germany, West 1951–	Sudan 1956–
Ghana 1957–	Sweden 1919–
Greece 1919–	Switzerland 1919–
Guatemala 1919–38, 1945–	Syria 1947–
Guinea 1959–	Taiwan 1919–
Guyana 1966–	Tanzania 1962–
Haiti 1919–	Thailand 1919–
Honduras 1919–38, 1955–	Togo 1960–
Hungary 1922–	Trinidad and Tobago 1963–
Iceland 1945–	Tunisia 1956–
India 1919–	Turkey 1932–
Indonesia 1950–	Uganda 1963–
Iran 1919–	Ukraine 1954–
Iraq 1932–	USSR 1934–40, 1954–
Ireland 1923–	UAR (Egypt) 1936–
Israel 1949–	UK 1919–
Italy 1919–39, 1945–	US 1934–
Ivory Coast 1960–	Upper Volta 1960–
Jamaica 1962–	Uruguay 1920–
Japan 1919–40, 1951–	Venezuela 1919–57, 1958–
Jordan 1956–	Viet-Nam, South 1950–
Kenya 1964–	Yemen Arab Republic 1965–
Kuwait 1961–	Yugoslavia 1919–49, 1951–
Laos 1964–	Zambia 1964–

5 STRUCTURE

The principal organs of the ILO are the International Labor Conference, the Governing Body, and the International Labor Office.

THE INTERNATIONAL LABOR CONFERENCE

The International Labor Conference, the policy-making body of the ILO, is the organization's supreme authority. It regularly meets once a year at ILO headquarters in Geneva. Its first session, however, was held in Washington in 1919 at the invitation of President Wilson, and full sessions have been held in Philadelphia, 1944, Paris, 1945, and San Francisco, 1948. For several years during World War II, the conference was unable to convene.

Tripartite Representation. Each member country sends a national delegation to the International Labor Conference consisting of four delegates, two representing the government, one representing the country's employers, and one representing the country's workers. Alternates and advisers may be sent out as well. Each delegate has one independent vote. Discussing this system of tripartite representation in 1959, the Director-General noted that the ILO is "the only intergovernmental agency in whose work non-government delegates take part on an equal footing with Government representatives as a matter of constitutional right. Representatives of employers' and workers' organizations are included in its policy-making, standard-setting, and executive machinery and participate, with full voting rights, in all these aspects of its work."

The government, employers', and workers' representatives to the conference act in many respects as three separate groups, functioning somewhat as political parties function in a national legislature. The three groups meet separately for informal discussions of strategy; they hold caucuses; and, voting separately, they elect the government, the employers', and the workers' delegates to the Governing Body and to tripartite committees. If the tripartite system is to function as intended, it is essential that employers' and workers' delegates be true spokesmen for their respective points of view. The ILO constitution provides that governments must appoint these delegates in agreement with the "most representative" organizations of employers or workers, "if such organizations exist."

Since each government can select only one delegate as spokesman for all its workers, the problem of which workers' organization in a given country is to be regarded as "most representative" has often proved difficult and has led to considerable controversy. In recent years, the French government has chosen the labor delegate by rotation from the CGT (Conféderation Générale du Travail), the Force Ouvrière, and the French Confederation of Christian Workers, although the CGT has protested that it, as the largest and most representative of the French trade union organizations, should be represented more frequently. Even before World War II, the interpretation of the governing phrase in the ILO constitution, "the most representative organization," was considered significant enough to warrant its submission to the Permanent Court of International Justice. The eagerness of rival groups of unions to furnish the national workers' delegate shows the importance that they attach to the ILO.

The question of which employers' organization in a given country is the "most representative" has not led to much controversy, since in most countries with a free-enterprise economy a single federation of employers has usually enjoyed more or less unchallenged leadership. In the US, however, the National Association of Manufacturers challenged the government's practice of relying on nominations submitted by the US Chamber of Commerce; and after 1946 the US employers' representative was selected in agreement with both organizations until, in 1961, the NAM withdrew from participation in the ILO and ceased to select its candidate.

THE 1969 INTERNATIONAL LABOR CONFERENCE

The following description of the 1969 session illustrates how the International Labor Conference goes about its work:

The three-week conference at Geneva, 4 to 25 June, was attended by nearly 1,400 delegates and technical advisers from 116 member nations. Some 130 cabinet-level ministers and vice-ministers attended the conference. The UN, several specialized agencies, and other official and nongovernmental organizations were represented by observers.

The conference elected as its president a Swiss labor leader, Jean Mori, a break with tradition in that no one but a government delegate had ever before held the post. Vice-presidents elected were Angel Tzankov, First Deputy Minister of Labor and Social Assistance of Bulgaria, for the government group; Edwin Neilan of the United States for the employers' group; and Albert Monk of Australia for the workers' group.

As this was the 50th Anniversary Conference, world spiritual and political leaders participated, including United Nations Secretary-General U Thant; Pope Paul VI; Dr. Eugene Carson Blake, General Secretary of the World Council of Churches; Emperor Haile Selassie of Ethiopia; President Kenneth Kaunda of Zambia; and El Hadj Ahmadou Ahidjo, president of the Federal Republic of Cameroon.

As is customary, the conference opened with a discussion of the Director-General's Annual Report. The report, which is distributed to the delegates in advance, concentrates each year on specific problems of international significance. The 1969 report proposed a World Employment Program. More than 200 speakers took part in the discussion. The conference formally adopted the program. Also adopted were new international labor standards in the form of conventions and recommendations on labor inspection in agriculture and on sickness insurance.

First drafts of conventions were approved on holidays with pay and minimum wages. In addition, a first draft of a recommendation was approved for special youth employment and training programs for development purposes.

The ILO's new Governing Body was elected for a term of three years.

For the first time in its history, the ILO adopted a budget for a 2-year period, in the amount of approximately $61,500,000. United Nations Development Program funds are received separately.

THE GOVERNING BODY

The Governing Body is the executive council of the ILO. It is composed of 48 members, 12 representing employers, 12 representing workers, and 24 representing governments.

Members of the Governing Body are elected by the corresponding groups in the International Labor Conference, except that ten of the government representatives are appointed by countries that do not participate in the election of the other government representatives since these ten countries are entitled to permanent seats as "states of chief industrial importance." The ten governments permanently represented on the Governing Body are Canada, China (Taiwan), France, West Germany, India, Italy, Japan, USSR, UK, and US. Elections are held every three years.

Employers' representatives on the Governing Body elected for three years by the 1969 conference included leading industrialists or ranking employers' association officers from Ghana, Sweden, Brazil, West Germany, Niger, Iran, UK, Lebanon, US, India, France, and Mexico. The 12 members of the workers' group were ranking trade union officials from West Germany,

Tunisia, UK, US, Cameroon, Switzerland, Canada, USSR, Mexico, Japan, Morocco, and Norway. The government members included the Canadian deputy minister of labor, a member of the Council of Ministers of the USSR, a UK deputy secretary in the ministry of labor, and the US deputy undersecretary of labor for international affairs.

Meeting several times a year, the Governing Body coordinates and in many ways shapes the work of the organization. It draws up the agenda for each session of the International Labor Conference, and while the conference is empowered to change this agenda it rarely does. The Governing Body appoints the Director-General of the International Labor Office. It examines the proposed budget submitted to it each year by the Director-General and approves it for adoption by the conference. The Governing Body is also responsible for convening the scores of other conference and committee meetings held under ILO auspices every year in various parts of the world and decides what action ought to be taken on their resolutions and reports.

At a special session in May 1970 the Governing Body appointed Wilfred Jenks of the UK as director-general, to succeed David A. Morse of the US, who had resigned after 22 years in the post.

At the regular spring 1970 session the Governing Body dealt with the following matters, among others: Meeting of experts on control of atmospheric pollution in the working environment; meeting of joint ILO/WHO expert committee on personal health and social security; a comprehensive capacity study of the UN Development system; the contribution of the ILO to the UN Second Development Decade; use of the Nobel Peace Prize money awarded to the ILO; and reports submitted by the Governing Body Committee on Freedom of Association.

INTERNATIONAL LABOR OFFICE AND THE DIRECTOR-GENERAL

The International Labor Office in Geneva, headed by the ILO Director-General, is the organization's world headquarters and its permanent secretariat. Its staff consists of about 2,000 persons of over 80 different nationalities. During World War II, when for a time Switzerland was entirely surrounded by Axis forces, the International Labor Office and a skeleton staff were temporarily moved to Montreal where, thanks to the hospitality of the Canadian government and McGill University, the office was able to continue its more urgent work. The International Labor Office services the sessions of the conference, the Governing Body, and the various subsidiary organs and committees. It prepares the documents for these meetings; publishes periodicals, studies, and reports; and collects and distributes information on all subjects within ILO's competence. As directed by the conference and the Governing Body, it carries out ILO operational programs that have been decided on in various fields.

The ILO has had five Directors-General—Albert Thomas, France: 1919–1932; Harold Butler, UK: 1932–1938; John G. Winant, US: 1938–1941; Edward J. Phelan, Ireland: 1941–1948; David A. Morse, US: 1948–1970; Wilfred Jenks, UK: 1970–.

REGIONAL, BRANCH, AND FIELD OFFICES

On 1 January 1970 there were 3 regional offices, in Addis Ababa for Africa, Lima for the Americas, and Bangkok for Asia; 8 branch offices, in Washington, Ottawa, Tokyo, Paris, Bonn, Rome, Moscow, and London; 17 field offices, in Algiers, Yaoundé, Lagos, Dakar, Dar-es-Salaam, Cairo, Lusaka, Buenos Aires, Rio de Janeiro, Santiago de Chile, San José, Mexico City, Port-of-Spain, Montevideo, New Delhi, Beirut, and Istanbul.

THE ISSUE OF INDEPENDENT WORKER AND EMPLOYER REPRESENTATION

Since its early days, the ILO has been troubled by a basic constitutional issue: can the organization, without violating its own principles, countenance the seating of workers and employers' delegates from countries where workers and employers' organizations are not free from government domination or control?

Challenges to the Credentials of Workers' Delegates

When in the early 1920's a member of the Italian Fascist labor corporations appeared at Geneva to take his seat as the workers' member of the Italian delegation to the ILO, his credentials were challenged, though unsuccessfully, by the workers' group, which maintained that he was not a true spokesman for Italian labor. Every session of the conference from 1923 to 1938 saw the credentials of one or more workers' delegates challenged on the ground that these delegates did not represent an independent labor point of view. Among them were workers' delegates from Austria, Bulgaria, Germany, Greece, Italy, Latvia, Lithuania, and Poland. In all cases, however, the delegates were seated.

Since World War II, the conference has on several occasions actually refused to seat a workers' delegate whose credentials had been challenged. In 1945, it refused to seat the workers' delegate chosen by the Perón regime in Argentina on the ground that workers' organizations in Argentina did not at that time enjoy freedom of association, action, or speech. In 1950, it refused to seat the workers' delegate appointed by the government of Venezuela on the ground that the delegate could not have been nominated in agreement with the country's most representative workers' associations since the government had at that time dissolved all trade unions. Challenges to the credentials of Argentinian and Venezuelan workers' delegates on other occasions were overruled by the credentials committee, however, as was a 1955 challenge to the credentials of the Chilean workers' delegate.

The Question of Employers' Delegates from Communist Countries

Much greater difficulties have arisen over the seating of employers' delegates from Communist countries. When the first employers' delegate from the USSR, Mr. Kaoulin of the People's Commissariat of Water Transport, appeared at the 1936 maritime conference, the employers' group acquiesced in his seating but requested an examination of the constitutional questions involved. A study duly carried out by the International Labor Office concluded that the ILO constitution did not require an employer to be a private person, and that in countries where the state was the chief employer it was for the state to choose the employers' delegate. The employers' group at the conference voted unanimously to reject this interpretation.

At the 1945 ILO Conference, held in Paris shortly after the close of World War II, two constitutional amendments were proposed that aimed at increasing the size of the national delegations so as to give representation to both the public and private sectors of the economy. Both proposed amendments were, for a variety of reasons, rejected by the conference. The employers' group, however, issued a declaration stating that in the event that the USSR, which had withdrawn from the ILO in 1940, were to resume membership "it would naturally appoint as employers' delegate a representative of the socialized management of the USSR."

At the 1953 conference, the employers' group challenged the credentials of the Czechoslovakian employers' delegate and, when the USSR did rejoin the organization in 1954, challenged those of the Soviet employers' delegate as well. On both occasions the group was overruled by the credentials committee, which held that the delegates in question performed executive and managerial functions corresponding to those normally exercised by employers under other economic systems.

The McNair Report

When the Governing Body met in November 1954, it was sharply divided on the question of employers' delegates from countries with a nationalized economy. In hopes of facilitating a compromise, it appointed a special fact-finding committee, headed by Sir Arnold McNair, former president of the International Court of Justice, to report on the "extent of the freedom of employers' and workers' organizations" in ILO member countries "from government domination or control." The lengthy report, which the committee submitted in February 1956, was based on a study of the situation in 59 countries, including 5 in the Soviet bloc.

The report recognized at the outset that the unique feature of the ILO—cooperation between government, employers', and workers' spokesmen—can only be meaningful if the latter represent their constituents in the true sense of the word and have the right "to speak and vote freely without government control." On the other hand, the report noted, major changes had occurred in the economic structure of many countries since 1919, with governments participating in their countries' economic and social life in a wide variety of new ways. The ILO had long maintained that the principle of freedom of association is violated if the right to organize is subject to government authorization. Yet, the report found, the constitutions of no less than 21 ILO countries subjected the right of association to statutory regulation. No attempt was made to minimize the difficulty of reconciling the principle of universality of ILO membership, regardless of political and economic differences, and the principle that workers' and employers' representatives should be independent of government control; but the report at least made it clear that the problem was not limited to countries of the Soviet bloc. For example, it was found that in the less developed non-Communist countries trade unions and employers' associations were generally "not so strong vis-à-vis their governments as in the leading industrial countries" and that many opportunities existed for government domination.

A possible line of compromise was suggested in the committee's discussion of the role of management in the socialist economies. "The difference in function between the employing class in the majority of countries and the managerial class in the USSR and similar countries is that, while both are concerned with ensuring efficient management and development of industry, the latter are not concerned with the protection of the interests of private capital because there is no private capital to protect." Yet, the report noted, the managers of socialist enterprises "have extensive powers and discretions and responsibilities" and by reason of their experience should be capable of making "a distinct contribution" to the deliberations of the ILO.

Subsequent Developments

If anything, the controversy over the right of certain workers' and employers' delegates to be seated sharpened after the McNair Committee submitted its fact-finding report. At the 1956 ILO conference, the employers' group proposed a constitutional amendment requiring all employers' and workers' delegates to the ILO to be designated by organizations independent of their governments. The government and workers' groups opposed the move. An Italian government delegate, Roberto Ago, noted that a good third of the ILO member states could not appoint workers' and employers' delegates if the proposed amendment were strictly enforced. The proposed amendment

was rejected by the Governing Body in November 1956 by a vote of 29 to 11.

The Hungarian uprising of 1956 had sharp repercussions in the ILO, which were reflected in the credentials dispute. The Governing Body expressed solidarity with the Hungarian workers "who were struggling to secure their fundamental rights," and the 1957 conference rejected the credentials of the employers' and workers' delegates appointed by the Kádár government, which had, in effect, restored the Hungarian *status quo ante*. In 1958 and 1959, the ILO conference took the unprecedented step of rejecting the credentials not only of the Hungarian workers' and employers' delegates, but of the Hungarian government delegates as well.

In the meantime, various attempts were made to find a general solution to the problem that would satisfy all concerned, including the Western employers' delegates. Involved in the problem was the fact that, under the conference rules, the government, the employers', and the workers' group could refuse to seat delegates whose credentials it did not accept. In 1959, acting on a plan proposed by a tripartite committee headed by Roberto Ago of Italy, the ILO established a five-man Appeals Board composed of persons of "internationally recognized independence and impartiality" to rule on such matters. However, when the Appeals Board decided at the 1959 conference to seat the employers' delegates from the Soviet bloc countries on certain technical committees, the chairman of the employers' group, Pierre Waline of France, announced "on behalf of the free employers of the Conference" that he and his colleagues could no longer take part in the work of those committees. Later, the free employers' group resumed participation in these technical committees under protest.

In the past few years, an uneasy truce has been observed over the seating of workers' and employers' representatives from Eastern Europe. Their credentials are usually challenged by one or more of the Western groups, but increasingly these challenges are becoming a kind of opening-day formality, for it is becoming clear that if the ILO is to operate as a world organization, it cannot bar representatives from states with centrally directed economies. In a sense, the truce was broken at the 1966 session of the International Labor Conference, when the workers' group from the US staged an informal boycott of the proceedings to protest the election of a representative of a Communist country, Leon Chajn of Poland, as president of the conference. The boycott was not official, however, and ended before the conclusion of the conference.

6 BUDGET

ILO's activities are financed by a budget determined on a biennial basis for the first time for the 1970–1971 period, changed from an annual basis theretofore. The budget is fixed by the International Labor Conference and raised from the governments of member states according to a scale of contributions approved by the conference.

For 1971 the scale ranges from 0.08% for a number of smaller countries to 10.45% for the USSR and 25% for the US. For the 1970–71 biennium the conference voted a budget of approximately $61.5 million.

In addition, the ILO receives for its technical assistance programs a share of the funds raised from voluntary government contributions to the United Nations Development Program. ILO's share of these funds came to over $20 million in 1969.

7 ACTIVITIES

A. INTERNATIONAL LABOR CODE

One of the principal achievements of the ILO in its first 50 years of existence has been the formulation of an extensive international labor code through the drafting and adoption of various standard-setting conventions and recommendations. The first international convention adopted was the 1919 Hours of Work Convention establishing the eight-hour day and the six-day week in industry. By the end of 1969, the various sessions of the International Labor Conference had built up the edifice of the international labor code through the adoption of 130 conventions and 134 recommendations, covering such questions as the following:

Employment and unemployment: employment services, national development programs, provisions for unemployment.

Various aspects of conditions of work: wages, hours, weekly rest periods, annual holidays with pay, and allied topics.

Employment of children and young persons: minimum age of admission to employment, medical examination for fitness for employment, vocational training and apprenticeship, and night work.

Employment of women: maternity protection, night work, and employment in unhealthy work.

Industrial health, safety, and welfare.

Social security.

Industrial (i.e., management-labor) relations.

Labor inspection.

Social policy in nonmetropolitan areas and concerning indigenous and tribal populations.

Protection of migrants.

Trade unionism and collective bargaining.

INTERNATIONAL LABOR CONVENTIONS ADOPTED BY THE ILO AND NUMBER OF MEMBER STATES TO RATIFY EACH, I JANUARY 1970

CONVENTION	RATIFICATIONS
1. Hours of Work, Industry, 1919	32
2. Unemployment, 1919	46
3. Maternity Protection, 1919	26
4. Night Work, Women, 1919	56
5. Minimum Age, Industry, 1919	60
6. Night Work of Young People, Industry, 1919	51
7. Minimum Age, Sea, 1920	41
8. Unemployment Indemnity, Shipwreck, 1920	39
9. Placing of Seamen, 1920	28
10. Minimum Age, Agriculture, 1921	39
11. Right of Association, Agriculture, 1921	87
12. Workmen's Compensation, Agriculture, 1921	53
13. White Lead, Painting, 1921	48
14. Weekly Rest, Industry, 1921	77
15. Minimum Age, Trimmers and Stokers, 1921	58
16. Medical Examination of Young Persons, Sea, 1921	56
17. Workmen's Compensation, Accident, 1925	52
18. Workmen's Compensation, Occupational Diseases, 1925	52
19. Equality of Treatment, Accident Compensation, 1925	85
20. Night Work, Bakeries, 1925	14
21. Inspection of Emigrants, 1926	29
22. Seamen's Articles of Agreement, 1926	41
23. Repatriation of Seamen, 1926	25
24. Sickness Insurance, Industry, 1927	22
25. Sickness Insurance, Agriculture, 1927	17
26. Minimum Wage-Fixing Machinery, 1928	77
27. Marking of Weight, Packages Transported by Vessels, 1929	45
28. Protection Against Accidents, Dockers, 1929	4
29. Forced Labor, 1930	105
30. Hours of Work, Commerce and Offices, 1930	22
*31. Hours of Work, Coal Mines, 1931	2
32. Protection Against Accidents, Dockers, Revised, 1932	31
33. Minimum Age, Nonindustrial Employment, 1932	23
34. Fee-Charging Employment Agencies, 1933	10
35. Old-Age Insurance, Industry, etc., 1933	11
36. Old-Age Insurance, Agriculture, 1933	10
37. Invalidity Insurance, Industry, etc., 1933	9
38. Invalidity Insurance, Agriculture, 1933	8
39. Survivors' Insurance, Industry, etc., 1933	7
40. Survivors' Insurance, Agriculture, 1933	6
41. Night Work, Women, Revised, 1934	36
42. Workmen's Compensation, Occupational Diseases, Revised, 1934	45
43. Sheet-Glass Works, 1934	9
44. Unemployment Provision, 1934	13
45. Underground Work, Women, 1935	74
*46. Hours of Work, Mines, Revised, 1935	2
47. Forty-Hour Week, 1935	4
48. Maintenance of Migrants, Pension Rights, 1935	8
49. Reduction of Hours of Work, Glass-Bottle Works, 1935	7
50. Recruiting of Indigenous Workers, 1936	26
*51. Reduction of Hours of Work, Public Works, 1936	0
52. Holidays with Pay, 1936	45
53. Officers' Competency Certificates, 1936	21
*54. Holidays with Pay, Sea, 1936	6
55. Shipowners' Liability, Sick and Injured Seamen, 1936	10
56. Sickness Insurance, Sea, 1936	9
*57. Hours of Work and Manning, Sea, 1936	5
58. Minimum Age, Sea, Revised, 1936	42
59. Minimum Age, Industry, Revised, 1937	22
60. Minimum Age, Nonindustrial Employment, Revised, 1937	10
*61. Reduction of Hours of Work, Textiles, 1937	0
62. Safety Provisions, Building, 1937	23
63. Statistics of Hours and Wages, 1938	30
64. Contracts of Employment, Indigenous Workers, 1939	23
65. Penal Sanctions, Indigenous Workers, 1939	26
*66. Migration for Employment, 1939	0
67. Hours of Work and Rest Periods, Road Transport, 1939	4
68. Food and Catering, Ships' Crews, 1946	14
69. Certification of Ships' Cooks, 1946	17
*70. Social Security, Seafarers, 1946	6
71. Seafarers' Pensions, 1946	8
*72. Paid Vacations, Seafarers, 1946	5
73. Medical Examination, Seafarers, 1946	19
74. Certification of Able Seamen, 1946	16
*75. Accommodation of Crews, 1946	5
*76. Wages, Hours of Work, and Manning, Sea, 1946	1
77. Medical Examination of Young Persons, Industry, 1946	21
78. Medical Examination of Young Persons, Nonindustrial Occupations, 1946	21
79. Night Work of Young Persons, Nonindustrial Occupations, 1946	15
80. Final Articles, Revision, 1946	50
81. Labor Inspection, 1947	72
82. Social Policy, Non-Metropolitan Territories, 1947	4
*83. Labor Standards, Non-Metropolitan Territories, 1947	1
84. Right of Association, Non-Metropolitan Territories, 1947	4
85. Labor Inspectorates, Non-Metropolitan Territories, 1947	4
86. Contracts of Employment, Indigenous Workers, 1947	16
87. Freedom of Association and Protection of Right to Organize, 1948	77
88. Employment Service, 1948	51
89. Night Work, Women, Revised, 1948	48
90. Night Work of Young Persons, Industry, Revised, 1948	32
91. Paid Vacations, Seafarers, Revised, 1949	15
92. Accommodations of Crews, Revised, 1949	18
*93. Wages, Hours of Work, and Manning, Sea, Revised, 1949	5
94. Labor Clauses, Public Contracts, 1949	43
95. Protection of Wages, 1949	64
96. Fee-Charging Employment Agencies, Revised, 1949	28
97. Migration for Employment, Revised, 1949	30
98. Right to Organize and Collective Bargaining, 1949	90
99. Minimum Wage-Fixing Machinery, Agriculture, 1951	34
100. Equal Remuneration, 1951	69
101. Holidays with Pay, Agriculture, 1952	35
102. Social Security, Minimum Standards, 1952	20
103. Maternity Protection, Revised, 1952	13
104. Abolition of Penal Sanctions, Indigenous Workers, 1955	22
105. Abolition of Forced Labor, 1957	88
106. Weekly Rest, Commerce and Offices, 1957	30
107. Indigenous and Tribal Populations, 1957	23

108. Seafarers' Identity Documents, 1958   20
*109. Wages, Hours of Work, and Manning, Sea, Revised, 1958   7
110. Plantations, 1958   8
111. Discrimination, Employment and Occupation, 1958   71
112. Minimum Age, Fishermen, 1959   24
113. Medical Examination, Fishermen, 1959   15
114. Fishermen's Articles of Agreement, 1959   15
115. Radiation Protection, 1960   23
116. Final Articles Revision, 1961   59
117. Basic Aims and Standards of Social Policy, 1962   19
118. Equality of Treatment, Social Security, 1962   21
119. Guarding of Machinery, 1963   23
120. Hygiene, Commerce and Offices, 1964   24
121. Employment Injury Benefits, 1964   8
122. Employment Policy, 1964   29
123. Minimum Age, Underground Work, 1965   21
124. Medical Examination of Young Persons, Underground Work, 1965   18
125. Fishermen's Certificates of Competency, 1966   4
126. Accommodation on Board Fishing Vessels, 1966   5
127. Maximum Weight   4
128. Invalidity, Old-Age and Survivors' Benefits   5
*129. Labor Inspection (Agriculture)   0
*130. Medical Care and Sickness Benefits   0

*Convention that on 1 January 1970 had not yet received the number of ratifications required to bring it into force.

At first, the effort to build up minimum labor and social standards that would be internationally valid was considered by many as utopian. In these fields, international action used to be virtually unknown. But the freely accepted conventions and recommendations and the ILO machinery of mutual supervision have helped to improve working conditions and management-labor relations, to protect the fundamental rights of labor, to promote social security, and to lessen the frequency and intensity of labor conflicts. The 1969 International Labor Conference, which marked the ILO's 50th anniversary, showed that the organization continues to enjoy overwhelming support. President Nixon and Premier Kosygin were among the 21 chiefs of state or prime ministers who sent congratulatory messages. Some 130 cabinet level and subcabinet level officials were present at the conference.

The international labor code is continually being revised and extended, not only to broaden its scope but to keep pace with advancing concepts of social and economic welfare. In 1960, for example, the conference adopted a convention and a recommendation on the protection of workers against ionizing radiations. These instruments, in essence, provide for the establishment of maximum permissible doses and amounts of radioactive substances that can be taken into the body. Appropriate radiation levels are to be fixed for workers over 16 years of age. Under these international instruments, workers under 16 years of age are prohibited from doing work that involves direct contact with ionizing radiations.

In pursuit of ILO efforts to help extend the scope of social security coverage throughout the world and eliminate discrimination based upon nationality, the 1962 conference adopted a convention on the equal treatment of nationals and non-nationals in social security. Under this convention, a ratifying country shall give to nationals of other ratifying countries, within its territory, equal treatment with its own nationals under its social security legislation.

Countries may accept the obligations of the convention in any or all of the following types of social security: medical care; sickness benefits; maternity benefits; unemployment benefits; and family allowances. The instrument states that equal treatment with respect to benefits shall be accorded without any condition of residence. The convention applies to migrant workers, refugees, and stateless persons.

B. OBLIGATION OF MEMBER GOVERNMENTS AFTER ADOPTION OF INTERNATIONAL LABOR STANDARDS

The ILO, it should be borne in mind, is not a world lawgiver. The International Labor Conference cannot pass legislation that by itself is binding on any country. However, ingenious arrangements have been written in the ILO constitution to make sure that conventions and recommendations adopted by the International Labor Conference are not regarded as mere pious pronouncements.

Member governments must report back to the ILO the measures taken to bring the ILO convention or recommendation before their competent legislative authorities and the decisions made by the latter.

Supervision of Application of Ratified Conventions

Once a convention has been ratified and has come into force, every country that has ratified it is obligated to take all necessary measures to make its provisions effective.

By ratifying a convention, a country automatically agrees to report every year to the International Labor Office on how the convention is being applied in its territory. These reports are much more than a formality. For each convention, the Governing Body formulates a number of questions. They always include requests for information on the results of labor inspection, relevant court decisions, and statistics on the number of persons covered. Copies of each annual report prepared by a government are to be sent to the country's most representative employers' and workers' organizations, and the report as finally submitted to the ILO has to state whether the government has received any comments from them on the practical implementation of the convention in question.

These annual reports on the application of ratified conventions are first considered by a committee of independent experts and then by an employer-worker-government committee, which in turn reports to the full International Labor Conference. The object of this whole system of supervision is to enable the conference to determine what progress has been made from one year to the next by various countries in implementing the standards set forth in the conventions. On the basis of the intelligence it receives, the conference may, if it feels this to be necessary, make "observations" to governments, that is, suggest to them ways in which they may overcome discrepancies between the provisions of the conventions they have ratified and existing laws or practices.

How well does this system work? A study carried out in 1954 covered some 600 ratifications of a total of 22 conventions. In 71% of the instances, legislation conformed to the conventions ratified. In 29% of the instances, shortcomings had been found and had been brought to the attention of the governments concerned. In the latter case, the ILO's suggestions had been heeded in 13% of the instances; in 10% they had not yet been heeded, and in the remaining 6% the subsequent information had been inconclusive.

The effectiveness of this supervisory machinery depends naturally on the cooperation of member governments in submitting their annual reports. On the whole, an increasing percentage of governments have been living up to their obligations in this respect. If required reports are not forthcoming or if the reports submitted by certain countries are not really informative, the ILO supervisory committees express their dissatisfaction in polite but quite unmistakable terms. These criticisms are included in the printed reports of the committees and may occasion debates in the conference itself, thus giving the matter further publicity.

The ILO constitution provides two other procedures that may be followed to induce governments to carry out the provisions of conventions they have ratified. First, workers' or employers' organizations may make representations to the International Labor Office if they believe that any government, even their own, has failed to live up to a convention it has ratified. If the government concerned fails to provide a satisfactory answer to the allegation, the Governing Body may decide to publish the allegation, and, if one has been submitted, the government reply. Second, any ILO member government may file a complaint against any other member for alleged noncompliance with a ratified convention. The ILO constitution provides that in this event a commission of inquiry shall examine the matter, report on its findings, and recommend such remedial steps as it thinks proper. The fact that the ILO constitution provides for specific machinery to take up such complaints itself has contributed to the observance of ratified international labor conventions on the part of member governments.

Reports on Recommendations and Unratified Conventions

Recommendations adopted by the International Labor Conference, unlike the conventions it adopts, are not international treaties and are not subject to ratification. Hence these recommendations can never be binding on a member government in the sense that the provisions of a ratified convention are binding. Nevertheless, the recommendations constitute an important part of the International Labor Code; and since 1948 the Governing Body of the ILO has had the right periodically to ask member governments to what extent they have given or intend to give effect to conventions not ratified and to recommendations. In such case, the governments also have to state the reasons that have so far prevented or delayed the ratification of conventions and the modification of national law and practices according to recommendations.

Ratifications

By January 1970, the number of individual ratifications had passed the 3,500 mark, as shown in the accompanying table. A decade earlier, only about 1,900 had been effected. The geographical areas of states filing ratifications are widespread.

NUMBER OF INTERNATIONAL LABOR CONVENTIONS RATIFIED BY ILO MEMBER STATES, 1 JANUARY 1970

Afghanistan	10	Chad	19
Albania	17	Chile	37
Algeria	48	China (Taiwan)	35
Argentina	57	Colombia	41
Australia	28	Congo (Brazzaville)	13
Austria	37	Congo (Kinshasa)	27
Barbados	25	Costa Rica	25
Belgium	70	Cuba	65
Bolivia	9	Cyprus	28
Brazil	51	Czechoslovakia	44
Bulgaria	77	Dahomey	17
Burma	21	Denmark	35
Burundi	17	Dominican Republic	24
Byelorussia	26	Ecuador	31
Cambodia	4	El Salvador	4
Cameroon	10	Ethiopia	8
Eastern Cameroon	6	Finland	47
Western Cameroon	8	France	80
Canada	24	Gabon	27
Central African Republic	35	Germany, West	40
Ceylon	20	Ghana	36
Greece	36	Norway	64
Guatemala	37	Pakistan	30
Guinea	39	Panama	15
Guyana	25	Paraguay	33
Haiti	21	Peru	59
Honduras	16	Philippines	18
Hungary	39	Poland	59
Iceland	12	Portugal	29
India	30	Romania	23
Indonesia	7	Rwanda	15
Iran	6	Senegal	33
Iraq	33	Sierra Leone	32
Ireland	46	Singapore	21
Israel	35	Somali Republic	4
Italy	67	Former Trust Territory of Somaliland	6
Ivory Coast	25	Former British Somaliland	4
Jamaica	20	South Africa	12
Japan	26	Southern Yemen	13
Jordan	14	Spain	55
Kenya	27	Sudan	5
Kuwait	13	Sweden	48
Laos	4	Switzerland	31
Lebanon	7	Syria	38
Lesotho	11	Tanzania	18
Liberia	14	Tanganyika	6
Libya	11	Zanzibar	4
Luxembourg	50	Thailand	11
Malagasy Republic	26	Togo	12
Malawi	28	Trinidad and Tobago	10
Malaysia	8	Tunisia	38
States of Malaya	5	Turkey	21
States of Sabah	5	Uganda	20
State of Sarawak	9	Ukraine	27
Mali	21	USSR	40
Malta	27	UAR (Egypt)	34
Mauritania	36	UK	65
Mauritius	31	US	7
Mexico	51	Upper Volta	23
Mongolia	6	Uruguay	58
Morocco	30	Venezuela	24
Nepal	0	Viet-Nam, South	15
Netherlands	66	Yemen Arab Republic	2
New Zealand	45	Yugoslavia	53
Nicaragua	35	Zambia	19
Niger	23		
Nigeria	24		

The ILO attaches great importance to application of conventions in the nonmetropolitan territories of member states that have ratified them. To extend the application of a ratified convention to such an area, a country need make only a declaration to that effect. In mid-1970, 1,119 declarations were in effect, a figure lower than in previous years because countries which become independent and join the ILO agree to continue to apply ratified conventions previously in force in their territory, so that the declarations are transformed into ratifications.

The relative number of ratifications a given convention has received is not, in itself, an accurate measure of its acceptance or impact. The fact that a convention has not been ratified by a particular country does not necessarily mean that the country in question has not met the standards prescribed in the convention. The UK, for example, advised the ILO that it did not intend to propose parliamentary ratification of the convention requiring a minimum 24-hour weekly rest period for commercial and office workers. It explained that such workers in the UK were already assured a rest period of at least that length through established custom, and that it was not the policy of the government to intervene in matters that had already been satisfactorily settled by the parties concerned themselves. New Zealand, which in many ways has pioneered in labor legislation, waited until 1938 to ratify the eight-hour-day, six-day-week convention of 1919. On the same day, New Zealand also ratified the more restrictive 40-hour-week convention of 1935 and, in fact, remained for 18 years the only country ratifying it. Ratifications may be withheld for various reasons by a country for a number of years, after which a number of ratifications may be approved at once. Thus, in 1962 alone Peru ratified 31 different International Labor Conventions.

Very often countries do not ratify conventions on subjects that they feel do not concern them. The various maritime conventions, for example, are primarily of interest to nations with sizable merchant marine fleets. Occasionally, however, countries as a matter of principle ratify conventions on conditions quite alien to them. Thus, Switzerland ratified the 1957 Convention on the Abolition of Forced Labor on the recommendation of the Swiss Federal Council, which called for the convention's ratification because of its great humanitarian significance, although "forced labor in any of the forms mentioned in the Convention has never existed in Switzerland."

For a growing number of workers in an increasing number of countries, wages, working conditions, vacations, and so-called fringe benefits are being determined, not through government legislation, but through collective bargaining. The international standards embodied in the ILO's conventions, even though they may not show on the statute book, frequently serve as guides for labor-management agreements. The widening impact of ILO standards owes much to the various arrangements that have been worked out to make the provisions of the International Labor Code more widely known to employers' and workers' organizations.

The significance of the sharply increased rate at which governments have been ratifying ILO conventions in recent years remains, however, very great. Ratification, particularly in the case of a newly developing country, regularly signifies a definite step forward.

C. THE ILO AS PROMOTER OF HUMAN RIGHTS

Freedom of Association

World War II stimulated the growth of trade unions and increased their responsibilities. In many countries labor was recognized as an equal partner in the effort that won the war. Nevertheless, in various parts of the world the position of unions was far from secure, and in many countries such a basic freedom as the worker's right to join a union of his choice was respected neither in law nor in practice.

In 1948 the International Labor Conference adopted a Convention on Freedom of Association and the Right to Organize, and in 1949 it adopted a Convention on the Right to Organize and Collective Bargaining. These conventions stipulate that all workers and employers shall possess the right to establish and join organizations of their own choosing without having to obtain government authorization. Such organizations shall have the right to function freely and without interference from the public authorities; they may be dissolved or suspended only by normal judicial procedure and never by administrative authority. Workers must be protected against discrimination on the grounds of union membership or activities; thus a worker may not be discharged because he joins or is active in a union. Employers and workers must not interfere in the establishment or operation of one another's organizations, a provision that outlaws such devices as employer-dominated unions.

By 1 January 1970, the first of the two conventions had been ratified by 77 countries and the second by 90. Ratifications,

the Director-General has noted, "have come from countries in all stages of development."

The ILO has been particularly concerned with safeguarding the rights enumerated in these two conventions. It has made full use of its regular procedure to ascertain whether all member states have presented the conventions to the appropriate domestic authorities for ratification and to supervise the implementation of the conventions by states that have ratified them. In addition, the International Labor Conference has conducted four special reviews, in 1953, 1956, 1957, and 1959, concerning the extent to which member states, whether bound by the conventions or not, have given effect to their provisions. In 1969 a special review was made, in connection with the 50th anniversary of the ILO, of the problems and prospects of ratification of 17 key conventions, including these two conventions. Special machinery has been set up to deal with complaints that governments had violated trade union rights: a committee of the Governing Body, known as the Committee on Freedom of Association, composed of government, employer, and worker representatives; and a quasi-judicial Fact-Finding and Conciliation Commission, composed of ten independent persons serving as individuals. The Fact-Finding and Conciliation Commission is authorized to make on-the-scene investigations, but it cannot consider a case unless the government concerned gives its consent. Japan in 1964 was the first to do so; Greece was the second, in 1965. The government-employer-worker Committee on Freedom of Association, however, not being a semijudicial body, may consider complaints whether or not the government concerned gives its consent. Between 1951 and 1969, 612 cases were submitted to the committee, which issued definitive conclusions on 391 of them. The committee considers the full merits of each accusation and where it finds remedial measures appropriate recommends them. As former French Premier Ramadier stated during one of the frequent discussions of these matters in the Governing Body, the Committee on Freedom of Association has induced several governments to revise their trade union legislation and in other very delicate cases has obtained "the liberation of considerable numbers of arrested trade unionists."

Feeling that fuller factual information was needed about conditions in various countries affecting freedom of association, the ILO Governing Body decided in 1958 to inaugurate a worldwide survey to be carried out through on-the-spot studies. The first country to invite such a survey was the US, the second was the USSR. In the spring of 1959, an ILO survey mission visited the US. It traveled to various parts of the country and carried on discussions with government officials, employers, trade unionists, and others. In the fall of 1959, the mission visited the USSR. At the invitation of the governments of Sweden, the UK, Burma, and Malaya, surveys on freedom of association in those countries were made in 1960 and 1961.

Forced Labor

Before World War II, ILO's efforts in this field, including the 1930 Convention on Forced Labor and the 1936 Convention on Recruiting of Indigenous Workers, were directed primarily toward stamping out abuses in nonself-governing territories. A convention adopted in 1939 prescribed that contracts for the employment of indigenous labor must always be made in writing, and an accompanying recommendation called for regulation of the maximum period of time for which a native worker could bind himself under contract. Another convention adopted in 1939 required all penal sanctions exacted against indigenous labor for breach of contract to be progressively abolished "as soon as possible"; when applicable to juvenile workers these sanctions were to be abolished immediately.

Since the war, emphasis has shifted from protection against exploitation in colonial areas to the abolition of systems of forced labor wherever they may occur, as part of the promotion of human rights.

The first step in this broader attack was an impartial inquiry into the nature and extent of forced labor, including prison labor, gang labor, labor service, and the like. A joint UN-ILO committee studied the existence in the world of systems of forced or "corrective" labor as means of political coercion or as punishment for political views. In 1953, the committee reported that it had found two principal forms of forced labor existing in fully self-governing countries: one used mainly as a means of political coercion or political punishment, the other used mainly for economic reasons.

In 1957, the International Labor Conference, by a vote of 240 to 0, with one abstention, adopted the Abolition of Forced Labor Convention. The convention outlaws any form of forced or compulsory labor (a) as a means of political coercion or education or as punishment for political or ideological views, (b) as a means of obtaining labor for economic development, (c) as a means of labor discipline, (d) as punishment for participation in strikes, or (e) as a means of racial, social, national, or religious discrimination. The convention, one of the farthest-reaching adopted by the ILO, has been in force since 17 January 1959 and had been ratified by 88 states by 1 January 1970. At its 1965 session, the International Labor Conference adopted a "Resolution condemning the Government of Portugal on the grounds of the forced labor policy practiced by the said Government in territories under its administration," and requested the Portuguese Government to give effect without delay to the recommendations of the Commission of Inquiry in all territories under Portuguese administration.

Also in 1961, Portugal filed a complaint concerning Liberia's observance of the Forced Labor Convention (1930). The Commission of Inquiry appointed to examine the case based its report largely on hearings held in Geneva and on a careful examination of all pertinent Liberian legislation. Its report noted that Liberian laws had been inconsistent with the provisions of the Convention, which Liberia had ratified in 1931. But in February and May 1962, radical changes were made in the relevant legislation, eliminating all major discrepancies between the laws of Liberia and the requirements of the Convention. The Commission recommended that the remaining anomalies be removed during the 1963/64 legislative session. The governments of both Liberia and Portugal accepted the recommendations contained in the Commission's report in March 1963.

Later, Portugal filed a complaint concerning Liberia's observance of the Forced Labor Convention (1930).

In 1962 the ILO again conducted a world survey of forced labor and concluded that it "continued to exist in a number of countries."

Discrimination in Employment and Occupation

The Convention on Discrimination in Employment and Occupation, adopted by the International Labor Conference in 1958, constitutes another effort to promote the principle of equal rights. The convention defines such discrimination as any distinction, exclusion, or preference based on race, color, sex, religion, political opinion, national extraction, or social origin that impairs equal access to vocational training, equal access to employment and to certain occupations, or equal terms and conditions of employment. Measures affecting a person justifiably suspected of being engaged in activities prejudicial to the security of the state are not to be deemed discrimination, provided such a person is guaranteed the right of appeal. Furthermore, special measures of protection or assistance

required because of sex, age, disablement, family responsibility, or social or cultural status are not to be considered discriminatory, but workers' and employers' organizations must in certain cases be consulted on such measures.

Every state ratifying the convention thereby undertakes to declare and pursue a national policy designed to promote, by methods appropriate to national conditions and practice, equality of opportunity and treatment in respect of employment and occupation, with a view to eliminating any discrimination in this respect. This is to be done through cooperation with employers' and workers' organizations, through legislation, and through educational programs. Ratifying states also agree to pursue nondiscriminatory public employment policies and to ensure the observance of such policies by public vocational guidance, training, and placement services. By 1 January 1970, the convention had been ratified by 71 states.

A worldwide survey of the effect given to the Discrimination Convention was made by the ILO in 1963. Commenting on the broad degree of acceptance by member states of the 1958 convention, the survey report concluded that in the majority of countries the principle of equality is today a fundamental element of public law. But it was recognized that equality before the law was not enough, and that the convention required the application of a positive policy to promote equal opportunity and treatment for all social groups, not only in law but also in practice. Particular emphasis was placed on the need to guarantee to all categories of persons the means of obtaining the vocational education and training that open the way to all levels of employment.

D. MARITIME QUESTIONS: THE MERCHANT MARINE

The problems of merchant sailors differ in many respects from those of other workers. When plans for an international labor organization were being worked out in 1919, the world's seamen's organizations urged the creation of a separate "permanent general conference for the international regulation of maritime labor" and of a separate "supervisory office for maritime labor." Although it was eventually decided to include maritime questions as falling within the purview of ILO, special ILO machinery was established to deal with them, including special maritime sessions of the International Labor Conference and a Joint Maritime Commission.

Maritime sessions of the International Labor Conference are periodic full-scale sessions of the conference devoted exclusively to maritime questions. The first such conference was held in 1920 and the seventh, at which 97% of the world's shipping tonnage was represented, in 1958. By 1 January 1970, 29 conventions and 16 recommendations concerning seafarers had been adopted by international labor conferences pertaining to conditions of employment, health and safety, welfare, and social security. Together, these conventions and recommendations form the International Seafarer's Code which is binding on all subscribing countries.

The Joint Maritime Commission keeps questions regarding the merchant marine under review on a year-to-year basis. Since it began its work in 1920, the commission has been enlarged several times, mainly to provide wider geographical representation. It now consists of 33 persons: the chairman of the commission, 15 shipowners' representatives, and 15 seafarers' representatives, selected respectively by the shipowners' and seafarers' groups of the last maritime session of the conference, plus one representative each of the employers' and the employees' group in the Governing Body. The commission's composition reflects the belief that, wherever possible, agreement should be obtained between employers and employees on a maritime question before it is submitted to government representatives for their consideration.

Conditions of Employment

The first of the ILO's maritime conventions, adopted in 1920 and ratified by 43 countries by 1 January 1970, forbids the employment of children under 14 at sea, except on family-operated vessels. A convention adopted in 1936 and now in force in 40 countries raises the minimum age to 15. A convention adopted in 1926 and by 1 January 1970 ratified by 41 countries prescribes the standard form and content of seamen's articles of agreement or employment contracts, signing procedures, and the conditions under which such contracts may be terminated. A 1926 convention subsequently ratified by 25 countries guarantees that no seaman shall be abandoned in a foreign port and provides that a seaman put ashore through no fault of his own must be repatriated at no expense to himself. A 1920 convention, designed to abolish many abuses and now in force in 28 countries, stipulates that seamen must be hired not through private, fee-charging agencies but through free public employment offices operated either jointly and under public control by shipowners' and seafarers' organizations or, in the absence of such machinery, by the government itself.

Social Security for Seamen and Their Families

The first step toward social insurance for seamen was taken by a 1920 convention, now in force in 39 countries, which requires a shipowner to pay two months' wages to crew members of a lost or foundered vessel. Two conventions of much wider scope were adopted 16 years later. The 1936 Shipowners' Liability Convention ratified by 10 states entitles a sick and injured seaman to medical care and maintenance during a maximum period of 16 weeks. The Sickness Insurance Convention, ratified so far by only 9 countries, gives a sick seaman who is incapable of work and deprived of his wages a cash benefit and, with certain exceptions, medical treatment for at least the first 26 weeks of such incapacity.

The 1946 Social Security (Seafarers) Convention had not by mid-1970 received enough ratifications to enter into force. The Seafarers' Pensions convention had been ratified by eight states by the middle of 1970 and had entered into force. The standards set by these conventions, even when not ratified by many countries, have an influence on collective agreements, national statutes, and regulations.

Hours of Work and Minimum Pay

Of all technical questions concerning the merchant marine, that of the hours of work has had the roughest sailing. The 1919 Hours of Work Convention, establishing the eight-hour day and the six-day week for industry and transport in general, specifically excluded the merchant marine service, which presented a complex problem.

After World War II, with the contribution of the merchant marine to the war effort fresh in mind, the related questions of wages, hours, and manning were taken up together. After heated debate, the 1946 maritime session of the International Labor Conference adopted a convention which, among other things, (a) sets the minimum monthly basic wage for an able seaman at US$64 or £16 sterling (or their equivalent in other currencies), and provides for an adjustment if more than the normal crew is employed on a ship; (b) limits hours of work to eight hours a day for ships trading with distant ports and 112 hours in two consecutive weeks for ships trading with nearby ports; and (c) requires sufficient manning to ensure safety to life at sea and make possible the prescribed limits on normal working hours.

The 1946 convention on maritime wages, hours, and manning was adopted only after 26 years of efforts to establish such international standards. It was revised in certain respects in 1949. Bringing the convention as adopted into actual force has proved another serious problem. Because of fear of unequal competition if a large part of the world's shipping were to remain outside the convention's reach when it came into force, stringent conditions were laid down: the convention was to enter into force 6 months after ratification by 9 or more countries having among them an aggregate merchant marine of at least 15 million tons and including among them at least 5 countries, each with 1 million tons or more of merchant shipping. Since by 1958 there seemed to be no chance of these conditions being fulfilled in the foreseeable future, the maritime conference of that year further revised the convention to permit ratifying states to exclude the provisions on wages from their ratification. Most of the shipowners' delegates opposed the convention even as so modified or abstained from voting on it. By 1 January 1970 only five states—Australia, Brazil, Cuba, the Philippines, and Uruguay—had ratified the 1949 convention, and six states—France, Guatemala, Mexico, Norway, Sweden, and Yugoslavia—had ratified it under the eased conditions approved in 1958. Despite the formidable hurdle still to be surmounted before the convention can come into force, its effects have not been negligible. Shipowners, union leaders, and government spokesmen agree that the convention, like those pertaining to maritime social security, has had a marked influence on labor contracts reached through collective bargaining in all countries.

A convention adopted in 1946 providing for a minimum annual paid holiday of 18 working days for ships' masters and officers and 12 working days for other crew members ran into comparable ratification trouble. However, a 1949 amendment making pay during such holidays optional rather than obligatory has come into force by receiving the requisite ratifications.

E. TECHNICAL SERVICES: EXPERT ASSISTANCE AND EDUCATION

ILO's activities are not limited to drawing up international standards in the field of labor and social policy, encouraging their adoption, and supervising their application by countries subscribing to them. ILO provides expert assistance and advice to help countries translate these standards into reality; and, to make better wages, hours, and working conditions economically feasible, it provides international assistance to increase workers' skills in order to raise the level of industrial productivity.

Between 1950 and 1969, for example, over 120 countries and territories received such ILO assistance; more than 2,900 experts recruited from almost 90 countries were sent on some 5,000 technical assistance missions; over 3,000 worker-trainees were sent abroad, and over 5,000 served training periods and attended ILO seminars.

These operational activities of ILO, as distinguished from that part of its work that is carried out around conference tables, have multiplied since the inception of the UN's Expanded Program of Technical Assistance in 1950 and the UN Special Fund in 1959—the two assistance programs that were merged in 1966 to form the UN Development Program. ILO's share of the technical assistance funds allocated under these programs grew from $300,000 in 1950/51 to $20.4 million in 1969. Some of these UN development programs are very large projects, which require a number of years to execute, and in 1969 the total value of UN development programs being executed by the ILO came to approximately $110 million. Today technical assistance and other operational activities account for well over half the agency's work. The major fields of ILO operational activity are: manpower organization, including vocational training; productivity and management development; cooperation, small-scale industries, and handicrafts; social security; and labor conditions and administration. ILO's technical assistance activities have taken many forms and have been carried out in almost every part of the world.

Productivity

Poverty goes hand in hand with low productivity. Increased productivity, which may be roughly defined as greater output per man-hour worked through the more efficient use of human and technological resources, is the key to higher living standards. When the UN decided to make technical assistance one of the main concerns of its family of organizations, it stated that the object of the entire program was to increase the productivity of material and human resources, to obtain a wide and equitable distribution of the benefits of such increased productivity, and thereby to raise the standard of living of the people in all countries.

The first step in a typical ILO-assisted project to increase productivity is to enlist the interest and cooperation of employers, workers, and all others concerned in advanced concepts of management. The ILO stresses the fact that systematic fact-finding and scientific analysis of production methods must replace haphazard planning and partisan argument if output is to be improved and accelerated. It also urges all parties concerned to accept the proposition that efficient operations depend on good working conditions and properly enforced safety procedures. As government interest in encouraging higher productivity has increased, ILO has assisted in setting up and operating many productivity institutes and pilot projects.

ILO experts sent to India on a productivity mission in 1952–54 gave more than 100 lectures and carried out extensive practical demonstrations in mills and factories. The *Indian Labor Gazette* reported in November 1955 that the activities of the mission contributed to a sharp rise in productivity in many plants. A National Productivity Center was established in India with ILO assistance. Advice given by the center to a typewriter factory and to the workshops that service several thousand buses for the state of Bombay led to an eightfold to twelvefold increase in output for certain operations without any plant increase. In 1957, the Indian government established a National Productivity Council composed of government, employers', and workers' representatives with ILO organizational and technical assistance.

By the end of 1957, the Israel Productivity Institute, established with ILO assistance in 1951, had trained more than 6,000 persons, among them some 600 workers' representatives. Its staff included at various times one to four ILO specialists. The institute has trained personnel of virtually all the country's sizable public or private enterprises, including the cooperative farms (*kibbutzim*). Citrus fruit is Israel's principal export, and the institute's work that led to the organization of the citrus industry may have been essential in enabling it to survive its foreign competition: its productivity more than doubled, and as early as 1952–53 workers' earnings had risen by 20% to 40%.

Results out of all proportion to the relatively small amount of international assistance involved have been achieved by the ILO-aided Egyptian Productivity and Vocational Training Center, founded in 1955. In the center's first year of operation some 300 higher-echelon management personnel attended courses in industrial engineering and management and a much larger number of middle-echelon management personnel attended special ten-week courses. To cite one example of the results of the center's work: a silk weaving plant at Helwan, the Société pour tissage de la soie, within 8 months increased its labor productivity by 208% and increased production by 23% to 40% while cutting its labor force in various sections of the mill by one-fourth to a half. When the Egyptian government established a ministry of labor with a separate department of productivity and vocational training, the ILO productivity mission to Egypt was attached to that department. The ILO mission concentrated on training the technical staff of the new department in production and quality control, management accounting, and related fields. It also assisted in training industrial executives and helped set up permanent productivity units in selected plants.

Good results were achieved by a productivity demonstration mission that paid short visits to Sudan and to several countries in Southeast Asia. The mission's visits had considerable impact and led in the cases of Burma, Indonesia, and Thailand to arrangements for long-term ILO productivity assistance.

Government interest in this phase of ILO's program has been steadily growing. Though ILO's work in this field is carried out mainly among higher echelon personnel, its effects spread downward to influence the working lives of large numbers of people. Among its other activities, ILO publishes a number of practical handbooks on techniques for increasing productivity.

Management Development

As indicated by the illustrations cited above, management training became an increasingly prominent part of the ILO's technical assistance program in the field of productivity as carried out from 1952 through 1969. In 1958, the International Labor Conference decided to set up a special program of technical assistance in management development and training and to give this program a high priority, especially where countries less developed industrially were involved. ILO officials consulted with leading schools of business administration on the management development problems of countries in various stages of economic development. The experience gained by the ILO productivity missions was useful in setting up the new program, which aims to "assist industrialists and managers, including directors and managers of public undertakings, in the less developed countries to acquire or to develop further the insight and the managerial skills which will permit them to make the best possible use of the resources at their disposal for the benefit of their undertakings, the people employed in them, and the community as a whole."

At the beginning of 1970, the ILO had management development projects operating in 54 countries. The Middle East and Asia were the first main regions of operation, but activities now reach around the world. An increasing feature is that a number of management development experts are now being recruited from countries that themselves have been assisted by the ILO in this field.

Manpower Organization and Vocational Training

The basic objective of ILO's work in the field of manpower organization is (a) to give workers the maximum opportunity to find jobs, qualify for promotions, and obtain advancement, and (b) to enable employers to find qualified workers in the numbers they need. ILO may assist a country in assessing its manpower resources and needs, in setting up a national employment service or a network of local employment offices, in establishing facilities for market analysis, employment counseling, occupational testing, job analysis, and the like. Its extensive program of assistance in the field of vocational training complements these activities.

By the end of 1969 improvement of manpower organization, including vocational training, made up over 50% of all ILO technical assistance operations. The ILO considers that as a matter of policy vocational training should be planned on a countrywide level to meet the needs of a given country's employment markets. Training methods should be dynamic and should be adaptable to changing technological and economic conditions. Training programs should take into account not only the requirements of employers, the interests of the economy, and the general level of education prevailing, but also the workers' occupational interests and cultural requirements, which should be made integral parts of the programs.

ILO-assisted vocational training projects emphasize the training of strategic personnel—supervisors, foremen, technicians, instructors—people who, when trained, will train others. When a training institute is fully developed, the ILO experts withdraw, relinquishing all responsibility to the national authorities. The ILO helps set up institutes to train not only industrial workers, but also office workers, handicraftsmen, and agriculturalists. The ILO helps train youth—through apprenticeship programs and in-plant training—and adults, both the employed and unemployed. In 1969 more than 120 training projects were in operation in about 65 countries. ILO may be called on to assist in improving and reorganizing apprenticeship training in various industries of a given country, for example, or in preparing new legislation on the rights and duties of apprentices, or in drafting model apprenticeship working conditions and work contracts.

The ILO is also devoting substantial efforts to vocational training for indigenous and tribal populations, especially in agriculture, handicrafts, and small-scale industries. The largest and most comprehensive effort of this kind is the 16-year-old Andean Indian program, aimed at bringing 8 million Indians living in the isolated Andean highlands of Bolivia, Ecuador, Peru, Chile, Colombia, and Argentina into the mainstream of the modern economic and social life of their countries. Under the program, six international organizations—the United Nations itself, UNICEF, UNESCO, WHO, FAO, and the ILO—under the coordinating leadership of the ILO, are helping these Latin American governments in a simultaneous and coordinated effort to improve all aspects of Indian living conditions. The ILO, in addition to coordinating the entire program, provides experts in vocational training, handicrafts, cooperatives, housing, and resettlement.

Two special centers for advanced training for the developing countries have been established by the ILO:

The International Institute for Labor Studies, inaugurated in Geneva in 1961, serves as an advanced staff college for responsible officials drawn from the public service, management, trade unions, the professions, and universities. The Institute conducts research, sponsors research conferences, and holds study courses on the labor and social problems of economic development.

The International Center for Advanced Technical and Vocational Training opened the doors of its headquarters in Turin, Italy, in 1965. This center provides technical and vocational training more advanced than that which participants from the developing nations could obtain from institutions in their own countries.

The ILO also provides worldwide information on current developments in vocational training through the International Vocational Training Information and Research Center established in 1960.

Among other ILO manpower activities is the program for employment creation and development. For example, two long-term pilot projects for rural employment promotion have been started in India and Western Nigeria, with FAO cooperation.

Twenty countries received help in manpower assessment and planning in 1965. The *International Standard Classification of Occupations,* published in 1958, and which has proved to be an essential analytical tool in manpower assessment, was revised and updated in 1968 in preparation for use in the 1970 population censuses.

A growing trend in 1969 was the marked increase in the number of countries receiving expert assistance in introducing aptitude testing and other selection techniques, primarily for the purpose of choosing trainees for large-scale vocational training programs. Vocational rehabilitation projects also continued on the upswing in 1969.

Cooperatives, Small Industries, and Handicrafts

ILO has furnished direct assistance in organizing new cooperatives, in reorganizing existing ones along more efficient lines, and in improving government services in cooperatives. It also provides advice on management and personnel training. A number of publications on cooperatives are put out by ILO: in 1958 the 11th edition of its *International Directory of Cooperative Organizations* was published, and a reference list of films dealing with cooperatives had been prepared. A booklet, *Cooperative Information,* continues to be published and widely distributed.

The following are a few of the aspects of this field. In 1965, two teams of experts gave technical assistance in cooperative training in Madagascar and the Philippines; experts on cooperative marketing helped in Burma and Ceylon, experts on cooperative distribution and retailing in Nigeria and Tanzania. In the Ivory Coast, Sa'udi Arabia, Tunisia, and the Latin American region, experts provided advice on general cooperative organization and development. As part of its continuing program of meetings on cooperatives, the ILO, in association with the government of Denmark and the FAO, sponsors an annual seminar on cooperatives.

ILO technical cooperation in the field of small industries and handicrafts continues to expand; there were projects in 41 countries in 1969. Small industries promotion can play a significant part in employment creation, especially in rural areas. With their small capital outlay and heavy dependence on man power rather than machines, small industries are particularly suited to rural areas. These areas provide the agricultural products for them to process, the consumers who want their goods, and the workers who need their jobs. Handicrafts, if age-old practices are modernized, can ease entry of less developed rural areas into the commercial economy, provide a new source of employment, and meet a real consumer need for goods and services. An ILO expert set up a national ceramic center in Dahomey, for example; another set up small industry centers in Libya. In Thailand, experts have helped increase the productivity of the ancient lacquerware industry. In 1969 experts on small-scale industries were assigned to most of the developing areas of the world.

Social Security

With the coming of industrialization, social needs in newly developing countries can no longer be met on a family, village, or tribal basis, and new problems appear, such as industrial accidents and unemployment. As the ILO Director-General pointed out in a recent survey, *The ILO in a Changing World,* most of these countries are well aware that a comprehensive social security system is the only real answer to many of their new social needs. The financial, statistical, administrative, actuarial, and technical problems involved in setting up a new social security system are, however, formidable.

The ILO has helped most of the countries in the developing world with their social security systems. This assistance has been concerned with: the planning of social security and its various branches; the extension of existing systems to new groups of persons or to new risks; the financing of social security; administration; organization of medical care; and accounting and financial control. Technical assistance includes expert missions, fellowships for study in Geneva or other locations, and seminars and training courses. A great deal of technical literature has also been published.

Labor Conditions and Administration

Under its occupational safety and health program, the ILO gives expert advice, helps set up safety research institutes, and sponsors courses and meetings of experts. The International Occupational Safety and Health Information Center (CIS), established in 1960 as an autonomous unit within the ILO, works in cooperation with national centers in 34 countries to collect and disseminate information in this area.

Technical assistance is also provided in the fields of labor legislation, labor relations, labor administration, and workers' education. A number of nations have received help in drafting or revising their labor codes and in training labor department officials. Two training centers for officials were set up in 1965: the Advanced Training Center for Labor Administrators in Africa at Yaoundé, Cameroon, organized in cooperation with the French government at the request of 15 French-speaking African states; and the Inter-American Labor Administration Center in Lima, Peru, which not only organizes advanced training, but also carries out studies, sends advisory missions, and distributes information.

In the field of workers' education, or trade union training, the ILO's program is aimed at helping trade unions and workers' education groups to train their members in leadership.

F. PROBLEMS OF CERTAIN KEY INDUSTRIES; THE ILO INDUSTRIAL COMMITTEES

During World War II, and even earlier, it was felt that a gap existed in the structure of the ILO: special machinery was needed for the detailed and continuing study of specific industries by persons with thorough practical knowledge of their particular problems. Acting on a plan prepared by the British Minister of Labor and National Services, Ernest Bevin, and submitted in 1943 by the UK government, the Governing Body in 1945 established seven ILO industrial committees "to provide machinery through which the special circumstances of the principal international industries [could] receive special and detailed consideration." By 1946, when an eighth committee was set up, industrial committees had been created to deal with problems of the following key international industries: inland transport; coal mines; iron and steel; metal trades; textiles; petroleum; building, civil engineering, and public works; and chemical industries.

Other ILO committees that deal with special problems of great international significance include the Advisory Committee on Salaried Employees and Professional Workers, the Permanent Agricultural Committee, and the Committee on Work on Plantations. The ILO has also established the Asian Advisory Committee, African Advisory Committee, and the Inter-American Advisory Committee, which provide information on special regional problems. The ILO industrial committees are, in effect, small-scale, specialized international labor conferences.

Resolutions adopted by these committees may call for further action on the part of the ILO. On the other hand, they may be designed for the guidance of employers' associations and trade unions in their collective bargaining; and they may contain suggestions addressed to the UN, to other specialized agencies, or to governments. The following are a few examples of subjects concerning which important resolutions or recommendations have been adopted:

Inland Transport Committee: prevention of accidents involving dock labor; inland transport working conditions in Asia and Africa; automatic coupling of railway cars; transport and handling of dangerous goods; limitation of loads carried by one man; marking of weights on loads; interport competition.

Coal Mines Committee: principles for incorporation in a coal miners' charter; coal miners' housing; productivity in coal mines; safety in coal mines; social consequences of fuel and power consumption trends.

Iron and Steel Committee: regularization of production and employment at a high level; dismissal pay and payment for public holidays; cooperation at the industry level.

Metal Trades Committee: Regularization of production and employment at a high level; long-term estimates of raw material requirements.

Textiles Committee: disparities between wages in the textile industries of different countries.

Building, Civil Engineering, and Public Works Committee: reduction of seasonal unemployment in the construction industry; social aspects of the world timber situation and outlook; national housing programs.

Committee on Work on Plantations: the place of the plantation in the general economy of the countries concerned; living and working conditions as related to plantation productivity; the need for international action on commodity regulation.

Advisory Committee on Salaried Employees and Professional Workers: rights of the inventor who is an employed person; migration of salaried and professional workers; hygiene in shops and offices; employment problems of musicians, actors, and other public performers; employment conditions of teachers; professional problems of journalists; problems involved in collective bargaining for white-collar and professional workers; wages and working conditions of hospital and health-service staff; wages and working conditions of civil servants.

8 BIBLIOGRAPHY

The Cost of Social Security, 1958–1960. 1964. 296 pp. $5.00.
International Labour Review. Monthly. Covers subjects relating to labor, and social and economic problems; contains summaries of official reports and results of surveys. A supplement, inserted in each issue, gives statistics on employment, unemployment, consumer prices, hours of work, etc. One year, $6.50; single copies, $.65.
Legislative Series. The most important laws and regulations on labor and related matters issued in all parts of the world. Issued bimonthly in loose-leaf binders. One year. $7.50.
Official Bulletin. Quarterly. Contains documents, information, and articles concerning ILO. One year, $5.50; single copies, $1.65.
Studies and Reports. New Series. Since 1946, over 70 titles. Other series include *Monographs on Vocational Training and Retraining in Different Countries; Systems of Social Security; National Employment Services; Workers' Education Manuals.*
The Trade Union Situation in the United States (1960); *The Trade Union Situation in the U.S.S.R.* (1960); *The Trade Union Situation in the United Kingdom* (1961); *The Trade Union Situation in Sweden* (1961); *The Trade Union Situation in Burma* (1962); *The Trade Union Situation in the Federation of Malaya* (1962). $1.00–$1.25.
Training for Progress. Quarterly. One year, $2.80.
Year Book of Labour Statistics. Includes statistics on population, employment, hours of work, consumer price indices, family living costs, industrial injuries, unemployment, wages and labor income, social security, industrial disputes, migration. $12.00 cloth; $10.00 paper.

FOOD AND AGRICULTURAL ORGANIZATION OF THE UNITED NATIONS (FAO)

"To the millions who have to go without two meals a day the only acceptable form in which God dare appear is food."
Mahatma Gandhi.

1 BACKGROUND : Hunger is still the most urgent problem confronting the greater part of the human race. It is estimated that about half of the world's inhabitants are seriously and chronically undernourished. Not only is their diet quantitatively insufficient, it is qualitatively insufficient as well, lacking the high protein foods such as meat, fish, and milk essential to health and vigor. About one quarter of the world's population are adequately but not well fed. Furthermore, they are forced to spend an exorbitant amount of time to produce their food, since the methods they use are antiquated, arduous, and inefficient. Only about one person in four in the world is really well fed and adequately nourished.

Unless startling increases in food and agricultural production can be obtained in coming years, the situation will become even more serious, since the world's population is now growing by over 50 million persons per year. Addressing the Second World Food Congress, The Hague, 1970, Addeke H. Boerma, director general of FAO said: "It would be futile and unrealistic to attempt to discuss hunger and malnutrition in isolation from other evils of our age such as the stifling clamp of poverty, the flood of overpopulation, the paralysis of unemployment, the deformities of trade. We must look at the economic and social problems of the world in their totality if we are to come to grips with them individually. . . ."

BEGINNINGS OF INTERNATIONAL COOPERATION

From the mid-19th century, reflecting a growing recognition of the interdependence of nations in agriculture and associated sciences, international conferences were held at which there were exchanges of knowledge relating to biology, biochemistry, crop diversification, and animal health. But it was not until 1905 that these individually valuable but unrelated efforts were coordinated with the founding of the International Institute of Agriculture.

One of the institute's aims, which were necessarily modest because of public and governmental apathy, was "to get the farmer a square deal." The words were those of David Lubin, a prosperous California dry-goods dealer, ghetto-born in Poland, who almost singlehandedly founded the institute.

Depressed by the plight of his farmer customers during the agricultural crisis of the 1890's, he bought and managed his own fruit farm in order to study their problems. Rebuffed in his adopted country, he toured the chancelleries of Europe, preaching the importance of a healthy agriculture as a requisite of a healthy international society.

Finally, Lubin found a sympathetic listener in King Victor Emmanuel III of Italy. Under his patronage the institute started functioning in Rome in 1908 as a center for the dissemination of farming news, trends, prices, statistics, and techniques. Though lacking the capacity to initiate or directly assist projects in the field, IIA's experience as a "head office" for the collection, collation, analysis and redissemination of data formed a useful platform for the launching, later, of FAO's similar but much larger activities in agriculture.

LEAGUE OF NATIONS WORK ON NUTRITION

The League of Nations did not directly concern itself with agriculture, but work done under its auspices in the relatively new field of nutrition proved of great practical significance. Ironically, Nazi Germany, although a sardonic critic of the League, was the first country to base its wartime rationing system on the scientific standards of diet drawn up by the League for heavy workers, expectant mothers, children, and others. Soon other countries did the same, often with striking results. In the UK, for example, the meager, often uninteresting but balanced diet dictated by the ration card, actually led to an improvement in the nation's nutritional health. Between the two wars, however, the idea of international action, advice, and assistance to improve the conditions of rural populations or of a frontal attack on the twin problems of food surpluses and starvation was no more than an interesting but remote concept.

2 CREATION

FAO was the end product of a series of conferences held during World War II. In 1941 the US Nutrition Conference for Defense, attended by 900 delegates, resolved that it should be a goal of the democracies to conquer hunger, " . . . not only the obvious hunger that man has always known, but the hidden hunger revealed by modern knowledge of nutrition." Other discussions on methods to improve the world's food situation, held in Washington in 1942, were attended by specialists who had been active in the League's work on nutrition.

The UN Conference on Food and Agriculture, called by President Franklin D. Roosevelt at Hot Springs, Virginia, in May and June 1943, was the first full United Nations conference, antedating the UN Charter Conference itself by two years. Roosevelt felt that a conference on food, a relatively noncontroversial topic, offered a good opportunity for testing whether the Allies would be able to cooperate on postwar problems.

The conference, attended by 44 nations, agreed that a permanent international organization should be set up, and an interim commission, headed by Lester B. Pearson of Canada, drew up a draft constitution for FAO. This constitution was accepted by more than 20 governments. The first session of the FAO Conference was convened in Quebec, and FAO came into being on 16 October 1945.

3 PURPOSES

As expressed in the preamble to the FAO constitution, member states are pledged to promote the common welfare through separate and collective action to raise the levels of nutrition and standards of living, to improve the efficiency of the production and distribution of all food and agricultural products, to better the conditions of rural populations, and thus to contribute toward an expanding world economy and ensure humanity's freedom from hunger. Specifically, FAO is charged with collecting, evaluating, and disseminating information relating to nutrition, food, and agriculture and its derivatives, including fisheries, marine products, forestry, and primary forestry products.

FAO is committed to promote and, where appropriate, to recommend, national and international action with respect to:

(a) scientific, technological, social, and economic research relating to nutrition, food, and agriculture;

(b) the improvement of education and administration relating to nutrition, food, and agriculture and the spread of public knowledge of nutritional and agricultural science and practice;

(c) the conservation of natural resources and the adoption of improved methods of agricultural production;

(d) the improvement of the processing, marketing, and distribution of food and agricultural products;

(e) the adoption of policies for the provision of adequate agricultural credit, national and international;

(f) the adoption of international policies on agricultural commodity arrangements.

It is also the function of FAO:

(g) to furnish such technical assistance as governments may request;

(h) to organize, in cooperation with the governments concerned, such missions as may be needed to assist them to fulfill the obligations arising from their acceptance of the recommendations of the UN Conference on Food and Agriculture and of its constitution; and

(i) generally, to take all necessary and appropriate action to implement the purposes of the organization as set forth in the preamble.

4 MEMBERSHIP

The 45 countries represented on the interim commission were entitled to original membership. One of these, the USSR, had not taken up its membership by December 1969 but could do so at any time by depositing an act of ratification. There is, however, an unofficial exchange of publications and statistical data, and the USSR adheres to the International Plant Protection Convention. FAO as an executing agency for the UN Development Program receives Soviet funds and employs some Soviet technicians.

Any nation may withdraw after four years. Czechoslovakia did so in December 1950 but rejoined in November 1969, Hungary in January 1952 but rejoined in November 1967. The former mainland government of China (now Taiwan) withdrew in July 1952 and South Africa in December 1964. Poland withdrew in April 1951 but rejoined in November 1957. Indonesia gave notice of withdrawal in 1965 but later decided to remain a member.

Despite withdrawals, FAO's membership continued to increase as new nations came into being, particularly on the African continent. By January 1970, FAO had 119 members and 2 associate members:

Afghanistan	Laos
Algeria	Lebanon
Argentina	Lesotho
Australia	Liberia
Austria	Libya
Barbados	Luxembourg
Belgium	Madagascar
Bolivia	Malawi
Botswana	Malaysia
Brazil	Mali
Bulgaria	Malta
Burma	Mauritania
Burundi	Mauritius
Cambodia	Mexico
Cameroon	Morocco
Canada	Nepal
Central African Republic	Netherlands
Ceylon	New Zealand
Chad	Nicaragua
Czechoslovakia	Niger
Chile	Nigeria
Colombia	Norway
Congo (Brazzaville)	Pakistan
Congo (Kinshasa)	Panama
Costa Rica	Paraguay
Cuba	Peru
Cyprus	Philippines
Dahomey	Poland
Denmark	Portugal
Dominican Republic	Romania
Ecuador	Rwanda
El Salvador	Sa´udi Arabia
Ethiopia	Senegal
Finland	Sierra Leone
France	Somalia
Gabon	Southern Yemen
Gambia	Spain
Germany, West	Sudan
Ghana	Sweden
Greece	Switzerland
Guatemala	Syria
Guinea	Tanzania
Guyana	Thailand
Haiti	Togo
Honduras	Trinidad and Tobago
Hungary	Tunisia
Iceland	Turkey
India	Uganda
Indonesia	UAR
Iran	UK
Iraq	US
Ireland	Upper Volta
Israel	Uruguay
Italy	Venezuela
Ivory Coast	Viet-Nam, South
Jamaica	Yemen
Japan	Yugoslavia
Jordan	Zambia
Kenya	**Associate Members**
Korea, South	Bahrayn
Kuwait	Qatar

5 STRUCTURE

The supreme body of FOA is the all-member FAO Conference, which holds its regular biennial sessions in Rome in the fall of odd-numbered years. The conference determines the policy of FAO and adopts its budget. It makes recommendations relating to food, agriculture, fisheries, forestry, and associated matters to member nations and to other international organizations. It approves conventions and agreements for submission to member governments. It may establish commissions, working parties, and consultation groups and may convene special conferences. It elects the director general as well as the member nations to be represented on the FAO Council. Each FAO member, except associate members, has one vote in the conference.

FAO COUNCIL

The council, the executive organ of FAO, acts as the governing body in the interim between meetings of the conference. It was created in 1947 with a complement of 18 representatives of member nations under an independent chairman appointed by the conference. Its complement at the beginning of 1970 was 34. The nations represented on the council are elected for staggered two-year terms and are eligible for reelection. The council meets at least three times between the conference's biennial sessions.

DIRECTOR GENERAL

Under the supervision of the conference and the council, the director general has full power and authority to direct the work of the FAO. The post has been held by Sir John Boyd Orr (later Lord Boyd Orr) of the UK from 1945 to 1948; Norris E. Dodd of the US from 1948 to 1954; Philip Vincent Cardon of the US from 1954 to 1956; and Binay Ranjan Sen of India, who was elected in 1956 and reelected in 1959 and 1963. Addeke H. Boerma of the Netherlands was elected in 1967.

SECRETARIAT

The international secretariat of FAO consisted of some 3,700 at the end of April 1970, of whom about 3,150 were stationed at Rome headquarters and the remainder in regional and subregional offices.

In addition to secretariat staff, FAO had 1,810 technical experts in the field in more than 100 countries, at the end of April 1970, working on UN Development Program projects and other projects associated with FAO.

HEADQUARTERS

FAO headquarters were in Washington until 1951. Since then, they have been located in Rome in a large modern building, in extraterritorial grounds of 28,700 square meters near the Colosseum and the extensive ruin of the public baths of Emperor Caracalla. The building was planned originally by Mussolini for his ministry for governing conquered Ethiopia and other Italian overseas territories, but construction was halted by World War II. Completed after the war, it was leased by the Italian government for the "permanent use and occupancy" of FAO at an annual rental of $1, payable in advance. With the increase in FAO's operations, extra office space has had to be rented in Rome outside the headquarters' confines.

REGIONAL AND LIAISON OFFICES

Regional Office for Africa: North Maxwell Road (P.O. Box 1628), Accra, Ghana

Regional Office for Asia and the Far East: Maliwan Mansion, Phra Atit Road, Bangkok 2, Thailand

Regional Office for the Middle East: 110 Sharia Kasr El Aini (P.O. Box 2223), Cairo, UAR

Regional Office for Europe: c/o FAO Headquarters, Via Delle Terme di Caracalla, Rome, Italy

Regional Office for Latin America: Oficina Regional de la FAO, Avenida Providencia 871 (Casilla 10095), Santiago, Chile

Regional Office for North America: 1325 C Street Southwest, Washington, DC 20437, US

Liaison Office with the United Nations: Room 2258, UN Headquarters, 42d Street and 1st Avenue, New York, N.Y. 10017, US

Liaison Office with UN Economic Commission for Africa: Africa Building, P.O. Box 2001, Addas Ababa, Ethiopia

6 BUDGET

FAO's budget is voted by the conference, the funds to actuate it deriving from contributions by member nations in amounts roughly proportional to their national product. Among the many qualifying factors is that of capacity to pay. Associate member governments pay four-tenths less.

The budget voted for the biennium 1970–71 was $70.6 million. In addition, FAO was the executing agency in 1969 for some $18 million of aid under the UN's Expanded Program of Technical Assistance and for some $50 million under the UN's Special Fund, the latter to finance major projects beyond the scope of EPTA. Such projects include surveys of resources, pilot and demonstration programs, preinvestment planning for large development works, and the creation and strengthening of educational and research institutes.

From the beginning of 1966, EPTA and Special Fund were consolidated into the UN Development Program. EPTA, which started operations in 1950 with a budget of $46,000, had by 1969 entrusted to FAO projects costing a total of $167,968,000. The Special Fund, which started operations in 1960 with a budget of $649,000, had advanced to FAO a total of $388,710,000 for projects through 1969.

7 ACTIVITIES

A. A GLOBAL STRATEGY AGAINST HUNGER

Ever since FAO was born in the fall of 1945, shortly after the end of hostilities in World War II, it has been consistently occupied with the problem of preventing famine.

To distribute food to war-ravaged, hungry countries was not the task of the FAO. This work, which required huge operations in various parts of the world, was one of the main functions of the United Nations Relief and Rehabilitation Agency (UNRRA). Other important tasks in this connection were performed by the US–UK–Canadian Combined Food Board and the Emergency Economic Committee for Europe. At that time, FAO had only begun to recruit a staff and set up shop; its budget amounted to but a fraction of that of UNRRA. Yet one of FAO's first tasks was to help set up machinery to stave off widespread starvation.

EARLY VOLUNTARY COOPERATION

At the first meeting of the UN General Assembly, a few weeks after the creation of FAO, deep concern was expressed that the liquidation of emergency postwar relief agencies, particularly UNRRA, would precipitate a food catastrophe. A special meeting on urgent food problems was called at Washington in May 1946 by Sir John Boyd Orr, FAO director general. This emergency meeting established the International Food Council (IEFC), in which 34 countries were members within a few months. Representatives of participating governments recommended that specific allocations of foodstuffs and agricultural supplies be made available for import by countries facing a serious food shortage.

As Gove Hambidge, North American regional representative, FAO, points out in *The Story of FAO*, the IEFC "was able to perform a vital function during the postwar food shortage on a purely voluntary basis. . . . The IEFC could not increase food supplies, but it could help assure reasonably fair distribution of available food among countries in need and forestall a scramble for scarce food in which the highest bidders would have taken all they could get, the devil taking the hindmost."

The IEFC became an FAO committee in mid-1948 and continued work on a reduced scale. It was abolished as the world food situation improved and as alternative means of handling emergencies developed.

PLANS FOR A WORLD FOOD RESERVE

While perhaps 60% of the people in the less-developed countries were chronically undernourished, malnourished, or both, the postwar world was faced with the anomaly of embarrassing food surpluses in some of the economically developed countries—

"embarrassing" because shipping these surpluses to food-deficient countries without adequate forethought or planning could disrupt international commodity trade and impede agricultural development in the countries aided. Plans to create world food reserves were discussed as early as the Hot Springs conference of 1943. The UK proposed that FAO be empowered to buy and sell food on the open market and to hold "buffer stocks" of strategic commodities. The US proposed a system of international commodity agreements to regulate production, stocks, trade, and prices of important foodstuffs—with surpluses transferred to an international food pool. No agreement could be reached at that time, however. The problem was no nearer solution when FAO in 1945 held its founding conference, which issued this sharp reminder: "It is hypocritical to lament the wide extent of malnutrition while quantities of food are not reaching consumers. . . ."

The overriding fear was that the creation of world food reserves would depress agricultural prices. Director general Boyd Orr proposed to the 1947 FAO conference an international trading and financing agency to buy, store, and sell agricultural products so as to keep the world market in balance, but his proposals were rejected. Norris E. Dodd, who became director general the following year, proposed the creation of an international commodity clearinghouse, but in 1949 his plan was also rejected. However, the FAO conference of that year did establish an intergovernmental committee to coordinate commodity policies (see below).

Despite the discouraging fate of these proposals, neither the FAO nor the UN General Assembly, which was equally concerned, had abandoned the search for an acceptable formula for converting troublesome surpluses in agriculturally advanced countries into useful world reserves. FAO and the UN, along with many governments, and especially the US, worked progressively toward a solution that, to use the formulation proposed by B. R. Sen, who was named FAO director general in 1956, would replace the concept of "surplus food *disposal*" with "surplus food *utilization*."

Logical as this idea appears to be, the debates in the 1960 General Assembly, again showed the difficulties involved. How, for example, were the legitimate interests of food exporters to be protected? The latter included not only wealthier nations but also underdeveloped countries that were short of certain foods but feared that wider distribution of surpluses might jeopardize their particular food exports, which were vital to their economy.

FOOD FOR DEVELOPMENT

With these and related problems in mind, the FAO as early as 1956, in a basic study (*Functions of a World Food Reserve: Scope and Limitations*) prepared at the request of the UN General Assembly, put forth a proposal that attracted much attention. Linking the concept of food reserves with assistance to economic development, it proposed a world food capital fund—the capital not money but surplus food. This food would go to assist underdeveloped countries.

The UN General Assembly in 1960 unanimously endorsed international assistance for the establishment of national food reserves in the food-deficit countries and international arrangements for the "mobilization of available surplus foodstuffs and their distribution in areas of greatest need." At the request of the assembly, FAO experts prepared a study, *Development Through Food*, suggesting means whereby developing countries could utilize surplus foods worth up to $12 billion without unduly disturbing commodity markets. The idea was basically a simple one. Surplus foods would be used to stimulate new activities in the developing countries. For example, labor-intensive projects, such as road building, would increase a country's food requirements (people who do hard manual labor need more food than those who do not) and could be paid for in part through food. Also advocated were projects to improve the nutrition of underprivileged groups, since these groups were not in a position to buy food at market prices. Gains in health and productivity, the study pointed out, would enable the people of the countries aided to be self-sufficient sooner.

THE WORLD FOOD PROGRAM

In 1961 both the FAO Conference and the UN General Assembly approved without a dissenting vote an experimental three-year World Food Program to put agricultural surpluses to work in the cause of development. For the original three-year period, governments pledged $100 million in food, money, and services to launch development projects, meet local emergencies, build up national food reserves, and feed children of preschool and school age. In 1965 it was decided to put the World Food Program on a continuing basis. A new pledging conference was held in January 1966 and another in 1969.

The World Food Program is a joint UN–FAO venture, directed by an intergovernmental committee composed of 20 nations, 10 elected by the FAO and 10 by the UN's Economic and Social Council. Operations commenced in January 1963, and by the end of 1969 the World Food Program had approved 400 development projects in some 80 countries, involving expenditures of some $739 million. It had helped meet more than 100 emergencies.

A large part of the work of the World Food Program was aimed at developing more adequate supplies of livestock, and a number of projects included the provision of feed grains. Projects using food in partial payment of wages included land reclamation, irrigation, the settlement of new lands, afforestation, road building, housing, and industrial and mining ventures.

THE COMMITTEE ON COMMODITY PROBLEMS

The same FAO Conference of 1949 that turned down the Dodd plan for an international commodity clearinghouse established much more modest machinery to deal with commodity problems, namely a committee of government representatives. The Committee on Commodity Problems (CCP) does not itself undertake any operations. It neither buys nor sells food, nor does it maintain stocks or food reserves. Rather, it endeavors through exchange of information and discussion to coordinate the policies of surplus countries and deficit countries, and it can, if it finds this desirable, recommend international action. Over the years it has become one of FAO's busiest and most important bodies.

In 1954 the CCP established an intergovernmental subcommittee to concern itself specifically with the problems of surpluses. This group, the Consultative Subcommittee on Surplus Disposal, which has its seat in Washington, has become a center for full and frank discussion of surplus disposal. It deals with matters that affect not only international trade but the very income and living conditions of millions of persons. In the 1950's and early 1960's this subcommittee was instrumental in coordinating large-scale surplus disposal operations in such a manner that their effect on world commodity prices was minimal.

The CCP, however, has by no means restricted its interest to the matter of surpluses from the developed countries. By 1966, which was a year of intensive intergovernmental consultation on commodity questions, both within FAO and within such international bodies as GATT and UNCTAD, the CCP devoted a major share of its attention to increasing the exports of tropical commodities. Of the committee's ten commodity study groups (grains; rice; citrus; jute; kenaf and allied fibers; bananas; hard fibers and oilseeds; oils and fats; wine and vine products; and tea), all but one deal with products of which the developing countries are the leading producers. The study groups analyze production and trade trends; review national commodity policies and their international effects; examine approaches to international stabilization of exports and prices; and seek improvements in such fields as statistics, marketing, and product standardization.

The activities of the CCP are reinforced by a great deal of statistical and intelligence work in the FAO secretariat, ranging from the monthly "Commodity Notes" in the *FAO Bulletin* to systematic studies. The secretariat is also at the disposal of governments, research workers, and experts to answer inquiries and requests for information on commodity problems.

The Commodities Division prepared a new study on commodity projections for the period 1970–80. The study analyzes past and present trends in production, consumption and trade of agricultural commodities, and projects national and world demand to 1980.

FREEDOM FROM HUNGER CAMPAIGN

In 1958 the director general of FAO recommended that the UN and all UN-related organizations join FAO in a special campaign to help free the world from hunger. The Freedom From Hunger Campaign (FFHC) was launched in the fall of 1960 with the active participation of governments and of national and international nongovernmental organizations.

The campaign's main objective is to make governments and persons in all walks of life truly comprehend two facts: that hunger is an increasingly crucial world problem, which, unless understood and combated, is bound to have evermore serious worldwide repercussions; and that, if much greater efforts are made, hunger can be banished from the earth.

Originally designed to last for five years, the campaign was extended by the FAO Conference in 1969 to run at least until 1980. The early years were devoted to establishing national committees throughout the world and through them organizing publicity drives to increase general knowledge about the world food problem and to sponsor projects.

In 1965 the Young World Appeal (now called the Young World Program) was launched to enlist the support of young persons for FFHC and to formulate an action program with the cooperation of young leaders and youth groups.

A four-part program, drawn up by FFHC at the end of the first five years, emphasizes organization, education and information, action projects for development, and involvement of youth.

The FFHC acts as an information bureau for the national committees (95 by 1970). It produces a liaison bulletin with news of current national activities and has published a series of 24 basic studies aimed at giving the general reader a greater knowledge of the problems involved in the fight against hunger. It also arranges lectures, film shows, exhibitions, school programs, and various other events in scores of countries.

In the developing countries it has concentrated on education, particularly in nutrition, and has established a number of such projects. By the end of 1969, FAO–FFHC had 400 field projects in operation or completed. A total of $25 million had been contributed to FFHC from participating countries. Through bilateral aid within the framework of the campaign about $100 million was spent in developing countries between 1965 and 1969.

Among the numerous projects that had been undertaken, one of the earliest—the Fertilizer Program—was still in operation at the end of the first decade of the FFHC.

In the developed countries action has mainly been in fund raising and mobilizing resources on behalf of development. The Canadian Miles for Millions program in 1967 was supported by 100,000 marchers and raised well over $1 million. The 1969 spring walks attracted 350,000 marchers and raised $4 million.

Zambia and India had their first fund-raising walks in 1970.

THE WORLD FOOD CONGRESS

The first World Food Congress was held in Washington from 4 to 18 June 1963. It did much to bring hunger and malnutrition to the forefront of world concern. The congress declared that hunger could be vanquished only through a worldwide strategy aimed at harnessing "all human and natural resources to ensure a faster rate of economic and social growth." The Indicative World Plan was a direct outcome of this meeting.

The second World Food Congress, held in The Hague 16 to 30 June 1970, was attended by 1,800 delegates, including 300 young persons and 600 adults from developing countries. It established a new precedent for UN agency congresses, in that persons were invited to speak as individuals and not as representatives of their government or organization. This congress called for the fullest possible involvement of the public.

THE INDICATIVE WORLD PLAN FOR AGRICULTURAL DEVELOPMENT

Despite the dominant role played by agriculture in the developing world—nearly 70% of the people depend directly upon agriculture for their livelihood—half of the Third World's population is underfed or malnourished, or both.

To help change this course, FAO has produced an Indicative World Plan for Agricultural Development (IWP), which proposes a strategy to meet the needs of an additional billion people expected in the developing countries by 1985. The idea of the IWP came from the first World Food Congress, when some 1,200 delegates called on FAO to survey the world food situation in relation to population and overall development and produce a plan of action. In 1965, FAO's governing conference of member states endorsed this idea but decided that the organization should take an even broader approach and produce "a world plan for agricultural production trade and development."

FAO in October 1969 completed the unprecedented study, which fills 3 volumes totaling 744 pages. The global plan embodies the results of four provisional studies on the Middle East, South America, Africa south of the Sahara, and Asia and the Far East. It updates and, in some respects, modifies the conclusions of those studies—which covered 64 countries—and incorporates material on Central America and Northwest Africa. In terms of both population and gross domestic product (GDP), the plan covers 85% of the developing countries.

The IWP concludes that five key objectives must be achieved if agriculture in the developing world is to grow at the rate and in a manner necessary to meet the challenges of population growth from 1971 to 1985: (1) securing the staple food supplies required by a population growing at about 2.5% a year; (2) improving the quality of the diet; (3) earning and saving foreign exchange, which is crucial to overall development; (4) providing employment in agriculture and related industries; and (5) reducing waste.

The plan states that the key medium-term objective in achieving a staple food supply is a breakthrough in cereal production. This would have to rise from about 230 million tons in the developing countries surveyed in 1962—the base year for the plan's analysis—to some 500 million tons, representing a 3.5% annual growth rate. High-yielding varieties of cereals, primarily rice and wheat, will spearhead the production drive.

To combat malnutrition, a broad-based program is proposed. In the short term, emphasis is placed on animals with a fast reproductive rate to narrow the meat gap envisaged in regional studies. This would be supplemented by measures to increase output of vegetable protein, notably by growing more leguminous crops.

In discussing the foreign exchange problem and possible

ways of solving it, the IWP raises questions concerning the extent to which the exports by developing countries could be improved by changes in production, consumption, and trade policies in the developed world.

Because of lack of adequate base-year data on unemployment and underemployment, the IWP has not set specific objectives for employment. Instead it has concentrated on a labor-intensive approach to its production objectives that would give reasonable assurance of adding to the total man-hours required in the agricultural sector of the developing countries.

The IWP also emphasizes the need to raise productivity through more intensive use of land and water resources. An increase from 562 million hectares cultivated in the developing regions in 1962 to 660 million hectares in 1985 is proposed. The IWP places even greater importance on better use of lands already cultivated.

In conclusion, the IWP cautions that its objectives will be attained only as a "result of actions, both at the national and the supra-national level and to bring them about will require careful, long-term and coordinated planning."

THE FAO–IBRD COOPERATIVE PROGRAM

In 1945 the International Bank for Reconstruction and Development (IBRD) was set up to lend money to rebuild war-torn areas and to develop neglected areas of the world. In 1964 the FAO–IBRD Cooperative Program was established to assist the progress of agriculture in developing countries by advising the bank on possibilities for investment in agriculture.

The International Finance Corporation (IFC), an affiliate of IBRD, seeks to assist less-developed member countries by helping to promote growth of the private sector.

The International Development Association (IDA), another affiliate of IBRD, makes loans for long-term projects on softer terms than the bank itself. IBRD–IDA lending to agriculture in 1969 alone was some $265 million in 20 countries, as against an annual average of $32 million 10 years before. Country investments in these projects totaled $556 million.

FAO INDUSTRY PROGRAM

A cooperative effort between FAO and major industrial firms was developed in 1966 to strengthen and expand those industries most closely related to agriculture in the developing countries. The fertilizer industry, the agricultural equipment industry, and the various food and other industries dependent upon agricultural products have taken part. By 1970 some 88 industries joined the program, volunteering their technical and managerial support and capital resources for developing projects prepared through FAO's preinvestment work in developing countries. For example, a livestock production project in Central America became operational in 1969. Two agrochemical industries provided experts for FAO assignments related to a pesticide project in Brazil and a grain-storage project in India.

B. AID TO AGRICULTURAL DEVELOPMENT

Over the years FAO has become increasingly involved in providing direct aid to agricultural development. It furnishes technical assistance in a variety of ways, both through its own regular program and through the UN Development Program. Technical assistance activities include expert advice, cooperative assistance to governments, the provision of fellowships, and actual work in the field (often in the literal sense). FAO experts frequently travel great distances, sometimes on foot, to reach remote areas. To influence farmers is often difficult, since they are frequently poorly educated, conservative, and slow to accept changes. FAO does not expect sudden and dramatic results. Technical assistance fieldwork is often experimental and of long duration. Nevertheless, this approach is considered indispensable and, in the end, effective.

ORGANIZING FOR AGRICULTURAL DEVELOPMENT

Until recently, many governments had no agencies or services to deal with agriculture, which had remained a depressed sector of the economy, and farming methods had lagged far behind the results of scientific research. In many instances FAO has assisted in establishing and strengthening governmental agricultural services.

It is now commonly recognized that the centuries-old methods of farming cannot provide adequate food for the growing populations of these areas. Through the collection, analysis, and dissemination of agricultural data, through the preparation and publication of studies, through the research programs it fosters, and through the many conferences, study groups, and study centers it sponsors and assists, FAO aids governments in organizing modern agricultural programs and in bringing scientific discoveries to the attention of individual farmers.

ECONOMIC ANALYSIS

The Division of Economic Analysis in the FAO secretariat keeps the world food and agricultural situation under constant review. Since 1965 it has collaborated closely with other FAO divisions on the Indicative World Plan (see above). The division has conducted an increasing amount of operational work to help developing countries plan the economic aspects of their agricultural development. In 1969 the division had some 65 agricultural planning economists and marketing experts posted in the field under arrangements financed through the UNDP and other special accounts, and it had operational responsibility for 4 UNDP preinvestment (formerly Special Fund) projects, with a further 12 in preparation.

Requests for technical aid are scrutinized closely to determine their technical and economic feasibility and the priority that should be accorded to them. The Economic Analysis Division in the FAO secretariat is responsible for the preliminary economic appraisal of proposed projects and for interim and final evaluation of the results achieved. In 1969 the division carried out the economic appraisal of some 160 FAO field projects backed by the UNDP and of nearly 100 requests to the World Food Program for food aid.

RURAL INSTITUTIONS

To meet the increasing demands of governments for assistance in mobilizing human resources and improving organizational structure, FAO has provided worldwide services in agricultural education and research, rural youth programs, land tenure and settlement, cooperatives, credit, marketing and distribution, and rural social development.

In 1969, FAO's Rural Institutions Division managed 25 such projects financed by the UNDP Special Fund and supervised 25 other projects funded by the Freedom From Hunger Campaign (FFHC) and other sources.

Since the early 1950's one of the tasks has been to assist governments with land reform—notably, abolishing antiquated and unproductive systems of land tenure. The division has advised governments and has promoted the direct exchange of views and experiences among governments of different regions of the world by organizing meetings. It has also assisted in the establishment of permanent regional land-reform centers.

FAO has collaborated in the preparation of the UN three-year reports on progress in land reform which present to governments and other interested parties a great volume of comparative data. In 1970 a special committee on land reform comprising ministers of agriculture in the developing countries met in Rome to decide a strategy of action for the second development decade.

The division also gives close support to the activities aimed at the introduction of high-yielding cereal varieties, one of FAO's five areas of concentration. The organizational and administrative problems to be solved range from seed multiplication and distribution, organizing supplies of fertilizer and pesticides, and providing extension services to the marketing of increased production.

Continuing emphasis has been given to training youth and enlisting their effective participation in rural development. A three-year training project in Thailand, and a Young Farmer Cooperative in Uganda, are regarded as forerunners of similar programs in other countries. FAO was host to the 1969 Inter-Agency Meeting on Youth.

Also in 1969, FAO launched an agricultural school project in Burundi and an accelerated training project in Algeria. National training centers were conducted for agricultural teachers and farmer training centers staffs in several other countries.

RATIONAL USE OF LAND AND WATER
Water

Since water shortage is one of the world's major agricultural problems, most land conservation and development plans involve water-resources development as well. Though water is found over most of the earth, it varies greatly in distribution and quality. Attention has centered on the improvement of existing irrigation projects, the development of underground reserves, efficient drainage of irrigated land, and better management of water. As funds became available through the UN for preinvestment studies, the Rural Institutions Division sent its first experts into the field under the technical assistance program. By September 1970 the division, under the UNDP, was carrying out a total of 58 Special Fund projects employing 226 experts; there were also 35 technical assistance posts. Thus new scope and emphasis was brought to the division, which until then was mainly occupied with advisory and informational activities.

Land

Great progress has been made in the field of soil and soil fertility because it has been recognized that the amount of available land will not become much greater in the future. In the past, larger populations were fed mainly by putting more land to the plow. In some of the most populated areas of the earth, this option has run out. A more intensified use will have to be made of the land in addition to better inputs (seed, fertilizer, and chemicals for controlling pests and diseases). Particular attention has been paid to soil fertility and its improvement.

The division in cooperation with UNESCO has been instrumental in preparing a soil map of the world showing, on a scale of 1:5,000,000, the distribution and quality of 103 major soil types in all countries of the earth. The map, the first of its kind, should be completed by 1973.

The IWP points to the need for 30 million hectares of new irrigated land over the next 20 years to meet the foreseeable demand for agricultural products. As preliminary support for this huge task, FAO is carrying out a program of preinvestment studies, financed by the UNDP Special Fund, covering irrigation development, improved water use, drainage, and swamp and tidal land development.

A Regional Applied Research Program for Soils and Water in the Middle East was initiated in 1969. FAO is participating in the International Hydrological Decade and is providing the technical secretariat for the relevant working groups.

In-service training of local technicians, short training courses, and fellowships are essential elements in all field operations. In 1969, 66 fellowships were awarded, and nearly 100 fellowships awarded in previous years were still current.

FAO's development program calls for considerable applied research and opens up new areas of technical knowledge and practice. Experts have pioneered the latest scientific methods for determining the most effective techniques of fertilizer and water application. Radioactive isotopes have been used in tracing the movements of underground water. Computerized operations have revealed patterns for optimal use of water resources in complex studies on multipurpose river basin development.

FAO has also entered the fight against pollution, which is ruining so much of the world's water and endangering fish resources. In December 1970 it held an international conference on marine pollution and a seminar on methods of detection, measurement, and monitoring of pollutants.

PROMOTING THE USE OF FERTILIZERS

World fertilizer consumption has increased rapidly since 1945. The increase has been most spectacular in the developing countries, although they still use only 18% of the world's total.

The Indicative World Plan for Agricultural Development proposes fast rates of growth in the production and use of fertilizers. An overall annual rate of increase of 14.3% is envisaged by 1975. In 1968/69 the world increase was less than 7%; in the previous 4 years it had been 10%. This reflected a less rapid increase in Western Europe and North America and in India. Twelve major developing countries, however, reported fertilizer consumption in 1968/69 at 25% or more above the year before. A number of these countries had special crop intensification programs or were carrying out large-scale fertilizer schemes.

Because of high production costs in medium-sized factories serving a limited market, the developing countries produce very little fertilizer—less than 10% of the world total. But they are increasing production rapidly. The Republic of Korea has reached the stage where it can even export nitrogenous fertilizers. India is also producing nitrogenous fertilizers.

It is of primary importance for farmers to know which fertilizers are correct and most economical to spread and how much to use for various crops under different conditions. One of the quickest ways of finding out, while at the same time teaching the effective use of fertilizers, is to put down trial plots and carry out demonstrations in the farmers' own fields.

FERTILIZER

Within the framework of the FFHC, FAO launched a fertilizer program financed by the World Fertilizers industry in 1961. The annual contribution amounting to $1.2 million in 1970 came not only from the fertilizer industry but also from the sponsoring governments and nongovernmental organizations. To impress upon peasant farmers the usefulness of fertilizer, simple trials and demonstrations are carried out to show concretely the often spectacular difference between the fertilized and unfertilized crops. As a world average, the quantitative and qualitative improvement of the crops show that for every dollar spent on fertilizer, the sale value of the crop yields an extra $3.3.

The FAO Fertilizer Program in 1970 was operational in 22 countries, covering Africa, Latin America, and the Far East. By 1970, 160,000 simple trials and demonstrations had been carried out. The average yield of crops with the recommended fertilizer is 60% over that without fertilizer. Average rate of increase in fertilizer consumption is about three times as fast as that of comparable countries not carrying out such a program.

GENERAL ASSISTANCE TO HORTICULTURE

FAO's assistance in the field of horticulture is handled by its Division of Plant Production and Protection. Experts from this division also participate in FAO–UNICEF "applied nutrition projects" aimed at improving children's nutrition through greater production and consumption of fruits, vegetables, and the like at the village level. This division played a key role in drawing up the Indicative World Plan for Agricultural Development (see above) by gathering basic information on crop, grassland, and fodder production and by seeking realistic estimates on what crop production targets should be in the light of future nutritional requirements and economic demand.

Besides providing expert advice on specific country projects, the division generally concerns itself with the diversification of agricultural production, the expansion of the use of better seeds, and campaigns against plant pests and diseases.

In the field of crop protection, great attention is paid to the safety aspect of the widespread application of pesticides. Increasing emphasis is placed on integrated control measures in order to overcome the problem of resistance to pesticides. Together with the World Health Organization (WHO), the division has undertaken studies on the toxicity and residual effects of commonly used pesticides, especially those that cause problems in international trade. Guidelines for legislation governing the registration and marketing of pesticides have been jointly issued.

THE "GREEN REVOLUTION"

In the field of plant improvement a virtual "green revolution" has taken place. The original high-yielding strains of wheat, rice, and other vital staples were produced by private foundations. But much of the work of disseminating them in the developing countries—of demonstrating how they should be planted, irrigated, fertilized, harvested, and stored—has been supported by FAO field experts.

The World Fertilizer Program, initiated under the Freedom From Hunger Campaign is one essential of the green revolution (see above).

Results such as those in India have been achieved in varying degrees in a dozen other countries. A few years ago India was often said to be incapable of feeding itself. Yet in 1967–68, thanks largely to the new high-yielding varieties, India brought in a grain harvest of just under 100 million tons. It repeated the feat the following year and was expected to do even better in 1970.

In West Pakistan there has been much the same story. Seed imports in 1965 were 350 metric tons. These imports, allied to a successful seed multiplication and distribution program, so speeded the expansion of the whole project that by 1968 the national wheat production goal was not merely achieved but exceeded. From 4.2 million tons before the beginning of the changeover, the country's harvests rose to 6.5 million tons.

In Afghanistan, Iran, Turkey, and the United Arab Republic, large-scale plantings of improved cereal varieties are also under way, and smaller programs have begun in Ethiopia, Iraq, Kenya, Nigeria, and Syria.

In Chile newly developed wheat varieties can yield 5 to 7 tons per hectare, and new wheat varieties in Uruguay are yielding about 4 tons per hectare. In Colombia improved, open-pollinated corn varieties are yielding up to three times as much as traditional varieties, while new hybrids have yielded 7 tons per hectare under normal field conditions. In Kenya corn production has risen to the level where supplies are available for fattening livestock. In Malawi hybrid corns have increased the average yield fourfold. New breeds of sorghum promise to double yields in Senegal.

Yet many problems remain. Production of high-yielding varieties (HYV) demands a sophistication of technique and quantities of water, fertilizer, and pesticides far beyond those required for traditional crops. FAO's activities in aiding and encouraging HYV programs will be concentrated largely on the follow-up efforts that are so important—the so-called problems of plenty.

THE INTERNATIONAL RICE COMMISSION

Rice is the staple food of approximately half the human race. For over 1.4 billion persons in the Far East, where 90% of the world's rice is grown and consumed, it provides the main dietary source of energy. During the 1960's, an increasing share of FAO's attention has been devoted to ways of improving rice yields in developing countries, as one of the immediate measures

that can be taken to alleviate world hunger. Following an Indian proposal, FAO in May 1957 convened an International Rice Conference in Tribandrum, India, at which representatives of ten governments discussed plans and proposals to increase rice production in the Far Eastern region. Suggestions were made for tentative production goals and for cooperation in breeding better varieties of rice. The meeting set the stage for the creation of a new FAO subsidiary organ, the International Rice Commission, with headquarters in Bangkok. Its members are the rice-producing and rice-consuming countries of Asia and the Far East, some European nations, among them the UK, and some countries of the Americas, including the US.

The International Rice Commission is concerned with all problems related to the production, conservation, distribution, and consumption of rice. Continuous work is carried out in hybridization and testing of improved rice strains, which may result in increased yields.

THE INTERNATIONAL PLANT PROTECTION CONVENTION

FAO has taken over five international conventions concluded before World War II under IIA auspices: locust control; the marketing of eggs in international commerce; standardization of methods of keeping and utilizing herdbooks; standardization of cheese analysis; and standardization of wine analysis. The international convention adopted by FAO was the International Plant Protection Convention (1951). This convention prescribes cooperative action to prevent the introduction and spread of plant pests and diseases and to promote measures for their control.

Each government party to the convention agrees to establish national services for plant protection, which include providing for inspection of fields, plantations, gardens and nurseries; inspection of plants and plant products moving in international traffic; and other measures to control plant pests and diseases and prevent their spread. The convention establishes uniform procedures to prevent the spread of such pests and diseases without hampering international trade, and it prescribes relatively simple standard phytosanitary considerations.

The convention obligates adhering governments to report to FAO any outbreaks of economically important pests or diseases and to describe control methods they have found most effective. FAO's world reporting service on plant diseases and pests circulates this information through its *FAO Plant Protection Bulletin*. In emergency situations FAO alerts its regional offices and the countries cooperating in its work by radio. Its prompt warnings have helped check the spread of such pests as the migratory locust and related species in the Middle East, the Arabian Peninsula, Central and South America, Africa, Asia, and the Far East that once devastated entire regions.

The convention provides that supplementary agreements may be drawn up to apply to specific regions, pests, or diseases. Under this provision, the Plant Protection Agreement for Southeast Asia and the Pacific Region was drafted by an FAO meeting in Singapore in 1954, and later endorsed by the FAO Conference. It has been in force among 16 countries in that region since 1956.

In addition two other FAO plant protection bodies have been established—one in the Middle East and the other in the Caribbean. FAO also collaborates with four other autonomous plant-protection bodies.

THE FIGHT AGAINST THE DESERT LOCUST

Destructive insects destroy enough food crops each year to nourish millions of people. Among the most destructive of all insects is the grasshopper, particularly the desert locust of the Middle East and northern Africa. The desert locust may lead a solitary existence for years, doing no great damage to crops, but at intervals the insect becomes gregarious. During these gregarious periods, locusts multiply rapidly and gather into migrating swarms that may cover as much as 50 square miles. Traveling as rapidly as 40 miles a day, some swarms are known to migrate up to 3,000 miles. These swarming phases may last several years, and as many as 700 tons of insects may settle on a single acre of ground. Every green thing in their path is destroyed. The Arabian peninsula is the principal gathering place for these migratory swarms of desert locusts, but they attack areas as far removed as India, the southern USSR, and Kenya.

Yet up-to-date coordinated locust control campaigns began only during World War II, with UK, USSR, and Indian experts participating. Such campaigns have been greatly stepped up since the war, under FAO auspices. International conferences were held, and a special center established by FAO in Jeddah, a Saʿudi Arabian port on the Red Sea, coordinates field operations against the Middle Eastern desert locust.

Campaigns against the desert locust had to be repeated every year. Particularly intensive campaigns were called for in 1957 and 1958. Fortunately, these severe infestations had been predicted in advance through international cooperation, so that international action against them was organized in advance with FAO assistance.

In 1957 a coordination center for antilocust activities in northeast Africa was established in Addis Ababa, and FAO-directed activities were extended to northwest Africa in the same year. By 1958, 17 governments were actively participating in the large-scale campaigns against the desert locust: India, Iraq, Jordan, Pakistan, Saʿudi Arabia, and the Sudan through joint operations; the UAR and Yemen through operations on their own territory; and Ethiopia, Bahrayn, Kuwait, Lebanon, France, Poland, Turkey, Qatar, and the USSR through donations in cash or kind.

The International Desert Locust Information Service, located in London, was established in 1958 under FAO sponsorship and is partially financed by FAO. Functioning as a worldwide intelligence center, the service collects information, publishes monthly summaries of the locust situation, and issues special warnings when dangerous swarms are gathering.

In 1958 the UN Special Fund decided to contribute to the costs of the most comprehensive antilocust program to date, which was proposed by the fourth (1958) FAO Regional Conference for the Far East. The six-year program involved ecological surveys, research, training, and pilot projects. By the end of 1962 the Special Fund's contributions to FAO's part in the program had been increased to almost $4 million, and 28 governments were participating in it by contributions in cash and kind.

At first, FAO organized trial operations with the most advanced methods, including the use of dieldrin, a new poison which when sprayed on the ground kills the insects in the larva to nymph stages—that is, before they can fly. Successful experiments on the India-Pakistan border permitted further improvements in equipment and techniques. By early 1963, FAO reported that the principal breeding areas and breeding seasons in the region had been ascertained. Information on migrations was still incomplete (it appeared that they were governed mainly by prevailing winds), so that, the FAO warned, an area of some 23 million sq. km was still "under the threat of devastation overnight." The region includes many countries where food supplies are greatly deficient and which would be doubly hurt by the calamity.

When another locust plague struck in 1967, after an exceptionally long recession of six years, FAO's battle plan immediately came into action.

The ensuing campaign was an unprecedented international operation fought with every modern technique available. The regional groupings covered dangerous locust outbreaks in West Africa, eastern Africa, parts of the Sudan, and the Arabian Peninsula. Locust invasions of Morocco, the United Arab Republic, Pakistan, and India and a great explosion of locusts in Sudan were dealt with largely by national organizations.

The result was the shortest locust plague in recorded history—18 months, compared with the 14 years of the previous plague.

At FAO headquarters, after two consecutive breeding seasons had passed with no further flare-ups, FAO's locust specialists cautiously noted that at least 85% of the swarms must have been brought under control by human action—the use of poisonous sprays, dusts, and baits. The locusts' natural predators—birds, small rodents, various wasps, and beetles—apparently took care of the rest. However, the 14th session of FAO's Desert Locust Control Committee in Rome, in 1970, confirmed that policing the area was still a vital necessity to prevent further outbreaks. An amount of $40,000 was earmarked for further experimental work on the detection of nonswarming locusts by aerial photography.

Otherwise work on the Desert Locust Project as far as FAO's field operations are concerned is being concluded. The participating governments are taking over the responsibility themselves.

COMBATING OTHER DESTRUCTIVE INSECTS

The locust is by no means the only insect adversary that makes serious depredations on agriculture, and FAO's assistance in combating other insect pests, though not as dramatic as its locust control work, has been important. A team of FAO entomologists has been seeking an effective method to control the olive fly, the larva of which causes losses to the olive crop of the Mediterranean area estimated at millions of dollars annually. The fall webworm, an insect somewhat like the tent caterpillar, frequently strips the leaves from trees throughout an entire area and had proved a serious pest in parts of Eastern Europe. The FAO is experimenting with natural parasites to destroy the webworm. The FAO is also experimenting with natural parasites to control the sunn pest, an insect that attacks cereal crops in Iran, Iraq, Syria, Turkey, and parts of Afghanistan and the USSR.

One of the newer control techniques is the sterilization of male insects through irradiation to prevent productive breeding. So far the method has given positive, if not conclusive, results in limited experiments against the Mediterranean fruit fly on the island of Capri and in Central America. Such a method has eradicated the melon fly on Rota Island in the Pacific and the screwworm fly in Curaçao and the US.

ANIMAL HUSBANDRY

FAO carries out studies and sponsors projects on animal breeding, animal fertility, and livestock and poultry management.

Animal disease-control programs inaugurated with FAO assistance in many countries produce and distribute vaccines, administer quarantine regulations, and carry out education and field services. In cooperation with WHO and UNICEF, FAO has been consistently concerned with increasing the production of safe milk and improving milk processing and distribution. All these activities come under FAO's Division of Animal Production and Health.

The division has also prepared an agricultural study on contagious bovine pleuropneumonia, and discussions on its control have taken place between representatives of FAO, OIE, and the Organization for African Unity. Research into bovine paralytic rabies is being conducted in Mexico under a UNDP–Special Fund project. As part of the WHO–FAO Coordinated Research Program on Wildlife Rabies in Central Europe, FAO arranged a meeting in 1969 of fox ecologists in Denmark to compare field experience.

In the field of poultry, FAO has helped many countries to build up their poultry industries to a high level of efficiency.

India, for instance, virtually tripled its egg production in ten years. A new method for hatching eggs at high altitude has been developed by two FAO poultry scientists working in the Peruvian Andes.

Since 1965, FAO has given increasing attention to pig production, working in Thailand, India, Singapore, Taiwan, and Indonesia on improved management, feeding, housing, health, and breeding, which will help to play an important role in closing the protein gap in these countries.

Experiments with the introduction and cross-breeding of improved breeds of sheep and goats have been conducted extensively. Much of FAO's work in livestock improvement has related to the better utilization of natural pastures, the introduction of new fodder crops, and the use of feed concentrates.

The Fight Against Rinderpest

Rinderpest, also known as cattle plague and steppe murrain, has long been the scourge of cattle in tropical and subtropical Asia and Africa. When FAO began its fieldwork, rinderpest control was one of its first concerns.

In many cases, FAO workers met with little or no initial enthusiasm from cattle owners. In Afghanistan, farmers hid their cattle, suspecting that the veterinarian was a tax collector in disguise. In other cases, rumors spread that vaccination killed animals, since cattle suffering from rinderpest sometimes died before the slow-acting vaccine took effect. Terrain proved a formidable difficulty. Some infected herds could not be reached by vehicles carrying refrigerated vaccines. Teams were compelled to proceed by foot or on horseback and had to pack their flasks in snow.

Yet in spite of obstacles, rinderpest campaigns have been successful. Thailand, once a beef-deficit country, is now a beef exporter. Much success has been achieved in parts of India and Burma. No recent serious outbreaks have been reported in Ethiopia, where as many as a million head of cattle were sometimes killed by rinderpest in a single year.

In 1969–70 a serious outbreak occurred again in the Middle East, affecting Afghanistan, Iran, Bahrayn, and Lebanon. Kuwait and Syria too had suspected cases. FAO has about 40 animal health experts in the Middle East, keeping watch for outbreaks of various animal diseases. In cooperation with local veterinary services they help identify and control the diseases. In Nepal in 1969, a project to fight rinderpest achieved the vaccination of 3 million head of buffalo and cattle, and a vaccine production laboratory was established in Kathmandu.

The Fight Against Foot-and-Mouth Disease in Europe

Foot-and-mouth (or hoof-and-mouth) disease is a contagious illness that affects cloven-footed animals, especially cattle. A serious outbreak in Europe in 1950–51 affected every country except Iceland, causing damages conservatively estimated at $400 million. Although some new vaccines have been developed, the disease is still difficult to combat, since it is caused by several different viruses, and vaccine made from one virus gives no protection against the other viruses. Three types—O, A, and C—are found in Europe, but any of the three African types or the one Asian type may also appear in Europe, and each type appears in different variants. Thus FAO's work in controlling the disease is similar to WHO's efforts to control influenza: whenever an outbreak occurs, the virus must be identified and a vaccine developed.

The Animal Virus Research Station at Pirbright, UK, has been designated by the FAO as the world reference center for the identification of viruses. It keeps strains of antiserums against various types of viruses.

A European Commission for the Control of Foot-and-Mouth Disease, with headquarters in Rome, was created by the 1953 FAO Conference. Through the commission, over a dozen countries exchange information on outbreaks, determine what virus or viruses are involved, inform each other on available vaccines, coordinate research on diagnosis and control, and set up training centers for research. The commission has broad powers to produce and store vaccines for emergency distribution. Each member country is pledged to a rigorous program of vaccination of threatened animals and slaughter of infected animals. By 1969 there were 19 member countries in the European commission.

The systematic vaccination of entire cattle populations in seven Western European countries and of cattle in exposed frontier areas helps to act as a buffer for the disease. A buffer region has also been set up in Thrace against a strain that appears to move into Greece via Turkey and other countries. Permanent vaccine production and diagnostic installations have been set up in Ankara under a UNDP project.

REGIONAL ACTIVITIES IN THE FIELD OF AGRICULTURE

FAO has encouraged a regional approach to agricultural problems by the creation of the European Commission on Agriculture and the periodic convening of regional FAO conferences. Regional conferences are attended by ministers and other high officials of the region's member states and by observers from other international agricultural organizations. These conferences discuss FAO's program as it pertains to their respective regions and consider other regional economic, technical, and social developments relating to agriculture and food.

The European Commission on Agriculture is composed of the European member nations of FAO plus Israel, the only non-European country to belong. In contrast to the looser regional cooperation on the other continents, the commission has a permanent structure and has established a number of subcommittees, also on a continuous basis. They deal with agricultural research, land and water use, extension and vocational training, home economics, and rural youth work. These subcommittees hold frequent meetings. Their findings are forwarded to the annual sessions of the full commission, which in turn formulates recommendations to governments and to the FAO Council and Conference. The European commission promotes cooperation of governmental agencies and such nongovernmental organizations as farmers' and dairymen's associations. Annual conferences are held under the commission's auspices to coordinate their activities.

C. FISHERIES

Fish are an excellent and comparatively economical source of high-grade protein. Annual production has been about 62 million metric tons of marine and freshwater fish. But even countries with very highly developed fisheries, and which largely depend on products of the sea, have only made a beginning in estimating the maritime resources that await development. Important new resources are still being discovered, sometimes unexpectedly, and efforts are under way by FAO to tap the little-utilized fisheries of the Indian Ocean, about which very little is known.

For many years the FAO has collected, collated, and disseminated information and statistics on various aspects of the world's fisheries. Its *Yearbook of Fishery Statistics, World Fisheries Abstracts,* and *Fishery Study* series embody material collected on a worldwide scale. Three world fishing-boat conferences have been sponsored by the FAO—the first in 1953; the second, attended by some 300 naval architects, boat designers, builders, owners, and marine engineers, as well as government officials, in 1959; and the third in 1965. These conferences have led to significant practical results. Fishing boat design has been included in the naval architecture curriculum in some universities, and impetus has been given in general to the movement to replace the old rule-of-thumb methods of building small fishing boats with modern methods stressing improved hull design and greater seaworthiness. Two conferences on research craft were held in 1961 and 1968. A world fishing gear conference, convened at Hamburg in 1957, spurred the international exchange of knowledge and experience concerning improved fishing equipment. Two other meetings were held in 1963 and 1970. A 600-page book based on the papers and discussions of this congress was published in 1959. Other important matters have been dealt with at FAO-sponsored fishery conferences. In May 1966, for example, 17 nations drafted an international treaty for the conservation of Atlantic tuna at an FAO-sponsored conference in Rio de Janeiro. The treaty went into effect in 1969. Another convention for conserving fisheries in the southeast Atlantic off Africa was drafted under FAO auspices in 1969.

FAO's work in this field is conducted by its Department of Fisheries, comprising three divisions dedicated to fishery resources, economics, and industries. Policy matters are decided by a 34-nation Committee on Fisheries, which meets annually. As of 1970 there were about 250 FAO fishery experts working in some 60 developing countries, about two thirds of them engaged in long-range UNDP projects. FAO also assists in training programs for fishermen and for others involved in getting the catch to the consumer. Fish culture in inland waters has received considerable emphasis. For example, the stocking of carp, tilapia, and other fast-growing fish in village irrigation ponds is a prominent feature of a number of the nutrition projects that FAO is assisting in collaboration with FFHC.

THE WORK OF REGIONAL FISHERIES BODIES

Six important regional bodies have been established under the FAO to further the development of fishing. In 1947 the FAO Conference recommended the formation of such regional bodies for the scientific exploration of the sea and its resources. The Indo-Pacific Fisheries Council was the first organized, growing out of an FAO fisheries meeting held in Baguio, Philippines, in 1948. The General Fisheries Council for the Mediterranean was created in 1952. Other bodies followed: the Regional Fisheries Advisory Commission for the Southwest Atlantic (1961); the European Inland Fisheries Advisory Commission (1957); the Indian Ocean Fishery Commission (1967); and the FAO Fishery Committee for the Eastern Central Atlantic (1967).

TECHNICAL ASSISTANCE IN THE FIELD OF FISHING

FAO technical assistance projects in fisheries are carried out in many countries. They include research on aquatic stocks; the development of pond culture; fish processing; improvements in fishing boats, gear, and techniques; improved government services to fisheries; distribution and marketing; and related subjects.

For instance, in Peru, FAO fisheries experts from five countries were assigned in 1960 to help establish the Fisheries Research Institute at Callao, the port of Lima. The problem was to strengthen, by systematic research, an already flourishing export trade in fishery products. FAO is helping Peru to develop fisheries for internal consumption as well as for export.

The Peruvian catch, relatively insignificant in 1956, by 1962 exceeded that of any other country and in 1968 came to 10.5 million tons, or nearly one sixth of the world total. Peru's commercially most valuable fish is a tiny anchovy called the anchoveta, which is processed into fishmeal and oil for export. The aims of the institute (staffed entirely by Peruvian scientists) include learning the unknown spawning habits of the anchoveta and of other fishery resources in the area. In addition to work in fish biology, plankton chemistry, and other subjects, the institute is engaged in research to control and maintain the balance between fish

and birds. Peru's seabirds, which nest by the million on the coastal cliffs and islands, feed mainly on anchoveta.

D. FORESTRY

Almost one third of the world's land area is forest. The trees on this land act as a protective cover that secures the maximum absorption of rainfall, regulates streamflow, and prevents flooding and silting. They give protection against erosion, act as barriers against landslides and avalanches, furnish shade and fodder for livestock, and provide a habitat for wildlife as well as a setting for public recreation. Each year, wood from the world's forests is turned into thousands of industrial products—from explosives to chairs and paper.

In 1969 more than 2,000 million cubic meters of wood were removed—by gigantic machines devouring whole trees as well as by loincloth-clad laborers slowly sawing through trunks as thick as factory smokestacks in the tropical jungles of Southeast Asia. By 1975, FAO has estimated, world consumption of wood and wood products will have climbed to about 2,700 million cubic meters. FAO also sees the export of wood and wood products as a particularly promising field for developing countries, which, in general, have rather poor opportunities for export expansion.

Annual exports of forest products from developing to developed countries rose from $280 million in 1955 to more than $1,000 million in 1968, and may reach $1,500 million by 1975.

In the industrialized countries, rapidly changing technology is compelling a radical rethinking of forest policies and management and much closer integration of forest production with the industries and trade based upon it.

FAO's forestry activities fall into two major segments. A Forest Resources Division is concerned with forest management, wildlife and forest conservation, forest logging and transport, and forestry institutions and education. A Forest Industries and Trade Division is concerned with mechanical wood products, pulp and paper, and forest economics and statistics.

Government participation in FAO forestry activities is channeled mainly through regional forestry commissions for Europe, Asia and the Pacific, Africa, Latin America, the Middle East, and North America. Each regional commission is open to all FAO member states located wholly or partially within that region. A joint Southern European and Middle Eastern commission, the Silva Mediterranea, deals with forest problems of the Mediterranean basin. Within these commissions, specialized working parties deal with national parks, forest fire control, forest insects and diseases, avalanch control, and so on. An International Poplar Commission concerns itself with this economically important species. A series of specialized world committees deals with such problems as forest development in the tropics, pulp and paper, forestry education, the conservation of forest resources, and the like.

FAO has placed increasing emphasis on training of forest workers. There are roughly 90,000 professionally trained personnel working in world forests, and the need is for many more. FAO's Indicative World Plan has estimated that the developing regions as a whole will need four to five times as many forest professionals and technicians in 1985 as in 1965. For example, in Latin America there were about 1,500 professional foresters and 6,500 technicians in 1965. The region's needs in 1985 will be about 6,500 professionals and 30,000 technicians.

Typical of educational activities of FAO's Forestry Department was the establishment of Brazil's first National Forestry School, at Curitiba, which later became an independent faculty of the Federal University there. By the end of 1969, when the UN Development Program project executed by FAO had ended, the school had graduated 156 professional foresters who all found immediate employment in forestry. The project also established four research centers in other parts of the country and directly inspired the establishment of two other training centers. In India, five logging training centers were set up under a 4-year project in the course of which over 1,000 trainees were taught the operation and maintenance of log handling, transport, and milling equipment.

Overall, FAO's Forestry Department was operating 27 forestry education and training projects in all developing regions by early 1970. The department is also widely concerned with surveys of forest resources. For example, a five-year project successfully completed in Ecuador has enabled the government to grant concessions over an area of 400,000 hectares and to start new forest industries with national and foreign investment capital. The project also helped to train field staff and to establish demonstration centers that will continue in operation under the Ecuadorian Forest Service. The project area comprises one million hectares situated between the Colombian border and the western slopes of the Andes.

As well as concerning itself with existing forest areas, FAO is also taking a part in the creation of new forests. By planting young trees to replace destroyed forests, or by starting brand-new forests, man can protect the soil, control water flow, and challenge the scarcity of wood and wood products that plagues many parts of the world. In Madagascar, for example, FAO is supporting a pilot project for testing tree varieties and training the technicians who are to bring approximately 55,000 hectares under pine trees.

E. NUTRITION

Not only is actual hunger widespread in the world, but hundreds of millions of people who eat a sufficient quantity of food do not eat the right kind. This lowers their working capacity and impairs their health. FAO's first objective, as stated in the preamble to its constitution, is to raise levels of nutrition. Indeed, the final test of all FAO's work to increase food production and improve distribution is whether it provides enough of the right kind of food to eat.

In the field of nutrition FAO is concerned with the study and appraisal of food consumption patterns throughout the world, changes and development in food production and food supply, basic physiological requirements in terms of calories and nutrients, and the practical application of advancing knowledge in these matters. FAO is particularly concerned with encouraging the most effective use of available foodstuffs. It has devoted much attention to food technology, supplementary feeding programs such as milk distribution to children, pregnant women, and nursing mothers, and to education in nutrition. The improvement of nutrition through home economics and extension courses designed to reach people at the family level is stressed, and direct assistance is given to governments wishing to develop such services.

Much of FAO's work in nutrition has been done in collaboration with WHO, which is concerned with medical aspects of nutrition. FAO has cooperated closely with UNICEF in developing dairy plants and in encouraging greater production and consumption of eggs, garden vegetables, and other nutritious foods at the village and community level. The joint FAO–WHO–UNICEF Protein Advisory Group meets yearly to review developments in new high-protein foods, such as peanut butter, cotton-seed- and soy-cereal mixtures, and fish protein concentrate.

By the end of 1969 the FAO Nutrition Division was responsible for 194 assistance projects in Africa, the Middle East, the Far East, and Latin America. Assistance was given to ten countries in the establishment of nutrition services. Aid to nutrition education was provided to 35 countries, and assistance was given to 63 school gardens and feeding projects. The Nutrition Division has provided to FAO member countries considerable advice on the revision of food laws and regulations. Frequent meetings have been held on the *Codex Alimentarius,* a joint FAO–WHO program whose aims are the establishment of international standards to facilitate trade in food products and the protection of consumers against frauds and adulterations.

F. STATISTICAL AND WORLD CENSUSES OF AGRICULTURE

FAO functions as an international intelligence service on matters of food and agriculture. This entails the continuous collection of pertinent statistics, largely from governments, the collating and analysis of these data, and their dissemination. FAO's *Monthly Bulletin of Agricultural Economics and Statistics* contains current statistics on all major crop and livestock products, data on land area and use, agricultural populations, and farm requisites. Quarterly tables show quantities and values of important commodities. The *Yearbook of Food and Agricultural Statistics,* in two volumes, one on production and one on trade in food and agricultural products, is a basic reference. The annual publication *The State of Food and Agriculture* analyzes developments and world trends in agricultural production, consumption, demands, trade, prices, and investment, and reviews plans and policies. This information is designed to assist various FAO bodies, governments, producers, and commercial interests to plan development with a full knowledge of the issues involved and to discover and, if possible, prevent surplus situations, price depressions, and other unfavorable developments.

Reliable agricultural statistics are essential for sound planning. FAO sponsored a worldwide agricultural census in 1950 and in 1960. The first world census was carried out by the IIA in 1930. The 1970 census is now being carried out. It has involved, in some cases, setting up the administrative machinery for collecting the data, giving technical assistance-statistical experts and regional training centers in developing countries.

8 BIBLIOGRAPHY

Animal Health Yearbook. $3.50.
Annual Review of World Production, Consumption and Trade of Fertilizers. $1.50.
Ceres—FAO Review.
Cocoa Statistics. Quarterly. One year, $2.50.
Current Food Additives Legislation. Ten issues annually. One year, $6.00; single copies, $0.60.
FAO Fisheries Bulletin. Quarterly. One year, $1.00.
FAO Plant Protection Bulletin. Information received by the World Reporting Service on Plant Diseases and Pests; plant quarantine measures; etc. One year (six issues) $4.00; single copies, $0.75.
Food and Agricultural Legislation. Quarterly. One year $3.50; single copies, $1.00.
Indicative World Plan for Agricultural Development.
Monthly Bulletin of Agricultural Economics and Statistics. One year, $5.00; single copies, $0.50.
Series: *Agricultural Studies; Agricultural Development Studies; Atomic Energy Series; Commodity Policy Studies; Forestry and Forest Products Studies; Forestry Development Papers; Marketing Guides; Nutritional Studies.*
The State of Food and Agriculture. Annual World Survey. $6.00.
Unasylva. An International Review of Forestry and Forest Products. Quarterly. One year. $2.50; single copies, $0.65.
World Grain Trade Statistics. Annual. $0.50.
World Fisheries Abstract. Bimonthly review of the world's technical literature on fisheries and related subjects. One year, $4.00; single copies, $0.75.
Yearbook of Fishery Statistics. Various.
Yearbook of Food and Agricultural Statistics. Various.
Yearbook of Forest Products Statistics. $3.00.

WORLD HEALTH ORGANIZATION (WHO)

¹BACKGROUND:

A century ago, communicable diseases that were impervious to known methods of treatment swept through communities, nations, and continents. The first discovery of bacterial vaccine, Pasteur's for anthrax, was not made until 1881. Since then, progress toward the control of communicable diseases has made great strides. Nevertheless, it cannot be said that all disease-producing organisms have been conquered. Smallpox is still with us, cholera has spread again to countries from which it had been absent for decades, and in many countries tuberculosis is still the chief public health problem.

By the mid-20th century, however, the discoveries of vaccines, residual insecticides, antibiotics, and a host of other drugs had equipped medical science with an imposing array of weapons for the battle against communicable disease. With the retreat of these diseases, other problems are everywhere coming to the fore: cancer and heart disease, accidents, environmental pollution. The task of making available the advantages of medical science to governments and individuals in all parts of the world has been undertaken by WHO.

SMALL BEGINNINGS: INTERNATIONAL SANITARY CONFERENCES

During the 19th century, waves of communicable diseases swept Europe, accompanying the growth of railways and steam navigation. Cholera struck Russia, Poland, Prussia, and Austria in the 1820's and appeared in Western Europe in 1831 for the first time in history. Yet the first international sanitary conference, attended by 12 governments, was not until 1851. An international convention on quarantine was drawn up, but it was ratified by only three states, of which two withdrew in 1865. An increasing number of governments participated in subsequent sanitary conferences, but progress was slow. The comparative lack of success of these conferences is not surprising in view of the scanty and often inaccurate information then available regarding communicable diseases. The delegates had little to contribute but unverified and often contradictory hypotheses on the character and communication of diseases. At the 1851 conference a committee actually warned against quarantining passengers from cholera-infected ships and wanted such persons to be dispersed by all possible means. In 1881, Dr. Carlos Finlay made the historic discovery that yellow fever was transmitted through a mosquito, but this met with general incredulity until confirmed by the US Army Yellow Fever Commission 19 years later.

Two main ideas dominated international sanitary conferences in the 19th century: the removal of hindrances to trade and transport, and the "defense of Europe" against exotic pestilences. The limited objectives of the nations participating in these conferences also militated against the success of early international health efforts. International public health did not come of age until the 20th century.

The distinction of having established the first international health bureau with its own secretariat belongs to the republics of the Americas, which in 1902 founded the International Sanitary Bureau. The name was changed in 1923 to the Pan American Sanitary Bureau.

The International Office of Public Health (OIHP)

The idea of a permanent international agency to deal with health questions was seriously discussed for the first time at the 4th conference (1874), but it was not until the 11th conference (1903) that the establishment of such an agency was recommended. By that time, scientific discoveries concerning cholera, plague, and yellow fever had been generally accepted. The agency, known as the Office International d'Hygiène Publique (OIHP), was created in December 1907 by an agreement signed by 12 states (Belgium, Brazil, Egypt, France, Italy, Netherlands, Portugal, Russia, Spain, Switzerland, the UK, and the US). The OIHP was located in Paris, and its first staff consisted of nine persons, including two messengers. It had a budget of only 150,000 French francs. Its Permanent Committee, functioning through biennial meetings of medical experts, recommended the destruction of rats on ships and the prevention of rats' ship-to-shore and shore-to-ship migrations as a means of preventing plague, which is transmitted by rat fleas. Quarantine for yellow fever was first prescribed by the 12th International Sanitary Convention (1912). Originally a predominantly European institution, OIHP had grown to include nearly 60 countries and colonies before the outbreak of World War I.

World War I left in its wake disastrous pandemics. The influenza wave of 1918–19 was estimated to have killed 15 to 20 million people, and in 1919 almost 250,000 cases of typhus were reported in Poland and more than 1.6 million in the USSR. Other disasters also made heavy demands on OIHP.

Division of Work Between the League of Nations and OIHP

In these circumstances, OIHP found itself overburdened with work. Early in 1920 a plan for a permanent international health organization, drafted by an international health conference in London, was approved by the League of Nations. United official action to combat the typhus epidemic then raging in Poland was urged by the League council and the London conference. Such direct assistance would have been an altogether new venture.

OIHP, however, was unable to participate in an interim combined League—OIHP committee. This was partly because the US, which was not a member of the League, wished to remain a member of OIHP but could not if OIHP were absorbed into a League-connected agency. OIHP continued to exist for another generation, maintaining a formal relationship with the League of Nations. The Permanent Committee of the OIHP acted as the General Advisory Health Council of the League's Health Organization, although the two bodies maintained their parallel existence.

The OIHP Between the World Wars

OIHP's main concern continued to be supervision and improvement of international quarantine measures. Smallpox and typhus were added to the quarantinable diseases by the International Sanitary Convention of 1926. Also adopted were measures requiring governments to notify OIHP immediately of any outbreak of plague, cholera, or yellow fever, or of the appearance of smallpox or typhus in epidemic form.

The Health Work of the League of Nations

Recalling the tremendous loss of lives from pandemics following World War I, the League took steps to prevent other such disasters. It established a permanent epidemiological intelligence service to collect and disseminate worldwide data on the status of epidemic diseases of international significance. Its Eastern Bureau was established in 1925 to perform this function in Asia. The Malaria Commission was founded, which adopted a new international approach: to study and advise on control of the disease in regions where it exists rather than to work out the conventional precautions to prevent its spread from country to country. The annual reports of the League's Cancer Commission on such matters as results of radiotherapy in cancer of the uterus became an important vehicle of international information on that disease. Other technical commissions included those on typhus, leprosy, and biological standardization. An important report on nutrition was published by the League's Health Organization in 1936.

World War II and Its Aftermath: UNRRA

Most of the work of OIHP and the League's health units was cut short by World War II, although the *Weekly Epidemiological Record* continued to be published. Fear of new postwar epidemics, however, prompted the Allies to draw up plans for action long before the end of hostilities. At its first meeting in 1943 the newly created United Nations Relief and Rehabilitation Administration (UNRRA) put health work among its "primary and fundamental responsibilities."

2 CREATION

At its first meeting, in 1946, the UN Economic and Social Council (ECOSOC) decided to call an international conference to consider the establishment of a single health organization of the United Nations. The conference met in New York and on 22 July adopted a constitution of the World Health Organization, which would carry on the functions previously performed by the League's Health Organization and OIHP.

Because of precarious health conditions in many parts of the world, many had hoped that UNRRA would continue its work in the health field, at least until the new organization was able to take over. But WHO did not come into existence until April 1948, when its constitution was ratified by the required 26 UN member states. In the meantime UNRRA had liquidated its activities. In the intervening period a WHO Interim Commission, operating on a very small budget, could carry out only the most indispensable of UNRRA's health functions. The first WHO assembly did not convene until June 1948, almost two and a half years after the first UN General Assembly.

Among the severe problems that beset the Interim Commission was a cholera epidemic in Egypt in 1947. Three cases were reported on 22 September, and by October 33,000 cases were reported in widely separated areas on both sides of the Red Sea and the Suez Canal. Urgent calls for vaccine were sent out by the Interim Commission within hours after the first three cases were reported, and by means of a history-making cholera airlift, 20 million doses of vaccine were flown to Cairo from the US, the USSR, India, and elsewhere, one third of them outright gifts. Various other emergency measures were also organized by the Interim Commission. The cholera epidemic claimed a toll of 20,472 lives in Egypt before Egyptian health authorities declared the country cholera-free in February 1948. During the epidemic the number of countries ratifying WHO's constitution increased by almost 50%.

3 PURPOSES

WHO's objective, as stated in the first article of its constitution, is "the attainment by all peoples of the highest possible level of health." It is designed to be "the directing and co-ordinating authority on international health work." It cooperates with national health administrations, the UN, other specialized agencies, and professional groups and other organizations concerned with health. Its constitution permits it, upon request, to assist governments to strengthen their own health services and to furnish them with technical assistance and aid in emergencies. Other important functions are to establish and maintain epidemiological, statistical, and other required services; to stimulate and advance work to eradicate epidemic, endemic, and other diseases; to sponsor and conduct research in the field of health and promote cooperation among scientific and professional groups that contribute to the advancement of health; to propose conventions, agreements, and regulations and make recommendations with respect to international health matters; to promote the improvement of nutrition, housing, sanitation, recreation, economic and working conditions, and other aspects of environmental hygiene; to foster activities in the field of mental health; to assist in developing an informed public opinion among all peoples on matters of health; to establish an international nomenclature of diseases, causes of death, and public health practices; and to develop international standards with respect to food, biological, pharmaceutical, and related products.

4 MEMBERSHIP

UN members can join WHO by unilateral, formal notification to the UN secretary-general that they accept the WHO constitution. Non-UN members may be admitted if their application is approved by a simple majority vote of the World Health Assembly. A special feature of the constitution, important before many new countries attained their independence, is that territories or groups of territories "not responsible for the conduct of their international relations" may be admitted as associate members upon application by the WHO member state or other authority responsible for their international relations.

As of June 1970, WHO had 128 member states and 3 associate members:

Afghanistan	Cuba
Albania	Cyprus
Algeria	Czechoslovakia
Argentina	Dahomey
Australia	Denmark
Austria	Dominican Republic
Barbados	Ecuador
Belgium	El Salvador
Bolivia	Ethiopia
Brazil	Germany, West
Bulgaria	Finland
Burma	France
Burundi	Gabon
Byelorussia	Ghana
Cambodia	Greece
Cameroon	Guatemala
Canada	Guinea
Central African Republic	Guyana
Ceylon	Haiti
Chad	Honduras
Chile	Hungary
Colombia	Iceland
Congo (Brazzaville)	India
Congo (Kinshasa)	Indonesia
Costa Rica	Iran

Iraq
Ireland
Israel
Italy
Ivory Coast
Jamaica
Japan
Jordan
Kenya
Korea, South
Kuwait
Laos
Lebanon
Lesotho
Liberia
Libya
Luxembourg
Madagascar
Malawi
Malaysia
Maldives
Mali
Malta
Mauritania
Mauritius
Mexico
Monaco
Mongolia
Morocco
Nepal
Netherlands
New Zealand
Nicaragua
Niger
Nigeria
Norway
Pakistan
Panama
Paraguay
Peru
Philippines

Poland
Portugal
Romania
Rwanda
Sa'udi Arabia
Senegal
Sierra Leone
Singapore
Somalia
South Africa
Southern Yemen
Spain
Sudan
Sweden
Switzerland
Syria
Taiwan
Tanzania
Thailand
Togo
Trinidad and Tobago
Tunisia
Turkey
Uganda
Ukraine
USSR
UAR
UK
US
Upper Volta
Uruguay
Venezuela
Viet-Nam, South
Western Samoa
Yemen
Yugoslavia
Zambia

Associate Members:
Bahrayn
Qatar
Rhodesia

5 STRUCTURE

The principal organs of WHO are the World Health Assembly, the Executive Board, and the Secretariat.

WORLD HEALTH ASSEMBLY

All WHO members are directly represented in the World Health Assembly. Each member has one vote but may send three delegates. According to the WHO constitution, the delegates are to be chosen for their technical competence and preferably should represent national health administrations. Delegations may include alternates and advisers. The assembly meets annually, usually in May, for approximately three weeks. Except for five sessions (1949 Rome; 1955 Mexico City; 1958 Minneapolis; 1961 New Delhi; 1969 Boston), all assemblies have been held in Geneva. The president of the World Health Assembly is elected by each assembly.

The World Health Assembly determines the policies of the organization and deals with budgetary, administrative, and similar questions. By a two-thirds vote the assembly may adopt conventions or agreements on matters within WHO's competence. While these are not binding on member governments until accepted in accordance with their constitutional procedures, WHO members have to "take action" leading to their acceptance within 18 months. Thus each member government, even if its delegation voted against a convention in assembly, must act according to its country's constitutional requirements; for example, it must submit the convention to the legislature for ratification. It must then notify WHO of the action taken. If the action is unsuccessful, it must notify WHO of the reasons

for nonacceptance. This system, combining respect for noninterference in domestic affairs with direct pressure, is modeled on provisions in the constitution of the International Labor Organization.

In addition, the assembly has quasi-legislative powers to adopt regulations on important technical matters specified in the WHO constitution. Once such a regulation is adopted by the assembly, it applies to all WHO member countries (including those whose delegates voted against it) except those whose governments specifically notify WHO that they reject the regulation or wish to accept it with certain reservations.

WHO is empowered to introduce uniform technical regulations on the following matters: (1) sanitary and quarantine requirements and other procedures designed to prevent international epidemics; (2) nomenclature with respect to disease, causes of death, and public health practices; (3) standards with respect to diagnostic procedures for international use; (4) standards with respect to safety, purity, and potency of biological, pharmaceutical, and similar products in international commerce; (5) advertising and labeling of biological, pharmaceutical, and similar products in international commerce.

The assembly at its first session, in 1948, adopted World Health Regulation No. 1, *Nomenclature with Respect to Diseases and Causes of Death*. This regulation guides member countries in compiling statistics on disease and death and, by providing for a standardized nomenclature, facilitates their comparison. World Health Regulation No. 2 deals with quarantinable diseases (see below).

Each year, the assembly doubles as a scientific conference on a specific topic of worldwide health interest, selected in advance. These technical discussions are held in addition to and separate from the other business of the assembly. They enable the delegates, who as a rule are top-ranking public health experts, to discuss common problems more thoroughly than formal committee debates would permit. Governments are asked to contribute special working papers and studies to these discussions and, if practicable, to send experts on the matters to be discussed with their delegations. Conclusions need not be put in the form of precisely worded resolutions. Matters discussed have included health education of the public (1959), the role of immunization in communicable disease control (1960), advances in tuberculosis control (1961), mental health programs in public health planning (1962), education and training of physicians for the preventive and social aspects of clinical practice (1963), the influence of community water supply programs on health and social progress (1964), health planning (1965), the collection and use of health statistics in national and local health services (1966), the challenge to public health of urbanization (1967), national and global surveillance of communicable diseases (1968), the application of technology to health needs (1969), and education for the health professions—regional aspects of a universal problem (1970).

EXECUTIVE BOARD

Regarding the composition and selection of WHO's Executive Board, the WHO constitution does not distinguish between "great" and "small" powers. Instead, the World Health Assembly may elect any 24 member countries (the only rule being equitable geographic distribution) for 3-year terms, and each of the countries elected designates 1 person "technically qualified in the field of health" to the WHO Executive Board. The countries are elected by rotation, eight every year, and are reeligible. Board members, once designated, serve as individuals and not as representatives of their governments.

The Executive Board is the executive organ of the World Health Assembly. One of its important functions is to prepare the assembly's agenda. It meets twice a year, for sessions of a few days to several weeks, but it may convene in a special meeting at any time. The WHO constitution authorizes the board "to take emergency measures within the functions and financial resources of the Organization to deal with events requiring immediate action. In particular, it may authorize the director general to take the necessary steps to combat epidemics and to participate in the organization of health relief to victims of a calamity."

THE SECRETARIAT: HEADQUARTERS AND REGIONAL OFFICES

The Secretariat comprises the technical and administrative personnel of the organization. It is headed by a director general, appointed by the assembly. The first director general of WHO was Dr. Brock Chisholm of Canada. He was succeeded in 1953 by Dr. Marcolino G. Candau of Brazil.

WHO headquarters are in Geneva. WHO's activities have been progressively decentralized. There are six regional offices, each covering a major geographic region of the world. These are located in Alexandria for the Eastern Mediterranean area, population approximately 282 million; in Manila for the Western Pacific area, 270 million; in New Delhi for the Southeast Asia area, 718.8 million; in Copenhagen for Europe, 753.4 million; in Brazzaville for the African area, 229 million; and in Washington, where the directing council of the Pan American Health Organization acts as the regional committee of WHO in the Americas, 487.8 million.

While all work of direct assistance to individual member governments is decentralized to the regional offices, the Geneva headquarters is the nerve center of the organization. There the work of the regions is coordinated and worldwide technical services are organized, including collection and dissemination of information. Headquarters cooperates with the UN, specialized agencies, and voluntary organizations and is responsible for the medical research program.

At the beginning of 1970 the total staff of WHO including headquarters, regional offices, country, area, and zone offices totaled 2,281, both internationally and locally recruited. Some 1,065 of this total were working at headquarters. In addition, 402 technical assistance experts were working for WHO in different parts of the world (including 24 agents in the Democratic Republic of the Congo), 42 were employed on projects financed by voluntary funds, and 52 by the International Agency for Research on Cancer, at Lyons, France.

FROM REGIONAL COMMITTEE MEETINGS TO WHO PROGRAMMING

WHO assistance is given in response to a request from a government. Member governments meet annually in regional committees to review and plan WHO activities for their areas. Requests are consolidated by the regional directors and forwarded to the director general, who incorporates regional programs and their estimated costs into the overall WHO draft program and budget. The program and budget, after review by the Executive Board, is submitted to the World Health Assembly.

6 BUDGET

For 1949, the first year of WHO's existence, its regular budget amounted to $5 million. By 1962 its annual budget had risen to $24.7 million, and a regular budget of $73,230,000 was approved by the World Health Assembly for 1971.

By far the largest part of the budget is to cover WHO's operating program (91.86%). This leaves 1.24% for organizational meetings, 6.07% for administrative services, and 0.83% for other purposes including the headquarters building fund.

A breakdown by major program headings of the activities of the organization for 1971 gives the following percentages:

Communicable diseases control	29.87
Environmental health	7.89
Public health services	29.60
Health protection and promotion	8.56
Education and training	13.26
Biology, pharmacology, and toxicology	4.75
Noncommunicable diseases	2.00
Health statistics	3.17
Other activities	0.90

WHO's regular budget is fixed each year for the following year by the World Health Assembly. It is financed through available income and contributions by member states in accordance with a scale of assessments based on that of the UN.

In addition to the regular budget, WHO's share in the UN Special Fund amounts to some $8 million a year. UNICEF's contribution to the 1971 joint projects was $16 million.

7 ACTIVITIES

The world is beset by such a complexity of health problems that WHO's activities range over many fields important to the governments whose representatives decide on the organization's programs. Some of WHO's most important work includes the least dramatic—for example, the preparation of an international pharmacopoeia and the establishment of uniform names for chemicals used in medicines which are of high significance to physicians, health workers, and the pharmaceutical industry.

Also unspectacular but of basic importance are WHO's efforts to alleviate the worldwide shortage of doctors, nurses, and other health workers, to improve professional education, and to stimulate the growth of health services. The most dramatic programs are those directed against mass communicable diseases, especially the worldwide eradication campaigns against malaria and smallpox.

A. COMBATING DISEASES
Malaria

Malaria, though now principally a disease of tropical and subtropical areas, has existed in most countries from northwestern Russia to southern Argentina. During the first half of the 20th century it was endemic in areas inhabited by over two thirds of the world's population. In 1947 an estimated 300 million people suffered from attacks, and the disease was the direct cause of about 3 million deaths annually.

Despite these high figures, and though malaria is often a major cause of infant mortality, particularly in highly endemic areas, even more important is that it produces chronic invalidism in rural populations. It impairs physical and mental development and leads to an increased number of deaths from other causes. It has been the world's greatest single cause of disablement.

Malaria is caused by a protozoan parasite of the genus *Plasmodium* and normally is transmitted from person to person through the bite of an infected female mosquito of certain *Anopheles* species. In exceptional cases, the disease may be transmitted at birth through the placenta from an infected mother, or following transfusion of blood from a donor who has had malaria, or through the use of contaminated syringes or needles, particularly in drug addicts.

From the beginning of the 20th century various attempts had been made in many countries to control malaria, but with limited success. However, the advent of DDT, the first residual insecticide that would remain lethal for several months, offered great possibilities for widespread and economically feasible malaria control.

Research has shown that the mosquito, after gorging itself with blood, generally flies only a short distance before it rests, usually by alighting on the walls or hangings of a dwelling. If this resting place is covered with a lethal dose of insecticide, the mosquito dies. The parasite that is sucked up has to mature or develop in the mosquito for 10 to 12 days before it can infect man. During this period the mosquito takes four to five blood meals. Thus it has many chances of being killed by insecticide before transmitting the disease, and the cycle of transmission from man to mosquito to man may be broken.

The World Health Organization and Malaria Control and Eradication

The World Health Organization had inherited a long tradition of international cooperation in the fight against malaria, from the establishment of the Pan American Sanitary Bureau in 1902 to the Malaria Commission of the League of Nations. Therefore, the importance of malaria as a public health problem and the need to give priority to antimalaria activities were recognized from the inception in 1946 of the Interim Commission of WHO. The first World Health Assembly, in July 1948, decided to provide malaria-control demonstration teams to countries requesting such assistance. DDT residual spraying was recommended as the main method of control. By the end of 1949, seven malaria-control demonstration teams were in operation in different parts of Asia, and in 1951, 22 projects were undertaken in cooperation with UNICEF.

The employment of this insecticide was considered generally an advanced method of control, and its continued use year by year was envisaged. However, experience soon indicated that eradication of malaria could be achieved even without the complete extermination of the vector, by ensuring, through residual insecticides, that the infected mosquitoes were killed off before the developing infection reached the stage where it could be passed on to man. With transmission halted for a period of about three years, most of the parasite reservoir in man would die out even without treatment, and the remaining parasitemia could be eliminated by case detection and treatment.

The concept of a time-limited program for completely eliminating malaria was born of experiences in different parts of the world. Such a program could now be undertaken in rural areas, where the disease was of the highest public health importance, as a capital investment and not a permanently recurring cost.

In 1951 the development of resistance of the vector *Anopheles sacharovi* to DDT was reported in Greece, which reinforced the desirability of adopting a time-limited approach to eradicating malaria and demonstrated that the residual insecticides could not be depended on to continue their effectiveness indefinitely. Confirmation that this was not an isolated instance became evident when the same resistance was reported for *Anopheles quadrimaculatus* in the US, and reports from other parts of the world showed that it was likely to become widespread. With the danger of resistance developing, it was obvious that the larger the area in which eradication techniques could be rapidly and effectively adopted the greater would be the success of eliminating the disease on a wide basis and preventing its reestablishment.

In 1955 the eighth World Health Assembly, meeting in Mexico, resolved that the organization should take the initiative in implementing a program of worldwide eradication of malaria rather than continue developing more efficient controls. Thus the organization became instrumental in stimulating and guiding the most extensive public health operation ever undertaken.

On the basis of experience developed in several countrywide malaria eradication programs in 1956, the principles and practice of malaria eradication were laid down. These were defined as halting the transmission of malaria and eliminating infected cases in a time-limited campaign, which if carried out to perfection would prevent possible future transmission.

Year by year, as experience with the eradication program accumulated, the methodology recommended was reviewed and continuously adapted to the needs. In 1969 the 22d World Health Assembly, at Boston, while reaffirming global eradication of malaria as a long-term goal, adopted a revised strategy. This envisaged the diversification of employment of the methods available and adapting them to local conditions, especially in relation to the replanning, wherever necessary, of malaria eradication programs so as to obtain optimum results and to provide measures for sustaining eradication in areas under maintenance. It recognized malaria control as a valid and indispensable interim step where eradication would seem impracticable. Prior to the development of an antimalaria program, following a survey of the epidemiological and general health situation of the country with reference to prevailing socioeconomic conditions and studies of available resources, the technical and operational feasibility of eradication had to be demonstrated through pilot studies.

Malaria eradication programs are planned in four phases. The first, or preparatory, phase consists of surveys, the drawing up of detailed plans, and the recruitment and training of personnel. The second, or attack, phase requires infinite attention to detail: for about three to four years, every habitation within the area must be completely sprayed with insecticide at intervals of 6 to 12 months. Teams traveling by jeep, horseback, water buffalo, canoe, or on foot must find their way to even the most remote huts. In the third, or consolidation, phase all remaining malaria cases must be found and treated. Eradication may be considered successful if, after three years, no new locally contracted cases are found in the area. The final, or maintenance, phase which is continued until global eradication is achieved, is normally a routine health service function. It consists of checks for any signs of recurrence of malaria in the area and of measures against importation of the disease through infected outsiders to prevent the reestablishment of endemicity.

The malaria eradication program is the greatest campaign against a single disease the world has ever known both in the number of persons engaged in it and in the number of persons affected by it. At the height of the world effort, over 250,000 physicians, engineers, entomologists, spray men, surveillance staff, and microscopists were engaged. In the organization's programs for evaluating and testing new insecticides, more than 1,300 compounds were reviewed. A number of effective residual insecticides were developed and made operational, but few are as safe to use and none as cheap to produce nor, in the long term, as effective in their residual action as DDT, the most widely used insecticide. Hence any action that limits the availability of DDT for the control of malaria in developing countries could lead to a public health disaster.

By the end of 1969, of the 1.8 billion persons living in originally malarious areas in 145 countries of the world, 39% were in areas where malaria had been eradicated, and 40% in areas where eradication programs were in progress. In 36 countries all the previous malarious areas have been completely freed of the disease. Progress has been marked, especially in Europe—where the transmission of malaria has ceased—in the Americas, and in Southeast Asia. In India, where the program covers a population of 555 million people, less than 300,000 cases of malaria were reported in 1969, compared with 100 million 30 years before. In the Eastern Mediterranean and Western Pacific regions, programs with reasonable prospects of success cover large portions of the population.

Tuberculosis

Although tuberculosis has ceased to be a mass killer in economically advanced countries, it continues to be a major infectious disease. Perhaps half of the world's population, about 1.5 billion persons, still carry tubercle bacilli. In about 99% of these, the disease is dormant because of natural resistance. However, the quiescent bacilli may suddenly become active if the body's equilibrium is upset by physical, mental, or social stress. In about 1% of all infected persons, some 15 million, the bacilli multiply and cause disease, which spreads to others. The annual toll of this process is some 2 to 3 million new infectious cases and about 2 million deaths. Studies in rural Asia have shown that approximately 90% of the persons diagnosed as suffering from infectious tuberculosis in random surveys are aware of chest symptoms, that 70% actually worry about them, and that slightly more than 50% have sought medical help, usually in vain.

If tuberculosis is to be controlled, emphasis needs to be placed upon a systematic reduction in the transmission of the disease. This epidemiological approach has been the major concept of WHO's tuberculosis program, which has two objectives: the prevention of new cases of tuberculosis and the detection and cure of infectious cases. The principal tools for accomplishing this on a worldwide basis are BCG vaccination, to reduce the danger of bacilli invading susceptible persons, and drug treatment (chemotherapy), to reduce the spread of infection from diseased persons.

BCG Vaccination. The protective value of vaccination with bacillus Calmette-Guérin (BCG) has been well established. Controlled trials demonstrated that susceptible persons who have been vaccinated have an 80% better chance of escaping tuberculosis than those who have not, and that this protection lasts for many years.

When, shortly after WHO's creation, it was first realized that international action was needed to reduce tuberculosis in underprivileged countries, the initial step was mass BCG vaccination because of its relatively low cost and its easy administration.

Through WHO- and UNICEF-assisted projects in 49 countries, by the end of 1965 more than 445 million persons were given preliminary tuberculin tests to determine whether they had been infected with tubercle bacilli, and 189 million susceptibles (persons who had never been infected) were given BCG vaccination.

Treatment and Prevention Through Drugs: Chemotherapy and Chemoprophylaxis. The applicability of BCG vaccination is limited because a large proportion of the people in many developing countries are already infected with tuberculosis. Fortunately, another breakthrough occurred with the dramatic discovery in the 1950's of powerful antituberculosis drugs such as streptomycin, and isoniazid. This suggested the possibility of using such drugs on a mass scale for neutralizing infectious cases (chemotherapy) and preventing dormant cases from becoming active and infectious (chemoprophylaxis).

The WHO-assisted Tuberculosis Chemotherapy Center in Madras, India, was set up in 1956 to provide answers to certain fundamental questions about the mass application of the new drugs. Trials showed that taking the drugs for one year at home was as effective as taking them for one year in a hospital, and that this did not expose persons living with the patients to any special risk of infection.

The Control of Tuberculosis. In spite of remarkable advances in the treatment and prevention of tuberculosis, not a single country has reached the point in control where the proportion of natural reactors to tuberculin among children in the 14-year age group is less than 1%. Tuberculosis is not declining everywhere—there have been local increases, even in some developed countries. The situation is not due to any inadequacy in the control measures but to poor planning, coordination, and evaluation, according to a WHO expert committee on tuberculosis.

WHO's assistance to national tuberculosis programs is provided through teams assigned to a particular country for several years. The composition of the teams varies. It may include a medical officer, a statistician, a laboratory technician, a public health nurse, and, in some instances, an X-ray technician. In addition to these permanently assigned WHO staff members, countries are served by advisory teams, on request, to assess the efficacy of the national program. Such a program usually lasts two to four years. WHO has established a number of regional epidemiological and training centers for the pooling of experience, in-service training, and the centralization of complex statistical work. Over 1,000 fellowships have been awarded by WHO, and interregional as well as regional training courses have been organized for medical officers in key positions in various governments. Apart from these activities, the training of paramedical and auxiliary personnel is largely taken care of by WHO staff members in the field and by seminars and symposia organized by the regional offices.

Syphilis and Yaws

Yaws, a disfiguring and disabling disease that causes open sores and attacks the bones, has many similarities to syphilis. Both diseases can be cured with penicillin. Syphilis is caused by the spirochete *Treponema pallidum* and it can be transmitted by flies as well as by contact. In the late 1940s there were an estimated 40 million cases of syphilis in the world, and some 200 million persons in the tropics were exposed to yaws or other treponemal infections. In many rural areas the infection rate ranged from 30% to as high as 70% and the number of active cases exceeded 25%.

WHO, in cooperation with UNICEF, inaugurated mass campaigns against treponema-caused diseases in 49 countries. A single injection of long-acting penicillin (PAM) or benzathine penicillin has proved very effective and can deliver a patient from lifelong misery.

The first campaign to eradicate yaws was undertaken in Haiti in 1950, assisted by WHO and UNICEF. The campaign began with a survey, which classified any person with lesions of any kind as a yaws case and the remainder of the population as contacts. It was found that 36.5% of the country's 3.5 million inhabitants were infected. Subsequent studies showed that the incidence of yaws had fallen to 0.57% of the population. A successful yaws campaign also took place in Nigeria, where it was combined with a survey for leprosy and mass immunization against smallpox and yellow fever.

The world's largest campaign against treponemal diseases was launched in Indonesia in 1950. It was a difficult undertaking because a large proportion of the population is scattered over hundreds of islands. Nevertheless, the incidence of yaws dropped from an initial 11% of persons examined to less than 1% by June 1961.

A WHO world survey of syphilis and gonorrhea from 1960 to 1970 showed a persistent increase of both diseases in all regions of the world, including an increase of gonorrhea among teenagers in a number of countries. The trend has continued and is also reflected in data on seamen. This development indicates a need for renewed vigilance and intensified control, particularly since the spread of venereal disease is increasingly governed by social, behavioral, and other environmental factors. For instance, increasing use of contraceptive measures has tended to remove fear of pregnancy, intensify sexual activity, and increase the risk of acquiring a sexually transmitted disease.

Influenza

The wave of influenza that swept over the world in 1918–19 was the greatest epidemic in history. Approximately 1 billion persons were affected, of whom perhaps as many as 1 out of 50 died. Epidemic influenza often attacks 30% to 40% of a country's population, and it frequently is accompanied by secondary complications such as bacterial pneumonia.

There are several types of influenza. The virus of human influenza A was discovered in 1933, and that of influenza B in 1940. A horse influenza and a swine influenza have been identified. Each influenza has many subtypes, strains, and variants. No variant immunizes against any other, and new ones may appear at any time. For effective vaccination, the virus causing a specific epidemic must be known. Hence, science must constantly be on the alert for new strains and data on influenza, including reliable and internationally comparable virus tests, which must be continuously exchanged.

Reports on influenza outbreaks can be interpreted correctly only through laboratory studies of the virus responsible. This is one of the main considerations that led to the setting up of the WHO network of national influenza laboratories, with international centers in London and Atlanta. The functions of the laboratories are to report with all speed the occurrence of influenza within a country and to isolate and identify the type of virus involved. The viruses are then dispatched by air to London or Atlanta for further study and for comparison with strains isolated elsewhere. Strains that show unusual characteristics are exchanged without delay so that they are available in both hemispheres for vaccine production if required. The WHO network, which consists of 87 collaborating laboratories in all parts of the world, keeps track of influenza epidemics.

Trachoma

Trachoma, an eye disease that is the main cause of loss of vision, is endemic in many regions of the world. According to an estimate in 1956, cases of this communicable virus disease totaled 400 million. Estimates in 1970 were even larger, despite effective campaigns against the disease. There are two reasons for the increased estimates: trachoma has been found in population groups not previously surveyed, and larger numbers of children who are surviving other diseases are being exposed to infection.

Trachoma can be cured by sulfonamides and various antibiotics, but treatment is relatively long and difficult to administer on a large scale. Nevertheless, mass treatment campaigns assisted by WHO and UNICEF in 21 countries in Africa, Asia and Europe have had significant success.

In 1959 isolation of the trachoma virus in culture revived widespread interest in laboratory research. A number of institutions in every continent have been studying various aspects of the problem. Attempts to produce an effective vaccine have been disappointing, but work is continuing together with basic research, which may lead to new therapeutic or preventive approaches. Epidemiological studies are aimed at obtaining a better understanding of the natural history of the disease. The WHO International Reference Center for Trachoma in California collects and stores strains of the agent and distributes them as required together with standardized reagents to other laboratories working on this disease. Specialized training of trachomatologists is another important function of the California center, which maintains contacts with other laboratories taking part in collaborative studies.

Leprosy

Data published by WHO in 1966 about the world leprosy problem showed that there were some 11 million estimated cases in 1965. The number of treated cases was over 1.9 million, which represented 68% of the registered (2.8 million) and 18% of the estimated cases. About 2,097 million people lived in areas with leprosy prevalence rates of 0.5 per 1,000 or higher. The data represented an attempt to indicate the magnitude of the leprosy problem in order to provide a better approach to its epidemiological, human, and socioeconomic aspects.

In 1965–70 over 500,000 cases were detected and registered in 107 countries. Reports from 51 countries indicate that 131,987 leprosy patients were released from control during the same period, and 217,878 treated cases in 54 countries were considered inactive (disease arrested). Following WHO recommendations in 1958, compulsory segregation of leprosy patients was abolished, and emphasis was given to out-patient care.

Progress in leprosy control has been hampered by the shortcomings of antileprosy drugs, limited development of health services in endemic areas, and gaps in knowledge about the disease. WHO gives technical advice to UNICEF-assisted leprosy control projects in many countries and to government and private agencies throughout the world. It also arranges for and assists in the training of technical personnel. In addition, WHO promotes and coordinates research on drug trials, chemoprophylaxis, cultivation and experimental transmission of *Myobacterium leprae*, epidemiology, immunology, and pathology, with priority for investigations that can most rapidly bring improvement in leprosy control.

Schistosomiasis

This disease, also known as bilharziasis ("snail fever"), is caused by trematode worms that live in the human veins. There are three main forms, produced by three different species of the genus *Schistosoma*. The disease is endemic in many tropical and subtropical regions of Africa, Asia, South America, and the Carribean. The parasite spends part of its life cycle in freshwater snails, and human beings contract the debilitating disease through wading or swimming in contaminated water. Schistosomiasis has been spreading with the development of water resources for irrigation and hydroelectric power. The number of persons infected is estimated to be 200 million.

Recent developments in chemotherapy and molluscicides are likely to give great assistance in campaigns against schistosomiasis. But in spite of these advances, schistosomiasis still takes a heavy toll in human health and continues to thwart economic development in many countries.

International Health Regulations and the Reporting of Cases or Outbreaks

International health regulations are intended to ensure maximum security against the international spread of disease and avoid interference with world traffic. Unfortunately, many international health policies were founded on a defensive, legalistic attitude. The inherent element of compulsion was expressed in the word "quarantine," which implied some type of police action at the national level. Experience has shown that these defensive policies were not a sufficient deterrent against the introduction of serious communicable diseases into any given nation. It has become apparent that a more positive scientific and technical approach, as opposed to a legalistic and regulation-minded one, must be adopted both nationally and internationally.

Resolutions were adopted that changed the name of the old Committee on International Quarantine to a new Committee on International Surveillance of Communicable Diseases. Also, the International Sanitary Regulations are now the International Health Regulations. The latter, which became effective on 1 January 1971, have further important changes, reflecting the new approach of international surveillance rather than regulation and quarantine. These changes are expected to facilitate the development of integrated national epidemiological surveillance services as a part of the general health services of a country. Gradually, better understanding and more sincere cooperation should develop among the epidemiological services of the various countries. As a natural extension of this, the development of international surveillance responsibility and resources would include early notification of cases and outbreaks and coordination of measures preventing the export or import of communicable diseases.

Only four diseases are subject to the new International Health Regulations: yellow fever, plague, cholera, and smallpox. The regulations for reporting cases and outbreaks of these diseases are specified in Articles 3 to 9. All initial cases or suspects, including those transferred or imported into a country, should be reported immediately and directly to WHO, Geneva, by telegram, telex, or telephone within 24 hours of receipt of the first information by a national health administration. These reports are to be supplemented by laboratory diagnosis, clinical findings, and pertinent epidemiological details as soon as they become available. When an epidemic is in progress, weekly summaries are to be forwarded to WHO. Instructions on declaring an area free of infection are given in Article 7, and they vary with each disease. In addition to the specific notifications, which may be sent at any time, the regulations request member governments to prepare and send to WHO each week summaries of the cases and deaths that have occurred in the preceding week for any of the diseases under the regulations. If none has occurred, a negative report is requested by airmail letter. In the case of plague, health administrations are to undertake collection and regular examination of rodents and their ectoparasites in areas infected or suspected of being infected by rodent plague. With respect to yellow fever, each health administration shall notify WHO of those areas within its territory where the presence of the vector would permit the development of the disease if the yellow fever virus were introduced. Finally, each health administration is requested to furnish an annual summary of the status of the diseases subject to the regulations, concurrent with other information submitted annually to WHO.

The Epidemiological Surveillance and Quarantine unit of WHO prepares and transmits a daily epidemiological bulletin by radio-telegraph.

The Weekly Epidemiological Record (WER)

The WER publishes notes on communicable diseases of international importance and information concerning the application of the International Health Regulations. In the past the publication was chiefly a summary of the weekly or daily notifications of diseases under the regulations with declarations of infected areas or of freedom from infection when attained. It then became the vehicle for timely reports, narrative summaries, and interpretive comments on a variety of communicable disease topics. Annual, semiannual, or quarterly summaries are published of major trends in diseases receiving special attention, such as malaria and smallpox. Data from special surveillance programs, such as smallpox eradication, the global influenza program, the European program for salmonella, and dengue hemorrhagic fever surveillance, are summarized and published at appropriate intervals. The *WER* also communicates important changes in the International Health Regulations or the changing policies of the member states.

Yellow Fever

An acute and often fatal disease, yellow fever occurs in certain tropical and semitropical countries, including parts of Central and South America and tropical Africa. There was a major outbreak in Ethiopia in 1961, in Senegal in 1965, and in five other countries of West Africa in 1969. This mosquito-borne disease has never been known in Asia, although conditions for its propagation seem favorable in many areas of that continent.

Much progress has been made in the Western Hemisphere through an eradication campaign against *Aedes aegypti,* the mosquito that spreads yellow fever, carried out in cities under the auspices of the PASB. Outbreaks of jungle yellow fever continue to occur in countries in the Americas, but the number of cases is generally small. Yellow fever has not been reported north of the Panama Canal since 1957.

Plague

The incidence of plague in humans has been dramatically reduced, but a serious danger still exists as long as there are plague-infected rats, mice, and wild rodents at large. Plague deaths fell from a yearly average of 170,000 in the 1920's to less than 288 by 1958 and 169 in 1961.

In 1964, however, a fairly large outbreak occurred in Tanzania, and in 1965 a higher incidence was observed both in South America and in Southeast Asia. In 1966, 3,809 cases and 214 deaths were reported to WHO, the bulk of them in Viet-Nam.

The geographical distribution of plague in the world has remained more or less the same. This indicates that plague is far from vanishing and will continue to present an important problem whenever man has to penetrate into areas where wild-life plague exists.

Cholera

Since 1961, cholera caused by the *El Tor vibrio* has spread from its endemic foci and gradually invaded practically all countries in the Western Pacific and Southeast Asia regions, most of which had been free from cholera for many years. Cholera continued to spread westward, reaching West Pakistan, Afghanistan, Iran, and Uzbekistan (USSR) in 1965 and Iraq in 1966. The spread of cholera in 1969 and in the summer of 1970 created great problems in the Middle East, North and West Africa, and in Europe. Numerous field and laboratory studies, organized mostly by WHO, showed that current control measures are rather ineffective. The anticholera vaccines in use, when tested in controlled field trials, were shown to protect at most about half of the persons vaccinated and for less than six months. Some vaccines provided no protection at all. Furthermore, it was shown that one third or more of the persons who come in contact with cholera victims can become carriers of the disease. Persons recovering from cholera may remain carriers for four months to eight years or more.

In view of these findings, WHO has intensified its research activities. With modern treatment, case fatalities should be no more than 1% to 3%.

Smallpox

WHO has adopted an all-out worldwide eradication policy against smallpox. This disease lends itself particularly well to eradication, for it is directly transmitted from man to man, there are no animal reservoirs or vectors, and the disease is quickly detected. Furthermore, the victim of the disease transmits the virus for only about two weeks and is immune against further attacks.

Eradication is achieved by programs of systematic vaccination coupled with special surveillance activities to detect, investigate, and contain outbreaks. Vaccination reduces the number of persons susceptible to the disease, while surveillance is designed to break the remaining chains of transmission.

A global program of eradication was initiated in 1959, but progress was limited because of lack of funds and other support. To intensify its activity WHO, in 1967, was provided with a special budget for smallpox eradication, and considerable additional bilateral and multilateral support was offered by many countries, particularly the US and the USSR. It was hoped that the task might be completed in 10 years.

In 1959, 94,603 cases were reported. The number fluctuated over succeeding years, reaching a maximum of 132,773 in 1963. In 1967, the first year of the intensified program, 131,160 cases were recorded. Since then, the incidence of smallpox has declined steadily. In 1969, 53,814 cases were reported, the lowest in history. The number of countries reporting smallpox has also decreased—from 61 in 1959 to 43 in 1967 and to 29 in 1970. As of July 1969, 17 countries remained endemic; 1 in South America (Brazil); 5 in Asia (Afghanistan, Indonesia, India, Nepal, Pakistan), and 12 in Africa (except for Nigeria and Dahomey, all in eastern and southern Africa).

Transmission from these countries to the rest of the world remains a problem. Imported cases continue to be reported each year from many parts of the world. Until smallpox is eradicated on a worldwide basis, countries free from smallpox must continue to pay a high cost for remaining free through vaccination campaigns and quarantine measures. For example, Czechoslovakia spends more than $1 million per year and the US $20 million a year on maintenance vaccination.

The World Health Organization provides to countries in

endemic areas freeze-dried vaccine that remains stable even in the tropics, vaccination instruments, vehicles, camping equipment, and technical personnel. In addition, more than 30 countries have contributed vaccine, financial support, and technical personnel. Even so, the endemic countries themselves have been the supporters of the program through provision of personnel, transportation costs, and so forth.

From the results of successful programs already conducted in many countries of the Americas, Asia, and Africa, no technical problems seem insurmountable in realizing the goal of global smallpox eradication.

Diseases of Undernourishment and Malnutrition

Active international interest in the public health aspects of nutrition dates only from the 1930's, when reports on nutrition and its physiological bases were prepared and circulated by the Health Organization of the League of Nations. Food shortages during World War II focused attention on the subject, and in 1948 the first World Health Assembly gave high priority to nutrition in the program of the newly founded World Health Organization.

The work of WHO has been devoted principally to the following areas: protein-calorie malnutrition (PCM) in young children, relationship between PCM and infection, development and testing of new protein-rich foods, nutritional anemias, vitamin A deficiency, endemic goiter, rickets, assessment of nutritional status, nutritional requirements, nutrition activities in health services, coordinated applied nutrition programs, and training of personnel.

In this comprehensive program WHO coordinates its activities with those of other specialized agencies in relationship with the UN. From the outset there has been close collaboration with FAO and UNICEF, particularly in promoting local production of protein-rich foods and encouraging mothers and young children to use them.

Diseases Transmissible Between Animals and Man (Zoonosis)

Several diseases and infections that are interchangeable between human beings and animals are being studied and combated by WHO in cooperation with FAO. These include brucellosis, which affects sheep, swine, goats, and cattle, causing great losses in milk and meat production. When transmitted to humans, brucellosis takes the form of a prolonged disease known as undulant fever. One strain, carried by sheep and goats, causes the highly virulent Malta fever. The chief hope for combating this disease appears to be the elimination of infected animals. When this is not possible for economic reasons, development of better vaccines and vaccination procedures is the best interim measure. Rabies, invariably fatal once the clinical signs appear, is being attacked by WHO-sponsored and coordinated research programs in several countries. More potent and less cumbersome vaccination procedures for man are being developed. Other projects deal with ecological factors, surveillance, and control of wildlife rabies. Among the other zoonoses that WHO is studying are toxoplasmosis, hydatidosis, and cysticercosis.

Mental Health

Two ten-year programs of research in psychiatry were inaugurated in 1965—one concerned with psychiatric diagnosis, classification, and epidemiology, and the other with biological aspects of psychiatry.

International seminars have concentrated each year on a different category of psychiatric disorders with a view to improving international agreement on diagnosis and classification. Diagnostic exercises using case histories and filmed or videotaped interviews have been used. The first part of an international pilot study of schizophrenia has been carried out with nine collaborating field centers using agreed research methods, schedules, and follow-up studies.

Four scientific groups have convened to consider the state of knowledge and the further research required concerning genetics in psychiatry, psychopharmacology, neurophysiological and behavioral research in psychiatry, and the biochemistry of mental disorders. Their recommendations have led to the establishment of international collaborative research on specific aspects of these subjects. Regional and international reference centers have been set up to collect information on psychotropic drugs. In 1969 a scientific group on schizophrenia considered both epidemiological and biological research in this category of mental disorders.

WHO is attempting to interest governments in establishing the mechanisms for carrying out operational research on psychiatric services as a whole and on services for prevention and treatment of problems having mental health repercussions, such as mental retardation, dependence on alcohol and other drugs, suicide prevention, and delinquency.

B. MEDICAL EDUCATION AND TRAINING

Almost all WHO activities have an educational aspect. Moreover, as a sure means of moving toward the solution of the immense health problems facing the world, WHO has devoted a large part of its resources to the education and training of health workers. The world lacks sufficient doctors, nurses, and other health personnel. For a total population of about 3.2 billion there are only 1.5 million doctors. Although some countries have 1 doctor for every 500 inhabitants, the proportion in others is 1 to 50,000 or more. The lack of medical personnel no doubt is the greatest obstacle to health progress. There is also the question of quality.

Visiting Professors and Teams

WHO encourages the creation of medical teaching institutions in the developing countries and provides teachers for limited periods. In 1969, 233 visiting teachers were provided to schools in 58 countries and territories for an average of 9 months each. The subjects taught included environmental health, nursing, pediatrics, basic and clinical medical services, public health, and preventive medicine. A visiting professor is expected to train national staff, so that at least one qualified person may take over when WHO assistance ends.

Training of Medical Auxiliaries

Since so few doctors are available in most developing countries, and since it will take many years to train the requisite number of new doctors, it is essential that auxiliary personnel take over all the routine work that can be entrusted to them under qualified supervision. Medical assistants and other auxiliary staff can perform many of the duties required in basic health services, and considerable effort is devoted to the training of such personnel in the developing countries. Great importance is attached to adapting the training to the work required from every category of health personnel. Consequently, attention is paid to careful description of jobs that serve as a basis for the design of curricula. Research projects have been supported in various universities in the UAR, Brazil, and Hungary.

WHO Fellowships

WHO organizes or assists training courses for government-sponsored candidates in specialized fields such as anesthesiology, human genetics, and viral laboratory techniques. It holds many international meetings, which, through exchange of information, serve educational purposes. WHO fellowships are granted on government request through the regional offices and go mainly to qualified health workers for studies not available in their own countries. From 1 December 1968 to 30 November 1969 the number of individual fellowships granted by WHO was over 3,400. WHO also concerns itself with standards of education and the contents of curricula, on which it makes recommendations.

Nursing

As stated in the *Second World Health Situation Report,* "In the last analysis nothing is more important for the future of the health services than the training of personnel and not least of women in all branches of nursing, including midwifery. . . ."

Due to increases in population and to expanding health services, there continues to be a shortage of qualified nursing personnel in practically all countries. To overcome this shortage greater attention is being given to devising ways in which all categories and levels of nursing personnel can be most effectively utilized. To this end, the allocation of activities and tasks according to the level of skill and responsibility involved and the preparation required for each level are important. Emphasis is also placed on the systematic and scientific study of problems relating to nursing service, education, practice, and postbasic nursing education.

An overall view of WHO's program for 1969 shows that 95 countries received assistance in nursing through the provision of over 280 professional nursing or midwifery personnel in 223 projects.

C. PUBLIC HEALTH SERVICES
Most of the WHO member states receive assistance from WHO in one form or another. Central health administrations in a number of countries are assisted with planning, coordinating multilateral or bilateral aid, and training high-level public health staff.

Planning Health Services
WHO frequently is called upon by countries to assist in assessing their health situation and for advice on planning their health plans and shaping them into a form acceptable to their governments; to advise on the type and amount of health manpower required as well as their education and training; and to evaluate plans that are either completed or being implemented. Planning, whether in the economic or the health field, concerns not only politicians and health experts at the center but also men and women in every town and village and health workers in the field.

The utmost importance of health manpower planning is widely recognized. In any plan to established a network of health services, it is essential to determine the necessary categories of health personnel and to develop a suitable training program to provide them. No realistic health plan draft can ignore the fact that in 1965 at least 14 countries with populations far in excess of 3 million had no medical schools. The situation is particularly grave in Africa. The creation of educational and training facilities must receive the highest priority if the emerging nations are to organize their own medical and public health services. In the developing countries, education and training of health personnel must be conceived as an integral part of their national health plans.

Environmental Health
In the field of environmental health WHO promotes the planning and organization of national environmental health programs. It gives advice on community water supplies, wastes disposal, environmental pollution (air, water, soil, and food), the health aspects of housing, and environmental health problems arising from urbanization and industrialization. It collects, appraises, and disseminates technical information, encourages and promotes research, and assists in the education and training of personnel.

The community water supply program is designed to help developing countries assess their needs, formulate policies and programs for meeting those needs, and create national and regional organizations for planning, financing, constructing, managing, and operating community water supplies. Most developing countries lack funds for the construction of waterworks. WHO, although not itself a financing agency, assists member governments in this respect. Preinvestment surveys financed by the Special Fund component of the United Nations Development Program have been undertaken, with WHO assisting both in the preparation of the government's request and as executing agency for the project.

WHO emphasizes the need for planning for wastes disposal and for water supplies simultaneously and has assisted a number of countries in the preparation of requests to UNDP (SF) for preinvestment surveys. Wastes management projects are in progress in China (Taiwan), Iran (Teheran), Nigeria (Ibadan), Philippines (Manila), and in the Central African Republic (Bangui).

WHO's environmental pollution program aims at assisting countries by determining those levels of pollution that are incompatible with health and by advising on measures to prevent pollution from becoming a major hazard in the course of economic and social development. Almost every country is faced with the problem of water pollution. In the developed countries the demand for water is growing continually. Even if the rate of increase is as low as 4% a year, the water requirements and the need for new purification plants will double every 20 years.

Research and development activities in various fields of environmental health are stimulated by WHO international reference centers together with regional and national centers and collaborating laboratories. The outcome is expected to provide, particularly for developing countries, some new approaches to problems. International reference systems are being established for community water supply, wastes disposal, air pollution, water pollution, and environmental radiation protection.

WHO, on request, provides assistance to governments in the planning, organization, and strengthening of environmental sanitation services and the training of sanitation personnel. Training of sanitary engineers and sanitarians has been going on for several years in India, Lebanon, Morocco, Tanzania, and elsewhere. In fact, most WHO country projects dealing with public health and sanitation include classroom or in-service training of local sanitation workers. Seminars and training courses are also organized on various subjects.

The findings of groups of experts convened by WHO have been published in the *Technical Report Series* of the organization and in a number of guides and manuals.

Health Laboratory Services
In 1969, WHO provided assistance to 105 national projects in 61 countries and 22 intercountry projects in the planning and organization of public health laboratory services, training of personnel (mainly technicians), and provision of equipment. The International Committee on Laboratory Animals, which is supported mainly by WHO, provides advice to countries on the rearing and maintenance of laboratory animals for diagnostic, control, and research purposes and promotes international cooperation through seminars and research studies. WHO also cooperates with the International Committee for Standardization in Hematology.

Health Aspects of Population Dynamics
The health aspects of population dynamics are numerous and varied. On the one hand, health services contribute to shaping patterns of natality, mortality, and migration. On the other, changes in population size, composition, and distribution create health problems and demand changes in health services. Health services thus play a role as determinants and consequences of population changes.

Generally, better health is correlated with changes from wasteful patterns of high mortality and high natality to more productive patterns of low mortality with natality regulated as desired, irrespective of increase or decrease over previous levels. Childbearing patterns are deeply influenced when health measures give greater assurances that children will survive. Historically, a high birthrate is associated with high infant mortality. A minimal level of health seems to be necessary for a family to realize that it can control its own "demographic" behavior.

Health factors and health services thus are important components of the equations that determine population outcome. At the same time, population changes bring with them increasing need for new approaches to health services. Regardless of what else is done to change current population trends, medical and public health services will need to intensify their activities to meet the challenges of growing population trends in many countries—rapidly expanding urbanization in some, growing populations in many others, and so forth. There is an urgent need for large-scale planning to create "mass" networks of basic health services as soon as possible.

The entire work of WHO thus becomes relevant to the health aspects of world population. Population projections regarding birthrates, patterns of mortality and morbidity, migration, and age composition and life expectancy are necessary for the planning and implementation of health services. The relevant statistics to provide such information are urgently needed. The training of manpower is probably the most important factor in the implementation of health programs to meet the needs produced by changes in world population.

Health Education
WHO defines health education as helping people to achieve better health through their own efforts. Health education services, when properly planned, organized, and implemented within the organizational framework of national health programs, can be of importance in helping to enlist the active participation of the people concerned in making better use of available health services and related resources. WHO assists the health ministries of its member states to establish or reorganize their technical health education services and to recruit and train their own professional specialists. Another major concern of WHO includes assistance in improving the preparation in health education of all professional and auxiliary health workers. In addition, WHO has continued to work with UNESCO and UNICEF in fostering health education as an important component of programs of primary and secondary education, teacher education, and colleges and universities. Health education has been the subject of several meetings of experts, scientific groups, and technical seminars.

D. PHARMACEUTICAL QUALITY CONTROL
International Pharmacopoeia
In 1865 the first attempt was made to establish international standards for therapeutic and other agents. Limited agreements concerning certain potent drugs were reached in the first decades of the 20th century, and in 1937 the compilation of an international pharmacopoeia was begun under League of Nations auspices.

The first volume of *Pharmacopoeia Internationalis* was completed by a WHO committee in 1951, a second volume in 1955, and a supplement in 1959. These volumes contain specifications for physical and chemical properties, identification tests, permissible limits for impurities, usual and maximum doses to be prescribed, and other important information for over 400 pharmaceutical products, including insulin preparations, antibiotics, and synthetic drugs. A second edition of the pharmacopoeia, published in 1967, contains 555 monographs and 69 appendices. A supplement is in preparation. The World Medical Association, the International Pharmaceutical Federation, the International Union of Pure and Applied Chemistry, and other nongovernmental and national organizations are cooperating in this major undertaking.

Although the specifications of the *International Pharmacopoeia* are not binding upon member states, they are used increasingly for domestically manufactured and imported products.
International Nonproprietary Names for Drugs
Many pharmaceutical substances are known not only by their nonproprietary or scientific names but by various trade names as well. For instance methadone hydrochloride is also known

as Amidone, Miadone, Diadone, Diaminon, Mephenon, and Symoron. WHO has set up a procedure to rectify this situation (without jeopardizing legitimate commercial interests) by proposing lists of international nonproprietary names for pharmaceutical substances. Such names are published regularly in the *WHO Chronicle*. By the end of 1970 over 2,500 names had been proposed and published in 24 lists. A second cumulative list comprising lists 1–17 was published in 1967.
WHO Center for Chemical Reference Substances, Stockholm
As a further service, the WHO Center for Chemical Reference Substances was established at the Apotekens Centrallaboratorium in Stockholm in 1955. Its function is to collect, assay, and store chemical reference substances and to make them available, free of charge, to national and nonprofit laboratories and institutes and, for a nominal fee, to commercial firms. About 40 chemical reference substances needed for tests and assays described in the *International Pharmacopoeia* are available.
International Biological Standardization
A number of substances used in prophylactic and therapeutic medicine require testing, on either animals or microorganisms, to evaluate their potency. This is known as biological assay, and the substances that need to be assayed are called biological substances. Many complexities are involved, including varying susceptibilities of animals in different parts of the world or even at different times in the same laboratory. This necessitates the determination of potency relative to an established standard, national or international.

Much work in this field was done under League of Nations auspices, so that by 1945, 34 international biological standards were established for such substances as vaccines, antitoxins, antisera, some antibiotics, enzymes, and hormones. Since then, WHO had enlisted the collaboration of more than 100 laboratories to conduct international collaborative biological assays. Speed is sometimes an important consideration, so that international standards for newly developed substances may be introduced before many varying units of potency are designated and accepted at national levels.

The work on biological standardization has expanded considerably and comprises a number of new activities, including the establishment of international reference reagents for the purpose of diagnosis and identification. By 1970, 22 years after the inception of WHO, there were over 250 international biological standards, reference preparations, and reference reagents established and nearly 70 others under consideration.

A further activity has been the formulation of sets of requirements for the manufacture and testing of certain biological products used in medicine. These are intended to help member states ensure at least a minimum level of efficacy and safety of these products. By the end of 1965, 21 such sets of requirements were published.
International Blood Group Reference Laboratory
In 1952 the Blood Group Reference Laboratory of the United Kingdom Medical Research Council in London was designated as a WHO international center. It is concerned mainly with techniques and reagents related to blood groups and other factors that are of special interest in blood transfusion, medicolegal work, genetics, and anthropology.

E. FOOD ADDITIVES: A NEW PROBLEM
The widespread use of chemical substances to improve the appearance, flavor, or durability of food products presents a new health problem. WHO has found that many additives are used without adequate previous testing to determine possible harmful effects. Legislation controlling their use is meager or virtually nonexistent in many countries; nor is their use governed by international agreement on uniformity, procedures, testing, and standards.

A conference on food additives was convened by FAO and WHO in 1956. Since that time, the Joint FAO-WHO Expert Committee on Food Additives has made toxicological evaluations of many food additives and has prepared specifications for their identity and purity.

F. ATOMIC ENERGY IN RELATION TO HEALTH

The work of WHO in the field of radiation began in 1954. It has been concerned with three main areas: radiation effects on man—in particular the genetic and somatic health problems associated with the uses of radiation; radiation protection measures dealing with the public health aspects of atomic energy and the use of radiation and radioactive isotopes in medicine, research, and industry; and radiation medicine—that is, the use of X-rays, other ionizing radiations, and radionuclides in medicine and health work. WHO has concentrated on assisting national programs in radiation protection within the framework of public health services, encouraging the sound use of radiation and radioactive materials in health work, and helping to initiate and coordinate research in radiobiology and radiation genetics. Increased attention has been devoted to the education and training of professional and technical personnel in radiation medicine, considering that the greatest contribution to man-made radiation exposure of populations is by the medical use of radiation, particularly for X-ray diagnosis, and that the extent of such exposure depends primarily on the knowledge and experience of the persons handling these radiations. A number of guidelines and manuals have been published, particularly in cooperation with the IAEA. WHO in its activities has collaborated with FAO, ILO, and IAEA; the UN Scientific Committee on the Effects of Atomic Radiation; and the International Commissions on Radiological Protection and Radiological Units and Measures, as well as with other intergovernmental and nongovernmental organizations.

G. MEDICAL RESEARCH

WHO medical research is directed toward problems that by their nature cannot be investigated adequately on the national level. The organization has no laboratories of its own but works with individuals and institutions all over the world, stimulating the coordinating projects where an acute need for further information has appeared or where it may be possible to formulate and test a new and potentially useful hypothesis. Thus important studies of the genetics, physiology, and biochemistry of insects have been being made in close cooperation with numerous centers and laboratories throughout the world. Through these studies it is hoped that new methods of controlling disease-bearing insects that have developed resistance to insecticides will result.

WHO also works in the field of chronic degenerative diseases such as cancer. The trend of mortality rates for cancer is steadily rising all over the world. Therefore, the problems of cancer as a disease become more and more important, particularly in developed countries. Present diagnostic and therapeutic facilities enable final cures to be achieved in many cancer sites where there is early detection. One of WHO's activities in cancer is focused on the implementation of early detection measures, such as mass screening procedures for those cancer sites for which it is possible—for example, for cervical cancer. A coordinated international approach is clearly indicated for comparative studies, a basis for which is an agreed terminology for different types of tumors. To this end, WHO has set up 17 international reference centers that work with more than 200 collaborating laboratories in 46 countries. For exploring the best diagnostic and therapeutical procedures, 4 international reference centers with 54 collaborating laboratories in 26 countries have been established. Besides this, WHO supports international comparative studies that are intended not only to elucidate the striking differences in incidence between some countries but also to broaden the avenues for better understanding of cancer.

Other examples of WHO-sponsored international collaborative research ventures include investigations into the adaptation of the human organism to extremes of heat, cold, and altitude, the toxicity of insecticides to mammals, adverse reactions to drugs, and the development of high blood pressure in different environmental conditions.

WHO's research program is constantly expanding. This is reflected in the increasing number of research training grants awarded and of scientific groups that are called to advise on specific problems. Extensive use is made of their published reports on subjects such as cholera, dental health, environmental pollution, and virus diseases. New collaborative research projects include the biology of human reproduction, human genetics, and immunology. The WHO Advisory Committee on Medical Research, composed of some 20 distinguished scientists, reviews work done and gives advice to the director general.

WHO reference centers have been set up essentially for providing services to medical research: they act as the final courts of appeal for the identification of unusual variants of disease-producing organisms; they distribute standard substances to serve as international yardsticks; they encourage the use of uniform techniques; and, in general, they help to make the results of medical research internationally comparable. Most of them also provide specialized training. In all, there are 191 regional or international reference centers spread over 34 countries. Together with their many collaborating laboratories, they form a network of scientific cooperation spanning the globe.

8 BIBLIOGRAPHY

Bulletin of the World Health Organization. The principal scientific periodical of the WHO. 2 vols. (12 numbers) annually. One year, $25.00; single copies, $2.25.

Chronicle of the World Health Organization. Monthly. Describes all public health activities undertaken under WHO auspices or with WHO participation. Also reviews all WHO technical publications. One year, $3.00; single copies, $0.30.

Epidemiological and Vital Statistics Report. Monthly. Statistics on notifiable infectious diseases, natality, mortality, causes of death, etc. One year, $16.00; single copies, prices vary.

The First Ten Years of the World Health Organization. 1958. vii + 538 pp. $5.00.

The Second Ten Years of the World Health Organization. 1968. viii + 413 pp. $8.75

International Digest of Health Legislation. Quarterly. One year, $10.00.

Series: *Monograph Series* ("essentially textbooks for post-graduate workers," published after examination by internationally recognized authorities); *Public Health Papers* (for wider circulation), for example, Nos. 26–31: "Domestic Accidents" ($2.00); "Trends in the Study of Morbidity and Mortality" ($2.75); "Aspects of Family Mental Health in Europe"; ($1.75); "Mass Campaigns and General Health Services" ($1.25); "Noise: An Occupational Hazard and Public Nuisance" ($2.00); "A Guide for Staffing a Hospital Nursing Service" ($1.25); and *Technical Report Series* (prepared by, or summarizing the work of, committees and study groups), for example, Nos. 330–345: "Trachoma Research"; "The Midwife in Maternity Care"; "Basic and Clinical Aspects of Intra-Uterine Devices"; "Chemistry and Physiology of the Gametes"; "Immunological Aspects of Human Reproduction"; "Expert Committee on Onchocerciasis"; "Sampling Methods in Morbidity Surveys and Public Health Investigations"; "Training and Preparation of Teachers for Medical Schools with Special Regard to the Needs of Developing Countries"; "Haemoglobinopathies and Allied Disorders"; "Specifications for the Identity and Purity of Food Additives; and Their Toxicological Evaluation"; "Methods of Planning and Evaluation in Applied Nutrition Programs"; "Principles for Pre-Clinical Testing of Drug Safety"; "Prevention of Rheumatic Fever"; "Expert Committee on Dependence-Producing Drugs"; "Immunotherapy of Cancer"; "Training of Health Laboratory Personnel"; "Research on Genetics in Psychiatry."

Weekly Epidemiological Record. Contains notifications and other information relating to diseases designated as "quarantinable" in the International Sanitary Regulations. For the guidance of national health administrations and quarantine services. One year, $15.00; single copies, $0.30.

World Directory of Medical Schools. 3d ed., 1963. 348 pp. $6.75

World Health. Illustrated WHO periodical for the nontechnical reader. One year, $5.00; single copies, $0.50.

UNITED NATIONS EDUCATIONAL, SCIENTIFIC AND CULTURAL ORGANIZATION (UNESCO)

1 BACKGROUND : "Since wars begin in the minds of men," the preamble to the UNESCO constitution states, "it is in the minds of men that the defences of peace must be constructed." Education, science, and cultural institutions have not always been enlisted to serve peace and the ennoblement of man; indeed, they have sometimes been employed to advance the most ignoble ends. As also stated in the preamble, "the great and terrible war which has just ended was a war made possible by the denial of the democratic principles of the dignity, equality and mutual respect of men, and by the propagation, in their place, through ignorance and prejudice, of the doctrine of the inequality of men and races." World War II was too recent an event when UNESCO was created for its founders to forget that. UNESCO's purpose as an autonomous member of the UN family of organizations is "to contribute to peace and security by promoting collaboration among the nations through education, science and culture in order to further universal respect for justice, for the rule of law and for the human rights and fundamental freedoms which are affirmed for the peoples of the world, without distinction of race, sex, language or religion, by the Charter of the United Nations."

INTERNATIONAL INTELLECTUAL COOPERATION DURING THE LEAGUE OF NATIONS PERIOD

Occasional attempts at international cooperation in educational, scientific, and cultural matters were made before World War I, but no machinery existed to promote these efforts on a worldwide scale. Even the League of Nations Covenant, when it was drawn up after the war, failed to mention international cooperation in these matters. However, thanks in a great part to the efforts of the Belgian delegate Henri La Fontaine, a League of Nations Committee on Intellectual Cooperation was formed. Composed of 12 eminent persons, the committee met for the first time in the summer of 1922 under the chairmanship of the French philosopher Henri Bergson. Among those who served on the committee were Marie Curie, Gilbert Murray, and Albert Einstein. The intellectual atmosphere that prevailed in the committee was a lofty one, but at the same time the committee established precedents in practical matters that have proved useful to UNESCO. Thus, the 40-odd national committees on intellectual cooperation whose creation it promoted were a precedent for the national commissions now operating in 94 countries to further the work of UNESCO. The International Institute of Intellectual Cooperation, established with the aid of the French government, and located in Paris, began work early in 1926 and provided a permanent secretariat for the Committee on Intellectual Cooperation.

Through the Committee on Intellectual Cooperation, the permanent institute in Paris, and the national committees on intellectual cooperation, collectively known as the International Organization for Intellectual Cooperation, the League was provided with a technical body to promote international activity in this field. Although modest in size and handicapped by an inadequate budget, the organization was active in many fields, especially those of interest to scholars, professional men, learned societies, librarians, and the like. It promoted studies on a variety of subjects, including such practical matters as the employment situation in the academic world. Numerous conferences and symposia were held under the auspices of the International Institute in Paris. Among the topics taken up by these conferences as the world situation became more menacing were the psycho-logical causes of war and methods of promoting peaceful change as a substitute for war. Although education did not originally come under the organization's purview—governments tended to look rather doubtfully on discussions about their educational systems—it was later to have a prominent place in its work. For example, the Organization for Intellectual Cooperation conducted a worldwide survey of higher education, became a center for studies on secondary education and textbook revision, and concerned itself with the use of radios, films, and audio-visual aids in schools.

2 CREATION

More intensive international cooperation in the field of educational problems began during World War II itself. A Conference of Allied Ministers of Education (CAME) was convened in London in November 1942 to consider how the devastated educational systems of the countries under Nazi occupation could be restored after the war. The first meeting of the conference was attended by representatives of eight governments in exile and the French National Committee of Liberation. CAME met at frequent intervals throughout the war, with the participation of a growing number of representatives of other allied governments. The US delegation to the April 1944 meeting of the conference included William Fulbright, then congressman and later senator from Arkansas, and the poet Archibald MacLeish, at that time Librarian of Congress, who was later to participate in the drafting of UNESCO's constitution.

Before the US delegation left for the San Francisco Conference of 1945, which was to draft the UN Charter, two resolutions of the US Congress, the Mundt Resolution in the House of Representatives and the Fulbright-Taft Resolution in the Senate, recommended the creation of an international educational agency. It was decided at San Francisco that one of the objectives of the UN should be to promote international cultural and educational cooperation, and a number of delegates, notably the Chinese and French, stressed the need for a separate specialized agency to devote itself exclusively to this task. Addressing the closing plenary session, President Harry S Truman declared: "We must set up an effective agency for constant and thorough interchange of thoughts and ideas. For there lies the road to a better and more tolerant understanding among nations and among peoples.''

The conference that created UNESCO met, at the invitation of the UK and French governments, in London in November 1945. It was attended by all but 7 of the 51 governments that had signed the UN Charter. Among governments not attending was that of the USSR, which maintained that the conference should have been called by the UN Economic and Social Council. Important decisions were made at the London conference. It was decided that the new organization should deal not only with the transmission of existing knowledge, that is, with education, but with the pursuit of new knowledge as well. Hence, the encouragement of natural and social sciences through international cooperation was one of the principal tasks assigned UNESCO. UNESCO's constitution was adopted by the London conference after only two weeks of discussion and entered into effect on 4 November 1946 when 20 states had deposited instruments of acceptance with the UK government.

3 PURPOSES

UNESCO's functions as prescribed in its constitution are to "(a) Collaborate in the work of advancing the mutual knowledge and understanding of peoples, through all means of mass communication. ... (b) Give fresh impulse to popular education and to the spread of culture by collaborating with Members, at their request, in the development of educational activities; by instituting collaboration among the nations to advance the ideal of equality of educational opportunities without regard to race, sex or any distinction, economic or social; by suggesting educational methods best suited to prepare the children of the world for the responsibilities of freedom; (c) Maintain, increase, and diffuse knowledge ... by assuring the conservation and protection of the world's inheritance of books, works of art, and monuments of history and science ... ; by encouraging cooperation among the nations in all branches of intellectual activities, including the international exchange of persons active in the fields of education, science, and culture, and the exchange of publications, objects of artistic and scientific interest, and other materials of information; by initiating methods of international cooperation calculated to give the people of all countries access to the printed and published materials produced by any of them.''

In short, UNESCO is to promote on the one hand the democratization of education, science, and the arts, and thus help to give the people a fuller and more meaningful life; and on the other hand, to promote the progress of all sciences and altogether all branches of intellectual activity, which again aims at improving the material as well as spiritual life of the people.

At the same time, UNESCO's constitution specifically emphasizes the need to preserve "the independence, integrity and fruitful diversity of the cultures and educational systems" of the member states. The organization cannot impose any particular standard either on all its members or on any of them, and it is "prohibited from intervening in matters which are essentially within their domestic jurisdiction.''

4 MEMBERSHIP

Any UN member may join UNESCO. Other states may be admitted to UNESCO membership upon the recommendation of the organization's executive board and the approval of the UNESCO general conference by a two-thirds majority. Austria, Hungary, and Japan joined UNESCO years before being admitted to membership in the UN. Five states still not UN members in 1970 had belonged to UNESCO for a number of years: West Germany, South Korea, Monaco, Switzerland, and South Viet-Nam. The USSR joined in 1954.

A state may withdraw from UNESCO by notifying the organization's Director-General of its intention to do so; the withdrawal takes effect as of the end of the respective calendar year. The Union of South Africa so withdrew as of 31 December 1956. Czechoslovakia, Hungary, and Poland suspended their participation in UNESCO activities in 1952, but returned as active participants in 1954.

Under a UK-proposed amendment to the constitution adopted in 1951 territories or groups of territories not responsible for their international relations can be admitted as associate members upon application of member states or other authorities responsible for their international relations. Associate members do not have the right to vote. At the end of 1946, UNESCO had 27 members; in 1970 UNESCO had 125 members and 3 associate members:

Afghanistan	Ivory Coast
Albania	Jamaica
Algeria	Japan
Argentina	Jordan
Australia	Kenya
Austria	Korea, South
Barbados	Kuwait
Belgium	Laos
Bolivia	Lebanon
Botswana	Lesotho
Brazil	Liberia
Bulgaria	Libya
Burma	Luxembourg
Burundi	Madagascar
Byelorussia	Malawi
Cambodia	Malaysia
Cameroon	Mali
Canada	Malta
Central African Republic	Mauritania
Ceylon	Mauritius
Chad	Mexico
Chile	Monaco
China (Taiwan)	Mongolia
Colombia	Morocco
Congo (Brazzaville)	Nepal
Congo (Kinshasa)	Netherlands
Costa Rica	New Zealand
Cuba	Nicaragua
Cyprus	Niger
Czechoslovakia	Nigeria
Dahomey	Norway
Denmark	Pakistan
Dominican Republic	Panama
Ecuador	Paraguay
El Salvador	Peru
Ethiopia	Philippines
Finland	Poland
France	Portugal
Gabon	Romania
Germany, West	Rwanda
Ghana	Sa'udi Arabia
Greece	Senegal
Guatemala	Sierra Leone
Guinea	Singapore
Guyana	Somalia
Haiti	Spain
Honduras	Sudan
Hungary	Sweden
Iceland	Switzerland
India	Syria
Indonesia	Tanzania
Iran	Thailand
Iraq	Togo
Ireland	Trinidad and Tobago
Israel	Tunisia
Italy	Turkey

Uganda
Ukraine
USSR
UAR (Egypt)
UK
US
Upper Volta
Uruguay
Venezuela

Viet-Nam, South
Yemen
Yugoslavia
Zambia

Associate Members
Bahrayn
British East Caribbean Group
Qatar

⁵STRUCTURE

UNESCO is an autonomous organization affiliated with the UN through a relationship agreement signed in 1946. Its three principal organs are the General Conference, the Executive Board, and the Secretariat, the latter headed by the organization's Director-General.

THE GENERAL CONFERENCE

All UNESCO members have the right to be represented in the General Conference, which determines UNESCO's policies and decides on its major undertakings. Each member state has one vote in the conference but may be represented by five delegates. UNESCO's constitution requires that member governments are to consult with national educational, scientific, and cultural bodies before selecting these delegates; in countries where national UNESCO commissions have been established, these too are to be consulted.

From 1946 through 1952, the General Conference met every year. Since then it has met in alternate even-numbered years only. As a rule, the conference takes place in Paris, but the 1947 session was held in Mexico City, the 1948 session in Beirut, the 1950 session in Florence, the 1954 session in Montevideo, and the 1956 session in New Delhi. Important international artistic and cultural events are often scheduled to accompany sessions of the UNESCO General Conference. In 1966 the General Conference saw the celebration of the 20th anniversary of the founding of UNESCO.

Decisions of the General Conference are made by a simple majority vote except for certain constitutionally specified matters that require a two-thirds majority, such as to amend the UNESCO constitution or to adopt an international convention. Member nations are not automatically bound by conventions adopted by the UNESCO General Conference, but the UNESCO constitution requires them to submit such conventions to their appropriate national authority or authorities for ratification within one year after the close of the respective session of the General Conference. The same applies to recommendations, which the UNESCO General Conference can adopt by simple majority.

THE EXECUTIVE BOARD

The 34-member Executive Board, chosen by the General Conference from the conference delegates, supervises the execution of UNESCO's program. It meets in regular session at least twice a year. Before the General Conference convenes, the Executive Board reviews the budget estimates and work program for the following two-year period as prepared by the Director-General. It submits these, with any recommendations it may make, to the conference and prepares the agenda for the conference. No member state is entitled to permanent representation on the Board and nothing in its rules of procedure corresponds to the big-power veto in the UN Security Council.

The UNESCO constitution provides that "Although the members of the Executive Board are representatives of their respective governments, they shall exercise the powers delegated to them by the General Conference on behalf of the Conference as a whole." In the case of other international organizations, countries rather than individuals are named to their executive bodies, it then being the prerogative of those countries to appoint whatever individuals they choose to represent them. In the case of UNESCO, the General Conference itself elects from among the delegates attending the session the individuals who are to sit on UNESCO's executive body. UNESCO's constitution instructs the conference to select these individuals with due "regard to the diversity of cultures and a balanced geographical distribution" and to "endeavor to include persons competent in the arts, the sciences, education and the diffusion of ideas."

Following a constitutional amendment adopted by the General Conference in 1968, Board members elected since that date serve for six years and are not immediately reeligible for a second term. At each of its biennial sessions the General Conference elects the number of members required to fill the vacancies occurring at the end of the session. Elections during the 1968 session of the General Conference were conducted in accordance with an experimental system of electoral groups. For the two-year period 1969–70, the Board consisted of a chairman from Italy, four vice-chairmen from Czechoslovakia, India, Peru, and Tanzania with members also from Afghanistan, Algeria, Argentina, Brazil, Canada, Ceylon, Chile, Congo, Costa Rica, Ethiopia, Finland, France, Hungary, Israel, Ivory Coast, Japan, Lebanon, Mali, Mexico, Netherlands, Nigeria, Pakistan, Senegal, Switzerland, United Arab Republic, UK, US, USSR, and Zambia.

DIRECTOR-GENERAL AND SECRETARIAT

The secretariat carries out UNESCO's program of action. It is headed by a Director-General, nominated by the Executive Board and appointed by the General Conference for a six-year term. The staff are appointed by the Director-General. Julian Huxley of the UK was UNESCO's first Director-General, serving from 1946 to 1948. He was succeeded by Jaime Torres Bodet of Mexico, who resigned in 1952. John W. Taylor of the US served as acting Director-General from November 1952 until July 1953, when Luther H. Evans of the US was appointed Director-General. He was succeeded in office by Vittorino Veronese of Italy, who served from 1958 to 1962. He was followed by René Maheu (France), appointed in 1962, and reelected for a further term in 1968.

HEADQUARTERS

UNESCO's first headquarters were in the Hotel Majestic in Paris, a building which, ironically, had served as headquarters for the Gestapo during the German occupation of France. In November 1958 the organization's headquarters were transferred to three new buildings of striking architectural design on a seven and a half acre site, which was donated by France.

The UNESCO headquarters group consists of a conference building, a secretariat building, and a building for the permanent delegations assigned to UNESCO. The architectural plans were drawn up by Marcel Breuer of the US, Pier Luigi Nervi of Italy, and Bernard Zehrfuss of France. They were approved by an international panel of leading architects including Le Corbusier of France, Walter Gropius of the US, Ernesto Rogers of Italy, Sven Markelius of Sweden, and Lucio Costa of Brazil. Works by contemporary artists are an integral part of the architectural setting of the new headquarters group. These include murals by Pablo Picasso of Spain and Rufino Tamayo of Mexico; ceramic murals by José Llorens-Artigas and Joan Miró of Spain; a sculpture by Henry Moore of the UK; a bronze relief by Jean Arp of France; a mobile by Alexander Calder of the US; and paintings by Afro Basaldella of Italy, Karel Appel of the Netherlands, and Roberto Matta of Chile. A Japanese garden in the court was designed by the American sculptor Isamu Noguchi.

The continued growth of UNESCO made a fourth building necessary and Bernard Zehrfuss drew up plans for an "underground" structure, which was inaugurated on 4 November 1965. The new building is a two-story office and conference room structure laid out around six patios, the whole complex being sunk below street level to comply with zoning restrictions. The patios were designed by Burle Marx, Brazilian landscape architect; in each there are pools, fountains, and beds of varied plants, shrubs, and grasses. A fifth building, also designed by Zehrfuss, was inaugurated in 1970. Situated just over 300 yards from the other UNESCO buildings, the 550-office block is decorated with works by Giacometti, Chillida, Kelly, and Soto.

REGIONAL OFFICES

UNESCO has regional offices at Havana, Cuba; and Santiago, Chile. It maintains regional centers for science and technology for the Arab states, South Asia, Southeast Asia, and Africa, and the Latin American Center for the Development of Science. These centers serve regions "remote from the main centers of science and technology," and are staffed by "scientific men" who do "every type of liaison work which will assist the scientists of the region." The activity of these offices has increased over the years. They aid in promoting the international exchange of scientific personnel, information, and materials.

NATIONAL COMMISSIONS FOR UNESCO

The UNESCO constitution requests every member state to "make such arrangements as suit its particular conditions for the purpose of associating its principal bodies interested in educational, scientific, and cultural matters with the work of the Organization, preferably by the formation of a National Commission. . . ." By October 1970, 118 UNESCO member states had established such broadly representative national commissions to collaborate with UNESCO in attaining its objectives. These commissions are not official UNESCO organs, but they provide a vital link between UNESCO and the public at large. They advise their governments and the delegations that attend the UNESCO General Conference on pertinent matters and serve as liaison agencies and information outlets.

The national commissions play an important role in furthering the work of UNESCO, which, by its very nature, is a cooperative undertaking. Addressing the 1948 General Conference, Julian Huxley, then Director-General of UNESCO, remarked: "It has often—and rightly—been said that UNESCO can only operate efficiently with the active cooperation of Member States, through their governments, their National Commissions, their specialists and experts in the field of education, science and culture, and the general mass of their peoples."

The various national commissions vary greatly in size and composition. Often the country's minister of education is the commission's president, and its members may include high government officials, leaders in the fields of education, science, and the arts, and representatives of professional organizations. Through meetings, publications, broadcasts, contests, and exhibitions the commissions stimulate public interest in specific UNESCO projects.

National UNESCO commissions of several countries often meet together for regional conferences. For example, in 1970, the Fifth Regional Conference of Asian National Commissions was held in Tehran and the 7th Regional Conference of Arab State National Commissions met in Khartoum. The 4th Regional Conference of Western Hemisphere National Commissions was convened in Mexico in 1967 and the 5th European meeting was held in Monaco in 1965. The first meeting of African National Commissions took place in Kampala in 1963.

National commissions are frequently given contracts to translate UNESCO publications and to handle the printing and distribution of these translations. To cite a few recent examples, *Education and Agricultural Development* has been brought out

in Turkish (Turkey), *Buddhism and the Race Question* in Sinhalese (Ceylon), *Unesco and Human Rights* in Hebrew (Israel), *Racial Myths* in Portuguese (Brazil), and *Education and Mental Health* in Arabic (UAR).

COOPERATION WITH NONGOVERN- MENTAL ORGANIZATIONS

Like the other specialized agencies of the UN family, UNESCO maintains consultative arrangements with international nongovernmental organizations (NGO's) in its field. Through them, it is in contact with numerous affiliated national organizations, with the institutions belonging to these organizations, and ultimately with the thousands of specialists and professionals who are individual members and with the institutions that are the corporate members of the various societies.

Workers in education, the sciences, and cultural fields have long realized the advantages of professional cooperation. Even before UNESCO was founded, a number of international roof-organizations of professional associations, learned societies, and the like had been established. By July 1970, 181 such international nongovernmental organizations had been granted consultative status with UNESCO. Both UNESCO and the organizations concerned profit from the relationship. Observers from appropriate NGO's are invited to attend most of the specialized conferences and meetings convened by UNESCO and to assist in the work of UNESCO's advisory committees. UNESCO, on its part, assists the various NGO's with documentation and special studies and may otherwise service and participate in their conferences. Through its own publications, UNESCO gives worldwide publicity to the gatherings of various associations of professional and learned groups and reports their achievements.

UNESCO also encourages the formation and growth of new professional societies and associations. As a result of UNESCO's initiative, four new organizations for the international promotion of the social sciences, a field in which international cooperation had been relatively meager, were established between 1949 and 1951: the International Association of Legal Science, the International Economic Association, the International Political Science Association, and the International Sociological Association. The establishment of the International Social Science Council followed in 1952. UNESCO also helped in the establishment of the Union of International Engineering Organizations and the Council of International Organizations of Medical Science (CIOMS).

UNESCO delegates certain of its own tasks to such international nongovernmental organizations of specialists and scholars. The number of NGO's so collaborating varies according to UNESCO's program but generally is between 35 and 40. At UNESCO's behest, these organizations set up international meetings, symposia, conferences, and working groups; they undertake inquiries on many topics of concern to UNESCO member nations. For example, the World Confederation of Organizations of the Teaching Profession undertook a worldwide investigation on the access of women to teaching positions; the International Center for Films for Children set up an information center and publishes an international bulletin regarding films for children; the International Association of Legal Science assumed the tasks of studying the influence of the principle of sovereignty on world affairs, the development of domestic laws on peaceful uses of atomic energy, and the legal problems of nationalization. Projects such as the International Social Science Council's investigation of the social implications of technical change, and meetings such as the International Union of Geodesy and Geophysics Symposium on the general circulation of the oceans draw on a cumulative specialized knowledge that UNESCO could otherwise assemble only with great difficulty if at all.

While organizations thus cooperating receive subsidies from UNESCO—$863,535 to 36 NGO's in 1970—the cost to UNESCO is substantially less than it would be if UNESCO attempted to carry out these programs singlehandedly.

The number of UNESCO-subsidized conferences and meetings organized through these cooperating NGO's has constantly increased, and these international gatherings have become important vehicles for the promotion of UNESCO's objectives. A list of the topics discussed even in a single year at such events by the UNESCO-connected associations would fill many pages. In 1962 they ranged from "environmental problems of man in space" to the organization of an "International Quiet Sun Year," that is, of carefully coordinated geophysical research by many countries in 1965, when solar activities were at a cyclical minimum, and the best conditions for observation prevailed. Preparations for this vast undertaking included the construction of observatories in different parts of the world.

One example of the growth of professional associations is the International Association of Universities (IAU), which was established under UNESCO auspices in 1950, at a time when there were few systematic worldwide contacts among institutions of higher learning. By 1970, 530 universities and other institutions at university level in 103 different countries were IAU members, and 8 other international associations participated in the IAU's work: the Association of Universities of the British Common-wealth, the Federation of Catholic Universities, the Union of Latin-American Universities, the Association des Universités entièrement ou partiellement de langue française, the Association of Southeast Asian Institutions of Higher Learning, the Permanent Conference of Rectors and Vice-Chancellors of European Universities, the Association of Arab Universities, and the Association of African Universities.

In 1962 the IAU, under a joint research program with UNESCO, carried out a world study on university admission and a second study on the role of institutions of higher education in countries of Southeast Asia. Two volumes have now been produced by UNESCO on admission and access to higher education and four volumes on higher education and development in Southeast Asia.

The IAU offers in other respects, too, a good example of how a cooperating NGO may assist in furthering the objectives of UNESCO. The association's central office, located at UNESCO House in Paris, serves as a world documentation center for information on universities and other institutions of higher learning. It publishes a biennial *International List of Universities*, and an *International Handbook of Universities*.

6 BUDGET

For the 2-year period 1969–70, the 1968 General Conference voted a regular budget of $77,413,500, an increase of $15.9 million over the 1967–68 two-year budget. The $38.7 million per year that UNESCO now spends compares with the one-year budgets of $7 million voted in 1946 and $10 million in 1954, but UNESCO's membership has increased at least proportionately. The size of UNESCO's budget has been the subject of much controversy between economy-minded delegates to the General Conference and delegates who wish to expand the organization's activities. Of the $77,413,500 voted for 1969–70, $16,837,907 was spent on program operations and services in education; $10,495,053 on natural sciences; $8,367,620 on social sciences, human sciences and culture; $9,519,176 on communication; and $895,525 on international standards, relations, and programs.

UNESCO's budget is financed through contributions assessed against member states on a sliding scale. For the 1969–70 period, these assessments ranged from a minimum of 0.04% of the total amount to be raised, assessed against such countries as Afghani-

stan, Honduras, and Zambia to 5.65% for France, 6.6% for West Germany, 13.75% for the USSR, and 29.73% for the US.

Like other UN specialized agencies, UNESCO participates in the UN Development Program (UNDP). UNESCO's approved program for operational assistance to member states in 1969–70 amounted to $59,763,000 from UNDP.

7 ACTIVITIES

UNESCO's work is principally carried out through its four operational sectors: education; science; social science, human science, and culture; and communication. These sectors are responsible for nearly all UNESCO's regular and extrabudgetary activities. Since the 1950 General Conference adopted a "basic program" in 1950, it has concentrated on selected long-range major goals; among the long-range major projects carried through are: primary education in Latin America, arid zone research, and the promotion of understanding between Orient and Occident.

A. EDUCATION

According to statistics published by UNESCO, about half of the world's children do not go to school at all. Of those attending, 40% complete no more than a few years of elementary schooling; and only 10% are in a position to receive secondary or higher education. The number of illiterate adults in the world far exceeds the number of children without schooling, and it is estimated that 55% of all persons over 10 years of age have never been to school at all. UNESCO, since its creation, has labored to promote education on all levels and of every type.

The annual International Conference on Public Education, organized jointly by UNESCO and the International Bureau of Education (IBE), serves as a world forum for the consideration of educational problems of all sorts. The central educational authority of each participating country submits a report on national educational developments to the conference. These reports are discussed at the conference and form the basis for UNESCO's *International Yearbook of Education*. Recommendations by the conference are submitted to all participating governments and to the international organizations concerned. They are published in Arabic, English, French, Russian, and Spanish and are distributed to all participating states for wide dissemination among teachers and educators. Each year, the conference concentrates on specific issues of international significance, for example, curricula for secondary schools; the one-teacher school; education for mentally retarded children. The recommendations arrived at may then be elaborated by regional UNESCO conferences, by working groups, teachers' associations, etc.

Up-to-date methods of teacher training, curricula adapted to changing requirements, modernized textbooks and other teaching tools, and techniques of learning that do away with the painful routines of rote memorization are among the means promoted by UNESCO to advance popular education. UNESCO also encourages the use of radio, films, and television in education and emphasizes the importance of linking education with the realities of community life. An important concern of UNESCO—one, in fact, prescribed in its constitution—is to foster education for mutual and international understanding. UNESCO may pursue its aims in the fields of education in a number of ways. Thus, its interest in opening up educational opportunities to women may be furthered by working out recommendations for educational reforms, through studies and the publication of information, by supporting international women's organizations, or by entrusting some of its training missions to women experts.

Since 1960, when the UNESCO General Conference decided to give priority to its educational programs, an increasing proportion of the organization's efforts has been channeled into this field.

Regional Educational Programs

The preparation of programs for entire regions begins with the collection and the analysis by experts of many facts and figures. Hence, UNESCO, in cooperation with the countries concerned, carries out surveys to determine the size of the school-age population, the number of teachers and other personnel needed, the particular skills required for social and economic development plans, and other basic data. Furthermore, UNESCO experts are sent into the regions to provide assistance in surmounting the many complex problems connected with actual educational development, beginning with such primary tasks as educational planning, teacher training, establishment of administrative machinery, and the production of textbooks.

Funds for some of this work come from UNESCO's regular budget, but the larger projects are financed mainly under the United Nations Development Program. Growing financial assistance is now coming from the International Bank for Reconstruction and Development.

Ten-Year Major Project for the Spread of Primary Education in Latin America

This 10-year major project, launched in 1957, was the first large-scale international undertaking in the field of education. UNESCO is cooperating with 20 Latin American states to attain the goal of making free, compulsory primary education available to all children in the region. It was estimated when the project began that some 17 million children of school age in Latin America were without schooling. Since the region's population was increasing at an annual rate of about 2.5%, the problem was aggravated by the rapid growth of the school-age population. More than two fifths of the population of Latin America is under 15 years of age, and the burden of providing educational facilities falls on the other three fifths of the region's inhabitants.

Work toward the goal of universal compulsory primary education accordingly concentrated on rapidly increasing the number of teachers. It was estimated that 400,000 new teachers and other educational personnel would be needed to bring primary education to all the children of Latin America. UNESCO cooperated with the universities of São Paolo, Brazil, and Santiago, Chile, in the training of teachers, administrators, inspectors, and experts on teaching methods and curricula. Study courses and in-service training for teachers in rural normal schools were prepared by UNESCO. Selected normal schools, with the assistance of UNESCO experts and UNESCO-provided funds for research and equipment, serve as pilot institutions for the training of teachers from the participating countries. UNESCO grants have been awarded to more than 350 Latin American educators for studies outside their own countries and to nearly 2,000 for studies within their countries.

As a result of these increased efforts in teacher training, 354,000 new teaching posts were filled between 1956 and 1965 and an additional 12 million children were enrolled in primary schools. UNESCO efforts then concentrated on improving the quality of education and the training of better qualified teachers, expert missions visiting nine Latin American countries to advise on measures since 1969. Looking ahead to continued school-population expansion, many countries sought UNESCO help in planning educational television to be relayed by satellite.

When the Latin American regional project was at the halfway mark, UNESCO's General Conference, meeting late in 1962, asked the organization to concentrate not only on primary education in Latin America, but also to initiate integrated planning for all levels of education. As a result, UNESCO began a series of studies and surveys on educational planning in relation to economic and social development and is assisting the Latin American Institute for Economic and Social Planning established by the UN Economic Commission for Latin America.

Beginning in 1967, UNESCO experts were also assisting in the creation of a Latin American Institute for Planning and Administration, at Santiago, Chile.

Twenty-Year Plan for Educational Development in Asia

The strides made in Latin American elementary education in connection with that major project led UNESCO in 1959–60, at the request of Asian member countries, to conduct surveys of educational systems, needs, and problems on that continent. A conference called by UNESCO at Karachi, Pakistan, in 1960 adopted a 20-year plan for educational development. Eighteen Asian countries are participating. The objective of the Asian program adopted in Karachi is free and compulsory education of at least 7 years duration for over 160 million children and adolescents by 1980, necessitating the hiring and training of more than 5 million teachers and the building of some 5 million classrooms. The total cost is estimated at $56 billion. In 1962 a Tokyo conference of ministers and high officials of education and economic planning extended the Karachi plan to cover all levels of education: primary, secondary, higher, and technical, without overlooking adult education. The Tokyo conference agreed that appropriate educational targets should be integrated into the national development plans of the Asian countries and that each country should count on allocating about 5% of its gross national product to education by 1980. UNESCO has cooperated in establishing a regional center for training educational planners, administrators, and supervisors in New Delhi, and an institute for training teacher educators at Quezon City, Philippines. In addition, a regional school-building research center was set up, first at Bandung, but subsequently moved to Colombo. A regional education bureau was established by UNESCO in Bangkok in 1961 to aid Asian countries by providing research and educational documentation and information and to help in the creation of national education bureaus.

UNESCO experts have been sent to a number of Asian countries to assist education and government authorities in such fields as planning, demographic studies, educational statistics, administration and finance, textbooks, teaching aids, language teaching, and education of girls.

Emergency Program for Africa

In 1960, UNESCO's General Conference decided on a special program of aid for Africa. Ministers and directors of education from 34 countries were called to the Conference of African States on the Development of Education in Africa, held at Addis Ababa, Ethiopia, in May 1961.

The resulting Addis Ababa Plan placed education among Africa's highest priorities, emphasizing the central role of education in African economic and social development and its importance as a productive investment. Hence, among many other measures, the plan calls for an increase of expenditures for education by the participating countries from 3% of the gross national product (a figure already reached in most of them at that time) to 4% by 1965, and 5% by 1970. The plan also calls for universal primary education on the African continent by 1980; by the same date, 20% of all children leaving primary schools are to be enrolled in secondary schools; and university enrollments are to reach a total of 300,000 compared with 31,000 in 1961 (18,000 in Africa, 13,000 abroad). To meet these targets, it was calculated that expenditures on education would have to rise from $450 million in 1960 to $2,200 million by 1980. African states anticipated that education and other efforts would so far improve their economies that they could gradually assume all financial burdens by the 1980's.

Following on the Addis Ababa meeting, UNESCO convened further meetings of African ministers of education in Paris in 1962 and at Abidjan in 1964. Another meeting was scheduled for 1968. At these meetings progress achieved is evaluated and programs amended or adapted as necessary.

Under an emergency program to help the African countries implement the Addis Ababa Plan, UNESCO has aided in the creation of a regional school construction bureau in Khartoum, Sudan, and a regional textbook production center at Yaoundé, Cameroon. Work at these centers has constantly expanded. Khartoum now concentrates on documentation, research, training, and the promotion of building development groups in African countries. In Dakar, a regional center set up in 1970 took over the organization of regional activities, holding training courses and assisting national undertakings. Mobile teams on the staff are ready to visit other countries at need. Yaoundé produces teaching aids and "Africanized" instructional manuals putting the emphasis on the needs, the cultural background, and the habits of African children. The complexity of the problems involved can be seen from the fact that over 500 separate languages are spoken in Africa and that many vernacular tongues still lack a written form; hence the importance of the studies—in which UNESCO experts participate—to determine the local language or languages in which education is to be conducted (in addition to instruction in English or French).

Since 1961, UNESCO has dispatched teams of experts to African countries, at their request, to help them frame educational systems corresponding to their aims and aspirations. Sometimes, these teams have made one or two return visits. Planning sections, with their advice, have been set up in nearly all ministries of education. Help is also available from the UNESCO International Institute for Educational Planning, in Paris, as well as from the newly created UNESCO regional group for educational planning and administration at Dakar, Senegal.

Another priority field of UNESCO assistance has been teacher training, particularly for secondary education, where African states have still to rely largely on foreign staff. From 1965 to 1970, 21 higher and secondary-teacher training colleges had been set up in middle Africa with the aid of the UN Development Program and 3 such colleges had been established in North African Arab states. For the training of primary teachers a center was set up at Bangui, Central African Republic (in cooperation with UNICEF). Similar projects for primary or rural education are being carried out in 15 other French- and English-speaking African countries. Engineers, geologists, and other technicians are being trained at the Institute of Higher Learning in Tripoli, Libya; the Engineering School at Rabat, Morocco; and the Technical Institute in Kampala, Uganda.

In most developing countries, higher education has reached a critical phase of growth and change, and nowhere is this more evident than in Africa. UNESCO continues where possible to provide expert assistance to institutions, such as, for example, the newly created Federal University of East Africa, one of the 35 institutions of higher learning in middle Africa. In conjunction with the International Association of Universities (IAU), UNESCO promotes cooperation between African universities on teaching methods and the comparability of degrees.

Education in the Arab States

Total school enrollment in the Arab states at the three levels—primary, secondary, and higher—increased from 8.7 million in 1960/61 to 14 million in 1967/68, making an increase of about 60% in the 8-year period.

Nevertheless, it is estimated that 10 million Arab children between the ages of 6 and 14 still do not go to school, and of the 11 million enrolled at the preprimary and primary level only a little more than a third are girls.

Thus, the main tasks remain help in the provision of schooling for all primary children, the training of skilled manpower for development, and the eradication of illiteracy.

The third regional conference of Arab states education, held in Marrakech in 1970, decided on a number of measures to promote further educational development, namely: increased attention to scientific and technological development, to overcome shortages and gaps in the training of scientific, technical, and managerial staff; greater use of new technological methods and equipment in education; expanding girls' education at all levels; special attention to the education of Palestinian refugee children; and greater efforts towards the eradication of illiteracy.

In educational planning, UNESCO has been working in close collaboration with the International Bank for Reconstruction and Development (IBRD) and the International Development Association, which have provided sizable loans to Morocco, Sudan, and Tunisia for improving and widening their educational systems. In Kuwait, Libya, Sa'udi Arabia and Sudan, UNESCO experts have participated with the economic planning boards and ministries of education in the elaboration of new educational policies and plans.

To extend and improve teacher training, UNESCO has set up secondary and higher teacher training colleges in Libya, Morocco, Sa'udi Arabia, Sudan, and Tunisia. In Algeria, Iraq, Libya, Morocco, Sudan, Syria, South Yemen, Tunisia, UAR, and Yemen, efforts, often in collaboration with UNICEF, have centered on the provision and upgrading of primary teachers by accelerated training courses and the improvement of the quality of primary education through the revision of curricula. A regional workshop was organized by UNESCO in 1969 at Beirut to examine problems and needs for further and improved training of primary teachers.

Algeria was one of the first three countries to receive aid under the Experimental World Literacy Program for a pilot project in functional literacy whose execution is entrusted to UNESCO. Some 100,000 industrial and agricultural workers in 3 separate regions will be affected by the project. A similar project has recently started in Sudan and in Syria; an experimental literacy project is being carried out with joint UNESCO/FAO assistance.

The program for education of Palestinian refugees was begun in 1950 in cooperation with UNRWA. Under this program, about 283,000 children are at present receiving instruction, the greater part in 480 UNRWA/UNESCO elementary and preparatory schools. A further 2,600 refugee students are attending technical and vocational training centers, and some 1,600 are at preservice teacher training colleges. In 1964 an institute of education was created at Beirut by UNESCO and UNRWA, with help from the Swiss government, to train teachers at these schools. In 1969, as a result of long and patient negotiation, UNESCO arranged for students in the Gaza Strip to take the entrance examination to Arab universities; later, just over 1,000 successful candidates were ferried to Cairo during a truce operation organized with the help of the Red Cross.

Out-of-School Education

UNESCO's program for education outside of schools covers three main fields: literacy training and rural adult education; general adult education activities; special projects with youth organizations. For a long time, UNESCO activity in this area of "out-of-school education" was limited to making studies, providing technical assistance in national literacy programs, and initiating pilot projects for research and training, such as fundamental education centers for rural adult education and community development. Two of these were established by UNESCO. The first, CREFAL (Centro Regional de Educación Fundamental para la América Latina) in Pátzcuaro, Mexico, was established in 1951. Many of its students are already experienced teachers, nurses, social workers, or agricultural engineers. The second center, ASFEC (Arab States Fundamental Education Center) in Sirs-el-Layyah, UAR, offers, in addition to regular courses, special short training courses for officials and technicians. Furthermore, UNESCO has set up national training centers in some 20 member states.

Rural adult education is often called "fundamental education," because it aims to provide elementary knowledge to people who have no or very little schooling, so as to help them improve their health, food supply, and family life. Fundamental education is primarily to benefit people who cannot read or write. Teaching these skills to them is not the most urgent task of fundamental education, however. Usually they are first taught elementary facts about nutrition and sanitation, the manufacture and use of improved tools, improved methods of agriculture, more profitable ways to use their spare time, their basic rights and duties as citizens, and the like. Literacy classes may be postponed until the participants, stimulated by the new ideas with which they have been brought in contact, ask to be taught reading and writing.

At present, however, it is literacy training that rates the highest priority in UNESCO's "out-of-school" programs. In many countries people are classified as literate by the census-takers if they can sign their names, write a few simple sentences, and distinguish among the different candidates on a ballot. UNESCO is concerned not with this kind of nominal literacy but with what it calls "functional literacy": the ability to impart and acquire useful knowledge through the written word—for it is this kind of literacy that the masses of the developing countries must acquire in order to make lasting progress in raising their standards of living.

In 1961, the UN General Assembly asked UNESCO to prepare a report on the illiteracy situation throughout the world. Since then, UNESCO has amassed knowledge and helped mobilize public opinion for an eventual world campaign aimed at eradicating illiteracy altogether. A worldwide investigation revealed that at least 700 million adults in the world—2 out of every 5—are illiterate and that the number of adult illiterates is increasing at the rate of several millions a year (by as many as 20 million a year, according to one estimate). Other studies revealed that 97 countries have an illiteracy rate of over 50% and 20 of 95% or more.

Following the world congress on literacy in Tehran in 1965, where this crucial problem was studied by 88 national delegations, and following approval from the UN General Assembly that year, UNESCO launched its experimental literacy program to pave the way for a world campaign. Under this plan, 12 experimental literacy projects were started in selected countries, with assistance from the UN Development Program. The effort is directed toward organized sections of the community where motivation is likely to be strongest.

By 1970 the first results from the 12 experimental projects where literacy instruction was given as part of industrial and agricultural development schemes had begun to demonstrate the validity of the functional approach, and more than 50 countries had asked for aid in starting similar projects.

Other out-of-school educational fields in which UNESCO has also been active include education for youth, especially involving the participation of young people in development schemes and activities designed to promote international cooperation. UNESCO also promotes physical education, sports, and science education for youth. UNESCO seeks ways and means to promote the implementation of the convention against discrimination in education, especially as regards the education of girls and women. In its adult education activities in recent years, UNESCO has strongly supported the idea of "lifelong" education—the growing realization that education should not stop at the end of formal schooling.

Production of Reading Materials for New Readers. Literacy campaigns for adults are often received with great enthusiasm.

Nevertheless, such experiments have failed in many countries because of the dearth of reading matter suitable to the adult with a meager reading vocabulary. The habit of reading will not be firmly acquired unless it is practiced over a period of years, and a newly acquired ability to read may eventually be lost if simple books and pamphlets are not available.

In 1955, UNESCO inaugurated a program for the production of texts for new readers in Burma, Ceylon, India, and Pakistan, with good results. In 1963 the program was extended to Afghanistan, Nepal, Thailand, and other countries.

Human Rights and International Understanding

UNESCO works for the equality of educational opportunity and for the extension of education for mutual understanding and cooperation. The organization has carried out this work—often in cooperation with the UN, with other specialized agencies, and with professional educational organizations—through meetings of experts, surveys, reports, travel grants, fellowship awards, and special projects.

Through its associated school projects, UNESCO encourages educational institutions to undertake experimental activities relating to the study of the United Nations, human rights, and to the understanding of other countries, peoples, and world problems. In 1966 there were more than 500 primary and secondary schools and teacher-training institutions in 54 countries participating in this project.

Status of Teachers

The rapid expansion already achieved in education enrollments, especially in the developing areas, has often resulted in a crucial shortage of qualified teachers and an urgent need to upgrade the whole teaching profession. For some time, UNESCO, in collaboration with the International Labor Organization (ILO), has been preparing an international recommendation on the professional, social, and economic status of teachers. An "international instrument" to this effect was approved in October 1966 by delegates from UNESCO member states. It is hoped that, by setting minimum standards, this instrument will help governments and teachers' organizations to improve professional standing, qualifications, training, and working conditions.

B. THE NATURAL SCIENCES

Like nearly everything else in a world of sovereign nation-states, knowledge acquired through scientific investigation has to be brought out of the national context and placed where it is accessible to all for the well-being of all. One of the tasks assigned to UNESCO by its constitution is to "maintain, increase and diffuse knowledge . . . by encouraging cooperation among the nations in all branches of intellectual activity," including the natural sciences.

Efforts to realize international cooperation in science have been made for hundreds of years by farsighted individuals and, more recently, by groups of individuals whether working through private institutions, national governments, or international agencies.

Scientists themselves appear to have always had an instinct besides a need for cooperation. Given the natural tendency of scientists to come together and the universality of science itself, it was by no means accidental that the founders of UNESCO gave a high-priority role to science and to international cooperation in science.

In the past 25 years of UNESCO's existence various steps have been taken to ensure that effective international cooperation in science becomes a reality rather than a wishful thought. One of these steps has been the development of "mechanisms" designed to further cooperation at the international level. For example, since its very beginning UNESCO has established, or has helped to establish, several autonomous intergovernmental organizations such as the European Organization for Nuclear Research (CERN, Geneva) or the Latin American Center of Physics (Rio de Janeiro). In more recent times, an outstanding example of UNESCO's support to a semiautonomous body, is the International Center for Theoretical Physics (Trieste). This center, jointly sponsored with the International Atomic Energy Agency and a member state (Italy) furthers close collaboration among the world's scientists, particularly between those of the advanced and the less developed countries.

But other types of mechanisms also have been created by UNESCO to coordinate and stimulate the activities in science of national governments as well as of other organizations both inside and outside the UN system. The prime example in this connection is the Intergovernmental Oceanographic Commission that was set up in 1960 under the auspices of UNESCO. The success of this commission is reflected in the fact that it (financed by UNESCO at less than $500,000 per year) has encouraged and coordinated international research on the high seas worth as much as $15 million annually. The second intergovernmental coordinating body in question is that for the International Hydrological Decade, a ten-year program which began in 1965 to seek the scientific information needed for rational management of water resources.

Besides developing, or helping to develop, machinery at the international level for international cooperation in science, UNESCO has served for 24 years as a type of international "clearinghouse" for scientific information, science periodicals and journals, and for scientists themselves who have worked in the Secretariat as staff members or as consultants. Furthermore, UNESCO has served as an "international meeting place" where scientists from all parts of the world come together for an open exchange of information and views. Many of these meetings, which range from small groups of experts to ministerial conferences such as the European Conference of Ministers Responsible for Science Policy (MINESPOL, June 1970), are organized by the UNESCO Secretariat.

UNESCO has developed its own programs in science. These programs are largely formulated by the UNESCO Secretariat, discussed and approved by UNESCO's member states, and administered and guided by the organization's staff, both at headquarters and in the field. There is probably no single answer to why UNESCO's program in science has taken the form it has. On the one hand UNESCO is a "development organization" which aims to help developing member states in their economic and social development plans. From this naturally springs "development programs" that include the training of technicians, engineering education, science policy studies, the sending of experts and teams of experts in different fields to developing countries on missions, the establishment of training and information centers in developing countries, and the examination of the science component of agricultural education. On the other hand, UNESCO's mandate in science requires that fundamental research be carried out and initiated. Thus, UNESCO supports programs and projects in the life sciences, in ecology and natural resources research, in surveys of technological innovations, in marine sciences, in hydrology, and in the establishment of field science cooperation offices that can serve as monitors on scientific advances in any area of the world.

Many of the projects connected to the various program activities mentioned above are financed by the United Nations Development Program with UNESCO serving as the "executing agency". These operational development-oriented projects include such areas as a National Center for Planning of Scientific and Technological Research in Senegal and a Mekong River Delta Model Study in Cambodia and South Viet-Nam.

There are approximately 29 such projects in Africa, 28 in Asia, and 21 in Latin America.

In addition to the aforementioned science programs in which development aspects and pure science aspects become entwined, UNESCO has developed programs that more explicitly help meet the challenge to science. The importance of the biosphere cannot be overestimated, particularly in an age when entire lakes are polluted from industrial waste materials and huge urban centers have become dangerous places to live and work in due to air and water pollution. In view of the importance of ecology and the earth sciences UNESCO has promoted scientific research in these areas and has trained specialists in related disciplines through the creation of research institutions, postgraduate training courses, and the development of centers of integrated studies. Also, the organization has prepared natural resources maps, launched an International Geological Correlation Program, has studied the causes of natural disasters, and is ready to launch a large program on "Man and the biosphere."

Without adequate exchange of scientific information and a system of documentation common to all science communities, development through science and technology would be greatly hampered. Recognizing this, UNESCO has undertaken to assist its member states by establishing national documentation and information centers in science and technology. Perhaps more important, though, has been the initiative taken by UNESCO to study the possibility and feasibility of a world science information system (UNISIST). The working groups set up by UNESCO to look into this question recently concluded that such a system is in fact feasible.

Undoubtedly one of the principal reasons that science and its technologies have come under heavy attack by the world public is the lack of understanding by man of the aims and function of science. To help bridge this gap UNESCO has formulated science-teaching programs designed for all levels of the learning process. To date this problem has been pursued by a series of pilot projects in the developing countries aimed at modernizing science-teaching methods and producing new learning materials.

No organization works in a vacuum. A large part of UNESCO's program is therefore carried out under contract or through subvention to various nongovernmental organizations such as the International Council of Scientific Unions (ICSU), the International Cell Research Organization (ICRO), the International Brain Research Organization (IBRO), and the World Federation of Engineering Organizations. In many instances UNESCO gives several hundreds of thousands of dollars to these organizations to help the implementation of their programs and to advise on UNESCO's activities. Also, by being a specialized agency of the United Nations system, UNESCO works closely with, e.g., the World Health Organization in matters concerning cell and brain research and the biosphere, the World Meteorological Organization concerning hydrology, the Food and Agriculture Organization concerning agricultural education and marine sciences, the International Labor Organization concerning agricultural education and the status of scientific workers, and the United Nations concerning the biosphere and the application of science and technology to development.

The regular science budget of UNESCO was considerably increased in 1964 when the General Conference approved an estimate for the next biennium 57% higher than in the last. Supplemented by far greater resources from the UN Development Program, UNESCO expenditure on science and technology in 1965–66 was over $16 million a year. For 1971–72, this figure was expected to be nearly $22 million a year.

C. THE SOCIAL SCIENCES

Since UNESCO was founded in 1946, it has participated in the growth of the social sciences. It was realized at that time that the social sciences suffered from a lack of organization. To remedy this, UNESCO began to build "bridges" between nations by encouraging the establishment of professional associations on the international level in comparative law, political science, sociology, economics, and documentation. At the same time, it supported such existing organizations as the International Institute of Administrative Sciences and the International Statistical Institute. Finally, an international and an interdisciplinary body that was set up began to function in 1952 in Paris: the International Social Science Council (ISSC), subsidized by UNESCO.

A new factor has played a role in the evolution of the social science program. Beginning in the 1960's, a number of young nations, particularly the newly independent countries of Africa, joined the organization. UNESCO's programs underwent a shift toward increasingly concrete and technical activities aimed at helping these countries to develop. Other UN specialized agencies were also affected by this new situation. To avoid overlapping, part of UNESCO's social science program had to be revised. These combined factors led UNESCO to place utmost importance on the training of counterparts in the field to replace the organization's experts at the earliest possible moment.

Starting in 1950, social science experts held posts in Science Cooperation Offices set up by UNESCO in 1947 and 1948 at Cairo, New Delhi, and Havana. At the same time, experts were sent on missions and symposia were organized to deal with specific regional problems. Permanent centers were set up, such as the European Coordination Center for Social Sciences Research and Documentation at Vienna, the Latin-American Center for Social Science Research at Rio de Janeiro, and the Research Center on Social and Economic Development in Southern Asia, now part of the New Delhi Institute of Economic Development. An African center for training and research for development was set up in Tangier in 1965.

A meeting held in 1950 on university social science teaching resulted in 15 studies that were published. Annual seminars have been held since 1962 on the use of mathematical methods in the social sciences. Seminars and training courses for university teachers and researchers have been organized in Africa and Asia under the UN Development Program. In 1966 a long-term program was begun to promote the teaching of management sciences and international law.

All these activities have resulted in numerous specialized publications. *The Dictionary of Social Sciences* appeared in English in 1964. Standardized terminology is one of the major aims of this work. In cooperation with the International Committee for Social Science Documentation, UNESCO continues to publish international bilingual bibliographies, lists, periodical catalogs, and other reference works for scholars and researchers. Equally useful is the series *Social Science Reports and Documents*, in which 22 publications have already appeared. The quarterly *International Social Science Journal*, successor since 1959 to a "bulletin" with the same purpose, devotes each of its issues to a thorough study of a major scientific theme.

UNESCO's most ambitious project in the social sciences, launched in 1963, is an international study of the main trends in research in the social and human sciences. Coming under both the department of social sciences and the department of culture, it covers the entire spectrum of disciplines, from economics to history and from demography to literary criticism. A collection of 32 studies entitled *The Social Sciences: Problems and Orientations* arising from this work appeared in 1968.

UNESCO carries out programs of research applying social science to development problems such as the "brain drain," youth and society, rural development, the access of women to scientific and technical careers, and demography and family planning from the educational point of view and the environ-ment. Within this program, an international seminar on the role of social sciences in development was held in 1970. Among the most notable projects has been the series of studies on racism and racial prejudice. The Declaration on Race and Racial Prejudice of 1967 was based on the work of geneticists, anthropologists, ethnologists, sociologists, historians, and lawyers, and produced a series of works such as *The Racial Questions Before Modern Science, The Racial Question and Modern Thought,* and *Race and Society* as well as a report on apartheid.

D. CULTURE

The Universal Declaration of Human Rights asserts that everybody has the right to participate freely in the cultural life of the community and from this follows the right to share in the heritage and the activity of the world community. It also implies, as the Venice Intergovernmental Conference on Cultural Policies recognized in 1970, that culture cannot be the privilege of an elite but must be regarded as a dimension of human life. This conference, attended by representatives of 85 countries and acknowledging the obligation of governments to provide and plan for the cultural needs of their citizens, was the first of its kind. It gives a clue to the cultural policy pursued by UNESCO since its inception.

UNESCO serves culture in two ways. The first is the encouragement of creative work or, at least, an understanding of it; the protection of creative artists and their works; and the dissemination of these works within the societies for which they are destined. The second is the stimulation of intercultural relations and the study of the significance of these relations.

UNESCO has taken care since its inception to facilitate the collaboration of specialists. A large network groups these specialists into national and worldwide federations and maintains continuous contact with them. These organizations receive financial support from UNESCO, and UNESCO often relies upon them in carrying out its program.

For example, the International Council for Philosophy and Humanistic Studies (CIPSH), founded on UNESCO's initiative in 1949, promotes research and the cooperation of scholars in many fields, as indicated by the names of its member associations: International Academic Union; International Federation of Societies of Classical Studies; International Union of Anthropological and Ethnological Sciences; International Committee for the History of Art; International Federation for Modern Languages and Literatures; International Union of Orientalists; International Society of Musicology; International Union for Prehistoric and Protohistoric Sciences; International Congress of Africanists.

Other international nongovernmental organizations—such as the International Theater Institute, the international councils of music, museums, and monuments and sites, the International Association of Plastic Arts, the International Union of Architects, the International Pen Club,—help composers, writers, film and theatrical directors, sculptors, architects, etc. For example, the International Music Council organizes each year an international tribune of composers in which various broadcasting networks take part. These networks agree to include in their season's programs at least six of the works submitted to the tribune. In addition, UNESCO administers fellowships for creative artists.

Artistic Creation and Protection of the World's Cultural Heritage

Contemporary creative activity is closely linked to three aspects characteristic of modern life: technical innovations (for there is often a connection between new communications media and present-day art and literature); an ever-increasing public; and new forms of aesthetic expression. UNESCO concerns itself with these problems and is currently engaged in a widespread study of the present situation and the future tendencies of artistic creation, beginning with cinema, radio, and television.

One of UNESCO's constitutionally prescribed tasks is to ensure "the conservation and protection of the world's inheritance of books, works of art, and monuments of history and science" and to recommend "to the nations concerned the necessary international conventions."

World War II caused irreparable losses to the world's heritage of artistic and cultural treasures, and one of UNESCO's first concerns was to promote an international agreement to protect this heritage against the consequences of armed conflict. After several years of preparation, a special international conference adopted a convention on this subject in 1954. It is to apply in the event of any type of armed conflict, including civil war. UNESCO has also produced recommendations to be applied to archaeological excavations, public access to museums, the safeguarding of monuments and sites, and measures to curb the illicit export, import, and transfer of cultural properties. A draft international instrument for the protection of sites and monuments of universal interest was presented to the 1970 General Conference.

Efforts to Save Works of Art and Monuments from Deterioration

It is often true that public works endanger the cultural heritage of a country, even when these works, such as dams or highways, are designed to improve living conditions. Time, weather, accidents, and nature itself raise threats. Frescoes, paintings, and manuscripts all suffer from the ravages of weather and humidity; temples and shrines become engulfed by tropical vegetation. They all need protection. Since its founding in Rome in 1955, an international center for the conservation and restoration of such cultural artifacts has been supported by UNESCO.

However, the most spectacular job done by UNESCO in this field remains the international campaign, launched in 1960, to save the monuments of Nubia from submersion by the waters of the Nile upon completion of the UAR's Aswan High Dam. In six years, all monuments, inscriptions, and rock carvings in both Egyptian and Sudanese Nubia were inventoried and photographed, all frescoes from the Christian period were removed to safety, and all archaeological sites reconnoitered and prospected. Twenty-two temples were moved, including the Abu Simbel shrines. These were first cut up into 1,035 blocks weighing 20 to 39 tons each and rebuilt on a higher level where the Nile can no longer threaten them.

The total cost of "Operation Abu Simbel" was reckoned at $36 million but thanks to contributions from 50 member states, UNESCO was able to raise $20.5 million of this. The last objective of the campaign—dismantling and removal of the temples of Philae to a safe place—calls for a further $6 million by the end of 1974, the UAR financing some of the work itself.

To show its gratitude, the government of the UAR allocated a large collection of antiquities to foreign museums and some complete temples to countries contributing to the campaign, including the temples of Dendur to the US, Ellesya to Italy, Debod to Spain, and Taffeh to the Netherlands.

It was in the same spirit of international solidarity that UNESCO launched in 1964 an international monuments campaign, which has since led to a number of initiatives by member states, and, on 2 December 1966, to the campaign for Florence and Venice. When opening the 1964 campaign, the Director-General of UNESCO recalled the lack of understanding encountered in past efforts to restore monuments, considered by some as a costly luxury. Since then, the idea has gained ground that preserving these vestiges of the past is not merely a cultural preoccupation but also has a solid economic basis. It is now recog-

nized that these monuments can stimulate the tourist industry and bring in foreign exchange. Since 1967, UNESCO has given technical assistance to countries undertaking the preservation of their monuments and their development as tourist attractions.

In cooperation with the International Council of Museums, UNESCO encourages the development and modernization of museums. Toward this end, a regional training center for museum technicians from African countries was set up at Jos, Nigeria, in 1963. At that time, it was the first of its kind. Another such center was opened in Mexico in 1966.

In these efforts, UNESCO's assistance to member states takes on such forms as documentation, expert meetings, missions, and administration of fellowships. The magazine *Museum*, published by UNESCO, enables specialists to keep abreast of the latest advances in the field. Finally, the organization encourages exchanges of original objects between museums, and the reassembly of works of art that have been dismembered.

Bringing Literature and Art to More People

Another tool indispensable to librarians, publishers, and translators, the *Index Translationum*, brought out each year by UNESCO, is an international catalog of translations. The first volume, which appeared in 1949, had 8,570 listings from 30 countries; the most recent edition had 36,800 from over 74 countries.

To bring world literature to a broader public, UNESCO encourages the publication of translated works that might otherwise never reach a wide audience because of commercial considerations. The UNESCO *Collection of Representative Works* today amounts to more than 300 titles translated into widely spoken languages—mainly English and French—from Burmese, Chinese, Indian, Indonesian, Japanese, Korean, Pakistani, Persian, Thai, and Vietnamese literature. At the same time, to enable the public in Asia to appreciate Western letters, a number of books have been translated into Oriental languages. To these are added works in little-known languages of the USSR, Central Asia, and Africa.

In the plastic arts, the "imaginary museum" is obviously the best solution. UNESCO has brought out two catalogs of color reproductions of paintings, one devoted to works before 1860, the other to works painted since that time, and revised regularly since 1949. The plates for these catalogs are chosen by international experts and they contribute to the encouragement of reproductions of quality. In addition, UNESCO has organized nine traveling exhibitions of reproductions, which have circulated or are circulating in 100 countries.

Then there is the UNESCO World Art Series aimed at drawing attention to works still too little known despite their importance to the history of art and existing, for example, in Egypt, Australia, Ceylon, Mexico, Ethiopia, and Poland.

Cultural films are another of UNESCO's preoccupations, and catalogs have been produced of films on architecture, musical education and operas, theater and the art of mime, painting and sculpture, ballet and classical dance. The organization encourages the use of cultural films in museums, libraries, and universities. And it supports two musical anthologies, one of Oriental music and the other of African. Among recordings already brought out are albums devoted to Afghanistan, Cambodia, India, Iran, Japan, Laos, Tibet, Ethiopia, Rwanda, to the Dans in the Ivory Coast, and to the music of the Ba-Bonzélé Pygmies.

The Universal Copyright Convention

Inadequate or, in some cases, nonexistent legal protection has long plagued not only publishers but also authors, composers, and other creative artists, whose works have often been plagiarized and pirated even within their own countries. The first international convention for the protection of copyright was the Berne Convention, adopted in 1886. The Berne Convention was an important step forward, but neither Czarist Russia nor the USSR adhered to it, and of the Western Hemisphere countries only Canada and Brazil became parties to the convention. Beginning in 1889, a separate system of copyright conventions grew up in the Western Hemisphere. Hence, the world was divided into three copyright camps: countries adhering to the Berne system; countries adhering to the Western Hemisphere system; and countries adhering to neither.

As a culmination of efforts started by the League of Nations' Institute of Intellectual Cooperation and, after World War II, continued by UNESCO, a special conference convened at Geneva in 1952 at length produced a Universal Copyright Convention to provide "copyright protection appropriate to all nations of the world." Designed to "facilitate a wider dissemination of works of the human mind and increase international understanding," the universal convention does not replace the Berne and Western Hemisphere copyright systems; it is an additional international agreement affording further and more universal protection to copyright holders.

Any state bound by the convention must "provide for the adequate and effective protection of authors as well as of other copyright owners [the author's heirs, for example] in literary, scientific and artistic works, including writings, musical, dramatic, and cinematographic works, and paintings, engravings and sculpture." Copyright is a very complex matter and is regulated very differently under the diverse legal systems of the world. As a result, the convention is a complex technical instrument. Standing out clearly, however, is the principle of unequivocal reciprocity: "Published works of nationals of any Contracting State and works first published in that State shall enjoy in each other Contracting State the same protection as that other State accords to works of its nationals first published in its own territory."

Copyright protection for works covered by the convention must never be for less that 25 years following first publication, except for photographs and works of applied art where under certain conditions the protection may be reduced to 10 years or to even shorter periods. Preferably, the period of protection "shall not be less than the life of the author and 25 years after his death."

Under the convention, the formalities necessary to claim copyright are reduced to a minimum. Normally it is sufficient to place the simple symbol introduced by the convention, the letter "c" surrounded by a circle, on each copy of the work followed by the name of the copyright owner and the year of first publication.

In its provisions regarding translations, the problem that caused the greatest difficulties, the convention endeavors to protect the interests of authors without unduly restricting widest international diffusion. The author is guaranteed the exclusive right to make or authorize translations of his work for a period of seven years following first publication. After seven years, if no translation has appeared in the national language or languages of a country where the convention is in force, such country may restrict this right.

Fifty-eight countries had become parties to the Universal Copyright Convention by 1970, when a meeting of the Intergovernmental Copyright Committee agreed to hold a conference on its revision in 1971. Draft amendments were prepared to benefit developing countries.

Mutual Appreciation of Cultural Values

The most widely extended and ambitious UNESCO project in the field of cultural exchange was the so-called East-West Major Project, which took ten years and covered the vast area from Beirut to Tokyo on one side of the globe as well as the countries of Western culture on the other. It involved specialists and the general public, universities and schools, libraries, museums, and the mass media. It gave rise to the creation of specialist institutions and to the improvement of textbooks as well as to the extension of studies of foreign culture.

It also prompted a series of studies of cultures to be undertaken, such as those on the civilizations of Central Asia, on the contribution of Japan to contemporary art, on Buddhist art, modern Arab culture, Tamil studies, and the preparation of a guide to Asian historical sources. Study of Latin American cultures covers such subjects as the influence of African culture in the continent and study of European cultures includes the Balkans and Scandinavia.

A whole new dimension has already been added to the East-West program by the emergence of the African countries, most of which have gained their independence since 1960. Acutely aware of their rich cultural heritage, these nations have been receiving the support of UNESCO.

In 1960, at a UNESCO-organized symposium on the history, the values, and the prospects of African cultures, Africans from various parts of the continent discussed their common cultural heritage and its development. Further to this meeting, UNESCO helped set up a network of institutes—ten are currently at work—that deal with various aspects of African history, ethnology, languages, and arts.

Under the current UNESCO program for Africa, a *General History of Africa* has been undertaken and, it is hoped, will be completed in 1975; this basic work should fill a serious gap in the study of human history. The organization is also currently working on a program of African linguistics—involving transcriptions of alphabets, basic vocabularies, and dictionaries—on which Africanist linguists, experts in literacy, and educators cooperate closely.

Another UNESCO undertaking without precedent is the *History of the Scientific and Cultural Development of Mankind.* This six-volume work on culture and science from prehistoric times to the 20th century, was prepared by a group of historians from various countries working under the supervision of an international commission set up by UNESCO in 1952 and has been published in English, Spanish, French, Serbo-Croatian, and Slovene.

E. COMMUNICATION

UNESCO is enjoined by its constitution to "collaborate in the work of advancing the mutual knowledge and understanding of peoples, through all means of mass communication. . . ." It is also authorized to recommend international agreements to facilitate "the free flow of ideas by word and image" and to encourage the international exchange of persons active in intellectual affairs and the exchange of "publications, objects of scientific interest, and other materials of information." UNESCO considers all these activities part of its work in the field of mass communications.

Aid in Developing Information Media

A survey carried out by UNESCO for the UN between 1960 and 1962 showed that some 2 billion persons, living in more than 100 countries in Africa, Asia, and Latin America, and representing 70% of the world's population, lack the barest minimum of information facilities in press, radio, film, and television. Poverty in information media, it was shown, goes hand in hand with other types of poverty in those regions.

A program to develop the media, prepared by UNESCO on the basis of this survey, was endorsed by the UN General Assembly, which emphasized the importance of the media in education and in economic and social progress generally. Governments of the developed countries, as well as public and private organizations, were urged to support the program as part of the UN Development Decade. The cost of providing the developing countries with minimum press, radio, and film facilities was estimated at $3.4 billion, of which 30% would need to come from external sources. UNESCO itself contributes to this program, notably by organizing expert missions, by awarding fellowships, and by holding seminars and training courses. Support for the program has been reflected in the economic development plans of various individual nations.

Since the advent of communication satellites vastly extended the range and potentialities of communication media, UNESCO has worked to ensure the maximum use of space communication for education and for cultural exchanges. Missions have advised the governments of India, Pakistan, and of eight Latin American countries on the use of satellites for these purposes. In addition, UNESCO convened a meeting of governmental experts in 1969 to consider the means of protecting rights that may be affected by the widespread use of satellite transmissions.

Agreement for Facilitating the International Circulation of Visual and Auditory Materials of an Educational, Scientific, and Cultural Character

Adopted by the 1948 UNESCO General Conference in Beirut, this agreement is designed to foster the easy and inexpensive importation of audiovisual materials that have become increasingly important to science and education: films, microfilms, recordings, slides, models, charts, maps, and posters. Countries adhering to the agreement are not only to exempt these materials from import duties but also to exempt them from all quantitative restrictions such as import quotas or licenses. The imported visual or auditory materials are also to be exempted from all internal fees and charges not levied against comparable domestically produced materials and must be guaranteed treatment no less favorable than that accorded the latter regarding transportation, distribution, processing, and exhibition.

To qualify for these benefits the auditory or visual materials must fulfill three conditions. Their main purpose must be to instruct, or to inform, or to promote the spread of knowledge and international understanding. They must be "representative, authentic, and accurate." They must be of adequate technical quality. Furthermore, they must carry a certificate stating that these criteria are fulfilled.

F. AGREEMENT ON THE IMPORTATION OF EDUCATIONAL, SCIENTIFIC, AND CULTURAL MATERIALS

The states parties to this treaty, adopted at the 1950 UNESCO General Conference in Florence, exempt all the following materials from customs duties and any other importation charges: books, newspapers, periodicals; various other categories of printed or duplicated matter; manuscripts including typescripts; music; geographic, hydrographic, and astronomical maps and charts, etc., all irrespective of language and destination; works of art (paintings, drawings, sculpture, etc.) and antiques, defined as articles more than 100 years old; visual and auditory materials, such as films, filmstrips, microfilms, sound recordings, glass slides, models, wall charts, posters, of an educational, scientific, or cultural character; scientific instruments and apparatus, under condition that they be (a) intended exclusively for educational purposes or pure scientific research; (b) consigned to public or private institutions approved by the importing country as entitled to exemption from customs duty; and (c) that instruments or apparatus of equivalent scientific value is not manufactured in the importing country; and finally, books and other publications for the blind, and other materials of an educational, scientific, or cultural character for the use of the blind.

In other words, any individual living in a country where the agreement is in force may import duty free books, works of art, or antiques from any other country where the agreement is in force. Other materials, such as educational films and scientific equipment, may be imported duty free only by organizations approved by the importing country.

G. THE UNESCO COUPON PLAN

UNESCO coupons are a type of international money order permitting persons living in countries with foreign-exchange restrictions to purchase from abroad books and many other articles of a scientific or cultural nature.

A person living in a country that participates in the UNESCO coupon plan, who wishes to obtain from another participating country an item covered by the plan buys the required UNESCO coupons (which come in denominations from $1 to $1,000 and in blank coupons to be filled out for amounts below $1), pays for them in local currency at the official rate, and mails them abroad without having to go through any formalities. To redeem the coupons, the seller sends them to a designated agency in his own country or to UNESCO in Paris. They are redeemed in the seller's national currency at the official exchange rate, after the deduction of a handling charge. In September 1970, 45 countries were participating in the UNESCO coupon plan, and more than $87.7 million in coupons had been redeemed since the project was launched in 1948.

H. ENCOURAGEMENT OF INTERNATIONAL TRAVEL AND PROGRAMS FOR EXCHANGE OF PERSONS

As a means of promoting education, research, and international understanding, UNESCO aids and encourages the exchange of persons between member states. It acts as a clearinghouse for governments as well as international organizations on all questions of exchange. It administers UNESCO's own program of fellowships and exchange of experts. It promotes study, training, and teaching abroad with the cooperation of governments and organizations.

The principal publications issued by the exchange service are: *Study Abroad*, a trilingual publication, issued every two years, listing more than 170,000 individual opportunities for subsidized study and travel abroad through a wide variety of fellowships, scholarships, and educational exchange programs of some 1,700 awarding agencies in 120 different countries and territories. It also includes an annual statistical roundup of persons studying abroad.

Handbook for International Exchanges, a standard reference work in the field of exchange, issued every two years, presents information previously published in separate volumes, including such subjects as travel abroad and frontier formalities and an index of cultural agreements.

In the past 22 years, UNESCO has awarded approximately 12,000 international fellowships in connection with various UNESCO projects. Since 1961, fellowships have been awarded every two years in four categories:

(1) Regular Program Fellowships; (2) UNESCO-Sponsored Fellowships; (3) United Nations Development Program (Technical Assistance and Special Fund sectors) Fellowships; and (4) Participation Program Fellowships.

I. THE UNESCO GIFT COUPON PLAN

The gift coupon plan enables such groups as schools and charitable and fraternal organizations to make personalized gifts to schools, libraries, and other educational institutions abroad, particularly those in the less-developed parts of the world. A group wishing to make a gift will first request from the UNESCO Public Liaison Division a catalog describing the various institutions eligible for such gifts, the items they need, and the cost of these items. Once the group has decided on a project, it buys gift coupons for the amount it wishes to donate, and sends those coupons directly to the project. There, school books or educational and scientific equipment can be exchanged for them.

Donations through the gift coupon plan have come to more than

$2 million since its inception, but its significance is more than a matter of money. Direct "people to people" relationships are established between donors and recipients that have often developed into lasting friendships. In addition, the program has a special appeal for school groups because it can be used to give a practical focus to history and geography classes, language courses, and other studies.

One year, for example, schools at Amsterdam, the Netherlands, organized a city-wide campaign for the benefit of a crippled children's home in Bombay, India. The campaign included exhibitions, meetings, and discussion groups, publication of a "Bombay Project" newspaper by students, and lectures by technical assistance experts. Altogether, $12,500 was raised in a few months, and the gift coupons were sent to Bombay along with 50 "painted letters," drawings by Dutch schoolchildren depicting life in Amsterdam. Since 1970 the gift coupon program has highlighted such projects as literacy, education for the handicapped, women's education, and education for refugees.

8 BIBLIOGRAPHY

Copyright Bulletin. Quarterly. $3.00.

Impact of Science on Society. Quarterly. One year, $2.50; single copies, $1.00.

International Social Science Journal. Quarterly. Emphasizes multidisciplinary approach (anthropology, economics, political science, psychology, sociology) toward social problems of international significance, and is intended to satisfy the interest of industry and commerce in the social sciences. One year, $7.00; single copies, $2.00.

International Yearbook of Education. Annual. $13.00.

Museum. Quarterly. One year, $10.00; single copies, $3.00

UNESCO Bulletin for Libraries. Six issues yearly. One year, $4.00; single copies $0.75.

UNESCO Chronicle. Monthly. Information on current UNESCO activities and problems with which it deals. One year, $3.00; single copies, $0.30.

The UNESCO Courier. An illustrated monthly review intended for teachers, students, and the general public. One year, $5.00; single copies, $0.40.

UNESCO Source Book for Science Teaching. Describes scientific experiments and the making of simple apparatus. 1967. 252 pp. Illus. $3.50.

Reference Books: *World Survey of Education,* Vol. IV: *Higher Education.* $42.00. *Handbook on the International Exchange of Publications.* 1964. 766 pp. $8.50. *Index Translationum: International Bibliography of Translations.* Annual. Lists translations published in preceding year in over 74 countries. $40.00. *Study Abroad.* Lists some 75,000 fellowships and scholarships, educational exchanges in 129 countries and territories, and necessary information for applicants. $6.00.

Series of publications includes: *Arid Zone Research: Documentation and Terminology of Science; Educational Studies and Documents; Monographs on Fundamental Education; Museums and Monuments; Natural Resources Research; Press, Film and Radio in the World Today; Problems in Education; The Race Question; Reports and Papers on the Social Sciences; Reports and Papers on Mass Communication; Science Policy Studies and Documents; UNESCO Bibliographical Handbooks; UNESCO Library Manuals.*

INTERNATIONAL MONETARY FUND (IMF)

¹BACKGROUND : The 1930's saw a decade not only of great political upheavals but also of grave financial and economic difficulties. There was widespread abandonment of the gold standard. There were sudden changes in currency exchange rates. Economic chaos was aggravated by lack of coordination between governments imposing controls over international financial transactions and by ruthless economic warfare.

During World War II, more and more countries knew that they would emerge from the conflict with their economic resources depleted at a time when they would be confronted by a reconstruction effort of staggering dimensions. It was also known that the UK would emerge from the war as the world's principal debtor nation and the US, the only major power whose productive capacity had greatly increased during the war, as the world's principal creditor nation.

²CREATION

THE 1943 PLANS OF THE US AND THE UK

The UK, the US, and their allies were convinced that international economic and financial cooperation through intergovernmental institutions expressly established for that purpose was required to prevent a more serious recurrence of the economic and monetary chaos of the 1930's. Two plans were proposed almost simultaneously in 1943: a US plan for an International Stabilization Fund, frequently referred to as the White plan, after H. D. White, then assistant to the US Secretary of the Treasury, and a British plan for an International Clearing Union, frequently referred to as the Keynes plan, after the British economist John Maynard Keynes. Both plans called for international machinery to stabilize currencies and—a radical innovation—a prohibition against altering exchange rates beyond narrow limits without international approval. Both would have introduced a new international currency unit defined in terms of gold. In other respects the plans differed widely. The American plan called for participating nations to contribute to a relatively limited stabilization fund of about $5 billion, on which they would be permitted to draw in order to bridge balance-of-payments deficits. The British plan did not call for advance contributions on the part of participating states; it would have established a system of international clearing accounts, under which each member country could borrow up to its own quota limit, while its creditors would be credited with corresponding amounts, expressed in international currency units. Both plans were discussed with financial experts of other powers, including China, the French Committee for Liberation, and the USSR. The IMF as finally constituted more closely resembled the US-suggested stabilization fund than it did the Keynes plan. The proposal (in both plans) to establish a new international monetary unit was dropped.

THE 1944 BRETTON WOODS CONFERENCE

A full-fledged conference, called by President Franklin D. Roosevelt and attended by delegates from all 44 of the United and Associated Nations, was held from 1 to 22 July 1944 at Bretton Woods, New Hampshire. The Bretton Woods Conference, known officially as the United Nations Monetary and Financial Conference (since the UN did not yet exist the expression "United Nations" referred to the anti-Axis coalition), produced the constitutions, or Articles of Agreement, of two agencies conceived as sister institutions: the International Monetary Fund (IMF) and the International Bank for Reconstruction and Development (IBRD, or World Bank).

The IMF came into existence on 27 December 1945, when 29 governments representing 80% of the quotas to be contributed to the Fund signed the IMF Articles of Agreement in Washington, D.C. An agreement with the UN, under which the International Monetary Fund became an agency related to the UN, came into force on 15 November 1947.

³PURPOSES

The purposes of the IMF are ambitious and far-reaching. They can be summarized as follows:

1. To promote international monetary cooperation.

2. To facilitate the expansion and balanced growth of international trade and contribute thereby to the promotion and maintenance of high levels of employment and real income.

3. To promote exchange stability, maintain orderly exchange arrangements among member states, and avoid competitive currency depreciations.

4. To assist in establishing a multilateral system of payments in respect of current transactions among members and in eliminating foreign exchange restrictions that hamper the growth of world trade.

5. To alleviate any serious disequilibrium in members' international balance of payments by making the resources of the Fund available to them under adequate safeguards, so as to avoid their resort to measures endangering national or international prosperity.

⁴MEMBERSHIP

The original members of the IMF were the 29 nations whose governments ratified the Articles of Agreement by 31 December 1945. Any other state, whether or not a member of the UN, may become a member of the IMF in accordance with terms prescribed by the Board of Governors. IMF membership reached 115 by 30 April 1970. The USSR, which according to the Bretton Woods formula would have been the Fund's third-largest contributor, with a quota of $1.2 billion, did not join. Membership corresponds approximately to that of the UN minus the Soviet-bloc countries and plus West Germany, South Korea, and South Viet-Nam. Switzerland is the only important free-market power that does not belong. Membership in the IMF is a prerequisite to membership in the World Bank.

A member may withdraw from the IMF at any time, and its withdrawal becomes effective on the day a written notice to that effect is received by the Fund. Poland voluntarily withdrew from the Fund on 14 March 1950, Czechoslovakia on 31 December 1954, Cuba on 2 April 1964, and Indonesia on 15 August 1965. Indonesia was subsequently readmitted to the Fund.

If a member state fails to fulfill any of its obligations under the IMF Articles of Agreement, the Fund may declare that country ineligible to use its resources. If, after a reasonable period has elapsed, the member state persists in its failure to live up to its obligations, the Board of Governors may require it to withdraw from membership. On 28 September 1954, the Board of Governors adopted a resolution requiring Czechoslovakia to withdraw from the IMF as of the close of business on 31 December 1954 unless it was willing to take steps to comply with certain of its obligations under the IMF agreement. The Czechoslovakian government did not take the prescribed steps and ceased to be a member of the Fund on 31 December 1954.

In January 1948, France failed to obtain IMF approval for a proposed plan for exchange adjustment, including a devaluation of the French franc that, in the opinion of the Fund, involved discriminatory currency practices. When the French government nevertheless carried out the plan, France became ineligible to use the resources of the Fund. This ineligibility was removed in 1954, and at no time had there been any talk of requesting France to withdraw from the organization.

The full membership of the IMF is listed in a table of quotas and subscriptions of member states in the section "Transactions Between the Fund and Its Members."

5 STRUCTURE

The Fund has a board of governors, composed of as many governors as there are member states; 20 executive directors; a managing director; and a staff.

BOARD OF GOVERNORS

All powers of the IMF are vested in its Board of Governors, on which all member states are represented. Each member state appoints one governor and one alternate governor, who may vote when the principal governor is absent. A government customarily appoints its minister of finance, the president of its central bank, or other high-ranking official as its governor. For example, in April 1970 the US governor was Secretary of the Treasury David M. Kennedy, and his alternate was Deputy Undersecretary for Economic Affairs Nathaniel Samuels.

The principle that applies in most international bodies, one nation one vote, does not apply in the IMF Board of Governors. Multiple votes are assigned IMF member states, more votes being assigned those subscribing larger quotas to the Fund's resources. Each member has 250 votes plus one additional vote for each $100,000 of its quota. The total number of votes of all IMF members was 242,236 on 30 April 1970; of these the US held about 21% and the UK about 10%. (See table in section "Transactions Between the Fund and Its Members.")

Each governor is entitled to cast all the votes allotted to his country as a unit. On certain matters, however, voting power varies according to the use made of the Fund's resources by the respective member. IMF decisions are made by a simple majority of the votes cast, unless otherwise stipulated in the constitution.

The Board of Governors regularly meets once a year, usually at the IMF's Washington headquarters, but not always; its 19th annual meeting, for example, was held in Washington in September 1969. The Board may also be convened for other than annual meetings.

Except for such basic matters as admission of new members, quota changes, and the like, the Board of Governors delegates most of its powers to the Executive Directors of the Fund.

EXECUTIVE DIRECTORS

The 20 Executive Directors of the IMF are responsible for the Fund's general operations and exercise for this purpose all the powers delegated to them by the Board of Governors. The Executive Directors "function [as the IMF constitution says] in continuous session" at the Fund's headquarters and meet as often as the business of the Fund may require.

Each of the five member nations that have the largest quotas—US, UK, France, West Germany, and India—is entitled to appoint one director; each of these five directors casts only the votes of the country that appointed him. Italy has also appointed an executive director under a Fund provision in recognition of the large use of Italian lire by the Fund. The 14 other executive directors are elected by the governors of the other IMF member countries. Each elected director casts as a unit all the votes of the countries that elected him, thus representing a number of different countries.

MANAGING DIRECTOR

The Managing Director, who is chosen by the Executive Directors, is responsible for the conduct of the ordinary business of the Fund. He is appointed for a five-year term and may not serve concurrently as governor or executive director of the IMF. The Managing Director chairs meetings of the Executive Directors but may vote only in case of a tie. There have to date been four Managing Directors: Camille Gutt of Belgium, 1946–51; Ivar Rooth of Sweden, 1951–56; Per Jacobsson, also of Sweden, 1956–63; and Pierre-Paul Schweitzer of France, since September 1963.

HEADQUARTERS AND STAFF

Permanent headquarters of the IMF are at 19th and H Streets, N.W., Washington, D.C. As of 30 April 1970, the staff consisted of about 1,100 persons of 81 nationalities.

6 BUDGET

The approved budget for the fiscal year 1969/70 was $27,900,000. In recent years, the Fund's income has considerably exceeded its administrative expenditures. This income is derived principally from charges on the Fund's transactions and from certain short-term investments.

7 ACTIVITIES

Since the activities of the IMF are designed to help member nations in monetary matters, it requires very substantial financial resources itself. The first matter to be explained, therefore, is the method by which it obtains those resources.

A. RESOURCES OF IMF
Quotas, Subscriptions, and Borrowing

The Fund obtains its necessary financial resources from the accumulated subscriptions made by its members. How much a member government subscribes to the Fund's resources is determined by the quota assigned that country. As mentioned, the quota also determines the country's voting strength in the IMF. Furthermore, the quota determines the amounts the country may draw from the Fund's currency pool.

In determining a member's quota, the IMF considers the country's national income, its holdings of gold and convertible currencies, and its volume of imports and exports.

The standard rule is that 25% of a member's subscription is to be paid in gold and 75% in its own currency. A country must have agreed with the Fund on the establishment of a "par value" for its currency and must have paid its subscription in full to be eligible for exchange transactions with the Fund. The Executive Directors, however, may permit, under certain prescribed conditions, exchange transactions with a country that has not established a par value. but such member will be required to complete payment of its subscription on the basis of an agreed-upon provisional rate of exchange for its currency.

The Fund is required by its constitution to review its members' quotas every five years and to propose called-for adjustments in these quotas, based on its findings. Furthermore, any member may at any time propose a change in its own quota. All quota changes must be approved by a four-fifths majority of the total voting power represented in the Board of Governors, and a country's quota may not be changed without its consent. Two general reviews of the adequacy of members' quotas have led to general and selective increases. The first, in 1958, brought a $5.5 billion rise in total quotas. The second, conducted early in 1965, was followed by a $5 billion increase. The total of members' quotas stood at $21.3 billion on 30 April 1970. Another general review is in progress. This could result in bringing total quotas to approximately $28.9 billion by 1971.

The Fund also can, under its Articles of Agreement. supplement its resources by borrowing. In January 1962, a 4-year agreement was made with 10 industrial members for loans up to $6 billion in their own currencies, if needed by the Fund to forestall or cope with their own impairment of the international monetary system. These General Arrangements to Borrow (GAB) have since been extended until 1975. They were used to help finance large drawings in 1964, 1965, 1968, 1969, and 1970. Fund borrowings from the GAB up to May 1965 have been repaid. On 30 April 1970 the amount available under the arrangements was $5.1 billion. The 10 industrial countries in the GAB and the amounts they undertook to lend the Fund are as follows (equivalent in US$ millions): Belgium 150; Canada 200; France 550; Germany 1,000; Italy 550; Japan 250; Netherlands 200; Sweden 100; UK 1,000; and US 2,000.

Composition and Use of the Fund's Resources

The Fund's transactions in its general account consist of (1) sales to member states of convertible and other needed foreign currencies to help them stabilize their national currencies and overcome short-term balance-of-payments difficulties, and (2) members' repurchases later of their own currencies from the Fund with gold or convertible currencies. Whenever the Fund sells an amount in one currency, it obtains an equivalent amount in another currency; and when, as has happened, it sells gold, it obtains an equivalent amount in some currency or currencies. The system is ingenious, enabling the Fund to engage in large-scale financial transactions without putting a heavy burden on the treasuries of member states. Since the IMF resources are used like a revolving fund, their overall total suffers no depletion through the agency's operations. In fact, as new members join the agency or as quotas (subscriptions) of old members are raised, these resources increase.

However, it is not only the aggregate total of these resources that counts. The composition of that total at any given time, particularly the amount of gold and convertible currencies held, is also of great importance to the Fund and its members. The composition of the Fund's resources varies according to its transactions: thus, whenever the Fund sells US dollars to a member country, its dollar assets decrease while its holdings in that member's currency increase.

Depositories for the Fund's Resources

The gold subscriptions paid into the Fund by member governments are held in IMF gold depositories. IMF regulations provide for such depositories in the US, the UK, France, and India. The institutions that act as depositories for the Fund's gold are designated by these governments. The location is determined in agreement with the IMF.

Each member country pays its national currency subscription to the IMF account at its own central bank or, if it has no central bank, at some other institution acceptable to the Fund. The Articles of Agreement specifically provide that "all the Fund's holdings" in a particular country's currency must be deposited in such bank or institution. Where any part of the Fund's holdings of a member country's national currency is not deemed necessary for Fund operations, the member country may deposit instead noninterest-bearing notes payable to the IMF at par value on demand. Such notes may total as much as 99% of the Fund's holdings of a country's national currency.

B. GENERAL OBLIGATIONS OF IMF MEMBERS

The economic philosophy of the Bretton Woods Agreement holds that monetary stability and cooperation, and the unhampered movement of money, especially in payment of current international transactions, will promote national and international prosperity. This principle is reflected in certain general obligations that countries undertake by accepting the IMF's Articles of Agreement. The Articles favor stabilization measures to help overcome short-term balance-of-payments difficulties and they discourage exchange controls under normal conditions. The Agreement also enables the Fund to help governments in short-term payments difficulties.

Each member undertakes to establish and maintain an agreed par value for its currency and to consult the Fund on any change exceeding 10% of initial parity. Countries retaining excessive controls must consult annually with the Fund on the restrictions in use, the balance of payments justification for these restrictions, and the possibilities for their removal. To aid the Fund's deliberations, members supply data on their holdings of gold and foreign currencies, international trade investment and payments, national income and prices, and other relevant matters.

Under IMF rules, the par value of a country's currency is always expressed in terms of gold and of US dollars (the US dollar is valued at $35 per troy ounce of pure gold). For example, the par value of the Australian dollar is 0.995310 gram of fine gold or $0.385. As of 30 April 1970, par values had been agreed upon by 81 members of the Fund.

C. CONSULTATIONS AND ASSISTANCE

Countries joining the Fund accept certain standards for the conduct of their financial affairs. These standards have rendered the world monetary situation in the post-World War II era different from that in the 1930's when practices such as competitive devaluation were common. In the years following World War II, inflation (a serious problem after any major war) was limited to relatively manageable proportions, thanks to the IMF and other international agencies and arrangements.

Since 1952, the Fund has held annual rounds of consultations with member states that have continued exchange restrictions permitted by the Articles of Agreement during the transitional period. In the course of these discussions, the members' fiscal and monetary policies are examined, as well as the plans for reducing restrictive practices. Under the post-World War transitional provisions of the Fund's constitution, exchange restrictions still obtained in most IMF member countries in the late 1950's. By 1960, only 10 members had accepted the obligations for the convertibility of their currencies. By 30 April 1970, 34 members had done so; today all major currencies used to finance world trade are convertible.

D. TRANSACTIONS BETWEEN THE FUND AND ITS MEMBERS

Little use was made of the Fund's resources in the first years of its existence, when progress toward its goals was impeded by the severe postwar economic difficulties and by widely used exchange restrictions and other import controls. The international payments situation, characterized by a large continuing surplus earned by the US in its trade with other countries, suggested that the need for grants and long-term credits was greater than for the short-to-medium-term financing of the Fund. The Marshall aid program, which was established to meet unusual needs, became a channel for large amounts of US foreign assistance from 1948 through January 1951.

During this period and later, substantial economic recovery was achieved in the UK, Western Europe, and Japan, with favorable effects upon world economy. Production increased in many countries, inflationary pressures were met with firmer policies, and governments began to relax their restrictions on the international flow of goods and services. This economic strengthening of many member countries was reflected in the establishment of convertibility for their currencies.

As members moved toward its objectives, the Fund found opportunities for supporting their efforts in many ways. Some countries requested assistance during seasonal declines in their agricultural production, or when world market prices were unfavorable for their principal export commodities. Domestic inflationary pressures have aggravated the problems of some countries, and speculative movements of capital have at times created further difficulty.

Members may draw up to 50% of their quota in compensation for temporary export short-falls beyond their control, and up to 50% of quota to finance participation in commodity buffer stocks organized under international agreements (see below).

By 30 April 1970, 70 countries had drawn from the Fund's resources the equivalent of over $20 billion in 23 currencies.

Members' repayments by repurchase of currency on 30 April 1970 totaled about $10.5 billion: this means that member countries had to that extent repaid the amount of currencies they had purchased from the Fund, which in turn gave them the equivalent amounts in their own currencies.

QUOTAS, VOTES, AND EXCHANGE TRANSACTIONS
(through 30 April 1970 in US$ millions)

MEMBER	QUOTA	NUMBER OF VOTES	DRAWINGS	REPAYMENTS
Afghanistan	29.00	540	45.8	22.7
Algeria	75.00	1,000	—	—
Argentina	350.00	3,750	425.0	349.1
Australia	500.00	5,250	225.0	225.0
Austria	175.00	2,000	—	—
Belgium	422.00	4,470	199.5	104.5
Bolivia	29.00	540	45.4	30.4
Botswana	3.00	280	—	—
Brazil	350.00	3,750	578.4	478.4
Burma	48.00	730	46.5	15.0
Burundi	15.00	400	19.4	12.8
Cambodia	19.00	440	—	—
Cameroon	18.20	432	—	—
Canada	740.00	7,650	726.0	310.4
Central African Republic	9.50	345	—	—
Ceylon	78.00	1,030	155.3	53.1
Chad	10.00	350	3.8	—
Chile	125.00	1,500	348.0	275.7
China (Taiwan)	550.00	5,750	—	—
Colombia	125.00	1,500	351.9	249.5
Congo (Brazzaville)	10.00	350	—	—
Congo (Kinshasa)	90.00	1,150	—	—
Costa Rica	25.00	500	40.8	37.5
Cyprus	20.00	450	2.9	2.9
Dahomey	10.00	350	—	—
Denmark	163.00	1,880	89.2	44.2
Dominican Republic	32.00	570	49.6	31.5
Ecuador	25.00	500	58.2	40.0
El Salvador	25.00	500	69.5	49.3
Equatorial Guinea	6.00	310		
Ethiopia	19.00	440	.6	.6
Finland	125.00	1,500	103.2	99.2
France	985.00	10,100	2,249.6	505.9
Gabon	9.50	345	—	—
Gambia	5.00	300	—	—
Germany, West	1,200.00	12,250	880.0	—
Ghana	69.00	940	106.4	33.5
Greece	100.00	1,250	—	—
Guatemala	25.00	500	36.6	18.6
Guinea	19.00	440	4.8	.5
Guyana	15.00	400	—	—
Haiti	15.00	400	29.1	21.3
Honduras	19.00	440	32.5	32.5
Iceland	15.00	400	21.8	6.8
India	750.00	7,750	1,090.0	954.9
Indonesia	207.00	2,320	283.2	172.5
Iran	125.00	1,500	167.5	136.2
Iraq	80.00	1,050	40.0	40.0
Ireland	80.00	1,050	42.5	10.0
Israel	90.00	1,150	61.2	16.2
Italy	625.00	6,500	225.0	65.3
Ivory Coast	19.00	440	—	—
Jamaica	38.00	630	—	—
Japan	725.00	7,500	249.0	249.0
Jordan	16.00	410	—	—
Kenya	32.00	570	—	—
Korea, South	50.00	750	12.5	10.7
Kuwait	50.00	750	—	—
Laos	10.00	350	—	—
Lebanon	9.00	340	—	—
Lesotho	3.00	280	—	—
Liberia	20.00	450	26.5	17.2
Libya	19.00	440	—	—
Luxembourg	19.00	440	—	—
Malagasy Republic	19.00	440	—	—
Malawi	11.25	362	—	—
Malaysia	125.00	1,500	—	—
Mali	17.00	420	21.2	10.9
Malta	10.00	350	—	—
Mauritania	10.00	350	—	—
Mauritius	16.00	410	4.0	—
Mexico	270.00	2,950	112.5	112.4
Morocco	90.00	1,150	73.1	13.1
Nepal	10.00	350	—	—
Netherlands	520.00	5,450	144.1	139.1
New Zealand	157.00	1,820	159.2	119.9
Nicaragua	19.00	440	70.5	53.7
Niger	10.00	350	—	—
Nigeria	100.00	1,250	9.2	3.1
Norway	150.00	1,750	9.6	9.6
Pakistan	188.00	2,130	150.5	64.6
Panama	28.00	530	12.1	4.2
Paraguay	15.00	400	8.1	8.1
Peru	85.00	1,100	112.0	68.1
Philippines	110.00	1,350	158.8	58.3
Portugal	75.00	1,000	—	—
Rwanda	15.00	400	12.0	6.0
Sa'udi Arabia	90.00	1,150	—	—
Senegal	25.00	500	—	—
Sierra Leone	15.00	400	6.9	3.5
Singapore	30.00	550	—	—
Somalia	15.00	400	18.9	17.0
South Africa	200.00	2,250	211.9	133.7
Southern Yemen	22.00	470	—	—
Spain	250.00	2,750	216.0	53.7
Sudan	57.00	820	79.4	32.8
Swaziland	6.00	310	—	—
Sweden	225.00	2,500	—	—

Syria	38.00	630	61.4	42.4
Tanzania	32.00	570	—	—
Thailand	95.00	1,200	—	—
Togo	11.25	362	—	—
Trinidad and Tobago	44.00	690	4.8	1.0
Tunisia	35.00	600	46.7	24.9
Turkey	108.00	1,330	230.5	169.5
Uganda	32.00	570	—	—
UAR	150.00	1,750	276.7	206.2
UK	2,440.00	24,650	7,284.0	3,973.9
US	5,160.00	51,850	1,840.0	185.4
Upper Volta	10.00	350	—	—
Uruguay	55.00	800	51.3	29.5
Venezuela	250.00	2,750	—	—
Viet-Nam, South	39.00	640	—	—
Yugoslavia	150.00	1,750	269.4	201.6
Zambia	50.00	750	—	—
TOTALS	21,348.70	242,236	20,875.1	10,547.3

Drawings and Stand-by Arrangements

A currency transaction between the Fund and a member government may take either of two forms, straight drawings or stand-by arrangements. These forms may also be combined. A member may request a straight drawing of a given amount of foreign exchange in a lump sum against payment of an equivalent amount in its own currency. In 1952, the Fund made an arrangement whereby a country can obtain stand-by credit involving a given amount of foreign exchange. Within a specified period, usually one year, that country can draw on the Fund's resources up to the total amount of that credit against an equivalent amount in its own currency. Such stand-by credit arrangements are more flexible than straight drawings and do away with the need for separate negotiations for each transaction.

The largest stand-by credits extended by the Fund have been to the UK—three $1 billion authorizations (in 1962, 1963, and 1964), and one of $1.4 billion in 1967 and another of $1 billion in 1969. (The first two were not touched as the UK did not find it necessary to make withdrawals against them). Stand-by agreements have been increasingly made in recent years by Latin American, European, Asian, and African countries. In a number of cases, these members did not have to draw on the Fund credits. This shows that the mere availability of IMF's assistance may suffice to strengthen a country's financial position.

Conditions and Purposes of Fund Transactions

The maximum amount of currency a member country may purchase from the Fund is limited by the condition that the IMF will not normally hold that country's currency in an amount more than double its quota. As a country makes repayments, it again becomes eligible for purchases within the prescribed limits. Furthermore, amounts in the "borrowing" country's currency purchased from the Fund by another country are considered repayments.

Requests to purchase foreign currency equivalent to a country's gold subscription, commonly called the "gold tranche," are automatically approved. Requests for drawings within the next 25% of quota (the so-called "first credit tranche") are treated liberally. Other requests are approved only when the countries requesting assistance are making reasonable efforts to solve their own problems. For larger drawings, substantial justification is required. The requesting country must show that purchases from the Fund are used to support programs to establish or maintain the stability of its currency at a realistic rate of exchange and establish conditions leading to convertibility.

The Fund's resources are made available in a variety of circumstances. Emergencies such as natural disasters may seriously drain gold and exchange reserves. Growing balance-of-payments difficulties may bring Fund assistance in the form of stand-by arrangements, through which the Fund takes part in members' longer-range programs of fiscal and monetary reform, both in the planning and in subsequent financing.

Countries may also turn to the Fund when faced by temporary exchange difficulties due to exports short-falls beyond their control, such as failure of a major export crop. This is known as the compensatory financing facility. The Fund recently liberalized this assistance, first introduced in 1963, by allowing members to draw up to 50% of their quota to compensate for temporary exports short-falls beyond their control. In 1969 the Fund further decided to allow drawings up to 50% of quota to permit member countries to finance participation in commodity buffer stocks organized under international agreements. But such drawings plus compensatory financing cannot exceed 75% of quota. However, ordinary drawing possibilities are not affected.

The conditions the Fund attaches to use of its resources cover undertakings regarding repurchase and those aspects of international behavior subject to Fund jurisdiction, such as maintenance of exchange stability, simplification of multiple exchange rate systems, reduction or removal of bilateral payments arrangements, and reduction or removal of exchange restrictions. The conditions also include undertakings or declarations of intention regarding such other aspects of international good behavior as the adoption of sound domestic financial policies and the limitation of trade restrictions. Practice has shown that, unless countries hold in check inflationary tendencies, they can neither repay their drawings from the Fund within due time nor progress toward the achievement of such Fund objectives as exchange stability and removal of restrictions on current international transactions. Therefore, drawings and stand-by arrangements are often made conditional upon the adoption of programs of financial stabilization, including rather precise undertakings with respect to public finance, quantitative limitations on central bank credit expansion, and minimum reserve requirements for commercial banks.

The Fund's charges on its ordinary transactions are a service charge of one-half of 1% on most drawings, with charges ranging from 2% to 5% on holdings beyond a 3-month period of a member's currency in excess of quota, graduated according to time held.

E. TECHNICAL ASSISTANCE

Technical assistance is a major activity of the Fund. Staff officials are sent to member countries, sometimes for extended periods, to give advice on stabilization programs or on the simplification of exchange systems, the modification of central banking machinery, the reform of fiscal systems and budgetary controls, or the preparation of financial statistics. The Fund collects and publishes a considerable amount of statistics supplied by members. As part of its technical cooperation the Fund established the IMF Institute in May 1964 to coordinate and expand its training program for staff members of finance ministries and central banks.

F. SPECIAL DRAWING RIGHTS

In September 1967 at the Fund's Annual Meeting in Rio de Janeiro, the Board of Governors approved an outline of a plan to establish special drawing rights (SDRs) in the Fund. The governors asked the Executive Directors to prepare the necessary Amendment to the Fund's Articles of Agreement. The proposed Amendment was approved by the governors in May 1968, and went into effect on 28 July 1969, after acceptance by the required majority of three-fifths of the membership representing four-fifths of the total voting power in the Fund. The Special Drawing Account, through which all operations and transactions pertaining to SDRs are channeled, was established in July 1969 and is open to all Fund members accepting its obligations. In September 1969, the Managing Director of the Fund proposed that the Board of Governors allocate to member countries SDRs totaling $9.5 billion for a first basic period of three years. The first allocation of SDRs, close to $3.5 billion, was made to 104 participants in the Special Drawing Account on 1 January 1970. Subsequent allocations close to $3 billion each are to be made on 1 January 1971 and 1 January 1972.

With the first allocation of SDRs, the total stock of international reserves as well as its rate of growth now reflects deliberate international decisions, rather than being determined solely by the availability of gold for official reserves and the accumulation of balances of reserve currencies. The Fund has become an important source of unconditional liquidity, or reserves that countries can use without being subject to any commitment or decisions as to policy. It continues to provide unconditional liquidity, as in the past, through the General Account of the Fund.

8 BIBLIOGRAPHY

Annual Report on Exchange Restrictions. Free.

Balance of Payments Yearbook. Published as a series of looseleaf sections. $7.50.

Direction of Trade. Monthly. Trade-by-country statistics of some 100 countries and summaries by geographic and monetary areas. Compiled by the IMF and the IBRD, and published jointly by the Fund, the Bank, and the UN. One year, $10.00; single copies, $1.00.

Exchange Restrictions Report. Annual. Free.

Fund and Bank Review—Finance and Development. Quarterly. Free.

International Financial News Survey. Weekly. In addition to financial news, carries reports of press releases and other special statements of the Fund. Free.

International Financial Statistics. Monthly. Statistics on all aspects of domestic and international finance (exchange rates, gold and foreign exchange holdings, money supply, bank assets, international trade, prices, production, interest rates, etc). One year, $10.00; single copies, $1.50.

INTERNATIONAL BANK FOR RECONSTRUCTION AND DEVELOPMENT (IBRD)

¹**BACKGROUND**: The International Bank for Reconstruction and Development, like its sister institution, the International Monetary Fund, was born of the realization on the part of the Allies during World War II that tremendous difficulties in reconstruction and development would face them in the postwar transition period and that international economic and financial cooperation on a vast scale would be required to overcome these difficulties. As early as February 1943, US Undersecretary of State Sumner B. Welles urged preparatory consultations aimed at reaching agreements for the establishment of agencies to finance such reconstruction and development. Subsequently, the US and the UK took leading roles in the negotiations that were to result in the formation of the IBRD and the IMF.

²**CREATION**

The IBRD, or World Bank, as it is commonly called, emerged from the 1944 Bretton Woods Conference as the sister organization to the International Monetary Fund. Like the IMF, the Bank came into existence on 27 December 1945, when its constitution (the "Articles of Agreement") was signed in Washington, D.C., by representatives of 28 governments. The Bank and the Fund have their headquarters side by side in Washington, D.C. Membership in the Fund is a prerequisite to membership in the Bank.

³**PURPOSES**

The principal purposes of the IBRD as set forth in its Articles of Agreement are to assist in the reconstruction and development of member territories by facilitating the investment of capital for productive purposes, thus promoting the long-range balanced growth of international trade, increased productivity, higher standards of living, and better conditions for labor. It is to supplement private investment when private capital is not available on reasonable terms by providing financing out of its own resources. It is to coordinate its own lending with other international loans so that the most urgent and useful projects will receive priority, with due regard for the effect its investments may have on business conditions in member territories. One of the Bank's early functions was to assist in bringing about a smooth transition from wartime to peacetime economies. Within a few years, however economic development, rather than reconstruction, became the object of all its operations.

⁴**MEMBERSHIP**

Membership in the World Bank rose gradually from 41 governments in 1946 to 113 as of June 1970. Some that attended the 1944 Bretton Woods Conference waited a long time to join—New Zealand until August 1961, Liberia until March 1962—and the USSR did not join at all. The Bank's membership now includes almost all the developing countries and all the major industrial or financial powers except Switzerland and those belonging to the Soviet bloc.

A government may withdraw from membership at any time by giving notice of withdrawal. Poland did so in March 1950, Cuba in November 1960, and Indonesia in August 1965. Indonesia rejoined in April 1967. Membership also ceases for a member suspended by a majority of the governors for failure to fulfill an obligation, if that member has not been restored to good standing by a similar majority within a year after the suspension.

Czechoslovakia ceased to be a member in December 1954. The Dominican Republic, which had ceased to be a member, rejoined in 1961.

The members of the IBRD are listed in the table of subscriptions by member states, in the section on "Resources."

⁵**STRUCTURE**

Board of Governors

All powers of the Bank are vested in its Board of Governors, composed of one governor and one alternate appointed by each member state. Ministers of finance, central bank presidents, or persons of comparable status usually represent member states on the IBRD Board of Governors. The IBRD Board of Governors meets annually in joint session with the Board of Governors of the IMF.

The IBRD is organized somewhat like a corporation. According to an agreed-upon formula, its member countries subscribe to various numbers of shares of the Bank's capital stock, each share representing a subscription of $100,000. Each governor is entitled to cast 250 votes plus one vote for each share of capital stock to which his country has subscribed. Botswana and Lesotho, which have each subscribed to 32 shares of the capital stock, valued at $3.2 million, are the smallest shareholders; and the US, which has subscribed to 63,500 shares, valued at $6,350,000,000, is the largest. Thus Botswana and Lesotho are each entitled to 250 votes plus 32, or 282, while the US is entitled to 250 votes plus 63,500, or 63,750.

Executive Directors

The IBRD Board of Governors has delegated most of its authority to 20 executive directors. Five of these directors are appointed by the 5 largest IBRD shareholders and each of these directors disposes of the votes of the country that appointed him; on 30 June 1970 the 5 largest voters were: US 63,750; UK 26,250; Germany 13,050; France 10,750; India 8,250. The other directors are elected for two-year terms by the governors of the remaining member states. Each of these directors casts the combined votes of the countries he is elected to represent. Thus an Australian elected as director by Australia, New Zealand, and South Africa casts the 9,880 votes to which the 3 countries together are entitled.

On 30 June 1970, when subscriptions to the Bank's authorized capital stood at $24 billion, the number of votes of IBRD members totaled 259,838.

President and Staff

The president of the Bank, elected by the executive directors, is also their chairman, although he is not entitled to a vote, except in case of an equal division. Subject to their general direction, the president is responsible for the conduct of the ordinary business of the Bank. Action on IBRD loans is initiated by the president and the staff of the Bank. The amount, terms, and conditions of a loan are recommended by the president to the executive directors; and the loan is made if his recommendation is approved by them.

Since April 1968, Robert S. McNamara has been the president of the IBRD. Under him, there is a staff of about 2,250 persons of close to 85 nationalities.

Earlier presidents of the Bank were: Eugene Meyer, June to December 1946; John J. McCloy, March 1947 to June 1949; Eugene R. Black, July 1949 to December 1962; and George D. Woods, January 1963 to March 1968.

Headquarters

The IBRD's headquarters are at 1818 H Street, N.W., Washington, D.C. Most annual meetings of the Board of Governors have so far been held at headquarters; others have taken place in London, Paris, Mexico City, Istanbul, New Delhi, Vienna, Tokyo, and Rio de Janeiro. The Bank's New York office, which helps in the execution of programs for the marketing of World Bank Bonds and arranges sales from the Bank's portfolio securities, is located at 120 Broadway, New York City.

The European office of the Bank is located in Paris. There is also a small office in London. The Bank maintains permanent missions at Nairobi, Kenya; and Abidjan, Ivory Coast. There are resident missions or staff in New Delhi, India; Djakarta, Indonesia; Bogotá, Colombia; Lagos, Nigeria; Addis Ababa, Ethiopia; Kinshasa, the Democratic Republic of the Congo; Islamabad and Dacca, Pakistan; and Kabul, Afghanistan.

6 BUDGET

The IBRD's administrative budget has gradually risen from $2.1 million in fiscal year 1947 to $61.2 million in fiscal year 1970. The administrative expenditures are met from the Bank's income.

7 ACTIVITIES

A. FINANCIAL RESOURCES

Authorized Capital

At its establishment, the Bank had an authorized capital of $10 billion. Countries subscribing shares were required to pay in only one-fifth of their subscription on joining, the remainder being available on call, but only to meet the Bank's liabilities if it got into difficulties. Moreover, not even the one-fifth had to be paid over in hard cash at that time. The sole cash requirement was the payment in gold or US dollars of 2% of each country's subscription. A further 18% of the subscription was payable in the currency of the member country concerned, and although this sum was technically paid in, in the form of notes bearing no interest, it could not be used without the member's permission. Only the US and Canada were in a position for some time after the war to allow these notes to be cashed. Most of the other industrialized countries have since freed the national currency part of their subscriptions on a convertible basis, but the subscriptions of many of the less-developed members of the Bank are still largely frozen in this way.

Upon actually joining the Bank a country pays in 10% of its subscription. One percent of this amount is paid in gold or United States dollars and is freely usable in the Bank's operations. The other 9% is paid in the country's own currency, and is available for use only with the consent of the member. The remaining 90% is not paid in but may be called by the Bank if required to meet its obligations arising out of borrowings or guaranteeing loans.

SUBSCRIPTIONS TO CAPITAL STOCK, 30 JUNE 1970

MEMBER	TOTAL SUBSCRIPTION (in millions of US dollars)	MEMBER	TOTAL SUBSCRIPTION (in millions of US dollars)
Afghanistan	30.0	Laos	10.0
Algeria	80.0	Lebanon	9.0
Argentina	373.3	Lesotho	3.2
Australia	533.0	Liberia	21.3
Austria	186.7	Libya	20.0
Belgium	450.0	Luxembourg	20.0
Bolivia	21.0	Malagasy Rep.	20.0
Botswana	3.2	Malawi	15.0
Brazil	373.3	Malaysia	133.3
Burma	50.7	Mali	17.3
Burundi	15.0	Mauritania	10.0
Cameroon	20.0	Mauritius	10.0
Canada	792.0	Mexico	208.0
Central African Republic	10.0	Morocco	96.0
Ceylon	82.7	Nepal	10.0
Chad	10.0	Netherlands	550.0
Chile	93.3	New Zealand	166.7
China	750.0	Nicaragua	8.0
Colombia	93.3	Niger	10.0
Congo, Brazzaville	10.0	Nigeria	106.7
Congo, Kinshasa	86.0	Norway	160.0
Costa Rica	10.7	Pakistan	200.0
Cyprus	21.3	Panama	9.0
Dahomey	10.0	Paraguay	6.0
Denmark	173.3	Peru	63.5
Dominican Republic	13.3	Philippines	117.3
Ecuador	17.1	Portugal	80.0
El Salvador	10.7	Rwanda	15.0
Ethiopia	10.0	Sa'udi Arabia	96.0
Finland	133.3	Senegal	33.3
France	1,050.0	Sierra Leone	15.0
Gabon	10.0	Singapore	32.0
Gambia, The	5.3	Somalia	15.0
Germany, West	1,280.0	South Africa	213.3
Ghana	73.4	Southern Yemen	23.5
Greece	66.7	Spain	266.7
Guatemala	10.7	Sudan	60.0
Guinea	20.0	Swaziland	6.4
Guyana	16.0	Sweden	240.0
Haiti	15.0	Syria	40.0
Honduras	8.0	Tanzania	33.3
Iceland	15.0	Thailand	101.3
India	800.0	Togo	15.0
Indonesia	220.0	Trinidad and Tobago	46.7
Iran	128.6	Tunisia	37.3
Iraq	64.0	Turkey	115.0
Ireland	85.3	Uganda	33.3
Israel	95.9	UAR	142.1
Italy	666.0	UK	2,600.0
Ivory Coast	20.0	US	6,350.0
Jamaica	40.0	Upper Volta	10.0
Japan	772.6	Uruguay	28.0
Jordan	16.3	Venezuela	186.7
Kenya	33.3	Viet-Nam, South	42.7
Korea, South	53.3	Yemen	8.5
Kuwait	66.7	Yugoslavia	106.7
		Zambia	53.3

Financial Resources for Lending Purposes

The subscriptions of the Bank's members constitute the basic element in the financial resources of the Bank.

Altogether, the paid-in portion of the subscriptions now amounts to a little more than $2.3 billion. But this is only part of the total funds available to the Bank for lending. It draws much more money from other sources: from borrowings in the market and from earnings.

The Bank's outstanding borrowings amount now to roughly $4.5 billion, raised in the capital markets of the world and most particularly from private investors of the US, Canada, and western Europe. In western Europe it has made public bond issues in the capital markets of Austria, Belgium, West Germany, Italy, the Netherlands, Switzerland, and the UK, and has borrowed privately in these and many other countries. Somewhat more than half of the total debt is owed to non-US investors. It has been possible for the Bank to raise this large sum, at interest rates little or no higher than are paid by governments themselves, for two basic reasons. One is the confidence in the Bank engendered by its record of operations over the past 25 years. The other is that investors know that the Bank has available still larger sums it can call upon to repay its borrowings, should it ever be in difficulty. These sums are the portions of the member countries' subscriptions that have not been paid in, but remain on call. The US guarantee alone amounts to $5,715 million or more than the Bank's outstanding borrowings, and when the guarantees of the other industrialized countries are added, the cover for its debt rises to roughly five times.

The Bank's uncalled subscriptions are the final guarantee for its borrowings. As a very substantial first line of defense, however, the Bank can call upon over $1,300 million of accumulated earnings. A part of these earnings is required to be kept in liquid form as an immediately accessible special reserve against losses, and this reserve now exceeds $290 million. The remainder of its net income, besides providing the Bank with a cushion against possible losses, consitutes a third major source of funds for lending. The lendable earnings are now over $1,000 million.

These three sources—capital, borrowings, and earnings—make up the original pool of funds for the Bank's lending. There are some further contributions that supplement this pool. Repayments of principal on earlier loans have allowed the Bank to turn over and re-lend about $2,126 million. In addition, the Bank sells to financial institutions in Europe and America portions of its loans (usually installments that are due to be repaid within a fairly short time), and thus replenishes its cash resources. These sales have provided $2,350 million.

Together, these various sources of funds have enabled the Bank to undertake loan commitments of approximately $14.5 billion, of which over $10 billion have been disbursed.

B. LENDING OPERATIONS

Under the Bank's declared purposes, its main function is to make loans according to specific principles: first, on condition that private capital is not available on reasonable terms; second, that the borrower will be able to repay the loan; third, that the project or program to be financed will benefit the economy sufficiently to justify borrowing the foreign exchange; and fourth, that the program or project is well designed and feasible of execution.

The World Bank makes loans to governments of member countries or, with the respective government's guarantee, to political subdivisions such as a province or overseas territory, or to public or private enterprises.

The Bank's first loan, $250 million for postwar reconstruction, was made in the latter part of 1947. Altogether it lent $497 million for postwar reconstruction, all to European countries. The Bank's first development loans were made in the first half of 1948, and it pursued its development loan program cautiously in the next few years, lending $109 million for that purpose in the fiscal year 1948/49 and $134 million in 1949/50. By the end of the calendar year 1952, the Bank had made 74 loans totaling $1,524 million in 28 countries and territories. Lending increased

to an average of $800 million by the end of 1968. Thereafter it increased sharply: in fiscal 1969 to $1,399 million; and in fiscal 1970 to $1,680 million.

As of 30 June 1970, the aggregate gross total of loans made by the Bank since its inception came to over $14 billion for 705 individual projects in 104 countries.

WORLD BANK LOANS AS OF 30 JUNE 1970
(IN US DOLLARS)

COUNTRY	BANK LOANS Net Amounts
AFRICA	
Algeria	$ 80,500,000
Botswana	—
Burundi	4,800,000
Cameroon	37,100,000
Central African Republic	
Chad	—
Congo (Brazzaville)	30,000,000
Congo (Kinshasa)	91,582,854
Dahomey	—
Ethiopia	97,800,000
Gabon	54,788,722
Gambia, The	—
Ghana	53,000,000
Guinea	64,500,000
Ivory Coast	48,491,567
Kenya	197,524,026
Lesotho	—
Liberia	15,249,812
Malagasy Republic	11,100,000
Malawi	—
Mali	—
Mauritania	66,000,000
Mauritius	6,973,119
Morocco	143,049,041
Niger	—
Nigeria	241,600,000
Rhodesia	86,950,000
Rwanda	—
Senegal	7,500,000
Sierra Leone	7,700,000
Somalia	—
South Africa	241,800,000
Sudan	134,000,000
Swaziland	6,950,000
Tanzania	12,200,000
Togo	—
Tunisia	76,835,481
Uganda	8,400,000
UAR	56,500,000
Upper Volta	—
Zambia	131,550,000
	$2,014,444,622
ASIA	
Afghanistan	$ —
Burma	33,123,943
Ceylon	89,712,258
China	244,072,087
India	1,087,653,602
Indonesia	—
Iran	447,397,565
Iraq	25,293,946
Israel	134,412,479
Japan	857,041,004
Jordan	—
Korea, South	110,000,000
Lebanon	27,000,000
Malaysia	237,878,513
Nepal	—

COUNTRY	BANK LOANS Net Amounts
Pakistan	633,470,130
Papua and New Guinea	11,500,000
Philippines	217,020,336
Singapore	114,243,457
Syria	—
Thailand	358,364,939
	$4,628,184,259
Australia	$ 417,730,000
New Zealand	$ 96,923,771

EUROPE

Austria	$ 104,860,083
Belgium	76,000,000
Cyprus	34,194,412
Denmark	85,000,000
Finland	243,526,846
France	250,000,000
Greece	32,500,000
Iceland	25,914,000
Ireland	14,500,000
Italy	398,028,000
Luxembourg	11,761,983
Malta	6,040,080
Netherlands	236,451,985
Norway	145,000,000
Portugal	57,500,000
Spain	224,161,832
Turkey	144,184,967
Yugoslavia	475,490,547
	$2,565,114,735

AMERICAS

Argentina	$ 357,602,049
Bolivia	23,250,000
Brazil	838,034,660
Chile	232,695,818
Colombia	727,652,840
Costa Rica	84,876,251
Dominican Republic	25,000,000
Ecuador	63,300,000
El Salvador	57,918,024
Guatemala	46,500,000
Guyana	8,819,017
Haiti	2,600,000
Honduras	52,317,613
Jamaica	44,012,988
Mexico	978,705,679
Nicaragua	59,858,828
Panama	60,047,426
Paraguay	21,838,549
Peru	214,102,066
Trinidad and Tobago	46,390,424
Uruguay	108,463,116
Venezuela	298,266,783
	$4,352,252,131

Purposes of the Loans

Electrification and improved transportation are fundamental for economic development, yet private capital is often not available for these purposes. Hence, the major portion of World Bank loans has been in these two fields. For example, of 70 loans totaling $1,680 million granted in its fiscal year 1970, $502 million was for electric power and $516 million for transport facilities. In recent years the Bank made specific and significant shifts to contribute to the optimal development of the developing nations. The number of agricultural projects in 1969 and 1970 alone totaled half as many as in the entire previous history of the Bank. Lending for education in these two years was greater than in all the previous years put together. The first loan ever for a family-planning project was made in June 1970. The following is a summary of loan distribution by uses:

	(In millions of US dollars)
Post-World War II reconstruction (no loans granted since 1948)	496.8
Electric power generation and distribution	4,642.2
Transportation railroads, roads, ports and inland waterways, airlines and airports, shipping, pipelines for natural gas and oil	4,405.4
Industry iron and steel, pulp and paper, mining, fertilizer and other chemicals, other industries, mining, other extractive industries, development finance companies	2,165.8
Agriculture irrigation and flood control, farm mechanization, land clearance and improvement, livestock improvement, credit, crop processing and storage, forestry and fishing	1,294.1
General development industrial import	552.3
Communications	243.9
Water supply	127.1
Education	144.4
Family planning	2.0
Financing loan IFC	200.0

In most cases, it should be noted, the impact of a loan extends well beyond the particular category under which it is listed; thus loans for transportation, agriculture, or electric power development stimulate other sectors of the economy as well. World Bank loans, furthermore, may encourage a much larger inflow of other capital for various projects planned with the Bank's assistance.

Loan Currencies

Normally, the Bank supplies the currency the borrower requires for a specific purchase or expenditure. This also determines the currency or currencies in which the borrower repays the loan principal. If the Bank provides a currency from its own holdings, repayment is made in that currency; if the Bank spends another currency to buy the currency required, the repayment is made in the currency that the Bank expended.

Loan Terms and Interest Rate

The Bank normally makes long-term loans, with the repayments commencing after a certain period. The length of the loans is generally related to the estimated useful life of the equipment or plant being financed. For example, the cost of a hydroelectric power plant consists partly of installations that last a very long time and partly of generating equipment that has a shorter economic life. The term for such loans may be 20 to 25 years. On the other hand, loans for the purchase of less durable goods, such as farm machinery, could be for shorter terms.

Since in the long run the IBRD must raise money in order to lend money, it uses as a basis for determining its own standard interest charge the estimated rate the Bank itself would have to pay as a borrower at the time of the loan. Hence, the level of the Bank's interest rate reflects rather closely the fluctuations in the main capital markets of the world. The Bank's standard rate, at present, is 7.25%.

Where World Bank Loans Are Spent

The IBRD collects information on the geographic distribution of orders financed by its borrowers with Bank loan funds. The normal procedure is for borrowers to place their orders on the basis of international competition. The accompanying table shows the main countries from which imports were financed by Bank loans.

LOAN EXPENDITURE IN INDIVIDUAL COUNTRIES
(IN MILLIONS OF US DOLLARS)

DISBURSEMENTS BY BORROWERS FOR IMPORTS FROM:	CUMULATIVE TOTAL TO 30 JUNE 1970
Belgium	176.1
Canada	198.8
France	404.2
Germany, West	909.2
Italy	481.8
Japan	475.9
Netherlands	83.9
Sweden	205.9
Switzerland	225.3
UK	1,125.6
US	2,683.5
All other countries	426.7
TOTAL	7,396.9
Other Disbursements	2,957.9
GRAND TOTAL	10,354.8

C. ILLUSTRATIONS OF LOAN USES
Loans in Africa

In June 1970, the African continent was represented in the Bank's membership by 41 states or more than one-third of the total membership. In 1962 only 10 of the then 75 members were countries in Africa. Of the African countries that have attained independence since 1955, Nigeria with a total of $241.6 million has been the largest recipient of World Bank financing. In fiscal 1970, for example, it got a $25-million loan for transportation rehabilitation, aimed primarily at maintaining the flow of imports and exports. The projects will assist in relieving congestion at the port of Lagos, the only major port in operation at the time the loan was granted, by reactivating the second-largest port, Port Harcourt, and its connections with its hinterland. The loan will also be used for the purchase of urgently needed materials and equipment for ports and railways, the rebuilding of up to 500 miles of highway, and replacement of damaged bridges.

The nature of the problem facing African countries is exemplified by the case of Mauritania, which is twice the size of France but nearly all desert. In 1960, shortly before Mauritania's transition to independence, France guaranteed a 15-year, 6.25% World Bank loan equivalent to $66 million made to a mining company to exploit the large high-grade iron ore deposits (proven estimated reserves: 250 million tons) deep in the interior of Mauritania and to build a 350-mile railway to transport the ore to the ocean. Similarly, in 1959, France guaranteed a 15-year, 6% World Bank loan of $35 million made to a mining company in Gabon. The loan helped to mine and process Gabon's large open-pit manganese ore deposits and to build a 45-mile cableway over the difficult terrain to the Congo (P.R.) frontier and from there a new 180-mile road to link up the existing Congo-Ocean road. The first Gabon ore was exported in mid-1962 and the first shipments of Mauritanian ore were made by mid-1963.

The Hassi Messaoud oil field lies 375 miles southeast of Algiers. In December 1959, the Bank made a $59-million, 12-year, 6% loan to the Société Pétrolière de Gérance to provide about half the funds required to finance further construction and operation of the 24-inch pipeline that extends 412 miles across the desert and brings crude oil from the Hassi Messaoud field to the Algerian port of Bougie on the Mediterranean coast. Primary reserves at Hassi Messaoud are estimated at about 170 million metric tons, with a probable reserve of another 150 million metric tons. The pipeline, which crosses a mountain pass at an elevation of 3,400 feet, came into limited operation in December 1959. By 1961, additional pumps and pumping stations were installed to bring the pipeline up to an annual capacity of about 14 million tons.

Schoolchildren in the Ivory Coast will learn through television, thanks to a new educational project for which the Bank granted a loan of US$11 million in fiscal 1970. For the first time in its history, the Bank is helping to finance construction of a nationwide instructional television production center in Bouaké, the second-largest city of that nation. Pilot programs are expected to be offered in 1971. Ultimately, more than 700,000 pupils, grade 1 through 6, will have televised instruction.

Loans in Asia

India. India is the largest single client of the World Bank and its affiliate, the International Development Association (IDA). By the end of June 1970 the two institutions had provided $2,351 million—$1,087 million in 39 Bank loans and $1,264 million in 28 IDA credits—to assist development projects and programs crucial to India's economic growth. India has accordingly accounted for almost 8% of all Bank lending and about 45% of all IDA lending to date. In addition, the Bank's other affiliate, the International Finance Corporation (IFC), has undertaken investment commitments totaling $42 million in 13 industrial projects. The overall commitment of $2,393 million must be looked at against the background of the immense task of raising living standards in India, a country with a population of over 525 million persons whose average income is among the lowest in the world.

During fiscal 1970, India received $267.5 million—1 loan of $40 million from the World Bank and 5 credits for a total of $227.5 million from IDA—of which $97.5 million were for agriculture, $55 million for railways, $40 million for industrial projects (development finance company) and $75 million for industrial imports.

In the earlier years the Bank helped to build a number of irrigation projects like tubewells in Uttar Pradesh, the Salandi in Orissa, the Sone in Bihar, the Purna in Maharashtra, and the Shetrunji in Gujarat. In recent months Bank and IDA assistance has been directed toward assisting India's efforts to expand her foodgrain output through the adoption of modern technology and inputs. IDA is assisting agricultural credit and farm mechanization projects in Gujarat and the Punjab, and the Bank is assisting a project to increase the production of seeds of the high-yielding varieties in the Tarai area of Uttar Pradesh.

Pakistan. Pakistan is the third-largest borrower in Asia with 31 Bank loans for $633,470,130 and 36 credits from IDA for $453,218,054. In fiscal 1970 Pakistan received $96.4 million, of which $27.0 million was for agriculture; $8.0 million for education; $15 million for telecommunications; $19.2 million for a natural gas pipeline; $23.0 million for industry; and $4.2 million for project preparation.

For example, Pakistan's new educational development policy is aimed at relating the educational system to manpower needs and emphasizes technical and vocational educators. The education loan of $8 million will make possible an increase of about 650 in the combined undergraduate engineering enrollment of 2 leading engineering schools at Lahore and Karachi.

Thailand. Thailand has received 21 loans with a net amount of $358 million.

In fiscal 1970, Thailand received a loan of $46.5 million for a project to increase its electric power generating capacity by 560,000 kw. The new installations form part of a continuing expansion program to meet Thailand's unusually high demand for electricity that has been growing at an annual rate of 30% in recent years. Other loans in earlier years have covered the fields of railways, ports, roads, irrigation, education, industry, and power.

Loans in Europe

During fiscal 1970, the World Bank granted 7 loans totaling $160.5 million for projects in Europe.

Of these, 3 loans totaling $98.5 million were to Yugoslavia. The first one of $18.5 million was for industrial development. Three important industrial enterprises in Yugoslavia—producers of cars, steel tubes, and automotive wheels—will modernize and expand their productive facilities with the assistance of the World Bank. The loan was made to the Yugoslav Investment Bank and guaranteed by the Socialist Federal Republic of Yugoslavia for a term of 14 years, including a 2½-year grace period, with interest at 7%. The Investment Bank will re-lend the funds on the same terms with interest at 8% to Zavodi Crvena Zastava, Yugoslavia's largest and only integrated car manufacturer ($10 million); to Zeljezara Sisak, the largest producer of steel tubes ($6.2 million) and to Industria Poljoprivrednih Masina, Yugoslavia's only producer of combine harvesters and of automobile, truck, and tractor wheels ($2.3 million).

The second one, of $40 million, will help finance the expansion and modernization of Yugoslavia's national long-distance and international telecommunication systems. The project forms part of a 7-year $470 million development program that will bring about a significant improvement in Yugoslavia's domestic and international telephone and telegraph services. The rapid growth of the economy, particularly of industry and tourism, has brought about a demand for telecommunications service far beyond the capacity of existing installations. There are some 800,000 potential subscribers awaiting telephone connections, and during business hours the long-distance lines are heavily congested.

Promoting economic growth and increasing foreign exchange earnings from tourism are the major aims of a $40 million World Bank loan to Yugoslavia for highways, the third one granted in fiscal 1970. The loan will help finance the second phase of a major highway construction program initiated in 1968, involving the construction of 6 sections of 4 major highways, totaling 140 miles. Yugoslavia is giving increasing priority to highway development, particularly since road transport has become the prime mode of passenger travel and is enlarging its share of freight traffic. More than half of the country's paved highways, extending to about 11,500 miles, have been built since 1962. The project is the fourth highway project to be assisted by the Bank in Yugoslavia, bringing Bank lending for highways to $115 million.

Other loans made to European countries were $5 million to Cyprus for electric power; $20 million to Greece for industry; and $37 million to Spain, of which $25 million was for livestock and $12 million for education.

Loans in Latin America

Since its inception, the World Bank Group has helped finance a wide variety of development projects in Latin America. The Bank's first loan for development was made in the region. The first credit extended by the Bank's soft-loan affiliate, the International Development Association, helped build a road in Honduras. The International Finance Corporation, another Bank affiliate, also made its first investment in private industry there.

The volume of lending to Latin America has risen rapidly in recent years—from $385 million in fiscal 1968 to $702.9 million in fiscal 1970.

As of 30 June 1970 the World Bank had made 246 loans totaling over $4.3 billion to 22 countries of Latin America and the Caribbean area. The largest amount ($978 million) was lent to Mexico. Next came Brazil, with $838 million, and Colombia with $727 million.

More than half of the total amount lent in Latin America has been for electric power. During the last 20 years or so, the World Bank has been the principal source of external financing for the development of electric power in the 17 countries in which it has financed power projects, increasing the generating capacity by nearly 15,000,000 kw. The new capacity that has already come into operation is giving a strong impetus to the development of industry and other sectors of the economy.

After power, the largest sector of Bank lending in this region has been transportation. The Bank has lent about $1.1 billion for such projects as building or improving roads, railways, ports, and pipelines. Agriculture, education, water supply, and industry are among the other sectors that have been supported by World Bank loans. In fiscal 1970, Colombia received loans of $18.3 million for livestock, $6.5 million for education, $32 million for roads, $52.3 million for electric power, and $18.5 million for water supply.

During fiscal 1970 the Bank's very first loan for a family-planning project was made to Jamaica. The Bank's interest in the population field arises from its awareness that the high rates of population growth in many member countries can severely impede their economic development efforts. The loan to Jamaica, of $2 million, will help the government develop a postpartum family-planning program by financing an extension to Jamaica's largest maternity hospital in Kingston and the construction of rural maternity centers. The Bank is making intensive efforts to increase its expertise in the field of population problems. Staff members keep in close touch with other organizations working in this field; international consultants have served on the Bank's missions. The Bank expects to expand its operational and analytical activities in the coming years, in line with member countries' requirements for technical and financial assistance.

D. ADVISORY ASISTANCE AND OTHER SERVICES

Technical Assistance

The Bank renders its members a wide variety of technical assistance. It conducts full-scale surveys of their economic potential, undertakes economic studies in depth, and advises on individual sectors in the economy or on specific projects. The Bank pays continuous attention to the economic performance of its borrowers. Each proposal for a loan or a credit is considered in the context of the Bank's assessment of the economic position, policies, and prospects of a borrowing country. The Bank's technical assistance activities are directed not only toward assuring sound lending but also toward assisting developing countries to maximize their resource utilization. Many of the Bank's loans have been instrumental in the establishment of more efficient management and in introducing better administrative methods.

General Survey Missions

Since 1949 the Bank, at the request of the governments, has organized general survey missions. All the missions were to assist in development planning; some, like those to Ceylon (1951) and Somalia (1956), were undertaken shortly before or after the country became independent. Frequently, since a few years ago, these missions include, in addition to World Bank experts, specialists in such fields as agriculture, water resources, public health, and education, who are recruited with the help of other UN-related agencies, such as FAO, WHO, and UNESCO.

In quite a few countries, the surveys have constituted the first attempt to analyze all aspects of the economy and to help in framing a comprehensive development strategy for a number of years ahead. Sometimes the Bank urges wide dissemination of its survey reports in the countries concerned and publishes them in book form through The Johns Hopkins Press, Baltimore, Md.

The Bank also carries out sector reviews. Recent individual studies have dealt with the industrialization of Iran and Pakistan, agriculture in Brazil, and mining and manufacturing in Morocco. In addition to conducting project and sector studies, the Bank acts as executing agency for the relatively large-scale preinvestment projects financed by the UN Development Program that fall within its field of specialization. These range from studies of the feasibility of building a multipurpose dam on the Niger River (Nigeria) and a new port in Thailand to surveys on siltation at the port of Georgetown, Guyana; hydroelectric resources of the state of Minas Gerais, Brazil; irrigation in Guatemala; mineral deposits in Surinam; port siltation in Bangkok; and a railway to transport iron ore from the interior of Gabon to the Atlantic coast.

Many of the less-developed countries need assistance in bringing project plans to a stage where they can be considered for international financing. To help African states in this task, in 1965, the Bank established permanent missions in Abidjan, Ivory Coast, and Nairobi, Kenya, to serve member countries in west and east Africa, respectively. These missions concentrate their activities on the agricultural and transportation sectors. The least formal but frequently employed method of assistance consists of discussions and exchanges of views at headquarters and in the field between Bank staff and officials and technicians engaged on the project that the Bank has financed or contemplates supporting.

During the fiscal year 1970, six project preparation credits were extended to four countries for studies in the sectors of agriculture, transportation, and electric power. A $2.5 million IDA credit to Botswana will finance consultants' services and design coordination work for the infrastructure needed to support a proposed nickel mining development project. Credits of $0.4 million and $1.5 million were provided to Burundi and Ghana respectively for highway engineering and (in the case of Burundi) maintenance studies. Two credits to Pakistan, of $0.8 million and $2.4 million, will provide funds for engineering studies designed to help lay the foundations of an adequate irrigation system in East Pakistan: these studies are associated with the East Pakistan Agriculture and Water Development Program. A third credit to Pakistan, of $1 million, will help finance studies relating to the development and expansion of the port of Karachi. This work will be closely integrated with other studies of the port's future development, which are being financed by the UNDP and being carried out under Bank supervision as Executing Agency.

Training
An Economic Development Institute was established in 1955, with initial financial support from the Ford Foundation and the Rockefeller Foundation, to determine whether the experience of the World Bank in dealing with problems of economic development in many countries could be used to broaden the perspective and competence of senior officials of developing countries, who are concerned with these problems.

This activity soon passed the experimental stage and is now an integral part of the World Bank program. By the end of fiscal 1970 over 1,100 such officials had attended EDI courses. The 150 participants in the 6 courses offered during the last fiscal year came from 68 developing countries and 2 international organizations. The number of nominations, always greatly in excess of the number of participants who can be accommodated, has steadily increased. The Bank's 1970 budget allotted almost $1.6 million (against $400,000 in 1962) for the institute and an

expansion for 1971 is foreseen with expenditures up to $1.9 million.

Coordinating Development Assistance
Effective financial and technical assistance demands coordination. At the aid-giving end, closer consultation among the providers helps to assure that all are supporting consistent development goals and that financial and technical aid is applied to priority needs. At the receiving end, better planning and execution make assistance more effective in bringing about increased productivity.

The Bank's experience in coordinating aid from several sources to a single recipient country began as an emergency matter in the summer of 1958, when a consortium of interested governments met under the chairmanship of the Bank to provide assistance needed to avert a foreign-exchange crisis in India. It is currently sponsor of two Consortia, eleven Consultative Groups, and the Aid Group for Ceylon. During the fiscal year 1970 the Bank took over from the International Monetary Fund the chairmanship of the Ghana Aid Group. In addition, the Bank provides staff support for the Inter-Governmental Group for Indonesia (IGGI) and the coordination groups convened by the governments of Guyana and Honduras; it is also a member of the OECD-sponsored Consortium for Turkey.

Eleven meetings of Bank-sponsored aid groups were held in fiscal 1970. For the East Africa Consultative Group, separate meetings were held for Uganda, Kenya, and Tanzania; the India Consortium met in November 1969 to consider the United Nations report on "Evaluation of the Family Planning Program of the Government of India," and again in May 1970; the Consultative Group for Tunisia met in October 1969 and June 1970. Single meetings were held of the Pakistan Consortium, the Consultative Groups for Korea and Morocco, and of the Ceylon Aid Group. The Bank makes periodic comprehensive reports on the recipient country's development possibilities, problems, and performance, comments on the country's estimates of its aid requirements, and recommends what types and terms of aid seem most appropriate. It also helps the recipient country in its development programming, the execution of projects, the arrangement of feasibility studies, and other forms of technical assistance, and in the identification and preparation of projects.

Several developing countries depend largely on a few cash crops for their foreign exchange earnings. Disadvantageous trends in the world market might disrupt their economies and make it impossible for them to go ahead with their development plans, which normally are framed several years ahead. The Bank Group took a number of steps during fiscal year 1970 to implement the decisions of the Executive Directors regarding the role the group could feasibly play in helping to solve problems related to the stabilization of prices of primary products. The directors' decisions related mainly to policies for the diversification of productive activity in the primary producing countries, for strengthening the competitive position of primary products, and for assistance to appropriate international commodity arrangements. The first of these objectives was furthered by the group's lending during the year in a number of project areas—in particular its lending for livestock, fisheries and forestry development, and for industrial projects—and also by the economic analysis undertaken during the year of national economies, vital sectors of activity, and other specialized topics. Efforts to meet the second objective included discussions with other international organizations concerned with commodity production and consideration by the Bank Group of possibilities for its participation in programs of research into key aspects of agricultural commodity production, and into new types of end use. As to the third main objective, Bank/IDA staff members participated as observers in the meetings of major commodity groups, furnishing them with Bank commodity studies and other relevant material and discussing with them, where appropriate, opportunities for cooperation in financing specific projects. Arrangements were also made to receive authoritative data relating to problems of market access.

Mediation and Insurance

Legal and political uncertainties often deter foreign private capital from being used in developing countries. To improve the private investment climate, the Bank has set in motion two conventions aimed to facilitate the flow of foreign capital. The first convention concerns the action that can be taken in case disputes arise between a private foreign investor and the country in which he has invested. The convention, which was submitted by the Bank to its member governments in March 1965, foresees the establishment of machinery, under the auspices of the Bank, through which states and nationals of other states can settle disputes by arbitration or conciliation. Adherence to the machinery is voluntary in each separate investment operation, but once agreed upon it is compulsory. By the end of fiscal 1970, 57 states had become parties to the Convention on the Settlement of Investment Disputes between States and Nationals of Other States;

a further 7 states had signed but have not yet ratified the Convention.

8 BIBLIOGRAPHY

The World Bank Group. Illustrated description of loans made by IBRD and IDA. Free.

The World Bank, IDA and IFC. Policies and Operations. Free.

World Bank. 100 Questions and Answers. Free.

Recent World Bank publications (published by The Johns Hopkins Press) include:

Experience with Agricultural Development in Tropical Africa, by John de Wilde and others (1967, 2 vols., $15.00). *Development Finance Companies* by William Diamond and others (1968, 119 pages, $3.00); *Water and Power Resources of West Pakistan,* by Pieter Lieftinck and others (1968, 3 vols., $28.50).

Reappraisal of a Road Project in Iran, by Herman G. van der Tak and Jan de Weille (1969, 152 pages, $3.00).

Automotive Industries in Developing Countries, by Jack Baranson (1969, 106 pages, $3.00).

Manufacture of Heavy Electrical Equipment in Developing Countries, by Ayhan Cilingiroglu (1969, 122 pages, $3.00).

INTERNATIONAL FINANCE CORPORATION (IFC)

1 BACKGROUND : The International Finance Corporation is the member of the World Bank Group that promotes the growth of the private sector in less-developed member countries. IFC's principal activity is helping to finance individual private enterprise projects that contribute to the economic development of the country or region where the project is located. The Corporation is one of the very few international development organizations that can supply equity financing as well as provide loans and make underwriting and standby commitments. In addition, IFC helps identify and promote promising projects; encourages the flow of domestic and foreign capital in productive investments in developing countries; assists development finance companies and other institutions with goals similar to IFC's; helps improve investment conditions in the developing countries by assisting in establishment of institutions that marshal funds for investments or provide a liquid market for investments; and assist banks and companies that have difficulty in making a viable financial plan for a sound project by making available the needed finance.

2 CREATION

Within a few years of the founding of the World Bank (IBRD), it became evident that sufficient provision had not been made for financing the development of the private sector in countries looking to the UN system for aid. The Bank's charter restrained it from making equity (capital stock) investments or from lending money, directly or indirectly, to a private company without a governmental guarantee. Yet "venture capital" was the very thing needed in many developing countries to get a variety of productive enterprises under way, and the amount of venture capital available through private banking and investment channels was inadequate.

The first public suggestion for an international institution to close this gap appeared in a report, "Partners and Progress," which Nelson Rockefeller (then chairman of the advisory board of the Point 4 Program) had submitted to President Harry S Truman in 1951. The matter was taken up by the staff of the World Bank, and in 1952 the Bank submitted proposals for such an institution to the Economic and Social Council of the UN. Some members of the council, including the UK and the US, voiced the fear that the proposed institution might deter the flow of private capital to the developing countries. They also objected in principle to an intergovernmental organization's having the right to purchase shares in private companies.

The majority of ECOSOC members, however, strongly endorsed the idea of an international financial institution to aid the private sector of development, and by late 1954 a compromise was worked out. The International Finance Corporation, as originally established, could lend money to private enterprises without government guarantees, but it was not empowered to make equity investments, though loans with certain equity features, such as stock options, were allowed. The 31 countries necessary to launch the IFC pledged their consent over the next 18 months and IFC formally came into existence on 24 July 1956 as a separate legal entity affiliated with the World Bank.

The IFC's early investments often included such features as stock options and other profit-sharing devices in lieu of direct equity financing, but the terms were complex and difficult to negotiate, and it soon became apparent to all concerned that the IFC's effectiveness was severely circumscribed by the restriction on equity investment. Proposals to amend the charter

so as to permit IFC to hold shares were put to the Board of Directors and the Board of Governors, and approved, in 1961 — with the support, this time, of both the UK and the US. The revision of IFC's charter to permit investment in equities has made it possible to broaden and diversify operations as well as to simplify the terms of investment. With the demand for IFC's services steadily expanding, the Board of Directors amended the charter again in 1965 to permit the IFC to borrow from the World Bank up to four times its unimpaired subscribed capital and surplus—at present about $428 million.

3 PURPOSES

In its simplest form, IFC's purpose is to assist its less-developed member countries by promoting the growth of the private sector of their economies. It does this by providing venture capital for productive private enterprises in association with local investors and management, by encouraging the development of local capital markets, and by stimulating the international flow of private capital. The Corporation is designed to supplement, rather than replace, private capital. It provides financial and technical assistance to privately controlled development finance companies. IFC attempts to recruit foreign capital for a project and encourages the participation of other private investors in its own commitments.

4 MEMBERSHIP

Membership in IFC is open to all members of the World Bank. On 30 June 1970, membership included the following 94 countries.

Afghanistan	Congo (Kinshasa)	Greece	Ivory Coast
Argentina	Costa Rica	Guatemala	Jamaica
Australia	Cyprus	Guyana	Japan
Austria	Denmark	Haiti	Jordan
Belgium	Dominican	Honduras	Kenya
Bolivia	Republic	Iceland	Korea, South
Brazil	Ecuador	India	Kuwait
Burma	El Salvador	Indonesia	Lebanon
Canada	Ethiopia	Iran	Liberia
Ceylon	Finland	Iraq	Libya
Chile	France	Ireland	Luxembourg
China, Taiwan	Germany, West	Israel	Madagascar
Colombia	Ghana	Italy	Malawi

Malaysia	Pakistan	South Africa	Uganda
Mauritania	Panama	Spain	UAR
Mauritius	Paraguay	Sudan	UK
Mexico	Peru	Swaziland	US
Morocco	Philippines	Sweden	Uruguay
Nepal	Portugal	Syria	Venezuela
Netherlands	Sa´udi Arabia	Tanzania	Viet-Nam, South
New Zealand	Senegal	Thailand	Yemen
Nicaragua	Sierra Leone	Togo	Yugoslavia
Nigeria	Singapore	Tunisia	Zambia
Norway	Somalia	Turkey	

5 STRUCTURE

The structure of the IFC is similar to that of the World Bank. The IFC's Board of Governors consists of those governors of the World Bank whose countries are also members of IFC. Its Board of Directors is now composed of all the Executive Directors of the World Bank. IFC headquarters, like those of the World Bank, are at 1818 H Street N.W., Washington, D.C. The Corporation also has an office in Paris and a special representative in Tokyo.

The Annual Meeting of the IFC Board of Governors is held in conjunction with the Annual Meeting of the Board of Governors of the World Bank.

IFC's president is appointed by the Board of Directors. The first president was Robert L. Garner, formerly vice-president of the World Bank. Since 1961, the president of the World Bank also has been the president of the Corporation: Eugene R. Black until the end of 1962, George D. Woods from January 1963 to April 1968, and Robert S. McNamara since April 1968. The immediate direction of the Corporation is the responsibility of the executive vice-president, William S. Gaud, who has served in that post since October 1969.

6 BUDGET

The administrative expenses of IFC, which are met from income, were $5,360,288 in 1969/70.

7 ACTIVITIES

A. FINANCIAL RESOURCES
Capital Subscriptions
The authorized capital of IFC is $110 million. Each member country subscribes to it, and the amount of the subscription determines voting power. As of 30 June 1970, $107.0 million had been subscribed. The largest subscriptions were by the US ($35.2 million); the UK ($14.4 million); France ($5.8 million); India ($4.4 million); China ($4.2 million); Germany ($3.7 million); Canada ($3.6 million); the Netherlands ($3.0 million); Japan ($2.8 million); Belgium ($2.5 million); Australia ($2.2 million); and Italy ($2.0 million).

Earnings, Profits, and Other Resources
By investing its subscribed capital, revolving its funds, borrowing from the World Bank, and ploughing back its earnings, IFC's cumulative resources available for loans and equity commitments have increased more than fourfold. In its 14 years of operations, IFC's net cumulative earnings (including profits on the sale of investments) came to $58.8 million. During the same period, the Corporation recovered $173.9 million from its commitments through repayment of investments, sales of investments, and acquisition by others of securities covered by IFC standby and underwriting commitments. The World Bank has agreed to lend $200 million to IFC for use in its lending operations. The total funds available to the IFC for its operations from 1956 to 1970 thus came to $539.7 million, of which all but $86.7 million had been committed by 30 June 1970.

B. INVESTMENT POLICIES
IFC provides risk capital for a wide variety of productive private enterprises and will consider investments in utilities, agriculture, mining, tourism and other fields, as well as manufacturing industry, which has been and remains its dominant field of operation. IFC is prepared to assist companies to expand, modernize, or diversify their operations as well as to help finance new projects. Generally the Corporation will invest only in the less developed of its member countries and will finance only ventures in which there is room for local participation. IFC will not invest in undertakings that are government owned or controlled, though it may be prepared to help an enterprise in which the government has a minority interest. The IFC does, however, advise the government concerned of any proposed investment in a country and will not proceed if that government objects.

Direct Investments
IFC will provide loan capital, equity capital, or a combination of the two. IFC financing may be used to acquire fixed assets or for working capital and is available for foreign exchange as well as local currencies. Funds are not tied to procurement from specific countries, except to the extent that goods and services must be procured in a member country of the World Bank or in Switzerland. IFC's direct investments are made in association with local or foreign investors, and the Corporation welcomes projects combining both.

IFC Underwritings
IFC provides financing through standby or underwriting arrangements in support of public offerings or private placements of shares, debentures, or other corporate securities. It is prepared to act as sole underwriter or as principal in an underwriting group. The same standards as for direct IFC investments apply to underwritings.

Revolving Portfolio
IFC is ready to sell all or part of any of its investments whenever it can do so on satisfactory terms, unless the Corporation's partners in the enterprise concerned object to a potential purchase for valid business reasons.

C. DEGREE AND MANNER OF IFC PARTICIPATION
IFC expects other investors to provide a substantial part of the capital required for a project. Where a new enterprise is concerned, the Corporation's participation will be less than 50%, though a larger proportion of funds required may be provided in the case of expansion of an existing enterprise. Normally IFC will not provide more than $20 million nor less than $1 million for a single enterprise.

IFC does not assume management responsibilities and will not expect to hold more than 25% of the share capital of any company. The Corporation neither seeks nor accepts board representation in companies in which it invests, except in the case of certain development finance companies. Only in exceptional circumstances will IFC exercise the voting rights of shares it holds.

Periodic progress reports, other information as may be necessary, and the right to visit plants and other property and consult with management are required by IFC. In this, as in the provision of its regular investment agreements, IFC carries on its business in the manner of a private investor. It neither seeks nor accepts government guarantees for its investments.

D. DEVELOPMENT FINANCE COMPANIES
The principal contribution of the World Bank Group to the building of financial institutions in the developing countries has been its support of development finance companies. These institutions can perform many important services, such as:
  providing medium and long-term capital to local private enterprises;
  mobilizing domestic private savings for investment purposes;
  acting as a channel for foreign capital;
  identifying and promoting new investment opportunities;

carrying out underwritings; and

selling their more seasoned portfolio securities to local investors.

IFC has played a key role in creating or substantially reorganizing a number of privately owned development finance companies. It is a shareholder of such companies, is now represented on the boards of 13 of them, and has engaged in a wide range of activities designed to improve their management, staff, policies, and operations.

There are many kinds of investment companies. Some operate in a single country, others regionally and still others worldwide. Some are locally owned and controlled, while others are owned and controlled by private interests in capital exporting countries. All are eligible for IFC support if they need it, are well managed, contribute to the development of the countries in which they are doing business, and follow policies generally consistent with with those of IFC.

E. INTEREST RATES AND OTHER CONDITIONS

There is no fixed interest rate for IFC loans. Each case is determined on its own merits, taking into account the risk involved and the prospective return on the whole of the investment. A commitment fee of 1% per annum is charged by IFC on the undisbursed loan portion of its investments. Repayment is usually in 5 to 15 annual installments and generally starts after a certain period of time so as to allow the project to become profitable.

F. INVESTIGATION OF INVESTMENT PROPOSALS

There is no standard form of application for IFC financing.

However, the Corporation requires certain preliminary information. This usually includes a description of the enterprise and sponsor, financial forecasts, and in some cases certain technical details.

G. IFC INVESTMENTS

In the 14 years of operations to 30 June 1970, IFC made investment commitments totaling $476.5 million to 152 enterprises in 43 countries. It has also made one investment in a regional development institution. The pace of the Corporation's business has quickened in recent years and more than one-half of commitments have been made in the last three years. Most investments have been made in enterprises of economic priority, such as iron and steel, pulp and paper, textiles, cement and fertilizers, as well as in development finance companies. IFC has acted as a catalyst in the financing of projects involving a total capital cost of more than $2.6 billion. On average, other investors have provided over $4 for every $1 invested by IFC.

As of 30 June 1970, $189.8 million had been invested in the Western Hemisphere in 111 operations, compared with $147.2 million in Asia and the Middle East in 45 commitments, and $85.8 million in Africa in 26 commitments. IFC has made 25 commitments in 6 European countries, involving a total of $52.7 million, and 3 commitments in Australia in the Corporation's early years totaled $975,000.

8 BIBLIOGRAPHY

Annual Report—IFC. Free.

Facts about IFC. Quarterly. A current summary of IFC operations. Free.

IFC–General Policies. A description of general policies. Free.

INTERNATIONAL DEVELOPMENT ASSOCIATION (IDA)

¹**BACKGROUND :** The world's poorer countries have gone heavily into debt to finance their development. The total outstanding external debt of the developing countries rose from an estimated $ 10 billion in 1955 to $ 53.4 billion in 1968, and by 1968 the annual interest and amortization charges on this debt had reached a level of $ 4.7 billion. Many countries have long since arrived at the point where they can no longer afford to raise all the development capital they are in a position to make good use of at ordinary rates of interest and in the time span of conventional loans, World Bank loans included. The function of the International Development Association, an affiliate of the Bank and the youngest member of the World Bank Group (IBRD, IFC, and IDA), is to supply financing for high priority purposes on terms that will permit such countries to pursue their development without adding excessively to their debt-servicing burden. IDA's loans are interest free and repayable over very long terms, with extended grace periods. As a result, IDA's resources, unlike the resources of a regular lending institution, must be regularly replenished through contributions if the agency is to continue in business.

²**CREATION**

The creation of an international agency such as IDA was discussed in the UN at various times during the 1950's. A report drawn up by a group of experts on financing and economic development in 1951 referred to the need for an "international development authority." Although such proposals were at first opposed by the US, IDA as it was finally launched was largely the result of US initiative. In 1958 the US Senate passed a resolution introduced by Senator A. S. (Mike) Monroney calling for cooperative international action along these lines. Eventually, on 1 October 1959, the World Bank's Board of Governors approved, without objections, a motion of US Secretary of the Treasury Robert Anderson that a new agency, under the name International Development Association, be established as an affiliate of the World Bank.

The debate that preceded the Board's action revealed potential disagreements between different members of the Bank on a number of points, such as the terms IDA should set for its loans, permissible restrictions that countries subscribing to IDA's capital could place on the use of funds supplied in their national currencies, and related matters. Rather than decide these matters itself, the Board of Governors asked the Executive Directors of the World Bank to draw up a constitution ("Articles of Agreement") for IDA, which would then be submitted to the Bank's member governments.

IDA's Articles of Agreements were accordingly drafted by the Executive Directors of the World Bank and early in 1960 transmitted to the member governments of the Bank. The next step was for those governments desiring to join IDA to take whatever legislative or other action might be required to accept membership and to subscribe funds. The new lending association came into existence in September 1960, when governments whose subscriptions to its capital aggregated $ 650 million, or 65% of the projected $ 1 billion goal, had accepted membership. IDA started operations in November of that year.

³**PURPOSES**

In the preamble to the Articles of Agreement, the signatory governments declare their conviction that mutual cooperation for constructive economic purposes, healthy development of the world economy, and balanced growth of international trade foster peace and world prosperity; that higher standards of living and economic and social progress in the less-developed countries are desirable, not only in the interest of the latter, but also for the international community as a whole; and that achievement of these objectives would be facilitated by an increase in the international flow of capital, public and private, to assist in the development of the resources of less-developed countries. Hence, as stated in its Articles of Agreements, the purposes of IDA are "to promote economic development, increase productivity and thus raise standards of living in the less developed areas of the world included within the Association's membership, in particular by providing finance to meet their important developmental requirements in terms which are more flexible and bear less heavily on the balance of payments than those of conventional loans, thereby furthering the developmental objectives of the (IBRD) and supplementing its activities."

⁴**MEMBERSHIP**

For the purposes of IDA, members are divided into two categories. Part I members, of which there are 18, are economically advanced countries. These countries pay their entire initial subscriptions in gold or freely convertible currency and have made further agreed contributions to replenish the Association's resources. Part II members are the less-developed countries, which pay 10% of their subscriptions in usable form and 90% in their own currencies, which can be used by IDA only with their consent. A list of members in the two categories, with their subscriptions, is given in the section on financial resources.

⁵**STRUCTURE**

IDA is administered by the same officers and staff who administer the affairs of the World Bank. The president of the Bank also serves as the president of IDA, and the governors and executive directors of the Bank serve in the same capacity in IDA.

Voting Power of Member Governments. As in the World Bank, a government's voting power in IDA is roughly proportionate to its capital subscription. As of 30 June 1970, the 18 Part I countries had 62.37% of the total votes, including 25.28% for the US, 10.47% for the UK, and 4.34% each for France and West Germany. The 87 Part II countries had 37.63% of the total votes, ranging from 3.36% for India and 2.57% for China (Taiwan) down to 0.20% for Iceland and Panama.

6 BUDGET

Since IDA relies entirely on the World Bank's staff and facilities for all its activities, IDA reimburses the Bank through a management fee for administrative expenses incurred on its behalf. The management fee was established at $15.8 million for the fiscal year ending 30 June 1970.

7 ACTIVITIES

A. FINANCIAL RESOURCES

IDA's funds have been obtained from five sources: members' subscriptions, periodic "replenishments" provided by its richer members, special contributions made by some members, transfers of income from the World Bank, and IDA's own accumulated net income.

Members' Subscriptions

Members' subscriptions to IDA have totaled about $1,014 million thus far. Of this total, $795 million has been subscribed in dollars or other currencies that IDA can use in its lending operations, while $219 million has been paid in the currencies of less-developed members, which are not yet available for lending.

Replenishments

Initial subscriptions alone were never envisaged as the sole source of IDA's lending funds. From the beginning it was expected that IDA would have to obtain further funds from the Part I countries from time to time, to enable it to continue operations.

In 1964 agreement was reached on the first general replenishment of IDA's resources. This totaled about $750 million equivalent, paid in by the 18 Part I countries over a 3-year period.

In July 1969 a second replenishment came into effect. Under this agreement, about $1,200 million is being added to IDA's funds by the 18 Part I countries, plus Switzerland, a nonmember. Approximately $1,188 million equivalent is to be made available by the Part I countries in 3 annual installments, of which 2 have been paid, and the 3d is payable in November 1970, while the Swiss Confederation has made IDA a 50-year interest-free loan equivalent to approximately $12 million.

Special Contributions

Aside from their contributions under the replenishment agreements, 3 Scandinavian countries have made special supplementary contributions to IDA in the following amounts: Sweden $49.5 million, Denmark $15 million, and Norway $1.32 million.

Transfers from the World Bank

By the autumn of 1969, the World Bank had made 6 grants totaling $385 million to IDA out of its net income.

IDA's Net Income

Accumulated net income of IDA totaled $31.8 million as of 30 June 1969. This total amount was allocated for further use in IDA commitments. IDA's operating income has been derived from the service charge of 3/4 of 1% on the disbursed portion of credits and from short-term investments of liquid funds.

SUBSCRIPTIONS TO THE CAPITAL OF IDA
(EXPRESSED IN US$ MILLIONS)

PART I MEMBERS' SUBSCRIPTIONS PAYABLE IN GOLD OR FREELY CONVERTIBLE CURRENCIES:

Australia	20.2	Kuwait	3.4
Austria	5.0	Luxembourg	.4
Belgium	8.2	Netherlands	27.7
Canada	37.8	Norway	6.7
Denmark	8.7	South Africa	10.1
Finland	3.8	Sweden	10.1
France	53.0	UK	131.1
Germany, West	53.0	US	320.3
Italy	18.2		
Japan	33.6	TOTAL PART I MEMBERS	751.3

PART II MEMBERS' SUBSCRIPTIONS PAYABLE 10% IN GOLD OR FREELY CONVERTIBLE CURRENCIES AND 90% IN THE NATIONAL CURRENCY OF THE COUNTRY CONCERNED

Afghanistan	1.0	Laos	0.5
Algeria	4.0	Lebanon	0.45
Argentina	18.8	Lesotho	0.2
Bolivia	1.1	Liberia	0.8
Botswana	0.2	Libya	1.0
Brazil	18.8	Malagasy Republic	1.0
Burma	2.0	Malawi	0.8
Burundi	0.8	Malaysia	2.5
Cameroon	1.0	Mali	0.9
Central African Republic	0.5	Mauritania	0.5
Ceylon	3.0	Mauritius	0.9
Chad	0.5	Mexico	8.7
Chile	3.5	Morocco	3.5
China (Taiwan)	30.3	Nepal	0.5
Colombia	3.5	Nicaragua	0.3
Congo (Brazzaville)	0.5	Niger	0.5
Congo (Kinshasa)	3.0	Nigeria	3.4
Costa Rica	0.2	Pakistan	10.1
Cyprus	0.8	Panama	0.02
Dahomey	0.5	Paraguay	0.3
Dominican Republic	0.4	Peru	1.8
Ecuador	0.65	Philippines	5.0
El Salvador	0.3	Rwanda	0.8
Ethiopia	0.5	Sa'udi Arabia	3.7
Gabon	0.5	Senegal	1.7
Gambia	0.3	Sierra Leone	0.8
Ghana	2.4	Somalia	0.8
Greece	2.5	Spain	10.1
Guatemala	0.4	Sudan	1.0
Guinea	1.0	Swaziland	0.3
Guyana	0.8	Syria	0.95
Haiti	0.8	Tanzania	1.7
Honduras	0.3	Thailand	3.0
Iceland	0.1	Togo	0.8
India	40.35	Tunisia	1.5
Indonesia	11.1	Turkey	5.8
Iran	4.5	Uganda	1.7
Iraq	0.8	UAR	5.1
Ireland	3.0	Upper Volta	0.5
Israel	1.7	Viet-Nam, South	1.5
Ivory Coast	1.0	Yemen	0.4
Jordan	0.3	Yugoslavia	4.0
Kenya	1.7	Zambia	2.7
Korea, South	1.3		
		TOTAL PART II MEMBERS	263.0

Supplementary resources of IDA, as of 30 June 1970, amounted to $1,579,950,000 paid-in, and $370,240,000 not yet due from members listed in Part I.

B. TERMS OF IDA LENDING

The terms of IDA's development credits are discretionary. All so far have been extended for 50 years without interest, but with an annual service charge of 3/4 of 1% on amounts disbursed. Repayment begins after a 10-year period of grace, with 1% of the principal payable each year for the second 10 years and 3% each year for the remaining 30 years.

C. IDA'S OPERATIONS

While IDA's financial terms are liberal, its economic and technical criteria for development credits are exactly the same as those applied by the World Bank in lending on conventional terms. Each credit must be justified by the borrowing country's economic position, prospects, and policies. Credits are extended only for high priority purposes that, in the words of IDA's Articles of Agreement, will "promote economic development, increase productivity and thus raise standards of living in the less developed areas of the world."

Since IDA's resources have been considerably less than the need of developing countries for additional external finance on easy terms, they must be carefully rationed on the basis of need and prospects for their most effective use. With a few exceptions, IDA credits have been extended to countries whose per capita GNP is below a level of about $300 a year equivalent. Thus, IDA funds have helped to finance projects in 32 countries in Africa, 11 in the Western Hemisphere, 12 in Asia and the Middle East.

By the end of June 1970, IDA had committed $2,773 million for 221 projects in 55 countries. About 71% of the total had been lent to countries of Asia and the Middle East, and of that amount more than 86% had been extended to 2 of the Association's most populous members, India and Pakistan, with combined populations of about 647 million and per capita of approximately $100 per year.

Thirty-seven of the 55 countries that have received IDA credits have also borrowed from the World Bank, since the Bank's analysis has shown them credited for conventional lending to meet some, though not all, of their development needs. India, for example, has borrowed a total of $1,087 million from the Bank and $1,264 from IDA. In this way, IDA provides the Bank Group with greater flexibility in "blending the terms of its lending to meet the widely differing needs of its less developed members."

Reflecting the development priorities of the poorest among the less-developed countries, the emphasis in IDA lending is considerably different from that of the World Bank. For example, over 20% of IDA's financing has been for agriculture, compared with less than 10% of the Bank's; while more than 30% of the Bank's lending has assisted power generation and transmission projects, less than 6% of IDA's assistance has been for this purpose. Beginning in 1962, IDA was the first member of the World Bank Group to enter the field of financing for educational development, with a credit of $5 million to help expand Tunisia's secondary school system. Since then it has advanced an additional $174 million for education projects, while the Bank has made loans totaling $144 million since its inception. IDA's support of industrial development has been confined chiefly to credits to India and Pakistan to enable the maintenance of production in existing plants through the import of essential equipment and supplies for which foreign exchange was otherwise unavailable, and to provide capital for lending by finance companies.

Since the IDA is managed and directed as an affiliate of the World Bank, all its operations are closely coordinated with those of the Bank, and a joint annual report is issued covering the work of the two institutions.

Amongst other things, IDA credits made as of the end of fiscal year 1970—alone or with supplementary finance from the World Bank or other lenders, and together with the contribution of the borrowing country—are helping to finance projects for:

Bringing under cultivation or improving more than 22,000,000 acres for agricultural purposes, including: 6,127,000 acres through irrigation in the Republic of China, India, Pakistan, Ceylon, the Sudan, and Turkey; 12,672,000 acres through flood protection and drainage in India, Pakistan, the United Arab Republic, and Indonesia; and 1,797,840 acres through land development (mechanization, cooperatives, plantations) in Africa and Asia.

Construction or improvement of more than 15,000 miles of roads in Asia, Africa, Latin America, and the Middle East; the engineering of more than 3,700 miles of roads; and the improvement of road maintenance operations in many of the countries involved.

Improvement and expansion of railroads in 4 countries by the provision of more than 5,440 freight cars, 250 passenger cars, track signaling devices, electrification and workshop equipment, as well as components for the domestic construction of hundreds of locomotives, thousands of freight and passenger cars.

Port improvements in six countries by construction of ship berths and passenger and cargo building and by provision of new dredgers, harbor craft, navigation aids, and other equipment.

Installation of about 919,000 kw of electric generating capacity and the extension of transmission lines in seven countries.

Improvement and expansion of water supply systems in 16 cities with a total population of over 6,000,000 located in 6 countries.

Construction, expansion, and/or equipping of 627 general secondary and specialized training schools, 52 teacher-training colleges, and eight agricultural universities. These projects, in 11 African, 3 Asian and 2 South American countries, will enable enrollment to expand by 148,900 in general secondary schools; 31,100 in technical and agricultural training schools; 7,700 in teacher training colleges; and 6,200 in agricultural universities.

8 BIBLIOGRAPHY

Facts about the World Bank and IDA. Quarterly. Includes summaries of IDA credits in each country and area, with total amounts and disbursements. Free.

Statement of Development Credits (IDA). Quarterly. Listings of borrowers, dates, purposes, and amounts from beginning of operations. Free. *IDA. 50 Questions and Answers.* Free.

GENERAL AGGREEMENT ON TARIFFS AND TRADE (GATT)

1 BACKGROUND : Efforts to foster international trade go back to antiquity: so do national efforts to expand exports to the detriment of competitors and to restrict or even prohibit imports. Wars have been fought over such issues, and for long periods of time in many countries controversy between protectionists and free traders has dominated the political scene. In the 1930's, when the world was suffering from an intense economic depression, many governments attempted to find shelter behind protective trade barriers: high tariff walls, quota restrictions on imports, exchange controls, and the like. If anything, these uncoordinated and mutually antagonistic policies prolonged the international economic crisis. During World War II serious thought was given to ways and means of preventing such restrictive trade practices from becoming permanently fastened upon the world. Postwar attempts to create a full-fledged international agency to foster and liberalize world trade failed. The General Agreement on Tariffs and Trade (GATT) is today the major result of the efforts that were made in this direction. In the absence of a true international trade organization, it serves as the only intergovernmental instrument that lays down rules for trade and harmonizes trading relations among the nations of the international community.

2 CREATION

The starting point for the General Agreement on Tariffs and Trade can be traced to the Atlantic Charter and to the lend-lease agreements in which the wartime allies bound themselves to seek a world trading system based on nondiscrimination and aimed at higher standards of living to be achieved through fair, full, and free exchange of goods and services.

Three agencies to operate in the specialized field of economic affairs were contemplated: an International Monetary Fund (IMF), an International Bank for Reconstruction and Development (IBRD), and an International Trade Organization (ITO). The IMF and the IBRD were duly established at the Bretton Woods Conference of 1944, but for various reasons, including the complexity of the problems involved, the drafting of the ITO charter was delayed. The UN Economic and Social Council took the matter up at its first session, in February 1946, and appointed a 17-nation preparatory committee to draft such a charter. The committee's draft was submitted to a 56-nation conference that met in Havana from 21 November 1947 to 24 March 1948 and, after considering some 800 separate amendments, hammered out a document known as the Havana Charter to serve as the constitution of the ITO.

The Havana Charter dealt not only with the reduction of trade barriers but with a number of other complex (and sometimes controversial) matters, including employment and investment policies, mutual cooperation for economic development, commodity control agreements, and the control of international cartels. In view of the preponderant economic position of the US at that time, American participation in the proposed agency was indispensable. The US government favored ratification, but opinion in the country and in Congress was sharply divided. Some opponents argued that the Havana Charter contained too many escape clauses to be effective; others argued that it was too strong and would stifle private enterprise. In December 1950, the President of the United States decided not to submit the Havana Charter to the US Senate for ratification, since it was evident that the requisite two-thirds majority could not be obtained. After it became clear that the US would not join the ITO, the plan to create the agency was quietly buried.

While the draft charter of the ITO was being worked out prior to the Havana Conference, the governments of the 17-member preparatory commission had agreed to sponsor negotiations for an interim agreement aimed at lowering customs tariffs and reducing other trade restrictions among themselves. The first tariff negotiating conference was held in Geneva in 1947. The tariff concessions resulting from these special negotiating sessions were embodied in a multilateral treaty called the General Agreement on Tariffs and Trade (GATT), which included a set of rules designed to prevent the tariff concessions from being frustrated by other protective devices. The agreement was signed on 30 October 1947 and came into force on 1 January 1948. GATT was originally intended as no more than a stopgap arrangement pending the creation of the ITO, but as events have worked out, it has functioned since 1948 as a kind of quasi-agency fulfilling some of the proposed ITO's most important functions.

3 PURPOSES

The General Agreement on Tariffs and Trade is a multilateral trade treaty embodying reciprocal rights and duties. It contains the world's first common code of commercial conduct and fair trading, the objective of which is to expand the production and exchange of goods and so to promote economic development, full employment, and higher standards of living. Under the agreement, all parties are to accord to one another the same "most-favored-nation" treatment in the application of import and export duties and charges and in their administration. Protection is to be afforded to domestic industries exclusively through custom tariffs, import quotas being specifically outlawed as a protectionist device (though they may be used for certain other purposes, such as redressing a country's balance of payments). Countries adhering to GATT agree to avoid, through consultations, damage to the trading interests of any of the contracting parties. GATT itself provides a framework within which negotiations can be held for the reduction of tariffs and other barriers to trade and within which the results of such negotiations can be embodied in a legal instrument. The importance of this "fair trading" code can be measured by the fact that it is accepted and applied by countries accounting for well over 80% of the world's total volume of foreign trade.

4 MEMBERSHIP

Since GATT is a treaty rather than an organization, adhering governments are designated not as members but as "contracting parties."

When the agreement was brought into operation on 1 January 1948, it was applied by eight governments only. Four years later, their number had grown to twenty-two. As of September 1970, there were 78 contracting parties to the General Agreement and 13 others to which it applied in some manner.

CONTRACTING PARTIES TO THE GATT (78)

Argentina	Ghana	Niger
Australia	Greece	Nigeria
Austria	Guyana	Norway
Barbados	Haiti	Pakistan
Belgium	Iceland	Peru
Brazil	India	Poland
Burma	Indonesia	Portugal
Burundi	Ireland	Rhodesia
Cameroon	Israel	Rwanda
Canada	Italy	Senegal
Central African	Ivory Coast	Sierra Leone
Republic	Jamaica	South Africa
Ceylon	Japan	Spain
Chad	Kenya	Sweden
Chile	Korea, South	Switzerland
Congo (Brazzaville)	Kuwait	Tanzania
Cuba	Luxembourg	Togo
Cyprus	Madagascar	Trinidad and Tobago
Czechoslovakia	Malawi	Turkey
Dahomey	Malaysia	Uganda
Denmark	Malta	UAR
Dominican Republic	Mauritania	UK
Finland	Mauritius	US
France	Netherlands	Upper Volta
Gabon	New Zealand	Uruguay
Gambia	Nicaragua	Yugoslavia
Germany, West		

COUNTRIES WHICH HAVE ACCEDED PROVISIONALLY (1)

Tunisia

COUNTRIES TO WHOSE TERRITORIES THE GATT HAS BEEN APPLIED AND WHICH NOW, AS INDEPENDENT STATES, MAINTAIN A DE FACTO APPLICATION OF THE GATT PENDING FINAL DECISIONS AS TO THEIR FUTURE COMMERCIAL POLICY (12)

Algeria	Equatorial Guinea	Singapore
Botswana	Lesotho	Southern Yemen
Cambodia	Maldives	Swaziland
Congo (Kinshasa)	Mali	Zambia

The General Agreement encourages the adherence of additional countries. However, in order to gain acceptance and thus to obtain the tariff concessions in force among the GATT parties, an applicant must itself make tariff concessions. The concessions will vary, in particular in accordance with the height of the country's tariff walls. The terms under which a country applying for accession will be accepted are not set once and for all; they are fixed for each specific case by a two-thirds majority of the GATT countries. The normal procedure is for such a country first to negotiate with GATT countries toward an exchange of tariff concessions.

Under a special provision (Article XXXV) of the General Agreement, a GATT country that has not yet entered into tariff negotiations with another GATT country is permitted to declare that the GATT obligations will not apply between the two of them.

Thus, although Japan was accepted unanimously into GATT in September 1955, a number of GATT countries invoked this provision and thereby freed themselves from GATT obligations toward Japan, and vice versa. Subsequent negotiations between Japan and the other governments concerned have, however, improved Japan's position in this respect.

Provisional Accession

There may be preliminary stages before a country becomes a full contracting party. Switzerland, for example, now a full contracting party, was listed as having "provisionally acceded" to GATT for a number of years until certain questions regarding Swiss agricultural imports were ironed out through negotiations. Tunisia occupied this position in 1970.

Special Arrangements

A special problem arose in 1960 when a considerable number of territories that, as French and British colonies, had been covered by the agreement attained independence. The parties to the General Agreement decided that the previous trading arrangements that had applied to these countries could be continued on a *de facto* basis pending their own determination of their future commercial policy. As of 1970 all but two of the countries originally included in this arrangement, Congo (Kinshasa) and Mali, had become full contracting parties to the General Agreement, but the arrangement had been extended to a number of more recently independent countries.

5 STRUCTURE

SESSIONS OF THE CONTRACTING PARTIES AND THE COUNCIL

The central forum in which GATT countries act collectively is provided by the GATT sessions, officially called "Sessions of The CONTRACTING PARTIES (sic) to the General Agreement on Tariffs and Trade." As need arises, the sessions establish GATT committees and panels, set up study groups, convoke meetings of experts, and the like. As a rule, the contracting parties meet once a year, although in a few instances they have met twice, and the meetings almost always take place in Geneva. The twenty-sixth session of the contracting parties was held in the spring of 1970. Lasting two or three weeks on the average, the sessions are attended not only by representatives of the countries that have fully acceded to GATT but also by representatives of countries that have provisionally acceded to or entered into special arrangements with GATT. Certain international and regional organizations are also represented.

In 1960 a council of representatives was established to take care of routine matters and to deal with any urgent situations that might arise between sessions. The council meets when there is appropriate business to be transacted—about six times a year.

At the GATT sessions, each GATT country has one representative who may be accompanied by alternates and advisers. Each GATT country has one vote. Decisions are taken by simple majority except where the General Agreement itself requires unanimity or a two-thirds majority.

At these sessions, the representatives of the GATT countries review developments and trends in international commerce; review the operation of the General Agreement and decide on changes in it; discuss and decide whether and under what conditions individual GATT countries may make use of the various exceptions allowed to their general obligations as set forth in the General Agreement. They may agree on recommendations to GATT countries aiming at liberalization of trade and removal of trade barriers; decide the terms on which countries outside GATT may accede to it; and consider all other pertinent topics.

The GATT sessions may also deal with complaints by GATT

countries alleging violations of GATT obligations by other GATT countries and set the dates for new multilateral tariff negotiations.

SECRETARIAT AND HEADQUARTERS
The GATT is administered by a secretariat under Director-General Olivier Long. This secretariat was established in 1948, after the Havana Conference, to prepare for the International Trade Organization, but for many years it has been wholly engaged on work for the contracting parties to the General Agreement.

Headquarters are in the Villa Le Bocage, Palais des Nations, Geneva.

⁶BUDGET
Governments that are parties to GATT contribute to its administrative expenses according to a scale of assessments based on their countries' share in the total trade of the contracting parties and participating governments. Contributions for 1970 were set at a total of $3,678,000.

⁷ACTIVITIES
MAIN PROVISIONS OF THE GENERAL AGREEMENT
Since GATT is not an agency but a multilateral treaty, it is strictly proper to speak not of "GATT activities" but of activities of the contracting parties within the framework of the General Agreement. The agreement contains 38 articles, whose provisions may be briefly summarized as follows:

Articles I and II are the articles that deal directly with tariffs. The first article is the mutual guarantee of most-favored-nation treatment among all contracting parties. It states that any "advantage, favour, privilege or immunity" in regard to duties, payments, and formalities in connection with imports and exports granted by a GATT country to another must automatically be extended to all other GATT countries. Article II provides for actual tariff reductions. These reductions are set forth in detail in the schedules annexed to Article II by the periodic tariff reduction conference held among the contracting parties.

Article III prohibits the use of internal taxes to protect domestic products against imports, once these imports have cleared customs.

Articles IV to X—known as the technical articles—provide general rules and principles relating to transit trade, to anti-dumping duties, to customs valuation, customs formalities, and marks of origin. For example, all countries adhering to GATT are required to grant freedom of transit to goods en route to or from other GATT countries; and if a country can prove that another country is injuring its industry by dumping a product on its markets at less than normal value, it may level a special duty on the product in question.

Articles XI to XIV include a general prohibition of quantitative import restrictions except to safeguard balance of payments, while Article XV deals with relations between contracting parties and the International Monetary Fund.

Further articles deal with the progressive elimination of export subsidies (XVI), state trading (XVII), emergency measures (XIX), and general and security exceptions (XX and XXI). Article XVIII, which comes midway in this "qualifying" group, recognizes that the less-developed countries need to maintain a special degree of flexibility in their tariff structure in order to protect vulnerable new industries. It also recognizes that they may need to apply quantitative restrictions on certain groups of imports in order to have sufficient foreign exchange for imports vital to their development program.

The important provisions for action by contracting parties

to settle differences arising out of the application of the General Agreement are contained in Articles XXII and XXIII. Article XXIV, which has assumed great importance since the establishment of the European Economic Community ("Common Market"), lays down conditions under which a customs union or free-trade area is accepted as a basis for an exception to the most-favored-nation principle.

Article XXVIII deals with the general principles of tariff negotiation and sets forth the arrangements under which contracting parties can, by negotiation, modify existing tariff concessions. Other articles deal with technical matters relating to the agreement, such as acceptance, accession, and withdrawal.

One of the most important provisions is that in Article XXV, which provides for joint action by the contracting parties. This is the legal basis for the "agency functions" that GATT, as a collective enterprise, has assumed in working toward the expansion of international trade and serving as a forum for the discussion of international trade problems.

In February 1965 a chapter on Trade and Development, consisting of Articles XXXVI to XXXVIII, was added to the General Agreement. These articles provide a legal basis for collective action on the part of the contracting parties aimed at furthering economic progress in the less-developed countries through the growth of their export trade.

A. REDUCTION OF TARIFFS AND OTHER BARRIERS TO TRADE
The reduction of tariffs is laid down in the General Agreement as one of the principal means of obtaining its broad objectives. Prior to the coming into force of the agreement, tariffs were generally established by simple unilateral action, each government acting independently or through bilateral negotiations, in which one government would trade reciprocal concessions with another. The General Agreement provides the first machinery for multilateral tariff negotiations, aimed at reducing tariffs simultaneously among all the contracting parties, in accordance with the most-favored-nation principle.

The multilateral tariff conferences are called "rounds" of negotiations, for the participating countries simultaneously negotiate in pairs, each setting forth the export items on which it it is willing to grant such concessions. (Since some countries entered GATT with much higher tariffs than others on particular products, a "concession" is not always an agreement to reduce or abolish a duty; it may also be an agreement to freeze the duty on an item or not to raise it past a certain level.) The best concessions agreed to by each country are incorporated into the schedules annexed to Article II of the agreement. A conference produces as many new national tariff schedules as there are governments granting concessions. All concessions must be extended to all GATT countries.

Tariff Negotiating Conferences in GATT
Prior to the important "Kennedy Round" negotiations, which took place between 1964 and 1967, there were five major tariff negotiating conferences: 1947 (Geneva), 1949 (Annecy, France), 1951 (Torquay, England), 1956 (Geneva), and 1960/61 (Geneva). Smaller-scale negotiations preceded the accessions of individual countries such as Japan and Switzerland. As a result of these conferences, the tariff rates for thousands of items entering into world commerce were reduced and rates for thousands of other items were frozen to prevent their being increased ("bound," in GATT parlance).

The Kennedy Round of Trade Negotiations
In May 1963, a meeting of ministers of GATT countries laid down directives looking toward more comprehensive and even broader reduction of trade barriers. They agreed to negotiate on linear, across-the-board tariff reductions for broad categories

of products, as opposed to the previous procedure of negotiating concessions on a product-by-product basis. They further agreed that the new negotiation should cover all classes of products, including agricultural and primary products, and that every effort should be made to reduce barriers to exports from the less-developed countries. The trade negotiations that began in 1964 were known as the Kennedy Round, because it was President Kennedy's Trade Expansion Act of 1962 that enabled the United States for the first time to participate in a scheme of across-the-board tariff reductions.

The negotiations were long and arduous. Opened formally in May 1964, they were concluded three years later. They resulted in by far the most extensive reductions in tariffs ever achieved. The participants, who accounted for some 75% of world trade, exchanged concessions valued at some $40 billion. The principal industrialized countries agreed to make tariff reductions on 70% of their dutiable imports (cereals, meat, and dairy products excluded). Two thirds of these cuts were of 50% or more, and around another one fifth were of between 25% and 50%. The cuts are being put into force over five years; at mid-1970 the first three equal instalments were in force, and the remaining two cuts were to take place at the beginning of 1971 and 1972. In addition, an agreement, incorporated in the International Grains Agreement 1967, was reached on basic minimum and maximum prices for wheat, and on the provision of grains as food aid for developing countries.

Current GATT Work Program
In the autumn of 1967, shortly after the Kennedy Round negotiations ended, the member countries of GATT met to establish the basis for a further effort aimed at freeing international trade. This effort took the form of a coordinated work program, which it was agreed should be undertaken in stages. The first stage, carried out mainly in 1968, was the assembly of the necessary basic information and documentation. The second, largely completed in 1969, was concerned with the identification of problems. The third stage, on which GATT was embarked in 1970, was the search for mutually acceptable solutions to the problems identified. This third stage should eventually, when the appropriate decisions are taken by GATT member governments, lead to actual negotiations.

Work in progress in 1970 on industrial products falls into two parts: on the one hand, concerned with tariffs, and on the other with non-tariff and para-tariff barriers to trade. In the tariff field, the main task is to analyze the situation that will exist when the Kennedy Round concessions have been fully implemented. The analysis, of a kind never before attempted, involves the recording on computer tape of an immense amount of data about the tariffs and trade of the developed member countries of GATT. It will provide a powerful tool both in defining problems and in seeking solutions to them.

The second main focus of GATT activities with regard to industrial products is currently to make ready for negotiations to reduce non-tariff barriers to trade, whose effects have increasingly been felt as tariffs have been progressively lowered over the past twenty years. Member countries, invited to report barriers that they believe have hampered their exports, have provided the basic information for compiling an inventory of some 800 non-tariff barriers. These notifications have been studied to establish their precise nature and effects and have been classified according to whether they concern government participation in trade, customs and administrative entry procedures, standards involving imports and domestic goods, specific limitations on imports and exports, or restraints on imports and exports through the price mechanism.

A similar approach is being followed in GATT with regard to agricultural products. Here problems are exceptionally severe, largely because there are grave social difficulties involved in adaptation of the structure of agriculture to changing economic circumstances, and because government intervention, for this and other reasons, is widespread in both agricultural production and trade. As in the case of non-tariff barriers, GATT action concentrated initially on the identification of problems, which have been classified in the broad categories of measures affecting exports, measures affecting imports, national policies for agricultural production, and other relevant measures.

Removal of Quantitative Restrictions on Imports
The general prohibition on the use of quantitative restrictions on imports, together with the rule of nondiscrimination, is one of the basic principles of the General Agreement. The main exception allows a contracting party to apply import restrictions for the purpose of safeguarding its balance of payments and monetary reserves and, in certain circumstances, to use such restrictions in a discriminatory way. Such restrictions must not be applied beyond the extent necessary in the circumstances and must be progressively reduced and eliminated as soon as they are no longer required. Countries applying import restrictions on balance-of-payments grounds are required to consult with the organization at regular intervals (once a year for an industrialized country and once every two years for a less-developed country); countries introducing new restrictions or substantially intensifying existing restrictions are required to consult; and any country that considers that another country is applying restrictions inconsistently with the provisions of the agreement and that its trade is adversely affected has the right to bring the matter up for discussion and ask for redress.

Over the years, a considerable number of consultations have been held. They have had a large part in ensuring that restrictions have been relaxed or removed, as rapidly as improvements in the balance of payments of individual countries permitted.

Following the moves toward convertibility of currencies early in 1959, contracting parties (other than less-developed countries) declared their intention of proceeding to the dismantling of the remaining import restrictions, and significant progress has since been made toward this objective. At present, only a few developed countries are still applying restrictions on balance-of-payments grounds. A number of other contracting parties, however, still maintain certain "residual restrictions." Under the present GATT work program, renewed efforts are being made to remove the remaining quantitative restrictions, with particular attention being paid to those restrictions that affect exports of the less-developed countries.

Regional Arrangements
If two or more countries form a customs union or free-trade area, goods moving between them are liberated from import and export duties and other trade barriers. Under a free-trade area arrangement, the participating countries maintain their right to determine separate customs tariffs toward the outside. Under a customs union, the participating countries go further; they set up a common customs tariff for trade with the outside. Clearly, both arrangements affect the commercial interests of third countries.

Beginning with the European Economic Community (EEC), or "European Common Market," which was launched in 1958 to integrate the economies of Belgium, France, West Germany, Italy, the Netherlands, and Luxembourg, a growing number of countries that are party to GATT have become members of regional customs unions or free-trade areas. The EEC and the European Free Trade Association (EFTA), which includes Austria, Denmark, Iceland, Norway, Portugal, Sweden, Switzerland, and the UK, with Finland as a close associate, are the two regional arrangements that have posed the greatest problems in respect to the most-favored-nation principles of the General Agreement, since the countries belonging to EEC and EFTA are all parties to the agreement and since their combined foreign commerce accounts for a very high proportion of total world trade.

The rules in the General Agreement relating to customs unions and free-trade areas are contained in Article XXIV. This article states that integration of national economies is conceived of as a means of contributing to the objectives of the GATT. It lays down the conditions under which a customs union or a free-trade area is accepted as a basis for an exception to the most-favored-nation clause. It sets out a series of rules designed to ensure that a customs union or a free-trade area shall in effect lead to the reduction and elimination of barriers within the area without raising new barriers to trade with the outside. The general purpose of these rules is to ensure that a grouping of this kind is a movement toward liberalism and not an attempt to create preferential arrangements.

From the time the first of the progresssive internal EEC tariff reductions went into effect, at each GATT session the Common Market spokesman (the representative of the Commission of the European Economic Community) has reported on EEC developments, and these reports have formed the basis for intensive discussion and for negotiation of concessions and counter-concessions. The Common Market representative has endeavored to alleviate the anxieties of outside GATT countries about the effects of the customs union by emphasizing that the economic growth that the EEC has stimulated has increased trade, not only within the EEC area, but with the rest of the world, too, and that this is to be expected also in the future.

One objective of the EEC, achieved in 1968, was a common tariff structure vis-à-vis the rest of the world. To effect this, some of the EEC countries were obliged to raise their tariffs on certain items. This necessitated the renegotiation of a number of concessions agreed on between individual EEC countries and other GATT countries. Thus the first eight months of the GATT negotiations that began in September 1960 were devoted to renegotiations to secure appropriate "compensations" to GATT countries outside the EEC for tariff increases effected by EEC members.

More recently, some members of GATT have expressed disquiet about the preferential agreements which have been negotiated between the European Economic Community and certain Mediterranean and African countries, maintaining that that agreements do not fully satisfy the requirements of the General Agreement. For their part, the EEC and its associates maintain that the agreements are covered by Article XXIV of the GATT.

Tariff reductions among members of the European Free Trade Association began in 1960 and were effectively completed in 1966. These developments, too, have been closely examined within the framework of the General Agreement. Unlike the EEC countries, however, the EFTA countries have not set up common tariffs for imports from outside countries; hence there were fewer "exceptions" to negotiate than in the case of the EEC countries.

Among other regional trading arrangements that the contracting parties regularly examine within the framework of Article XXIV of the General Agreement are the Latin American Free Trade Association, the New Zealand-Australia Free Trade Area, the UK-Ireland Free Trade Area, the Central American Common Market, and the Central African Customs Union.

B. SETTLEMENT OF DIFFERENCES

Among the matters that are referred to the sessions of the contracting parties are trade disputes over the application of the agreement. If a GATT country considers that a benefit that should accrue to it is being nullified or impaired (or that the attainment of any objective of the agreement is being impeded), it is first expected to seek redress through diplomatic channels. If no satisfactory adjustment can be reached through diplomatic consultations, then the country may lodge a complaint with the GATT collectivity. The contracting parties, acting as a collective body, are then required to carry out prompt investigations and to make recommendations or rulings. In recent years, the practice has grown of submitting such trade differences as are not settled through diplomatic consultations to a group of experts chosen from countries that have no direct interest in the matter. These Panels of Consultation, as they are called, have frequently succeeded in bringing about an agreement between the disputants.

C. TRADE PROBLEMS OF DEVELOP-ING COUNTRIES

About two thirds of the member countries of GATT are in the early stages of economic development. It is an urgent objective of GATT to help the economic growth of these countries by working for policies that will contribute to a sustained expansion of their export earnings.

GATT follows a twin approach to the problems of trade and development. In the first place, the developing countries take a full part in its general work. This ensures that their voice is heard and that their interests are taken into proper account. Their presence underlines the fact that their hopes of economic progress are closely bound up with the continued expansion of world trade, which in turn is largely dependent on the maintenance under GATT of a fair and open trading system. In the second place, a number of the particular problems of the developing countries are tackled through institutions set up for this purpose. This approach is consistent with the working methods of GATT as a whole, whereby the longer-term effort to liberalize trade on a broad front is supplemented by seizing any opportunities that may present themselves to make more rapid progress on a narrower front.

Part IV of GATT on Trade and Development

In 1965 a new Part IV was added to the General Agreement, to provide a contractual and legal basis for commitments on individual and joint action by the GATT contracting parties, aimed at ensuring that the less-developed countries can increasingly find the means to raise standards of living and promote economic development through participation in international trade and through the sustained growth of their export earnings. It provides for new approaches to the trading problems faced by developing countries in the light of changing world trade or economic conditions, and specifically establishes the principle that the developed countries will not expect reciprocity for their own efforts to reduce barriers to the trade of developing countries. A committee on trade and development was established to keep the implementation of the Part IV provisions under continuous review.

Residual Restrictions

The removal of quantitative import restrictions on products of export interest to the developing countries has been an important preoccupation of GATT since 1958, and steady progress has been achieved. In the industrial sector, cotton textiles excepted, few products are still subject to import restrictions in developed countries. Quantitative restrictions remain more widely used against unprocessed and processed agricultural products, including many of interest to developing countries. With the aim of securing removal of the remaining restrictions, GATT consults regularly with individual developed countries maintaining quantitative restrictions, and also carries out a product-by-product examination of the problems involved in speeding-up the dismantling of these restrictions.

Tariffs and Taxes on Products of Developing Countries

Progress has also been made in the framework of GATT in reducing and removing import duties and taxes on products of export interest to developing countries. This has been achieved through pressure in various bodies of GATT, as well as in the framework of general trade negotiations. The Committee on Trade and Development on several occasions reviewed the progress of the Kennedy Round negotiations in their relation to the trade interests of developing countries, in order to achieve the highest possible concessions in favor of these countries. Following the negotiations, many of the participating countries put into force ahead of schedule, and without the phasing agreed upon for the majority of the tariff reductions, those concessions that had been negotiated on products of export interest to developing countries.

Trade Negotiations among Developing Countries

GATT members have agreed that the establishment of preferences among developing countries, appropriately administered and subject to the necessary safeguards, could make an important contribution to the expansion of trade among these countries. First initiatives, aimed at negotiations for the reduction of tariff and other barriers to their mutual trade were taken by these countries in the context of the Kennedy Round. Subsequently, in November 1967, a trade negotiations committee of developing countries was set up to provide a framework for an exchange of tariff and trade concessions between these countries. By mid-1970, a broad consensus had been reached on certain working hypotheses on the basis of which requests and offers for concessions in these negotiations might be formulated and discussed. Thirty-three developing countries (of which 10 were not members of GATT) were taking part in the work, and 15 had presented lists of specific requests to other participants.

Preferences by Developed for Developing Countries

At their sessions in 1968, and again in 1970, contracting parties expressed their readiness to take appropriate action when the general nondiscriminatory scheme of preferences in favor of developing countries, under discussion in UNCTAD and the OECD, had been negotiated.

Technical Assistance and Training

Since 1955, GATT has provided training in commercial policy for over 300 officials from developing countries at its headquarters in Geneva; other courses have been organized in conjunction with the Regional Commissions of the UN. Technical assistance is also provided to some developing countries to enable them to take full advantage of their membership in GATT, for example in the trade negotiations among developing countries.

The International Trade Centre UNCTAD/GATT

In 1964, GATT established the International Trade Centre to provide trade information and trade promotion advisory services for developing countries. Since January 1968 the center has been jointly operated by GATT and UNCTAD. Its work program and activities are determined by the governing bodies of UNCTAD and GATT on the basis of recommendations made annually by a joint intergovernmental advisory group of experts on trade promotion drawn from the member states of both agencies.

The trade center responds to requests from developing countries for assistance in the formulation and implementation of export promotion programs. To this end, it provides these countries with information and advice on export markets and marketing techniques and helps them both to develop their export promotion and marketing services and to train the personnel required for these services. While some of this assistance is provided from its regular work program financed from its own budgetary resources, the center serves as a base organization for programming assistance projects designed to meet the needs of individual countries or groups of countries; such projects are financed from United Nations Technical Co-operation programs or voluntary contributions by developed countries.

The headquarters of the center is organized in four main services: Market Research Service and Export Promotion Techniques Research Service (Research Services); Training Service and Trade Promotion Advisory Service (Operational Services). In addition, there is a publications service that disseminates information that is of general utility for the export promotion efforts of many developing countries through the center's journal, *International Trade Forum,* and through the publication of market surveys and handbooks on export promotion techniques.

Trade in Cotton Textiles

In June 1961 the GATT Council agreed to a request by the US to convene a meeting of countries substantially interested in the importation and the exportation of cotton textile products, "with a view to reaching agreement on arrangements for the orderly development of the trade in such products, so as progressively to increase the export possibilities of less-developed countries and territories and of Japan, while at the same time avoiding disruptive conditions in import markets." The meeting was held in July 1961, and the participating governments drew up the arrangements regarding international trade in cotton texiles. These comprised, first, a short-term arrangement, designed to deal with immediate problems and applying to the twelve-month period starting 1 October 1961. The Cotton Textiles Committee was created in order to undertake work looking toward a long-term solution. This task was concluded in 1962 with the completion of a Long-Term Arrangement for Cotton Textiles. The arrangement entered into force on 1 October 1962 for a period of five years thereafter; with minor changes, it was renewed for a further period of three years in 1967, and renewal for another three-year period was under consideration in mid-1970. Some thirty countries are signatories to the arrangement. Its purpose is to allow orderly development of international trade in cotton textile products, on the one hand progressively opening up export possibilities for the developing countries, and on the other avoiding disruption of markets in the importing countries. The arrangement allows a country suffering from disruptive imports to request the exporting country to restrict its shipments to a certain level. If agreement is not reached, the importing country may impose import restrictions to this level. The permitted level must be regularly increased, and existing quotas must also be enlarged.

D. PUBLICATIONS

GATT publications are set out in the *List of Publications,* available free of charge from the GATT secretariat. This list gives full details concerning the text of the General Agreement, the *Basic Instruments and Selected Documents* series, Tariff Schedules, Reports on International Trade; *International Trade Forum* and other publications of the International Trade Centre are included.

8 BIBLIOGRAPHY

GATT: What it is, what it does. Information brochure. Free.

GATT Activities. Annual report on the work of GATT, and account of developments of the year under review. 1969/70. 47 pp. $1.50.

International Trade Forum. Bimonthly. Published by the GATT International Trade Centre, $3.00 a year.

International Trade. Annual. Report on developments in world trade. $5.00.

INTERNATIONAL ATOMIC ENERGY AGENCY (IAEA)

¹BACKGROUND: The UN came into existence at the beginning of the atomic age. Man's success in harnessing atomic energy has made the UN's objectives not only vital but absolutely indispensable. The primary purpose of the UN is to prevent war. A major war involving the use of atomic weapons would be not simply catastrophic but very probably suicidal. The second objective of the UN is to promote the economic and social welfare of peoples throughout the world. Atomic energy promises to contribute greatly to worldwide prosperity. Although "atoms for peace" has been a continuing concern of the UN itself, and although a number of organizations of the UN family such as the FAO and WHO have been concerned with specific aspects of peaceful uses of atomic energy, it was not until 1957 that a special organization, the International Atomic Energy Agency, came into being for the express purpose of accelerating and enlarging the contribution of atomic energy to peace, health, and prosperity throughout the world.

²CREATION

Addressing the UN General Assembly in December 1953, President Eisenhower of the United States called for the establishment of an international atomic energy organization to "serve the peaceful pursuits of mankind." The President said that he hoped the atomic powers, through such an organization, would dedicate "some of their strength to serve the needs rather than the fears of mankind."

Mr. Eisenhower stated that the USSR "must, of course, be one" of the countries principally involved in the proposed organization. Accordingly, as a first step, the US State Department in the spring and summer of 1954 submitted a series of memoranda to the USSR suggesting the principles that should be incorporated in the statute of such an agency. It was, however, impossible for the two powers to reach agreement at that time. The USSR maintained that the issues of disarmament and peaceful uses of atomic energy were inseparable and that agreement on a general prohibition of nuclear weapons would have to precede the creation of the agency. The US countered with the argument that effective international control of nuclear weapons would have to precede their prohibition, and announced that it was prepared to go ahead with international negotiations even without the participation of the USSR.

In the summer of 1954 the US issued invitations to seven other countries, including both "atomic powers" and important uranium-producing states—Australia, Belgium, Canada, France, Portugal, the Union of South Africa, and the UK—to meet with it in Washington to prepare a draft statute for the proposed agency. In September the USSR reversed its previous position. It announced its willingness to separate the issues of disarmament and peaceful uses of atomic energy and to accept the eight-power draft statute as a basis for further negotiations and guidance.

In December 1954 the UN General Assembly unanimously adopted an "Atoms for Peace" resolution expressing the hope that the International Atomic Energy Agency would be established "without delay" in order to assist "in lifting the burdens of hunger, poverty and disease." An international conference on the statute was convened at UN headquarters in New York on 20 September 1956, with the participation of 81 nations, including some, such as West Germany, that were not members of the UN itself. After adopting a number of amendments, proposed for the most part by the atomic "have not" powers,

the conference unanimously adopted the statute as a whole on 26 October.

On 29 July 1957 the statute entered into force after 26 states had deposited instruments of ratification, and the International Atomic Energy Agency officially came into existence. The first General Conference of the IAEA was held in Vienna in October 1957, at which time it was decided to make Vienna the permanent headquarters site of the agency.

³PURPOSES

According to the statute of IAEA, "The Agency shall seek to accelerate and enlarge the contribution of atomic energy to peace, health and prosperity throughout the world. It shall ensure, so far as it is able, that assistance provided by it or at its request or under its supervision and control is not used in such a way as to further any military purpose."

The IAEA acts as a clearinghouse for the pooling and coordination of experience and research in the peaceful uses of nuclear power and radioisotopes. It helps its member countries acquire the necessary skills and materials to share in the benefits of the atomic age. In practice the IAEA has been particularly concerned with bringing the advantages of atomic energy to underdeveloped regions.

The IAEA is obliged under its statute to "ensure, so far as it is able," that all the activities in which it takes part are directed exclusively to civilian uses. A second important task of the IAEA, then, is to establish a system of supervision and control to make certain that none of the assistance programs it fosters, none of the materials whose distribution it supervises, is used for military purposes. This aspect of the work has assumed significance far beyond its primary objective, with the entry into force in March 1970 of the Treaty on the Non-Proliferation of Nuclear Weapons, for which the IAEA is the body responsible for the necessary control system.

⁴MEMBERSHIP

Any member of the UN or of any of the specialized agencies that signed the statute within 90 days after 26 October 1956 thereby became a charter member of the IAEA upon ratification of the statute. Other countries, even if not members of the UN or any of the specialized agencies, may be admitted by the General Conference upon recommendation of the Board of Governors.

As of 15 November 1970, 103 states had become members of IAEA:

Afghanistan	Kuwait
Albania	Lebanon
Algeria	Liberia
Argentina	Libya
Australia	Liechtenstein
Austria	Luxembourg
Belgium	Madagascar
Bolivia	Malaysia
Brazil	Mali
Bulgaria	Mexico
Burma	Monaco
Byelorussia	Morocco
Cambodia	Netherlands
Cameroon	New Zealand
Canada	Nicaragua
Ceylon	Niger
Chile	Nigeria
China (Taiwan)	Norway
Colombia	Pakistan
Congo (Kinshasa)	Panama
Costa Rica	Paraguay
Cuba	Peru
Cyprus	Philippines
Czechoslovakia	Poland
Denmark	Portugal
Dominican Republic	Romania
Ecuador	Sa'udi Arabia
El Salvador	Senegal
Ethiopia	Sierra Leone
Finland	Singapore
France	South Africa
Gabon	Spain
Germany, West	Sudan
Ghana	Sweden
Greece	Switzerland
Guatemala	Syria
Haiti	Thailand
Hungary	Tunisia
Iceland	Turkey
India	Uganda
Indonesia	Ukraine
Iran	USSR
Iraq	UAR
Ireland	UK
Israel	US
Italy	Uruguay
Ivory Coast	Vatican
Jamaica	Venezuela
Japan	Viet-Nam, South
Jordan	Yugoslavia
Kenya	Zambia
Korea, South	

5 STRUCTURE

The three organs of the IAEA are the General Conference, the Board of Governors, and the Secretariat, headed by a director general.

GENERAL CONFERENCE

The General Conference consists of all members, each having one vote. It meets once a year, in the fall, at IAEA headquarters in Vienna. Special sessions may be convened by the director general at the request of the Board of Governors or a majority of the IAEA members. The General Conference elects 12 of the 25 members of the Board of Governors. It considers the board's annual report and approves reports for submission to the UN and agreements with the UN and other organizations. It approves the budget recommended by the board and the appointment of the director general. The General Conference may discuss any matter concerning the IAEA and may make recommendations to the Board of Governors or to any of the member states.

The General Conference in most matters is less powerful than the Board of Governors. Concerning the ordinary business of the IAEA, it can do little more than approve decisions of the Board of Governors or suggest changes. However, one very important power is vested in the General Conference: the power to act on amendments to the statute. Amendments come into force when approved by a two-thirds vote of the General Conference and ratified by two thirds of the member states. In other words, a two-thirds majority of the IAEA member states could always make its will prevail, even if it had to amend the statute to accomplish this. In 1962 the General Conference voted to increase the size of the governing body from 23 to 25 in order to give increased representation to African and Asian nations. Ratification was completed in 1963.

Decisions of the General Conference are made by a majority vote of members present and voting, except decisions on financial questions, amendments to the statute, and suspension of members, which require a two-thirds majority.

BOARD OF GOVERNORS

The Board of Governors is the body actually vested with the "authority to carry out the functions of the Agency in accordance with [the] Statute." It consists of 25 members, 12 named by the General Conference and 13 designated by the preceding board. Its composition represents a delicately balanced compromise—first, between the atomic powers themselves and, second, between the atomic powers and the atomic "have-nots."

The statute requires the outgoing Board of Governors to designate 13 member nations of the IAEA to the succeeding board as follows:

1. The five members of the IAEA "most advanced in the technology of atomic energy including the production of source materials." The preparatory commission designated Canada, France, the USSR, the UK, and the US as the five top atomic powers. These countries are designated for terms of one year but they may succeed themselves on the board as long as they retain their atomic leadership (the board alone determines whether or not they do).

2. The member nation most advanced in atomic technology from each of five major geographic areas not represented by the atomic big five. Australia (Southeast Asia and the Pacific); Brazil (Latin America); India (South Asia); Japan (Far East); and South Africa (Africa and the Middle East) were the nations so designated by the preparatory commission. The Latin American seat has alternated between Argentina and Brazil.

3. Two of the following "producers of source materials"—Belgium, Czechoslovakia, Poland, and Portugal—to serve one year and to be succeeded by the other two the following year. Czechoslovakia and Portugal have alternated with Belgium and Poland as rotating board members from this category. (Since Belgium and Portugal were originally designated as producers of source material by virtue of their African holdings, there has been some pressure to review their status.)

4. "One other member as a supplier of technical assistance," also to serve no more than one year at a time. To date this seat has rotated among Denmark, Norway, and Sweden.

The General Conference has nothing to do with the appointment of the 13 governors described above. It does, however, independently elect the remaining 12 members of the board, these members serving staggered 2-year terms. The 12 members chosen by the conference are so selected as to include at all times 3 representatives of Latin America, 3 of Africa and the Middle East, and 1 each from Western Europe, Eastern Europe, South Asia, Southeast Asia and the Pacific, and the Far East.

Moves are in progress to bring representation more into line with modern requirements. Following the Conference of Non-Nuclear Weapon States at Geneva in 1968, supported by views at the IAEA General Conference in 1969, the board was asked to review its statute dealing with the subject. It approached the problem by setting up a committee of the whole to which all member states were invited to send representatives. An increase of at least six is expected.

The Board of Governors is so organized as to enable it to function continuously and to meet at the IAEA headquarters in Vienna as often as necessary. It is required to meet at the request of any of its members or of the director general, and, after the General Conference has referred a matter to it, it must meet within 48 hours. Furthermore, it must meet at the request of any of the members of the IAEA to consider "any matter of an urgent character" arising out of its right of inspection under the safeguards provision of the statute.

Each member of the board has one vote. Decisions on the amount of the budget and the appointment of the director general are made by a two-thirds majority of the members present and voting. Governors who abstain from voting are considered as not voting, and decisions on other questions are by a simple majority. There is no big power "veto" right such as exists in the UN Security Council.

The Board of Governors for 1969/70 was composed of Argentina, Australia, Brazil, Canada, Czechoslovakia, France, Hungary, India, Iran, Italy, Japan, Morocco, Nigeria, Pakistan, Portugal, Singapore, South Africa, Spain, Sweden, USSR, UK, US, Uruguay, Venezuela, and South Viet-Nam.

THE DIRECTOR GENERAL AND THE STAFF

The staff of the IAEA is headed by a director general. He is appointed by a two-thirds vote of the Board of Governors, with the approval of a majority vote of the General Conference, for a term of four years. The statute describes the director general as "the chief administrative officer of the Agency," but it closely limits his independent powers by providing that he "shall be under the authority of and subject to the control of the Board of Governors." The director general is "responsible for the appointment, organization, and functioning of the staff," but in practice he has been required to clear important staff appointments with the board.

The first director general, who held the post from 1957 to 1961, was Sterling Cole of the US. Mr. Cole, a former congressman, served as chairman of the Joint Committee on Atomic Energy of the US Congress. In 1961, Dr. Sigvard Eklund, Swedish physicist and administrator, was elected director general, to serve until 1965. He was reelected in 1965 and in 1969.

The statute requires that the IAEA's "permanent staff shall be kept to a minimum." Considering the complexity and scope of its work, the secretariat of the IAEA is relatively small. At the end of June 1970 its staff numbered 1,081, of which 354 were in professional categories. The statute provides that the first consideration in recruiting should be "to secure employees of the highest standards of efficiency, technical competence, and integrity. Subject to this consideration due regard shall be paid to the contributions of members to the agency and to the importance of recruiting the staff on as wide a geographical basis as possible." By 1970, 55 nationalities were represented.

SCIENTIFIC ADVISORY COMMITTEE

The Scientific Advisory Committee of the IAEA was established by the Board of Governors in September 1958. It is "a standing scientific advisory council composed of scientists of international eminence." The committee meets periodically—about twice a year at the present time—to advise the director general and through him the Board of Governors on specific scientific and technical questions arising out of the IAEA's program.

The members of the committee are appointed by the director general with the concurrence of the board. They serve not as representatives of their governments but "in their individual capacity." The committee, it should be noted, is independent of the IAEA secretariat.

The members of the committee in 1970 were: M. A. El-Guebeily (UAR), Bertrand Goldschmidt (France), Hans Kronberger (UK), W. B. Lewis (Canada), I. Malek (Czechoslovakia), S. Mitsui (Japan), L. C. Prado (Brazil), Isidor I. Rabi (US), Homi N. Sethna (India), and V. I. Spitsyn (USSR).

POSITION IN THE UN SYSTEM

The IAEA is not an organ of the UN, nor is it, properly speaking, one of the specialized agencies. It is an autonomous international organization occupying its own position in the UN family of organizations.

Under the relationship agreement between the UN and the IAEA, the IAEA is recognized as being "responsible for international activities concerned with the peaceful uses of atomic energy." Under the agreement the IAEA is to submit an annual report on its activities directly to each regular session of the General Assembly. (The specialized agencies report to ECOSOC.) The IAEA is to transmit its annual budget to the UN "for such recommendations as the General Assembly may wish to make on the administrative aspect thereof." But the IAEA's operational budget—that is, the costs of activities under its program—is not subject to UN review.

The IAEA (unlike any of the specialized agencies) has the right and obligation to report directly to the UN Security Council in certain cases. One of the statutory objectives of the IAEA is to ensure that none of the assistance it gives to member states is "used in such a way as to further any military purpose," and the IAEA is empowered to establish a staff of inspectors to report violations of this rule. If it finds that such a violation has occurred, the IAEA is required to report the matter to the General Assembly and the Security Council.

Under a resolution passed by the UN General Assembly in 1957, the General Conference and the Board of Governors are both empowered to "seek an advisory opinion of the International Court of Justice on any legal question arising within the scope of the activities of the Agency." Furthermore, it is required to submit to the court "any question or dispute concerning the interpretation or application of [the] Statute" that is not settled by negotiation.

For some time, a number of the specialized agencies have been concerned with various aspects of the peaceful uses of atomic energy. Thus, WHO is concerned with atomic health standards and the medical use of radioisotopes, the ILO with safety standards for workers in atomic industry, and UNESCO with reactor physics. To provide for continuous exchange of information, the IAEA has negotiated agreements with a number of the specialized agencies.

The IAEA is a member of the Inter-Agency Consultative Board of the UN Development Program.

The IAEA also has "informal contacts and consultations" with regional organizations not a part of the UN system that are concerned with the peaceful uses of atomic energy. These include the European Organization for Nuclear Research, the Joint Institute for Nuclear Research, the European Nuclear Energy Agency of the OEEC, the European Atomic Energy Community (EURATOM), the Council for Mutual Economic Aid (COMECON), the Commission for Technical Co-operation in Africa South of the Sahara, and the Inter-American Nuclear Energy Commission of the OAS.

Finally, the IAEA maintains informal contacts with a number of nongovernmental organizations to enable it to draw upon their scientific services. Seven such organizations, among them the International Commission on Radiological Protection and the World Power Conference, have been granted consultative status with the IAEA.

6 BUDGET

The IAEA 1970 estimated budget was $14,837,000, divided, according to IAEA practice, into two parts.

The regular budget, amounting to $12,250,000, was intended to cover scientific and technical services and laboratory charges, distribution of scientific information, the organization of seminars, symposia, conferences, and scientific panels, the dispatch of special missions, and certain other activities, as well as administrative expenses. The regular budget was to be financed mainly from the assessed contributions of member states, set at $11,853,000.

The operational budget allocations for 1970, intended to cover the cost of the agency's laboratory facilities, exchange and training, technical assistance, and research contracts, was set at $2,587,000. Of this total, $2 million was to come from voluntary contributions of member states. The same target figure of $2 million had been set every year until 1969, but the deficit was such that in recent years only about one fourth of requests for assistance could be met. In 1970, however, there was an encouraging increase in contributions, and it was decided to set the target figure at $2.5 million.

7 ACTIVITIES

In broad terms, there are two ways in which atomic energy may be used to further the peace, health, and prosperity of the world. First, the heat generated by nuclear reactions may be used to produce electric power and to distill fresh water to satisfy the world's rapidly increasing requirements. Second, the various radioisotopes that can be produced in nuclear reactors may find a number of practical applications in industry, agriculture, medicine, and research. For example, radioactive tracers are widely used to detect leaks in pipelines, to plot the flow of underground water, and to measure the intake of nutrients by plants. Radioactive "labeling" has helped biologists understand the chemical transformations in living cells and to crack the genetic code that determines the structure of all living creatures, man included.

The first objective of the IAEA is to encourage the worldwide advance of the peaceful use of atomic energy.

Certain dangers have to be considered, however. Even the most peaceful uses of atomic energy raise serious health and safety problems, and there is always the possibility that nuclear facilities or materials may be used to produce weapons of destruction.

A. ASSISTANCE TO MEMBER STATES

The initial program of the IAEA, unanimously adopted by the 1957 General Conference, emphasized activities that could be undertaken while the IAEA's experience and resources were still relatively limited. A high priority must be given "to those activities which will give the maximum possible benefit from the peaceful applications of atomic energy in improving the conditions and raising the standard of living of the peoples in the under-developed areas."

In the light of these considerations, two of the IAEA's major initial objectives are to help member states prepare for the eventual use of nuclear power, particularly in economically underdeveloped areas, and to encourage them in the wider use of radioisotopes. Although it cannot undertake actual programs of development for its members, it can assist them in initiating and carrying out such programs.

Technical Assistance

Since 1957, 11 preliminary assistance missions and further "follow-up" missions have been sent to 70 countries. The findings of these missions are taken into account in providing technical assistance.

In 1969, 65 countries received technical assistance. Requests for assistance mainly related to the application of isotopes and radiation in agriculture; nuclear engineering and technology; nuclear physics and nuclear chemistry; and the use of radioisotopes in medicine, industry and hydrology.

The assistance was provided through the service of 230 experts, lecturers or visiting professors, the award of 484 fellowships, and the supply of equipment in the amount of $882,800.

Provision of Materials

Under the IAEA statute, any member desiring to set up an atomic energy project for peaceful purposes "may request the assistance of the Agency in securing special fissionable and other materials."

The IAEA acts, on request, as an intermediary in arranging the supply of reactors, reactor fuel, and other specialized equipment from one member state to another. The Congo (Kinshasa), Finland, Japan, Mexico, Pakistan, Yugoslavia, Norway, Argentina, and Uruguay have been beneficiaries of such arrangements. Small quantities of special fissionable materials have also been supplied to a number of countries for research purposes.

Training of Technical Personnel

This part of the IAEA's program has grown rapidly, not only because of the pressing needs of member states for trained technicians but also because less elaborate preparations are required for assistance of this kind than for more complex technical assistance operations.

To meet the shortage of scientific and technical workers that, particularly in the less developed areas of the world, is a major obstacle to "atoms for peace" progress, the IAEA has initiated a fivefold program:

1. Fellowships. Fellowships are awarded in nuclear physics; production, handling, and application of isotopes; nuclear chemistry; research and power reactors; and health physics and protection. Fellows receive a monthly stipend to cover room, board, and incidentals, ranging from $100 to $300, according to the local cost of living.

2. Assignment of professors, experts and consultants. The program provides for the exchange of scientists to lecture on nuclear physics, radiochemistry, and related subjects.

3. Survey of available facilities in member states. The IAEA collects detailed information from its member states about their training and research programs, training facilities, and the experts they are prepared to make available to the IAEA. It is thus in a position to act as an international clearinghouse for training in atomic energy.

Regional Training Centers

The IAEA helped to set up a Middle Eastern Regional Radioisotope Center for the Arab countries, which is now fully established and operating independently. The scientific program of the center consists of training specialists in the application of radioisotopes in science, industry, agriculture, and medicine. In addition, research using radioisotope techniques in hydrology, agriculture, entomology, and medicine is being conducted.

5. Special training courses. The organization of these courses for participants from various countries requires elaborate preparation and cooperation with other organizations, national governments, universities, and scientific institutions. Such courses, which are given continuously in different parts of the world, vary in duration from a few weeks to a few months. In 1965, 12 regional and interregional courses were organized: 6 devoted to the application of radioisotopes in agriculture, 2 to health, safety and waste disposal, 1 to the application of radioisotopes in medicine, 1 to nuclear metallurgy, and 1 to the general application of radioisotopes.

B. EXCHANGE OF INFORMATION AND CONFERENCES

While its assistance programs are directed primarily to the needs of economically underdeveloped areas, the IAEA's program of exchange of information and conferences is designed to benefit all of its members, even the most technically advanced.

So rapidly has new scientific and technical information in the nuclear field accumulated in recent years, it would be impossible, without the aid of modern, high-speed electronic computer systems, to keep abreast of more than a small fraction of the developments relating to the peaceful uses of atomic energy. Widely scattered computer centers in a number of countries now assimilate, analyze, store, and disseminate nuclear data. The nuclear-data unit at IAEA headquarters in Vienna has its own electronic computer. Data from all over the world are fed into this computer, and the information is available to all member states.

The IAEA also plays a leading role in promoting the more time-honored methods of disseminating scientific information— meetings and publications. Some dozen international scientific conferences, seminars, and symposia are arranged annually. The large conferences cover a wide range of topics, such as nuclear electronics and the use of radioisotopes in industry. The IAEA was entrusted with the scientific aspects of the Third International Conference on the Peaceful Uses of Atomic Energy, held in Geneva in 1964. This conference, which concentrated on reactor technology and power development, was attended by 1,800 delegates and consultants from 75 states and specialized agencies and more than 2,000 observers. The fourth conference was scheduled to be held in Geneva in September 1971.

The IAEA publishes more than 30,000 printed pages each year. In addition to the proceedings of scientific meetings, the publications include technical directories on reactors and other equipment, specialized bibliographies, a list of nuclear references based on books, reports, etc., and a guide to scientific conferences, meetings, and training courses. The Technical Reports Series consists of reports on the findings of meetings of experts on various subjects and similar material. The Safety Series features manuals on the safe handling and transport of radioactive materials and reports on such matters as the disposal of radioactive wastes. Two scientific journals, *Nuclear Fusion* and *Atomic Energy Review*, appear four times a year. The *IAEA Bulletin*, published six times a year, gives information intended for laymen. It is printed in English, French, Russian, and Spanish and is available free on request.

An important service initiated in 1970 is the International Nuclear Information System (INIS), in which member states cooperate to make information published in all parts of the world readily available. They, and a number of international and regional organizations that also assist, scan relevant literature and report to the IAEA, which processes it and issues a magnetic tape service for participating governments and organizations; the *INIS Atomindex*, produced directly by computer from the tapes, available on subscription; abstracts for every item on microfiche, also available on subscription; and full texts on microfiche at small fees.

A technical service in operation involves collaborative use of computer centers in Western Europe, the USSR, and the US to enable requests for specialized nuclear data to be met from any part of the world.

C. RESEARCH

In 1964 the IAEA set up the International Center for Theoretical Physics in Trieste. It has achieved great success in bringing together specialists from developing and developed countries to carry out research and to enable scientists from developing countries to keep abreast of progress without having to leave their own countries permanently or for long periods. Fellowships from developing countries are awarded for training and research and an international forum is provided for personal contacts. Associate memberships are awarded by election to enable distinguished physicists to spend one to three months every year at the center. Senior and junior positions are offered by invitation, and a federation scheme is designed to forge a partnership with institutions in developing countries. Assistance has been given by Italy and by the University and city of Trieste. Further aid has come from the Ford Foundation and UNESCO, which in 1970 undertook joint management of the center. Many of the IAEA's technical assistance activities involve work with isotopes and radiation sources. The development of the practical uses of atomic energy, rather than fundamental research, is the statutory task of the IAEA. Nevertheless, it very soon became clear that in order to develop a practical "atoms for peace" program the IAEA would have to concern itself with certain serious gaps in existing knowledge concerning the use of radioisotopes. In particular, additional research was required concerning safeguards, radiation safety and protection, and radiation health problems. Accordingly, the IAEA allocates funds for research to be carried out at IAEA headquarters or to be contracted out to research institutions in member states.

The IAEA has three laboratories: a small one at its headquarters in Vienna, the main laboratory at Seibersdorf (20 miles from Vienna), and one at Monaco for research on the effects of radioactivity in the sea. The laboratories undertake work in agriculture, hydrology, medicine, physics, chemistry, and low-level radioactivity.

A research contract program has been established with various institutions in member states. The subjects include nuclear power and reactors, waste treatment, physics and chemistry; radioisotope and radiation applications in agriculture, food technology, industry and medicine; water resources development; protection of man against ionizing radiation, radiation biology, medical and biological radiation dosimetry, health physics and radiation protection; environmental contamination and waste disposal.

To keep abreast of scientific developments, members of the IAEA's scientific staff visit institutions in member states and conduct various studies. The IAEA has made a survey of research trends in the sterilization of food and drugs by ionizing radiations, a problem of considerable interest to both developed and the less-developed countries.

D. NUCLEAR POWER STUDIES

Nuclear power promises to be a prime source of electrical energy, particularly in areas lacking conventional sources of energy— coal, petroleum, and hydropower.

Many developing countries are taking an interest in nuclear power. Nuclear centers and research reactors are used increasingly to study nuclear engineering and basic sciences. From a general review of national and regional plans it can be expected that 20% of all newly installed electric capacity between 1970 and 1980 will be nuclear.

The agency has assisted a number of countries by making preliminary assessments of nuclear power requirements. It has also helped several countries to secure research reactors.

A number of countries are interested in dual-purpose reactors that can be used both to desalt water and generate electricity. Panels of experts are convened periodically under IAEA auspices to review progress in this direction.

A considerable number of scientific meetings on nuclear power have been organized. They have discussed such matters as integration of nuclear plants in nuclear power grids, operating experience, the possibilities for small and medium power reactors, development of fast breeder reactors, and many aspects of safety and waste management and siting. Proceedings of these meetings are published.

The IAEA has organized regional study-group conferences on research reactor use and has held meetings on various scientific and technological considerations in the design of new reactor types.

Cooperation in research programs in reactor physics is promoted by the IAEA. For example, an agreement has been in effect for some years between the IAEA, Norway, Poland, and Yugoslavia. In the Far East a joint research and training program involving the use of a neutron crystal spectrometer was organized under IAEA auspices.

International study courses held in Vienna in 1969 and 1970 have proved of value as a means of reviewing the current status of nuclear power.

E. HEALTH AND SAFETY REGULATION

Since the basic raw materials of atomic energy are radioactive and since all ionizing radiation is potentially dangerous, a very important duty of the IAEA is to establish standards of safe practice for activities carried out under its auspices or with its assistance. The statute specifically authorizes the IAEA to establish and adopt "standards of safety for protection of health and minimization of danger to life and property (including such standards for labour conditions)" and to provide for the application of these standards to its own operations and operations carried out with its assistance. If requested, the IAEA may also provide for the application of these standards to a state's own nuclear activities or to any bilateral or multilateral arrangement between states.

The IAEA has formulated basic safety standards, which have taken account of recommendations of the International Commission on Radiological Protection (ICRP), and it has issued model regulations and technical guidance on particular types of operations. Such standards are proving to be a useful basis for international regulations and national legislation.

Plans have been worked out by the IAEA for emergency assistance to countries in the event of radiation hazard. This is mainly for those countries without sufficient experience or resources to deal with the consequences of such incidents.

The Nordic Mutual Emergency Assistance Agreement in connection with Radiation Accidents was signed by Denmark, Finland, Norway, Sweden, and the IAEA in 1963.

A number of manuals on safe practice have been issued by the IAEA in its Safety Series. Manuals of guidance on environmental monitoring in emergencies and the control of atmospheric pollutants that could result from the operation of nuclear plants are also under preparation.

F. NUCLEAR LAW

From its inception, the IAEA has been faced with the need for international coordination and harmonization of the principles governing third-party liability in the event of nuclear damage. The absence of special legislation might leave injured victims without redress. Great difficulties might arise if different nations were to incorporate different principles and procedures in their legislation concerning third-party liability.

Some steps toward standardization have already been taken in respect of compensation for damage arising from nuclear operations through the conclusion of two international conventions: the Brussels Convention on the Liability of Operators of Nuclear Ships (1962) and the Vienna Convention on Civil Liability for Nuclear Damage (1963). These two conventions set the minimum standards concerning the liability of individual states in the event of accidents that occur during the operation of nuclear ships and installations or during transport of nuclear materials.

Growing awareness of the necessity for developing both special and general law in relation to nuclear energy has been demonstrated by the activities of the Legal Division. These have included symposia, training courses in Vienna (1968) and in Athens (1970), and a seminar in Bangkok (1970). There was widespread demand for the book *Nuclear Law for a Developing World,* issued after the Vienna course.

G. SAFEGUARDS AGAINST MILITARY USE OF NUCLEAR MATERIALS

The basic science and technology of nuclear energy are the same for both peaceful and military purposes. Therefore, the IAEA statute requires the agency "to establish and administer safeguards" to ensure that no materials, services, equipment, facilities, or information that the IAEA makes available are used "in such a way as to further any military purpose." Such safeguards may also be applied, "at the request of the parties, to any bilateral or multilateral arrangement, or, at the request of a State, to any of that State's activities in the field of atomic energy."

Under the safeguards system, which was first developed by the Board of Governors on the basis of these statutory provisions in 1961, and continuously revised to cover all major aspects of the fuel cycle, control may be exercised either over assistance provided directly by the agency or under its auspices, or over items placed voluntarily under IAEA control by any country or group of countries—for instance, over reactors, their fuel, and fuel-reprocessing plants.

The safeguards consist of the agency's right to review the design of a nuclear installation to ensure that it will not further any military purpose and that it will lend itself to the exercise of safeguards; maintenance of records by the state, to which the IAEA has full access; progress reports made by the state; the IAEA's right to approve means of chemical processing of spent reactor fuel and to require the deposit of fissile material produced. A major development in international statesmanship greatly affecting the significance of the agency's work was the coming into force in 1970 of the Treaty on the Non-Proliferation of Nuclear Weapons, under which many nations not in possession of nuclear weapons have agreed to devote their atomic work to peaceful purposes and to accept the control system of the IAEA for this purpose. All parties to the treaty have undertaken to pursue negotiations relating to cessation of the nuclear arms race and to nuclear disarmament and on a treaty of general and complete disarmament under international control. The non-nuclear states will in due course complete agreements with the agency for safeguards aimed at preventing diversion to military purposes. The experience gained by the agency under 40 previous agreements with 30 countries will thus be of great value in the task of expanding safeguards work and in training the new staff members required. Considerable effort is being made to improve the techniques and increase efficiency with the greatest economy in cost and manpower. A number of research contracts have been placed for this purpose.

In addition, the IAEA may send inspectors into the state with the right of "access at all times to all places and data and to any person" as may be necessary for its purpose.

IAEA's Right of Inspection. The statute provides that "the Agency shall, as necessary, establish a staff of inspectors." These inspectors would be charged with the responsibility of supervising all operations conducted by the IAEA to ensure that they complied with prescribed health and safety standards and that the agency was taking adequate measures to prevent the diversion of fissionable materials to military purposes. The IAEA would have the right to send these inspectors into the territory of any "recipient State or States" to "account for source and special fissionable materials supplied [by the agency] and fissionable products." The inspectors would be responsible for determining whether the prescribed safeguards against diversion of any of these materials were being complied with. They would be required to report "any non-compliance" to the director general who in turn would report it to the Board of Governors.

At this juncture, certain corrective measures would go into effect. The statute requires that "the Board shall call upon the recipient State or States to remedy forthwith any noncompliance which it finds to have occurred. The Board shall report the non-compliance to all Members and to the Security Council and the General Assembly of the United Nations. In the event of failure of the recipient State or States to take fully corrective action within a reasonable time, the Board may take one or both of the following measures: direct curtailment or suspension of assistance being provided by the Agency or by a Member, and call for the return of materials and equipment made available to the recipient Member or group of Members. The Agency may also . . . suspend any non-complying Member from the exercises of the privileges and rights of membership."

H. VOLUNTARY APPLICATION OF IAEA SAFEGUARDS

The statute provides that IAEA safeguards can be applied to a member country's atomic energy program upon request and that they can be applied to a bilateral arrangement "at the request of the parties."

Japan was the first country to accept IAEA safeguards controls when in 1959 it requested a supply of nuclear fuel. By the beginning of 1970, IAEA controls were accepted by all member states in Latin America, Africa south of the Sahara, and Southeast Asia and the Far East. In February 1967, 21 states meeting in Tlatelolo, Mexico, adopted a Treaty for the Prohibition of Nuclear Weapons in Latin America. This envisaged that the IAEA would apply safeguards on request.

8 BIBLIOGRAPHY

More than 400 books on various aspects of nuclear science and agency responsibilities have been published to date. Titles are listed in the IAEA publications catalogue. Other subjects include life sciences; health, safety and waste management; physics, chemistry, geology and raw materials; reactors and nuclear power (including directories); industrial applications; and nuclear law. Periodicals are:

Atomic Energy Review—6 times a year, annual subscription $14.

INIS Atomindex—monthly, annual subscription $20.

International Atomic Energy Agency Bulletin—6 times a year, free.

Meetings on Atomic Energy—quarterly, annual subscription $3.

Nuclear Fusion—6 times a year, annual subscription $16.

INTERNATIONAL CIVIL AVIATION ORGANIZATION (ICAO)

1 BACKGROUND : In December 1903 the first heavier-than-air craft, designed by the Wright brothers, managed to fly a few hundred yards under its own power carrying one person. In 1969 scheduled airlines alone flew 216 billion passenger miles, carrying 287 million passengers. Total operating revenues (passenger, cargo, mail) of the world's airlines had reached $3.7 billion a year by 1958 and $15.3 billion by 1969. The average aircraft speed increased from 214 miles an hour in 1959 to 242 miles an hour in 1961, 270 miles in 1963, and 350 miles in 1969. These compare with an average speed of 155 miles an hour 20 years earlier, when the DC 3 was the backbone of most airlines fleets. Although in a number of countries machinery to regulate domestic flights was established fairly soon, little was accomplished until 1944 to solve the multifarious technical, economic, and legal problems posed by international civil aviation.

2 CREATION

The first international civil aviation conference, held in 1910 and attended by European governments only, since trans-ocean flight was then regarded as no more than a wild dream, was a failure. Almost another decade elapsed before 1919, when an international convention, signed in Paris, created the International Commission for Air Navigation (ICAN). The commission was to meet at least once a year and concern itself with technical matters. An international committee of jurists was also established, to concern itself with the intricate legal questions created by cross-border aviation. In 1928 a Pan American convention on commercial aviation was adopted at a conference held in Havana to deal with problems then emerging as international flights became more frequent in the Western Hemisphere. Although some progress in obtaining agreement on international flight regulations had been made by the end of the 1930's, most nations still granted very few concessions to each other's airlines, and no agreement existed permitting foreign planes to fly nonstop over the territory of one country en route to another country.

THE CHICAGO CONFERENCE OF 1944

World War II greatly accelerated the development of long-distance aerial navigation, and a high degree of cooperation on technical matters was achieved among the Allied nations. As the war drew to a close, however, there still was no general body of law that would regulate international flight under normal, peacetime conditions.

In November and December 1944 delegates of 54 nations met at the International Civil Aviation Conference in Chicago to plan for international cooperation in the field of air navigation in the postwar era. It was this conference that framed the constitution of ICAO.

In essence, the conference was faced with two questions: (1) whether universally recognized navigational signals and other navigational and technical standards could be agreed upon; (2) whether international rules concerning the economics of air transport could be established. One group of countries, led by the US, wanted an international organization empowered only to make recommendations regarding standard technical procedures and equipment. In its economic aspects, these countries believed, air transport should be freely competitive. This would also best serve the interests of the "consumer nations" that had no international airlines of their own. Another group of countries, led by the UK, favored a stronger organization, which would have a great deal to say about the economics of civil aviation. It would be empowered to allocate the international routes that the airlines of different countries would be allowed to fly, regulate the frequency of such flights, and fix rates. A radical proposal, advanced by New Zealand and supported by Australia, called for international ownership and operation of international air transport.

The convention on international aviation finally adopted by the conference was something of a compromise between the American and British positions. The convention established for the first time an independent international body, the International Civil Aviation Organization, to supervise "order in the air," obtain maximum technical standardization for international aviation, recommend certain practices that member countries should follow, and carry out other functions. Countries ratifying or acceding to the convention thereby agree in advance to conform to ICAO-adopted civil aviation standards and to endeavor to conform to ICAO-adopted recommendations.

In the economic field, the organization has no regulatory powers, but one of ICAO's constitutional objectives is to "prevent economic waste caused by unreasonable competition." Furthermore, under the convention member states undertake to have their international airlines furnish ICAO with traffic reports, cost statistics, and financial statements showing, among other things, all receipts and the sources thereof.

The Chicago convention affirms every state's "complete and exclusive sovereignty over the airspace above its territory." It provides that nonscheduled flights may, subject to certain permissible conditions and limitations, be made by the civil aircraft of one country into or over the territory of another. Scheduled international air service, however, may be operated from one country into or over the territory of another country only with the latter's authorization. Furthermore, member states are permitted to establish areas prohibited to foreign aircraft as long as these regulations are nondiscriminatory. Pilotless aircraft as well as conventional aircraft are covered by these provisions. The term "airspace" is not precisely defined, however, and with the development of rockets and long-range missiles the problem of deciding where a country's airspace ends and where outer space begins has become a matter of practical concern.

An important matter considered by the Chicago conference was the question of the exchange of commercial rights in international civil aviation. It was not possible to reach an agreement satisfactory to all states attending the conference. Hence, the question was covered, not in the Convention on International Aviation that serves as ICAO's constitution, but in two supplementary agreements adopted by the conference: the International Air Services Transit Agreement and the International Air Transport Agreement. These two treaties do not form part of the ICAO constitution and are binding only on the ICAO member states that have ratified them.

The International Air Services Transit Agreement guarantees (1) the freedom of civil aircraft to fly over foreign countries and territories as long as they do not land, and (2) the freedom of civil aircraft to make nontraffic landings, for refueling or overhaul only, in foreign territory. The agreement, which thus established for the first time the principle of automatic right of transit and of emergency landing, had come into force between 73 countries by 31 December 1965.

The International Air Transport Agreement, also known as the Five Freedoms Agreement, affirms, in addition to the two freedoms covered by the transit agreement, three other freedoms of the air: (3) freedom to transport passengers and cargo from an aircraft's homeland to other countries, (4) freedom to transport passengers and cargo from other countries to an aircraft's homeland, and (5) freedom to carry air traffic between countries other than the aircraft's homeland.

Since the Chicago convention was adopted in December 1944, ICAO has the distinction of possessing a constitution older than the UN Charter. Countries were much slower in ratifying the Chicago convention, however, than they were in ratifying the UN Charter, and ICAO did not actually come into being until 4 April 1947, 30 days after the convention had been ratified by the required 26 states.

3 PURPOSES

ICAO's aims and objectives, as stated in the Chicago convention, are to foster the planning and development of international air transport so as to:

(a) ensure the safe and orderly growth of international civil aviation throughout the world;

(b) encourage the arts of aircraft design and operation for peaceful purposes;

(c) encourage the development of airways, airports, and air navigation facilities for international civil aviation;

(d) meet the needs of the peoples of the world for safe, regular, efficient, and economical air transport;

(e) prevent economic waste caused by unreasonable competition;

(f) ensure that the rights of contracting states are fully respected and that every contracting state has a fair opportunity to operate international airlines;

(g) avoid discrimination between contracting states;

(h) promote safety of flight in international air navigation;

(i) promote generally the development of all aspects of international civil aeronautics.

4 MEMBERSHIP

Countries that in World War II were members of the United Nations (i.e., the anti-Axis coalition) or remained neutral during the conflict may join ICAO by ratifying the Chicago convention of 1944. Others must be accepted by a four-fifths vote of the ICAO assembly and must also obtain the approval of the UN General Assembly. On 1 September 1970, ICAO membership was 119:

Afghanistan	Austria
Algeria	Barbados
Argentina	Belgium
Australia	Bolivia

Brazil	Madagascar
Bulgaria	Malawi
Burma	Malaysia
Burundi	Mali
Cambodia	Malta
Cameroon	Mauritania
Canada	Mauritius
Central African Republic	Mexico
Ceylon	Morocco
Chad	Nepal
Chile	Netherlands
Colombia	New Zealand
Congo (Brazzaville)	Nicaragua
Congo (Kinshasa)	Niger
Costa Rica	Nigeria
Cuba	Norway
Cyprus	Pakistan
Czechoslovakia	Panama
Dahomey	Paraguay
Denmark	Peru
Dominican Republic	Philippines
Ecuador	Poland
El Salvador	Portugal
Ethiopia	Romania
Finland	Rwanda
France	Sa'udi Arabia
Gabon	Senegal
Germany, West	Sierra Leone
Ghana	Singapore
Greece	Somalia
Guatemala	South Africa
Guinea	Southern Yemen
Guyana	Spain
Haiti	Sudan
Honduras	Sweden
Hungary	Switzerland
Iceland	Syria
India	Taiwan
Indonesia	Tanzania
Iran	Thailand
Iraq	Togo
Ireland	Trinidad and Tobago
Israel	Tunisia
Italy	Turkey
Ivory Coast	Uganda
Jamaica	UAR
Japan	UK
Jordan	US
Kenya	Upper Volta
Korea, South	Uruguay
Kuwait	Venezuela
Laos	Viet-Nam, South
Lebanon	Yemen
Liberia	Yugoslavia
Libya	Zambia
Luxembourg	

5 STRUCTURE
THE ASSEMBLY

The all-member assembly, which originally met annually, now meets less frequently. Since the mid-1950's, sessions have been held in Caracas, 1956; Montreal, 1958; San Diego, 1959; Montreal, 1961; Rome, 1962; Montreal, 1965; Buenos Aires, 1968. Every member state has one vote in the assembly, and decisions are made by a simple majority vote unless otherwise specified by the Chicago convention.

The assembly makes policy recommendations, reviews the work of ICAO, offers guidance to the other ICAO bodies, elects the council, and determines the budget. The assembly may amend the ICAO constitution by a two-thirds majority vote, and it has done so on several occasions. But amendments come into force for the states that ratify them only after they have been ratified by at least two-thirds of the ICAO member states as specified by the assembly. In other words, the assembly may feel that it would not be fair to introduce a particular innovation in international civil aviation unless certain states would abide by it. On the other hand, the assembly possesses a rather unusual prerogative to induce wide ratification of an amendment it has adopted: if a member state does not ratify a particular amendment within a given period of time, the assembly has the right to revoke that country's membership in ICAO.

Furthermore, the ICAO constitution leaves the door open for the organization to assume responsibilities, within its competence, on aviation matters "directly affecting world security." This could, for example, conceivably include the creation of an international air patrol. The ICAO assembly is authorized to "enter into appropriate arrangements" for such purposes with the UN or, as the Chicago convention states broadly because when it was written the United Nations did not yet exist, "with any general organization set up by the nations of the world to preserve peace."

THE ICAO COUNCIL

The council is a permanent body, composed of 27 member states elected by the Assembly for three-year terms. In selecting the membership of the council, the assembly is required by the Chicago convention to give adequate representation to nations of major importance in air transport, to nations that provide the largest share of facilities for international civil air navigation, and to nations whose inclusion on the council will ensure representation of all major geographical regions of the world. The following countries were elected by the 1968 assembly to be represented on the council until 1971.

Argentina	Italy
Australia	Japan
Belgium	Lebanon
Brazil	Mexico
Canada	Netherlands
Colombia	Nigeria
Congo (Brazzaville)	Senegal
Czechoslovakia	Spain
Denmark	Tanzania
France	Tunisia
Germany, West	UAR
Guatemala	UK
India	US
Indonesia	

The council's powers are unusually broad, as compared with those of the executive councils of most other specialized agencies. This body of 27 representatives adopts international standards and recommended practices regarding civil air navigation and transport. It may act as arbiter between member states on disputes relating to the interpretation or application of the Chicago convention and its annexes. It may investigate any situation that presents avoidable obstacles to the development of international air navigation. In general, it may take whatever steps are necessary to maintain the safety and regularity of operation of international air transport.

Since the spring of 1957, Walter Binaghi of Argentina has been president of the council. He was formerly in charge of experimental work in physics at the school of engineering of the University of Buenos Aires and was chairman of ICAO's Air Navigation Commission from 1949 to 1957.

SECRETARIAT

The ICAO secretariat is headed by a secretary-general, who is appointed by the council. The secretary-general appoints the staff of the ICAO secretariat and supervises and directs its activities. Albert Roper of France was the first secretary-general,

serving through 1951. He was succeeded by Ernst Carl Robert Ljundberg of Sweden (until 1959) and by R. M. Macdonnell of Canada (until 1964). B. T. Twigt of the Netherlands served as secretary-general until 1970. The present secretary-general is Dr. A. Kotaite of Lebanon.

HEADQUARTERS AND REGIONAL OFFICES

ICAO headquarters are located in the International Aviation Building, 1080 University Street, Montreal. The organization maintains six regional offices: the European office in Paris; the Far East and Pacific office, in Bangkok; the Middle East and East African office, in Cairo; the North American and Caribbean office, in Mexico City; the South American office, in Lima, and the African office, in Dakar. One of the most important functions of the regional offices is to assist member states in providing the aeronautical services expected of them under ICAO's regional air navigation plans (see below).

6 BUDGET

The 1968 assembly voted the following net budgets: 1969, $6,182,206; 1970, $6,215,384; 1971, $6,332,614 (all figures are in US dollars). Contributions from member states are assessed on a sliding scale determined by the assembly.

7 ACTIVITIES

A. ESTABLISHMENT OF INTERNATIONAL STANDARDS AND RECOMMENDED PRACTICES

By joining ICAO—that is, by accepting the Chicago convention—states undertake to collaborate in securing the highest practicable degree of uniformity in regulations, standards, procedures, and organization in all matters in which such uniformity will facilitate and improve air navigation. Hence, one of ICAO's chief tasks is to adopt such international standards and recommendations and to keep them up to date through modifications and amendments.

A standard, as defined by the first ICAO assembly, is "any specification for physical characteristics, configuration, material, performance, personnel, or procedures, the uniform application of which is recognized as *necessary* for the safety or regularity of international air navigation and to which Member States *will conform*." Standards may thus include specifications for such matters as the length of runways, the materials to be used in aircraft construction, and the qualifications to be required of a pilot flying an international route. A recommendation is any such specification, uniform application of which is recognized as "*desirable* in the interest of safety, regularity, or efficiency of international air navigation and to which Member States will *endeavor to conform*."

Preparing and revising these standards and recommendations is largely the responsibility of ICAO's air navigation commission, which plans, coordinates, and examines all ICAO's activities in the field of air navigation. The commission consists of 12 persons, appointed by the council from among persons nominated by member states. If the council approves the text, it is submitted to the ICAO member states. While recommendations are not binding, standards that thus become part of the convention automatically become binding on all member states, even those that may have opposed them. Countries finding it impossible to comply with a standard that has been adopted by ICAO must so notify the council, in which case the matter may be further discussed to find a solution.

The various standards and recommendations that have been adopted by ICAO are grouped into 15 technical annexes to the Chicago convention. Of the 15 annexes, 14 deal with navigational matters. The aim of the navigational annexes is to promote progress in flight safety, particularly by guaranteeing satisfactory minimum standards of training and safety procedures and by assuring uniform international practices that will minimize the risk of accidents resulting from misunderstanding. Annex 9, the only one not concerned with navigation, aims to facilitate air transport through the simplification of national entrance and exit formalities.

TECHNICAL ANNEXES TO THE CHICAGO CONVENTION
OF 1944

1. Personnel Licensing
   Licensing of flight crews, air-traffic control officers, and aircraft maintenance personnel.
2. Rules of the Air
   Rules relating to the conduct of visual and instrument flights.
3. Meteorology
   Provision of meteorological services for international air navigation and reporting of meteorological observations from aircraft.
4. Aeronautical Charts
   Specifications for aeronautical charts for use in international aviation.
5. Units of Measurement to be used in Air-Ground Communications
   Reduction in the variety of dimensional systems.
6. Operation of Aircraft—International Commercial Air Transport
   Specifications which will ensure in similar operations throughout the world a level of safety above a prescribed minimum.
7. Aircraft Nationality and Registration Marks
   Requirements for registration and identification of aircraft.
8. Airworthiness of Aircraft
   Certification and inspection of aircraft according to uniform procedures.
9. Facilitation
   Recommendation of uniform practices to simplify customs, immigration, and health inspection regulations at international airports.
10. Aeronautical Telecommunications
    Standardization of communications equipment and systems (Vol. I) and of communications procedures (Vol. II).
11. Air Traffic Services
    Establishment and operation of air-traffic control, flight information, and alerting services.
12. Search and Rescue
    Organization and operation of facilities and services necessary for search and rescue.
13. Aircraft Accident Inquiry
    Uniformity in the notification, investigation of, and reporting on aircraft accidents.
14. Aerodromes
    Characteristics and equipment for aerodromes used in international air navigation.
15. Aeronautical Information Services
    Methods for the collection and dissemination of aeronautical information required for flight operations.

In their original form these annexes came into force between May 1949 and April 1954. Almost all have since been amended, some very extensively.

The range of problems can be illustrated by the important amendments that were made to Annex 6, "Operations," as the result of a four-week Air Navigation Conference held in Montreal in late 1965. It was attended by representatives of 40 contracting states, 1 noncontracting state (USSR), and 7 international organizations. Special attention was paid to the needs of jet airliners, particularly in regard to radio equipment and flight crews. Other important amendments dealt with the carriage of dangerous goods, clarified and expanded the provisions on operational flight planning, and laid down regulations on the fuel and oil reserves that turbojet aircraft must carry. It was

decided that all flights should be required to carry two sets of very-high frequency survival radio equipment and that flight data recorders should be mandatory equipment on all aircraft weighing more than 12,500 pounds. Changing operational practices and technological development in the area of self-contained navigation aids also made it necessary for the conference to rewrite the existing statement of operational requirements for long-distance navigation.

B. FACILITATION OF INTERNATIONAL AIR TRANSPORT

Annex 9 to the Chicago convention deals with matters that are the primary responsibility of ICAO's air transport committee. The annex contains recommendations (since the required majority for standards binding on all ICAO member states could not be mustered) for uniform practices to simplify customs and health inspection regulations, to liberalize visa requirements and entry procedures for foreign visitors, to speed up the handling of and clearance procedures for air cargo, mail and baggage, and the like. Amendment 5 to Annex 9, "Facilitation," was adopted in November 1965. This recommends procedures to facilitate further the temporary admission of personnel required for search, rescue, repair, or salvage operations in connection with a lost or damaged aircraft and to expedite the movement of parts of such an aircraft between states for technical examination or testing.

The basic aim of the organization in this field is to achieve the greatest practicable freedom of passage for aircraft, crews, passengers, cargo, mail, and baggage involved in international flights. ICAO has received considerable cooperation from its member states in this "facilitation" program, as it is called, and there has been a great decrease in the red tape involved in entering and leaving countries by air. During the 1960's, members of the ICAO headquarters staff have visited many states to discuss air transport facilitation problems with governments and airline officials and to assist in simplifying local procedures and practices. The organization has emphasized the need for expediting the handling of air cargo and has suggested that preflight passenger check-in times be reduced.

C. REGIONAL PLANNING FOR AIR NAVIGATION

While worldwide uniformity is desirable for certain matters pertaining to aviation, others are best approached on a regional basis, since operating conditions vary a great deal from region to region. In the North Atlantic region, for example, long-range ocean flying predominates, whereas in Europe many international flights are short overland jumps. To deal with these different conditions and to facilitate detailed planning, ICAO has mapped out eight geographic regions. At meetings held in each of them, detailed plans for the facilities, services, and procedures appropriate to that flight area are drawn up. Altogether the eight regional plans specify more than 50,000 air navigation facilities and services that are required, and the locations where they are required: communications and meteorological facilities, airports, aerodromes, search and rescue bases, and so on. The ICAO plans for the eight regions of the world are regularly revised or amended to meet the needs of increasing traffic and the demands of the jet age.

Difficulties in Implementing the Regional Plans. One of ICAO's main concerns has been to see these regional plans carried out and to help member governments provide the services called for. It cannot be said that so far the regional plans have been adequately implemented. The less serious shortcomings are taken up by the secretary-general and the ICAO secretariat with the governments concerned. More serious ones are studied by the Air Navigation Commission and sometimes even by the ICAO council itself. The problem of eliminating the more serious deficiencies in navigational services and facilities is one that ICAO considers critical. The organization in 1956 set up a special implementation panel, which in 1960 was succeeded by the council's standing group on implementation.

The major difficulties blocking better implementation of the regional plans are lack of funds to provide the recommended facilities and services, a shortage of trained personnel to man them, and poor administration on the part of certain national aviation authorities. Joint financing has been successful only in the North Atlantic region (see below). ICAO has encouraged governments to upgrade their facilities through loans for capital expenditures, technical assistance, and other means. The 1965 ICAO assembly suggested that governments approach UNESCO for its collaboration in establishing preliminary training schools. It also suggested that member governments consider establishing an aviation development fund under ICAO auspices.

The six regional offices are the organization's principal agents in advising and assisting states in the implementation of ICAO standards, recommended practices and procedures, and regional plans. The offices have directed as much of their resources as possible to giving practical help, with a resulting increase in the number of visits to states for this purpose by members of the technical staff.

Since 1960, ICAO has budgeted funds for advisory implementation missions to help member countries overcome local deficiencies.

D. JOINTLY OPERATED OR FINANCED AIR NAVIGATION SERVICES "JOINT SUPPORT"

Under the Chicago convention, every ICAO member state is required to provide air navigation facilities and services on its own territory. Navigational facilities and services must also be provided for air routes traversing the high seas and regions of undetermined sovereignty. The ICAO council is constitutionally authorized at the request of a member state to "provide, man, maintain, and administer any or all of the airports and other air navigation facilities, including radio and meteorological services, required in its territory for the safe, regular, efficient and economical operation of the international air services of the other contracting States." The council may also act on its own initiative to resolve a situation that might impair the "safe, regular, efficient, and economical operation" of international air services. Although ICAO has not yet undertaken the actual supervision of any nation's international air navigation facilities and services, several agreements are in effect to furnish such services and facilities in parts of the North Atlantic region through so-called "joint support" programs.

Under these joint-support agreements, the nations concerned contribute services, facilities, or cash payments based principally on the use by their own aircraft of the routes involved. Certain other benefits a nation may derive from a joint-support plan are also taken into consideration in calculating contributions.

North Atlantic Ocean Stations. Nine floating ocean stations in the North Atlantic are manned through a joint-support agreement coordinated by ICAO and participated in by more than 20 countries. Canada, France, the Netherlands, Norway, Sweden, the UK, and the US provide the 21 ships needed for the operation, while Australia, Belgium, Czechoslovakia, Denmark, West Germany, Iceland, Ireland, Israel, Italy, Japan, Mexico, Spain, Switzerland and Venezuela, all of whose aircraft fly the North Atlantic, support the program with cash payments. The floating stations provide radio navigation services and meteorological reports to aircraft, surface and upper air observations being broadcast at regular intervals, and also serve as floating search and rescue bases. They have rescued several hundred persons, victims of shipwrecks and air mishaps.

Joint-Financing Arrangements for Icelandic and Greenland Air Navigation Services. The vast majority of aircraft that utilize the special traffic control, navigational, and meteorological services furnished from Iceland and Greenland for transatlantic crossings are neither Icelandic nor Danish. Hence, 19 countries, including Iceland and Denmark, provide the funds necessary for the operation of these services.

Cable System for North Atlantic Point-to-Point Communications. A transatlantic cable, part of the Danish-Icelandic joint-financing arrangements, is a good example of the value of joint financing. The cable came about as the result of a determination by the ICAO implementation panel that the world's "most immediate and compelling need for aviation improvement" was the air traffic control and communications network in the North Atlantic region. The high frequency radio "point-to-point" network involving control centers at Prestwick in Scotland, Reykjavík in Iceland, and Gander in Newfoundland is liable to frequent disturbance by electronic emissions from the sun, such as those which cause the aurora borealis. These solar emissions also interfere with communications between aircraft in flight and ground stations. Frequent breakdowns in these point-to-point communications proved the greatest single obstacle to efficient aircraft operation in this heavily traveled region.

The best solution, it was agreed, was to link the North Atlantic control centers by cable, but existing cable facilities were inadequate to handle the required load. Consequently, a joint-financing agreement was worked out with commercial cable companies for a new transatlantic cable linking Newfoundland to Scotland via Greenland and Iceland, with one speech channel and four duplex teletypewriter channels reserved for exclusive aeronautical use. The new cable forms the spinal cord of a system interconnecting the flight control and navigational centers of the North Atlantic flightway. Air traffic controllers in any of these centers may speak directly to one another merely by lifting a telephone. An additional bonus is that the system provides alternate channels of communication with aircraft in flight.

E. OTHER PREPARATIONS FOR JET-AGE AND SUPERSONIC AVIATION

Jet transport planes run to a larger size than piston-driven transports; they fly at much faster speeds and cruise at much higher altitudes. A great many problems have therefore been posed by the increasing use of such aircraft in civil aviation. Runways have had to be lengthened and strengthened; there have been new communications, traffic control, and meteorological requirements to meet. Under ICAO auspices, many meetings have been held to study jet-age technological problems, and a special ICAO jet operations panel specified in considerable detail the requirements that had to be met before jet aircraft could operate economically and on dependable schedules.

With the era of supersonic civil aviation not far off, the ICAO assembly in 1959 requested the council to study the prospects of early development of supersonic aircraft and their availability for commercial use before 1975. The ICAO council assessed the probable technical, economic, and social consequences of these prospects. Specific problems, such as noise control and the increasing amount of land required for airports as longer and longer runways become necessary, were taken up as well. The purpose of the study was to help governments make coordinated plans for the age of supersonic flight—plans taking into account the interests of the general public, the interests of the airlines, and the views of the civil aviation authorities. The assembly adopted measures to make sure that the services and facilities required for the smooth and efficient operation of faster-than-sound civil aircraft are available before the introduction of such aircraft into commercial service. The ICAO council is keeping the organization's 119 member nations informed of supersonic developments and is working toward international agreement on critical operational standards. The council is also keeping states informed on traffic volume and patterns and on world demands for air transport, in order to assist in planning both subsonic and supersonic operations.

F. TECHNICAL ASSISTANCE

Economic progress in underdeveloped countries is heavily dependent on aviation. Not only are satisfactory alternative means of transportation frequently lacking, but exploration and survey operations often can be conducted most economically by air. Furthermore, the condition of a country's civil aviation is a matter of far more than local concern. The lives of airline passengers are frequently in the hands of foreign pilots, and aircraft flying to foreign countries must rely on local facilities, services, and personnel.

From its inception, therefore, ICAO's technical assistance has concentrated on matters that are essential to safe operation, such as air-traffic control, communications, pilot training, meteorological services, and airport facilities. ICAO experts have advised on the installation and improvement of facilities, on the reorganization of communication centers, on the establishment of approach and landing procedures, and on the construction of essential ground installations and elimination of unessential ones. In this way a variety of safety measures have been introduced in many countries; essential ground installations have been put up and unessential ones eliminated; governments have been assisted in the preparation of their civil aviation plans and budgets and in reorganizing national civil aviation administrations.

A major part of ICAO's technical assistance has been in the field of training. Experts have been sent to examine the technical competence of pilots employed by commercial airlines in countries with little experience in these matters and to help establish training programs where necessary to improve their skills. ICAO has helped establish schools for basic technical training in such subjects as air-traffic control, aeronautical meteorology, radio maintenance and operations, aircraft maintenance, repair, and overhaul, and power-equipment maintenance. ICAO experts serve as teachers in a number of these schools. On-the-job training is also encouraged. Some supplies and equipment for these training projects have been provided by ICAO.

In 1969 the organization's work in the field of technical assistance included activities carried out in connection with both the UN's Expanded Program of Technical Assistance and the Special Fund (since merged into a single UN Development Program—UNDP). Some technical assistance was financed by funds-in-trust provided by individual governments, and special aid was financed by funds provided by agreement between the UN and the US for operational services in the Congo (Kinshasa).

Technical Assistance and Special Fund Projects (now UNDP). Under the Expanded Program of Technical Assistance, ICAO aid was provided to some 53 countries in 1969. It included both the assignment of experts and the granting of fellowships and scholarships to national personnel. Most of these projects were continuations of previous technical assistance programs, since in aviation continuity is essential to success. Aid was given also to one regional project (Latin America) and two interregional projects (Africa–Middle East and Asia–Middle East) dealing with such matters as fire services, frequency search, flight safety, teletypewriter maintenance, communications, and operations.

The UN Special Fund was established in 1959 to accelerate economic development by creating conditions within the less-developed countries conducive to capital investment. Now administered as the "major preinvestment" section of the UNDP, Special Fund programs have been of particular interest to ICAO because among other things they provide for research and training centers in the field of civil aviation. Under this program, aviation training centers in Mexico City and Cairo were established by mid-1966 and their operation was taken over by the Mexican and UAR governments. Aid was continued to the development of civil aviation training centers in Bangkok, Casablanca, and Tunis, as well as to an aeronautical laboratory in Bangalore. A civil aviation institute, giving courses in air-traffic control, radio operation, and aircraft and radio maintenance, had begun to function at Kinshasa in the Congo. The civil aviation safety center in Beirut was fully functional, and had taken delivery of a large jet flight simulator.

At the country level, technical assistance work by the ICAO resident missions continues. In 1969 missions were located in Afghanistan, Algeria, Bolivia, Burundi, Cambodia, Cameroon, Central African Republic, Ceylon, Chile, Congo (Kinshasa), Costa Rica, Ecuador, El Salvador, Ethiopia, Ghana, Guatemala, Guinea, Guyana, Honduras, Indonesia, Iran, Iraq, Israel, Jordan, Kuwait, Laos, Lebanon, Liberia, Libya, Mali, Mexico, Morocco, Nepal, Nicaragua, Nigeria, Pakistan, Paraguay, Peru, Rwanda, Sa'udi Arabia, Somalia, Southern Yemen, Sudan, Surinam, Tanzania, Thailand, Trinidad and Tobago, Tunisia, Uganda, UAR, Upper Volta, Venezuela, and Yemen.

Operational Assistance in the Congo. ICAO assistance in the Congo began originally in 1960, when an ICAO technical assistance mission—as part of the UN operation in the Congo—was sent in to perform air-traffic control, communications, and other technical tasks on an emergency basis, as well as to train Congolese personnel to take over these responsibilities. ICAO aid continued through 1965 through the medium of the United Nations operation in the Congo, the subsequent UN–US–Congo agreement, and the technical assistance program. In addition, the ICAO training school became a special fund project in November 1964 and went into complete operation in 1966.

Experts in the Field. In 1969 there was a total of 235 ICAO experts in the field representing a wide range of specialization—electronics engineers, flight simulator operators and maintenance engineers, personnel licensing and fire-fighting experts, flying instructors, teletypewriter technicians, civil aviation advisers, aerodrome engineers, aircraft instrument technicians, mechanics, air-traffic controllers, aviation training and airworthiness experts, and economists and financial consultants. These experts came from 50 professions and from 37 countries—their nationalities included Argentinian, Australian, Belgian, Canadian, Chinese, French, German, Greek, Indian, Lebanese, Dutch, Norwegian, Portuguese, Spanish, Swedish, Egyptian, British, American, and Russian.

Examples of Technical Assistance in 1969

In Afghanistan, ICAO technical assistance provided civil aviation advice, workshop maintenance instruction, flight safety programs, radio maintenance instruction, and heavy vehicle maintenance instruction.

In Burundi, ICAO training school graduated 9 air-traffic controllers and 10 meteorological observers. As a result, the Bujumbura airport was enabled to be open 24 hours a day in 1970.

In Chile, aeronautical communications, airport management, personnel licensing, and operations control training and improvement were conducted.

In Honduras, preparation and promulgation of personnel licensing, operations regulations, development of administrative procedures, and fire control were dealt with by ICAO technical assistance.

In Laos, communications circuits between Vientiane and Bangkok and the installation of new equipment were explored.

In Liberia, a four-year civil aviation development program was formulated.

In Mali, technical assistance concentrated on strengthening of regulations, application of ICAO standards and advice on the implementation of the ICAO air navigation plan for the Africa-Indian Ocean region.

In Pakistan, fire prevention and rescue operations courses were conducted.

In Peru, advanced courses for the civil aviation school were planned. During 1969, 66 air-traffic service personnel and 16 radio technicians were graduated.

In Somalia, activities were conducted in the fields of aerodromes, aeronautical information services, air-traffic control, telecommunications, fire fighting, personnel licensing, air law, and search and rescue.

In Southern Yemen, assistance was given the department of civil aviation in the fields of air safety, facilitation, air-traffic control, communications, meteorological services, and training.

In Surinam, fire and rescue personnel were trained, and fire-fighting installations were planned.

G. SETTLEMENT OF DISPUTES BETWEEN ICAO MEMBER STATES

The Chicago convention vests important semijudicial powers in the ICAO council. In the event that a disagreement between ICAO member states concerning the interpretation or application of the Chicago convention or its annexes cannot be settled by negotiation, "it *shall,* on the application of any state concerned in the disagreement, be *decided*" by the ICAO council. Thus, once a particular party to a disagreement brings the matter before the council, the other state or states concerned cannot disclaim the council's jurisdiction. Under certain conditions, however, a member state may appeal the council's decision either to a special ad hoc tribunal (in agreement with the other party or parties) or to the International Court of Justice. If, once a decision is final, the council decides that a given airline is not complying with that decision, all ICAO members are pledged to deny the use of their air space to that airline. If a member state does not comply with a council decision, its voting rights shall be suspended.

A serious controversy settled under the auspices of the council, though it did not act as official arbiter, was a dispute between India and Pakistan concerning flights from India to Afghanistan. The countries finally agreed on the establishment of two 20-mile corridors through prohibited areas in Pakistan to allow direct India-Afghanistan flights.

H. INTERNATIONAL CONVENTIONS PREPARED UNDER ICAO AUSPICES

ICAO's legal committee prepared drafts for five international conventions that were subsequently approved either by the ICAO Assembly or by special diplomatic conferences.

The Geneva Convention of 1948. This convention deals with the international recognition of property rights and other rights pertaining to aircraft. It is designed to ensure the protection of these rights when an aircraft crosses an international frontier, and it is felt that its wide acceptance would encourage investments for the purchase of new aircraft. By 1 December 1969, this convention had been ratified or adhered to by 25 states.

The Rome Convention of 1953. This deals with damage caused by foreign aircraft to third parties on the ground. The economic aspects were considered by the air transport committee and the council prior to acceptance by a diplomatic conference on private air law in Rome. The convention includes the principle of absolute liability of the aircraft operator for damage caused to third parties on the ground but places a limitation on the amount of compensation. It also provides for the compulsory recognition and execution of foreign judgments. As of 1 December 1969, 22 states had become parties to the convention.

The Protocol of Amendment to the Warsaw Convention of 1929.

An international convention adopted in Warsaw in 1929 limits the liability of air carriers for death or other damage caused to passengers, except in cases of the carrier's willful misconduct, to 125,000 gold francs, equivalent to US$8,292 per person. A diplomatic conference sponsored by ICAO met in 1955 at The Hague and adopted a protocol that doubles the existing liability limit, making it the equivalent of $16,584. The protocol also provides that the carrier's liability is *unlimited,* not only in case of the carrier's willful misconduct but also whenever the death or other damage is proved to have resulted from an act or omission of the carrier or was done with intent to cause damage. More than 30 ratifications of the protocol were received by 3 May 1963; as a result, the Hague protocol came into effect between the ratifying states on 1 August 1963.

The position of the Warsaw-Hague agreements is in some doubt. As the result of a decision by the US government to withdraw if the limits were not increased considerably, the majority of the world's airlines have agreed to raise the limit of liability to US$75,000 (including lawyer's fees) for carriage of passengers on trips originating, terminating, or passing through the US.

The Guadalajara Convention of 1961. The Warsaw convention does not contain particular rules relating to international carriage by air performed by a person who is not a party to the agreement for carriage. Accordingly, as a result of the work of the legal committee on this subject, a diplomatic conference held at Guadalajara, Mexico, in 1961 adopted a convention, supplementary to the Warsaw convention, containing rules to apply in the circumstances mentioned. As of 1 December 1969, 30 states had become parties to the convention.

The Tokyo Convention of 1963. This convention provides that the country in which an aircraft is registered is competent to exercise jurisdiction over offenses and acts committed on board. Its object is to ensure that offenses, wherever committed, should not go unpunished. As certain acts committed on board an aircraft may jeopardize the safety of the aircraft or persons or property therein or may jeopardize good order and discipline on board, the aircraft commander and others are empowered to prevent the commission of such acts and to disembark the person concerned. In the case of unlawful and forcible seizure of an aircraft in flight by a person on board, the states parties to the convention are obliged to take all appropriate measures to restore control of the aircraft to its lawful commander or to preserve his control of it. Twelve ratifications were required to bring this convention into force. As of 1 December 1969, 20 ratifications had been received. The convention came into force on 4 December 1969.

[8] BIBLIOGRAPHY

Air Navigation Plans: African-Indian Ocean Region; Caribbean Region; European-Mediterranean Region; Middle East Region; North Atlantic Region; Pacific Region; South East Asia Region; South American-South Atlantic Region. $3.50 each.

ICAO Bulletin. Provides a concise account of the activities of ICAO and features additional information of interest to contracting states and the international aeronautical world. Monthly. One year, $5.00; single copies, $0.50.

Technical publications, subject to periodic amendments, include the following annexes to the ICAO convention: *Personnel Licensing; Rules of the Air; Meteorology; Aeronautical Charts; Dimensional Units to Be Used in Air-Ground Communications; Operation of Aircraft—International Commercial Air Transport; Aircraft Nationality and Registration Marks; Airworthiness of Aircraft; Facilitation; Aeronautical Telecommunications; Air-Traffic Services; Search and Rescue; Aircraft Accident Inquiry; Aerodromes;* and *Aeronautical Information Services.* Prices vary.

INTERNATIONAL TELECOMMUNICATION UNION (ITU)

¹BACKGROUND : The International Telecommunication Union (ITU) is the oldest of the intergovernmental organizations that have become specialized agencies related to the UN. In 1865, a convention establishing an International Telegraph Union was signed in Paris by the plenipotentiaries of 20 continental European states, including two extending into Asia—Russia and Turkey. Three years later, a permanent international Bureau for the Union was established in Bern, Switzerland. This bureau, which operated until 1948, was the forerunner of the present General Secretariat of the ITU. In 1885, at Berlin, the first regulations concerning international telephone services were added to the telegraph regulations annexed to the Paris Convention. By the end of the 19th century, radiotelegraphy, or "wireless," had been developed, and for the first time it was possible to communicate directly between shore stations and ships at sea. Rival wireless companies frequently refused to accept one another's messages, however. In 1903, an international conference was called to consider the problem, and in 1906, in Berlin, 29 maritime states signed the International Radiotelegraph Convention, establishing the principle of compulsory intercommunication between vessels at sea and the land. The International Radiotelegraph Conference which met in Washington in 1927 drew up for the first time a table of frequency allocations.

²CREATION

Two plenipotentiary conferences were held in 1932 at Madrid: one covering telephone and telegraph and the other radiotelegraph communications. The two existing conventions were amalgamated into a single International Telecommunication Convention (the word " telecommunication" signifying "any transmission, emission or reception of signs, signals, writing, images and sounds, or intelligence of any nature by wire, radio, visual, or other electro-magnetic systems"). The countries accepting the new Convention, which came into force in 1934, formed the International Telecommunication Union.

The International Telecommunication Convention of 1932 has been revised four times. The Plenipotentiary Conference of the ITU meeting in Atlantic City in 1947 made radical changes in the organizational structure of the Union to keep up with intervening developments in telecommunications; for example, a new permanent organ, the International Frequency Registration Board, was created to cope with the problem of the overcrowding of certain transmission frequencies; and an agreement was drawn up under which ITU was recognized by the UN as the specialized agency for telecommunications. The convention was further modified in certain respects by the plenipotentiary conferences of Buenos Aires, in 1952; Geneva, in 1959; and Montreux, Switzerland, in 1965.

³PURPOSES

The ITU has three objectives: to maintain and extend international cooperation for the improvement of telecommunications and their rational use; to promote the development of the most efficient operation of technical facilities; and to harmonize the actions of nations in the attainment of these goals.

⁴MEMBERSHIP

As of January 1970, the ITU had 137 members:

Afghanistan	Austria	Botswana	Ireland
Albania	Barbados	Brazil	Israel
Algeria	Belgium	Bulgaria	Italy
Argentina	Byelorussian SSR	Burma	Ivory Coast
Australia	Bolivia	Burundi	Jamaica
		Cambodia	Japan
		Cameroon	Jordan
		Canada	Kenya
		Central African Republic	Korea, South
		Ceylon	Kuwait
		Chad	Laos
		Chile	Lebanon
		China (Taiwan)	Lesotho
		Colombia	Liberia
		Congo (Brazzaville)	Libya
		Congo (Kinshasa)	Liechtenstein
		Costa Rica	Luxembourg
		Cuba	Malagasy Republic
		Cyprus	Malawi
		Czechoslovakia	Malaysia
		Dahomey	Maldives
		Denmark	Mali
		Dominican Republic	Malta
		Ecuador	Mauritania
		El Salvador	Mauritius
		Ethiopia	Mexico
		Finland	Monaco
		France	Mongolia
		French Overseas Territories	Morocco
		Gabon	Nauru
		Germany, West	Nepal
		Ghana	Netherlands
		Greece	New Zealand
		Guatemala	Nicaragua
		Guinea	Niger
		Guyana	Nigeria
		Haiti	Norway
		Honduras	Pakistan
		Hungary	Panama
		Iceland	Paraguay
		India	Peru
		Indonesia	Philippines
		Iran	Poland
		Iraq	Portugal

Portuguese Overseas Provinces	Togo
Rhodesia	Trinidad and Tobago
Romania	Tunisia
Rwanda	Turkey
Sa'udi Arabia	Uganda
Senegal	Ukrainian SSR
Sierra Leone	USSR
Singapore	UAR
Somalia	UK
South Africa (including South West Africa)	UK Overseas Territories
Southern Yemen	US
	US Territories
Spain	Upper Volta
Spanish Province in Africa	Uruguay
Sudan	Vatican City
Sweden	Venezuela
Switzerland	Viet-Nam, South
Syria	Yemen
Tanzania	Yugoslavia
Thailand	Zambia

5 STRUCTURE

THE PLENIPOTENTIARY CONFERENCE

The supreme body of the ITU is the Plenipotentiary Conference. It meets at intervals of five to seven years.

Each ITU Member has the right to be represented at the Plenipotentiary Conference and is entitled to one vote. Plenipotentiary conferences were held in Atlantic City in 1947, Buenos Aires in 1952, Geneva in 1959, and Montreux, Switzerland, in 1965. The next conference is scheduled for 1972 in Geneva. The principal functions of the Plenipotentiary Conference are to govern the Union's activities and to revise the International Telecommunication Convention where necessary. It establishes the general basis of the ITU's budget and approves the accounts of the Union.

ADMINISTRATIVE CONFERENCES

ITU administrative conferences are convened to consider particular telecommunications matters of worldwide or regional import. There are two regular world administrative conferences: one for telegraph and telephone, the other for radio and other forms of wireless transmission. One of the functions of these conferences is to revise the telegraph, telephone, and radio regulations annexed to the International Telecommunication Convention. The world administrative radio conference also elects the members of the International Frequency Registration Board (described below) and reviews its activities. Regional administrative conferences are convened to consider questions of a more restricted geographical scope, such as the assignment of television frequencies that have a relatively limited radius of transmission.

ADMINISTRATIVE COUNCIL

The Administrative Council, which normally meets once a year but may meet more frequently, is responsible for taking all steps to facilitate the implementation by member countries of the provisions of the Convention, of the decisions of the Plenipotentiary Conference, and, where appropriate, of the provisions of other conferences and meetings of the Union. The council was established by the Atlantic City conference of 1947. Originally it consisted of 18 members elected by the Plenipotentiary Conference. This number was increased to 25 in 1959 and to 29 in 1965. The Council ensures efficient coordination within the Union and in its relations with other international organizations.

INTERNATIONAL FREQUENCY REGISTRATION BOARD (IFRB)

The IFRB records all frequency assignments and furnishes advice to members and associate members with a view to operating the maximum practicable number of radio channels in those portions of the radio-frequency spectrum where harmful interference between stations is likely to occur. The IFRB is composed of five persons, each of a different nationality, elected by the administrative radio conference from a list of candidates nominated by ITU member states and territories. IFRB members serve not as representatives of countries or regions, but in their individual capacity as custodians of an international public trust. They are experts in the field of radio communications, with practical experience in the assignment and use of radio frequencies.

INTERNATIONAL CONSULTATIVE COMMITTEES

The ITU has two permanent consultative committees, whose function is to study and draw up recommendations on various problems in the field of telecommunications. The International Radio Consultative Committee (CCIR), in existence since the late 1920's, concerns itself with technical questions pertaining to radio communications and with operational problems arising out of technical considerations. The International Telegraph and Telephone Consultative Committee (CCITT) came into existence in 1957, replacing the separate telegraph and telephone consultative committees. Both the CCIR and the CCITT have their own secretariats and maintain laboratories.

At the head of each CCI is a director, elected by the plenary assembly of each CCI. The two ITU consultative committees have a very large membership that includes not only ITU member states and territories, but also international organizations, scientific and industrial organizations, and private agencies.

The consultative committees have considerable machinery of their own. They hold plenary assemblies, usually at four-year intervals. Programs of study are mapped and are carried out by specially constituted study groups. The work of the study groups is revised by the plenary assemblies of the consultative committees, which finally draw up and publish their own recommendations. These recommendations are not binding. The various governments, operating agencies, and private companies are free to follow or to ignore them. In practice, however, they readily comply with the recommended rules, since no system of international telecommunications is practicable without agreement on the technical means to be used. Many of these recommendations are implemented by ITU administrative conferences to form a part of ITU Regulations.

GENERAL SECRETARIAT AND HEADQUARTERS OF THE ITU

The General Secretariat works out of ITU headquarters in the Place des Nations, Geneva. It handles the arrangements of ITU conferences and meetings and maintains liaison with member states and territories and with the UN, the specialized agencies, and other international organizations. It also carries out the ITU's extensive publication program. It is headed by the Secretary-General, elected by the Plenipotentiary Conference. The present secretary-general is M. Mili of Tunisia, who succeeded M. B. Sarwate of India. Dr. Sarwate was elected by the Montreux Plenipotentiary Conference in 1965 and followed Gerald C. Gross of the United States as secretary-general. The present deputy secretary-general is Richard E. Butler of Australia. M. Mili was his immediate predecessor.

6 BUDGET

The ordinary expenses of the ITU are borne by all its members and associate members. Contributions roughly reflect the scale of telecommunications facilities maintained in the various member states and territories. Private operating agencies and international organizations contribute to the cost of the conferences and meetings in which they participate.

The total ITU budget came to 35,432,800 Swiss francs for 1971.

7 ACTIVITIES

In accordance with its basic objectives, the ITU functions in five ways: (1) It allocates radio frequencies to different types of radio-communication services and it registers the assignment of frequencies to particular stations so as to achieve an orderly use of the radio-frequency spectrum and avoid as far as possible interference between radio stations in different countries. (2) It seeks to establish the lowest rates for telecommunication services that are consistent with efficient service and sound financial administration. (3) It promotes measures for ensuring the safety of life through the coordination of telecommunication services, a function of particular interest to maritime countries. (4) It carries out studies, makes recommendations, and collects and publishes information for the benefit of all its members. (5) It provides technical assistance to developing countries for the expansion of telecommunications and the training of personnel.

A. FREQUENCY ALLOCATION AND RECORDING OF FREQUENCY ASSIGNMENTS, RADIO REGULATIONS

Although the range of frequencies (or wavelengths) used in wireless telecommunications is very great, it is, nevertheless, limited; and international traffic rules have become increasingly necessary to regulate the vast amount of broadcasting activity that now goes on all over the world. By the time the Plenipotentiary Conference met in Atlantic City in 1947, it was clear that the radio regulations drawn up by the conference at Cairo in 1938 were out of date. An administrative radio conference met concurrently with the Plenipotentiary Conference to revise these regulations, and subsequent conferences have revised them further to keep pace with the rapid technological advances in this field.

The 1947 Radio Conference prepared a new worldwide frequency allocation table covering frequencies from 10 kilohertz (KHz) up to the ultrashortwave channels ending at 10.5 gigahertz (GHz). The table adopted in 1938 extended only to 200 megahertz (MHz). Specific frequency bands were allocated to various essential radio services, such as maritime, air, coastal, and meteorological services. It was anticipated that operating frequencies would be assigned to individual broadcasting stations through the world through a series of special international and regional conferences. Unforeseen difficulties arose, however, and in 1951 an extraordinary administrative radio conference was convened in Geneva to review the situation. The conference drew up recommendations for the assignment of frequencies to particular broadcasting stations, and by 1958 the great majority of radio operations in member countries and territories had been adjusted to conform to these guidelines. Accordingly, the administrative radio conference meeting in 1959 in Geneva decided that the entire table of frequency allocations, as adopted in 1947, would come into force on 1 May 1961, together with all other parts of the revised radio regulations. Among others these include provisions relating to the operation of the maritime and aeronautical services, radio navigation, space services, and radio astronomy.

In accordance with the radio regulations, the IFRB maintains a Master International Frequency Register based on frequency assignments, including assignments for space communications and radioastronomy, reported to it by various countries and territories. This register, the contents of which are published as the *International Frequency List*, a service document of the ITU, includes particulars of about 370,000 frequency assignments to radio stations of various types. Summaries of monitoring information supplied by member countries are compiled by the IFRB from reports received from frequency monitoring centers in various parts of the world and are published monthly for the information of all frequency users.

The IFRB also does the technical planning for radio conferences and about every two years organizes seminars on the management of the radio-frequency spectrum. Over 70 officials from member countries participated in the 1968 seminar.

The radio regulations, as revised by the Geneva Radio Conference in 1959, were signed by 83 countries. They were partially revised in 1963 by a space radio conference, in 1966 by an aeronautical radio conference, and in 1967 by a maritime radio conference.

B. TELEGRAPH AND TELEPHONE REGULATIONS

The ITU, through its Administrative Telephone and Telegraph Conference, draws up regulations prescribing certain uniform practices and procedures for telephone and telegraph communications. A conference held in Geneva in November 1958 adopted a set of revised regulations that came into force on 1 January 1960. The telephone regulations, which were formerly applicable only to Europe, were made worldwide in scope. The revised telegraph regulations provide for a special telegraph rate for prisoners of war and for civilians interned in wartime. The telegraph regulations were signed by 64 countries and the telephone regulations by 61.

C. TELECOMMUNICATIONS IN SPACE

As early as 1957, the ITU noted in its annual report to the UN that with the advent of artificial satellites new international problems had been raised, especially in connection with radio frequencies, to which the ITU would have to give its attention.

An extraordinary conference was convened by the ITU in October and November 1963 in Geneva to make proposals for the regulation of telecommunications in space. This conference allocated over 6,000 megahertz (about 15% of the entire radio frequency spectrum) to outer space purposes and adopted a number of important resolutions and recommendations. The next World Space Telecommunications Conference will open in Geneva on 7 June 1971 and last for six weeks. A progress report is issued annually on the action taken by the ITU in the field of outer space.

D. STUDY AND EXCHANGE OF INFORMATION

A very large part of the regular activities of the ITU consists of continuous study of technical and administrative problems pertaining to telecommunications. In this respect, the ITU functions as an international university of telecommunications. Study groups are composed of experts from governmental telecommunication administrations, recognized private operating agencies, and national scientific and industrial organizations. The majority of them work under the aegis of the two international consultative committees, the CCIR and the CCITT.

Each year there are numerous meetings of study groups, subgroups, and working parties of the CCITT to discuss telegraph and telephone engineering, operating, and tariff problems. The plenary assemblies of the consultative committees review the findings of the study groups and draw up recommendations based on their inquiries. Joint meetings of the CCIR and the CCITT discuss problems of concern to both committees, such as long distance television transmission. Both also cooperate in the "Plan" committee, which, in conjunction with regional subcommittees, assembles data for the planning of international telecommunication networks. The CCIR is devoting attention to working out technical standards for all aspects of space telecommunications, in preparation for the World Space Telecommunications Conference. These technical standards involve aspects of microwave relay by way of satellites, positioning of satellites in the geostationary orbit, maritime and aeronautical communications by satellites, and possible uses of satellites for sound and television broadcasting.

One of the most important duties of the ITU Headquarters is to collect and collate essential telecommunications data and to edit and publish the numerous documents essential for the day-to-day operation of the various telephone, telegraph, and broadcasting systems of the world. The 1971 publications budget amounted to 3,694,000 Swiss francs. Among the documents regularly issued by the ITU are the *International Frequency List,* the quarterly *High Frequency Broadcasting Schedules,* yearly radio statistics, lists of coast, ship, and fixed stations, codes and abbreviations in general use, lists of radiolocation stations, an alphabetical list of call signs, summaries of international monitoring information, the *Telecommunication Journal,* and similar publications, all generally issued in separate English, French, and Spanish editions.

E. TECHNICAL ASSISTANCE

The ITU participates in both the Technical Assistance and Special Fund sectors of the United Nations Development Program (UNDP), providing assistance in any area of telecommunications contributing to economic and social progress in the developing countries. Among other things, ITU may provide experts to help a country improve its local telephone systems, set up a national television network, or analyze its future communications requirements. Besides assigning experts, the ITU conducts special seminars in the developing countries, awards fellowships, and provides some training and demonstration equipment. (Govern-ments desiring technical assistance relating to any aspects of telecommunications should address their requests to UNDP. Advice may be obtained from ITU headquarters in Geneva.)

Under the technical assistance program, ITU incurred obligations amounting to $1,468,166 for assistance to 69 countries in 1969. This included the services of 79 international experts, 219 fellowships, and $33,790 worth of training and demonstration equipment.

In 1969 the ITU was acting as the executing agency for 23 Special Fund telecommunications projects. Of these, 21 were projects to establish or expand telecommunication training centers in developing areas. Total expenditure incurred in 1969 under this component was $2,871,225. In 1969, 117 international experts were assigned to these special fund projects, 62 fellowships were dealt with, and equipment to the value of $619,833 was ordered.

Other ITU technical assistance in 1969 included the organization of 4 seminars and the provision of 19 experts under the "funds-in-trust" arrangements.

8 BIBLIOGRAPHY

Journal UIT: Journal des Télécommunications / Telecommunication Journal / Boletin de Telecomunicaciones. Monthly. Edited in three languages. One year, $5.79 for one language edition, $11.58 for two, and $17.37 for three separate language editions; single copy $0.58.

Publications of the General Secretariat of the International Telecommunication Union. Quarterly. Comprehensive list of all technical ITU publications. Free.

UNIVERSAL POSTAL UNION (UPU)

1 BACKGROUND: Every year some six billion pieces of mail cross international boundaries with a minimum of formalities and are safely delivered to their destinations. The orderly and economical movement of the international mail is made possible by the Constitution and Convention of the Universal Postal Union, the basic legislation under which the UPU operates. Under the Constitution, UPU countries, embracing almost the entire world, are united into a single postal territory.

2 CREATION

Although generally taken for granted, present-day postal service is of relatively recent origin. The use of postage stamps for pre-payment of postage was not introduced until 1840, when the UK established a unified internal postage charge, the famous penny rate, to be paid by the sender of a letter regardless of the distance which it had to travel. Until that year, the postal fee based on distance was often very high and was not paid by the sender but by the addressee. If the addressee could not pay, the letter was returned. Gradually, other countries introduced stamps and their use spread to international mail. In 1863 on the initiative of the US, representatives of 15 postal administrations met in Paris to consider the problem of standardizing international postal practices.

The decisive development came 11 years later with the meeting of the first international postal Congress at Berne in 1874 at the suggestion of the North German government. The Berne Congress was attended by delegates from 22 different countries: 18 Continental countries, including Russia, the UK, Egypt, Turkey, and the US. Congress adopted a treaty concerning the establishment of a General Postal Union—commonly known as the Berne Treaty—signed 9 October 1874. This was the forerunner of the series of multilateral Universal Postal Union conventions and came into force the following year, when the Union was formally established to administer its operative regulations.

The 1874 Convention provided for subsequent postal congresses to revise the Convention in the light of economic and technical developments. The second Postal Congress, held in Paris in 1878, changed the name of the General Postal Union to the Universal Postal Union (UPU). Four more congresses were held prior to World War I: Lisbon 1885; Vienna 1891; Washington D.C. 1897; Rome 1906; and 5 between the wars: Madrid 1920; Stockholm 1924; London 1929; Cairo 1934; and Buenos Aires 1939. The first post-World War II Congress met in Paris in 1947 and arranged for the UPU to be recognized as a specialized agency of the United Nations family in 1948. Other congresses met at Brussels 1952; Ottawa 1957; Vienna 1964; and Tokyo 1969. The legislation adopted at Tokyo will come into force on 1 July 1971. The centennial (17th) Universal Postal Congress is scheduled to be held in Switzerland in 1974.

3 PURPOSES

The basic objective of the Union as stated in the 1874 Convention has been reiterated in all successive revisions and embodied in the new Constitution adopted at Vienna in 1964: "The countries adopting this Constitution comprise, under the title of the Universal Postal Union, a single postal territory for the reciprocal exchange of letter-post items." The 1924 Congress added: "It is also the object of the Postal Union to secure the organization and improvement of the various international postal services" and the 1947 Congress added another clause: "and to promote the development of international collaboration in this sphere."

In recognition of the Union's continued interest and newly assumed responsibilities in the field of development aid, the Congress of Vienna in 1964 enlarged UPU's goals to include the provision of postal technical assistance to member states.

Under the single territory principle all the Union's member countries are bound by the Constitution and Convention to observe certain fundamental rules pertaining to ordinary mail. Ordinary mail (the letter post) under the Tokyo Convention includes letters, postcards, printed papers, small packets and literature for the blind such as books in Braille. Although the Convention lays down basic postage rates for ordinary mail sent to addresses in UPU territory, variations are permitted within generous limits. Postal authorities of all member states are pledged to handle all mail with equal care, regardless of its origin and destination, and to expedite mail originating in other UPU countries on a level comparable to the best means of conveyance used for their own mail. In principle, foreign mail is delivered to destination without charge to the country where it was posted and each country retains the postage collected on international mail. As of 1 July 1971, however, where there will be a considerable imbalance between mail sent and received, the postal administration of the country receiving the larger quantity will be authorized to ask for repayment at standard rates to offset its excess costs. Each country reimburses intermediary countries through which its mail passes in transit.

Freedom of transit—the basic principle of the Union—is guaranteed throughout UPU territory. Specific regulations provide for the dispatch of mail and returning undeliverable mail to the sender. Certain articles, such as opium and other drugs and inflammable or explosive agents are excluded from the international mails.

Eight optional postal agreements supplement the Convention. They cover parcel mail, insured letters and parcels containing valuable articles, money orders, giro transfer accounts, cash on delivery, savings bank service, subscriptions to periodicals, and settlement of personal debts.

For technical assistance and postal studies—see below: 7 E and F.

4 MEMBERSHIP

The original treaty allowed "overseas" countries to be admitted to the Union subject to the agreement of administrations having postal relations with them. The 1878 Congress decreed, however, that any country could accede directly to the Union merely by unilateral declaration. This system was revised by the Paris Congress of 1947, which ruled that applications had to be sent to the Swiss government. Approval is then required by at least two-thirds of the full membership. At the 1964 Vienna Congress, it was also decided that any member nation of the United Nations could accede directly to the UPU by a formal declaration addressed to the Swiss government.

Dependent territories were granted collective membership by a special postal conference held in Berne in 1876.

Membership in the UPU as of 1 August 1970 had reached 143, including 136 independent states (125 of them members of the UN) and 7 collective members of dependent territories:

Afghanistan	Guyana	Peru
Albania	Haiti	Philippines
Algeria	Honduras	Poland
Argentina	Hungary	Portugal
Australia	Iceland	Portuguese Provinces in
Austria	India	East Africa, Asia,
Barbados	Indonesia	and Oceania
Belgium	Iran	Portuguese Provinces in
Bhutan	Iraq	West Africa
Bolivia	Ireland	Qatar
Botswana	Israel	Romania
Brazil	Italy	Rwanda
Bulgaria	Ivory Coast	San Marino
Burma	Jamaica	Sa´udi Arabia
Burundi	Japan	Senegal
Byelorussia	Jordan	Sierra Leone
Cambodia	Kenya	Singapore
Cameroon	Korea, South	Somalia
Canada	Kuwait	South Africa
Central African	Laos	Southern Yemen
Republic	Lebanon	Spain
Ceylon	Lesotho	Spanish Territory in
Chad	Liberia	Africa
Chile	Libya	Sudan
China (Taiwan)	Liechtenstein	Swaziland
Colombia	Luxembourg	Sweden
Congo (Brazzaville)	Madagascar	Switzerland
Congo (Kinshasa)	Malawi	Syria
Costa Rica	Malaysia	Tanzania
Cuba	Maldives	Thailand
Cyprus	Mali	Togo
Czechoslovakia	Malta	Trinidad and Tobago
Dahomey	Mauritania	Tunisia
Denmark	Mauritius	Turkey
Dominican Republic	Mexico	Uganda
Ecuador	Monaco	Ukraine
El Salvador	Mongolia	USSR
Equatorial Guinea	Morocco	UAR
Ethiopia	Nauru	UK and Northern
Finland	Nepal	Ireland
France and French	Netherlands	UK Overseas
Overseas	Netherlands Antilles	Territories
Departments	and Surinam	Upper Volta
French Overseas	New Zealand	US
Territories	Nicaragua	US Territories
Gabon	Niger	Uruguay
Germany, West	Nigeria	Vatican
Ghana	Norway	Venezuela
Greece	Pakistan	Viet-Nam, South
Guatemala	Panama	Yemen
Guinea	Paraguay	Yugoslavia
		Zambia

RESTRICTED POSTAL UNIONS
Members of the UPU may participate in the various Restricted Unions—the African Postal Union, the African and Malagasy Postal and Telecommunications Union, the Arab Postal Union, the Asian-Oceanic Postal Union, the European Conference of Postal Telecommunications Administrations, the Postal Union of the Americas and Spain, and the Nordic Postal Union. These Unions may not prescribe rates higher than those of the UPU nor may they lay down provisions less favorable to the public than those of the UPU.

5 STRUCTURE
The organs of the UPU are the Universal Postal Congress, the Executive Council, the Consultative Council for Postal Studies, and the International Bureau.

THE UNIVERSAL POSTAL CONGRESS
The Congress meets generally at 5-year intervals to review the Acts of the Union. Special sessions may be called at the request of two-thirds of the Union's membership. UPU members are each entitled to one vote at sessions of the Congress.

In reviewing UPU legislation, Congress exercises quasi-legislative functions, and before a session of the Congress is convened member-states are instructed to give their delegates full power to discuss, negotiate, and conclude UPU legislation. Each Congress scrutinizes each article of the Universal Postal Convention then in force, considers all proposed amendments, and finally adopts a new Convention and agreements. Legislation supersedes rather than augments previous provisions. The Acts of Tokyo 1969 will come into force on 1 July 1971 and supersede on that date the Acts of Vienna 1964. The Constitution of the UPU was first adopted at Vienna in 1964; it does not have to be renewed by each Congress, but can be modified.

The fundamental principles of the 1874 Berne Convention have been maintained in all subsequent legislation, but every Congress has made changes in the system to meet changing conditions. Once a country has ratified the Constitution and the Acts as revised by the Congress, it is obligated to follow the new postal rules and agreements promulgated by the Convention, even if special national legislation is required.

Congress may decide on constitutional matters if the need arises. With respect to UPU's internal finances, Congress determines the ceiling for expenditure over the coming 5-year period. Congress reviews questions concerning technical collaboration, including aspects such as the general administration of projects, and is responsible for drawing up the program of the Consultative Council for Postal Studies.

THE EXECUTIVE COUNCIL
The Executive Council was created under the title Executive and Liaison Committee by the 1947 Congress to ensure the continuity of UPU activities during the long intervals between postal congresses. It is composed of 31 UPU members, elected by the Postal Congress on the basis of equitable geographical distribution. Only 15 of its members may be reelected by each Congress, and none may be elected by 3 congresses in succession. A slow rotation of membership is thus assured.

The Executive Council maintains the closest work relations with UPU members in order to improve international postal service; to study various postal questions; and, in general, to carry out the tasks entrusted to it by the Postal Congress. The Council is also responsible for general supervision of International Bureau activities especially as regards staff, finance, budget as well as for supervision of the technical assistance program. It appoints the Director-General of the UPU's International Bureau (its permanent secretariat) and approves the appointment of the Bureau's high officials.

THE CONSULTATIVE COUNCIL FOR POSTAL STUDIES
The UPU has been concerned that postal systems in general should benefit from technical studies that have been carried out under its auspices. To deal more efficiently with research relating to technical, operational, and economic aspects of the postal ser-

vice, the 1957 Ottawa Congress set up the Consultative Committee for Postal Studies. The Committee worked through a Management Council of 26 members meeting yearly. The 1969 Tokyo Congress replaced this arrangement with a 30-member Consultative Council for Postal Studies. This organ meets once yearly under the chairmanship of Belgium. Six standing committees deal with technical problems, use of modern methods and techniques in the postal service, modernization of postal operations in new nations, development of human resources (in particular, training and cost effectiveness of staff), and economic and other problems relating to postal operations.

THE INTERNATIONAL BUREAU OF THE UPU

The International Bureau, officially known as Bureau international de l'Union postale universelle, was founded in 1875 and serves as the UPU's permanent secretariat. It is located in Berne, Switzerland. The Bureau serves as a liaison organ for the postal administrations of UPU member countries and as an information and consultation center for them. It acts as a clearinghouse for the settlement of accounts relating to international postal service, such as transit charges and international reply coupons. The Bureau provides the secretariat for UPU meetings, publishes official records of meetings, postal handbooks, and other information on international postal matters. The Bureau also plays an important role in the organization and administration of technical assistance (see 7 F below).

6 BUDGET

The Postal Congress sets a ceiling for the ordinary annual expenditure of the UPU. For the years 1970 through 1975 the Tokyo Congress set a basic ceiling of 7 million Swiss francs for 1970, allowing for a maximum annual increase of 5% calculated on the previous year's total. UPU's expenses are shared by all members. They are assessed contributions of 1, 3, 5, 10, 15, 20, or 25 units each; in 1969 one unit amounted to 7760 Swiss francs or about $1800. In 1969, 57 countries contributed the minimum, one unit each; and 17 countries contributed the maximum, 25 units each. The maximum contribution was 194,000 Swiss francs, or about $45,000. UPU's regulations provide that Swiss authorities shall supervise the expenditure of the International Bureau and advance the funds it requires against later collections.

In 1969 the ordinary operating expenditures of the UPU totaled 6,164,800 Swiss francs, or $1,427,000, and extraordinary expenditures, including conferences and special work, totaled 2,693,400 Swiss francs ($623,500), for a total budget of 8,858,200 Swiss francs ($2,050,500). This was balanced by contributions from members totaling 7,356,500 Swiss francs ($1,702,900) and income from the sale of documents and other sources totaling 1,501,700 Swiss francs ($347,600).

7 ACTIVITIES

A. CLEARING ACCOUNTS FOR INTERNATIONAL SERVICES

In this, as in certain other respects, the UPU acts as a central office for the international postal traffic carried on by its members. In principle, UPU member states retain the revenue they derive from the sale of postage stamps and from other fees and charges for foreign-bound mail, but must reimburse one another for the transportation of foreign mail in intermediate transit. At the end of each year the Bureau draws up an annual general clearing account for transit charges, stating the balances due. For 1969, 93 postal administrations settled their transit charges through the Bureau's clearing account, 26 paying and 67 receiving balances.

The Bureau maintains a special clearing account for the international reply coupons that it supplies to facilitate payment of international correspondence. More than 100 countries now sell these coupons and all countries must accept them as payment for postage.

B. INFORMATION SERVICES

The UPU acts as an international clearinghouse for postal information. At the request of postal administrations, the International Bureau circulates inquiries concerning the operation of the various postal systems and makes the replies available to all UPU members. Inquiries may concern domestic as well as international postal practices and cover subjects as diverse as the texts of propaganda permitted on letters and packages, mobile post offices on motorboats, and national regulations covering the dispatch of radioactive substances. The following are examples of the subjects on which inquiries have been circulated in recent years: Acceptance of pressurized containers of butane or other gases (Australia); charge for collection of sums on behalf of air carriers (Iraq); late posting of air mail (South Africa); sale of official postage stamps to the public (Argentina); and handling of unpaid or underpaid air-mail correspondence (Kuwait).

The International Bureau publishes a number of useful and essential international postal handbooks, including the following: *Statistical data relating to the postal services (internal and international)*; *List of prohibited articles* (i.e., prohibited from the mails); *International list of post offices*; *List of kilometric distances*; and *List of shipping lines*. The Consultative Council for Postal Studies has prepared a *Multilingual Vocabulary of the International Postal Service*, an essential tool designed to ensure that terms used by different national postal services convey the identical meaning.

The Bureau also prepares an annotated edition of UPU legislation, which includes discussion of principles, opinions, decisions, and practices underlying current international postal procedures and the present organization of the Union. The *Genèse des Actes de l'UPU* is a compendium of analytic data on the evolution of UPU's legislative texts from 1874 to 1964. The Bureau publishes a monthly magazine, "Union Postale," in seven languages.

C. ARBITRATION AND INTERPRETATION OF INTERNATIONAL POSTAL RULES

If a difference of opinion on the interpretation of UPU legislation between two or more postal administrations cannot be resolved by direct negotiations, the matter is settled by arbitration. The countries concerned may also designate a single arbitrator, such as the International Bureau of the UPU.

D. REVISION OF RULES GOVERNING INTERNATIONAL SERVICES

The UPU periodically revises its Detailed Regulations governing international services. Amongst the 600-odd proposals adopted by the 1969 Tokyo Congress, the following illustrate the impact of UPU decisions upon the world's postal services:

Forms used in the international postal service are to be adapted to the use of office machines but without making it more difficult to fill out these forms by hand.

The tariff structure of the letter post is to be considerably simplified by reducing the number of categories of items and introducing progressive weight steps with retrogressive rates.

Since the Union's inception, administrations of origin have retained the proceeds of charges on letter-post items and administrations of destination have not been paid for the terminal services of conveying, sorting, and delivering incoming international mail. Countries that claim to receive more mail than they send are now to be compensated with a payment of 50 gold centimes (about 16 US cents) per kilogram of mail received over and above the weight of mail sent.

For the first time, sea and land rates for postal transit of parcels are to be determined on an objective basis and a direct correlation with the charges applicable to letter mail in transit is to be established.

E. TECHNICAL COLLABORATION AND TRAINING

For many years a traditional form of direct technical assistance consisting largely of exchange of visits of postal officials, of information, and of experience was practiced within the UPU and still exists on a bilateral basis. In 1963, however, the UPU, acting in its capacity as the UN agency specialized in the postal field, undertook to participate fully in the United Nations Development Program (UNDP). In this way the UPU now aids in the promotion of efficient postal services among developing nations. This task is particularly important in relationship to the economic, social, and cultural advancement of all nations, a goal that cannot be attained without a reliable system of basic communications of which the post is one of the cornerstones. UPU has consequently moved positively to cooperate with UNDP in the wider field of aid represented, for example, by the UN's Second Development Decade. In this regard four targets have been set for the evaluation of postal progress in the 1970's:

1) One post office to serve, on the average, either an area of 20–40 sq. km or 3,000 to 6,000 people.

2) Next day delivery of priority items within a radius of 500 km.

3) A progressive increase in the percentage of parcels forwarded by air in the international service, with a goal of 30% of the total.

4) Widespread introduction of financial services with the aim of increasing the ratio between the funds of the postal financial services (savings bank, giro and savings certificates) and GDP by 5%–10%.

Since 1963 postal projects have included some 130 missions carried out by UPU experts and 550 fellowships benefiting some 80 countries at a cost of some 3 million dollars.

Because of the rapid rate of development in the demand for postal services, and the general lack of qualified staff, special emphasis has been placed on the training of staff at all levels. A feature in this connection has been the organization of seminars and the development of training facilities. These activities have allowed a special concentration of the resources and abilities available from UNDP, postal administrations, and the International Bureau. During 1969, 14 experts were carrying out tasks under UNDP technical assistance schemes and 104 scholarships were awarded.

Important projects have included the reorganization of the Higher Arab Postal Institute at Damascus, several postal service modernization projects in the Caribbean area and in Mexico, the setting up of a national philatelic service in Nigeria, and numerous seminars for higher and middle grade staff.

F. POSTAL STUDIES

The 1969 Tokyo Postal Congress assigned the Consultative Council some 50 topics for consideration. Technical studies include such questions as the mechanization and automation of sorting mail and mechanical equipment of a large sorting office. Studies in the use of modern techniques in the postal service cover topics such as postal market research and automatic stamp vending machines. Problems relating to the modernization of operations in developing countries are receiving special attention.

8 BIBLIOGRAPHY

Report on the work of the Union. Résumé and general review of UPU activities. Annual. Two language editions: French, $2.10; English, $4.20.

Union postale. Monthly. Parallel text in Arabic, Chinese, English, French, German, Russian, and Spanish. Contains articles on postal services, information on UPU activities, and, in the French section, an illustrated feature listing new postage stamps. One year $2.25; single copies, $0.20.

The Universal Postal Union. Text in 4 languages: Arabic, English, French, and Spanish. A brief outline of UPU functions. Folder. Free in single copies.

Collection of Postal Studies. A series of publications concerning topics studied by the Consultative Council for Postal Studies. Prices on application.

Liste des publications du Bureau international. French. Free.

INTER-GOVERNMENTAL MARITIME CONSULTATIVE ORGANIZATION (IMCO)

1 BACKGROUND : The seven seas, accounting for about two-thirds of our planet's surface, are the only truly international part of our globe. Except for a marginal belt a very few miles wide, touching on the shores of countries, the greater part of the world's oceans and maritime resources are the common property of all nations. Since ancient times, however, "freedom of the seas" has too often been a theoretical ideal rather than a reality. In each historic era, the great maritime powers tended to use their naval might to dominate the sea. Some of those powers, while serving their own interests, served the world as a whole, as in the great explorations of unknown continents. Many sought to use the waters for purely national interests, particularly in matters affecting straits and other narrow waterways. Private shipping interests, often supported by their national governments, have been even more competitive, and international co-operation in maritime matters has been very limited.

The need for an international organization to develop and coordinate international maritime co-operation was best expressed by President Wilson, who called for "universal association of the nations to maintain the inviolate security of the highway of the seas for the common and unhindered use of all the nations of the world." However, it was not until after the creation of the United Nations that such an organization came into being.

2 CREATION

IMCO is the youngest of the specialized agencies related to the UN. Its Convention was drawn up in 1948 by the UN Maritime Conference, which met in Geneva from 19 February through 6 March. It was ten years, however, before the Convention came into effect. The conference decided that IMCO's success depended on participation by most of the nations with large merchant navies and specified that the organization would come into being only when 21 states, including 7 having at least 1 million gross tons of shipping each, had become parties to the Convention. On 17 March 1958, Japan became the 21st state, and the 8th with at least 1 million gross tons of shipping, to accept the Convention, and the Convention came into effect on that day. A committee of 12 IMCO member states carried out preparations for the first IMCO Assembly, which met in London in January 1959. The relationship of IMCO to the UN as a specialized agency was approved by the UN General Assembly on 18 November 1958 and by the IMCO Assembly on 13 January 1959.

During the long interval between the 1948 Maritime Conference and the date the IMCO Convention came into force, some of the functions to be undertaken by IMCO had been carried out by the UK and by the UN.

3 PURPOSES

The purposes of IMCO, as set forth in the Convention, are: (1) to promote cooperation among member governments engaged in international trade in solving technical problems of shipping; (2) to encourage general adoption of the highest practicable standards for the safety and efficiency of navigation; (3) to seek the removal by governments of discriminatory action and unnecessary restrictions on international shipping; and (4) to deal with unfair restrictive practices by shipping concerns.

4 MEMBERSHIP

Any state invited to the 1948 Maritime Conference or any member of the UN may become a member of IMCO by accepting the 1948 Convention. Any other state whose application is approved by two-thirds of the IMCO membership becomes a member by accepting the Convention. If an IMCO member responsible for the international relations of a territory (or group of territories) declares the Convention to be applicable to that territory, the territory may become an associate member of IMCO.

As of 15 June 1970 there were 72 IMCO members:

Algeria	Ivory Coast
Argentina	Japan
Australia	Korea, South
Barbados	Kuwait
Belgium	Lebanon
Brazil	Liberia
Bulgaria	Libya
Burma	Malagasy Republic
Cambodia	Maldives
Cameroon	Malta
Canada	Mauritania
China (Taiwan)	Mexico
Cuba	Morocco
Czechoslovakia	Netherlands
Denmark	New Zealand
Dominican Republic	Nigeria
Ecuador	Norway
Finland	Pakistan
France	Panama
Germany, West	Peru
Ghana	Philippines
Greece	Poland
Haiti	Romania
Honduras	Sa'udi Arabia
Hong Kong*	Senegal
Hungary	Singapore
Iceland	Spain
India	Sweden
Indonesia	Switzerland
Iran	Syria
Ireland	Trinidad and Tobago
Israel	Tunisia
Italy	Turkey

UAR   US
USSR   Uruguay
UK   Yugoslavia

*Associate Member

5 STRUCTURE

THE ASSEMBLY

The policy-making body of IMCO is the Assembly, which is composed of all IMCO members. The Assembly decides upon the work program, votes the budget to which all member states contribute, and approves the appointment of the secretary-general. The Assembly meets every two years.

THE COUNCIL

Between sessions of the Assembly, the Council performs all functions of the organization except that of recommending the adoption of maritime safety regulations, a prerogative of the Maritime Safety Committee. The Council also has an important policy-making role. Drafts of international instruments and formal recommendations must be approved by the Council before they can be submitted to the Assembly.

The Council is made up of 18 members elected by the Assembly on the following basis: 6 members representing states with the largest interest in providing international shipping services; 6 representing states with the largest interest in international seaborne trade; and 6 representing states, not elected under the foregoing categories, which have special interests in maritime transport or navigation and whose presence in the Council will ensure representation of the world's major geographic areas.

The Council meets as often as may be necessary, normally twice a year.

MARITIME SAFETY COMMITTEE

This committee, the third major body of IMCO, is made up of 16 members elected by the Assembly from those member states having an important interest in maritime safety. The IMCO Convention specifies that at least 8 of the 16 members are to be elected from among the 10 "largest shipowning nations"; 8 to be elected in such a manner that each of the major geographic areas (Africa, the Americas, Asia and Oceania, and Europe) is represented; and 4 to be elected from among those nations not otherwise represented in the committee. Members are elected for a term of four years, and are eligible for reelection.

The committee's field of work covers all technical matters relating to shipping (within the scope of IMCO) and includes the prevention of marine pollution. The committee also considers the construction, equipment, and manning of vessels from a safety standpoint; rules for preventing collisions and for handling dangerous cargoes; maritime safety procedures and requirements; hydrologic information, logbooks, and navigational records; marine casualty investigation; salvage and rescue; and any other matter directly affecting marine safety. In addition, the committee provides machinery for dealing with kindred matters that may be referred to it and for maintaining close relationship with other intergovernmental bodies concerned with transport and communications. It may appoint subcommittees, as required, to deal with specific problems.

The composition of the committee led to a constitutional controversy in the first IMCO Assembly, in 1959. Some delegates held that Liberia and Panama should have obtained mandatory seats on the committee since the gross tonnage registered under their flags placed them among the first eight "ship-owning nations." Other delegates questioned the existence of a genuine link between these states and the largely foreign-owned ships flying their flags. Thus, the so-called "flags of convenience" became an issue at the very beginning of the organization's existence. As it turned out, neither Liberia nor Panama was includ-ed in the committee named in 1959, but the Assembly agreed to refer the question to the International Court of Justice for an advisory opinion.

On 8 June 1960, that court, by a majority of nine to five, stated its advisory opinion that the "largest ship-owning nations" were those having the largest registered ship tonnage and that the question of a genuine link between a ship and a country was irrelevant. The second session of the IMCO Assembly (April 1961) accordingly dissolved its Maritime Safety Committee, although the measures taken by the committee since its formation in 1959 were confirmed. It elected a new committee that included Liberia but not Panama because the tonnage registered under its flag was not enough to rank Panama among the eight largest ship-owning nations. The membership of the Maritime Safety Committee now consists of Argentina, Canada, France, Germany (West), Greece, Italy, Japan, Netherlands, Norway, Pakistan, Spain, Sweden, UAR, USSR, UK, and US.

SECRETARIAT

The Secretariat consists of a secretary-general appointed by the Council with the approval of the Assembly; the Secretary of the Maritime Safety Committee; and an international staff. IMCO headquarters are at 104 Piccadilly, London.

The secretary-general is Colin Goad of the UK.

6 BUDGET

A budget of $2,706,994 was approved by the sixth IMCO Assembly for the period 1970/71.

7 ACTIVITIES

A. GENERAL ADVISORY AND CONSULTATIVE FUNCTIONS

IMCO's general functions, as stipulated in its Convention, are "consultative and advisory." It thus serves as a forum where members can consult and exchange information on maritime matters. It discusses and makes recommendations on any maritime question submitted by member states or by other bodies of the UN. IMCO advises other international bodies, including the UN itself, on maritime matters. Various intergovernmental agencies deal with specialized maritime matters, such as atomic propulsion for ships (IAEA), health at sea (WHO), maritime labor standards (ILO), meteorology (IMO), oceanography (UNESCO), and ship-to-ship and ship-to-shore communications (ITU). One of the functions of the IMCO is to help coordinate the work in these different fields.

IMCO is also authorized to convene international conferences when necessary and to draft international maritime conventions or agreements, which it may recommend to governments and to intergovernmental agencies.

B. ADMINISTRATION OF CONVENTIONS

IMCO is the depository for the following international instruments: the International Convention for the Safety of Life at Sea (1960); the International Regulations for Preventing Collisions at Sea (1948 and 1960); the International Convention for the Prevention of Pollution of the Sea by Oil (1954, as amended in 1962); the Convention on Facilitation of International Maritime Traffic (1965); the International Convention on Load Lines (1966); the International Convention on Tonnage Measurement of Ships (1969); the International Convention relating to Intervention on the High Seas in Cases of Oil Pollution Damage (1969); and the International Convention on Civil Liability for Oil Pollution Damage (1969).

C. CONFERENCES

IMCO has convened a number of diplomatic conferences: the international conference on the safety of life at sea, in 1960; on the prevention of pollution of the sea by oil, in 1962; on facilitation of travel and transport, in 1965; on load lines, in

1966; and on tonnage measurement of ships, in 1969. An international legal conference on marine pollution damage was also held in 1969. All these resulted in conventions that are administered by IMCO.

D. INTERNATIONAL STANDARDS AND STUDIES

IMCO's technical studies are handled initially by the various subcommittees of the Maritime Safety Committee. Work is in progress on the following: fire safety measures for tankers; construction and equipment of tankers so as to minimize the risk of collision or stranding and the resultant pollution; a code to cover design, construction, and equipment of bulk carriers of dangerous chemicals; stability standards for fishing vessels, and a code of safety for fishermen and fishing vessels; subdivision and stability standards for passenger ships; traffic separation schemes for areas of high density traffic; revision of the collision regulations; standards for lifesaving equipment for hydrofoils and air-cushion vehicles; a manual for search and rescue operations at sea; many aspects of marine pollution; and technical and safety aspects of container transport. Simplified formalities for tourists and transit passengers are being worked out by an ad hoc group formed in connection with the Convention on Facilitation of International Maritime Traffic. IMCO's legal committee has an extensive work program, in which high priority is given to the establishment of the International Compensation Fund for Oil Pollution Damage.

IMCO is an executing agency of the United Nations Development Program and provides technical assistance in the maritime field to developing countries.

8 BIBLIOGRAPHY

IMCO Annual Report. 1961-. Free.

IMCO Bulletin. Published at varying intervals. Free.

IMCO—What It Is, What It Does. Descriptive leaflet. Free.

IMCO information publications include *Charts of Prohibited Zones* (1967, $0.70); *IMCO Glossary of Maritime Technical Terms* (1963, $6.00); *Merchant Ship Position-Reporting Systems* (1965, $1.20); *Pollution of the Sea by Oil* (1964, $1.00); *International Legal Conference on Marine Pollution Damage,* 1969 (1970, $2.20).

WORLD METEOROLOGICAL ORGANIZATION (WMO)

1 BACKGROUND : The practical uses of meteorology are to instruct, advise, and warn mankind about the weather. Thus it can help prevent devastation caused by flood, drought, and storm; and it can assist the peoples of the world in best adapting their agriculture and industry to the climatic conditions under which they live.

For meteorology, international cooperation is indispensable. Expressed in the words of the late President John F. Kennedy:

". . . there is the atmosphere itself, the atmosphere in which we live and breathe and which makes life on this planet possible. Scientists have studied the atmosphere for many decades, but its problems continue to defy us. The reasons for our limited progress are obvious. Weather cannot be easily reproduced and observed in the laboratory. It must, therefore, be studied in all of its violence wherever it has its way. Here, new scientific tools have become available. With modern computers, rockets and satellites, the time is ripe to harness a variety of disciplines for a concerted attack.

. . . the atmospheric sciences require worldwide observation and, hence, international cooperation."

2 CREATION

The World Meteorological Organization has been in existence for only a few years, but behind it lies more than a century of international cooperation in the study of weather phenomena. Beginning in 1853, many of the world's leading maritime countries tried to establish an international tried system of collecting meteorological observations made by ships at sea.

The first international meteorological congress was held in Vienna in 1873; it led to the founding of the International Meteorological Organization (IMO), composed of directors of meteorological services of various countries and territories throughout the world. The IMO, while not formally an intergovernmental organization, carried out ambitious programs to perfect and standardize international meteorological practices.

As transport, communications, agriculture, and industry developed in the 20th century, they increasingly relied on meteorology. At the same time, meteorology itself relied to an increasing extent on advances in science and technology to perfect its methods of observing and predicting weather phenomena. Hence, the closest possible collaboration was called for between the IMO and other international organizations. By 1947, the need for cooperation with the UN family was recognized.

A conference of directors of national meteorological services met in Washington that year under the auspices of the IMO and adopted the World Meteorological Convention, establishing the World Meteorological Organization as a UN specialized agency. On 23 March 1950, after 30 signers had ratified or acceded to the Convention, it came into force. In 1951, final arrangements were completed for the transfer of the functions, activities, assets, and obligations of the IMO to the new organization. The first WMO congress opened in Paris on 19 March 1951. The headquarters of the WMO are in Geneva, Switzerland.

3 PURPOSES

As set forth in the World Meteorological Convention the purposes of the WMO are fivefold:

1. to facilitate worldwide cooperation in the establishment of networks of stations for meteorological observations or other geophysical observations related to meteorology, and to promote the establishment and maintenance of meteorological centers;

2. to promote the establishment and maintenance of systems for rapid exchange of weather information;

3. to promote standardization of meteorological observations and ensure the uniform publication of observations and statistics;

4. to further the application of meteorology to aviation, shipping, water problems, agriculture, and other human activities; and

5. to encourage research and training in meteorology and to assist in coordinating such research and training at the international level.

4 MEMBERSHIP

Membership in the WMO is not limited to sovereign states; it may include territories that maintain their own meteorological services. Membership is open to any of the 45 states and 30 territories attending the 1947 conference in Washington that signed the convention, or to any member of the UN with a meteorological service. Any of these automatically becomes a member of the WMO upon ratifying or acceding to the convention. Any other state, territory, group of territories, or UN trust territory maintaining its own meteorological services may become eligible for membership upon approval of two-thirds of the WMO membership. As of 1 March 1970, the WMO had 132 members including 122 states and 10 territories:

Afghanistan	Brazil
Albania	British Caribbean Territories
Algeria	Bulgaria
Argentina	Burma
Australia	Burundi
Austria	Byelorussia
Barbados	Cambodia
Belgium	Cameroon
Bolivia	Canada
Botswana	Central African Republic

Ceylon
Chad
Chile
China
Colombia
Congo (Brazzaville)
Congo (Kinshasa)
Costa Rica
Cuba
Cyprus
Czechoslovakia
Dahomey
Denmark
Dominican Republic
Ecuador
El Salvador
Ethiopia
Finland
France
French Polynesia
French Territory of the Afars
    and Issa
Gabon
Germany, West
Ghana
Greece
Guatemala
Guinea
Guyana
Haiti
Honduras
Hong Kong
Hungary
Iceland
India
Indonesia
Iran
Iraq
Ireland
Israel
Italy
Ivory Coast
Jamaica
Japan
Jordan
Kenya
Korea, South
Kuwait
Laos
Lebanon
Libya
Luxembourg
Madagascar
Malawi
Malaysia
Mali
Mauritania

Mauritius
Mexico
Mongolia
Morocco
Nepal
Netherlands
Netherlands Antilles
New Caledonia
New Zealand
Nicaragua
Niger
Nigeria
Norway
Pakistan
Panama
Paraguay
Peru
Philippines
Poland
Portugal
Portugese East Africa
Portugese West Africa
Rhodesia
Romania
Rwanda
Sa'udi Arabia
Senegal
Sierra Leone
Singapore
Somalia
South Africa
Southern Yemen
Spain
Sudan
Surinam
Sweden
Switzerland
Syria
Tanzania
Thailand
Togo
Trinidad and Tobago
Tunisia
Turkey
Uganda
Ukraine
USSR
UAR
UK
US
Upper Volta
Uruguay
Venezuela
Viet-Nam, South
Yugoslavia
Zambia

5 STRUCTURE

The WMO is headed by a President and three Vice-Presidents, elected by the World Meteorological Congress. The Congress is the supreme body of the organization, and is composed of the delegates representing its member states and territories. (According to the World Meteorological Convention, the principal delegate of each member "should be the director of its meteorological service.") The congress, which is required to meet at least once every four years, determines regulations on the constitution and function of the various WMO bodies, adopts regulations covering meteorological practices and procedures, determines general policies to carry out the purposes of the organization and related matters. It established the regional associations and technical commissions.

Each member of the congress has one vote. Election of individuals to serve in any capacity in the organization is by a simple majority of the votes cast: other questions are decided by two-thirds of the votes cast for and against. On certain subjects, only members that are states may vote. The executive committee has 24 members: the president and the 3 vice-presidents of the WMO; the presidents of the 6 regional associations; and 14 directors of meteorological services of its members selected by the congress. Meeting at least once a year, the committee carries out the activities of the organization and the decisions of the congress. Its own decisions are reached by a two-thirds majority.

There are six regional associations: one each for Africa, Asia, South America, North and Central America, the Southwest Pacific, and Europe. The regional associations are composed of the WMO members whose meteorological networks lie in or extend into the respective regions. They meet when necessary and examine from a regional point of view all questions referred to them by the executive committee. Each association has the responsibility of coordinating meteorological activity and promoting the execution of WMO resolutions within its region.

The technical commissions are composed of experts in meteorology. They study various meteorological problems and make recommendations to the Executive Committee and congress, which are then submitted to the executive committee and the congress for approval. The WMO has established eight of these commissions: for (1) agricultural meteorology; (2) maritime meteorology; (3) aeronautical meteorology; (4) synoptic meteorology; (5) atmospheric sciences; (6) climatology; (7) instruments and methods of observation; (8) hydrometeorology.

The secretariat, located in Geneva, completes the structure of the WMO. Its staff, under the direction of a secretary-general, undertakes studies, prepares publications, acts as secretariat during meetings of the various WMO bodies, and provides liaison between the various meteorological services of the world.

The first president of the WMO was F. W. Reichelderfer (US), who was succeeded in 1955 by A. Viaut (France). In 1963, A. Nyberg (Sweden) was elected president. The first secretary-general was Gustave Swoboda (Switzerland), succeeded in 1955 by D. A. Davies (UK).

6 BUDGET

Contributions to the WMO regular budget are apportioned among its members according to assessments determined by the congress. The estimates for 1970 approved by the 21st session of the executive committee amounted to US$ 3,418,216 (gross $ 3,803,224). In addition, budget estimates of $ 640,200 have been established for 1970 for the technical cooperation department of the secretariat. Further it is expected that expenditure on various extrabudgetary programs listed below will amount to approximately $ 8,200,000 (as they did in 1969), thus bringing the total expenditure of WMO to about $ 12,000,000. The extrabudgetary programs mentioned above include: the UNDP, Funds-in-Trust Programs, the WMO New Development Fund, the WMO Voluntary Assistance Program, the WMO Voluntary Contributions Account and the equipment and services provided under the WMO Voluntary Assistance Program.

7 ACTIVITIES
ACTIVITIES—WMO PROGRAMS

The program of scientific and technical activities of WMO authorized by the fifth congress (1967) falls into the following 4 broad categories: the World Weather Watch, the WMO research program, the WMO program on the interaction of man and his environment, and the WMO technical cooperation program.

WORLD WEATHER WATCH

WMO coordinates the development of networks of stations, with specified observational programs, to permit members to fulfill their responsibilities in the application of meteorology. At regular intervals, throughout the 24 hours of the day, weather stations the world over make meteorological observations at exactly the same time. The methods and practices are based on agreed decisions and are practically uniform everywhere. Every day, about 8,000 land stations, 3,000 transport and reconnaissance aircraft, and 4,000 ships make 100,000 observations for the surface of the earth and 10,000 observations relating to the upper air. Observations become more numerous from year to year as new stations are brought into service. International rules govern this work.

Every year, millions of observations of the surface and upper air, as well as forecasts, analyses, and warnings are transmitted by radio and other telecommunication links throughout the world. The exchange of weather reports is an important WMO responsibility. The information is transmitted in a series of internationally agreed figure-code groups that ensure its rapid and efficient exchange and its comprehension in all countries, regardless of language difference. The transmission schedules, their contents, times and frequencies of operation are controlled by WMO regulations. For the benefit of meteorological services, airlines and ships, WMO issues up-to-date information.

In view of the progress made in meteorology through the use of satellites, telecommunications for exchange of weather reports, and computers for weather analysis and forecasting, the Fourth World Meteorological Congress decided, in 1963, that there was urgent need for planning by WMO of a World Weather Watch. The secretary general presented a plan which was approved by the fifth congress in April, 1967. The plan outlines the location and functions of world and regional centers. These centers are to process observational data, weather analyses, and forecasts with computers and make the information available to national services. World centers have been established in Washington, Moscow, and Melbourne. Regional Centers are at 21 other locations. *The general characteristics of the global communications networks* required for the timely and coordinated collection and dissemination of weather data and of the processed information. This is based on a system in which every national service disseminates a definite part of the information it has collected and, in its turn, receives the global information it needs.

The basic engineering principles in the design of a global communication network have been established, particular emphasis being placed on the increased application of modern high-speed communications technology, including the potential of communications satellites in meteorological communications. Initial implementation of the high-speed main trunk circuit of the global telecommunication system is to take place in January 1971.

In addition to methods generally used in observing atmosphere (such as land and ship stations, radiosondes, and aircraft reports), the use of meteorological satellites, rockets, and horizontal sounding balloons is also envisaged. The present observational system is inadequate to meet *current* requirements; it will be necessary to increase the program at existing stations and to set up additional stations to satisfy the urgent need for more data. Also important is the making of more observations in ocean areas through the use of automatic weather stations and automated techniques for improving observational coverage. More than 80 detailed surveys and studies are being undertaken on the three basic components of World Weather Watch: the Global Observation System, the Global Telecommunications System, and the Global Data Processing System.

The approved plan of World Weather Watch includes the detailed design for the global observational, communications, and data-processing systems. Fifth congress also approved a program of research comprising further studies and investigations of new and promising techniques to ensure that by the end of the period, the next congress will be able to decide whether these techniques should be incorporated in the revised world system for the following four-year period. This principle of anticipating change in the world weather system is to be a continuing policy of WMO.

The World Weather Watch plan is being implemented through the application of the basic principle that each country will provide the facilities and services that fall within its territory. However, those developing countries that are unable to do this are being assisted, as far as possible, through the UNDP and through bilateral arrangements. A third means of assistance is the Voluntary Assistance Program, which is made up of financial contributions or equipment or services offered by members of WMO. In the case of regions outside the territories of individual countries (i.e., outer space, ocean areas, and Antarctica) implementation is based on the principle of voluntary participation of countries by providing facilities and services from their national resources. The Voluntary Assistance Program (VAP) to some extent replaces the WMO New Development Fund of $1.5 million that was established by the fourth WMO congress in 1963 to enable significant and prompt assistance to be rendered to members during the period 1965–1967. As of 1 March 1970 there were 86 projects approved for implementation in whole or part and from which 49 member countries will benefit. In financial terms these projects involve assistance to the amount of approximately $5 million. The total number of projects presently approved as eligible to qualify for VAP assistance is 288.

WMO RESEARCH PROGRAM

WMO has participated in worldwide research programs such as the International Geophysical Year, IGY (1957/1958), the International Years of the Quiet Sun (1964/1965), the International Indian Ocean Expedition, and the International Hydrological Decade.

During the IGY, the WMO data center collected and published several million meteorological observations that form the basis for research work in many countries. On the occasion of the International Indian Ocean Expedition, WMO contributed through its participation in UNDP to the establishment in India of an international meteorological center that collects and analyzes data, conducts research, and trains meteorologists. Further, WMO organizes symposia on subjects such as tropical meteorology and numerical weather prediction (based on the use of computers for weather analysis and forecasting).

WMO's main research effort, in collaboration with the International Council of Scientific Unions (ICSU) is centered on the Global Atmospheric Research Program (GARP) which aims at probing the scientific problems that prevent a fuller understanding of the atmosphere's structure and behavior.

GARP is being planned as a worldwide scientific effort in theoretical research and complex field experiments. It will enable the fundamental physical and mathematical bases of long-range weather prediction to be developed further and tested. Use will be made of what are known as numerical simulation models of the atmosphere's circulation.

It is hoped that GARP, besides helping provide weathermen with the scientific knowledge needed for prediction of large-scale weather movements for periods of ten days or even longer, may also establish the basis for methods of weather modification.

A joint WMO/ICSU Organizing Committee composed of 12 internationally known atmospheric scientists has been established to launch GARP.

WMO PROGRAM ON THE INTER-ACTION OF MAN AND HIS ENVIRONMENT

Part of WMO's scientific and technical program is aimed at applying meteorological knowledge to human activities. The range of this part of the program includes such activities as agriculture and food production, the use and development of water resources, services to different forms of transportation and the exploitation of the oceans, as well as efforts to modify the weather and to reduce tropical storm damage. Studies of atmospheric pollution and conservation of the environment are also receiving increased attention.

High among topics of direct concern to mankind is the problem of feeding the world's expanding population. The fifth congress recognized the obligation of meteorologists to help increase world food production by making the maximum possible use of meteorological knowledge. A number of agro-climatological surveys have been carried out in different parts of the world and an interagency group (FAO, UNDP, UNESCO, WHO, and WMO) has drawn up several projects to make use of the data collected.

The WMO Commission for Hydrometeorology has completed guidance material in hydrometeorology and hydrology, as well as several *Technical Notes*. WMO also supports the International Hydrological Decade, by providing the technical secretariat for a number of projects forming part of the program. An International Glossary of Hydrology has been published jointly by WMO and UNESCO in four languages.

The greatly increased scientific interest in all questions relating to the oceans has had important effects for WMO. The organization has become increasingly involved in plans for marine research and investigations of the oceans, and in marine pollution studies. One aspect of these activities is the Integrated Global Ocean Station System (IGOSS), which has been developed along lines similar to the World Weather Watch. The plan and implementation program for the first phase of IGOSS was completed in 1969 and agreed to by both the Intergovernmental Oceanographic Commission (IOC) and WMO.

The WMO is closely concerned with the need to plan the use of natural resources and to conserve the human environment; it is cooperating with other bodies involved in environmental problems.

WMO cooperates with the Economic Commission for Asia and the Far East in its program to reduce typhoon damage. Consultations have begun with countries in other areas affected by tropical storms to determine whether there is a need for similar projects to be initiated.

TECHNICAL ASSISTANCE IN METEOROLOGY

WMO has participated in the United Nations Development Program (UNDP) since 1952 and has provided assistance to many countries in developing their meteorological services, training, personnel, supplying equipment for observing networks, providing experts, and awarding fellowships for training abroad, and supporting training seminars. Advice has been given on subjects ranging from the application of meteorology in special fields (e.g., control of desert locusts or utilization of meteorological satellite data) to the establishment, organization, and operation of national meteorological services. WMO also participates in large-scale economic development projects under the UNDP that have been undertaken in a number of countries to enable them to provide information needed for the development of water resource potential (e.g., irrigation, hydroelectric power, and flood control projects) and agriculture, and to develop institutions for the training of personnel and the performance of research. During the 10-year period, 1960–1969, assistance at a cost of more than $30 million was provided under the UNDP. In that time period over 680 man-years of expert service had been provided and 800 fellowships had been awarded.

[8] BIBLIOGRAPHY

International Cloud Atlas. Vol. I, $3.75; Vol. II, $8.75. Abridged Atlas, $3.75.

International Geophysical Year 1957–1958. Meteorological Programme: General Survey. $2.50.

Meteorological Services of the World. 1959 edition. $6.00.

WMO Bulletin. Provides a summary of the work of the WMO and of developments in international meteorology. Quarterly. One year, $1.00; single copies, $0.25.

Informational booklets published by WMO include: *Meteorology in the Indian Ocean* ($0.50); *Weather and Food* ($0.50); *Weather and Man* ($0.50); *Weather and Water* ($0.50); *World Weather Watch* ($0.25); *Harvest from Weather* ($0.25); *How to Become a Meteorologist* ($0.25).

A catalog of all WMO publications is available on request.

GLOSSARY OF INTERGOVERNMENTAL ORGANIZATIONS (IGO'S)

The following is a glossary of international organizations, outside the United Nations system, in which nations cooperate on a governmental level. Known as intergovernmental organizations, or IGO's, such bodies have memberships representing governments only, both sovereign and nonself-governing. This glossary briefly summarizes their activities and supplements the information given in the *International Cooperation* section (18) of the individual country articles.

Initials generally refer to organization names in English. French, Spanish, or other language initials are given where there is no formal English abbreviation, or where an organization is commonly identified by such foreign abbreviation.

Bracketed numbers at the end of an organization's listing in the glossary refer to the accompanying table's numbers at top of page. By going down the specific numbered column, one can find all the countries that belong to a particular organization. Thus, for the membership of the International Relief Union (IRU), which has the number [145] at the end of its listing, follow column headed 145.

To find the organizations to which a particular country belongs, look up the country in the table's alphabetical listing, then follow the horizontal line opposite it across all the pages.

The dot appearing in the table indicates: member. The letters designate: **A** = associate member; **O** = observer.

Membership is given as of mid-1970. Cuba's membership in the Organization of American States and the OAS affiliates is marked with an asterisk (*) because Cuba as a country is included in the OAS, but its present government is excluded.

Administrative Center of Social Security for Rhine Boatmen
ACSSRB, Strasbourg, France

ACTIVITY: Assures the application of the Accord of 1950 concerning social security for Rhine boatmen. [1]

African and Malagasy Common Organization
OCAM, Yaoundé, Cameroon

ACTIVITIES: 1. Organizes and coordinates foreign policy. 2. Assures common security. 3. Develops the economics of member states. 4. Fosters cooperation and harmonization of economic and social policies of members. 5. Develops and harmonizes transportation and communications among members. [2]

African and Malagasy Council on Higher Education
CAMES, Ouagadougou, Upper Volta

ACTIVITY: Coordinates higher education and research of members. [3]

African and Malagasy Industrial Property Office
OAMPI, Yaoundé, Cameroon

ACTIVITY: Serves member states as a common office of patents, trade marks, and industrial designs and models. [4]

African and Malagasy Postal and Telecommunications Union

Agency of African and Malagasy Union. [5]

African Development Bank
Abidjan, Ivory Coast

ACTIVITIES: 1. Coordinates members' development finances. 2. Provides long-term, large-scale development loans. [6]

African Inter-State Office for Tourism
OIETA, Paris, France

ACTIVITY: Develops technical aspects of tourism in member countries. [7]

African Postal and Telecommunications Union
APTU, Pretoria, South Africa

ACTIVITY: Secures, by means of agreements, conferences, and other methods, the organization and improvement of telecommunication and postal services between member states. Nonself-governing members: Angola, Mozambique, South West Africa. [8]

African Postal Union
AfPU, Cairo, UAR

ACTIVITIES: 1. Coordinates and improves postal services among member states. 2. Ensures cooperation on present agreements. 3. Studies and recommends augmentation of postal services among members. [9]

Afro-Asian Rural Reconstruction Organization
AAPSO, New Delhi, India

ACTIVITIES: 1. Studies problems of hunger and poverty in rural areas of member states. 2. Explores possibilities for and coordination of actions to combat hunger and poverty in rural areas. [10]

Alliance for Progress: see Inter-American Committee on the Alliance for Progress

ANZUS Council (ANZUS Pact): see Security Treaty of Australia, New Zealand and the United States of America

Arab International Tourist Union
Cairo, UAR

ACTIVITIES: 1. Studies the tourist industry of member states. 2. Recommends to members measures for the development of tourism. [11]

Arab League: see League of Arab States

Arab Postal Union
UPA, Cairo, UAR

ACTIVITIES: 1. Develops cooperation between members. 2. Fosters the formation of a single postal territory encompassing all members. 3. Coordinates policy of members in relation to the Universal Postal Union and others. 4. Fosters exemptions from territorial transit taxes and promotes the free mailing of literature for the blind. 5. Engages in research, translation, and postal education.
NOTE: The Shaykhdoms of Dubayy, Qatar, Ras al-Khaymah, and Sharjah are members of UPA. [12]

Asian-African Legal Consultative Committee
New Delhi, India

ACTIVITIES: 1. Serves members as advisory body. 2. Studies legal problems presented to it by members. 3. Presents views to the International Law Commission. [13]

Asian and Pacific Council
ASPAC, Bangkok, Thailand

ACTIVITIES: 1. Maintains a registry of scientists and experts available to members. 2. Operates a cultural and social center to promote mutual interests. [14]

Asian Development Bank
Pasay City, Philippines

ACTIVITIES: 1. Studies and encourages economic growth in Asia and the Far East. 2. Participates in economic development of member states with emphasis on developing countries. [15]

Asian Industrial Development Council
AIDC, Bangkok, Thailand

ACTIVITIES: 1. Defines economic development projects of interest to its members. 2. Undertakes feasibility studies.
NOTE: Brunei and Hong Kong are members of AIDC. [16]

Asian-Oceanic Postal Union
AOPU, Manila, Philippines

ACTIVITIES: 1. Fosters cooperation in postal services among members. 2. Works for the augmentation and improvement of postal services.
NOTE: Hong Kong is a member of AOPU. [17]

Asian Productivity Organization
APO, Tokyo, Japan

ACTIVITIES: 1. Endeavors to increase productivity in member countries. 2. Researches, studies, exchanges, and disseminates information on techniques and methods. 3. Pools technical experts and trains personnel. 4. Stimulates developments conducive to effective adoption of methods of advanced productivity. [18]

Association of South East Asian Nations
ASEAN, Djakarta, Indonesia

ACTIVITIES: 1. Promotes economic cooperation among members. 2. Provides professional, technical, and administrative training. [19]

Baghdad Pact: see Central Treaty Organization

Bank for International Settlements
BIS, Basel, Switzerland

ACTIVITIES: 1. Promotes cooperation of central banks. 2. Provides facilities for international financial operations. 3. Acts as trustee or agent in international settlements. [20]

Benelux Customs Union: see Benelux Economic Union

Benelux Economic and Social Consultative Council
EUB, 13, The Hague, Netherlands

ACTIVITY: Provides forum for exchange of views of members for bettering economic and social collaboration. [21]

Benelux Economic Union
BENELUX, Brussels, Belgium

ACTIVITIES: 1. Strengthens economic ties of members by means of free movement of persons, goods, capital, and services. 2. Coordinates policies of members in economic, financial, and social fields. 3. Promotes a joint trade policy of members with nonmembers. 4. Publishes a statistical quarterly and a bulletin. [22]

Caribbean Economic Development Corporation
CODECA, Hato Rey, Puerto Rico

ACTIVITIES: 1. Is concerned with social, cultural, and economic interests of the Caribbean area. 2. Operates a clearing house on trade, tourism, and manpower information. 3. Endeavors to accelerate development of the area by mutual assistance projects.
Nonself-governing members: British Virgin Islands, French Guiana, Guadeloupe, Martinique, Netherlands Antilles, Puerto Rico, Surinam, US Virgin Islands. [23]

Caribbean Food and Nutrition Institute
CFNI, Kingston, Jamaica

ACTIVITIES: 1. Coordinates nutrition planning and studies through member governments. 2. Promotes training of nutrition personnel on community level. [24]

Caribbean Free Trade Area
Antigua

ACTIVITY: Promotes a free trade area among member states.
NOTE: Antigua is a member of the Caribbean Free Trade Area. [25]

Central African Customs and Economic Union
UDEAC, Bangui, Central African Republic

ACTIVITIES: 1. Establishes common customs and tariffs. 2. Works for the elimination of import duties and taxes among members. 3. Coordinates internal fiscal systems. [26]

Central American Bank of Economic Integration
BCIE, Tegucigalpa, Honduras

ACTIVITIES: 1. Promotes economic integration of member states. 2. Finances projects of interest to the Central American Common Market. [27]

Central American Institute of Public Administration
ICAP, San José, Costa Rica

ACTIVITIES: 1. Trains administrative and technical personnel. 2. Conducts research in and advises on administrative techniques. [28]

Central American Research Institute for Industry
ICAITI, Guatemala City, Guatemala

ACTIVITIES: 1. Serves as consultant to industry. 2. Undertakes technical research. 3. Promotes the application of modern methods of productivity. 4. Supplies market, feasibility, industrial process, application of materials, and other studies. [29]

Central Commission for the Navigation of the Rhine
CRC, Strasbourg, France

ACTIVITIES: 1. Holds diplomatic conferences concerning Rhine navigation and promotes uniform regulations for member states. 2. Safeguards freedom of navigation for all, equality of treatment without discrimination. [30]

Central Office for International Railway Transport
OCTI, Berne, Switzerland

ACTIVITY: Implements the 1952 International Conventions on the carriage of goods, passengers, and luggage by rail. [31]

Central Treaty Organization
CENTO, Ankara, Turkey

ACTIVITIES: 1. Based on the principles laid down in the Charter of the United Nations, plans collective regional defense. 2. Promotes intraregional communications, transportation, navigation aids, personnel training, and other technical assistance. [32]

Cocoa Producers Alliance
Lagos, Nigeria
ACTIVITIES: 1. Controls marketing of cocoa by allocation of supplies. 2. Promotes consumption of cocoa. 3. Serves as clearinghouse for technical and scientific information. [33]

Colombo Plan for Cooperative Economic Development
C-Plan, Colombo, Ceylon
ACTIVITIES: 1. Promotes technical cooperation of experts and equipment for economic development of the region. 2. Facilitates research and personnel training. 3. Cooperates with UN and others active in the area development. 4. Disseminates information. [34]

Common Afro-Malagasy Organization: see Organisation Commune Africaine et Malgache

Common Market: see European Common Market

Commonwealth Advisory Aeronautical Research Council
CAARC, Teddington, England
ACTIVITY: Encourages and coordinates aeronautical research throughout the Commonwealth, with view to avoiding duplication and ensuring complementary research, whenever possible. [35]

Commonwealth Agricultural Bureaux
CAB, Farnham Royal, Bucks, England
ACTIVITIES: 1. Maintains information service for research in the agricultural sciences. 2. Publishes reports, bibliographies, abstractions, etc. 3. Provides identification service of insects, mites, and pathogens injurious to plants and animals. British dependent territories are represented by UK. [36]

Commonwealth Economic Consultative Council
CECC, London, England
ACTIVITY: Facilitates consultations on and coordinates matters of economic interest to the Commonwealth. [37]

Commonwealth Education Liaison Committee
CELC, London, England
ACTIVITIES: 1. Provides a forum for the discussion of matters on Commonwealth cooperation in education. 2. Develops and improves Commonwealth cooperation in education. British dependent territories are represented by UK. [38]

Commonwealth Foundation
London, England
ACTIVITY: Administers a fund devoted to the promotion of professional cooperation among members. [39]

Commonwealth Scientific Committee
London, England
ACTIVITY: Promotes cooperation among scientific bodies of members. [40]

Commonwealth Secretariat
London, England
ACTIVITIES: 1. Arranges meetings of heads of state or ministers of the Commonwealth. 2. Serves as information center on Commonwealth matters. [41]

Commonwealth Telecommunications Board
CTB, London, England
ACTIVITY: Coordinates telecommunication services of the British Commonwealth. [42]

Commonwealth War Graves Commission
London, England
ACTIVITY: Cares for graves of fallen soldiers of member states killed in World Wars I and II. [43]

Conference of Heads of States of Equatorial Africa
Bangui, Central African Republic
ACTIVITY: Directs interstate service organizations, i.e., the Central African Foundation for Higher Education and the Trans-Equatorial Communications Agency. [44]

Council for Mutual Economic Aid (COMECON)
CMEA, Moscow, USSR
ACTIVITIES: 1. Develops jointly economic resources and trade of Eastern European countries. 2. Exchanges economic information and experience and fosters mutual technical aid. 3. Establishes special subsidiary bodies for jointly administered international enterprises, statistics, coordination of research, industrial design, etc. Albania has not participated in COMECON since 1961. [45]

Council of Europe
Strasbourg, France
ACTIVITIES: 1. Aims to achieve political unity between members through its Committee of Ministers and Consultative Assembly, whose work results in international agreements. 2. Develops and coordinates economic policy of members and relations with other regions. 3. Formulates legal policy in human rights, criminology, etc. 4. Fosters educational and cultural cooperation and exchange. 5. Develops public health programs. 6. Operates fund for resettlement of refugees. 6. Draws up a European nature conservation program. [46]

Council of Europe Resettlement Fund
Paris, France
ACTIVITY: Studies, and provides possible solutions for, problems of overpopulation. [47]

Council of Ministers of the European Communities
Brussels, Belgium
Supreme organ of European Economic Community (EEC), European Coal and Steel Community (ECSC), and European Atomic Energy Community (EURATOM). [48]

Council of the Entente
Abidjan, Ivory Coast
ACTIVITY: Coordinates aspects of foreign and domestic policies of member states and provides mutual aid through a Solidarity Fund. [49]

Court of Justice of the European Communities
Luxembourg, Luxembourg
ACTIVITY: Ensures the observance of law in the interpretation and application of the EEC, ECSC, and EURATOM treaties. [50]

Customs Cooperation Council
CCC, Brussels, Belgium
ACTIVITIES: 1. Aids the promotion of international cooperation in customs matters. 2. Studies customs procedures and the

harmonization of customs systems. 3. Supervises and prepares conventions on customs matters. 4. Makes recommendations on customs matters. [51]

Danube Commission
CD, Budapest, Hungary

ACTIVITIES: 1. Plans and executes large-scale improvements of navigation on the Danube River. 2. Coordinates hydrotechnical work on the Danube. 3. Assembles and publishes statistical, navigational, customs, health, and other information. [52]

Desert Locust Control Organization for Eastern Africa
DLCOEA, Asmara, Ethiopia

ACTIVITIES: 1. Promotes control of the desert locust by members. 2. Coordinates and reinforces national action. [53]

Diplomatic Conference of International Maritime Law
DCML, Brussels, Belgium

ACTIVITY: Fosters uniformity of maritime law.
NOTE: The Conference is not a membership organization. The Belgian government extends invitations to conferences to all countries and international organizations concerned with the subject.

East Africa Common Service Organization
Dar es Salaam, Tanzania

ACTIVITIES: 1. Develops common services for members' transportation and communications needs. 2. Unifies and standardizes customs tariffs. 3. Develops commercial and industrial aspects of members' economies. 4. Engages in social research. [54]

East African Agricultural and Forestry Research Organization
EAAFRO, Nairobi, Kenya

ACTIVITIES: 1. Serves as scientific advisory board on agriculture and forestry to member governments. 2. Conducts research in various aspects of agriculture and forestry. [55]

East African Medical Research Council
Arusha, Tanzania

ACTIVITY: Conducts research on diseases common to East Africa. [56]

Economic and Customs Union of Central Africa
UDE, Brazzaville, Congo

ACTIVITIES: 1. Coordinates and modifies custom tariffs of members. 2. Makes recommendations to members on fiscal policy. [57]

Economic and Social Committee
ESC, Brussels, Belgium

ACTIVITY: Assists, in a consultative capacity, the Councils of Ministers and the European Common Market and EURATOM commissions. Affiliated with the European Communities. [58]

European and Mediterranean Plant Protection Organization
EPPO, Paris, France

ACTIVITIES: 1. Advises and assists members on the technical, administrative, and legislative measures necessary to fight pests and diseases of plants and plant products. 2. Compiles and disseminates information on pests, diseases, and measures affecting free movement of plants and plant products. 3. Simplifies and unifies regulations and certification. Affiliated with the Food and Agriculture Organization of UN. Nonself-governing members: Guernsey, Jersey. [59]

European Atomic Energy Community—EURATOM
EAEC, Brussels, Belgium

ACTIVITIES: 1. Undertakes and coordinates nuclear research to develop economical nuclear energy for members. 2. Establishes a common market for nuclear materials, equipment, personnel, and capital. 3. Determines safety and health standards. 4. Prevents nuclear materials from being diverted from their declared purposes. 5. Operates four nuclear establishments. 6. Disseminates information to members. [60]

European Civil Aviation Conference
ECAC, Paris, France

ACTIVITY: Treats economic aspects of aviation. [61]

European Coal and Steel Community
ECSC, Luxembourg, Luxembourg

ACTIVITIES: 1. Maintains the Common Market through fair competition, guidance of production and consumption, opinions on private investments, and loans to firms. 2. Retrains, readapts, and resettles workers as required by development shifts in industries and locations. 3. Redevelops depressed industrial areas. 4. Researches production methods, security in mines, industrial health, etc. 5. Studies market and develops common energy policy. [62]

European Commission for the Control of Foot-and-Mouth Disease
ECCFD, Rome, Italy

ACTIVITIES: 1. Serves as monitor on developments in the foot-and-mouth disease. 2. Collects and disseminates information on quick identification of the disease. 3. Carries on research and helps members obtain vaccine.
Affiliated with the Food and Agriculture Organization of UN. [63]

European Commission of Human Rights
Strasbourg, France

ACTIVITIES: 1. Works in conjunction with the European Court of Human Rights. 2. Hears and considers petitions by individuals of member states. 3. Endeavors to effect out of court settlement. [64]

European Committee on Crime Problems
ECCP, Strasbourg, France

ACTIVITIES: 1. Develops and executes anticrime programs. 2. Studies and makes recommendations on penal reform, including questions such as capital punishment, treatment of prisoners, aftercare of prisoners. 3. Coordinates work of institutions and trains prison personnel, and organizes international courses.
Affiliated with the Council of Europe. [65]

European Committee on Legal Co-operation
Strasbourg, France

ACTIVITY: Promotes coordination of the legal program of the Council of Europe. [66]

European Company for the Chemical Processing of Irradiated Fuels
EUROCHEMIC, Mol, Belgium

ACTIVITIES: 1. Reprocesses fuel elements from the atomic reactors of members in order to extract and purify the plutonium formed during irradiation and the remaining uranium. 2. Undertakes research on chemical processing techniques. [67]

European Company for the Financing of Railway Rolling Stock
EUROFIMA, Basel, Switzerland

ACTIVITIES: 1. Obtains rolling stock for railway administrations, both sha   olders and others. 2. Seeks financial assistance, of loans and own   nds, to fulfill its operations. [68]

European Conference of Insurance Supervisory Services
Rome, Ita
ACTIVI   tudies insurance supervisory services and exchanges informa   among member states. [69]

European Conference of Local Authorities
Strasbourg, France
ACTIVITIES: 1. Fosters the participation of local authorities in the aims and activities of the Council of Europe. 2. Advises on attitudes of populace, local authorities, and governments, in respect to measures taken by the Council. 3. Informs and solicits the support of local authorit s on progress in European integration. Affiliated with the Council of Europe. [70]

European Conference of Ministers of Transport
ECMT, Paris, France
ACTIVI IES: 1. Promotes activities concerning transportation—railroad, roads, and inland waterways. 2. Encourages improvement, develop ent, coordination, and financing of investment in European main li s of communication. 3. Deals with general policy problems. 4. Standardizes railway rolling stock. 5. Promotes road safety, an antinoi   campaign, and coordinates road traffic regulations. Affiliated with the Organization for Economic Cooperation and Development. [71]

European Conference of Postal and Telecommunications Administrations
CEPT, Rome, Italy
ACTIVI IES: 1. Simplifies and improves postal and telecommunications. 2. Investigates questions on organization, technique, and operation of the communications services. 3. Studies proposals presented to it. 4. Exchanges information and officials. [72]

European Conference on Satellite Communications
London, England
ACTIVITY: Coordinates interests of member states in global communications. [73]

European Council for Cultural Cooperation
CCC, Strasbourg, France
ACTIVITIES: 1. Develops and coordinates educational programs for elementary and secondary schools. 2. Organizes courses in higher educati n, research, fellowships, exchange of teachers and students, translations, etc. 3. Fosters out-of-school cultural activities, including exhibitions, film awards, etc.
Affiliated with the Council of Europe. [74]

European Court of Human Rights
Strasbourg, France
ACTIVITY: Has jurisdiction in cases of interpretation or application of the European Convention for the Protection of Human Rights and Fundamental Freedoms that are referred to it either by the European Commission of Human Rights or by members. Affiliated with the Council of Europe. [75]

European Economic Community
EEC, Brussels, Belgium
ACTIVITIES: 1. Establishes the European Common Market. 2. Reduces and eliminates import and export duties with view of attaining complete economic unity of members by 1973. 3. Establishes and fosters common tariffs, commercial, agricultural, and transport policies, fair competition, coordination of economic policies, ap-

proximation of municipal laws, and the free movement of persons, services, and capital of members. [76]

European Forestry Commission
EFC, Rome, Italy
ACTIVITIES: 1. Advises on the formulation of forest policy and co-ordinates its implementation. 2. Exchanges information and advises on practices in technical and economic problems. Affiliated with the Food and Agriculture Organization of UN. [77]

European Free Trade Association
EFTA, Geneva, Switzerland
ACTIVITIES: 1. Works toward European economic integration, economic growth of members, and expansion of world trade. 2. Endeavors to reduce tariffs on industrial goods among members, aiming at elimination of tariffs by 1970. [78]

European Investment Bank
EIB, Brussels, Belgium
ACTIVITY: Contributes to the development of the Common Market by granting and guaranteeing loans for developing underdeveloped areas, modernization or creation of Common Market enterprises, and projects of common interest to several member countries. Affiliated with the European Communities. [79]

European Nuclear Energy Agency
ENEA, Paris, France
ACTIVITIES: 1. Builds and operates joint research installations. 2. Promotes scientific and technical cooperation between OECD countries. 3. Solves administrative and regulatory problems in health and safety, liability and insurance, transport of radioactive materials, and waste disposal. 4. Studies economic aspects of nuclear energy and assesses its role in meeting Europe's energy demands. Affiliated with the Organization for Economic Cooperation and Development. [80]

European Organization for Nuclear Research
CERN, Geneva, Switzerland
ACTIVITIES: 1. Provides for collaboration among European countries in peaceful uses of nuclear physics. 2. Publishes results of its experimental and theoretical work. 3. Has constructed a proton synchrotron for energies above 25 gigaelectronvolts and a synchro-cyclotron that can accelerate protons up to 600 million electronvolts. 4. Inaugurates research in new areas. [81]

European Organization for the Safety of Air Navigation
Brussels, Belgium
ACTIVITIES: 1. Studies systems and mechanical aspects of air navigation control. 2. Trains personnel. 3. Develops new techniques of air navigation control. [82]

European Parliament
Luxembourg, Luxembourg
ACTIVITIES: 1. Exercises control over, with powers to dismiss, the executive bodies of the European Communities (ECSC, EEC, EURATOM). 2. Prepares the parliamentary debates. [83]

European Pharmacopeia Commission
Strasbourg, France
ACTIVITIES: 1. Unifies pharmaceutical standards of member states. 2. Promotes pharmaceutical research. [84]

European Space Research Organization
ESRO, Paris, France
ACTIVITY: Researches space by launching satellites. [85]

European Space Vehicle Launcher Development Organization
ELDO, Paris, France

ACTIVITY: Launches satellites for peaceful uses. [86]

General Fisheries Council for the Mediterranean
GFCM, Rome, Italy

ACTIVITIES: 1. Formulates development and utilization of aquatic resources. 2. Encourages and coordinates research and use of improved methods in fishery and allied industries. 3. Disseminates scientific and technical information. 4. Promotes standardization of equipment, techniques, and nomenclatures.
Affiliated with the Food and Agriculture Organization of UN. [87]

General Treaty on Central American Economic Integration
SIECA, Managua, Nicaragua

ACTIVITIES: 1. Develops the Central American Common Market and the Central American Free Trade Area. 2. Fosters the development and integration of the economies of member states. [88]

Hague Conference on Private International Law
CODIP, The Hague, Netherlands

ACTIVITY: Promotes unification of private international law through the conclusion of treaties between member governments. [89]

Ibero-American Bureau of Education
OEI, Madrid, Spain

ACTIVITIES: 1. Seeks to strengthen collaboration of Spain and Latin American countries in the field of education. 2. Maintains institute for education research. 3. Serves as documentation and information center. 4. Develops technical aid and exchange of personnel. [90]

Indo-Pacific Fisheries Council
IPFC, Bangkok, Thailand

ACTIVITIES: 1. Formulates development and utilization of living aquatic resources. 2. Promotes and coordinates research, methods, development projects, and nomenclature. 3. Assembles, publishes, and disseminates oceanographical, biological, and technical aquatic information.
Affiliated with the Food and Agricultural Organization of UN. [91]

Institute of Nutrition of Central America and Panama
INCAP, Guatemala City, Guatemala

ACTIVITIES: 1. Studies and works out solutions to nutrition problems of the area. 2. Participates in research programs. 3. Publishes an annual and a quarterly bulletin. 4. Trains professional and auxiliary personnel. 5. Prepares material for nutrition education.
Affiliated with the Organization of American States and the World Health Organization. [92]

Inter-African Coffee Organization
IACO, Neuilly, France

ACTIVITIES: 1. Studies problems affecting African coffee. 2. Formulates common marketing policy. 3. Cooperates with national, regional, and international coffee organizations. [93]

Inter-American Children's Institute
ICI, Montevideo, Uruguay

ACTIVITIES: 1. Serves as center of research, documentation, and information about the life and welfare of children and the family. 2. Develops programs of technical cooperation and studies on child welfare and related fields. 3. Consults on matters relating to the protection of children and the family. 4. Publishes bulletins, magazines, etc.
Affiliated with the Organization of American States. [94]

Inter-American Commission of Women
IACW, Washington, D.C., US

ACTIVITIES: 1. Promotes extension of civil, political, economic, and social rights of American women. 2. Investigates women's problems and proposes solutions. 3. Maintains relations with other organizations dealing with related matters. Affiliated with the Organization of American States. [95]

Inter-American Committee for Agricultural Development
CIDA, Washington, D.C., US

ACTIVITIES: 1. Coordinates agricultural development, technical assistance in Latin America. 2. Assists governments in study and formulation of agricultural development. 3. Fosters training of agricultural personnel.
NOTE: The Committee is not a country-membership organization. Members are regional IGO's concerned with agricultural development. Affiliated with the Organization of American States.

Inter-American Committee on the Alliance for Progress
ICAP, Washington, D.C., US

ACTIVITIES: 1. Coordinates aid programs of members. 2. Directs economic planning. 3. Supervises training of personnel. 4. Initiates infrastructure projects. 5. Provides direct aid. [96]

Inter-American Conference on Social Security
CISS, Mexico City, Mexico

ACTIVITIES: 1. Develops cooperation among the social security authorities of American states. 2. Holds meetings, conducts seminars, and disseminates information.
Affiliated with the Organization of American States. [97]

Inter-American Defense Board
IADB, Washington, D.C., US

ACTIVITIES: 1. Plans military defense of Western Hemisphere. 2. Advises and counsels Inter-American Defense College, whose mission is to conduct a study of the essential components of inter-American defense.
Affiliated with the Organization of American States. [98]

Inter-American Development Bank
IDB, Washington, D.C., US

ACTIVITIES: 1. Provides technical assistance and financing of development projects of member countries, both individually and collectively. 2. Helps to orient the policies of members toward utilizing their resources, complementing their economies, and fostering foreign trade. [99]

Inter-American Indian Institute
III, Mexico DF, Mexico

ACTIVITIES: 1. Promotes Indian community development programs. 2. Investigates Indian matters. 3. Publishes scientific magazines and books. 4. Holds exhibitions of Indian arts and crafts. [100]

Inter-American Institute of Agricultural Sciences
of the Organization of American States
IAIAS, San José, Costa Rica

ACTIVITIES: 1. Deals with all aspects of agriculture, including teaching, research in natural resources, soils, crops, animal husbandry, forestry, agricultural economics, engineering, rural sociology, marketing, and land reform. 2. Operates a graduate school and tropical center, a center for the temperate zone, and several regional centers. [101]

Inter-American Music Council
CIDEM, Washington, D.C., US

ACTIVITIES: 1. Fosters interest in and the advancement of music in the Americas. 2. Cooperates with universities on the establishment of music centers. [102]

Inter-American Nuclear Energy Commission
IANEC, Washington, D.C., US

ACTIVITIES: 1. Holds meetings and sponsors symposia on peaceful applications of nuclear energy. 2. Cosponsors, with the US Atomic Energy Commission and member countries, workshops in utilization of nuclear energy information for scientific libraries and scientists. 3. Publishes proceeding of meetings, symposia, etc. Affiliated with the Organization of American States. [103]

Inter-American Peace Committee
IAPC, Washington, D.C., US

ACTIVITY: Keeps constant vigilance to ensure that member states having any dispute or controversy will solve it as quickly as possible. Affiliated with OAS.
NOTE: Membership consists of five countries, rotating one member in August of each year.

Inter-American Travel Congress
ITC, Washington, D.C., US

ACTIVITIES: 1. Coordinates promotional activities of national tourist offices. 2. Fosters tourist traffic studies. 3. Encourages unification of tourist travel laws and regulations. [104]

Inter-American Tropical Tuna Commission
IATTC, La Jolla, California, US

ACTIVITY: Studies the tropical tuna with view to securing sustained catch. [105]

Intergovernmental Committee for European Migration
ICEM, Geneva, Switzerland

ACTIVITIES: 1. Helps solve Europe's overpopulation and refugee problems. 2. Stimulates and creates new economic opportunities overseas. 3. Services movement, resettlement, and integration of emigrants. 4. Assists Latin America in attracting European emigrants. 5. Transports refugees from country of first asylum to country of permanent reestablishment. [106]

Intergovernmental Committee of the International Convention of Rome for the Protection of Performers, Producers, of Phonograms and Broadcasting Organizations
Geneva, Switzerland

ACTIVITY: Studies the application of the Convention of Rome for its possible revision. [107]

Intergovernmental Copyright Committee
IGC, Paris, France

ACTIVITIES: 1. Studies problems concerning application and operation of the Universal Copyright Convention. (UCC). 2. Prepares periodic revisions of the Convention. 3. Studies problems on the international protection of copyrights in cooperation with interested international organizations. 4. Informs IGC countries of its activities. Affiliated with UNESCO.
NOTE: Membership as indicated in column [108] denotes signatory parties and/or accessions to the Universal Copyright Convention as of August 1970. Philippine's accession to UCC is legally uncertain. [108]

Intergovernmental Oceanographic Commission
IOC, Paris, France

ACTIVITY: Promotes scientific exploration of the oceans by collective action of members.
Affiliated with UNESCO. Ukraine is a member of IOC. [109]

International African Migratory Locust Organization
OICMA, Bamako, Mali

ACTIVITIES: 1. Conducts research in the field of primary formation of locust. 2. Fosters controls and destruction of locust. [110]

International Bank for Economic Co-Operation
IBEC, Moscow, USSR

ACTIVITIES: 1. Fosters development of foreign trade by advancement of funds. 2. Accepts deposits in gold, transferable rubles, convertibles, and other currencies. 3. Performs multilateral settlements. [111]

International Bureau of Education
IBE, Geneva, Switzerland

ACTIVITIES: 1. Collects and disseminates information on education. 2. Researches, and publishes reports on, education. 3. Holds an annual international conference on public education. 4. Publishes bulletin, annual, and yearbook of education. 5. Maintains a library and a permanent international exhibition of public education.
NOTE: Byelorussia, Qatar, and Ukraine are members of IBE. [112]

International Bureau of Weights and Measures
IBWM, Sèvres, France

ACTIVITIES: 1. Establishes international standards of weights and measures. 2. Coordinates techniques for weighing and measuring. 3. Determines relationships of national to international standards. 4. Determines basic physical constants. [113]

International Center for Settlement of Investment Disputes
Washington, D.C., US

ACTIVITY: Facilitates the settlement of investment disputes between member states and foreign investors.
Affiliated with the IBRD. [114]

International Center for the Study of the Preservation and Restoration of Cultural Property
Rome, Italy

ACTIVITIES: 1. Researches, studies, gathers, and disseminates technical information on conservation and restoration of cultural property. 2. Assists in training specialized personnel. 3. Serves as center of information and documentation. 4. Renders consultation services on conservation and restoration of cultural properties. [115]

International Children's Center
ICC, Paris, France

ACTIVITIES: 1. Aids governments and international organizations in postgraduate training of school teachers and health and social personnel. 2. Gives international courses and postgraduate training courses for professional personnel. 3. Prepares individual study programs, grants research fellowships, and organizes seminars and conferences for professional personnel, especially for developing countries. 4. Publishes reports and monthly and quarterly reviews.
NOTE: ICC is not a membership organization.

International Coffee Agreement
ICA, Washington, D.C., US

ACTIVITIES: 1. Adapts the supply of coffee to demand. 2. Ensures the orderly placement of coffee in world markets. 3. Fosters coffee consumption throughout the world. [116]

International Coffee Organization
London, England

ACTIVITIES: 1. Fosters cooperation between coffee producing and consuming countries. 2. Encourages coffee consumption. [117]

International Commission for Agricultural Industries
ICAI, Paris, France

ACTIVITIES: 1. Researches technical and economic aspects of the food, agricultural, and biological industries. 2. Studies liquid residue, methods of analysis, antiparasitic products, dairy science. 3. Serves as center of information and documentation, including statistics. [118]

International Commission for the Northwest Atlantic
Fisheries
ICNAF, Halifax, Canada

ACTIVITIES: 1. Prepares international fisheries regulations for consideration by members. 2. Holds annual and special scientific meetings. 3. Collects statistical data and collaborates on research. 4. Publishes statistics and research results. [119]

International Commission for the Protection
of the Moselle Against Pollution
Paris, France

ACTIVITY: Investigates causes of pollution and recommends ways and means to lessen and avoid pollution of the Moselle waters. [120]

International Commission for the Protection of the Rhine
Against Pollution
Koblenz, Germany

ACTIVITY: Researches causes of pollution of the Rhine and recommends measures of combat to member states. [121]

International Commission for the Scientific Exploration
of the Mediterranean Sea
CIESMM, Paris, France

ACTIVITY: Studies and researches physical and chemical nature of the Mediterranean, including plankton, benthic animals, microbiology, flora, brine waters, underwater geology. [122]

International Commission of Civil Status
CIEC, The Hague, Netherlands

ACTIVITIES: 1. Researches simplification and unification of civil status administration and the rights of the individual. 2. Exchanges information and advises on civil status. 3. Publishes civil status card index. [123]

International Committee of Military Medicine and Pharmacy
ICMMP, Liège, Belgium

ACTIVITY: Fosters collaboration of members to maintain and improve care of war invalids. [124]

International Computation Center
ICC, Rome, Italy

ACTIVITIES: 1. Collects, evaluates, and develops existing theories and methods of scientific research and in the teaching of data processing. 2. Renders consulting and computation services. 3. Issues publications on computation, technical reports, and terminology. 4. Serves as clearinghouse for computer services.
Affiliated with UNESCO. [125]

International Copyright Committee:
see **Intergovernmental Copyright Committee**

International Cotton Advisory Committee
ICAC, Washington, D.C., US

ACTIVITIES: 1. Keeps abreast of and collects and disseminates statistics on world cotton production, trade, consumption, stocks, and prices. 2. Suggests measures for international collaboration. 3.

Holds monthly and annual meetings. 4. Publishes reviews, bulletins, and other cotton studies. [126]

International Cotton Institute
Brussels, Belgium

ACTIVITY: Fosters the demand for cotton and cotton products by means of market research, public relations campaigns, and sales promotion. [127]

International Council for the Exploration of the Sea
ICES, Charlottenlund, Denmark

ACTIVITIES: 1. Fosters and coordinates research of the sea. 2. Publishes reports. [128]

International Diplomatic Academy
Paris, France

ACTIVITY: Organizes study of international affairs by statesmen and diplomats. [129]
Details of membership could not be ascertained at time of publication.

International Exhibitions Bureau
BIE, Paris, France

ACTIVITIES: 1. Oversees the fulfillment of the Diplomatic Agreement rules by members. 2. Selects and registers applications for international exhibitions. 3. Regulates members' participation in international exhibitions held by nonmembers. Byelorussia and Ukraine are members of BIE. [130]

International Hydrographic Bureau
IHB, Monte Carlo, Monaco

ACTIVITIES: 1. Establishes association between members' hydrographic offices. 2. Coordinates members' work to promote easier and safer navigation. 3. Encourages uniformity in charts, hydrographic documents, and survey methods. 4. Encourages development of hydrographic science, theory, and practice. [131]

International Institute for Educational Planning
IIEP, Paris, France

ACTIVITIES: 1. Conducts training for educational planning and personnel research. 2. Cooperates with universities on basic studies. 3. Works in cooperation with UNESCO and other specialized agencies of the UN. [132]

International Institute for the Unification of Private Law
UNIDROIT, Rome, Italy

ACTIVITIES: 1. Prepares drafts of law with the object of establishing uniform legislation. 2. Prepares drafts of international agreements on private law. 3. Undertakes studies of comparative law. 4. Participates in allied projects of other organizations. 5. Organizes conferences and publishes works. [133]

The International Institute of Refrigeration
IIR, Paris, France

ACTIVITIES: 1. Develops research, teaching, and popularization techniques of the science, technology, and uses of refrigeration. 2. Maintains liaison with world organizations. 3. Prepares international codes, congresses, and recommendations. 4. Publishes bulletins, reports, directories. [134]

International Lead and Zinc Study Group
ILZSG, c/o UN, New York, US

ACTIVITY: Makes studies of lead and zinc, especially with respect to supply and demand, and considers solutions to special problems. [135]

International Moselle Company
SIM, Trier, West Germany
ACTIVITY: Finances and executes canalization of the Moselle River for navigation. [136]

International North Pacific Fisheries Commission
INPFC, Vancouver, Canada
ACTIVITY: Encourages conservation of fisheries resources of the North Pacific Ocean and promotes and coordinates scientific studies on conservation. [137]

International Office of Epizootics
OIE, Paris, France
ACTIVITIES: 1. Conducts research on contagious diseases of live-stock. 2. Serves as center of information and documentation on epizootic diseases and advises on means to combat them. 3. Makes recommendations for international agreements. 4. Maintains specialized commissions on foot-and-mouth disease, usages of biological products, fish diseases, and others.
Nonself-governing members: Angola, New Caledonia, Mozambique, and the Asian Portuguese dependencies, and French Somaliland. [138]

International Olive Oil Council
IOOC, Madrid, Spain
ACTIVITIES: 1. Administers the International Agreement on Olive Oil. 2. Promotes expansion of olive growing, consumption. 3. Endeavors to stabilize the olive market and prices. 4. Standardizes national olive oil regulations, contracts, standards and methods of analysis. 5. Promotes fair trade practices among producers, exporters, and consumers. [139]

International Organization of Legal Metrology
IOLM, Paris, France
ACTIVITIES: 1. Studies ways and means of unifying methods and regulations of measurement. 2. Serves as center of information and documentation on national methods of measurement. 3. Checks and verifies instruments of measurement. 4. Makes recommendations on characteristics and standards of measurement. 5. Publishes legal texts of members.
Nonself-governing members: overseas dependencies of France and Netherlands. [140]

International Patent Institute
IIB, The Hague, Netherlands
ACTIVITY: Carries out documentary research of patents for governments, persons, or corporations of member countries or of persons of any country that is a member of the Industrial Property Convention. [141]

International Poplar Commission
IPC, Rome, Italy
ACTIVITIES: 1. Studies the scientific, technical, social, and economic aspects of poplar and willow cultivation. 2. Promotes exchange of ideas and materials between research workers, producers, and users. Affiliated with the Food and Agriculture Organization of UN. [142]

International Red Locust Control Service
IRLCS, Abercorn, Zambia
ACTIVITIES: 1. Researches chemical and ecological methods for improvement of control of the red locust. 2. Maintains and equips active force to fight red locust.
Nonself-governing members: Angola, Mozambique. [143]

International Regional Organization against Plant and Animal Diseases
OIRSA, San Salvador, El Salvador
ACTIVITY: Studies and recommends to member states improved methods of detection and combat of plant and animal diseases. [144]

International Relief Union
IRU, Geneva, Switzerland
ACTIVITIES: 1. Furnishes, organizes, and coordinates aid in cases of natural calamities. 2. Encourages study of prevention of disasters. 3. Serves as center of information and documentation on natural calamities. 4. Promotes mutual international assistance. [145]

International Rice Commission
IRC, Bangkok, Thailand
ACTIVITY: Promotes national and international activity in production, conservation, distribution, and consumption of rice. Affiliated with the Food and Agriculture Organization of UN. [146]

International Rubber Study Group
IRSG, London, England
ACTIVITIES: 1. Provides a forum for production, consumption, and trading problems of natural and synthetic rubber. 2. Publishes statistical bulletins, news sheets, and others. [147]

International Secretariat for Volunteer Service
ISVS, Washington, D.C., US
ACTIVITIES: 1. Serves as clearinghouse for information and know-how on volunteer services. 2. Fosters assistance to developing nations in the field of volunteer services. 3. Provides technical assistance. [148]

International Sericultural Commission
ISC, Alès, France
ACTIVITIES: 1. Maintains Sericultural (silkworm) Documentation Center. 2. Publishes bulletins, meetings proceedings, and specialized publications. 3. Organizes international meetings on sericultural science. 4. Exchanges information and carries on research. 5. Develops and coordinates work which establishes sericeous insects as "biological types." [149]

International Sugar Council
ISC, London, England
ACTIVITIES: 1. Assures supplies of sugar to importing countries and markets to exporting countries, at equitable and stable prices. 2. Promotes sugar consumption. 3. Prepares for an establishment of an effective regulative agreement. [150]

International Tea Committee
ITC, London, England
ACTIVITY: Operates as a statistical and information center.
Nonself-governing members: Portuguese African dependencies. [151]

International Telecommunications Satellite Consortium
INTELSAT, Washington, D.C., USA
ACTIVITY: Operates telecommunications satellites, for commercial communications, available to all countries. [152]

The International Tin Council
ITC, London, England
ACTIVITIES: 1. Operates the Second International Tin Agreement. 2. Regulates maladjustments between supply and demand of tin with view to alleviating unemployment. 3. Endeavors to achieve fair and

stable tin prices and adequate supplies by the operation of buffer stock or export control. 4. Collects and publishes statistics on tin. [153]

International Tsunami Information Center
ITIC, Honolulu, Hawaii, US

ACTIVITIES: 1. Disseminates tsunami warnings. 2. Engages and encourages research of tsunami phenomena and data, including preparation of a mareographic atlas. [154]

International Union for the Protection of Industrial Property
UIPPI, Geneva, Switzerland

ACTIVITY: Studies and makes recommendations for international measures for the protection of industrial property.
Nonself-governing members: overseas dependencies of Denmark, UK, France, Netherlands, Portugal, and Spain. [155]

International Union for the Protection of Literary and Artistic Works
IUPLAW, Geneva, Switzerland

ACTIVITIES: 1. Fosters protection for authors and artists, and prepares an international agreement for the protection of performers, producers of phonograms, and of broadcasters. 2. Fosters international cooperation for the protection of literary and artistic works.
NOTE: Nonself-governing members: French overseas territories, Netherlands Antilles, Norfolk Islands, Papua, Spanish overseas territories, South West Africa, UK overseas territories. [156]

International Union for the Protection of New Varieties of Plants
Geneva, Switzerland

ACTIVITIES: 1. Identifies and secures rights for commercial application of new varieties of plants. 2. Serves as a forum of arbitration. [157]

International Union for the Publication of Customs Tariffs
ICTB, Brussels, Belgium

ACTIVITY: Publishes in English, French, German, Italian, and Spanish all the members' customs tariffs and modifications. [158]

International Vine and Wine Office
IWO, Paris, France

ACTIVITIES: 1. Collects, studies, and publishes information on scientific procedures and techniques of wine making and vine growing. 2. Endeavors to improve international wine matters. 3. Submits recommendations to members on matters of purity, authenticity, and suppression of fraud. [159]

International Whaling Commission
IWC, London, England

ACTIVITIES: 1. Makes recommendations for conservation and utilization of whale resources. 2. Organizes studies on whales and whaling. 3. Collects and analyzes statistics on whale stocks. 4. Studies and disseminates methods of maintaining and increasing whale populations. [160]

International Wheat Council
IWC, London, England

ACTIVITIES: 1. Administers the 1962 International Wheat Agreement regarding trade and prices. 2. Reviews the world wheat situation affecting international trade in wheat and flour. 3. Studies factors concerning wheat consumption and its increase, especially in developing countries.
NOTE: Western Samoa is a member of IWC. Nonself-governing members: overseas territories of Netherlands, Portugal, and UK. [161]

International Wine Office: see International Vine and Wine Office

International Wool Study Group
IWSG, London, England

ACTIVITIES: 1. Collects statistics on world wool trade. 2. Reviews world wool developments and considers possible solutions to any problems or situations of the world wool trade. [162]

Inter-Parliamentary Consultative Council of Benelux
ICPB, Brussels, Belgium

ACTIVITIES: 1. Advises members on matters related to the Benelux Economic Union. 2. Fosters cooperation in cultural and educational fields, unification of law, and foreign policy. [163]

Italian-Latin American Institute
ILAI, Rome, Italy

ACTIVITY: Fosters research and interchange in the cultural, socioeconomic, scientific, and technical fields. [164]

Joint Anti-Locust and Anti-Aviarian Organization
OCLALAV, Dakar, Senegal

ACTIVITIES: 1. Studies new techniques of fighting locust and bird pests. 2. Carries out antilocust and antibird pests operations. [165]

Joint Institute for Nuclear Research
JINR, Moscow, USSR

ACTIVITIES: 1. Conducts theoretical and experimental research in elementary particles, nuclear forces, nuclear structure, reactions, physics of solids and liquids and charged particle accelerators. 2. Carries out research of high and low energies. 3. Collaborates with national and international research establishments on peaceful uses of nuclear energy. [166]

Latin American Center for Monetary Studies
CEMLA, Mexico City, Mexico

ACTIVITIES: 1. Conducts research and accumulates information on banking, finance policies, and monetary problems. 2. Helps train banking personnel. 3. Serves as center of information and documentation. [167]

Latin American Center of Physics
CLAF, Rio de Janeiro, Brazil

ACTIVITIES: 1. Carries out physical science research. 2. Fosters the training of physical scientists. [168]

Latin American Common Market: see Latin American Free Trade Association

Latin American Educational Film Institute
ILCE, Mexico City, Mexico

ACTIVITIES: 1. Produces educational audiovisual films and other material. 2. Conducts a program of teacher training in audiovisual material. 3. Grants and fosters scholarships. [169]

Latin American Forestry Commission
LAFC, Santiago, Chile

ACTIVITIES: 1. Acts as forum for discussions of Latin American forest policies. 2. Advises and assists governments on problems of forest industries, and recommends action to promote forest development. 3. Promotes and coordinates education, training, and research in forestry and wood technology, and the norms in the use of forest land.
Affiliated with the Food and Agriculture Organization of UN. [170]

Latin American Free Trade Association
LAFTA, Montevideo, Uruguay
ACTIVITIES: 1. Eliminates barriers to intraregional trade and accelerates members' economic development by reduction of tariffs. 2. Calls on ECLA and OAS for technical aid. [171]

Latin American Institute for Economic and Social Planning
Santiago, Chile
ACTIVITIES: 1. Advises and trains personnel in the economic and social fields, at the request of members. 2. Conducts research in economic and social planning. [172]

League of Arab States
AL, Cairo, UAR
ACTIVITIES: 1. Coordinates national and international political and economic activities of members. 2. Revives and diffuses the cultural legacy of Arabs and develops Arab social consciousness. 3. Regulates legal relations between members. 4. Cooperates with UN and its agencies. 5. Disseminates information about members. [173]

Maghreb Permanent Consultative Committee
Tunis, Tunisia
ACTIVITIES: 1. Coordinates economic planning with view to establishment of a joint customs union. 2. Operates centers and bureaus in the fields of transportation, trade, esparto growing, industrial research. [174]

Mutual Assistance of the Latin American Government
Oil Companies
ARPEL, Lima, Peru
ACTIVITIES: 1. Fosters and organizes meetings, lectures, and other activities for the furtherance of technical and economic aspects of oil industry. 2. Promotes technical and economic agreements on the oil industry. [175]

Nordic Children's Film Council
Copenhagen, Denmark
ACTIVITIES: 1. Studies matters pertaining to children and the film medium. 2. Promotes children's educational and entertainment films for screen and TV. 3. Establishes standards of censorship. 4. Makes recommendations to members. [176]

Nordic Council
NC, Copenhagen, Denmark
ACTIVITY: Acts as consultative body on matters of common interests, and makes recommendations to parliaments and governments of members. [177]

North Atlantic Treaty Organization
NATO, Brussels, Belgium
ACTIVITIES: 1. Based on the principles laid down in the Charter of the United Nations, seeks to safeguard the freedom, common heritage, and civilization of members through collective defense. 2. Promotes unified political action. 3. Fosters cooperation in economic, scientific, and cultural activities. [178]

North-East Atlantic Fisheries Commission
London, England
ACTIVITY: Ensures the rational exploitation of fish reserves of the Northeast Atlantic. [179]

North Pacific Fur Seal Commission
Washington, D.C., US
ACTIVITIES: 1. Regulates the hunting of fur seals in the North Pacific. 2. Conducts research on conservation of the fur seal. [180]

Organisation Commune Africaine et Malgache
OCAM, Yaoundé, Cameroon
ACTIVITY: Fosters economic, political, social, technical and cultural cooperation among the African and Malagasy states. [181]

Organization for Cooperation and Coordination of Control
of Epidemic Disease
OCCCE, Bobo-Dioulasso, Upper Volta
ACTIVITY: Coordinates members' efforts against epidemic disease. [182]

Organization for Economic Cooperation and Development
OECD, Paris, France
ACTIVITIES: 1. Promotes economic growth, employment, a higher standard of living, and financial stability in member countries. 2. Contributes to sound economic expansion in member and nonmember countries. 3. Contributes to the expansion of world trade on a multilateral, nondiscriminatory basis. [183]

Organization for European Economic Cooperation (OEEC):
see Organization for Economic Cooperation and
Development (OECD)

Organization for the Collaboration of Railways
OSZhD, Warsaw, Poland
ACTIVITIES: 1. Develops international traffic and technical and scientific cooperation in the sphere of railway and road traffic. 2. Holds an annual Conference of Ministers of members. [184]

Organization of African Unity
OAU, Addis Ababa, Ethiopia
ACTIVITIES: 1. Promotes African unity and development. 2. Defends sovereignty and territorial integrity of members. 3. Eradicates colonialism. 4. Promotes international cooperation in accordance with the UN Charter and the Universal Declaration of Human Rights. 5. Coordinates members' economic, political, diplomatic, educational, cultural, health, scientific, and defense policies. [185]

Organization of African Unity Scientific and Research
Commission
OAU-STRC, Lagos, Nigeria
ACTIVITIES: 1. Holds symposia and conferences on technical and scientific matters. 2. Conducts fight against rinderpest. 3. Explores fisheries resources. 4. Conducts studies and campaign to improve cereal crops. [186]

Organization of American States
OAS, Washington, D.C., US
ACTIVITIES: 1. Seeks to achieve peace, security, justice, and the pacific settlement of disputes of members. 2. Promotes solidarity and economic, health, social, and cultural cooperation. 3. Strengthens defense collaboration against aggression and threat to the sovereignty, territorial integrity, and independence of members. 4. Has under its aegis agencies and subsidiary organizations dealing with specialized fields. 5. Disseminates information. [187]

Organization of Central American States (ODECA)
OCAS, San Salvador, El Salvador
ACTIVITIES: 1. Strengthens fraternal bonds among members and seeks to settle disputes by pacific means. 2. Develops economic, cultural, and social cooperation by joint action. [188]

Organization of the Development of African Tourism
ODTA, Paris, France
ACTIVITIES: 1. Offers technical services for development of tourist

industries of members. 2. Fosters joint representation abroad. [189]

Organization of Petroleum Exporting Countries
OPEC, Geneva, Switzerland
ACTIVITY: Coordinates and unifies policies of its members and determines the best means of safeguarding their interests.
NOTE: Abu Dhabi and Qatar are members of OPEC. [190]

Organization of Senegal Riparian States
OERS, Dakar, Senegal
ACTIVITY: Coordinates development and exploitation of the Senegal River basin. [191]

Pan American Health Organization
PAHO, Washington, D.C., US
ACTIVITIES: 1. Promotes eradication and control of communicable diseases. 2. Strengthens health services, such as maternal and child care, nutrition at local and national levels. 3. Encourages environmental sanitation, such as water supply. 4. Promotes education and professional training activities. 5. Supports biomedical research.
Affiliated with the Organization of American States. [192]

Pan American Highway Congress
PAC, Washington, D.C., US
ACTIVITY: Fosters regional integration of road construction in the Western Hemisphere. [193]

Pan American Institute of Geography and History
PAIGH, Mexico City, Mexico
ACTIVITIES: 1. Encourages, coordinates, and publicizes cartographic, geographic, and historical studies. 2. Initiates and executes studies requested by members. 3. Promotes cooperation among cartographic, geographic, and historical institutes.
Affiliated with the Organization of American States [194]

Pan American Sanitary Organization: see Pan American Health Organization

Pan American Union: see Organization of American States

Permanent Court of Arbitration
PC of A, The Hague, Netherlands
ACTIVITY: Promotes pacific settlement of international disputes. Byelorussia, and Ukraine are members of PC of A. [195]

Permanent International Bureau of Analytical Chemistry of Human and Animal Food
PIBAC, Paris, France
ACTIVITIES: 1. Verifies methods of analytical chemistry to determine national constituents of food. 2. Compares national methods with view to unification of analytical approaches. 3. Maintains specialized commissions for methods of estimating toxicity, antibiotics, pesticides and germicides, antiseptics, antioxydants, essences and aromatics. [196]

Picture and Sound World Organization
PSWO, Paris, France
ACTIVITIES: 1. Fosters interest in the social aspects of picture and sound. 2. Promotes supply of equipment to developing countries. [197]

Plant Protection Committee for the Southeast Asia and Pacific Region
Bangkok, Thailand
ACTIVITIES: 1. Determines procedures and arrangements necessary to implement the regional Plant Protection Agreement and makes recommendations to members. 2. Reviews members' progress reports. 3. Considers plant protection problems and mutual assistance.
Affiliated with the Food and Agriculture Organization of UN. [198]

Postal Union of the Americas and Spain
PUAS, Montevideo, Uruguay
ACTIVITIES: 1. Coordinates postal services among members. 2. Fosters common action of members in UPU congresses. 3. Serves as center of information and documentation. [199]

Provisional International Computation Center: see International Computation Center

Regional Co-operation for Development
CRD, Teheran, Iran
ACTIVITIES: 1. Fosters regional economic and cultural cooperation. 2. Initiates agreements among members in the fields of aviation, shipping, petroleum, trade development, finance, communications, and culture. [200]

Security Treaty of Australia, New Zealand and the United States of America
ANZUS, Canberra, Australia
ACTIVITIES: 1. Based on the principles laid down in the Charter of the United Nations, seeks to strengthen peace in the Pacific area by implementing their mutual security agreement. 2. Holds periodic consultations. [201]

Southeast Asian Ministers of Education Secretariat
SEAMES, Bangkok, Thailand
ACTIVITY: Institutes regional activity in the fields of medicine, biology, agriculture, science, mathematics, linguistics. [202]

South Pacific Commission
SPC, Noumea, New Caledonia
ACTIVITY: Assists members with their welfare, health, economic, and social programs by organizing research, training personnel, providing experts, financing study tours, and by collecting, preparing, and distributing information. [203]

Southeast Asia Treaty Organization
SEATO, Bangkok, Thailand
ACTIVITIES: 1. Based on the principles laid down in the Charter of the United Nations, seeks collective defense of members, and the settlement of international disputes by pacific means. 2. Fosters economic and social development, including technical assistance. [204]

Southwest Atlantic Fisheries Advisory Commission
SWAFAC, Rio de Janeiro, Brazil
ACTIVITY: Studies supplies of fish reserves in the South Atlantic with view to ensuring rational exploitation. [205]

Standing Technical Secretariat for the Conferences of Ministers of National Education in French-speaking African and Malagasy States
Dakar, Senegal
ACTIVITIES: 1. Ensures application of Conference resolutions. 2. Maintains relations with specialized educational and research organizations. [206]

Tripartite Commission for the Restitution of Monetary Gold
TCRMG, Brussels, Belgium
  ACTIVITY: Keeps record of war restitutions due members in monetary gold. [207]

Tripartite Commission on the Working Conditions
  of Rhine Boatmen
Strasbourg, France
  ACTIVITY: Arbitrates disputes arising from the agreements among members. [208]

Union of Central African States
UEAC, Bangui, Central African Republic
  ACTIVITY: Coordinates general policies of members with view to ensuring harmony in economic, social, and political spheres. [209]

UNESCO Research Center on Social and Economic
  Development in Southern Asia
Delhi, India
  ACTIVITIES: 1. Collects and interprets research material on social sciences. 2. Provides documentation for social scientists. 3. Promotes pilot studies, organization of symposia, and seminars. 4. Provides experts at request of governments. 5. Organizes research under contracts with governments and other institutions. [210]

Warsaw Pact: see **Warsaw Treaty Organization**

Warsaw Treaty Organization
WTO, Moscow, USSR
  ACTIVITIES: 1. Based on the principles laid down in the Charter of the United Nations, organizes collective defense of members. 2. Holds consultations on international questions of common interest. [211]

West African Customs Union
Abidjan, Ivory Coast
  ACTIVITY: Unifies and standardizes customs tariffs of members. [212]

West African Monetary Union
Nouakchott, Mauritania
  ACTIVITY: Assures members monetary unity. [213]

West African Postal and Telecommunications Union
Niamey, Niger
  ACTIVITY: Coordinates telecommunications and postal services between member states. [214]

Western European Union
WEU, London, England
  ACTIVITIES: 1. Promotes unity and progressive integration of Europe. 2. Ensures close cooperation with NATO and the adherence by members to agreed land, air, and sea force limits. 3. Develops cooperation between members in armament production and utilization of armament resources. [215]

Country	1	2	3	4	5	6	7	8	9	10	11	12	13	14	15	16	17	18	19	20
Afghanistan															•	•				
Albania																				•
Andorra																				
Algeria					•						•	•								
Argentina																				
Australia														•	•	•				
Austria															•					
Barbados																				
Belgium	•														•					
Bolivia																				
Botswana								•												
Brazil																				
Br Honduras																				
Bhutan																				
Bulgaria																				•
Burma													•			•				
Burundi								•												
Cambodia															•	•				
Cameroon		•	•	•	•	•														
Canada															•					
Cent. Afr. Rep.		•	•	•		•														
Ceylon		•	•	•	•										•	•				
Chad		•	•	•		•														
Chile																•				
China																•				
Colombia																				
Congo (Brazzaville)		•	•	•	•	•	•	•												
Congo (Kinshasa)		•	•			•														
Costa Rica																				
Cuba																				
Cyprus																				
Czechoslovakia																				•
Dahomey		•	•	•	•															
Denmark															•					
Dominican Rep.																				
Ecuador																				
El Salvador																				
Equat. Guinea																				
Ethiopia						•														
Fiji																				
Finland													•							•
France	•																			•
Gabon		•	•	•	•															
Gambia																				
Germany, East																				
Germany, West	•														•					•
Ghana						•			•	•			•							
Greece																				•
Guatemala																				
Guinea						•														
Guyana																				
Haiti																				
Honduras																				
Hungary																				•
Iceland																				
India										•				•	•	•		•		
Indonesia													•	•	•	•		•	•	
Iran														•	•	•				
Iraq											•	•	•							
Ireland																				•
Israel																				
Italy																				
Ivory Coast		•	•	•	•	•	•													
Jamaica																				
Japan													•	•	•	•		•		
Jordan											•	•	•							
Kenya						•				•										
Korea, North																				
Korea, South														•	•	•	•			
Kuwait											•	•								
Laos															•	•				
Lebanon											•	•								
Lesotho								•												

Country	1	2	3	4	5	6	7	8	9	10	11	12	13	14	15	16	17	18	19	20
Liberia						•														
Libya										•	•	•								
Liechtenstein																				
Luxembourg	•																			
Madagascar		•	•	•	•															
Malawi						•		•												
Malaysia																•	•	•		•
Maldives																				
Mali						•		•												
Malta																				
Mauritania			•	•	•	•														
Mauritius																				
Mexico																				
Monaco																				
Mongolia																	•			
Morocco						•			•		•	•								
Nauru																				
Nepal																•	•			
Netherlands	•														•					•
New Zealand															•	•	•			
Nicaragua																				
Niger		•	•	•	•	•	•													
Nigeria						•														
Norway															•					
Oman																				
Pakistan														•		•	•		•	
Panama																				
Paraguay																				
Persian Gulf Shay.																				
Peru																				
Philippines															•	•	•	•	•	
Poland																				•
Portugal																				
Rhodesia								•												
Romania																				•
Rwanda		•	•		•	•														
San Marino																				
Sa'udi Arabia										•	•									
Senegal		•	•	•	•	•														
Sierra Leone						•														
Singapore																•	•		•	
Somalia						•														
South Africa								•												
South Yemen												•								
Spain																				•
Sudan						•				•	•	•								
Swaziland								•												
Sweden															•					•
Switzerland	•																			•
Syria											•	•								
Taiwan														•	•		•	•		
Tanzania						•														
Thailand														•	•	•	•	•	•	
Togo		•	•	•	•	•														
Tonga																				
Trinidad & Tob.																				
Tunisia						•					•	•								
Turkey																				
Uganda						•														
USSR																				
UAR						•				•	•	•	•							
UK															•					•
US															•					
Upper Volta		•	•	•	•	•														
Uruguay																				
Vatican																				
Venezuela																				
Viet-Nam, North																				
Viet-Nam, South														•	•		•			
Western Samoa														•	•					
Yemen											•	•								
Yugoslavia																				•
Zambia						•														

Country	21	22	23	24	25	26	27	28	29	30	31	32	33	34	35	36	37	38	39	40
Afghanistan														•						
Albania																				
Andorra																				
Algeria																				
Argentina																				
Australia															•	•	•	•	•	•
Austria											•									
Barbados			•	•										•						
Belgium	•	•								•	•									
Bolivia																				
Botswana																				
Brazil													•							
Br Honduras																				
Bhutan														•						
Bulgaria											•									
Burma														•						
Burundi																				
Cambodia														•						
Cameroon						•							•							
Canada														•	•	•	•	•	•	•
Cent. Afr. Rep.						•														
Ceylon															•	•	•	•	•	•
Chad						•														
Chile																				
China																				
Colombia																				
Congo (Brazzaville)						•														
Congo (Kinshasa)																				
Costa Rica							•	•	•											
Cuba																				
Cyprus																•	•	•	•	
Czechoslovakia											•									
Dahomey																				
Denmark											•									
Dominican Rep.				•																
Ecuador																				
El Salvador							•	•	•											
Equat. Guinea																				
Ethiopia																				
Fiji																				
Finland											•									
France			•							•	•									
Gabon						•														
Gambia																•	•	•	•	
Germany, East																				
Germany, West										•	•									
Ghana													•		•	•	•	•	•	•
Greece																				
Guatemala							•	•	•											
Guinea																				
Guyana			•	•															•	
Haiti			•																	
Honduras							•	•	•											
Hungary											•									
Iceland																				
India														•	•	•	•	•	•	•
Indonesia														•						
Iran											•	•		•						
Iraq											•									
Ireland														A						
Israel																				
Italy											•									
Ivory Coast													•							
Jamaica			•													•	•	•	•	
Japan														•						
Jordan																				
Kenya																•	•	•	•	
Korea, North																				
Korea, South														•						
Kuwait																				
Laos														•						
Lebanon																				
Lesotho																				

Country	21	22	23	24	25	26	27	28	29	30	31	32	33	34	35	36	37	38	39	40
Liberia																				
Libya																				
Liechtenstein											•									
Luxembourg	•	•									•									
Madagascar																				
Malawi																•	•	•	•	•
Malaysia															•	•	•	•	•	•
Maldives																				
Mali																				
Malta																•	•		•	
Mauritania																				
Mauritius																				
Mexico																				
Monaco																				
Mongolia																				
Morocco											•									
Nauru																				
Nepal														•						
Netherlands	•	•	○							•	•									
New Zealand														•		•	•	•	•	•
Nicaragua							•	•	•											
Niger																				
Nigeria														•		•	•	•	•	•
Norway											•									
Oman																				
Pakistan														•	•	•	•	•	•	•
Panama										•										
Paraguay																				
Persian Gulf Shay.																				
Peru																				
Philippines														•						
Poland											•									
Portugal											•									
Rhodesia																		•	•	
Romania											•									
Rwanda																				
San Marino																				
Sa'udi Arabia																				
Senegal																				
Sierra Leone																•	•	•	•	
Singapore															•		•	•	•	•
Somalia																				
South Africa																				
South Yemen																				
Spain											•									
Sudan																				
Swaziland																				
Sweden											•									
Switzerland										•	•									
Syria																				
Taiwan																				
Tanzania																•	•	•	•	•
Thailand														•						
Togo														•						
Tonga																				
Trinidad & Tob.								•								•	•	•	•	•
Tunisia											•									
Turkey											•	•								
Uganda																•	•	•	•	•
USSR																				
UAR																				
UK			○							•	•	•		•	•	•	•	•	•	•
US			○											•						
Upper Volta																				
Uruguay																				
Vatican																				
Venezuela																				
Viet-Nam, North																				
Viet-Nam, South														•						
Western Samoa																				
Yemen																				
Yugoslavia											•									
Zambia																•			•	•

Country	41	42	43	44	45	46	47	48	49	50	51	52	53	54	55	56	57	58	59	60
Afghanistan																				
Albania					●															
Andorra																				
Algeria											●									●
Argentina																				
Australia	●	●	●								●									
Austria						●	●				●	●							●	
Barbados	●	●																		
Belgium				●		●	●	●		●	●							●	●	●
Bolivia					●															
Botswana	●	●																		
Brazil																				
Br Honduras																				
Bhutan																				
Bulgaria						●														
Burma																				
Burundi											●									
Cambodia																				
Cameroon											●						●			
Canada	●	●	●																	
Cent. Afr. Rep.				●													●			
Ceylon	●	●									●									
Chad				●													●			
Chile											●									
China																				
Colombia																				
Congo (Brazzaville)				●													●			
Congo (Kinshasa)																				
Costa Rica																				
Cuba																				
Cyprus	●	●				●	●				●								●	
Czechoslovakia					●						●	●							●	
Dahomey									●		●									
Denmark						●	●				●									
Dominican Rep.																				
Ecuador																				
El Salvador																				
Equat. Guinea																				
Ethiopia													●							
Fiji																				
Finland											●									
France						●	●	●		●	●	●						●	●	●
Gabon				●							●						●			
Gambia	●	●																		
Germany, East					●															
Germany, West						●	●	●		●	●							●	●	●
Ghana	●	●																		
Greece						●	●				●									
Guatemala																				
Guinea																				
Guyana	●	●																		
Haiti											●									
Honduras																				
Hungary						●					●								●	
Iceland						●	●													
India	●	●	●																	
Indonesia											●									
Iran											●									
Iraq																				
Ireland						●	●				●								●	
Israel											●								●	
Italy						●	●	●		●	●							●	●	●
Ivory Coast									●		●									
Jamaica	●	●									●									
Japan											●									
Jordan											●									
Kenya	●	●									●		●	●	●	●				
Korea, North																				
Korea, South																				
Kuwait																				
Laos																				
Lebanon											●									
Lesotho	●																			

Country	41	42	43	44	45	46	47	48	49	50	51	52	53	54	55	56	57	58	59	60
Liberia																				
Libya																				
Liechtenstein																				
Luxembourg						●	●	●		●	●							●	●	●
Madagascar											●									
Malawi	●	●									●									
Malaysia	●	●									●									
Maldives																				
Mali																				
Malta		●					●	●												
Mauritania																				
Mauritius	●																			
Mexico																				
Monaco																				
Mongolia																				
Morocco																				
Nauru																				
Nepal																				
Netherlands						●	●	●		●	●							●	●	●
New Zealand	●	●	●								●									
Nicaragua																				
Niger														●						
Nigeria	●	●									●									
Norway						●	●				●									
Oman																				
Pakistan	●	○	●								●									
Panama																				
Paraguay																				
Persian Gulf Shay.																				
Peru																				
Philippines																				
Poland						●													●	
Portugal											●									
Rhodesia																				
Romania						●							●							
Rwanda											●									
San Marino																				
Sa'udi Arabia																				
Senegal																				
Sierra Leone	●	●																		
Singapore	●	●																		
Somalia													●							
South Africa			●																	
South Yemen																				
Spain											●								●	
Sudan											●									
Swaziland																				
Sweden						●	●				●								●	
Switzerland						●	●				●								●	
Syria											●									
Taiwan																				
Tanzania	●	●									●		●	●	●	●				
Thailand																				
Togo														●						
Tonga																				
Trinidad & Tob.	●	●																		
Tunisia											●								●	
Turkey						●	●				●								●	
Uganda											●		●	●	●	●				
USSR					●						●	●								
UAR																				
UK	●	●	●			●	●				●									●
US																				
Upper Volta														●						
Uruguay																				
Vatican																				
Venezuela																				
Viet-Nam, North																				
Viet-Nam, South																				
Western Samoa																				
Yemen																				
Yugoslavia			●								●	●							●	
Zambia		●																		

Country	61	62	63	64	65	66	67	68	69	70	71	72	73	74	75	76	77	78	79	80
Afghanistan																				
Albania																				
Andorra																				
Algeria																				
Argentina																				
Australia																				
Austria	●		●	●	●		●	●	●	●		●	●	●	●			●		●
Barbados																				
Belgium	●	●	●	●		●	●	●		●	●	●	●		●	●			●	●
Bolivia																				
Botswana																				
Brazil																				
Br Honduras																				
Bhutan																				
Bulgaria																				
Burma																				
Burundi																				
Cambodia																				
Cameroon																				
Canada																				A
Cent. Afr. Rep.																				
Ceylon																				
Chad																				
Chile																				
China																				
Colombia																				
Congo (Brazzaville)																				
Congo (Kinshasa)																				
Costa Rica																				
Cuba																				
Cyprus			●	●	●			●			●	●	●	●			●			
Czechoslovakia	●																			
Dahomey																				
Denmark	●		●	●	●						●	●	●	●						
Dominican Rep.																				
Ecuador																				
El Salvador																				
Equat. Guinea																				
Ethiopia																				
Fiji																				
Finland							●			●	●		●	●			●	A		
France	●	●		●	●		●	●	●	●		●	●	●		●	●		●	●
Gabon																				
Gambia																				
Germany, East																				
Germany, West	●	●		●		●	●	●	●	●		●	●	●	●		●		●	
Ghana																				
Greece	●		●	●	●						●	●	●	●	●					
Guatemala																				
Guinea																				
Guyana																				
Haiti																				
Honduras																				
Hungary																				
Iceland			●	●	●			●				●	●	●			●			●
India																				
Indonesia																				
Iran																				
Iraq																				
Ireland	●		●	●	●				●	●	●						●			●
Israel																		●		
Italy	●	●	●		●	●	●	●		●	●	●	●	●		●	●		●	●
Ivory Coast																				
Jamaica																				
Japan																				A
Jordan																				
Kenya																				
Korea, North																				
Korea, South																				
Kuwait																				
Laos																				
Lebanon																				
Lesotho																				

Country	61	62	63	64	65	66	67	68	69	70	71	72	73	74	75	76	77	78	79	80
Liberia																				
Libya																				
Liechtenstein												●	●							
Luxembourg	●	●	●	●		●	●	●	●		●	●	●	●			●		●	●
Madagascar																				
Malawi																				
Malaysia																				
Maldives																				
Mali																				
Malta						●	●	●			●					●	●		●	
Mauritania																				
Mauritius																				
Mexico																				
Monaco												●	●							
Mongolia																				
Morocco																				
Nauru																				
Nepal																				
Netherlands	●	●	●	●		●	●	●	●	●	●	●	●	●	●		●			●
New Zealand																				
Nicaragua																				
Niger																				
Nigeria																				
Norway	●		●	●		●	●			●	●							●	●	●
Oman																				
Pakistan																				
Panama																				
Paraguay																				
Persian Gulf Shay.																				
Peru																				
Philippines																				
Poland	●																●			
Portugal	●						●	●	●		●	●	●				●	●		
Rhodesia																	●			
Romania																				
Rwanda																				
San Marino												●	●							
Sa'udi Arabia																				
Senegal																				
Sierra Leone																				
Singapore																				
Somalia																				
South Africa																				
South Yemen																				
Spain	●						●	●	●		●	●	●					●		●
Sudan																				
Swaziland																				
Sweden	●		●	●	●	●	●	●			●	●	●	●	●			●	●	●
Switzerland	●		●	●		●														
Syria																				
Taiwan																				
Tanzania																				
Thailand																				
Togo																				
Tonga																				
Trinidad & Tob.																				
Tunisia																				
Turkey			●	●	●		●				●	●	●	●			●			●
Uganda																				
USSR																				
UAR																				
UK	●		●	●		●					●	●		●	●			●	●	A
US																				A
Upper Volta																				
Uruguay																				
Vatican												●	●							
Venezuela																				
Viet-Nam, North																				
Viet-Nam, South																				
Western Samoa																				
Yemen																				
Yugoslavia	●		●			●			●			●					●			
Zambia																				

Country	81	82	83	84	85	86	87	88	89	90	91	92	93	94	95	96	97	98	99	100
Afghanistan																				
Albania																				
Andorra																				
Algeria							•													
Argentina											•				•	•	•	•	•	•
Australia						•					•									
Austria	•			•					•											
Barbados															•	•	•		•	
Belgium	•	•	•	•	•		•													
Bolivia															•	•	•	•	•	•
Botswana																				
Brazil															•	•	•		•	
Br Honduras																				
Bhutan																				
Bulgaria																				
Burma											•									
Burundi													•							
Cambodia											•									
Cameroon												•								
Canada																	○			
Cent. Afr. Rep.											•									
Ceylon											•									
Chad																				
Chile															•	•	•	•	•	•
China																				
Colombia											•				•	•	•	•	•	•
Congo (Brazzaville)													•							
Congo (Kinshasa)												•								
Costa Rica							•							•	•	•	•	•	•	•
Cuba														★	★		★			
Cyprus			•			•														
Czechoslovakia																				
Dahomey													•							
Denmark	•			•	•	○			•											
Dominican Rep.											•				•	•	•	•	•	•
Ecuador											•				•	•	•	•	•	•
El Salvador								•	•						•	•	•	•	•	•
Equat. Guinea																				
Ethiopia													•							
Fiji																				
Finland									•											
France	•	•	•	•	•	•	•			•	•									
Gabon													•							
Gambia																				
Germany, East																				
Germany, West	•	•	•	•	•		•			•										
Ghana	•				•			•		•										
Greece	•				•															
Guatemala								•			•				•	•	•	•	•	•
Guinea																				
Guyana																				
Haiti														•	•	•	•	•	•	•
Honduras							•					•	•		•	•	•	•	•	•
Hungary																				
Iceland				•																
India											•									
Indonesia											•									
Iran																				
Iraq																				
Ireland		•	•						•											
Israel								•	•											
Italy	•		•	•	•	•				•										
Ivory Coast													•							
Jamaica																				
Japan									•	•										
Jordan																				
Kenya													•							
Korea, North																				
Korea, South											•									
Kuwait																				
Laos																				
Lebanon						•														
Lesotho																				

Country	81	82	83	84	85	86	87	88	89	90	91	92	93	94	95	96	97	98	99	100
Liberia																				
Libya							•													
Liechtenstein																				
Luxembourg	•	•	•																	
Madagascar													•							
Malawi																				
Malaysia											•									
Maldives																				
Mali																				
Malta				•			•													
Mauritania																				
Mauritius																				
Mexico																•	•	•	•	•
Monaco																				
Mongolia																				
Morocco							•													
Nauru																				
Nepal																				
Netherlands	•	•	•	•	•	•			•		•									
New Zealand																				
Nicaragua							•		•			•			•	•	•	•	•	•
Niger																				
Nigeria																				
Norway	•								•											
Oman																				
Pakistan											•									
Panama								•				•			•	•	•	•	•	•
Paraguay								•							•	•	•	•	•	•
Persian Gulf Shay.																				
Peru								•							•	•	•	•	•	•
Philippines											•									
Poland																				
Portugal								•												
Rhodesia																				
Romania																				
Rwanda												•								
San Marino																				
Sa'udi Arabia																				
Senegal																				
Sierra Leone												•								
Singapore																				
Somalia																				
South Africa																				
South Yemen																				
Spain	•			•		•		•	•											
Sudan																				
Swaziland																				
Sweden	•			•	•				•											
Switzerland	•			•	•	○			•											
Syria																				
Taiwan																				
Tanzania													•							
Thailand											•									
Togo												•								
Tonga																				
Trinidad & Tob.																•	•		•	•
Tunisia							•													
Turkey				•		•			•											
Uganda												•								
USSR																				
UAR							•		•											
UK	•	•		•	•	•		•		•										
US								•								•	•	○	•	•
Upper Volta																				
Uruguay															•	•	•	•	•	•
Vatican																				
Venezuela														•	•	•	•	•	•	•
Viet-Nam, North																				
Viet-Nam, South											•									
Western Samoa																				
Yemen																				
Yugoslavia								•	•											
Zambia																				

	101	102	103	104	105	106	107	108	109	110	111	112	113	114	115	116	117	118	119	120
Afghanistan														●						
Albania															●					
Andorra								●												
Algeria									●			●								
Argentina	●	●	●	●		●		●	●			●		●			●			
Australia						●		●	●			●								
Austria						●		●	●			●	●			●				
Barbados			●	●																
Belgium						●		●	●			●	●	●	●					
Bolivia	●		●	●		●		●	●			●		●						
Botswana																				
Brazil	●	●	●	●		●		●	●			●	●	●	●					
Br Honduras																				
Bhutan																				
Bulgaria											●	●	●		●					
Burma																				
Burundi												●		●			●			
Cambodia								●			●			●						
Cameroon										●		●		●						
Canada		●						●	●			●	●				●			
Cent. Afr. Rep.										●				●						
Ceylon														●	●					
Chad										●				●						
Chile	●	●	●	●		●		●	●			●	●							
China																				
Colombia	●	●	●			●					●						●			
Congo (Brazzaville)								●		●	●			●			●			
Congo (Kinshasa)										●										
Costa Rica	●		●	●	●			●			●									
Cuba		●	★	★				●	●											
Cyprus														●	●					
Czechoslovakia								●			●	●	●							
Dahomey										●				●	●					
Denmark								●	●				●	●		●				
Dominican Rep.	●		●	●								●	●		●					
Ecuador	●	●	●	●	●	●	●	●	●			●					●			
El Salvador	●		●	●													●			
Equat. Guinea																				
Ethiopia														●						
Fiji																				
Finland								●	●			●	●	●						
France								●	●			●	●	●				●	●	●
Gabon										●				●						
Gambia											●									
Germany, East											●									
Germany, West						●		●	●			●	●	●	●				●	●
Ghana								●	●			●								
Greece						●		●	●			●								
Guatemala	●	●	●			●											●			
Guinea															●					
Guyana																				
Haiti	●		●	●		●											●			
Honduras	●		●	●		●														
Hungary												●	●	●						
Iceland								●	●					●				●	●	
India								●	●				●	●						
Indonesia									●					●						
Iran																				
Iraq								●							●					
Ireland								●				●	●	●						
Israel						●		●	●			●			●					
Italy						●	●	●	●			●	●	●	●		●	●		
Ivory Coast									●					●						
Jamaica																				
Japan								●	●			●	●	●			●			
Jordan												●		●						
Kenya									●	●				●			●			
Korea, North								●												
Korea, South								●				●	●	●						
Kuwait												●		●						
Laos								●												
Lebanon								●	●			●		●						
Lesotho																				

	101	102	103	104	105	106	107	108	109	110	111	112	113	114	115	116	117	118	119	120
Liberia								●				●		●	●			●		
Libya															●					
Liechtenstein								●												
Luxembourg						●	●	●	●					●				●		●
Madagascar													●	●						
Malawi								●												
Malaysia											●			●						
Maldives																				
Mali										●	●									
Malta															●					
Mauritania																				
Mauritius													●		●					
Mexico	●	●	●	●	●		●	●	●			●	●		●		●			
Monaco								●	●											
Mongolia											●									
Morocco								●					●	●			●			
Nauru																				
Nepal																				
Netherlands								●				●	●	●						
New Zealand																				
Nicaragua	●		●	●				●									●	●		
Niger										●				●						
Nigeria											●			●	●		●			
Norway						●		●	●				●	●					●	●
Oman																				
Pakistan								●						●						
Panama	●	●	●	●	●	●					●			●			●	●		
Paraguay	●		●	●		●														
Persian Gulf Shay.																				
Peru	●	●	●	●		●						●			●					
Philippines								●						●						
Poland								●			●	●	●		●	●				
Portugal								●				●	●		●	●				
Rhodesia																				
Romania								●			●	●	●							
Rwanda																	●			
San Marino																				
Sa'udi Arabia														●						
Senegal										●				●						
Sierra Leone										●		●				●				
Singapore											●									
Somalia																				
South Africa								●					●							
South Yemen																				
Spain						●		●	●			●	●					●	●	
Sudan											●			●						
Swaziland																				
Sweden						●		●	●			●	●	●	●					
Switzerland						●						●	●							
Syria																				
Taiwan								●					●	●			●			
Tanzania											●			●						
Thailand								●						●						
Togo														●			●			
Tonga																				
Trinidad & Tob.							●	●												
Tunisia								●	●						●					
Turkey																				
Uganda										●			●	●			●			
USSR											●		●	●						●
UAR								●				●		●						
UK						●	●	●	●			●	●	●	●			●	●	●
US	●	●	●	●	●		●	●	●			●	●	●					●	●
Upper Volta																				
Uruguay	●		●	●		●								●						
Vatican								●												
Venezuela	●		●	●		●		●	●			●	●	●		●				
Viet-Nam, North																				
Viet-Nam, South														●						
Western Samoa																				
Yemen																				
Yugoslavia								●				●	●	●	●		●			
Zambia							●													

	121	122	123	124	125	126	127	128	129	130	131	132	133	134	135	136	137	138	139	140
Afghanistan				●														●		
Albania																		●		
Andorra																				
Algeria	●		●											●	●			●	●	
Argentina			●	●		●					●			●				●	●	
Australia						●					●			●	●			●		●
Austria			●	●		●							●	●	●			●		●
Barbados																				
Belgium		●	●		●		●		●				●	●				●	●	●
Bolivia				●																
Botswana																				
Brazil				●									●	●						
Br Honduras																				
Bhutan																				
Bulgaria										●			●	●				●		●
Burma				●							●									
Burundi																				
Cambodia				●																
Cameroon																		●		
Canada						●		●		●	●			●	●		●	●		
Cent. Afr. Rep.														●						
Ceylon																				
Chad						●														
Chile						●					●	●								
China																				
Colombia				●		●						●	●							
Congo (Brazzaville)				●																
Congo (Kinshasa)				●																
Costa Rica																				
Cuba				●	●						●									●
Cyprus																		●		
Czechoslovakia				●					●					●	●					
Dahomey																				
Denmark				●		●		●		●	●		●	●	●			●		
Dominican Rep.				●							●								●	●
Ecuador			●	●								●								
El Salvador				●		●														
Equat. Guinea																				
Ethiopia																				
Fiji																				
Finland			●		●	●		●		●			●			●		●		
France	●	●	●	●	●		●			●			●	●				●	●	
Gabon														●						
Gambia																				
Germany, East																				
Germany, West	●		●	●		●		●		●	●	●	●	●	●		●	●	●	
Ghana			●	●																
Greece	●	●	●	●				●		●	●		●	●						
Guatemala				●		●														
Guinea														●						●
Guyana																				
Haiti				●							●									
Honduras				●																
Hungary				●						●			●	●				●		
Iceland								●			●									
India				●			●	●			●	●	●	●	●					
Indonesia				●							●		●	●				●		
Iran				●							●	●	●					●		
Iraq				●																
Ireland				●				●					●	●				●		
Israel	●	●		●	●				●				●	●				●	●	●
Italy	●	●	●	●	●			●			●		●	●				●	●	●
Ivory Coast				●										●						
Jamaica																				
Japan			●	●	●				●		●		●	●	●			●	●	●
Jordan																		●		
Kenya																		●		
Korea, North																				
Korea, South				●		●					●									
Kuwait																				
Laos				●																
Lebanon				●					●									●		●
Lesotho																				

	121	122	123	124	125	126	127	128	129	130	131	132	133	134	135	136	137	138	139	140
Liberia																				
Libya				●														●		
Liechtenstein																				
Luxembourg	●		●	●									●				●		●	
Madagascar				●										●				●		
Malawi																				
Malaysia																				
Maldives																				
Mali														●				●		
Malta				●																
Mauritania														●						
Mauritius																				
Mexico			●	●		●	●						●				●			
Monaco	●		●							●	●									●
Mongolia																				
Morocco	●		●								●			●	●			●	●	●
Nauru																				
Nepal																				
Netherlands	●		●	●		●		●		●	●		●	●			●		●	●
New Zealand			●								●	●		●						
Nicaragua				●								●								
Niger														●						
Nigeria				●										●	●					
Norway				●				●		●	●			●				●		
Oman																				
Pakistan				●		●					●	●								
Panama																				
Paraguay				●								●								
Persian Gulf Shay.																				
Peru				●		●						●		●						
Philippines				●																
Poland				●				●		●	●	●	●	●				●	●	
Portugal				●						●	●		●	●	●			●	●	
Rhodesia																				
Romania	●		●							●			●	●						
Rwanda																				
San Marino				●																
Sa'udi Arabia																				
Senegal				●									●	●						
Sierra Leone																				
Singapore																				
Somalia																				
South Africa													●	●	●					
South Yemen																				
Spain	●	●		●	●	●						●	●	●				●	●	●
Sudan				●		●	●													
Swaziland																				
Sweden				●			●			●	●		●	●	●			●		
Switzerland	●		●	●		●				●	●		●	●	●			●		
Syria				●																
Taiwan				●		●					●									
Tanzania				●	●						●									
Thailand				●							●							●		
Togo																				
Tonga																				
Trinidad & Tob.																				
Tunisia	●	●		●									●	●					●	●
Turkey	●	●	●			●					●			●					●	●
Uganda				●																
USSR								●	●	●		●		●	●			●		
UAR	●			●						●			●	●	●			●	●	●
UK						●	●			●	●	●	●	●	●		●	●	●	●
US							●	●			●	●	●	●	●		●			
Upper Volta																				
Uruguay				●										●						
Vatican				●								●								
Venezuela				●									●					●		
Viet-Nam, North																				
Viet-Nam, South				●										●				●		
Western Samoa																				
Yemen																				
Yugoslavia	●		●	●							●		●	●	●			●	●	
Zambia																				●

	141	142	143	144	145	146	147	148	149	150	151	152	153	154	155	156	157	158	159	160
Afghanistan					•													•		
Albania																		•		
Andorra																				
Algeria	•											•			•			•	•	
Argentina		•						•				•			•	•		•	•	•
Australia						•	•					•	•		•	•		•		
Austria		•					•	•				•	•					•		
Barbados																				
Belgium	•	•	•		•		•	•				•	•					•		
Bolivia													•							
Botswana				•																
Brazil							•	•					•		•					
Br Honduras																				
Bhutan																				
Bulgaria					•												•	•		
Burma						•	•													
Burundi				•																
Cambodia						•	•													
Cameroon						•						•				•				
Canada		•					•	•				•	•	•	•	•		•		•
Cent. Afr. Rep.																•				
Ceylon						•	•									•				
Chad																•				
Chile												•						•	•	
China																				
Colombia												•								
Congo (Brazzaville)																•				
Congo (Kinshasa)			•										•	•						
Costa Rica				•							•							•		
Cuba						•												•		
Cyprus																•	•			
Czechoslovakia								•						•		•				
Dahomey							•	•								•				
Denmark							•	•					•	•		•	•	•		•
Dominican Rep.						•	•									•				
Ecuador						•	•	•						•						
El Salvador				•			•	•												
Equat. Guinea																				
Ethiopia												•								
Fiji																				
Finland						•		•								•	•	•		
France	•	•			•	•	•	•	•			•	•	•	•	•	•	•	•	•
Gabon																•	•			
Gambia																				
Germany, East																				
Germany, West		•					•	•				•				•		•	•	
Ghana											•									
Greece												•				•	•	•		
Guatemala				•			•					•								
Guinea																				
Guyana						•	•													
Haiti									•						•			•		
Honduras				•					•						•			•		
Hungary								•								•	•	•	•	
Iceland																•	•			
India		•				•	•	•	•	•	•	•	•			•		•		
Indonesia							•	•				•	•	•				•		
Iran		•		•		•						•	•							
Iraq												•								
Ireland										•						•	•			
Israel								•				•				•	•	•		
Italy		•			•	•	•	•				•				•	•	•		
Ivory Coast							•	•				•				•	•			
Jamaica												•								
Japan						•	•	•	•	•		•	•		•			•		•
Jordan																•	•			
Kenya											•	•			•					
Korea, North																				
Korea, South						•							•	•						
Kuwait												•								
Laos						•									•					
Lebanon	•								•			•				•	•			
Lesotho																				

	141	142	143	144	145	146	147	148	149	150	151	152	153	154	155	156	157	158	159	160
Liberia						•	•	•												
Libya															•			•		
Liechtenstein									•			•				•		•		
Luxembourg	•							•				•				•		•	•	•
Madagascar							•		•	•						•	•			
Malawi																				
Malaysia							•	•	•			•	•		•					
Maldives																				
Mali							•													
Malta																•		•		
Mauritania																				
Mauritius																				
Mexico			•					•				•			•	•	•	•		•
Monaco	•			•								•				•	•			
Mongolia																				
Morocco	•	•				•						•								
Nauru																				
Nepal							•		•											
Netherlands	•	•				•	•	•				•			•	•		•	•	•
New Zealand								•							•	•				•
Nicaragua			•									•								
Niger																				
Nigeria						•	•	•				•			•	•		•		
Norway								•							•	•		•		
Oman																				
Pakistan		•				•	•					•			•	•				
Panama						•						•								
Paraguay																				
Persian Gulf Shay.																				
Peru												•				•		•		
Philippines						•						•			•	•		•		
Poland				•				•				•				•	•			•
Portugal	•	•				•						•				•		•	•	
Rhodesia		•																		
Romania	•								•							•		•		•
Rwanda																				
San Marino			•													•				
Sa'udi Arabia												•				•				
Senegal																				
Sierra Leone						•		•				•				•				
Singapore				•																
Somalia																				
South Africa		•								•					•	•				•
South Yemen																				
Spain	•								•			•			•	•		•		•
Sudan			•									•								
Swaziland																				
Sweden							•	•				•				•		•	•	•
Switzerland	•	•				•						•				•		•	•	•
Syria	•																			
Taiwan			•						•			•								
Tanzania		•					•			•	•		•							
Thailand						•	•	•		•		•	•			•		•		
Togo																				
Tonga																				
Trinidad & Tob.										•		•				•		•		
Tunisia	•						•					•				•		•		
Turkey	•	•		•								•				•		•		
Uganda							•							•	•	•		•		
USSR	•												•			•		•	•	•
UAR	•					•														
UK	•	•	•			•	•	•		•		•		•	•	•		•	•	•
US						•	•	•		•		•	•	•	•	•		•		•
Upper Volta																				
Uruguay																•				
Vatican																				
Venezuela						•	•	•								•				
Viet-Nam, North																				
Viet-Nam, South						•	•					•				•		•		
Western Samoa																				
Yemen												•								
Yugoslavia	•											•				•		•	•	
Zambia			•				•									•				

Country	161	162	163	164	165	166	167	168	169	170	171	172	173	174	175	176	177	178	179	180
Afghanistan		•																		
Albania					•															
Andorra																				
Algeria													•	•						
Argentina	•	•		•		•	•	•	•	•	•	•			•					
Australia	•	•																		
Austria	•	•																		
Barbados																				
Belgium	•	•	•															•	•	
Bolivia				•		•	•	•	•	•				•						
Botswana																				
Brazil	•		•			•	•	•	•	•				•						
Br Honduras																				
Bhutan																				
Bulgaria					•															
Burma																				
Burundi																				
Cambodia																				
Cameroon				•																
Canada	•	•											•		•					
Cent. Afr. Rep.																				
Ceylon																				
Chad				•																
Chile		•				•	•	•	•		•	•		•						
China					•															
Colombia	•	•				•	•	•	•	•				•						
Congo (Brazzaville)																				
Congo (Kinshasa)																				
Costa Rica	•		•			•	•	•	•											
Cuba	•	•	•				•	•	•											
Cyprus																				
Czechoslovakia		•																		
Dahomey				•																
Denmark		•														•	•	•		
Dominican Rep.	•		•					•	•	•										
Ecuador	•		•	•		•	•	•	•	•										
El Salvador	•		•																	
Equat. Guinea																				
Ethiopia																				
Fiji																				
Finland	•	•														•	•			
France	•	•							•									•	•	
Gabon																				
Gambia																				
Germany, East					•															
Germany, West	•	•																•		
Ghana																				
Greece	•	•															•			
Guatemala	•			•		•		•	•		•									
Guinea																				
Guyana																				
Haiti	•		•	•		•	•	•												
Honduras				•		•	•	•												
Hungary					•															
Iceland	•	•														○	•	•	•	
India	•	•																		
Indonesia																				
Iran		•																		
Iraq		•										•								
Ireland	•	•															•			
Israel	•																			
Italy	•	•		•						•										
Ivory Coast				•																
Jamaica									•											
Japan	•	•																		•
Jordan												•								
Kenya																				
Korea, North					•															
Korea, South	•																			
Kuwait												•								
Laos																				
Lebanon	•	•										•								
Lesotho																				

Country	161	162	163	164	165	166	167	168	169	170	171	172	173	174	175	176	177	178	179	180
Liberia																				
Libya	•	•											•	•						
Liechtenstein																				
Luxembourg	•		•															•		
Madagascar																				
Malawi																				
Malaysia																				
Maldives																				
Mali				•																
Malta																				
Mauritania				•																
Mauritius																				
Mexico	•	•		•			•	•	•	•	•									
Monaco																				
Mongolia					•															
Morocco														•	•					
Nauru																				
Nepal																				
Netherlands	•	•	•							•									•	•
New Zealand	•																			
Nicaragua				•			•	•	•	•										
Niger				•																
Nigeria	•																			
Norway	•	•														•	•	•	•	
Oman																				
Pakistan	•																			
Panama	•		•				•	•	•	•										
Paraguay	•		•				•	•	•	•										
Persian Gulf Shay.																				
Peru	•	•		•			•	•	•	•					•					
Philippines																				
Poland					•															
Portugal	•	•																	•	•
Rhodesia	•																			
Romania					•															
Rwanda																				
San Marino																				
Sa'udi Arabia	•												•							
Senegal				•																
Sierra Leone	•																			
Singapore																				
Somalia																				
South Africa	•	•																		
South Yemen													•							
Spain	•	•																		•
Sudan																				
Swaziland																				
Sweden	•	•																•	•	•
Switzerland	•	•	•																	
Syria	•												•							
Taiwan																				
Tanzania																				
Thailand																				
Togo																				
Tonga																				
Trinidad & Tob.	•									•										
Tunisia	•												•	•						
Turkey	•																•			
Uganda																				
USSR	•			•									•						•	•
UAR	•	•											•							
UK	•	•								•								•	•	
US	•	•								•										•
Upper Volta				•																
Uruguay		•		•			•	•	•	•	•				•					
Vatican	•																			
Venezuela	•			•			•	•	•	•	•									
Viet-Nam, North						•														
Viet-Nam, South																				
Western Samoa	•																			
Yemen													•							
Yugoslavia																				
Zambia																				

Country	181	182	183	184	185	186	187	188	189	190	191	192	193	194	195	196	197	198	199	200
Afghanistan																				
Albania			•																	
Andorra																				
Algeria				•		•														
Argentina							•					•	•	•	•	•		•	•	
Australia			•												•					
Austria			•																	
Barbados							•					•								
Belgium			•				•					•	•	•	•					
Bolivia							•					•	•	•				•		
Botswana				•	•															
Brazil							•					•	•	•				•		
Br Honduras																				
Bhutan																				
Bulgaria			•																	
Burma																•				
Burundi				•	•															
Cambodia															•					
Cameroon	•	•	•		•	•			•						•					
Canada														•	•					
Cent. Afr. Rep.	•	•			•	•			•						•					
Ceylon															•		•			
Chad	•	•			•	•			•							•				
Chile							•					•	•	•	•					
China			•																	
Colombia							•					•	•	•				•		
Congo (Brazzaville)	•	•			•	•			•						•					
Congo (Kinshasa)	•				•	•										•				
Costa Rica						•	•					•	•	•				•		
Cuba							★					★	★	•				•		
Cyprus																				
Czechoslovakia			•												•					
Dahomey	•				•	•									•					
Denmark			•																	
Dominican Rep.							•					•	•	•	•			•		
Ecuador							•					•	•	•	•		•	•		
El Salvador						•	•					•	•	•				•		
Equat. Guinea																				
Ethiopia				•	•															
Fiji																				
Finland			•												•					
France			•									•			•	•	•			
Gabon	•	•			•	•														
Gambia					•	•														
Germany, East			•																	
Germany, West			•												•					
Ghana					•	•														
Greece			•												•	•				
Guatemala							•	•				•	•	•				•		
Guinea					•	•					•									
Guyana																				
Haiti							•					•	•	•	•			•		
Honduras							•	•				•	•	•	•			•		
Hungary															•	•				
Iceland			•																	
India															•		•			
Indonesia										•										
Iran															•					•
Iraq															•					
Ireland			•																	
Israel															•	•				
Italy			•												•					
Ivory Coast	•				•	•			•											
Jamaica												•								
Japan			•												•					
Jordan																				
Kenya				•	•															
Korea, North				•																
Korea, South																				
Kuwait										•										
Laos															•		•			
Lebanon																				
Lesotho				•	•															

Country	181	182	183	184	185	186	187	188	189	190	191	192	193	194	195	196	197	198	199	200
Liberia					•	•														
Libya					•	•				•										
Liechtenstein																				
Luxembourg		•																•		
Madagascar	•				•	•														
Malawi					•	•														
Malaysia																			•	
Maldives																				
Mali					•	•					•									
Malta																				
Mauritania					•	•			•											
Mauritius																				
Mexico							•							•	•	•	•			•
Monaco																				
Mongolia		•																		
Morocco					•	•														
Nauru																				
Nepal																				
Netherlands		•												•	•					
New Zealand															•					
Nicaragua												•	•	•	•	•		•		
Niger	•				•	•														
Nigeria					•	•														
Norway		•																		
Oman																				
Pakistan															•			•		•
Panama							•							•	•	•				
Paraguay							•							•	•	•				
Persian Gulf Shay.																				
Peru							•							•	•	•		•		
Philippines																				
Poland		•													•					
Portugal		•													•	•	•			
Rhodesia																				
Romania		•													•					
Rwanda	•				•	•														
San Marino																				
Sa'udi Arabia					•				•	•										
Senegal	•				•	•			•								•			
Sierra Leone					•	•														
Singapore																				
Somalia					•	•														
South Africa																				
South Yemen																				
Spain		•													•				•	
Sudan					•	•									•					
Swaziland																				
Sweden		•													•					
Switzerland		•													•					
Syria																				
Taiwan																				
Tanzania					•	•														
Thailand					•	•									•					
Togo	•				•	•			•											
Tonga																				
Trinidad & Tob.							•						•	•						
Tunisia					•	•														
Turkey					•	•									•					•
Uganda					•	•									•					
USSR		•													•					
UAR					•	•														
UK		•													•			•		
US		•				•								•	•	•				
Upper Volta	•				•	•						•								
Uruguay							•							•	•	•		•		•
Vatican																				
Venezuela							•							•	•	•		•	•	
Viet-Nam, North		•																		
Viet-Nam, South																		•		
Western Samoa																				
Yemen																				
Yugoslavia		•													•					
Zambia					•	•														

	201	202	203	204	205	206	207	208	209	210	211	212	213	214	215
Afghanistan										•					
Albania											•				
Andorra															
Algeria															
Argentina				•											
Australia	•		•	•											
Austria															
Barbados															
Belgium								•							•
Bolivia															
Botswana															
Brazil				•											
Br Honduras															
Bhutan															
Bulgaria										•					
Burma									•						
Burundi															
Cambodia															
Cameroon						•									
Canada															
Cent. Afr. Rep.						•		•							
Ceylon						•			•						
Chad						•		•							
Chile															
China															
Colombia															
Congo (Brazzaville)						•									
Congo (Kinshasa)						•		•							
Costa Rica															
Cuba															
Cyprus											•				
Czechoslovakia															
Dahomey						•						•	•	•	
Denmark															
Dominican Rep.															
Ecuador															
El Salvador															
Equat. Guinea															
Ethiopia															
Fiji															
Finland															
France		•	•			•	•	•							•
Gabon						•									
Gambia															
Germany, East										•					
Germany, West								•							•
Ghana															
Greece															
Guatemala															
Guinea															
Guyana															
Haiti															
Honduras															
Hungary										•					
Iceland															
India									•						
Indonesia	•								•						
Iran															
Iraq															
Ireland															
Israel															
Italy															•
Ivory Coast						•						•	•	•	
Jamaica															
Japan															
Jordan															
Kenya															
Korea, North															
Korea, South															
Kuwait															
Laos	•								•						
Lebanon															
Lesotho															

	201	202	203	204	205	206	207	208	209	210	211	212	213	214	215
Liberia															
Libya															
Liechtenstein															
Luxembourg															•
Madagascar						•									
Malawi															
Malaysia		•							•						
Maldives															
Mali						•						•	•		
Malta															
Mauritania												•	•	•	
Mauritius															
Mexico															
Monaco															
Mongolia															
Morocco															
Nauru															
Nepal										•					
Netherlands								•							•
New Zealand	•		•	•											
Nicaragua															
Niger						•						•	•	•	
Nigeria															
Norway															
Oman															
Pakistan			•						•						
Panama															
Paraguay															
Persian Gulf Shay.															
Peru															
Philippines	•		•						•						
Poland															
Portugal															
Rhodesia															
Romania									•						
Rwanda						•									
San Marino															
Sa'udi Arabia															
Senegal						•						•	•	•	
Sierra Leone															
Singapore	•								•						
Somalia															
South Africa															
South Yemen															
Spain															
Sudan															
Swaziland															
Sweden															
Switzerland								•							
Syria															
Taiwan															
Tanzania															
Thailand	•		•			•				•					
Togo												•	•		
Tonga															
Trinidad & Tob.															
Tunisia															
Turkey															
Uganda															
USSR										•					
UAR															
UK		•	•	•			•								•
US	•		•	•			•								
Upper Volta						•						•	•	•	
Uruguay										•					
Vatican															
Venezuela															
Viet-Nam, North															
Viet-Nam, South	•									•					
Western Samoa		•													
Yemen															
Yugoslavia															
Zambia															

Index

Advisory Committee on Administrative and Budgetary Questions (GA): 4, 17
Advisory Committee on the Application of Science and Technology to Development: 78, 82
Africa:
  African refugees, 119
  apartheid question, 4, 115
  common market, 89
  Congo crisis, 46, 54
  denuclearization of, 63
  IBRD loans, 202
  see also: ECA; ONUC; South Africa; South West Africa; Southern Rhodesia; Statistics
Aggression:
  defining of, 134–135
  methods of dealing with, 5–6
  Security Council and, 26–27
Agreements: see Conventions (UN)
Agriculture:
  Association for the Advancement of Agricultural Sciences in Africa, 72
  Committee on Agricultural Problems (ECE), 69
  Committee on Work on Plantations (ILO), 152
  meteorological service for, 246
  see also: FAO
Alcoholism: 173
American Declaration of the Rights and Duties of Man: 114
Apartheid: 4, 115
Arbitration, procedure in: 135
Asia:
  Asian Coconut Community, 73
  Asian Development Bank, 72
  Asian Highway project, 74
  Asian Institute for Economic Development and Planning, 73
  Asian refugees, 119
  denuclearization of, 63
  IBRD loans, 202–203
  see also: ECAFE
Asylum, right of: 115–116
Atlantic Charter: 8
Atomic energy:
  control of, 58–59
  meteorological factors and, 245–246
  see also: IAEA
Atomic Energy Commission (UN): 58
Aviation: see ICAO

Bacteriological Methods of Warfare: 61
Barbiturates: 105
Bassow, Nikolai: 14
Bilharziasis: 171
Bretton Woods Conference: 192
British Imperial War Cabinet: 5
Brunfaut, Gaston: 14
Budget:
  FAO, 19, 155
  GATT, 214
  IAEA, 221
  IBRD, 199
  ICAO, 227
  IDA, 210
  IFC, 207
  ILO, 143
  IMCO, 241
  IMF, 193
  ITU, 233–234
  Office of the High Commissioner for Refugees, 117

Budget (cont.):
  UN, 17–19
    assessments for, 18
    contributions by nonmembers, 18
    extrabudgetary accounts, 17
    intergovernmental agencies, 19
    preparation of, 17
  UNESCO, 182
  UNRWA, 122
  UPU, 238
  WHO, 168
  WMO, 244
Building, Civil Engineering and Public Works Committee (ILO): 152

Cannabis: 104
Capital Development Fund (UN): 87
Caribbean Free Trade Association (CARIFTA): 76
CARIFTA: see Caribbean Free Trade Association
Central America:
  common market, 89
  ECLA projects, 75
  see also: ECLA
Charter (UN): 5, 6
  amending of, 9
  armaments, 58
  economic and social cooperation, 77
  equality of sex, 116
  human rights, 109
  on maintaining peace, 49
  on self-defense vs. war, 5–6
  on settlement of disputes, 26–27
  ratification of, 8–9
  UN aims, 10
  UN organs established by, 3
  UN Secretariat, 41
  welfare of colonial peoples, 123
Chemical Industry:
  ECE, work on, 70
Children: rights of, 115
China: representation of, in UN, 13, 44
Cholera: 172
Churchill, Winston: 8
Coal Committee (ECE): 69
Coal Mines Committee (ILO): 152
Coca leaf: 104
Cocaine: 104
Colonial territories:
  administration of, 6
  independence for, 4
Colonialism:
  Declaration of the Granting of Independence of Colonial Territories and Peoples, 125
  General Assembly, action on, 126
  outstanding issues, 126
  Southern Rhodesia, 127–128
  Trust Territory, 129
  see also: Committee of 24; Trusteeship Council; Trusteeship system
Commission for Social Development: 31
Commission for the Unification and Rehabilitation of Korea: 23
Commission on Human Rights: 31, 109–115
  Sub-Commission on Prevention of Discrimination and Protection of Minorities, 115
  see also: Human Rights
Commission on Narcotic Drugs: 31, 102; see also: Narcotic drugs
Commission on the Status of Women: 31

Committee for Coordination of Joint Prospecting for Mineral Resources in Asian Offshore Areas (CCOP): 73
Committee of 24 (UN):
    establishment, 125
    Oman question, 126
    Portuguese dependencies, 126–127
    South Africa, 126
    Southern Rhodesia question, 127–128
Committee on Contributions (GA): 3–4, 17
Committee on Water Problems: 69
Common Market:
    Arab, 89
    Central American, 89
    East African, 89
    European, 89
Conference of European Statisticians: 70
Conference of Non-Nuclear Weapon States at Geneva: 1968
Conference of the Committee on Disarmament: 61
Conference of the Eighteen Nation Disarmament Committee: 60–61
Conference on Human Environment: 108
Conference services, provided by UN: 14
Congo Crisis: 46; see also: ONUC
Conventions and Agreements (UN):
    Agreement on International Circulation of Audio-Visual Materials (UNESCO): 190
    Agreement Relating to Refugee Seamen, 118
    Convention and Agreements on Narcotic Drugs, 103
    Convention concerning Discrimination in Respect to Employment, 113
    Convention concerning the Abolition of Forced Labor, 112
    Convention on Consent to Marriage, 112
    Convention on Freedom of Information, 114
    Convention on International Aviation, 225–226, 228
    Convention on Privileges and Immunities of the UN, 15
    Convention on the Elimination of All Forms of Racial Discrimination, 113, 115
    Convention on the Elimination of All Forms of Religious Intolerance, 115
    Convention on the Freedom of Association, 112
    Convention on the International Right of Correction, 113
    Convention on the International Transmission of News, 113
    Convention on the Prevention and Punishment of the Crime of Genocide, 112
    Convention on the Status of Refugees, 112
    Convention on the Status of Stateless Persons, 112
    Convention on Transit Trade of Landlocked States, 90, 91
    Convention Relating to the Status of Refugees, 118
    Conventions (ICAO-related):
        Geneva Convention (1948), 231
        Guadalajara Convention (1961), 231
        Protocol of Amendment to the Warsaw Convention of 1929, 231
        Rome Convention (1953), 231
        Tokyo Convention (1963), 231
    Conventions on Slavery:
        League of Nations, 112
        UN, 112
    Covenant on Civil and Political Rights, 111
Copyright: see Universal Copyright Convention
Cormier, Ernest: 14
Cotton, textile trade: 217
Credentials Committee (GA): 4, 12
Crime:
    crimes against humanity, 114
    international criminal jurisdiction, 134
Cuba: Cuban refugees, 119
Culture, world: heritage of, 178, 187–189
Customs duties, UN and: 15
Cyprus question: 54–55

Dag Hammarskjöld Library (UN): 14
Declaration of the Elimination of Discrimination against Women 116

Declaration of the Granting of Independence of Colonial Territories and Peoples: 125
De Gaulle, Charles: 8
Demography: see Population
Development Decade (first): Proposals for Action, 78
Development, economic and social:
    aims of Development Decade (first), 78
    Committee for Development Planning, 78, 82
    financing
        Capital Development Fund, 87
        cooperative, 87–91
        external, 85–87
        sources for loans, 85
    human development, 80–81
    science and technology applied to, 82
    Second Development Decade, 79–81
        goals and objectives, 79
    see also: Economic development; Industrial development; Social development
Diplomatic relations: 136
Disarmament: 58–63
    atomic and conventional armaments, 58
    atomic energy control
        Baruch Plan, 58
        USSR proposal, 58
        West-East disagreement, 58
    Chemical and bacteriological weapons, 61
    Commission for Conventional Armaments, 58
    developments outside UN, 59
    General Assembly action:
        British plan, 60
        Conference of the Committee on Disarmament, 62
        Declarations on denuclearization of Africa and Latin America, 63
        strategic arms limitation (SALT), 61
        Treaty of Tlatelolco, 63
        Treaty on the Nonproliferation of Nuclear Weapons, 63
        US-USSR agreement, 60–61
        USSR plan, 60
    nuclear nonproliferation, 63
    nuclear test-ban treaty, 62–63
    Seabed pact, 62
    World Disarmament Conference, plans for, 63
    see also: Conference of the Eighteen Nation Disarmament Committee; Geneva Conference on Nuclear Testing
Disarmament Commission: 4, 58–61
    enlargement, 59
    establishment, 4, 58–59
    five-power discussions, 59
Discrimination:
    International Conventions against, 113
    see also: Racial discrimination; Religious intolerance; Status of Women
Disease: see UNICEF; under name of specific disease
Document services (UN): 14
Dominican Republic: US intervention, 47
Drug Supervisory Body: 102
Dumbarton Oaks Conference: 8

ECA: see Economic Commission for Africa
ECAFE: see Economic Commission for Asia and the Far East
ECE: see Economic Commission for Europe
ECLA: see Economic Commission for Latin America
Economic and Social Council (ECOSOC): 3, 30–32
    activities, 3, 30–32
        economic development, 30
        human rights, 30
        social problems, 30
        statistical techniques, 30
    economic commissions, 31, 67
    functional commissions, 31
    functions, 30
    International Conferences, 32

Economic and Social Council (cont.):
  membership, 30
  and NGO's, 32
  powers, 30
  sessions, 31
  specialized agencies, 30
  subsidiary bodies, 4, 31–32
  voting in, 31
Economic Commission for Africa (ECA): 31
  activities summarized, 70–72
  Association for Advancement of Agricultural Sciences in Africa 72
  Center for Economic Cooperation, 71
  development of science and technology, 72
  development of transport and communications, 72
  expansion, 71
  membership, 67–68
  Secretariat, 71
Economic Commission for Asia and the Far East (ECAFE): 31, 246
  activities summarized, 72–74
  membership, 67
Economic Commission for Europe (ECE): 31, 68–70
  activities summarize, 68–70
  membership, 67
Economic Commission for Latin America (ECLA): 31
  activities summarized, 74–76
  membership, 67
Economic commissions, regional:
  functions, 68
  headquarters, 68
  membership, 67–68
  publications, 68
  structure, 68
Economic development:
  Africa (ECA), 71–72
  ECAFE work in, 72–73
  ECLA activities, 74–76
  effect of disarmament on, 87
  through trade, 87
  UN programs, 70–91
Economic Development Institute (IBRD): 204
ECOSOC: see Economic and Social Council
Education:
  adult education, 184–185
  for international understanding, 185
  health education, 175
  in Arab states, 184
  in Africa, 183–184
  in Asia, 183
  in Latin America, 183
  medical training, 173–174
  teacher training, 185
    natural sciences, 185
  UNICEF programs, 101
  vocational training
    ILO program, 150–151
    UNICEF programs, 101
Electric Power Committee (ECE): 69
Emblem (UN): 16
Energy:
  atomic: see IAEA
  nonnuclear, 84
  nuclear: see IAEA
Environmental Problems: ad hoc interagency working group: 108
Europe:
  common market, 89
  IBRD loans, 203
  see also: ECE
European Commission of Human Rights: 114

FAO: see Food and Agriculture Organization
Far East: see Asia; ECAFE
Fedayeen: 120

Fellowships: UNDP program: 94
Fertilizers: 159
Films: on UN activities, 15
Finance, international: see IBRD; IDA; IFC; IMF
Finances (UN):
  Ad Hoc Committee of Experts to Examine the Finances of the UN, 19
  GA roll in, 20
  nonmember States and, 18–19
  peacekeeping operations, 55–57
  scale of contributions, 18
  Special Committee to examine peacekeeping questions and financial difficulties, 56
  see also: Budget
Fisheries: FAO work, 162–163
Flag (UN): 16
Flood control: ECAFE work on, 73
Food:
  additives, 175–176
  UNICEF programs, 100
  see also: FAO
Food and Agriculture Organization (FAO): 30, 153–164
  activities, 155–164
    agriculture, 158–162
      animal husbandry, 161–162
      application of science to, 158
      fertilizers, 159
      foot-and-mouth disease control, 162
      horticultural services, 159–160
      Indicative World Plan for Agricultural Development, 157–158
      insect control, 160–161
      International Plant Protection Convention, 160
      International Rice Commission, 160
      land fertility, 159
      land reform, 158–159
      locust control, 160–161
      plant protection, 160
      rice, 160
      rinderpest control, 162
      river basin projects, 159
      seed improvement, 160
      statistics, 164
      water resources and, 159
    FAO-IBRD cooperative program, 158
    FAO Industry program, 158
    fisheries, 162–163
      Committee on Fisheries, 163
      regional bodies, 163
      technical assistance, 163
    food development and distribution, 156
    food reserves, 155–156
    forestry, 163–164
    Freedom-from-Hunger Campaign, 157
    Latin American projects, 74
    nutrition, 164
    regional programs, 162
    World Food Program, 156
    World food reserve, 155–156
  background, 153
  budget, 19, 155
  Committee on Commodity Problems, 156–157
  Consultative Subcommittee on Surplus Disposal, 156
  establishment, 153–154
  headquarters, 155
  international cooperation, 153
  membership, 154
  offices, regional and liaison, 155
  purposes, 154
  Rural Institutions Division, 158
  structure, 154–155
    Conference, 154–155
    Council, 155
    Director-General, 155

Food and Agriculture Organization (cont.):
  structure
    Secretariat, 155
      Economic Analysis Division, 158
    World Food Congress, 157
Foot-and-mouth disease: 162
Ford Foundation: 14
Forestry: 163–164
Freedom-from-Hunger Campaign: 157
Freedom of Information, UN Conference on: 113
French Chamber of Deputies: 5
Fund of the UN for the Development of West Irian (FUNDWI):
      130

GA: see General Assembly
Gandhi, Mahatma: 153
Gas, Committee on (ECE): 69
GATT: see General Agreement on Tariffs and Trade
General Agreement on Tariffs and Trade (GATT): 4, 30,
      212–217
  activities, 214–217
    cotton textile trade, 217
    General Agreement (summarized), 214
    International Trade Center, 217
      publications of, 217
    Kennedy Round of trade negotiations, 214–215, 217
    publications, 217
    quantitative restrictions on imports, general prohibition
        of, 215
    regional arrangements, 216–217
    tariff negotiations, 214
    trade disputes arbitrated, 216
    trade problems of developing countries, 217
  background, 212
  budget, 214
  Committee on Trade and Development, 217
  establishment, 212
  headquarters, 214
  membership (listed), 213
    conditions for joining, 213
    provisional accession, 213
    special arrangements, 213
  purposes, 212–213
  secretariat, 214
  structure, 213–214
General Assembly (UN): 3, 4
  action open to, 24
  agenda, 22
    adoption of, 22–23
  Atomic Energy Commission, 58
  chemical and biological methods of warfare, 61
  committees, 3–4, 21
  Conference of the Committee on Disarmament, 62
  disarmament, 58
    seabed pact, 62
  Disarmament Commission, 61–62
  election of officers, 22
  functions of, 20
  General Debate, 21
  peacekeeping operations, 20–21
  plenary meetings, 21
  powers of, 20
  presidents (listed), 22
  resolutions, 23–24
  resolutions on disarmament, 61–62
  restrictions on powers of, 20
  seating of delegates, 22
  sessions, 21
  subsidiary organs, 3–4
  UN finances, 20
  UNCTAD and, 88
  Uniting for Peace Resolution, 20
  voting, 3
    compromise, 23

General Assembly (cont.):
  voting
    patterns in, 23
    procedure, 21–22
General Committee: 3
General Treaty on Central American Economic Integration
      (SIECA): 75
Geneva Conference on Nuclear Testing (1958): 59
Genocide: 112
Glossary of Intergovernmental Organizations (ICO's): 267

Hammarskjöld, Dag: 14, 41–42, 70, 77
  biography, 41–42
  death of, 47
  UN under, 45–47
Hammarskjöld Library (UN): 14
Headquarters (UN):
  Headquarters District, UN-US agreement signed, 15–16
    physical plant, 14
    temporary, 14
Headquarters and facilities (UN):
  capacity, 14
  Internal Services, 14
    Conference Services, 14
    Documents Services, 14
  Library, 14
    Telecommunications System, 14
High Commissioner for Refugees: see Refugees
Hitler, Adolf: 8
Housing and building: 83
  Building, Civil Engineering and Public Works Committee
      (ILO), 152
  Housing, Building and Planning Committee (ECE), 70
Human environment:
  pollution of, 108
Human rights: 109–116
  action taken by United Nations organs, 114–115
  Charter of the United Nations, San Francisco (1945), 109
  children's rights, 115
  conventions on the Rights of Women, 112
  Covenant on Civil and Political Rights, 111
  crimes against humanity, 114
  Declaration of the Rights of the Child, 115
  Declaration on Principles of International Law concerning
        Friendly Relations and Co-operation among
        States, 116
  Declaration on Territorial Asylum, 115–116
  elimination of discrimination against women, 116
  elimination of racial discrimination, 115
  equality of sex, 116
  Freedom of Association Convention, 112
  freedom of information and press, 113–114
  General Assembly, action for, 110
  genocide, 112
  Genocide Convention, 112
  Human Rights Committee, 111
  International Bill of Rights, 109
  International Conventions against Discrimination, 113
  International Covenant on Economic, Social and Cultural
      Rights, 109, 110
  racial discrimination, 113
  right of asylum, 115–116, 118
  slavery, 112
  social security, 110
  statelessness and refugees, 112
  Universal Declaration of Human Rights, 30, 109–111
  see also: Commission on Human Rights
Human Resources Development Division (ECA): 72
Humanities, cooperation in: 187–188
Hydrology: 186

IAEA: see International Atomic Energy Agency
IBRD: see International Bank for Reconstruction and Develop-
      ment

ICAO: *see* International Civil Aviation Organization
ICJ: *see* International Court of Justice
IDA: *see* International Development Association
IFC: *see* International Finance Corporation
IGOSS: *see* Integrated Global Ocean Station System
ILC: *see* International Law Commission
ILO: *see* International Labor Organization
IMCO: *see* Inter-Governmental Maritime Consultative Organization
IMF: *see* International Monetary Fund
Imports, restrictions on: 215
INCB: *see* International Narcotics Control Board
Indonesia: UN membership case, 12
Indian hemp: 102
Industrial development: 83–84
  ECAFE, work on, 73
  Special Industrial Services (SIS), 84
  UN Industrial Development Organization (UNIDO), 84
Industry and Natural Resources, Committee on (ECAFE): 73
Influenza: 170–171
Information: *see* Freedom of Information; Press; Public Information Office (UN)
Information Centers (UN): 15
INIS: *see* International Nuclear Information System
Inland Transport and Communications: ECAFE studies, 73–74
Inland Transport Committee (ECE): 70
Inland Transport Committee (ILO): 152
Insect control: 160–161
Integrated Global Ocean Station System (IGOSS): 246
Inter-Allied Declaration: 8
Inter-American Peace Force: 47
Inter-Governmental Maritime Consultative Organization (IMCO): 30, 240–242
  activities, 241–242
    administration of conventions, 241
    advisory role, 241
    conferences convened, 241–242
    international standards, development of, 242
  background, 240
  budget, 19, 241
  establishment, 240
  membership (listed), 240–241
  purposes, 240
  structure, 241
    Assembly, 241
    Council, 241
    Maritime Safety Committee, 241
    Secretariat, 241
Intergovernmental Organization (IGO's), glossary of: 247
International Atomic Energy Agency (IAEA): 4, 30, 218–224
  activities, 221–224
    assistance to member states, 221
    Conference of Non-Nuclear Weapon States at Geneva, 1968, 220
    conferences, 222
    exchange of information, 222
    International Nuclear Information System (INIS), 222
    nuclear power studies, 222–223
    research, 222
    safeguards system for nuclear installations, 223
    Treaty on the Non-Proliferation of Nuclear Weapons, 223
  background, 218
  budget, 19, 221
  establishment, 218
  membership (listed), 219
  purposes, 218
  relation to UN, 220–221
  Scientific Advisory Committee, 220
    members, 220
  structure, 219–220
    Board of Governors, 219–220
    Director General, 220
    General Conference, 219
  technical assistance, 221

International Bank for Reconstruction and Development (IBRD): 30, 198–205
  activities, 199–205
    advisory role, 203–205
    Africa, loans in, 202
    Asia, loans in, 202–203
    Economic Development Institute, 204
    Europe, loans in, 203
    investment insurance, 204–205
    Latin America, loans in, 203
    mediation role, 205
    survey missions, 203–204
    technical assistance, 203
  background, 198
  budget, 199
  financial resources, 199–200
  headquarters, 199
  lending operations, 200–202
    loan currencies, 201
    loans summarized, 200–201, 202
    purposes of loans, 201
    terms and interest rates, 201
  membership, 198
    listed, 199
  purposes, 198
  structure, 198–199
    Board of Governors, 198
    Executive Directors, 198
    President, 198–199
International Civil Aviation Organization (ICAO): 30, 225–231
  activities, 227–231
    air navigation facilities, 228–229
    arbitration of disputes between members states, 231
    facilitation of air transport, 228
    international conventions prepared under ICAO auspices, 231
    international standards for civil avaiation, establishment of, 227–228
    regional planning, 228–229
    supersonic aviation, 229–230
    technical assistance, 230–231
      examples of, 230–231
  background, 225
  budget, 19, 227
  Convention on International Aviation, annexes to, 225–226, 227–228
  establishment, 225–226
  headquarters, 227
  membership (listed), 226
  offices, regional, 227
  purposes, 226
  structure, 226–227
    Assembly, 226–227
    Council, 227
    Secretary-General, 227
International Council for Philosophy and Humanistic Studies: 187
International Court of Justice (ICJ): 3, 36–40
  advisory opinions, 38
  cases heard, 38–39
  establishment, 36
  extrajudicial functions, 38
  jurisdiction, 37–38
  legal disputes, 38
  members (judges), 36–37
  procedure, 37
  role reviewed by General Assembly, 39
  South West Africa case, 130–131
  Statute (constitution) of, 9
International Covenant on Civil and Political Rights: 111
International Covenant on Economic, Social and Cultural Rights: 112
International Covenants on Human Rights: 111
International Development Association (IDA): 30, 209–211
  activities, 210–211

International Development Association (cont.):
  budget, 210
  establishment, 209
  financial resources, 210
    capital subscriptions, 210
    supplementary resources, 210
  loans granted, 210–211
  membership, 209
  net income, 210
  purposes, 209
  structure, 209–210
  terms of lending, 210
International Finance Corporation (IFC): 30, 206–208
  activities, 207–208
  background, 206
  budget, 207
  development finance companies, assistance to, 207–208
  establishment, 206
  financial resources, 207
  investments, 207
    direct, 207
    interest rates, 208
    policies of, 207
    summarized, 208
    underwriting arrangements, 207
    membership (listed), 206–207
  purposes, 206
  structure, 207
International Frequency Registration Board (ITU): 233
International Labor Conference, 1969, World Employment Program: 141
International Labor Organization (ILO): 30, 139–152
  background, 139
  budget, 19, 143
  Director-General, 142
  establishment, 139
  headquarters, 142
  human rights, 147–148
    discrimination in employment, 148
    forced labor, 147–148
    freedom of association, 147
  industrial committees, 152
International Labor Code formulated, 143–145
    conventions adopted, 144–146
    maritime questions, 148–149
      employment conditions, 149
      hours and pay, 149
      social security, 149
    membership (listed), 140
    offices, regional, branch and field, 142
    purposes, 139–140
    questions considered, 144–145
    role in supervising application of ratified conventions, 145–146
    structure, 141–142
      governing body, 141–142
      International Labor Conference, 141
    technical assistance program, 149–150
      cooperatives, 151
      management, 150
      productivity, 150
      small business, 151
      social security, 151–152
      vocational training, 150–151
      working conditions, 152
    worker-employer representation issue, 142–143
    World Employment Program, 141
International Law Commission (ILC): 133–137
    activities,
      consular relations, 136
      Convention on Special Missions, 136
      defining aggression, 134–135
      Law of Treaties, 134
      work not completed, 136–137

International Law Commission (cont.):
    functions, 133
      codification of existing international law, 133
      development of new international law, 133
    organization, 133
    scope of work, 133–134
    topics dealt with, 133–137
      arbitral procedure, 135
      diplomatic relations, 136
      international criminal jurisdiction, 134
      Law of Treaties, 136
      Nuremberg Principles, 134
      rights and duties of states, 134
      statelessness, 135
International Monetary Fund (IMF): 30, 197
    activities, 193–197
      advisory role, 194
      borrowing by IMF, 194
      consultation and assistance on monetary matters, 194
      currency stabilization, 196
      par values of currencies, control over, 194
      technical assistance, 196
      transactions with members, 194–196
        conditions and purposes of, 196
    background, 192
    budget, 193
    establishment, 192
      Bretton Woods Conference, 192
    financial resources, 193–194
    headquarters, 193
    international liquidity, 197
    membership, 192–193, 195–196
      obligations of, 194
    policies and practices, 196
    purposes, 192
    structure, 193
      Board of Governors, 193
      Executive Directors, 193
      Managing Director, 193
International Narcotics Control Board (INCB): 102
International Nuclear Information System (INIS): 222
International Office of Public Health: 165–166
International Refugee Organization (IRO): 117
International Rice Commission (FAO): 160
International Telecommunication Union (ITU): 30, 232–235
    activities, 234–235
      exchange of information, 234–235
      frequency allocation, 234
      technical assistance, 235
      telecommunications in space, 234
      telegraph and telephone communications, 234
      World Space Telecommunications Conference, 234
    background, 232
    budget, 19, 233–234
    establishment, 232
    headquarters, 233
    membership (listed), 232–233
    purposes, 232
    structure, 233
      administrative conferences, 233
      administrative council, 233
      consultative committees, 233
      International Frequency Registration Board, 233
      Plenipotentiary Conference, 233
International Trade, General Assembly policy measures: 79–81
International Trade Center (GATT): 217
International Trade Organization: 4
Intolerance: see Racial discrimination; Religious intolerance
IRO: see International Refugee Organization
Iron and Steel Committee (ILO): 152
ITU: see International Telecommunication Union

Kashmir question: 53–54
Korean War: 45, 53

Labor: *see* ILO
Land reform: 83, 158–159
Latin America:
  IBRD loans, 203
  see also: ECLA
Law of the Sea Conference: 66
League of Nations:
  activities summarized, 6–7
  compared with UN, 5–7
  Covenant, 5–6, 27
  creation, 5
  cultural activities, 178
  ILO, 139
  mandate system, 33
  membership, 6
  narcotic drugs control, 102
  nutrition, 153
  Slavery Convention, 112
  voting system, 5
  world health activities, 165–166
Le Corbusier, Charles: 14
Leprosy: 171
Liang Ssu-ch'eng: 14
Lie, Trygve: 15, 102
  biography, 41
  resignation of, 45
  UN under, 44–45
Literacy: 185
Literature, world: 188
Locust control: 160–161
London Declaration: 8

Malaria: 168–169
  UNICEF, 100
  WHO, 100
Malnutrition: 173; *see also*: Nutrition
Maps: 84
Marijuana: 104
Maritime Consultative Organization: *see* IMCO
Maritime Safety Committee (IMCO): 241
Markelius, Sven: 14
Marriage: 112, 116
Marshall, George C.: 15
Mass communications: 189
Medical training: 173–174
Mekong River project: 73
Membership (UN):
  admission of new members, 11–12
  China representation question, 13, 44
  Credentials Committee, 12
  expulsion, 12
  Indonesia case, 12
  listed, 11
  method of representation of nations in UN, 12–13
  suspension, 12
  withdrawal, 12
Metal Trades Committee (ILO): 152
Meteorology: *see* WMO
Middle East Conflict:
  fedayeen, 120
  General Assembly emergency session, 51, 52
  June 1967 War, 52–53
  UN role, 48, 51–53
  withdrawal of UNEF units, 52
Military Staff Committee: 4
Mineral resources: 84
Mineral resources development, ECAFE surveys: 73
Moscow Declaration: 8

Narcotic drugs:
  addiction problem, 106–107
  control programs, 102–107
  Drug Supervisory Body, 102
  drugs not under international control,

Narcotic drugs (cont.):
  drugs not under international control
    barbituates, 105
    tranquilizers, 105
  drugs under international control,
    cannabis, 104
    coca leaf, 104
    opium, 103–104
  ECOSOC, action of, 106
  illicit traffic in, 106–107
  increasing drug abuse, 106
  international agreements,
    Opium Protocol, 103
    Paris Protocol, 103
    Single Convention on Narcotic Drugs, 103
  International Narcotics Control Board (INCB), 102
  League of Nations programs, 102
  Permanent Central Narcotics Board, 102
  Protocol on Psychotropic Substances, 104
  Psychotropic substances, 104
    identification of, 105
  scope of international control, 103
  synthetic drugs, 104
  UN programs, 102–103
  WHO and, 105
    WHO Expert Committee on Addiction-Producing Drugs, 102
  see also: Commission on Narcotic Drugs
Narcotic drugs control: 102
Natural resources:
  nonagricultural, 84
  survey of, 84
  see also: Agriculture; Mineral resources; Water resources
Natural sciences: 185–186
NGO's: *see* Non-Governmental Organizations
Niemeyer, Oscar: 14
Non-Governmental Organizations (NGO's):
  ECOSOC and, 32
  UNESCO and, 181–182
Nonself-governing territories: 123–128, 131–132
  Charter declaration on, 123
    territories included, 123
  Declaration on the Granting of Independence of Colonial Territories and Peoples, 125
  Committee of 24, 125
  independence for, 124
  reports on, to UN, 124
  status of, 131–132
  UN role, 123–124
Nuclear Arms Race: 62
Nuclear energy: *see* IAEA
Nuclear weapons:
  control of, 62–63
Nuremberg Principles, formulation of: 134
Nursing: 173–174
Nutrition:
  FAO work on, 164
  League of Nations work on, 153
  UNICEF work on, 100
  see also: Malnutrition

Oceanography: 186
Oman question: 126
ONUC (United Nations Organization in the Congo, nonmilitary operations): 54
  financing of, 55–56
  ICJ's advisory opinion, 56
Opium: 103–104
Opium Conference (UN): 103
Opium Protocol: 103
Organization of African Unity (OAU): 118
Outer space:
  Agreement on Rescue and Return of Astronauts and Objects Launched into, 65
  Committee on the Peaceful Uses of Outer Space, 64

Outer space (cont.):
    international conference, plans for, 65
    international cooperation in programs for, 64
    international law, 65
    Treaty of Principles, 65
    UN and, 64–65

Palestine refugees: 51, 119–122
Paris Peace Conference: 5
Paris Protocol: narcotic drugs, 103
Peace, crimes against: 134
Peaceful uses of outer space: see Outer Space
Peace-keeping operations of the UN: 49–57
    Congo, 54
    Cyprus, 54–55
    Czechoslovakia, 48
    financing of, 55–56
    Kashmir, 53–54
    Korea, 53
    Middle East, 48, 52–53
    Nigeria, 48
    Security Council responsibility in, 25–27
    Suez, 51–52
    types of UN action, 50–51
    UNEF, 55–56
    Uniting-for-Peace Resolution, 21
Permanent Central Narcotics Board: 102
Petroleum resources: ECAFE symposia, 73
Pharmaceuticals: 175
Photography: UN photo missions, 15
Plague: 172
Political role of the Secretary-General: 44–48
Population:
    health and, 174–175
    UN Conference on World Population, 32
    world problems, 83
Population Commission: 31
Population Program Center (ECA): 72
Portuguese dependencies question: 124
Portuguese refugees from colonial territories: 119
Postal administration (UN): 14–15
Press, freedom of: 113
Public Information Office (UN): 15
    Information Centers, 15
Public Information Services (UN):
    press, publications and photographic services, 15
    radio, TV, and film services, 15
Publications (UN): 15
    GATT program of, 217

Quarantinable diseases, regulations governing: 171–172

Racial discrimination: 113; see also: Apartheid
Radio:
    UN programs, 15
    see also: Mass communications
Refugees: 112, 117–122
    African, 119
    Asian, 119
    convention on statistics of, 118
    Convention relating to the Status of Refugees, 112
    Cuban, 119
    defined, 118
    High Commissioner for Refugees, 32
        budget for work of, 117
        election, 117
        headquarters, 117
        work of, 117–118
    IRO, 117
    Palestine refugees, 51, 119–122
    refugee problem summarized, 118–119
    repatriation, 117
    resettlement, 117
    right of asylum, 118

Refugees (cont.):
    seamen, 118
    Tibetan, 119
    UNRRA, 117
    see also: IRO; UNRWA
Regional economic commissions: see Economic commissions;
        under name of commission
Religious intolerance: 113, 116
Representation: see Membership (UN), method of representation
Rice: International Rice Commission (FAO), 160
Rinderpest: 162
Robertson, Howard: 14
Rockefeller, John D., Jr.: 14
Roosevelt, Franklin D.: 8, 9, 192

SALT: see Strategic Arms Limitation Talks
San Francisco Conference: 5, 8, 28, 36
    summarized, 9
Sanctions: 6
    types of, permitted to UN, 27
SC: see Security Council
Science:
    Advisory Committee on the Application of Science and Tech-
        nology to Development, 78, 82
    economic and social development, 82–84
    Scientific Advisory Committee, 220
    see also: Natural sciences: Social sciences
Scientific Advisory Committee (IAEA): 220
Sea, law of: 135
Seabed:
    Committee on the Peaceful Uses of the Seabed and the Ocean
        Floor Beyond the Limits of National Jurisdic-
        tion, 66
    exploration and exploitation of resources, 66
    Law of the Sea Conference, 66
        preservation of, 66
        General Assembly action, 66
Seabed pact: 62
Second Development Decade: 79–81, 91
Secretariat (UN): 3
    appointment of the Secretary-General, 41
    Charter (UN) on, 41
    composition, 41
    current structure and composition, 42
    evolving role, 43
    functions, 41
    organization, 42
    staff, 42–43
        geographical distribution, 42–43
        income assessment, 18
        privileges and immunities of, 15–16
    see also: Secretary-General
Secretariat building (UN): 14
Secretary-General (UN):
    appointment, 41
    political role, 44–48
    role of, Hammarskjöld on, 46
    "Troika" proposal, 46–47
    see also: Hammarskjöld, Dag; Lie, Trygve; Thant, U
Security Council: 3
    ad hoc committees, 4
    Charter provisions for UN armed forces, 27–28
    Committee on the Admission of Members, 12
    composition, 25
    elections to, 25
    functions of, 25–28
    peacekeeping responsibilities, 26–27, 49
    powers of, 3, 5–6, 25–28, 49
    representation in, 28
    sanctions, 27
    sessions of, 28
    standing committees, 4
    subsidiary organs, 4
    veto power, 8, 28–29

Security Council (cont.):
  voting in, 28–29
  ways of dealing with disputes, 26–27
Seed improvement: 160
Shipping: 90
Shotwell, James T.: 139
SIECA: *see* General Treaty on Central American Economic
      Integration
Single Convention on Narcotic Drugs: 103
  implementation, 103
Six Day War: *see* Middle East Conflict
Slavery,
  abolition of,
      UN, work on, 112
Smallpox: 172–173
Social development:
  ECAFE, work on, 74
  UN programs, 70–96
Social sciences: 186–187
Soileux, G. A.: 14
South Africa:
  apartheid, 4, 115
  colonialism question, 126
  racial discrimination, 110
South West Africa question: 130–131
  ICJ ruling, 130
Southern Rhodesia question: 127–128
Special Fund: 92
Specialized agencies: 4
Staff (UN): *see* Secretariat
Stalin, Joseph: 8
Stamps (UN): 14–15; *see also*: Postal Administration (UN)
Statelessness: 135
States, rights and duties of: 134
Statistical Commission (ECOSOC): 31, 82
Statistical Office (UN Secretariat): 82
Statistics:
  economic and social data, 82
  on Africa, 72
  statistical surveys under ECAFE, 73
  UN publications, 82
Status of women: 112, 116
Steel Committee (ECE): 69
Strategic Arms Limitation Talks (SALT): 61
Study, international: UNESCO program, 190
  Subcommission on Prevention of Discrimination and Protec-
      tion of Minorities: 31
Suez crisis: 45–46, 51–52
Surveys, aids for: 84
Syphilis: 170

Tariff: *see* GATT
Taxation, UN and: 15
Technical assistance:
  expanded program, 92
  IBRD program, 203
  ICAO program, 230–231
  ILO program, 149–152
  IMF program, 196
  Special Fund, 92
  UN program, 82, 96
  UNDP, 93–94
  UPU program, 239
Technology:
  Advisory Committee of Science and Technology, 78
  economic and social development, 82–84
Telecommunications system (UN): 14; *see also*: ITU
Textile trade, cotton: 217
Textiles Committee (ILO): 152
Thant, U: 129
  biography, 42
  role in Middle East crisis, 48, 52–53
  stand on Viet-Nam War, 47–48
  UN under, 47–48

Tibetan refugees: 119
Timber Committee (ECE): 69
Trachoma: 100, 171
Trade:
  Andean Subregional Integration Agreement, 76
  Caribbean Free Trade Association, 76
  East Caribbean Common Market, 76
  ECA activities, 71
  expansion, 80
  promotion of intra-African trade, 71
Trade, international:
  Committee on the Development of Trade (ECE), 70
  commodity trade and intergovernmental agreements, 89
  ECAFE activities, 74
  ECLA activities, 75
  economic development through, 87
  financing 89–90; *see also*: Economic development
  invisibles, 89
  land-locked countries, 90
  manufactures, 89
  semimanufactures, 89
  shipping, 90
  Trade and Development Board, 32, 90
  trends in, 90–91
  see also: GATT; United Nations Conference on Trade and
      Development
Trade Promotion Center (ECAFE): 74
Tranquilizers: 105
Transportation:
  Asian Highway Project, 74
  land-locked countries, 90
  shipping, 90
Travel, international: UNESCO program, 190
Treaties, law of: 136
Treaty for the Prohibition of Nuclear Weapons in Latin America
      (Treaty of Tlatelolco): 63
Treaty on the Nonproliferation of Nuclear Weapons: 63, 223
Treaty of Tlatelolco (Treaty for the Prohibition of Nuclear
      Weapons in Latin America): 63
Trusteeship Council: 3, 33–35, 129
  composition, 34
  functions, 34
  powers, 35
  sessions, 35
  voting in, 34
Trusteeship System: 33–34
  objectives, 33–34
  operation of, 35
  petitions, 35
  South West Africa problem, 130–131
  territories now independent, 129
  territories under trusteeship, 129
  West New Guinea problem, 129–130
Tuberculosis: 169–170
  UNICEF, 100

U Thant: *see* Thant, U
UNCTAD: *see* United Nations Conference on Trade and Devel-
      opment
UNDP: *see* United Nations Development Program
UNEF: *see* United Nations Emergency Force
UNICEF: *see* United Nations Children's Fund
UNIDO: *see* United Nations Industrial Development Organiza-
      tion
UNITAR: *see* UN Institute of Training and Research
United Nations (UN):
  admission of members, 11–12
  aims of, 10
  Charter, 33, 34
  compared with League of Nations, 5–7
  creation, 5
  establishment, 8–9
  headquarters and facilities, 14–16
  membership, 6

United Nations (cont.):
  membership (listed), 11
    expansion of, 14
  organs, 3–4
  purpose, 49
  related agencies, 4
  representation of nations, 12
  subsidiary organs, 3
  trusteeship system, 33–34; see also: Trusteeship Council, 33–34
  voting system, 6
  withdrawal from membership, 12
  see also: Charter (UN)
United Nations Capital Development Fund: 87
United Nations Children's Fund (UNICEF): 32
  and other UN agencies, 99
  and voluntary organizations, 98
  assisted projects, 99
  customs duties, 15
  finances, 98–99
  government contributions to, 98
  matching-funds principle, 99
  organization, 97–98
  purposes, 97
  scope, 97, 99
  work of, 99–101
    disease-control campaigns, 100
    education, 101
    vocational training, 101
    emergency aid, 101
    family welfare, 100–101
    integrated services, 101
    maternal and child health, 99–100
      environmental sanitation, 99
      family planning, 99–100
    nutrition, 100
    social services for children, 100–101
United Nations Conference on International Organization: see
        San Francisco Conference
United Nations Conference on Trade and Development
        (UNCTAD): 78, 79, 85
  established as organ of GA, 88–89
  second development decade, 91
  sessions summarized, 90–91
  summarized, 88
  trade financing, 90–91
United Nations Declaration: 8–9
United Nations Development Decade (first): 78–81
  aims, 78
  appraisal of, at mid-point, 78, 81, 83
  GA resolutions on, 78
  United Nations Development Decade Proposals for Action, 78
United Nations Development Decade, second: see Second Devel-
        opment Decade
UN Development Program (UNDP): 32, 91–96
  activities summarized, 94
  country programming, 94–95
  establishment of, 91–92
  executing agencies, 92–96
  experts, provision for, 93
  fellowships, 94
  financing, 93, 95
  functions, 92
  Governing Council membership, 92
  ICAO technical assistance and, 230–231
  preinvestment projects, 94
    funds for, 95
  structure, 92–93
  UN Capital Development Fund, 87
United Nations Educational, Scientific and Cultural Organiza-
        tion (UNESCO): 30, 178–191
  activities, 182–191
    coupon plan, 190
    culture, 187–189
      arts, promotion of, 187–188

United Nations Educational, Scientific and Cultural Organiza-
        tion (cont.):
  activities
    culture
      History of Mankind: Cultural and Scientific Development,
          189
      humanities, cooperation in, 187–188
      International Council for Philosophy and Humanistic
          Studies, 187
      literature promotion, 188
      mutual appreciation of cultural values project, 189
      Universal Copyright Convention, 188–189
      Venice Intergovernmental Conference on Cultural
          Policies, 187
      world's cultural heritage, conservation and protection
          of, 187–188
    education, 182–185
      adult education, 184–185
      Africa, 183–184
      Arab states, 184
      Asia, 183
      international understanding, 185
      Latin America, 183
      literacy, 185
      regional programs, 183
      special projects for youth, 185
      teachers, 185
    international style and travel, encouragement of, 190
    mass communications, 189
      agreement on international circulation of audiovisual
          materials, 190; customs duties and, 190; develop-
          ing media, aid to, 189–190
    natural sciences, 185–186
      application to development, 185–186
      budget, 186
      hydrology, 186
      oceanography, 186
      policy planning, 185–186
      research, 186
      teacher training, 186
    social sciences, 186–187
      professional societies, 187
      publications, 187
      research, 187
      setting up of permanent centers, 187
  background, 178
  budget, 19, 182
  cooperation with NGO's, 181–182
  establishment, 178–179
  headquarters, 180–181
  membership (listed), 179–180
  national commissions for, 181
  purposes, 179
  regional offices, 181
  structure, 180–182
    Director-General, 180
    Executive Board, 180
    General Conference, 180
    Secretariat, 180
United Nations Emergency Force (UNEF): 55–56
  financing of, 55–56
  ICJ's advisory opinion, 56
UN Flag Code and Regulations: 16
UN High Commissioner for Refugees: see Refugees
UN Industrial Development Organization (UNIDO): 32, 84
  Special Industrial Services (SIS), 84
UN Institute of Training and Research (UNITAR): 82
UN Monthly Chronicle: 15
United Nations Relief and Rehabilitation Administration
        (UNRRA): 117
United Nations Relief and Works Agency for Palestine Refugees
        (UNRWA): 119–122
  education, 120
  finances, 119–121

United Nations Relief and Works Agency for Palestine Refugees
    (cont.):
  refugees registered with, 121
  establishment, 119–120
  finances, 120
    budget, 122
  organization, 120
  refugees registered with UNRWA, 121
  services, 121–122
    clothing, 121
    education, 122
    food, 121
    health, 121–122
    shelter, 121–122
    vocational, 122
UN Trusteeship:
  territories under, 129
Uniting-for-Peace Resolution: 55
Universal Copyright Convention: 188–189
Universal Declaration of Human Rights: 30, 109–111
  significance, 110–111
Universal Postal Congress: 237
Universal Postal Union (UPU): 30, 236–239
  activities, 238–239
    arbitration role, 238
    central clearing house for international postal matters, 238
    information services, 238
    international mail regulations, revision of, 238–239
    postal studies, 239
    technical assistance, 239
  background, 236
  budget, 19, 238
  establishment, 236
  membership (listed), 237
  purposes, 236
  restricted postal unions, 237
  structure, 237–238
    Consultative Committee for Postal Studies, 238
    Executive Council, 237
    International Bureau of the UPU, 238
    Universal Postal Congress, 237
UNRRA: *see* United Nations Relief and Rehabilitation Administration
UNRWA: *see* United Nations Relief and Works Agency for Palestine Refugees
UPU: *see* Universal Postal Union
Use in War of Asphyxiating, Poisonous or Other Gases: 61

Veto power: 6
  use of, in Security Council, 28–29
Viet-Nam conflict: 47–48
  U Thant's stand, 47–48
Vilamajo, Julio: 14
Vocational training:
  ILO, 150–151
  UNICEF programs, 101

War crimes: 114
Water resources: 84
  ECAFE, work on, 73
  ECE, work on, 69
  FAO, 159
  WMO program for, 246
Weather: *see* WMO
West New Guinea question: 129–130
  role of U Thant, 47
WHO: *see* World Health Organization
Wilson, Woodrow: 5

WMO: *see* World Meteorological Organization
Women:
  marriage, 112, 116
  status of women, 112, 116
  see also: Commission on the Status of Women
Working Party on the Chemical Industry: 70
World Court: 36; *see also*: ICJ
World Economic Survey: 85, 87
World Food Program, 32, 156
World Health Organization (WHO): 30, 165–177
  activities, 168–176
    alcoholism, 173
    atomic energy and health, 176
    combating disease, 168–173
    diseases transmissible between animals and men, 173
    environmental health, 174
    food activities, 175–176
    health laboratory services, 174
    malnutrition, 173
    medical research programs, 176
    medical training, 173–174
    mental health, 173
    narcotic drugs, 105
    nursing, 173–174
    pharmaceutical-quality control, 175
    public health services, 174–175
    quarantine regulations, 171–172
    training medical auxiliaries, 173
    WHO fellowships, 173
  background, 165–166
  budget, 19, 168
  establishment, 166
  Expert Committee on Addiction-Producing Drugs, 102
  membership (listed), 166–167
  purposes, 166
  structure, 167–168
    Executive Board, 167
    Secretariat, 168
    World Health Assembly, 167
World Meteorological Congress: 244
World Meteorological Organization (WMO): 30, 243–246
  activities, 244–246
    Integrated Global Ocean Station System (IGOSS), 246
    meteorological service for agriculture, 246
    Program on the Interaction of Man and his Environment, 246
    research programs, participation in, 245
    technical assistance, 246
    water resources, development of, 246
    World Weather Watch, 245, 246
  background, 243
  budget, 19, 244
  establishment, 243
  headquarters, 244
  membership (listed), 243–244
  purposes, 243
  regional associations, 244
  structure, 244
    World Meteorological Congress, 244
  technical commissions, 244
  World Weather Watch, 65
World Population, UN Conference on: 32
World Weather Watch: 65, 245, 246

Yalta Conference: 8–9
Yaws:
  UNICEF, 100; WHO, 170
Yearbook of the United Nations: 15
Yellow Fever: 172

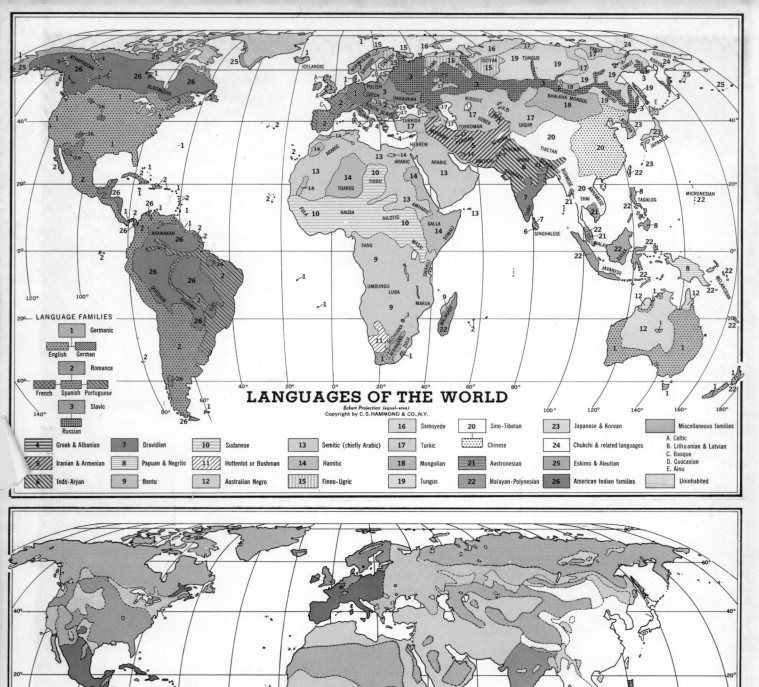

LANGUAGES OF THE WORLD

Eckert Projection (equal-area)
Copyright by C.S.HAMMOND & CO.,N.Y.

LANGUAGE FAMILIES

1 Germanic — English, German
2 Romance — French, Spanish, Portuguese
3 Slavic — Russian
4 Greek & Albanian
5 Iranian & Armenian
6 Indo-Aryan
7 Dravidian
8 Papuan & Negrito
9 Bantu
10 Sudanese
11 Hottentot or Bushman
12 Australian Negro
13 Semitic (chiefly Arabic)
14 Hamitic
15 Finno-Ugric
16 Samoyede
17 Turkic
18 Mongolian
19 Tungus
20 Sino-Tibetan
21 Austronesian
22 Malayan-Polynesian
23 Japanese & Korean
24 Chukchi & related languages
25 Eskimo & Aleutian
26 American Indian families

Miscellaneous families
A. Celtic
B. Lithuanian & Latvian
C. Basque
D. Caucasian
E. Ainu

Chinese
Uninhabited

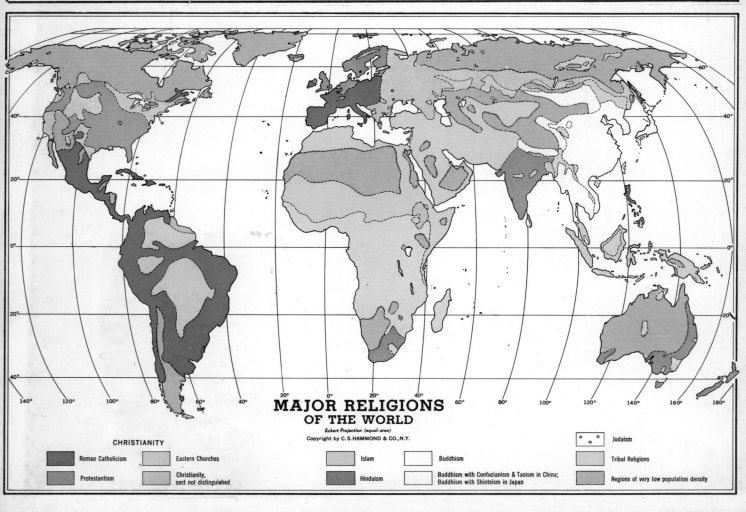

MAJOR RELIGIONS OF THE WORLD

Eckert Projection (equal-area)
Copyright by C.S.HAMMOND & CO.,N.Y.

CHRISTIANITY
Roman Catholicism
Protestantism
Eastern Churches
Christianity, sect not distinguished
Islam
Hinduism
Buddhism
Buddhism with Confucianism & Taoism in China; Buddhism with Shintoism in Japan
Judaism
Tribal Religions
Regions of very low population density